Computational Music Analysis

David Meredith

Editor

Computational
Music Analysis

 Springer

Editor
David Meredith
Department of Architecture, Design and
  Media Technology
Aalborg University
Aalborg
Denmark

ISBN 978-3-319-25929-1   ISBN 978-3-319-25931-4   (eBook)
DOI 10.1007/978-3-319-25931-4

Library of Congress Control Number: 2015954606

Springer Cham Heidelberg New York Dordrecht London
© Springer International Publishing Switzerland 2016

Printed on acid-free paper

Springer International Publishing AG Switzerland is part of Springer Science+Business Media
(www.springer.com)

Preface

The idea of putting together a book on computational music analysis emerged from a discussion that I had with Ronan Nugent (Senior Editor at Springer) at the Fourth International Conference on Mathematics and Computation in Music, held in Montreal in June 2013.[1] We talked about the fact that using mathematics and computing to advance our understanding of music (and, indeed, our understanding of how music is understood) would probably be considered a tiny niche area by most. However, those of us who devote our lives to this activity find ourselves split up into even tinier subdisciplines with names like "mathematical music theory", "computer music", "systematic musicology", "music information retrieval", "computational musicology", "digital musicology", "sound and music computing" and "music informatics". It must be almost incomprehensible to those working outside of the field that such a relatively small research area has become splintered into so many even smaller subdisciplines. What is more remarkable is how little communication and interaction takes place between these subdisciplines and, indeed, how much disagreement can arise when such interaction does occur.[2]

Ronan and I therefore agreed that the community would benefit from a book that gathered together papers by researchers from as many of these subdisciplines as possible, representing a wide range of current mathematical and computational approaches aimed at advancing our understanding of music. Such a book could showcase the technical and philosophical sophistication of these approaches, while also providing in-depth introductions to particular topics.

Work on this book started in April 2014 and it has taken seventeen months to get it into its final form. It consists of seventeen chapters, authored by thirty-two researchers from Europe and Japan. Each of the chapters was single-blind reviewed by at least two reviewers and the editor. The chapters are grouped into six parts: methodology, chords and pitch class sets, parsing large-scale structure (form and

---

[1] http://www.music.mcgill.ca/mcm2013

[2] See, for example, the special issue of the *Journal of Mathematics and Music* (Volume 6, Issue 2, July 2012), dedicated to a debate between leading figures in three of these subdisciplines.

voice separation), grammars and hierarchical structure, motivic and thematic analysis, and classification and distinctive patterns.

In the opening chapter, Alan Marsden explores the fundamental underpinnings of computational music analysis. He examines the nature of what exactly it is that we analyse, what the end result of an analysis should be and how one can evaluate a musical analysis. These issues are relevant to all aspects of music analysis and therefore prepare the ground for the remainder of the book.

Part II consists of three chapters focusing on chords, harmonic structure and pitch class set analysis. This part begins with a chapter by Emilios Cambouropoulos (Chap. 2), in which he challenges the usual assumption that the input to an analytical method should be a representation of a piece in terms of *notes*. Cambouropoulos argues that, from the perspective of music perception, it makes sense to start instead with a musical surface that encodes *chords* or 'vertical' pitch collections that are fused into Gestalts. Cambouropoulos proposes two novel, idiom-independent encoding schemes that can help with achieving this. The second chapter in Part II (Chap. 3), by Louis Bigo and Moreno Andreatta, also focuses on chords, but this time from a neo-Riemannian perspective in which relations between chords are represented geometrically and the chords themselves are modelled as pitch class sets represented as *simplices*. More specifically, they represent sets of chords closed under transposition and inversion (i.e., classes of T/I-invariant chords) as *simplicial complexes*. Pieces can then be represented as trajectories through such complexes and features of such trajectories can be used for analysis and classification. In the final chapter in Part II (Chap. 4), Agustín Martorell and Emilia Gómez present a complete method (implemented in software) for carrying out a multi-scale set-class analysis of a piece of music. They consider the problems of segmentation, description and representation, and introduce new data structures and visualization techniques to support their method.

Part III of the book is devoted to the analysis of large-scale structure. The two chapters in this part present methods for parsing whole pieces, on the one hand, into streams or voices and, on the other, into large-scale sections. In the first of these chapters (Chap. 5), Mathieu Giraud, Richard Groult and Florence Levé review the work that has been done on the computational analysis of musical form. They summarize the results they have obtained with systems designed for analysing fugues and movements in sonata form and they discuss the challenges associated with evaluating such systems. This is complemented by the second chapter in Part III (Chap. 6), by Tillman Weyde and Reinier de Valk, which focuses on parsing music into concurrent streams, that is, voice separation. Weyde and de Valk present and evaluate two contrasting approaches to voice separation: the note-to-note approach, where each note is assigned individually to a voice; and a chord-to-chord approach, where chords are treated as the basic units to be processed (as they are in the approach to harmonic analysis proposed by Cambouropoulos in Chap. 2).

Part IV consists of four chapters, presenting different aspects of and approaches to the analysis of hierarchical structure in music. In Chap. 7, Samer Abdallah, Nicolas Gold and Alan Marsden provide an in-depth introduction to the use of probabilistic grammars for analysing melodic structure. They review previous grammar-based approaches to music analysis as well as the foundations of their work in generative linguistics and information theory. They also present the results of experiments on learning the probabilities for simple grammars from two kinds of symbolic music corpora.

An important aspect of a reductive analysis of the hierarchical structure of a piece of music is identifying the relative structural importance of notes and the ways in which notes depend upon each other. The problem of designing an interactive tool that allows an analyst to do this effectively is addressed in Chap. 8 by David Rizo, Plácido Illescas and José Iñesta. Their proposed system learns from a user's corrections to an automatically generated analysis that classifies notes in a melody as either harmonic or one of six different types of non-harmonic elaboration (e.g., 'passing note' or 'neighbour note').

In the last two chapters of Part IV, Masatoshi Hamanaka, Keiji Hirata and Satoshi Tojo review their work on implementing parts of Lerdahl and Jackendoff's highly influential *Generative Theory of Tonal Music* (MIT Press, 1983). In Chap. 9, they present software implementations of Lerdahl and Jackendoff's theories of grouping structure and time-span reduction, that, like the system described by Rizo et al. in Chap. 8, is capable of learning from user-feedback in response to automatically generated analyses. In Chap. 10, the same authors present an algebraic formalization of Lerdahl and Jackendoff's theory of time-span reduction and develop a distance measure for comparing time-span trees, which they then evaluate against human judgements of similarity.

Part V of the book consists of three chapters presenting different approaches to the automatic discovery of repeated patterns in music. In the first of these chapters (Chap. 11), Olivier Lartillot presents an exhaustive approach to the discovery (or 'mining') of closed and cyclic patterns in sets of sequences representing melodies. Lartillot's system is capable of finding not only motives and themes in the conventional sense, but also 'heterogeneous' patterns that consist of sequences of items in several different musical dimensions (e.g., articulation, dynamics, pitch, rhythm). In the second chapter in this part (Chap. 12), Gissel Velarde, Tillman Weyde and I present a computational method for segmentation and clustering of segments, that relates closely to paradigmatic analysis. The method uses the continuous wavelet transform and self-similarity matrices. We also present and discuss the results obtained when the method was used for classifying folk songs into tune families and for identifying the parent pieces of excerpts from Bach's two-part inventions. In contrast to the essentially *sequential* approach adopted in Chaps. 11 and 12, the final chapter in this part of the book presents a *geometric* approach in which the music to be analysed is represented as a set of points in a multi-dimensional space. In this chapter (Chap. 13), I describe and analyse a number of pattern discovery and compression algorithms based on discovering maximal translatable patterns in such point-set representations. I give examples of the output of these algorithms on a Bach fugue and I also present the results of using the algorithms for folk song classification and the discovery of repeated themes and sections in polyphonic music.

The final part of the book concentrates on classification and the discovery of distinctive patterns. In the first chapter in this part (Chap. 14), Dorien Herremans,

David Martens and Kenneth Sörensen develop five types of classification model that can successfully distinguish between music by Bach, Haydn and Beethoven. They consider both comprehensible models, such as decision trees and rulesets, and black-box models such as support vector machines. The second chapter in this part (Chap. 15), by Kerstin Neubarth and Darrell Conklin, introduces the task and techniques of contrast pattern mining in the context of folk music analysis. Neubarth and Conklin identify two types of contrast patterns: sequential patterns and global feature patterns. They then recast previous work in quantitative folk music analysis as contrast pattern mining and show how subsumption applies equally to global feature and sequential patterns. In the third chapter in this part (Chap. 16), Darrell Conklin and Stéphanie Weisser report on a study of both frequent and rare motifs in Ethiopian bagana songs. They show that both over- and under-represented patterns can be discovered in a corpus of such songs that correspond with high significance to motifs that are well known within bagana performance practice. Finally, in Chap. 17, Tom Collins, Andreas Arzt, Harald Frostel and Gerhard Widmer present a method that uses geometric pattern discovery in combination with the viewpoint approach, symbolic fingerprinting and techniques from sequential pattern mining to discover patterns in polyphonic music that are distinctive of a particular composer and that are used across many works.

In September 2014, I had the pleasure of organizing a two-day special session on computational music analysis at the European Music Analysis Conference (Euro-MAC), at which many of the authors of chapters in this book gave presentations.[3] This proved to be a highly enjoyable event at which researchers from widely different backgrounds were able to interact constructively. My hope is that this book and events like the EuroMAC special session will help to establish computational music analysis as a recognized research area that *intersects* with many of the existing subdisciplines of computational and mathematical music research, and that possibly even assists in gluing these "sherds" back together. I would like to see computational music analysis become a sandbox, where researchers from different backgrounds can collaborate effectively with each other, united by the common goal of achieving a better understanding of music itself and how it is experienced and understood.

Aalborg, Denmark,   *David Meredith*
September 2015

---

[3] http://www.euromac2014.eu/programme/9a

Acknowledgements

As editor, I would like to thank the authors of the chapters in this book for the conscientiousness and diligence with which they worked on their respective chapters. I would also like to thank them for the careful and constructive anonymous reviews that they provided for chapters other than their own.

I would like to thank Teppo Ahonen, Justin Christensen, David Temperley, Costas Tsougras, Andrew Choi and Anna Jordanous for their constructive and helpful reviews of chapters.

I would like to thank Ronan Nugent at Springer for his steadfast support and for the confidence he has shown in me throughout this project.

I would like to thank my wife, Susanne Meredith, for her patience and support while I have been working on this book. I would also like to thank her for her feedback on the first draft of the preface.

Much of the editorial work on this book was carried out as part of the dissemination work package of the collaborative European project, "Learning to Create" (Lrn2Cre8). The project Lrn2Cre8 acknowledges the financial support of the Future and Emerging Technologies (FET) programme within the Seventh Framework Programme for Research of the European Commission, under FET grant number 610859.

Contents

List of Contributors

Samer Abdallah
Department of Computer Science, University College London, London, UK,
e-mail: s.abdallah@ucl.ac.uk

Moreno Andreatta
CNRS, France, and IRCAM, Paris, France, and Université Pierre et Marie Curie, Paris, France,
e-mail: moreno.andreatta@ircam.fr

Andreas Arzt
Department of Computational Perception, Johannes Kepler University, Linz, Austria,
e-mail: andreas.arzt@jku.at

Louis Bigo
Department of Computer Science and Artificial Intelligence, University of the Basque Country
UPV/EHU, San Sebastián, Spain, e-mail: louis.bigo@ehu.eus

Emilios Cambouropoulos
School of Music Studies, Aristotle University of Thessaloniki, Thessaloniki, Greece,
e-mail: emilios@mus.auth.gr

Tom Collins
Faculty of Technology, De Montfort University, Leicester, UK, e-mail: tom.collins@dmu.ac.uk

Darrell Conklin
Department of Computer Science and Artificial Intelligence, University of the Basque Country
UPV/EHU, San Sebastián, Spain, and IKERBASQUE, Basque Foundation for Science, Bilbao,
Spain, e-mail: darrell.conklin@ehu.eus

Harald Frostel
Department of Computational Perception, Johannes Kepler University, Linz, Austria,
e-mail: harald.frostel@jku.at

Mathieu Giraud
CNRS, France, and Centre de Recherche en Informatique, Signal et Automatique de Lille
(CRIStAL), Université de Lille 1, Villeneuve d'Ascq, France, e-mail: mathieu@algomus.fr

Nicolas Gold
Department of Computer Science, University College London, London, UK,
e-mail: n.gold@ucl.ac.uk

Emilia Gómez
Universitat Pompeu Fabra, Barcelona, Spain, e-mail: emilia.gomez@upf.edu

Richard Groult
Laboratoire Modélisation, Information et Systèmes, Université Picardie Jules Verne, Amiens,
France, e-mail: richard@algomus.fr

Masatoshi Hamanaka
Clinical Research Center, Kyoto University, Kyoto, Japan, e-mail: masatosh@kuhp.kyoto-u.ac.jp

Dorien Herremans
ANT/OR, University of Antwerp Operations Research Group, Antwerp, Belgium,
e-mail: dorien.herremans@uantwerpen.be

Keiji Hirata
Future University Hakodate, Hakodate, Hokkaido, Japan, e-mail: hirata@fun.ac.jp

Plácido R. Illescas
Universidad de Alicante, Alicante, Spain, e-mail: placidoroman@gmail.com

José M. Iñesta
Universidad de Alicante, Alicante, Spain, e-mail: inesta@dlsi.ua.es

Olivier Lartillot
Department of Architecture, Design and Media Technology, Aalborg University, Aalborg, Denmark,
e-mail: ol@create.aau.dk

Florence Levé
Laboratoire Modélisation, Information et Systèmes, Université Picardie Jules Verne, Amiens,
France, e-mail: florence@algomus.fr

Alan Marsden
Lancaster Institute for the Contemporary Arts, Lancaster University, Lancaster, UK,
e-mail: a.marsden@lancaster.ac.uk

David Martens
Applied Data Mining Research Group, University of Antwerp, Antwerp, Belgium,
e-mail: david.martens@uantwerpen.be

Agustín Martorell
Universitat Pompeu Fabra, Barcelona, Spain, e-mail: agustin.martorell@upf.edu

David Meredith
Department of Architecture, Design and Media Technology, Aalborg University, Aalborg, Denmark,
e-mail: dave@create.aau.dk

Kerstin Neubarth
Canterbury Christ Church University, Canterbury, UK, e-mail: kerstin.neubarth@canterbury.ac.uk

David Rizo
Universidad de Alicante, Alicante, Spain, and Instituto Superior de Enseñanzas Artísticas de la
Comunidad Valenciana (ISEA.CV), EASD Alicante, Alicante, Spain, e-mail: drizo@dlsi.ua.es

Kenneth Sörensen
ANT/OR, University of Antwerp Operations Research Group, Antwerp, Belgium,
e-mail: kenneth.sorensen@uantwerpen.be

Satoshi Tojo
Japan Advanced Institute of Science and Technology (JAIST), Nomi, Ishikawa, Japan,
e-mail: tojo@jaist.ac.jp

Reinier de Valk
Department of Computer Science, City University London, London, UK,
e-mail: r.f.de.valk@city.ac.uk

Gissel Velarde
Department of Architecture, Design and Media Technology, Aalborg University, Aalborg, Denmark,
e-mail: gv@create.aau.dk

Stéphanie Weisser
Université libre de Bruxelles, Brussels, Belgium, e-mail: stephanie.weisser@ulb.ac.be

Tillman Weyde
Department of Computer Science, City University London, London, UK,
e-mail: t.e.weyde@city.ac.uk

Gerhard Widmer
Department of Computational Perception, Johannes Kepler University, Linz, Austria,
e-mail: gerhard.widmer@jku.at

Part I
Methodology

Chapter 1
Music Analysis by Computer: Ontology and Epistemology

Alan Marsden

Abstract This chapter examines questions of what is to be analysed in computational music analysis, what is to be produced, and how one can have confidence in the results. These are not new issues for music analysis, but their consequences are here considered explicitly from the perspective of computational analysis. Music analysis without computers is able to operate with multiple or even indistinct conceptions of the material to be analysed because it can use multiple references whose meanings shift from context to context. Computational analysis, by contrast, must operate with definite inputs and produce definite outputs. Computational analysts must therefore face the issues of error and approximation explicitly. While computational analysis must retain contact with music analysis as it is generally practised, I argue that the most promising approach for the development of computational analysis is not systems to mimic human analysis, but instead systems to answer specific music-analytical questions. The chapter concludes with several consequent recommendations for future directions in computational music analysis.

1.1 Introduction

The nature of music analysis, as a discipline, if not as a practice, has been a topic of debate on several occasions (e.g., Nattiez, 1990; Pople, 1994; Samson, 1999). Researchers in computational music analysis, on the other hand, tend to take music analysis as a kind of 'given'. My aim here is to revisit this ontological and epistemological debate, with two objectives: first, to draw conclusions useful for those who would use computers for analysis or who write analytical software; and second, to explore what insights follow from taking an explicitly computational approach to the debate.

Alan Marsden
Lancaster Institute for the Contemporary Arts, Lancaster University, Lancaster, UK
e-mail: a.marsden@lancaster.ac.uk

© Springer International Publishing Switzerland 2016   3
D. Meredith (ed.), *Computational Music Analysis*,
DOI 10.1007/978-3-319-25931-4_1

Fig. 1.1 Analysis as a mapping from piece to analysis

Piece   Analysis

From a computational perspective, the simplest way of thinking of music analysis is as analogous to the working of a computer program. A piece of music is presented as input to a program, and this produces as output an analysis (Fig. 1.1). Music analysis, in this simple perspective, is effectively mapping from a piece to an analysis. As we will see below, this is too simplistic an account, but it will serve as a basis for the present. 'Mapping' here means there is a distinct relation between the piece and the analysis, involving also distinct relations between parts of the piece and parts of the analysis (see Sect. 1.4.1). It need not be a mapping in the mathematical sense, though it can often be expressed in that way. Different analyses of the same piece can exist because there can be different mappings, each corresponding to different programs. Any one program should always produce the same output for a given piece as input, unless it also takes input from some other, variable, source (such as a random-number generator). Human experts similarly map a piece to an analysis, and different experts produce different analyses. Different analyses arise through the application of different analytical approaches, whether these are gross differences between, say, analysis based on Schenkerian and Riemannian theories, or minor differences resulting from different interpretations of theory.

The following discussion will therefore be framed around three loci: the input or music, the output or analysis, and the mapping. Debates about analysis often go beyond discussion of the nature of music and analysis to also discuss the epistemology of the enterprise: how one comes to know what the mapping between music and analysis should be. In fact, although I say that the debate often goes beyond ontology, in writing about music analysis it often slips almost imperceptibly into epistemology. In what follows, I hope to make the move from one to the other more explicit, and also to draw out some definite conclusions and recommendations from the examination of ontological and epistemological questions.

1.2 Ontology of Pieces of Music

Questions of the ontology of music, of what it actually *is*, have generally focused on two issues. The first is whether music, or pieces of music, can properly be considered to have a distinct existence or not. At one extreme, a piece of music is considered to be a distinct 'object' with an abstract existence made manifest in various ways in the scores, recordings and performances of the piece, not to say also in the imagination of its composer and the memories of those who read the scores or hear the recordings and performances. At the other extreme, pieces of music are a kind of cultural fiction and music is ultimately an *activity* of which scores, recordings and performances are merely traces which exist only in certain cultural contexts (for discussion, see Goehr, 2007; Goodman, 1976; Levinson, 1980). Indeed, cultural context is of considerable importance in this debate, and it seems clear that different positions with respect to the nature of music, or at least the nature of pieces of music, are appropriate for different cultures and different periods of history. There are musical cultures in the world which have no scores, for example, and in which the notion of 'a piece', if it exists at all, is clearly something quite different from a symphony from nineteenth-century Europe.

The debate about the ontology of music, or of pieces of music, need not concern music analysts too deeply, though. Provided they show some due concern for the nature of the materials they use, they are able to proceed with their activities, and to produce useful insights, without having to commit themselves on the finer points of ontological debate. The computational music analyst, on the other hand, is not so free to use diffuse conceptions of a piece of music. The input to analytical software must be, ultimately, a binary code, in which every bit is unequivocally 0 or 1. Furthermore, every bit must be determined before the analysis begins, unless the analytical software is embedded in an interactive system which takes inputs from the user or other sources in the course of analysis, which is not typically the case for computational music analysis (see, however, Chap. 8, this volume, for an example of an interactive analysis system along these lines). The computational analyst is therefore effectively placed in a position at one extreme pole of the ontological debate, where pieces of music, or at least their manifestations used for analysis, are entities of which every feature is fixed. A human analyst can delay commitment about some features until part-way through the analysis. A curved line in a score, for example, might be interpreted as a slur or as a tie depending on the results of earlier stages of an analysis. One might object that the input to the analysis is then neither a slur nor a tie but a curved line, which is fixed in advance, but the example can then be moved down a level: is the curved line a proper part of the score or a printing error? There is no fixed boundary for the human analyst separating the information which can be used in the analysis from the information which cannot (see Sect. 1.2.1 below).

The upshot of this for computational analysis is that those who analyse pieces of music which clearly do *not* exist as fixed entities (e.g., from cultures without scores in which pieces are highly variable) should recognize that they do not analyse 'the piece', but rather some particular version or manifestation of it.

1.2.1 The Music Itself?

The classic contrast between music analysis and other areas of musicology used to be that analysis concerned itself with 'the music itself' rather than the music's context: historical, social, etc. This changed in the late twentieth century with the advent of 'new musicology' which questioned the entire notion that music could be extracted from its context. Whether or not this is always the case need not concern us here, but it is clear that at least the boundary between what one must include in 'the music itself' and what one can leave out is far from clear. In some music, from Europe in the early 18th century for example, it is clear that performers would regularly add ornaments. In some cases, especially later in that century, ornaments are written in scores. When analysing a piece of music, should one take into account the ornaments or not? And if one takes into account the written ornaments from later in the century, why not the unwritten ones from earlier? If the ornaments are not written in the score, how can one be sure what they are?

Even once such issues have been settled, there is still uncertainty over what properly constitutes the 'input' to analysis. Here the issue is not so much what is in the music itself, but whether analysis really considers *just* the music itself. One would normally analyse a piece from the twentieth century differently from the way one would analyse a piece of music from the Renaissance, but the date of composition of a piece is not normally considered to be part of 'the music'. Even if the focus of analysis is 'the music itself', it is clear that other information forms part of the input to the process.

Thus the boundaries for the input to the analytical process are indistinct in at least two ways:

- There is no clear definition of what information is included in 'the music itself' and what is excluded.
- It is not clear what additional information is required for proper analysis of a piece.

The simple diagram used in the introduction above should therefore be revised to show that the input to the analytical process, as traditionally conceived, has indistinct boundaries (Fig. 1.2). (Discussion of what a 'proper' analysis might be follows in later sections.)

As an example, consider the case of the '371 Bach chorales', which were considered a kind of dataset of good practice in harmony long before 'dataset' became a word. It has been known for some time that (a) there are not 371 distinct chorales (some are duplicates, with varying degrees of similarity), (b) they are not all by J. S. Bach, (c) independent instrumental parts are missing from some, and (d) the precise details of some are uncertain (sources differ). It has nevertheless been common for computational analysts to use the version available in 'Humdrum kern' format (Sapp, 2014) without questioning its validity.[1] When a source is large in size

Piece   Analysis

Fig. 1.2 Indistinct piece

---

[1] It must be acknowledged that the fault here is not Craig Sapp's. He clearly states the source used in compiling the version (down to the precise print and edition) and states its nature as a collection made by C. P. E. Bach and Kirnberger.

and easily available, it tends to be used in several studies, presumably because the researchers want to put time into analysis rather than into encoding sources. For a discussion of the adverse consequences of unquestioning use of such sources, see Sturm (2014).

1.2.2 Differences and Indeterminacy in Digital Data

While computational analysis must, because it deals with digital representations, take a definitive input, this does not mean that it deals with single definitive representations of pieces of music. An audio file in WAV format does not contain the same stream of digital data as the same audio in FLAC format. Yet we are right to say it contains *the same* audio because exactly the same information is encoded in both files: a rendition of both into streams of digital samples would produce identical streams. Such differences between input data are merely differences of format and have an effect only at an operational level; there is no reason to expect any difference in the analyses produced. We might consider the two representations to be two different 'projections' of the same data by analogy with the projection of graphical data from one co-ordinate space to another: the data is not changed but it is represented differently.

Other differences in input to computational analyses are more significant, and even when the word 'format' is used in connection with these, the differences constitute genuine differences in the information represented. An audio recording in a lossy compressed format such as MP3 is different from a recording in a non-compressed format because some of the information in the latter has been lost. A representation of a piece in a MIDI file and a representation of the same piece in a MusicXML file contain different information. For example, the MIDI file does not contain information about the location of barlines relative to the notes, whereas this information is essential in the MusicXML file. Differences of this kind are not so much ones of projection but ones of *selection* of data. Choosing to use one 'format' or another as input to the analytical process is tantamount to selecting some information about the piece and ignoring other information. Of course the data has to be present in the source which is being represented in order to be selected, so while one can take a MIDI file direct from the playing of a musician on a keyboard, one cannot directly derive a MusicXML file from that source. The location of barlines is not explicit in the musician's playing on the keyboard, but it is explicit in the score, and one can derive a MusicXML file from a score.

This difference with respect to sources underlines another kind of difference in different 'formats'. This is clearest with respect to the representation of pitch. A score shows the pitch of a note in a particular spelling (e.g., C♯ or D♭), and formats such as MusicXML contain similar information. A MIDI file, by contrast, contains pitch information only in relation to which key on a keyboard is pressed (so C♯ and D♭ are represented as the same pitch). On the other hand, a MIDI file contains information about precise timings, whereas a MusicXML file represents timings only by the notated durations of the notes and a generally imprecise indication of tempo. One can unequivocally derive the pitch information necessary for a MIDI file from a score, but one cannot derive the precise timing information required (unless the score indicates a precise tempo) without making a guess at an appropriate tempo, and using that as a basis for timings in the MIDI representation. Such an interpretative step is often required even when creating a MusicXML representation from a score, despite the fact that MusicXML was created precisely to represent score information (Good, 2001). When simultaneous notes occur, the format requires a distinction to be made between chords and simultaneous notes in different voices. Different people are likely to make different decisions about which is appropriate in some cases. We might use a single notated source as a guide to aim at definitive decisions, representing simultaneous notes as chords when they are attached to the same stem but in different voices when they are not. This does not overcome the problem of ambiguities in the assignment of notes to voices, however, and most obviously does not help in cases of simultaneous notes without stems such as semibreves (whole notes). Ideally, there would be conventions for making such decisions in a regular fashion, and so allowing the formation of canonical MusicXML files, but I am not aware of any such conventions.

In the cases of some computational music data, there is no evident interpreting agent. When scanning a score to generate a digital image, for example, the user places the score on the scanner and presses a button rather than taking a set of decisions on how to represent the information in the score. However, the resulting digital data is still contingent on factors which, like the decisions of an interpreting agent, are specific to the manner in which the scan is made rather than dependent solely on the score itself. The score might be placed at an angle, for example, so that the staff lines do not appear horizontal in the image. In the case of audio recordings, it is well recognized that factors like the placement of microphones and the acoustics of the recording space have a profound effect on the resulting data. Microphones and scanners, and indeed any sensing device, have an inevitable element of noise in their outputs, constituting another source of information effectively added to the original music data. Often one can go some way towards removing such unwanted data (often called noise or distortion)—a scan can be de-skewed, for example, or noise-reduction applied to a recording—but to do so relies on assumptions about the original data (e.g., that the staff lines are horizontal). There is no generalized way for distinguishing between original and introduced data on the basis of the data alone, and, perhaps more importantly, no way of distinguishing between introduced data which is possibly legitimate interpretation and introduced data which is spurious. In a recording, for example, how could one know if the sound of a particular instrument is prominent because the recording engineer has legitimately placed the microphone to best pick up the lead instrument, or because the resonance of the recording space happened to make it prominent?

There are thus three ways in which computational representations which form the input to computational analysis, while fixed in the sense that they have a definitive digital form, are nevertheless indefinite in the sense that there is not a single definitive form for the data representing a single piece:

- the projection of the data to a particular format,
- the selection of the data which is represented in that format, and
- some unavoidable element of extrinsically introduced information, or at least uncertainty about whether or not there is extrinsically introduced information.

The diagram of music analysis therefore needs revising once again, to reflect the varieties of possible inputs, even for a single, indistinct, piece of music. Unlike the indeterminacy discussed in Sect. 1.2.1 above, these are inputs which have distinct boundaries, but the indeterminacy arises from the impossibility of determining which is the proper input (Fig. 1.3).

In practical terms, the indeterminacy might be very low. We might, for example, decide to represent only the pitch and timing information from a score which we consider to be unequivocally given by the unambiguous placing of the notes vertically on the stave and horizontally in relation to barlines and each other. Of course we have selected information from the score, and we have implicitly assumed that the ignored information (articulation, for example) is not relevant to the analytical distinctions we aim to make, but at least we have not introduced anything which is not in the score. Or so we suppose, because while we might be confident that nothing has been introduced, we cannot be certain. Mistakes happen, and if we are using data generated by someone else, what information do we have about how likely it is to contain mistakes? More importantly, we cannot be certain that what is unequivocal in one musical source is unequivocal in another, so we cannot be confident that our procedure will generalize to all cases. For example, Don Byrd has given examples of standard music notation (by well known composers) where the timing of notes is ambiguous and some in which even the pitch is questionable (Byrd, 1984, 2013).

1.2.3 Error and Approximation

The solution to these issues is for computational music analysts to recognize that they operate with approximations. In the natural sciences, researchers are well used to dealing with input which contains noise and error. Every measurement is regarded as an approximation of the real value. Extremely reliable results can nevertheless be derived because researchers quantify the error in their measurements, take multiple measurements, and take these into account in calculating their conclusions. In the social sciences, too, the idea of multiple measurements to increase accuracy is common. To take an opinion poll, one asks not just one person their view, but many people, and one is careful to ask a variety of people so that the answers are not biased

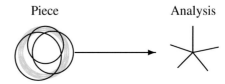

Fig. 1.3 Selected but definite input for analysis

to one point of view. The essential idea is that the overall properties of the *sample* one uses should match, within an acceptable degree of error, the overall properties one would find in the entire *population* if one were to actually measure everyone or everything in the domain.

In music analysis, one is generally concerned with the properties of a particular piece (sometimes even of a particular performance) and so some of the most obvious analogies of sampling from a population do not apply. However, a useful strategy might still be to consider different editions of a piece of music as sources, and perhaps performances as well as scores. It would be possible, too, to perform similar analyses on different formats of data, but since analytical software is usually specific to a particular format, and since it is not clear how 'the same' analysis can be ensured given data in different formats, this too is problematic.

The notion of error, however, is eminently applicable. In Fig. 1.3, error corresponds to the region within the fuzzy boundary of 'the piece' but outside the definite boundary of the particular digital representation used as input to the analytical process. Just as a natural scientist aims to minimize error, the computational analyst should aim to minimize the area of this region of the diagram. Of course, this cannot be done with certainty because the boundary of 'the piece' is indistinct. Furthermore, there is no definitive way of even estimating the area of the region. How much 'space' in the input domain is taken up by the pitch-spelling information which is not included in a MIDI representation, for example? The answer, if there is an answer, depends on the one hand on the nature of analysis undertaken, and on the other on the viewpoint, implicit or explicit, of the person judging its validity. A MusicXML file gives no information about the layout of a score on the page, and in many cases it is not regarded as significant: the area, in the sense of 'quantity of significant information' in the piece-as-score, which corresponds to the layout information missing from the MusicXML file will be close to zero. If the piece in question is *Eight Songs for a Mad King* by Peter Maxwell Davies, in which the staves of the third movement are arranged on the page in the shape of a birdcage, the area for information corresponding to layout will be greater.

A more effective way of quantifying error is to consider the effect on the analysis produced. How different are the analyses arising from different selections or interpretations of data from the piece? As indicated above, actually using different input formats will not always be realistic. However, one could simulate these differences to some degree. For example, as stated above, a MusicXML file, or indeed any input derived from a score, does not contain precise timing information. (Even if the score gives a metronome marking for the tempo, this is generally regarded as a suggestion for the tempo rather than a strict instruction to the performer.) When using analytical software such as Melisma (Sleator and Temperley, 2003) which requires timing information for input, it would be easy to make multiple runs of the software with variations in the timings in the input, made with the aim of producing a distribution of different timings similar to the distribution occurring in different likely interpretations of the information in the score. Comparison of the resultant outputs would then give good data on which to quantify the significance of error in the input. If the difference in the outputs is small, the error in the input can be considered to be small also.[2]

In some other cases, such as the Bach chorales mentioned above (Sect. 1.2.1), one can have some confidence in the smallness of the error even without this kind of testing. One could argue that (a) the number of duplicates is small in comparison to the number of chorales (371), (b) the number of known mis-attributions to J. S. Bach is tiny in comparison to the number of cases where J. S. Bach is confirmed as the composer, (c) very few chorales have missing instrumental parts which differ from the vocal parts, and (d) there are few differences between sources. However, even this kind of reasoning is usually absent from computational analyses, and researchers have tended to perform analyses as if there were no error in the input. The consequences of this oversight in the domain of genre recognition have been set out by Bob Sturm (2014). While researchers have claimed that their computational systems recognize the genre of audio recordings with a high degree of accuracy, an examination of the errors and inconsistencies in the dataset used and the effect of these on the measures of accuracy led Sturm to conclude that these claims are not supportable.

1.3 Ontology of Analysis as a Kind of Writing

The question of the ontology of an analysis is in some ways simpler and in some more complex than the ontology of a piece of music. It is simpler because the form is more distinct: analyses are pieces of writing or some other kind of discourse. They are communicated from one human being to another. (Or at least they were until computational analysis came along. It is entirely possible for the object of computational analysis to involve no human reading of the analytical outputs, but discussion of this will be left for later. For the present, it will be assumed that the objectives of computational analysis are the same as those of analysis without computers.)

The question of the ontology of an analysis is more complex because analyses are not surrounded by the same richness of data from patterns of use and context as are pieces of music. We have a clear idea of the situations in which music is typically created and listened to, we have information about what music is valued in which situations, and we have a large body of commentary to draw on. For music analyses, we know that these are published in books and journals, and discussed in conferences and classrooms, but clear information on the role of this activity within wider culture is not clear. Analysis has regularly been used as a tool in the teaching of composition, and analysts claim that their work can inform performance of a piece (Mawer, 1999), but there is precious little evidence of such influence in everyday practice.

---

[2] David Meredith followed a procedure somewhat like this to test the impact of tempo on pitch-spelling using Melisma, finding the effect to be quite large (Meredith, 2007, p. 205). This was over a range larger than the tempo variations one would typically find in performance, however.

1.3.1 Description and Explanation

Analysis is typically distinguished from other kinds of writing about pieces of music—commentary, criticism, hermeneutic exegesis, etc.—by claiming that it considers the piece itself (which as we have seen above is not entirely true), that it eschews the value judgements inherent in criticism, that it avoids the subjective perspective of hermeneutics, and that above all it provides not just a description of a piece of music but an *explanation*. The distinction between description and explanation, however, is not so easy to make, and might be only one of degree: if we can describe something very succinctly, then we can thereby, in a sense, explain it. (Applications of this idea using minimum-description-length coding, information theory and Kolmogorov complexity will be briefly reviewed in Sect. 1.5.1.)

In the domain of the natural sciences, a phenomenon is explained by demonstrating how general principles apply in a specific case. The characteristics of a species, for example, might be explained by demonstrating how the principles of the theory of evolution apply to the species in its particular environment. This kind of thing exists in music analysis also, where a piece is explained through a demonstration that it follows a particular model, e.g., Sonata Form. Herein lies a paradox, though. Music analysis is generally distinguished from music theory, and the distinction is that analysis is concerned with particular pieces of music whereas theory is concerned with generalities. An analysis, from this perspective, seeks not just to explain a piece by reference to a general model, but by reference also to *its particular properties*. While apparently seeking to *explain*, then, an analysis of a piece of music often takes a great deal of space to *describe* the particular and distinctive characteristics of that piece. Although I stated above that analysis eschews value judgement, value is rarely far from the surface. The apparent objective of many analyses (and in some cases, such as in some of the analyses of Schenker, the explicit objective) is to demonstrate how a piece of music is a masterwork. To do so requires pointing out its special characteristics, not just the ways in which it follows general models.

One response to this is for analysis to seek how a piece establishes its own explanatory principles, or it might seek to build an explanation either on scrutiny of listening experiences (one's own or others') or on information concerning the piece's creation. Nattiez famously distinguishes three levels for analysis: the poietic, which involves consideration of the process of creation; the esthesic, which involves consideration of the process of hearing; and between them a neutral level (Nattiez, 1990). Analysis at the neutral level examines the divisions and patterns in the neutral code, which in practice for most music analysis means the notes written in the score. An important component of the method of 'paradigmatic analysis' advocated by Nattiez is the discovery of 'paradigms' within the piece. These paradigms are, at first, based on evident similarities in the configuration of notes; but later, they take on a more generative role in determining which configurations count as occurrences of a particular pattern and which do not (for a large-scale example, see Nattiez, 1982). The basis for organization of the piece is thus established *in the course of analysis*. On the other hand, one does not start an analysis (and perhaps cannot start) from a blank, theory-free position and follow only the leadings of the information at the neutral level. Certain principles, usually unstated, govern the establishment of paradigms in the course of the analysis. The same thing can be seen in a simpler fashion in the manner of motivic analysis as practised by Réti, Keller, and others (Keller, 1965, 1985; Réti, 1962, 1967). They start from an underlying principle that pieces of music are organized by the use of melodic material which derives from a single basic motive. The nature of the motive and the methods of derivation will vary from piece to piece, and ad hoc arguments are presented in the course of the analysis to justify the analyst's decisions. Essentially, motivic analysis and paradigmatic analysis operate with a meta-theory which governs the generation, in the course of analysis, of a specific theory to explain the piece of music in question. Those familiar with machine learning, genetic programming and other inductive systems might see a similarity here: an overarching principle (the minimization of a particular error function, for example) is used to guide the development of the analytical process, the details of which are contingent on the properties of the actual data. (Other points of contact between machine learning and computational analysis will be explored further in Sect. 1.5.2.) In the case of motivic and paradigmatic analysis, however, the meta-theory is usually only vaguely expressed at the outset and is subject to revision in the course of making the analysis.

1.3.2 Limitations of Mechanistic Analysis

Nattiez (1990, p. 32), though, claims that analysis at the neutral level is descriptive, and that it is poietic and esthesic analyses which are explicative. Exactly why this should be so is not clear. One possibility is that explanation requires reference to wider realms of human meaning, and this is not possible without consideration of either the poietic or esthesic level. Another possibility (though probably not one Nattiez would endorse, for reasons set out below) is that analysis at the neutral level is mechanistic, and explanation by a mechanism is not possible, perhaps again because explanation requires some human reference.

Nattiez does consider the possibility of mechanistic analysis, but in the earlier article he goes beyond the assignation of mere description to call the result of a mechanistic operation an *inventory*, which he contrasts with an analysis. For Nattiez, analysis requires a step of deciding which relationships between musical units are to be considered transformations, placing the musical units into the same 'paradigm', and which relationships are to be considered distant enough to distinguish one paradigm from another.

> Given that not all possible forms of transformation are foreseeable, as soon as relationships are established between units that are not strictly identical we enter the realms of analysis. [...] The difference between an inventory and an actual analysis is that *it does not appear to be possible to deduce the latter from the sum of the information provided by the former.*
>
> (Nattiez, 1982, p. 256)

This is quite a strong challenge to computational analysis. Some will take heart from the fact that Nattiez's claim was made when computational analysis was in its infancy, and that Nattiez did not have a clear idea of what it was possible to do with a computer. Decisions on whether relationships count as class membership or not are now made many, many times a day by search engines. However, there is one further aspect of Nattiez's argument which will be readily recognizable to computer scientists. Later on in the same article, Nattiez acknowledges that mechanistic accounting can treat not just identity but any kind of relationship between musical units, expanding the inventory to accommodate these by adding extra 'columns' in a table to record the occurrence of particular units or transformed units. Extending the point quoted above that "not all possible forms of transformation are foreseeable", Nattiez points out that "[t]here is, therefore, no limit to the number of possible columns" (Nattiez, 1982, p. 257). Since every real computing machine has finite resources, we therefore can never be certain that the relationships required to make a proper analysis of the piece will be in the table.

There are, however, two flaws in this argument.[3] First, it is only true that the table of possible transformations will be infinite if the set of units to be related is itself infinite. If the representation of the piece at the neutral level is finite (e.g., a finite sequence of notes described in terms of pitch and duration), then the set of all possible relations between notes or sets of notes is finite (though large).[4] It would be possible for a computer with sufficient resources to make an inventory of all these relations and, given a mechanism for deciding which relations were of significance, to derive an analysis from this inventory, in Nattiez's terms. In most cases, however, the inventory would be impossibly large for this to be a realistic method of analysis.

The second flaw is not one which renders the argument invalid, but one which blunts its force. It was argued above (Sect. 1.2.3) that the fact that one cannot be certain that the input to computational analysis covers all the necessary information about the piece does not render analysis impossible. By a similar argument, the fact that one cannot be certain that all significant relations can be recognized by the analysing computer does not render analysis impossible. Once again it is a matter of statistics. How confident can one be that the significant relations can be taken account of? The fact that the same kinds of relationship seem to be regularly reported in music analyses suggests that it is possible to design analytical software a priori which is likely to encompass the significant relations. To extend this argument to quantify the degree of confidence would require some idea of what makes a relationship significant, which is moving towards questions of epistemology to be discussed below. As with the inputs, though, it would be possible to estimate confidence in the analysis on the basis of experiments using different sets of relationships in the early stages of analysis (the 'inventory' stage in Nattiez's terms). If the analysis

---

[3] It has to be acknowledged that Nattiez adumbrates rather than explicitly states this argument, so my interpretation of his meaning might be incorrect.

[4] Note that a relation in this sense is defined purely by the set of sets of notes which show that relation. There does not need to be a definition of the relation in terms which would allow us to determine, for any arbitrary set of notes which do not actually occur in the piece, whether they are in that relation or not. For example, if in a particular piece there is a relation consisting of the two pairs of notes with pitches (A, B) and (B, A), there is no necessity to define whether this relation is defined as 'transpose the first note up one step and the second down one step' or 'swap the first and second notes', or indeed in any other possible way.

uses pitch intervals as a basis for segmenting a sequence of notes, for example, one could experiment with runs of the software which use absolute intervals expressed in semitones or key-dependent intervals expressed in scale steps and investigate how much variation there is in the resulting segmentation.[5]

1.4 Ontology of Analysis: What Is It About?

An analysis is not adequately defined as a piece of writing; we want crucially to know what it is writing *about* when it describes or explains, and what kinds of things it says. Just as there are multiple answers to the question of the ontological nature of a piece of music, there are multiple perspectives on the ontology of an analysis.

1.4.1 Temporal Basis of Analysis

Before embarking on discussion of ontology proper, it is worth clarifying certain general characteristics of an analysis. As discussed above, an analysis contains information derived from a piece of music. This is not typically a single piece of information, or a piece of information which applies to the entire piece. There are other kinds of derivation of information from pieces which are not analyses, as for example determining who wrote a piece where there are disputed attributions, or determining the genre of a piece of music. Analysis can contribute to making this kind of determination, but the determination itself is not analysis. Even to say something like 'piece X is in Sonata Form' does not constitute an analysis, though it is a kind of analytical statement. The analysis would show us *how* the piece is in Sonata Form.

The distinguishing characteristic of an analysis is that, like the piece of music, it has a temporal structure (or at least a structure which maps onto time), and the mapping shown in Figs. 1.1–1.3 is not just from the piece to the analysis but from parts of the piece to parts of the analysis, and the temporal relations between the parts of the piece are reflected in some way in the relations between the parts of the analysis.

1.4.2 Information Content of Analysis

A second characteristic of analyses is that they contain, in a technical sense, less information than the piece analysed. An analysis does add information in the sense

---

[5] This resembles the approach of testing the effect of selecting different combinations of multiple viewpoints (Whorley et al., 2013) or of parameters (van Kranenburg, 2008), but generally this has been done in order to optimize the accuracy or efficiency of the result rather than in order to estimate its degree of error.

that someone reading an analysis will gain knowledge about the piece which they did not have before, but this is a gain for the reader brought about by directing his or her attention to aspects of the piece or derivations made from the information in the piece. Nothing is added which was not already latent in the piece, and a lot is left out because many alternative ways of structuring the piece have been excluded. On the other hand, whether one regards an analysis as always containing less information than the piece depends on one's view about what information is contained in 'the piece' in the first place and requires the questions about the ontology of a piece of music from Sect. 1.2 to be revisited.

As mentioned above (Sect. 1.2.2), the input to an analysis is already a *selection* from the information in the piece, but, as was also indicated above, analysis generally goes beyond this to reduce the quantity of information further. This is most obvious in a Schenkerian analysis, where the term 'reduction' is used explicitly, but it is evident in other kinds of analysis also, such as those which explain a piece in terms of a small set of melodic motives. Indeed, it can be argued that a necessary consequence of giving an explanation of the piece rather than merely a description will involve reduction in information. The discussion of significant relations in Sect. 1.3.2 is of relevance also: selection of significant relations will entail a reduction in information. This topic will be revisited in the discussion of epistemology below.

1.4.3 Analysis as Inherent Within the Piece

Analysis is often presented by its practitioners as demonstrating how a piece of music 'works' (Bent, 1987). Analogies are sometimes made to architecture (in phrases such as the 'plan' or 'structure' of a piece), to anatomy (the 'skeleton' of a piece) or to growth (the 'germ' of a piece). The analyst is like a surgeon dissecting a body to reveal its skeleton, ligaments and organs. Indeed, some find music analysis distasteful on similar grounds to dissection: to them the uncaring cutting and poking of a living thing, or at least a once-living thing, is a kind of violence. The common riposte is that, unlike dissection, the act of analysis does no damage to the piece which can, as it were, arise from the operating table and walk again. If music analysis does do damage to a piece, to my mind that is because some erroneously believe it prescribes a way of hearing. There is an important distinction between the act of analysis and the act of listening.

In the perspective of analysis as revealing structure, the analysis reveals what is already inherent in a piece, in the same way as a skeleton is inherent in a body. This follows also from the perspective of analysis as demonstrating how a piece 'works', which is not inconsistent with different analyses of a piece. We might encounter different descriptions of how a piece of machinery works, for example explanation of a hydraulic jack in terms of the incompressibility of the fluid and the volumes displaced or in terms of the conservation of energy, and we can see the correctness of both while still believing that there is *one* way in which the machine works. The different explanations offer different ways of accounting for how the machine works.

An analysis, in this perspective, has a relation to 'the piece' similar to scores or performances of the piece. There is a single entity which is 'the piece', and multiple manifestations which serve particular purposes, selecting information inherent in 'the piece' and projecting it to be presented in a particular way. These acts of selection and projection are themselves determined by other information, such as the date of composition of a piece, or a theory of tonal structure, but the information which the analysis presents is, essentially, information inherent in 'the piece' (Fig. 1.4).

1.4.4 Analysis and Cognitive Structures

Just as the objective existence of a piece of music is questionable, so too is the existence of a non-contingent analysis. The analysis itself might be a kind of document, which can have an existence as objective as a score, but the 'analysis' which this document conveys, the significant information, exists, perhaps, only in minds (Fig. 1.5).

There is a kind of analysis which tries to explain a piece by reference to the real or supposed processes and structures in the mind of its composer. This is Nattiez's poietic analysis, and we find analyses which take as supporting information such documents as composers' sketches. In recent decades we have set less store by the authority of composers, and so analysis which relates explicitly to cognitive structures more commonly now refers to the minds of listeners. This is like Nattiez's esthesic analysis, but the referents, at least for computational analysts, are generally not semiological but psychological. The approach of Lerdahl and Jackendoff, for example, explicitly aims to examine "the musical intuitions of a listener who is experienced in a musical idiom" (Lerdahl and Jackendoff, 1983, p. 1).

1.4.5 Analysis as Interpretation

One danger with the conception of analysis as revealing something of the cognitive structures engendered in listening to a piece of music is that it assumes that there is something fixed to reveal. The boundaries of 'the piece' in the listener's mind are likely to be even more fuzzy than those of an objective 'piece', and we have to contend also with multiple 'pieces' in the minds of multiple listeners.

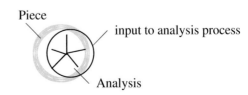

Fig. 1.4 Analysis reveals structure inherent in the piece

Piece   Analysis

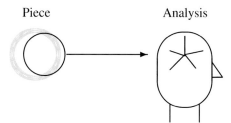

Fig. 1.5 Analysis as cognitive
structure

Several commentators, therefore, have abandoned any idea of analysis presenting
an authoritative explanation of how a piece 'works', and replaced this with either a
subjective 'works for me' or a shared or inter-subjective 'could work'. The analysis is
explicitly not *the* analysis of the piece, but one possible analysis. If we retain a stance
that the analysis shows structure in the piece, then we must abandon the analogies
of architecture and anatomy. The structure is no longer something definite in the
piece, but something which is *constructed* by the process of analysis. The relation
to listening persists, because listening too, in this perspective, constructs a structure,
and the structure in the analysis might match this one. A relation with the structure
latent or inherent in 'the piece' is not abandoned either: the configurations of notes
and sounds which convey the music to the listener, and which are the raw material
for the analyst, enable certain structures to be constructed, and hinder others.

One of the most eloquent advocates of this approach to analysis is Jim Samson,
who states that the reduction from 'surface' to 'structure' (the analytical process
under discussion here)

> far from providing an empirical explanation of a work, can only offer an interpretation of it,
> albeit one which may be constrained by something akin to a rule-governed system.
>
> (Samson, 1999, p. 45)

The resulting analysis depends on

> the role of observer, who [. . .] creates a theoretical predetermined and pre-analytic concept
> of the object to be analysed.
>
> (Samson, 1999, p. 46)

Samson goes on to relate this to the loss of faith within the natural sciences in 'the
stability of object description'. Some might therefore justifiably regard the difference
between theory-based 'explanation' offered by the natural sciences and theory-based
'interpretation' offered by music analysis to be just one of degree. There are several
important contrasts, however, that suggest that the difference lies not just in the degree
of impact of the observer's role, but also in a real divergence in method and focus.

1. The natural sciences generally examine many instances of a phenomenon; music
   analysis typically examines a single item.
2. The natural sciences derive principles to be applied in an objective and formulaic
   fashion; music analysis always presumes some degree of prior experience and
   understanding in the analyst and reader.

3. The principles of the natural sciences are tested by experiment in the real world; the principles of music analysis are generally tested against the agreement of other musicians.
4. Explanations in the natural sciences are acknowledged as imperfect, but the imperfections, embodied in differences between the outcomes of different plausible explanations, are minimized to a level where they can be safely ignored (to use Newtonian mechanics in the design of an aircraft is acceptable, for example, even though it is known that quantum mechanics is a more accurate explanation of physical phenomena); in music analysis, the differences between the outcomes of different plausible explanations are often the focus of debate, whose objective is not revision of principles to minimize error but rather to see one explanation prevail over another or, in more co-operative forums, to explore the different aspects of a piece explained by different analyses.

In music analysis, the analyst and reader are, or perhaps should be, always aware of what is *not* said, how the analysis might have been different, a point made strongly by Jonathan Dunsby in the editorial of the inaugural edition of *Music Analysis* (Dunsby, 1982).

In the conception of music analysis as interpretation, the structures shown are not simply 'discovered' in the piece but constructed, and the input to the process of analysis which is *not* part of the piece becomes crucial. (Note that, in practice, this input may not be recognized strictly as 'input' to the analytical process but may instead be embodied in the adaptation or design of the process itself prior to or in the course of analysis. It is nevertheless a kind of input, analogous in computation to the setting or modification of parameters.) Other perspectives on analysis do not deny that factors which are extrinsic to the piece are involved (as discussed above in Sect. 1.2.1), but these factors are regarded variously as a definite context or as the 'proper' environment of the piece. In the perspective of interpretation, the extrinsic factors are explicitly variable, and particular to the analysis: 'this is the way *I* hear this piece', or 'if we compare this piece to X (some other piece, or some theory of structure), the following pattern emerges'. To display this conception of analysis in graphical form, an additional arrow is required to show the crucial additional input to the analytical process, input which generally comes from the analyst herself or himself (Fig. 1.6).

I suspect most analysts follow this interpretative conception of analysis, even when they write as if they are revealing a structure intrinsic to the piece. (Perhaps

Piece   Analysis

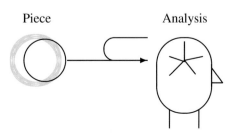

Fig. 1.6 Analysis as interpretation

they write in such a tone partly to imbue their writing with an aura of authority rather than because they believe other analyses are wrong.) Certainly this is how most analyses are used by their readers. Only students, I suspect, read an analysis to find the 'right' answers about the structure of a piece. Other analysts continually test their own conception of the piece's structure against what they read (at least, that is how I read analyses), and performing musicians seem to approach analyses with the same kind of curious but provisional approach taken to the performances of other musicians. Effectively, the analysis acts not to inform its readers of the piece's structure, but to propose a structure with which the readers may concur, often going so far as to seek to persuade readers to concur.

1.4.6 Computational Perspectives

Computational analysis, at first sight, seems most obviously to follow an ontology of analysis revealing the structure within a piece (Fig. 1.4). The input is data taken from the piece, and the analytical process generally finds specific structures (e.g., harmonies) or patterns (e.g., recurrences) within that data. Provided we accept the body of data as in some sense representing the piece, there is no reason to place the analysis in a locus different from the piece itself. On the other hand, there is also not necessarily any reason to believe that the particular structure in the output of the analytical process has a privileged status among the myriad other possible ways in which the input data could be structured. In other words, what authority does the computational process have to claim that the output is *the* structure of the piece or even that it is a significant, interesting or useful way of structuring the piece? (For some possible answers to the second half of this question, see Sect. 1.5.1.)

In the case of analysis by a human expert, the claim for a privileged, if not authoritative, status for the structure shown is implicit in the human's expertise. We tend not to ascribe expertise to computers, especially not in matters to do with the arts, so we are unlikely to regard computational analyses as carrying any particular authority. On the other hand, it is absolutely clear that the analysis which is the output of a computational analytical process *does* have a particular and unique status in the universe of possible analyses of the piece: it is the output of that particular analytical program when given that particular piece as input. If we know we want to find the structure which follows from a particular process, then a computational analysis, because it is free from bias, is *more* authoritative than a human one (provided the software properly implements the process). (In this regard, see also my analogy of computational analysis and forensic science in Sect. 1.5.2 below.)

Computational analysis can also sit comfortably with an ontology of analysis as revealing the structures of human musical cognition, though the epistemological issues around the correctness of the analysis are different from those arising from an ontology of analysis as revealing the structure in the piece (Sect. 1.5.1). The ontology with which computational analysis seems to sit least comfortably is that of analysis as interpretation. As discussed in Sect. 1.4.5, this kind of analysis places emphasis on the inputs to the process which are extrinsic to the piece and which cause one analysis to be different from another, even when the two share common music-theoretical bases. In the case of human expert analysis, these inputs come from multiple sources: the analyst's experience of listening to the piece, knowledge of other pieces and analyses, etc. To include all such possible inputs in a process of computational analysis would require modelling the entire human expert in all his or her aspects.

1.5 Epistemology

Some slippage from ontology to epistemology, which I remarked at the outset was a characteristic of writing on music analysis, can be detected also in the paragraphs above. From consideration of what an analysis *is*, one naturally and perhaps unavoidably moves to what it contains and why it contains what it does: from considering the nature of knowledge constituted by an analysis, one moves to considering the bases of that knowledge. The epistemology of music analysis in general is extremely fraught, so I will concentrate on some aspects of the epistemology of computational musical analysis only.

1.5.1 Correctness of Analysis

How do we know when a computational procedure produces a correct analysis? In one sense the analysis is always correct (provided the computer has not malfunctioned). That particular analytical procedure is not capable of producing any other output given the same input (remembering, in the case of stochastic procedures, that a random-number generator constitutes a kind of input). We are hardly likely, however, to set great store by the analysis of a piece produced by software which finds the structure of a melody in an entirely arbitrary manner such as to take every third note of the melody. The structures we want to find, as discussed above, have some special status which might be determined on one of several different bases. A more creditable analysis is likely to result from a procedure with a more sophisticated basis, and especially one where there are good grounds for believing that the basis implies musical significance also. A particularly promising approach involves a group of concepts around compression, minimum description length, information theory, and Kolmogorov complexity. As mentioned above (Sect. 1.3.1), there are good grounds for taking a parsimonious description of any phenomenon, including a piece of music, to be an explanation of it, and the more parsimonious the description the better the explanation. Software can find the description or 'analysis' of a piece which is the most parsimonious or at least close to the most parsimonious, and is therefore, in those theoretical terms, 'correct'. For applications of these ideas in computational music-analytical research, see Pearce and Wiggins (2012), Meredith (2012) and Chaps. 7 and 13 in this volume.

One way we might know if a computational analysis is correct is if its output matches analyses produced by human analysts. This is a path taken by several projects in computational analysis, for example (Anglade et al., 2010; Marsden, 2010; McVicar et al., 2011; Pauwels and Martens, 2014). In such cases, though, nothing is added by the computational analysis to explanation of the pieces analysed. An analytical dividend would come only from application of the same computational procedures to other pieces, and this step is rarely taken. The objective of this kind of research is not so much music analysis as the development of music theory, or at least of computational music theory.

Similar arguments apply if the objective of analysis is to reveal the structure of cognition of a piece. Here the comparator which the computer output is to match is not a ready-made analysis, but structures in the minds of listeners, and direct comparison is not possible. Instead some kind of indirect test is applied: listeners are asked to respond in a specific way; researchers infer what response would be expected if the cognitive structure matched the computational one, and determine a degree of match between the two accordingly. (An example can be seen in Pearce and Wiggins, 2012.)

One needs to be aware that a perfect match is almost certainly unobtainable in either case, if for no other reason than that the human-made analyses often do not match each other and human perceptions differ. Again we are faced with a question of approximation: how close to human analyses and perception do computational analyses need to be in order to be confident that the computational procedure can be applied to as-yet unanalysed pieces and produce useful results? To answer this question we need some way of quantifying the divergence between human analyses or perception and computational analyses, and we need to know how good is good enough. Solutions to the first of these—means of measuring divergence—are commonly proposed, and form the basis of the annual MIREX competitions (Downie, 2008) (in which the topics are by no means all strictly music-analytical) where program outputs are compared with a "ground truth" (i.e., pre-existing data which is taken to be correct). The second desideratum, however—knowing how good is good enough—is rarely addressed and cannot be, at least not without some better understanding of how analyses are to be *used*.

1.5.2 Usefulness of Analysis

If we follow the reasoning of Nattiez outlined above (Sect. 1.3.2), questions of the 'correctness' of computational analysis seem irrelevant. The computational step produces only an 'inventory' and the real analytical step follows from the application of other factors to select from the inventory and interpret what it shows. In this case the question is not so much whether the inventory is correct, but whether it is sufficiently complete: does it contain the information required to make a correct analysis of the piece? Even if the answer is affirmative, we cannot be confident of a good analytical outcome because that does not depend on the completeness alone. One way to maximize the completeness of the inventory is to maximize its size, but this also increases the quantity of useless information and makes finding the useful information more problematic. More realistically, we must ask how much useful information is present in comparison to how much useless information. A perfect outcome would be for the inventory to contain only the information which the analyst selects to construct the analysis (in which case the analytical step of selection becomes trivial and redundant, and we effectively return to the situation discussed above where an analysis is judged 'correct' by the degree to which it matches an analyst's conception). However, this perfection is unlikely to be achievable, and cannot reasonably be taken as a goal. Instead, if our objective is to use computer software as an aid in creating a 'good' analysis of a piece, and we will use our own judgement or that of some other expert to eventually determine a 'good' outcome, then our goal in software development should be a system which presents the user with an optimum which balances the risk of leaving out useful analytical information against the risk of obscuring the useful information by a heap of useless information.

If, on the other hand, we follow a conception of analysis as interpretation then we do *not* want the computational analysis to match a human analysis. Analyses are valued for their *difference* and for what is new that they can bring to our understanding of the piece analysed. It is highly unlikely, though, that any enriched understanding could come from merely random analyses. What bases are there for distinguishing a good analysis, meaning one capable of enriching understanding of a piece, from a poor analysis? (Indeed, how can we know whether or not someone's understanding of a piece has been enriched?) Would the understanding-enriching principles be different from the music-theoretic principles used in finding 'the structure' of a piece, as envisaged in Sect. 1.4.3 above?

One possibility is that there are principles which we can apply to determine whether or not an analysis is useful, but there is no known procedure which is guaranteed to produce an analysis which is useful. Certainly this is the case if the principle is whether or not a human reader finds the analysis useful. We might perhaps be able to predict this with some degree of accuracy, but we can never be certain. This is not a reason to discount such a course of development though. On the contrary, I suspect that in the long run the manner of computational analysis which will prove most profitable for analysis (rather than for the development of music theory) is one which is interactive, presenting a human user with the results of computational analysis and allowing that user to modify or intervene in the procedure to arrive at an acceptable or interesting result. An example of such an approach is the 'Automatic Timespan Tree Analyser' which implements Lerdahl and Jackendoff's method of analysis in interactive software (Hamanaka et al., 2006) (see also Chap. 9, this volume).

This and several earlier observations point to a potentially significant role in computational music analysis for machine learning, which could be applied in three ways. First, software might learn principles or parameter values from existing analyses (e.g., Pauwels and Martens, 2014). Second, following the idea that analysis seeks to uncover how a piece may be explained on principles which develop over the course of making the analysis (Sect. 1.3.1), the software might 'learn' the organization of the piece as it proceeds (see, e.g., Pearce and Wiggins, 2012). Third, the software might learn from the interactive input of the user. Fourth, the software might learn the probabilities of different musical configurations for use in an information-theoretic or minimum-description-length model of musical structure (see Chap. 7, this volume).

It was pointed out above (Sect. 1.4.6) that the authority of an analysis often derives from the expertise of the analyst. Machine learning has now advanced to the stage when computers can, within restricted domains, be *more* expert than humans. (In chess, for example, Garry Kasparov was beaten by IBM's Deep Blue computer in 1997, and more convincing computer victories against chess grand masters have followed.) This raises the intriguing prospect of computational music analysis which is, in some restricted sense, better than human analysis. Indeed, this appears to be the case already with software such as COSIATEC and SIATECCompress by David Meredith who presents evidence of the software finding patterns in pieces by Bach, Mozart and Chopin which can reasonably be claimed to be just as 'important' as other patterns in the same pieces identified by human analysts (Meredith, 2015).

Even in cases of super-human analysis, though, the extent to which the computer is doing 'music analysis' (as understood by musicologists) is uncertain. As suggested by the discussion above, we should probably re-imagine the objectives of the enterprise of computational music analysis. Instead of seeking a machine which analyses music automatically, we should think of computational music analysis as more like forensic science. Scientific examination of evidence can answer very specific questions, such as the likelihood that substances (e.g., DNA) found on the handle of a murder weapon came from the accused, with much greater accuracy than is possible without the application of scientific method. These answers can have a very significant role in court, but the scientific method does not ultimately determine the guilt or innocence of the accused; that continues to depend on the application of human judgement to the full range of evidence presented. Music-analytical computer software has advanced far beyond the stage of merely compiling an inventory of features or relations, as Nattiez envisaged, and can now answer complex questions about pieces of music. These answers are important and relevant for music analysis, but the final *musical* judgements, which determine how musicians might behave differently in future, will be made by people.

1.6 Conclusions

Music analysis is not a monolithic enterprise: different analysts do different things on different bases. Computational analysis therefore should also be multifarious. Most importantly, it should not and cannot be simply a machine reflection of the human activity. I conclude here with some reflections and recommendations about the ways in which computational analysis might profitably be used, and some recommendations on building software tools for music analysis.

1.6.1 Value of Computational Analysis

Computational music analysis needs to carve out a place for itself where it is not simply mimicry of human analysis, but a place which is not so distant from the human activity to prevent useful communication with musicians. We need to recall the potential value of computational analysis, the reasons we embark on this enterprise at all.

- Computational analyses have definite explicit bases, embodied in the analytical software used, whereas the bases for human analyses are, even when ostensibly explicit, subject to revision and reinterpretation.
- Computational analyses can handle large quantities of data, whether from within a single piece of music or from a large body of pieces of music.
- Computational analyses can formally test, try out or explore different hypotheses about musical structuring, without the risk of bias inherent in human analysis.
- Through techniques such as search and machine learning, computational analysis can find an 'explanation' for a piece which has a particular status among a well defined universe of alternative explanations, such as that it is the shortest possible, or most likely, description of the piece under certain assumptions.

The evidence that these can take music analysis into fruitful areas out of reach of human analysis has been emerging over the past decade or so. A clear sign is the two special issues of *Music Perception* dedicated to Corpus Methods (Temperley and VanHandel, 2013). In many of the papers in these two issues, conclusions were reported which would not have been possible without computational analysis. The level of sophistication in the analytical software used, however, was often at a much lower level than discussed in the contributions to this book. It would appear that we are still in the early stages of development of sophisticated analytical software capable of application to a large body of music to yield results in which we can have confidence. I suspect again that the reason is to do with error and approximation: research on a corpus usually involves conclusions based on statistics, and valid inference requires knowledge of the degree of error.

A second area in which computational analysis would show its distinctive value is by being embedded in other musical systems. As pointed out above (Sect. 1.4.5), music analysis rarely currently informs other musical activities. If an analysis really shows how a piece 'works', then could we not use that information to, for example, build a music recommendation system which offers us pieces of music which work well, or a system which adapts the music in a computer game to present coherently working segments of music aligned to the events in the game?

These possibilities might seem rather distant, but something similar is definitely within reach: the linking of analytical software to systems for rich visual display and sound output. Listening to music and reading an analysis are different activities, yet we do the second because we value the first. If we conceive of analysis as offering interesting interpretations of a piece of music (Sect. 1.4.5), then we should believe that analysis can influence our hearing of a piece, but for it to do so we have to somehow connect the analysis to the experience of listening. It is not at all self-evident how this should happen. To read something like 'bars 72 to 96 are dominant preparation' does not immediately translate to a way of hearing the piece. In illustration of this, I recount an event when I witnessed a visiting speaker at the university where I was a student. One of the staff of that university disagreed with the visiting speaker's interpretation of the harmony of a passage, and in response the speaker did not use logical argument to persuade his adversary but instead played the passage again, playing some of the chords louder. To cause someone to hear a passage in a particular way, one needs to give them a listening experience. One of the potential values of computational analysis is that its outputs can be readily rendered in sound or in many kinds of visual analogy using the same computational resources as in the making of the analysis.

1.6.2 Analytical Tool-Building

Those who make analytical software come up against the ontological and episte-mological issues of music analysis much more forcefully than do human analysts. The music expert can shift the analytical activity, select the material to consider and the conclusions to report, each in ways to soften the impact with ontological and epistemological problems. The computational researcher, by contrast, sets the software to work and cannot prevent it or its outputs from damage by such impact, except by once again rewriting the software, running it again and facing the same risks. It is for this reason that I believe computational researchers need to give these issues more explicit consideration than do human analysts.

- What is the input to the analytical software, and what is its status? Quantify, so far as possible, the differences between different possible inputs and the error inherent in them. What information comes from 'the piece' and what from elsewhere?
- What claim is being made about the analysis? Is it a structure with a particular status or property 'within the piece' (in which case be explicit about that status or property), or is it an image of the cognitive structures of the listener (in which case test it against psychological data), or is it some other kind of object?
- If the aim is to mimic some human analytical procedure, consider the degree of variance in human analysis. A perfect analysis from software of this kind is an impossibility if analysts do not agree in their analyses. Again, quantify error, and stop 'improving' the software when the error is close to the variance.
- If the aim is to offer possible interpretations of a piece, consider how the analyses will be presented to the user so that they can be usefully assessed. In particular, if the aim is to persuade the user of the benefit of hearing the piece in a particular way, use the computational resources to present the information in such a way as to make the transition from conceptual understanding to hearing more likely.

Finally, the objective of computational music analysis should probably not be to gen-erate 'an analysis' but rather, like forensic science, to answer specific music-analytical questions with a degree of complexity, speed and accuracy which is impossible by other means.

References

Anglade, A., Benetos, E., Mauch, M., and Dixon, S. (2010). Improving music genre classification using automatically induced harmony rules. *Journal of New Music Research*, 39(4):349–361.

Bent, I. (1987). *Analysis*. Macmillan.

Byrd, D. (1984). *Music notation by computer*. PhD thesis, Indiana University.

Byrd, D. (2013). Gallery of interesting music notation. http://homes.soic.indiana.edu/donbyrd/InterestingMusicNotation.html.

Downie, J. S. (2008). The music information retrieval evaluation exchange (2005-2007): A window into music information retrieval research. *Acoustical Science and Technology*, 29(3):247–255.

Dunsby, J. (1982). Editorial. *Music Analysis*, 1(1):3–8.

Goehr, L. (2007). *The Imaginary Museum of Musical Works: An Essay in the Philosophy of Music*. Oxford University Press, second edition.

Good, M. (2001). MusicXML for notation and analysis. In Hewlett, W. B. and Selfridge-Field, E., editors, *The Virtual Score: Representation, Retrieval, Restoration*, volume 12 of *Computing in Musicology*, pages 113–124. MIT Press.

Goodman, N. (1976). *Languages of Art: An Approach to a Theory of Symbols*. Hackett, second edition.

Hamanaka, M., Hirata, K., and Tojo, S. (2006). Implementing "A Generative Theory of Tonal Music". *Journal of New Music Research*, 35(4):249–277.

Keller, H. (1965). The chamber music. In Robbins Landon, H. and Mitchell, D., editors, *The Mozart Companion*, pages 90–137. Faber.

Keller, H. (1985). Functional analysis of Mozart's G minor quintet. *Music Analysis*, 4(1/2):73–94.

Lerdahl, F. and Jackendoff, R. (1983). *A Generative Theory of Tonal Music*. MIT Press.

Levinson, J. (1980). What a musical work is. *Journal of Philosophy*, 77(1):5–28.

Marsden, A. (2010). Schenkerian analysis by computer: A proof of concept. *Journal of New Music Research*, 39(3):269–289.

Mawer, D. (1999). Bridging the divide: embedding voice-leading analysis in string pedagogy and performance. *British Journal of Music Education*, 16(2):179–195.

McVicar, M., Ni, Y., Santos-Rodriguez, R., and De Bie, T. (2011). Using online chord databases to enhance chord recognition. *Journal of New Music Research*, 40(2):139–152.

Meredith, D. (2007). *Computing pitch names in tonal music: A comparative analysis of pitch spelling algorithms*. PhD thesis, Faculty of Music, University of Oxford.

Meredith, D. (2012). Music analysis and Kolmogorov complexity. In *Proceedings of the 19th Colloquio di Informatica Musicale (XIX CIM)*, Trieste, Italy.

Meredith, D. (2015). Music analysis and point-set compression. *Journal of New Music Research*, 44(3). In press.

Nattiez, J.-J. (1982). Varèse's 'Density 21.5': A study in semiological music analysis. *Music Analysis*, 1(3):243–340.

Nattiez, J.-J. (1990). *Music and Discourse: Towards a Semiology of Music*. Princeton University Press.

Pauwels, J. and Martens, J.-P. (2014). Combining musicological knowledge about chords and keys in a simultaneous chord and local key estimation system. *Journal of New Music Research*, 43(3):318–330.

Pearce, M. and Wiggins, G. (2012). Auditory expectation: The information dynamics of music perception and cognition. *Topics in Cognitive Science*, 4(4):625–652.

Pople, A., editor (1994). *Theory, Analysis and Meaning in Music*. Cambridge University Press.

Réti, R. (1962). *The Thematic Process in Music*. Macmillan.

Réti, R. (1967). *Thematic Patterns in the Sonatas of Beethoven*. Faber.

Samson, J. (1999). Analysis in context. In Cook, N. and Everist, M., editors, *Rethinking Music*, pages 35–54. Oxford University Press.

Sapp, C. (2014). 371 Four-part Chorales by J.S. Bach in the Humdrum file format. https://github.com/craigsapp/bach-371-chorales.

Sleator, D. and Temperley, D. (2003). The Melisma music analyzer. http://www.link.cs.cmu.edu/melisma/.

Sturm, B. L. (2014). The state of the art ten years after a state of the art: Future research in music information retrieval. *Journal of New Music Research*, 43(2):147–172.

Temperley, D. and VanHandel, L. (2013). Introduction to the special issue on corpus methods. *Music Perception*, 31(1):1–3.

van Kranenburg, P. (2008). On measuring musical style—The case of some disputed organ fugues in the J. S. Bach (BWV) catalogue. *Computing in Musicology*, 15:120–137.

Whorley, R. P., Wiggins, G. A., Rhodes, C., and Pearce, M. T. (2013). Multiple viewpoint systems: Time complexity and the construction of domains for complex music viewpoints in the harmonization problem. *Journal of New Music Research*, 42(3):237–266.

Part II
Chords and Pitch Class Sets

Chapter 2
The Harmonic Musical Surface and Two Novel Chord Representation Schemes

Emilios Cambouropoulos

Abstract Selecting an appropriate representation for chords is important for encoding pertinent harmonic aspects of the musical surface, and, at the same time, is crucial for building effective computational models for music analysis. This chapter, initially, addresses musicological, perceptual and computational aspects of the harmonic musical surface. Then, two novel general chord representations are presented: the first, the General Chord Type (GCT) representation, is inspired by the standard Roman numeral chord type labelling, but is more general and flexible so as to be applicable to any idiom; the second, the Directed Interval Class (DIC) vector, captures the intervallic content of a transition between two chords in a transposition-invariant idiom-independent manner. Musical examples and preliminary evaluations of both encoding schemes are given, illustrating their potential to form a basis for harmonic processing in the domain of computational musicology.

2.1 Introduction

Research in computational musicology and, more specifically, computational music analysis commonly assumes the fundamental concept of the *musical surface*, i.e., a minimal discrete representation of the musical sound continuum in terms of note-like events (each note described by pitch, onset, duration, and possibly dynamic markings and timbre/instrumentation). The musical surface is assumed to be merely an unstructured sequence of atomic note events, such as score notes or a piano-roll representation. Taking as a starting point this elementary musical surface, abstract structures may be determined, such as grouping/segmentation, metre, chords and motivic categories.

Emilios Cambouropoulos
School of Music Studies, Aristotle University of Thessaloniki, Thessaloniki, Greece
e-mail: emilios@mus.auth.gr

© Springer International Publishing Switzerland 2016   31
D. Meredith (ed.), *Computational Music Analysis*,
DOI 10.1007/978-3-319-25931-4_2

In this chapter we will focus on aspects of the musical surface that pertain to musical harmony. Challenging the 'standard' understanding (at least in the domain of computational musicology) of the musical surface as being the note level of a musical piece, it will be maintained that chords as wholes should be considered as an integral part of the musical surface. The emergence of this harmonic musical surface involves rather complex mechanisms that require, among other things, consonance/dissonance discrimination, chord-type abstraction, root-finding and function categorization (leaving aside non-harmonic factors such as rhythm, melody and voice separation).

A novel general representation of chord types is proposed that is appropriate for encoding tone simultaneities in any harmonic context whether it be tonal, modal, jazz, octatonic or even atonal. This *General Chord Type* (GCT) representation allows for the rearrangement of the notes of a harmonic simultaneity or pitch set, such that abstract, idiom-specific types of chords may be derived. The GCT algorithm finds the maximal subset of notes of a given note set that contains only consonant intervals, employing a user-specified consonance/dissonance classification; this maximal subset forms the base upon which the chord type is built. The proposed representation is ideal for hierarchic harmonic systems such as the tonal system and its many variations (actually the GCT is designed such that properties of the standard Roman-numeral encoding scheme are naturally accommodated), but adjusts to any other harmonic system such as post-tonal, atonal music, or traditional polyphonic systems. It thus allows for automatic chord-type labelling (resembling traditional Roman numeral encoding) in diverse musical idioms. The application of the GCT algorithm is illustrated on a small set of examples from a variety of idioms and tested on the Kostka–Payne harmonic dataset (Temperley, 2001b).

A proposal for representing chord transitions in an idiom-independent manner is also introduced. A harmonic transition between two chords can be represented by a *Directed Interval Class* (DIC) vector (this is an adaptation of Lewin's *interval function* between two collections of notes—see Sect. 2.4). This representation allows for the encoding of chord transitions at a level higher than individual notes that is transposition-invariant and idiom-independent (analogous to pitch intervals that represent transitions between notes). The proposed 12-dimensional vector encodes the frequency of occurrence of each distinct *directional* interval class (from 0 to 6 with $+/-$ for direction) between a pair of notes in two successive chords. Apart from octave equivalence and interval inversion equivalence, this representation preserves directionality of intervals (up or down). The proposed DIC representation has been evaluated on a harmonic recognition task (specifically, the identification of harmonic queries in a small database consisting of pieces from diverse idioms). The DIC vector representation is very general and may be useful in tasks such as chord pattern recognition tasks, but is rather too abstract to be used in tasks such as sophisticated harmonic analysis or melodic harmonization (for which the GCT representation is more appropriate).

In the following sections, the notion of musical surface will first be discussed in perceptual, musicological and computational terms. Then the GCT representation will be described. Finally, the DIC vector chord transition encoding will be presented.

2.2 The Harmonic Music Surface and Chord Representation Schemes

In this section, it is maintained that note simultaneities are perceived as chord types (e.g., major, minor, dominant seventh, etc.) prior to establishing more elementary aspects such as individual pitch octave information, note doubling, note omission and chord inversion. This intuition is reflected in established musicological theoretical typologies such as the standard guitar-like chord encoding or Roman numeral analytic labels or even pc-set categories. Advantages and shortcomings of such chord formalisms will be discussed primarily in relation to computational music analysis. A more extended discussion on representing the musical surface is given by Cambouropoulos (2010).

Jackendoff (1987), by analogy with the linguistic surface of phonemes, defines the *musical surface* as being the "lowest level of representation that has musical significance" (p. 219) and suggests that "standard musical notation represents the pitch-events of the musical surface by means of symbols for discrete pitch and duration" (p. 218). Sloboda (1985) suggests that the "basic 'phoneme' of music is a 'note'" (p. 24) and presents empirical evidence for categorical perception of pitch and duration. Should the *note*, however, be considered as the lowest level of representation that has musical significance and perceptual relevance?

In terms of co-sounding events, there is evidence that pitch intervals and chords are commonly perceived by listeners in a holistic manner, prior to their being perceived in terms of their constituent parts. Over eighty years ago, Vernon (1934), a Gestalt psychologist, suggested that ordinary listeners frequently perceive holistically a more or less complex auditory figure, such as a complex tone or a chord, without knowing or being able to analyse its constituent elements. Empirical research has shown that listeners perceive musical intervals categorically (see Burns, 1999; Handel, 1989; Smith et al., 1994). Categorical perception applies to chords as well, as has been shown by Locke and Kellar (1973). It is suggested that pitch intervals or chords are actually closer to the categorically perceived phonemic units of language than isolated notes.

Due to octave equivalence and transpositional pitch interval equivalence, harmonic pitch intervals and chords are considered 'equivalent' even though their constituent pitches may be placed in different octaves. Empirical research has shown that listeners confuse pairs of tones that are related by inversion (Deutsch, 2012) and that chord positioning does not affect recognizing components of a chord—i.e., that chords in different positions are essentially equivalent (Hubbard and Datteri, 2001).

Parncutt (1989) provides a psychoacoustic explanation of how chords are heard. Just as our perceptual mechanisms analyse a complex periodic sound into partials and then re-integrate them into a single percept, so chords can be heard as a single entity with a single perceived root, rather than three or more individual co-sounding tones. Parncutt suggests that the same factors that govern the perception of individual pitches govern the perception of chords. Parncutt (1997) proposes an extended model that calculates the perceptual root of a chord from its pitch classes, voicing, and the prevailing tonality. Parncutt's approach to chord perception is in line with the suggestion in this chapter that chords are perceived at the surface level as single integrated entities rather than sets of constituent atomic notes.

Identifying a set of co-sounding partials or notes as, for instance, a major, minor or diminished chord involves additional culture-specific knowledge that is acquired via exposure to a certain idiom. "Chord recognition is the result of a successful memory search in which a tone series is recognized as a pattern stored in long-term memory" (Povel and Jansen, 2001, p. 185). Template-matching models (Parncutt, 1994) are integrated in cognitive mechanisms of musical listening and are responsible for the extraction of musically pertinent entities from sound at the surface level (the musical surface is specific to a musical idiom in a similar way to that in which phonological structure is language-specific). The above discussion supports the idea that chords tend to be perceived at the surface level as single integrated entities, rather than agglomerates of independent atomic notes.

The reduction of the sound continuum into more abstract (symbolic) entities such as notes, chords, trills, and so on, may be attributed to general human cognitive mechanisms that aim to reduce sensory information into smaller more manageable discrete quantities (categorical perception). What are the grounding principles that enable this reduction? More specifically, what are the principles that allow the integration/segregation of distinct harmonics/tones into single entities or coherent 'wholes'? The basic perceptual mechanisms that enable the breaking down of the acoustic signal into more manageable units and successions of units (streams) have been investigated extensively in the field of auditory scene analysis (Bregman, 1994). These principles can be applied or adapted to account for musical practices of voice separation/integration and voice leading (Huron, 2001). For instance, principles such as tonal fusion, onset synchrony and pitch co-modulation (Huron, 2001) may play an important role in the fusion of co-sounding entities into larger percepts such as chords (e.g., greatest fusion in parallel motion of octave-related tones).

In recent years, a number of voice separation algorithms have emerged; these algorithms mostly attempt to separate polyphonic unstructured note complexes into a number of monophonic voices (see, e.g., Jordanous, 2008, and Chap. 6, this volume). Cambouropoulos (2008) adopts a different approach in which multi-note sonorities are allowed within individual 'voices'. Allowing both horizontal and vertical integration allows the algorithm to perform well not only in polyphonic music that has a fixed number of 'monophonic' lines, but in the general case where both polyphonic and homophonic elements are mixed together. In this sense, the musical surface is considered as consisting of both simple notes organized in melodic streams, and chords organized in chordal streams (such streams may appear independently, or in parallel, or may overlap).

A common underlying assumption in much cognitive and computational modelling of musical understanding is that musical structural processing starts at the musical surface and proceeds towards higher structural levels, such as metre, rhythmic patterns, melodic motives, harmonic structure and so on. Lerdahl and Jackendoff's (1983) influential theory is grounded on this assumption:

The musical surface, basically a sequence of notes, is only the first stage of musical cognition. Beyond the musical surface, structure is built out of the confluence of two independent hierarchical dimensions of organization: rhythm and pitch.

(Jackendoff and Lerdahl, 2006, p. 37)

It is often an underlying assumption in computational research that from audio the score may be extracted and then higher-level processing is possible.

However, as Cemgil et al. (2006) have pointed out,

one of the hard problems in musical scene analysis is automatic music transcription, that is, the extraction of a human readable and interpretable description from a recording of a music performance.

Indeed, research in automated music transcription has shown that a purely bottom-up approach (from audio to score) is not possible; higher-level music processing is necessary to assist basic multi-pitch and onset extraction techniques so as to reach acceptable transcription results. Ryynänen and Klapuri (2008, p. 73) have observed that

nowadays the concept of automatic music transcription includes several topics such as multipitch analysis, beat tracking and rhythm analysis, transcription of percussive instruments, instrument recognition, harmonic analysis and chord transcription, and music structure analysis.

Some of the 'higher level' musical processes that are necessary for transcription are addressed by Cambouropoulos (2010). It is suggested, not only that higher-level processing influences the formation of the musical surface, but that some processes that are considered 'higher-level' are actually necessary for the formation of the surface per se, which means, essentially, that they are at or below the musical surface. It is maintained that, for instance, beat structure, chord simultaneities and voice separation are internal 'primitive' processes of the musical surface, that are necessary for the surface to emerge.

For the sake of simplicity, in this chapter, we deal solely with purely symbolic, isorhythmic, homophonic textures (i.e., sequences of chords without secondary embellishment notes). Harmonic reduction (i.e., the abstraction of main chord notes from a musical work) is anything but a trivial task. Reduction relies not only on rhythm, metric position and melodic qualities (e.g., passing or neighbour notes), but also on harmony per se. That is, harmonic knowledge is paramount in establishing which notes are secondary and can be omitted. For instance, access to previously learned harmonic context in a given idiom (chord patterns) may assist the selection of appropriate chords that give rise to acceptable chord progressions (Mauch et al., 2010). The representation schemes presented in the following sections (especially the GCT) can be extended in the future so as to facilitate the recognition of harmonies in an unreduced collection of notes or unreduced stream of sounds (this is beyond the scope of the current chapter).

Researchers that work on symbolic music data (e.g., quantized MIDI or encodings of scores) commonly assume that the formation of the musical surface (i.e., the notes) from audio requires a potentially large amount of processing; once, however, the surface is formed, the road to higher-level processing (such as beat tracking, metre induction, chord analysis, pattern extraction, and so on) is open. On the other hand, researchers that work on music audio often leave aside the whole question of musical surface and attempt to extract high-level information (e.g., harmonic patterns, structural segmentation, music similarity, cover song identification) directly from audio. We suggest that the whole discussion on the musical surface, apart from being of theoretical interest, may make researchers more aware of the need to think more carefully when deciding which primitive starting representation to use for their systems (audio, expressive or quantized MIDI, pitch classes, notes, chords, etc.); how much processing is already implicitly 'embodied' in this primitive representation; and what kind of information can be extracted 'naturally' from the selected starting representation.

Computational systems developed for harmonic analysis and/or harmonic generation (e.g., melodic harmonization), rely on chord labelling that is relevant and characteristic of particular idioms. There exist different typologies for encoding note simultaneities that embody different levels of harmonic information/abstraction and cover different harmonic idioms. For instance, for tonal musics, chord notations such as the following are commonly used: figured bass (pitch classes denoted above a bass note—no concept of 'chord'); popular music guitar-style notation or jazz notation (absolute chord); and Roman numeral encoding (chord function relative to a key) (Laitz, 2012). For atonal and other non-tonal systems, pc-set theoretic encodings (Forte, 1973) may be employed.

For computational models of tonal music, Harte et al.'s (2005) representation provides a systematic, context-independent syntax for representing chord symbols which can easily be written and understood by musicians, and, at the same time, is simple and unambiguous to parse with computer programs. This chord representation is very useful for manually annotating tonal music—mostly genres such as pop, rock and jazz that use guitar-style notation. However, it cannot be automatically extracted from chord reductions and is not designed to be used in non-tonal musics.

Two question are raised and addressed in the remainder of this chapter. First, is it possible to devise a 'universal' chord representation that captures features of hierarchic pitch systems and adapts to different harmonic idioms? Is it possible to determine a mechanism that, given some fundamental idiom features, such as pitch hierarchy and consonance/dissonance classification, can automatically abstract chord types and encode pitch simultaneities in a pertinent manner for the idiom at hand? A second question regards chord transitions: is a relative pitch encoding of chords possible such that chord *transitions* (i.e., intervallic content) are captured without recourse to constituent chords? The first question will be addressed in the next section, the second in Sect. 2.4.

It should be noted that the representations and processes reported in the following sections do not explicitly deal with the issue of harmonic surface, but rather with two relatively simple schemes of chord encoding that capture different aspects of the harmonic surface. No explicit cognitive claims are made; however, it is suggested that these representations may capture some properties of chords that are cognitively relevant and are potentially linked to the notion of the harmonic surface. The main objective of the proposed representations is to provide appropriate, general encodings of aspects of the harmonic surface that may be useful in various computational music-analytic tasks, such as harmonic analysis, chord sequence similarity, and harmonic recognition. Hopefully, the proposed representations may be incorporated in more sophisticated music surface extraction and processing schemes, providing a useful step that links the sub-symbolic domain with higher-level musical structure.

2.3 The General Chord Type (GCT) Representation

Harmonic analysis focuses on describing the harmonic content of pitch collections and patterns within a given music context in terms of harmonic labels, classes, functions and so on. Harmonic analysis is a rather complex musical task that involves not only finding roots and labelling chords within a key, but also segmentation (points of chord change), identification of non-chord notes, metric information and other aspects of musical context (Temperley, 2001a, 2012). In this section, we focus on the core problem of labelling chords within a given pitch hierarchy (e.g., key). We assume, for simplicity, that a full harmonic reduction, identifying the main harmonic notes, is available as input to the model along with key and modulation annotations.

In trying to tackle issues of tonal hierarchy, a novel representation of chord types is proposed that is appropriate for encoding tone simultaneities (or more generally pitch sets) in any harmonic context (whether it be tonal, modal, jazz, octatonic or even atonal). The *General Chord Type* (GCT) representation, allows the rearrangement of the notes of a harmonic simultaneity such that abstract, idiom-specific types of chords may be derived; this encoding is inspired by the standard Roman numeral chord type labelling, but is more general and flexible. Given a consonance/dissonance classification of intervals (that reflects sensory and/or culturally-dependent notions of consonance and dissonance), and a scale, the GCT algorithm finds the maximal subset of notes of a given note simultaneity that contains only consonant intervals; this maximal subset forms the base upon which the chord type is built. The lowest note of the base is the root of the chord. The proposed chord type representation, takes as its starting point the common-practice tonal chord representation (for a tonal context, it is equivalent to the standard Roman-numeral harmonic encoding), but is more general as it can be applied to other non-standard tonal systems such as modal and even atonal harmony. This representation is based on notions drawn primarily from the domain of psychoacoustics and music cognition (such as octave equivalence, root, relative root, consonance, parsimony), and, at the same time, 'adjusts' to different culture-specific contexts of scales, tonal hierarchies and rankings of consonance and dissonance. Cambouropoulos et al. (2014) provide a more extended discussion on the background concepts underlying the GCT model.

At the heart of the GCT representation is the idea that the *base* of a note simultaneity should be 'consonant' (within some particular musical idiom). The GCT algorithm tries to find a maximal subset that is consonant; the rest of the notes that create dissonant intervals to one or more notes of the chord base form the chord *extension*. The GCT representation has common characteristics with the stack-of-thirds and the virtual pitch root-finding methods for tonal music, but has differences as well (see Cambouropoulos et al., 2014). Moreover, the user can define which intervals are considered consonant; thus giving rise to different encodings. As will be shown in the following subsections, the GCT representation naturally encapsulates the structure of tonal chords and, at the same time, is very flexible and can readily be adapted to different harmonic systems.

2.3.1 Description of the GCT Algorithm

Given a classification of intervals into the categories consonant and dissonant (i.e., binary values) and an appropriate scale background (i.e., scale with tonic), the GCT algorithm computes, for a given multi-tone simultaneity, the 'optimal' ordering of pitches such that a maximal subset of consonant intervals appears at the base of the ordering (left-hand side) in the most compact form. Since a tonal centre (key) is given, the position within the given scale is automatically calculated.

The input to the algorithm is the following:

Consonance vector The user defines which intervals are consonant/dissonant. A 12-dimensional vector is employed in which each value corresponds to a pitch interval from 0 to 11 (in the current version of the algorithm, Boolean values are used (i.e., consonant=1, dissonant=0).[1] For instance, the vector $[1,0,0,1,1,1,0,1,1,1,0,0]$ means that the unison, minor and major third, perfect fourth and fifth, minor and major sixth intervals are consonant; dissonant intervals are the seconds, sevenths and the tritone; this specific vector is referred to in this text as the 'common-practice' or 'tonal consonance' vector.

Pitch Scale Hierarchy The pitch hierarchy (if any) is given in the form of scale tones and a tonic. For instance, a D major scale is given as $2,[0,2,4,5,7,9,11]$ and an A minor pentatonic scale as $9,[0,3,5,7,10]$. Other more sophisticated encodings of

---

[1] The current version of the GCT algorithm requires a symmetric consonance vector for complementary intervals; for instance, if interval 2 is dissonant so is interval 10 (i.e., major second and minor seventh are both dissonant). This means, essentially, that the vector can be shortened to correspond to intervals from 0 (unison) to 6 (tritone). However, in principle, one may adjust the algorithm so as to allow different consonance values for complementary intervals (e.g., major seventh less dissonant than minor second). For this reason, the full 12-interval vector is retained. Additionally, non-binary consonance/dissonance values may be used, allowing for a more refined consonance vector. Instead of filling in the consonance vector with 0s and 1s, it can be filled with fractional values that reflect degrees of consonance derived from perceptual experiments (see, e.g., Hutchinson and Knopoff, 1978) or values that reflect culturally-specific preferences. Such values may improve the algorithm's performance and resolve some ambiguities in certain cases.

pitch hierarchies are possible, but this simple encoding suffices for the purposes of this study.

Input chord   A list of pitch classes (MIDI pitch numbers modulo 12).

The GCT algorithm, shown in Fig. 2.1, encodes most chord types 'correctly' in the standard tonal system. For instance, the note simultaneity [C,D,F♯,A] or $[0,2,6,9]$ in a G major key is interpreted as $[7,[0,4,7,10]]$, i.e., as a dominant seventh chord. Figure 2.2 shows an example of how the GCT algorithm labels a chord.

The algorithm successfully labels most tonal chords (see Sect. 2.3.2 and Cambouropoulos et al., 2014 for examples). However, it is undecided in some cases, and even makes 'mistakes' in other cases. In most instances of multiple encodings, it is suggested that these ideally should be resolved by taking into account other harmonic factors (e.g., bass line, harmonic functions, tonal context, etc.). For instance, the algorithm gives two possible encodings for a $[0,2,5,9]$ pc-set, namely minor seventh chord or major chord with added sixth (i.e., $[2,[0,3,7,10]]$ and $[5,[0,4,7,9]]$, respectively); such ambiguity may be resolved if tonal context is taken into account. For the $[0,3,4,7]$ pc-set with root 0, the algorithm produces two answers: a major chord with extension $[0,[0,4,7,15]]$ and a minor chord with extension $[0,[0,3,7,16]]$. This ambiguity may be resolved if key context is taken into account. For instance, $[0,4,7,15]$ would be selected in a C major or G major context and $[0,3,7,16]$ in a C minor or F minor context. Symmetric chords, such as the augmented chord or the diminished seventh chord, are inherently ambiguous; the algorithm suggests multiple encodings which can be resolved only by taking into account the broader harmonic

---

Algorithm 1 GCT algorithm (core)

Input: (i) the pitch scale (tonality), (ii) a vector of the intervals considered consonant, (iii) the pitch class set (pc–set) of a note simultaneity
Output: The roots and types of the possible chords describing the simultaneity
1: find all maximal subsets of pairwise consonant tones
2: select maximal subsets of maximum length
3: **for** all selected maximal subsets **do**
4:    order the pitch classes of each maximal subset in the most compact form (chord 'base')
5:    add remaining pcs ('extensions') above highest element of chord base (add octave, if needed)
6:    the lowest tone of the chord is the 'root'
7:    transpose the tones of the chord so that the lowest becomes 0
8:    find position of the 'root' with respect to the given tonal centre (pitch scale)
9: **end for**

Fig. 2.1 The GCT algorithm

Input: G major scale: $[7,[0,2,4,5,7,9,11]]$
Input: Consonance vector: $[1,0,0,1,1,1,0,1,1,1,0,0]$
  – Input $[50,60,66,69,74]$
    – Input converted to pc-set: $[0,2,6,9]$
    – Maximal consonant subset: $[2,6,9]$
    – Rewrite in narrowest range: $[2,6,9]$
    – Dissonant tone 0 goes to the end (i.e., by adding an octave): $[2,6,9,12]$
    – Lowest tone is root, i.e., 2 (note D)
    – Chord in root position: $[2,[0,4,7,10]]$ (i.e., major chord with minor seventh)
    – Relative position in key: root is 7 semitones above the tonic G
    – Chord in relative position: $[7,[0,4,7,10]]$
    – No other maximal subset exists.
Output: $[7,[0,4,7,10]]$ (i.e., dominant seventh chord)

Fig. 2.2 GCT chord labelling example

context (primarily the next chord). A half-diminished seventh chord $[0,3,6,10]$, is incorrectly encoded as $[0,3,7,9]$, i.e., minor chord with added 6th, since the base chord of the half-diminished chord is a diminished fifth interval (i.e., tritone) which is dissonant and should be avoided. A preliminary evaluation of the GCT algorithm was also carried out on the Kostka–Payne dataset (see Sect. 2.3.2).

Since the aim of this algorithm is not to perform sophisticated harmonic analysis, but rather to find a practical and efficient encoding for tone simultaneities (to be used, for instance, in creative, computer-assisted, harmonic generation that employs combination of harmonic components from diverse idioms—see Sect. 2.3.2), we decided to extend the algorithm by adding the additional steps shown in Fig. 2.3, so that it outputs in every case a single chord type for each simultaneity (no ambiguity).

The additional steps select chord type $[2,[0,3,7,10]]$ over $[5,[0,4,7,9]]$ for the $[0,2,5,9]$ pc-set (see above), as this encoding has maximal overlapping between the two maximal subsets. The maximal overlapping step of the GCT algorithm, in the case of the 'standard' tonal consonance vector, amounts to a preference for the 'stack of thirds' principle of common tonal chord labelling. The second additional step (if the first step gives more than one option) prefers a chord encoding where non-scale notes are at the end (this rule is not robust and requires further examination). The last step for finding a unique solution is just a simple temporary fix; ideally, the GCT algorithm should be extended to include other factors such as bass note, next chord and, more generally, harmonic context to resolve ambiguity.

2.3.2 Examples of Harmonic Analysis with GCT

An example harmonic analysis of a Bach Chorale phrase illustrates the proposed GCT chord representation (Fig. 2.4). For a tonal context, chord types are optimized

---

Algorithm 2 GCT Algorithm (additional steps)—for unique encoding

---
1: **if** more than one maximal subset **then**
2:      Overlapping of maximal subsets: create a sequence of maximal subsets by ordering them so as to have maximal overlapping between them and keep the maximal subset that appears first in the sequence as base of the chord.
3:      Avoid non-scale notes in the base: if more than one merged sequence, prefer maximal subset at the base that contains only pcs that appear in the given scale (tonal context).
4:      If the above do not give a unique solution, choose the consonant maximal subset that was calculated first as base.
5: **end if**
        Additional adjustment: for dyads, in a tonal context, prefer perfect fifth over perfect fourth, and prefer seventh to second intervals.

Fig. 2.3 The GCT algorithm: additional steps to generate unique encodings

such that pcs at the left-hand side of chords contain only consonant intervals (i.e., thirds and sixths, and perfect fourth and fifths). For instance, the dominant 7th chord is written as $[0,4,7,10]$ since set $[0,4,7]$ contains only consonant intervals whereas 10, which introduces dissonances, is placed on the right-hand side—this way the relationship between major chords and dominant seventh chords remains rather transparent and is easily detectable (Kaliakatsos-Papakostas et al., 2015). Within the given D major key context, it is simple to determine the position of a chord type with respect to the tonic. For example, $[7,[0,4,7,10]]$ means a dominant seventh chord whose root is 7 semitones above the tonic. This way we have an encoding that is analogous to the standard Roman numeral encoding (Fig. 2.4, top row). If the tonal context is changed, and we have a chromatic scale context (arbitrary 'tonic' is 0, i.e., note C) and we consider all intervals equally 'consonant', we get the second GCT analysis in Fig. 2.4, which amounts to normal orders (not prime forms) in a standard pc-set analysis. For tonal music, this pc-set-like analysis is weak as it misses out or obscures important tonal hierarchical relationships. Note that relative 'roots' to the 'tonic' 0 are preserved as they can be used in harmonic generation tasks (see comment on transposition values in the Messiaen example in Fig. 2.7 below).

Three further examples are presented below that illustrate the application of the GCT algorithm on diverse harmonic textures. The first example (Fig. 2.5) is taken from Beethoven's *Andante Favori*. In this example, GCT encodes classical harmony in a straightforward manner. All instances of the tonic chord are tagged as $0,[0,4,7]$; the dominant seventh (inverted or not) is $7,[0,4,7,10]$ and it appears once without the fifth $[7]$; the third-from-last chord is a minor seventh on the second degree encoded as $2,[0,3,7,10]$; the second and fourth chords are Neapolitan chords

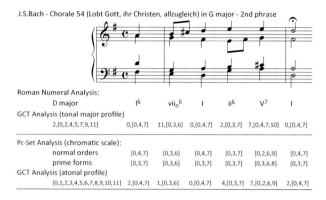

Fig. 2.4 Chord analysis of a Bach chorale phrase by means of traditional Roman numeral analysis, pc-sets and two versions of the GCT algorithm

encoded as $1, [0,4,7]$ (which means a major chord on the lowered second degree) with a secondary dominant in between.

The second example, in an extended chromatic style, is from Richard Strauss' *Till Eulenspiegel*. Piston (1978) provides a tentative partial analysis (Fig. 2.6). He suggests that "any generalized appearance of tonality breaks down under the weight of the rapid harmonic rhythm and distantly related harmonic functions" (p. 522). The GCT algorithm was applied to this excerpt for the standard tonal consonance vector, and for the key of F major $(5, [0,2,4,5,7,9,11])$. The algorithm assigns chord types correctly to all chords (in agreement with Piston's analysis) except for the seventh chord, which is a symmetric diminished seventh, for which the algorithm selects the wrong root. Additionally, the algorithm assigns chord types to all chords that have been left unanalysed by Piston. Of course, excluding some chords is an integral part of the analytic process (the analyst decides which chords are structurally important and should be labelled); the algorithm is not sophisticated enough to make such decisions. However, the chord types the GCT algorithm assigns to these chords are not arbitrary and may be potentially useful for an automated harmonic reasoning system.

In the third example, from a piece by Messiaen (Fig. 2.7), the second half of the excerpt is a transposed repetition (lowered by three semitones) of the first half.

Fig. 2.5 Reduction of bars 189–198 of Beethoven's *Andante Favori*. Top row: manual Roman numeral harmonic analysis; bottom row: GCT analysis. GCT successfully encodes all chords, including the Neapolitan sixth chord (the pedal G flat note in the third chord is omitted)

Fig. 2.6 Bars 1–3 of R. Strauss' *Till Eulenspiegel*. Partial harmonic analysis by W. Piston and chord types determined by the GCT algorithm (condensed GCT encoding—without commas)

The GCT can be used to capture transposition-invariant matching, if the 'roots' of chords are replaced by intervals between 'roots'. This way the representation becomes transposition-invariant. In this instance, the interval pattern between 'roots' of the first and second parts is $[+6, -3, +3, +3, -3]$ for the 'tonal' version, and $[-4, -3, +3, -2, -3]$ for the 'atonal' version. This is a reason for preserving the 'roots' (relative to an arbitrary reference pitch class: pc 0) in the atonal version. In pitch class set theory, normal orders do not have 'roots'; however, they have transposition values (T0-T11) in relation to a reference pc (normally pc 0). The normal orders with transposition values of pc-set theory are equivalent to the GCT for the 'atonal' consonance vector.

We tested the GCT algorithm on the Kostka–Payne dataset (Temperley, 2001b). This dataset consists of the 46 excerpts that are longer than 8 measures from the workbook accompanying Kostka and Payne's (1995) theory textbook. Given the local tonality (key), the GCT algorithm was applied to all the Kostka–Payne excerpts. Then, the resulting GCTs were compared to the Kostka–Payne ground truth (i.e., the Roman numeral analysis not taking into account inversions). From the 919 chords of the dataset, GCT encodes fully in compliance with the human analysis 846 chords, and 72 chords are labelled differently. This means that the algorithm labels correctly 92% of all the chords. Twenty-three mislabelled chords were diminished seventh chords—these symmetric chords can have as their root any of the four constituent notes; twenty-two half-diminished chords $[0, 3, 6, 10]$ were labelled as minor chords with added sixth $[0, 3, 7, 9]$; seventeen cases had a salient note missing (e.g., diminished chord without root, dominant seventh without third, half-diminished seventh without

Fig. 2.7 Reduction of the first six bars of O. Messiaen's *Quartet for the End of Time, Quartet VII*. The piece is based on the octatonic scale: $[0, 1, 3, 4, 6, 7, 9, 10]$. Top row: GCT encoding for standard common-practice consonance vector; bottom row: GCT encoding for atonal harmony—all intervals 'consonant' (this amounts to pc-set 'normal orders'). See text for further details

third) and this resulted in finding a wrong root; eight chords were misspelled because they appeared over a pedal note (the pedal note was included in the chord); two sus4 chords $[0, 5, 7]$ were written incorrectly as $[0, 5, 10]$ (e.g., [C,F,G] contains the dissonant interval [F,G] and is erroneously re-ordered as [G,C,F]).

In the context of tonal music, for the standard tonal consonance vector, the GCT algorithm makes primarily the following types of mistake: first, it is undecided with regard to the root of symmetric chords such as diminished seventh chords and augmented triads; second, it assigns the wrong root to chords that have 'dissonant' intervals at their base, such as diminished fifths in half-diminished chords or major second in sus4 chords; and, finally, tertian chords that have notes missing from their base (e.g., missing third in seventh chords) are misinterpreted as their upper denser part is taken as the chord's base and the lower root as an extension.

In order to correct such cases, a more sophisticated model for harmonic analysis is required. Such a model should take into account voicing (e.g., the bass note), chord functions (see Kaliakatsos-Papakostas et al.'s (2015) proposal for organizing GCTs into functional tonal categories), and, even, higher-level domain-specific harmonic knowledge (e.g., specific types of chords used in particular idioms). However, the aim of the current proposal is not a tool for tonal analysis, but a general chord representation that can be applied to different harmonic systems (including the tonal system).

The GCT algorithm captures reasonably well the common-practice Roman-numeral harmonic analysis encoding scheme (for the 'standard' consonance vector). Additionally, it adapts to non-tonal systems, such as atonal, octatonic or traditional polyphonic music. The question is whether the GCT representation works well on such non-tonal systems. The GCT representation has been employed in the case of traditional polyphonic music from Epirus (Kaliakatsos-Papakostas et al., 2014). In this study, song transcriptions were first converted to the GCT encoding, then a learning HMM scheme was employed to learn chord transitions and, finally, this knowledge was used to create new harmonizations in the polyphonic style of Epirus. Ongoing research is currently studying the application of GCT to various harmonic idioms, from mediaeval music to 20th century music, and various pop and folk traditions.

What might such 'universal' harmonic encoding systems be useful for? Apart from music-theoretic interest and cognitive considerations and implications, a general chord encoding representation may allow generic harmonic systems to be developed that may be adapted to diverse harmonic idioms, rather than designing ad hoc systems for individual harmonic spaces. This was the primary aim for devising the General Chord Type (GCT) representation. In the case of the project COINVENT (Schorlemmer et al., 2014) a creative melodic harmonization system is required that relies on conceptual blending between diverse harmonic spaces in order to generate novel harmonic constructions; mapping between such different spaces is facilitated when the shared generic space is defined with clarity, its generic concepts are expressed in a general and idiom-independent manner, and a common general representation is available (Kaliakatsos-Papakostas and Cambouropoulos, 2014).

Overall, the GCT representation and algorithm are an attempt to create a flexible and adaptable representation, capable of encoding different harmonic idioms. Clearly, the algorithm can be extended and improved in different ways, depending on the task at hand. Using it, for instance, for learning chord transition probabilities from different corpora, unambiguous results are handy (each chord receiving a unique encoding). On the other hand, if one wants to study human harmonic analysis or perception, it may be useful to retain ambiguity and compare results with human empirical data. The GCT representation attempts to capture commonly used properties of chords (root, basic type, extension) in diverse styles (giving, however, a privileged vantage point to hierarchic tonal systems). Various refinements of the algorithm are possible depending on the context of the particular music-analytic or creative task to which it is being applied.

2.4 Pitch Class Chord Transition Representation

Is it possible to devise a chord sequence representation that 'captures' the intervallic content of chord transitions in a transposition-invariant and idiom-independent way without recourse to the concept of a chord? Is it possible to define a harmonic equivalent to the idiom-independent transposition-invariant 'pitch interval'? In this section a proposal is made for a chord transition representation that encodes chord *transitions* independently of the absolute pitches of actual chords, or any other representation of the notion of a chord.

Chords are usually represented either as collections of pitch-related values (e.g., note names, MIDI pitch numbers, pitch class sets, chroma vectors, etc.) or as chord root transitions within a given tonality following traditional harmonic analysis (e.g., Roman numeral analysis, guitar chords, etc.). In the case of an absolute pitch representation (such as chroma vectors, i.e., pitch class profiles) transpositions are not accounted for (e.g., twelve transpositions of a given query are necessary to find all possible occurrences of the query in a dataset). On the other hand, if harmonic analytic models are used to derive harmonic descriptions of pieces (e.g., chords as degrees within keys or tonal functions), more sophisticated processing is possible; in this case, however, models rely on complicated harmonic analytic systems, and, additionally, are limited to the tonal idiom.

One obvious way to represent chord sequences in a transposition-invariant and idiom-independent way is to encode chord transitions as intervals between the first pitch classes in the prime forms of the transpositional equivalence classes of the pitch class sets of two chords (e.g., for transition C–F: $[5, [0, 4, 7], [0, 4, 7]]$). This works well but it relies on the conversion of chords into pitch class sets (prime forms)—that is, it requires encoding the two chords in some abstract form which implies various assumptions and processing steps (see discussion in Sect. 2.3.2 above, relating to Fig. 2.7, for a GCT example in the same vein). Another possible way is to employ voice-leading intervals following, for instance, Tymoczko's (2011) pitch-class voice-leading formalism. For example, for transition C–F, the voice-leading is represented by $(C,E,G) \xrightarrow{0,1,2} (C,F,A)$. This representation relies on coupling the first chord (i.e., the notion of chord is necessary) with voice-leading paths describing thus a chord transition; this formalism gets more complicated when successive chords do not contain the same number of notes, as this results in a non-bijective relation between pitch sets. All of the above encoding schemes require encoding one or both chords delimiting a chord transition. Is it possible to represent a chord transition solely in terms of pitch intervals? The proposed DIC vector representation provides one possible solution. This can be seen as a music-theoretic exercise per se, or as a practical encoding scheme that may be useful for certain tasks.

Most computational models of harmonic processing rely on some representation of individual chords. There are very few attempts, however, to represent chord transitions. For instance, de Haas et al. (2008, 2013) represent chord transitions as chord distance values, adapting a distance metric from Lerdahl's tonal pitch space (Lerdahl, 2001). This representation is geared towards the tonal system; additionally, a chord transition being represented by a single distance value may capture certain important properties of the transition but may abstract out other important information.

2.4.1 The Directed Interval Class (DIC) Vector Representation

A proposal for representing chord transitions in an idiom-independent manner is presented in this section. A harmonic transition between two chords can be represented by a *Directed Interval Class* (DIC) vector (Cambouropoulos, 2012; Cambouropoulos et al., 2013). This representation allows the encoding of chord transitions at a level higher than individual notes that is transposition-invariant and idiom-independent (analogous to pitch intervals that represent transitions between notes).

The proposed 12-dimensional vector is an adaptation of Lewin's (1959) interval function (see also Lewin, 2001, 2007). Lewin's function encodes the frequencies of occurrence of the pitch intervals (from 0 to 11) that occur between the notes in one pitch class set and the notes in another. In the current proposal, Lewin's function is modified such that the proposed vector encodes all pitch intervals (from 0 to 6 including $+/-$ for direction; 0 and 6 are always positive) between all the pairs of notes of two successive chords. The DIC vector is equivalent to Lewin's interval function; it is simply a re-ordering of Lewin's intervals using directed pitch interval classes. The proposed representation attempts to capture the fact that voice-leading practice involves mostly small intervals (e.g., unison, step-wise motion) connecting notes from one chord to another (cf. Tymoczko's (2011) pitch-class voice leading). From the left-hand side to the right of the proposed interval vector, we move from unison to small (up or down) intervals up to the tritone. The DIC vector simply makes the 'voice leading' character of a chord transition more apparent. As will be proposed toward the end of this section, it may be possible to shorten the proposed vector by keeping only the smaller intervals at the left-hand side of the vector without losing its expressivity.

The 12-dimensional DIC vector features the following directed interval classes in its twelve positions: 0 (unison), $+1$, -1, $+2$, -2, $+3$, -3, $+4$, -4, $+5$, -5, 6 (tritone). The reason for opting for this ordering is that the absolute size of intervals increases from left to right, and this places small intervals, that are thought to be most strongly connected with voice-leading, at the 'privileged' beginning of the vector. The proposed vector encodes the frequency of occurrence of all directional interval classes between all the pairs of notes of two successive chords. That is, from each note of the first chord, all intervals to all the notes of the second chord are calculated. Direction of intervals is preserved $(+, -)$, except for the unison (0) and the tritone (6) that are undirected. Interval size takes values from 0 to 6 (interval class). If an interval X is greater than 6, then its complement $12 - X$ in the opposite direction is retained (e.g., ascending minor seventh '$+10$' is replaced by its equivalent complement descending major second '-2').

As an example, the transition vector for the progression I–V is given by the DIC vector: $Q = < 1, 0, 1, 1, 1, 1, 0, 1, 0, 0, 3, 0 >$ (which means: 1 unison, 0 ascending minor seconds, 1 descending minor second, 1 ascending major second, etc.)—see Fig. 2.8, and further examples in Fig. 2.9.

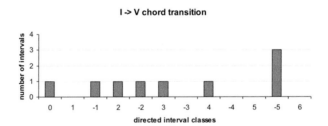

Fig. 2.8 The DIC vector, $< 1, 0, 1, 1, 1, 1, 0, 1, 0, 0, 3, 0 >$, for the chord transition I–V, depicted as a bar graph

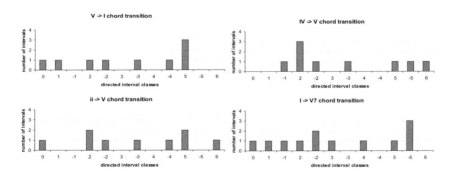

Fig. 2.9 DIC vectors for four standard tonal chord transitions: V–I, IV–V, ii–V, I–V7

For a given harmonic (e.g., tonal) context, the DIC vector is unique for many chord transitions. However, there are a number of cases where different tonal transitions have the same vector. For instance, the transitions I–V and IV–I share the same DIC vector as their directed interval content is the same; it should be noted, that, heard in isolation (without a tonal centre reference), a human listener cannot tell the difference between these two transitions. Another case is when one of the two chords is symmetric (e.g., an augmented triad or diminished seventh chord); this is actually an interesting case that agrees with music theory and intuition in the sense that, say, diminished seventh chords are considered ambiguous and can resolve to different chords leading to different tonal regions or keys.

In addition to the above cases of ambiguity (that are musically meaningful), the DIC vector encodes identically a chord transition and its retrograde inversion, i.e., any specific chord transition has the same DIC vector as its retrograde inversion. For instance, the retrograde inversion of a *major triad* progressing to a *major triad* by an interval X is a *minor triad* progressing to a *minor triad* by the same interval X; these two transitions share the same DIC vector. This is an inherent property of the DIC vector which reduces its descriptive power, and may have serious ramifications for certain tasks (see below).

Cambouropoulos et al. (2013) evaluated the proposed DIC representation on a harmonic recognition task, in which the accuracy of recognition of harmonic queries was tested in a small database of chord sequences (harmonic reductions) derived from diverse musical idioms and styles. More specifically, standard chord progressions were included from Bach chorales, along with harmonic progressions from modal Greek *rebetiko* songs, polyphonic songs from Epirus, Beatles songs and non-tonal pieces by Béla Bartók, Olivier Messiaen, Claude Debussy, and Erik Satie (31 chord reductions of pieces, collectively containing 957 chords in all). Both the query sequence and the chord progressions in the dataset were converted to DIC vectors and exact matching for recognition was employed (approximate matching was also considered using wildcards—see below). The results obtained with the algorithm were judged by human music analysis experts. For this small dataset, relatively longer sequences consisting of four or more chords were uniquely identified in the correct positions in the pieces where they originated. For instance, we examined exhaustively queries drawn from J. S. Bach's chorale, "Ein feste Burg ist unser Gott" (BWV 302), consisting of three or four chords; the longest sequence found in at least one other piece was a 4-chord sequence (the first four chords identified in position 26 of *Strawberry Fields* by The Beatles). Obviously, if the dataset is significantly extended we expect to find more occurrences of relatively longer harmonic queries. Many examples of harmonic queries and matches are reported and discussed by Cambouropoulos et al. (2013).

Overall, the harmonic recognition model behaves as expected, and has sufficient distinctive power to discern the harmonic individualities of these different harmonic languages. Almost all of the harmonic queries were correctly detected (see one problem below) and all queries containing at least three chords were identified without mistakes. Apparently the model is capable of finding repeating harmonic patterns even though pieces are in different keys (transposition invariance). Additionally, recall that the system has no knowledge of the different kinds of harmonic systems (tonal, modal, chromatic, atonal, etc.), and it is therefore interesting that it detects correctly any kind of harmonic query in diverse harmonic idioms.

Interestingly, the harmonic recognition model is equally successful and accurate when only the first five vector components are used. We tested all the above queries using only the first five vector entries $[0, 1, -1, 2, -2]$ (out of the 12) which correspond to unison (i.e., common pitches between two chords) and steps (i.e., ascending and descending semitones and tones); the resulting matches were the same in every case. These small intervals may be thought of as being mostly related to voice-leading as it is standard practice to try to connect chords avoiding larger intervals (using common notes and step movements). The reduction of the DIC vector to a 5-component subvector, enhances the cognitive plausibility of the proposed representation. Even though no cognitive claims are made in this chapter, we just mention that representing the transition between two chords as the small intervals that link adjacent pitches (being potentially part of individual harmonic voices) affords this representation potential cognitive validity. Finally, a mathematical analysis of the redundancy contained in the full DIC vector is needed; it is likely that, for example, for tertian chords, the larger pitch intervals can be recovered from the smaller ones. Both cognitive and mathematical properties of such a representation should be explored further in future studies. In any case, this reduced vector results in better computational efficiency.

As mentioned above, a chord sequence shares a DIC vector with its retrograde inversion. In the case of harmonic matching, this is not a serious problem if the sequences sought are relatively long (say, at least 3 chords). The reason is that the additional context of neighbouring chords often disambiguates the overall sequence. For instance, a query of two major chords an ascending fourth apart returns one hundred instances in our small dataset, some of which erroneously consist of two minor chords an ascending fourth apart; if, however, our query is preceded by a major chord one tone lower than the first chord, then we find only 12 instances of the sequence (corresponding to IV–V–I). In another example, the transition between two major chords an ascending tone apart returned 23 instances that correspond most likely to a IV–V chord progression (even though it may correspond to a ii–iii transition between minor chords). If the first chord is preceded by a diminished chord a semitone lower, then the whole sequence of three chords is found only once (in chorale BWV 302—the sequence is vii°–I–V/V). The specific context restrains the search drastically. Longer sequences are more unambiguous.

Finally, an important issue not explored sufficiently in this study is chord progression similarity, i.e., how similar two chord sequences are. As it stands, a IV–I transition and a V7–I transition are different (not matched) because their DIC vectors are not identical. Similarly, a V–I transition is not matched to another V–I transition if a note is missing such as the fifth of the first or second chord. Such relations can be captured if certain tolerances are allowed (approximate matching). For instance, if all entries of one vector are smaller than the corresponding entries of the other vector, and the sum of the differences is three or less, then sequences such as V–I and V7–I would be matched. This is a kind of approximate matching where the difference between individual DIC vector entries is less than or equal to δ and the sum of all differences less than γ (see Cambouropoulos et al. (2002) for another study of (δ, γ)-matching in music). The similarity relations between vectors is an open issue for further research.

In the current implementation, wild cards can be inserted in order to allow a certain tolerance in the matching. Disabling entries 6–12 in the vector, i.e., using only the first five components, did not seem to make a difference as mentioned earlier in this section. Trying out a more radical example, we queried the system with the vector $< 0, *, *, *, *, *, *, *, *, *, *, 2 >$; this means we are looking for a chord succession that contains no common notes but in which there exist two distinct tritone relations between different notes of the chords. The system returned 7 instances: 4 in the rebetiko songs; one in *Michelle* by The Beatles that corresponds to the transition of major chord to minor chord a tone lower (or the reverse); one in Bartók's fourth *Romanian Folk Dance* that corresponds to the transition of minor chord 7th to major chord a tone higher; and one in the first measures of Debussy's *Nuages* that corresponds to the transition of a perfect fourth harmonic interval to a perfect fifth a semitone lower. Such experiments allow the investigation of broader similarity relations.

Cambouropoulos (2012) attempted to test the effectiveness of the DIC vector representation in a harmonic progression similarity task. The main assumption there was that, if this representation encodes aspects of the harmonic content of chord progressions sufficiently well, then, given an appropriate distance metric, similarity between different chord progressions can be calculated and chord progressions can be clustered together in meaningful classes. We use the DIC vector representation as a basis for calculating the distance between simple chord progressions in two preliminary tests. In one case, we calculate the distances between 12 simple tonal triadic progressions; whereas in the second case, we have 11 jazz progressions. For this preliminary testing, we employed a very simple distance metric between the DIC vector sequences, namely the city block distance. In this initial experiment we employed phylogenetic trees (branching diagrams) to visualize the distance or similarity relations between the given chord sequences.

In the first preliminary test, we constructed a set of twelve triadic tonal chord progressions, each consisting of four chords (Fig. 2.10). The twelve chord progressions were constructed such that they were organized into three groups of four instances each, corresponding to the following harmonic function progressions: T–S–D–T, T–S–T–D, and S–T–D–T (T=tonic, S=subdominant, D=dominant). The simple similarity method employed in this study resulted in a phylogenetic tree branching that splits the twelve progressions into three groups that correspond with the expected harmonic function progressions (Fig. 2.10). This very simple method manages to group together successfully these chord progressions without any knowledge of tonality, keys, chord roots, scales or any other sophisticated harmonic concepts. Even if we transpose these progressions to various keys the proposed method would give exactly the same result. The mere intervallic content of these progressions is sufficient for finding similarities between them and organizing them into groups. It should be noted, however, that, if in this example more extensive substitutions of chords are introduced, the resulting tree is less successful, possibly because the distance metric

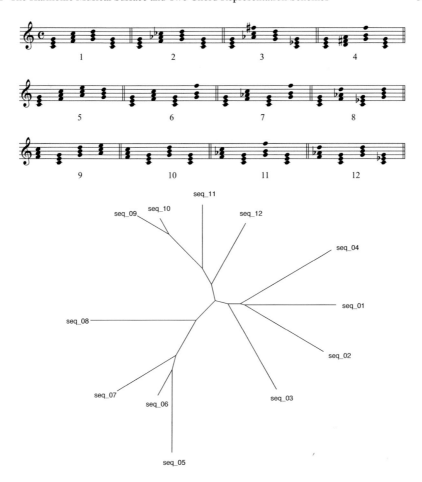

Fig. 2.10 The triadic chord progressions are organized into a phylogenetic tree that illustrates their similarities and grouping based on their DIC vector distances

is extremely elementary. The similarity relations between vectors is an open issue for further research.

In a second preliminary test, we asked an experienced jazz piano performer to write down some jazz chord progressions (same length) and, also, to let us know how she thought they related to each other. The jazz pianist prepared eleven jazz chord progressions, each consisting of 4 chords. As in the previous test, these were organized into an 11×11 distance matrix and, then, a phylogenetic tree was constructed (Fig. 2.11). The jazz musician examined the resulting phylogenetic tree and gave the following feedback:

> I think it is very nice and I agree with the main parts. The point on which I would disagree is placing 6 far away from 5, 7, 8; I would place them in [the] same class. Secondly, group 1, 3 is closer to 2 in my opinion; the rest of the tree is very convincing.

The harmonic similarity between these jazz chord progressions seems to be captured reasonably well, despite the simplicity of the proposed model and its total ignorance of jazz harmony. This is encouraging; however, more systematic research is necessary to improve the model and to test it more extensively (e.g., empirical data for the 11 progressions could be gathered from a larger number of jazz musicians).

One might argue that all the above harmonic recognition and classification tasks can be modelled equally well by employing a simple pc-set-based representation (e.g., chord transitions as intervals between the first pitch classes of the transpositional pitch class sets of two chords). This is true. Why, then, use the DIC vector representation at all? First, the DIC vector is very simple to compute (easier than normal orders and prime forms of pc-set theory). Second, it may allow more general distance metrics to be developed for the calculation of distances between chord sequences. Third,

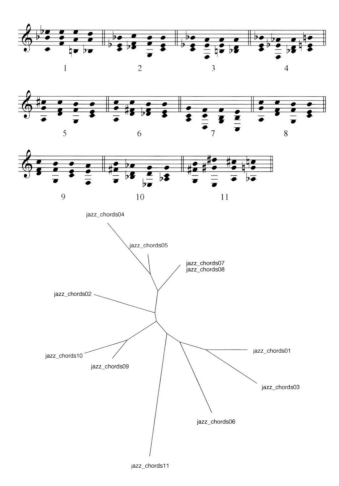

Fig. 2.11 The jazz chord progressions are organized into a phylogenetic tree that illustrates their similarities and grouping based on their DIC vector distances. See text for more details

it can be applied even in cases where it is not straightforward to compute prime forms. For example, it is not straightforward to convert chroma vectors extracted from audio into pitch class sets so that transitions between them may be represented in a transposition-invariant manner; whereas successive chroma vectors can readily be converted into weighted DIC vectors. Finally, the DIC vector (especially some abbreviated form containing, for instance, only small intervals) may afford cognitive relevance in the sense that, in some cases at least, listeners may abstract and categorize directly intervallic content of chord progressions (instead of applying more advanced processing that involves identifying pc-set classes and intervals between them). Further research is necessary to substantiate such claims. Herein only preliminary hints are given as to the potential of the proposed representation.

2.5 Conclusions

This chapter addresses issues of harmonic representation at the level of the musical surface. It is argued that selecting an appropriate representation for chords is crucial for encoding aspects of the musical surface that have perceptual pertinence, and at the same time is paramount for building efficient and meaningful computational models for music analysis. In the course of the chapter, two novel general chord representations were presented and their potential was discussed. The first, the GCT representation, generalizes the standard Roman-numeral representation in such a way as to apply to any idiom; whereas the second, the DIC vector, captures the intervallic content of a transition between two chords. The former is algorithmically more complex but embodies more structured harmonic information (consonance/dissonance, 'root', chord type, position in scale) and is thus adequate for music analytic/synthetic tasks in more sophisticated hierarchical musical idioms. It is suggested that both of the proposed chord representations may be used for representing harmonic relations in music from diverse musical idioms (i.e., they are not confined to tonal music) and, therefore, may provide a most appropriate framework for harmonic processing in the domain of computational musicology.

Acknowledgements The project COINVENT acknowledges the financial support of the Future and Emerging Technologies (FET) programme within the Seventh Framework Programme for Research of the European Commission, under FET-Open grant number: 611553. Special thanks are due to Costas Tsougras for the preliminary analysis of the Kostka–Payne dataset and for the harmonic reduction examples, Maximos Kaliakatsos-Papakostas for his practical support in preparing this manuscript, and two anonymous reviewers and David Meredith for providing most interesting suggestions on an earlier version of this chapter.

References

Bregman, A. S. (1994). *Auditory Scene Analysis: The Perceptual Organization of Sound.* MIT Press.

Burns, E. M. (1999). Intervals, scales and tuning. In Deutsch, D., editor, *The Psychology of Music*, pages 215–264. Academic Press, second edition.

Cambouropoulos, E. (2008). Voice and stream: Perceptual and computational modeling of voice separation. *Music Perception*, 26(1):75–94.

Cambouropoulos, E. (2010). The musical surface: Challenging basic assumptions. *Musicae Scientiae*, 14(2):131–147.

Cambouropoulos, E. (2012). A directional interval class representation of chord transitions. In *Proceedings of the Joint 12th International Conference for Music Perception and Cognition & 8th Conference of the European Society for the Cognitive Sciences of Music (ICMPC-ESCOM 2012)*, Thessaloniki, Greece.

Cambouropoulos, E., Crochemore, M., Iliopoulos, C. S., Mouchard, L., and Pinzon, Y. J. (2002). Algorithms for computing approximate repetitions in musical sequences. *International Journal of Computer Mathematics*, 79(11):1135–1148.

Cambouropoulos, E., Kaliakatsos-Papakostas, M., and Tsougras, C. (2014). An idiom-independent representation of chords for computational music analysis and generation. In *Proceeding of the Joint 11th Sound and Music Computing Conference (SMC) and 40th International Computer Music Conference (ICMC)*, ICMC–SMC 2014, Athens, Greece.

Cambouropoulos, E., Katsiavalos, A., and Tsougras, C. (2013). Idiom-independent harmonic pattern recognition based on a novel chord transition representation. In *Proceedings of the 3rd International Workshop on Folk Music Analysis (FMA2013)*, Amsterdam, Netherlands.

Cemgil, A. T., Kappen, H. J., and Barber, D. (2006). A generative model for music transcription. *IEEE Transactions on Audio, Speech, and Language Processing*, 14(2):679–694.

de Haas, W. B., Veltkamp, R. C., and Wiering, F. (2008). Tonal pitch step distance: a similarity measure for chord progressions. In *9th International Conference on Music Information Retrieval (ISMIR 2008)*, pages 51–56, Philadelphia, PA.

de Haas, W. B., Wiering, F., and Veltkamp, R. C. (2013). A geometrical distance measure for determining the similarity of musical harmony. *International Journal of Multimedia Information Retrieval*, 2(3):189–202.

Deutsch, D. (2012). The processing of pitch combinations. In Deutsch, D., editor, *The Psychology of Music*, pages 249–326. Academic Press, third edition.

Forte, A. (1973). *The Structure of Atonal Music.* Yale University Press.

Handel, S. (1989). *Listening: An Introduction to the Perception of Auditory Events.* MIT Press.

Harte, C., Sandler, M., Abdallah, S. A., and Gómez, E. (2005). Symbolic representation of musical chords: A proposed syntax for text annotations. In *Proceedings of the 6th International Conference on Music Information Retrieval (ISMIR 2005)*, pages 66–71, London, UK.

Hubbard, T. L. and Datteri, D. L. (2001). Recognizing the component tones of a major chord. *The American Journal of Psychology*, 114(4):569–589.

Huron, D. (2001). Tone and voice: A derivation of the rules of voice-leading from perceptual principles. *Music Perception*, 19(1):1–64.

Hutchinson, W. and Knopoff, L. (1978). The acoustic component of Western consonance. *Interface*, 7(1):1–29.

Jackendoff, R. (1987). *Consciousness and the Computational Mind*. MIT Press.

Jackendoff, R. and Lerdahl, F. (2006). The capacity for music: What is it, and what's special about it? *Cognition*, 100(1):33–72.

Jordanous, A. (2008). Voice separation in polyphonic music: A data-driven approach. In *Proceedings of the International Computer Music Conference 2008*, Belfast, UK.

Kaliakatsos-Papakostas, M. and Cambouropoulos, E. (2014). Probabilistic harmonisation with fixed intermediate chord constraints. In *Proceedings of the Joint 11th Sound and Music Computing Conference (SMC) and 40th International Computer Music Conference (ICMC)*, Athens, Greece.

Kaliakatsos-Papakostas, M., Katsiavalos, A., Tsougras, C., and Cambouropoulos, E. (2014). Harmony in the polyphonic songs of Epirus: Representation, statistical analysis and generation. In *4th International Workshop on Folk Music Analysis (FMA 2014)*, Istanbul, Turkey.

Kaliakatsos-Papakostas, M., Zacharakis, A., Tsougras, C., and Cambouropoulos, E. (2015). Evaluating the General Chord Type algorithm in tonal music and organising its output in higher-level functional chord categories. In *Proceedings of the 16th International Society for Music Information Retrieval Conference (ISMIR 2015)*, Malaga, Spain.

Kostka, S. and Payne, D. (1995). *Tonal Harmony*. McGraw-Hill.

Laitz, S. G. (2012). *The Complete Musician: An Integrated Approach to Tonal Theory, Analysis, and Listening*. Oxford University Press.

Lerdahl, F. (2001). *Tonal Pitch Space*. Oxford University Press.

Lerdahl, F. and Jackendoff, R. (1983). *A Generative Theory of Tonal Music*. MIT Press.

Lewin, D. (1959). Intervallic relations between two collections of notes. *Journal of Music Theory*, 3(2):298–301.

Lewin, D. (2001). Special cases of the interval function between pitch-class sets x and y. *Journal of Music Theory*, 45(1):1–29.

Lewin, D. (2007). *Generalized Musical Intervals and Transformations*. Oxford University Press.

Locke, S. and Kellar, L. (1973). Categorical perception in a non-linguistic mode. *Cortex*, 9(4):355–369.

Mauch, M., Cannam, C., Davies, M., Dixon, S., Harte, C., Kolozali, S., Tidhar, D., and Sandler, M. (2010). OMRAS2 metadata project 2009. In *Proceedings of the 11th International Society for Music Information Retrieval Conference (ISMIR 2010)*, Utrecht, The Netherlands.

Parncutt, R. (1989). *Harmony: A Psychoacoustical Approach*. Springer.

Parncutt, R. (1994). Template-matching models of musical pitch and rhythm perception. *Journal of New Music Research*, 23(2):145–167.

Parncutt, R. (1997). A model of the perceptual root(s) of a chord accounting for voicing and prevailing tonality. In Leman, M., editor, *Music, Gestalt, and Computing*, volume 1317 of *Lecture Notes in Computer Science*, pages 181–199. Springer.

Piston, W. (1978). *Harmony*. Norton. Revised and expanded by M. DeVoto.

Povel, D.-J. and Jansen, E. (2001). Perceptual mechanisms in music processing. *Music Perception*, 19(2):169–197.

Ryynänen, M. P. and Klapuri, A. P. (2008). Automatic transcription of melody, bass line, and chords in polyphonic music. *Computer Music Journal*, 32(3):72–86.

Schorlemmer, M., Smaill, A., Kühnberger, K.-U., Kutz, O., Colton, S., Cambouropoulos, E., and Pease, A. (2014). COINVENT: Towards a computational concept invention theory. In *5th International Conference on Computational Creativity (ICCC) 2014*, Ljubljana, Slovenia.

Sloboda, J. A. (1985). *The Musical Mind*. Oxford University Press.

Smith, J. D., Nelson, D. G., Grohskopf, L. A., and Appleton, T. (1994). What child is this? What interval was that? Familiar tunes and music perception in novice listeners. *Cognition*, 52(1):23–54.

Temperley, D. (2001a). *The Cognition of Basic Musical Structures*. MIT Press.

Temperley, D. (2001b). Kostka–Payne dataset. Available online at http://theory.esm.rochester.edu/temperley/kp-stats/. Last accessed 5 September 2015.

Temperley, D. (2012). Computational models of music cognition. In Deutsch, D., editor, *The Psychology of Music*, pages 327–368. Academic Press, third edition.

Tymoczko, D. (2011). *A Geometry of Music: Harmony and Counterpoint in the Extended Common Practice*. Oxford University Press.

Vernon, P. E. (1934). Auditory perception. I. The Gestalt approach. II. The evolutionary approach. *British Journal of Psychology*, 25:123–139, 265–283.

Chapter 3
Topological Structures in Computer-Aided Music Analysis

Louis Bigo and Moreno Andreatta

Abstract We propose a spatial approach to musical analysis based on the notion of a *chord complex*. A *chord complex* is a labelled simplicial complex which represents a set of chords. The dimension of the elements of the complex and their neighbourhood relationships highlight the size of the chords and their intersections. Following a well-established tradition in set-theoretical and neo-Riemannian music analysis, we present the family of T/I *complexes* which represent classes of chords which are transpositionally and inversionally equivalent and which relate to the notion of *Generalized Tonnetze*. A musical piece is represented by a trajectory within a given *chord complex*. We propose a method to compute the compactness of a trajectory in any *chord complex*. Calculating the trajectory compactness of a piece in T/I *complexes* provides valuable information for music analysis and classification. We introduce different geometrical transformations on trajectories that correspond to different musical transformations. Finally, we present HexaChord, a software package dedicated to computer-aided music analysis with chord complexes, which implements most of the concepts discussed in this chapter.

Louis Bigo
Department of Computer Science and Artificial Intelligence, University of the Basque Country
UPV/EHU, San Sebastián, Spain
e-mail: louis.bigo@ehu.eus

Moreno Andreatta
CNRS, France
IRCAM, Paris, France
Université Pierre et Marie Curie, Paris, France
e-mail: moreno.andreatta@ircam.fr

© Springer International Publishing Switzerland 2016
D. Meredith (ed.), *Computational Music Analysis*,
DOI 10.1007/978-3-319-25931-4_3

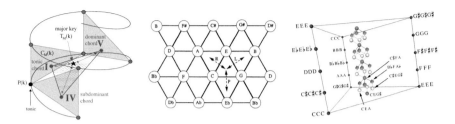

Fig. 3.1 Three symbolic spaces dedicated to musical representations: the spiral array (left), the *Tonnetz* (centre) and a voice leading space (right)

3.1 Introduction

This work concentrates on the harmonic aspect of musical sequences and introduces a spatial approach for its analysis. Musical analysis often requires specific tools when it focuses on a particular musical layer. For example, some theorists represent musical objects and their harmonic properties by (or in) symbolic spaces. When used in an analytic context, these spatial representations can reveal some strategies used to compose a piece. The spiral array (Chew, 2002), the *Tonnetz* (Cohn, 1997) and voice-leading spaces (Callender et al., 2008) are examples of such spaces. Among their numerous properties, they are well adapted for determining key boundaries, representing neo-Riemannian operations and voice-leading motions, respectively. Such spaces typically represent pitches or chords by vertices in a graph.

The chord spaces presented in this study include elements of higher dimension than vertices and edges. We represent *n*-note chords by geometrical objects of dimension $(n-1)$, called *simplices*. The faces of a *simplex* represent all sub-chords contained in the chord. Chord sets are represented by *simplicial complexes*. The possibly high dimension of a complex highlights specific neighbourhood relationships between chords and allows the space to represent more advanced musical properties.

A strong motivation of this work is the general desire to represent a collection of musical objects by a symbolic space governed by a set of neighbourhood relationships that reflect how represented objects interact. This general idea is inspired by the MGS project (Giavitto and Michel, 2001), which aims to provide tools for the modelling and simulation of (not necessarily musical) dynamical systems exhibiting dynamical structures.

Section 3.2 begins by briefly presenting the historical background of music representations, including a discussion of Pousseur's pioneering attempt to capture musical logic with geometric representations. We then present the notions of *T/I class* and *Generalized Tonnetze*. Section 3.3 introduces the notion of *simplicial complex* and explains how this concept allows for any set of chords to be represented by a symbolic space called a *chord complex*. This section finally introduces *T/I complexes* which are *chord complexes* representing chords of a *T/I class*. Section 3.4 introduces the idea of representing musical sequences as *trajectories* in *chord complexes*. We introduce the notion of the *d-compactness* of such a trajectory as a heuristic for selecting chord complexes for analysis or classification. We finally present a method to transform a musical sequence by applying some geometric transformations on its trajectory. *Chord complexes* and trajectories have been implemented in the HexaChord music analysis software, which is presented and discussed in Sect. 3.5.

3.2 Background in Musical Representations

We present two well-known notions in music theory: the *Tonnetz* and *T/I classes*. The first is a spatial organization of pitches that constitutes a well-established analytical tool in the so-called neo-Riemannian music-theoretical tradition (Cohn, 2012; Tymoczko, 2012). The second provides a classification of musical chords based on their equivalence up to transposition and inversion. These two representation tools constitute the musical starting point of this work.

3.2.1 The Tonnetz

One of the strongest motivations of this work is the wish to formalize a widely used tool in music theory, analysis and composition: the *Tonnetz*. The *Tonnetz* is a symbolic organization of pitches in the Euclidean space defined by infinite axes associated with particular musical intervals. It was first investigated by Euler (1739) for acoustical as well as graph-theoretical purposes[1] and rediscovered later by the musicologists A. von Oettingen and H. Riemann and by the composer and music-theorist H. Pousseur. More recently, music theorists have shown a strong interest in this model, in particular to represent typical post-romantic chord progressions (Cohn, 2012) currently called *neo-Riemannian transformations*. This model has also been used in musical composition, not only in contemporary musical styles (Chouvel, 2009) but also in more popular styles (Bigo and Andreatta, 2014).

The *neo-Riemannian Tonnetz* (on the left in Fig. 3.2) is a graph in which pitches are organized along the intervals of the perfect fifth (horizontal axis), major and minor thirds (diagonal axes). This representation has the interesting property that major and minor triads appear as triangles. Many theorists have investigated different derivations of the *Tonnetz*, often referred to as *generalized Tonnetze*. For instance, the three-dimensional *Tonnetz* introduced by Gollin (1998) is shown on the right in Fig. 3.2. This model corresponds to the one on the left side of Fig. 3.2 with some

---

[1] Euler's *Tonnetz* (*Speculum Musicum*) organizes pitches in just intonation along horizontal and vertical axes associated with the pure fifth and pure major third, respectively. Interestingly, the kind of music-theoretical problems he suggested could be approached via his *Speculum Musicum* deeply resonate with purely mathematical problems, such as the Königsberg Bridge Problem. This fact supports the idea that not only does mathematics apply to music but, conversely, music often anticipates some developments of mathematics (Andreatta, 2008).

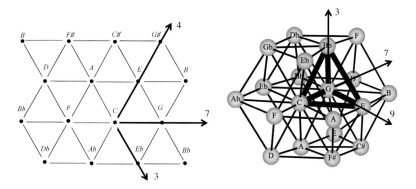

Fig. 3.2 On the left, a region of the neo-Riemannian *Tonnetz*. On the right, a three-dimensional derivation of the *Tonnetz* by Gollin (1998)

additional interval axes. Tetrahedra represent dominant seventh and half-diminished chords. Three-dimensional models are well adapted to the study of 4-note chord progressions. Similar structures can be built by associating axes with intervals that are diatonic instead of chromatic. In these *diatonic Tonnetze*, investigated by Cohn (2012), vertices and shapes only represent notes and chords belonging to a unique diatonic scale.

In this work, we limit ourselves to the context of equal temperament and octave equivalence, i.e., we are dealing with *pitch classes*. For example, the pitches C♯3, C♯4 and D♭4 are all members of the same *pitch class*. In particular, what we call *Tonnetz* more exactly refers to the *pitch-class Tonnetz*. In this context, the graph on the left of Fig. 3.2 repeats infinitely the 12 pitch classes along its axes. The pitch-class *Tonnetz* is frequently represented as a toroidal structure by merging the nodes representing the same pitch classes (Cohn, 1997).

Interestingly, this geometrical structure has also been rediscovered independently from the neo-Riemannian music-analytical tradition by the composer and music theorist H. Pousseur, one of the leading figures, with P. Boulez and K. Stockhausen, of European integral Serialism. Although Pousseur's model is much less well-known and rarely cited in neo-Riemannian music analysis, it contains the roots of the spatial approach that we present in this chapter. The point of departure of Pousseur's network theory is Rameau's (1722) *Traité de l'harmonie*, in which the latter introduces a bidimensional representation of the tone-space in just intonation as generated by the pure fifths (horizontal axis) and pure major thirds (descending vertical axis). This representation is equivalent to the *Speculum Musicum* which was introduced by Euler a few years later. Pousseur first presented his Rameau-inspired geometrical model in 1968 (Pousseur, 1968), but he provides several analytical examples of what he calls his "Network technique" in a more recent paper (Pousseur, 1998). In this analytical essay he goes back to the definition of a Network as a spatial distribution of pitches (and pitch classes) according to at least two axes which are characterized as a chain

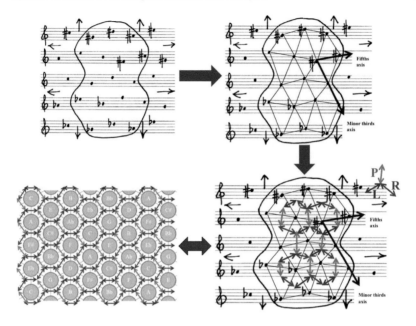

Fig. 3.3 The pitch network introduced by H. Pousseur in the late 1960s and accompanied by a triangulation showing its equivalence to the traditional *Tonnetz*

of a single interval. It is easy to show that his pitch distribution is equivalent to the traditional *Tonnetz* structure as generated by the fifths and minor thirds axes, as shown in Fig. 3.3. As clearly pointed out by Pousseur, this geometrical representation is one of the possible network configurations which can be utilized in music analysis. The basic principle of the Network technique, as he claims, resides in choosing the generating axes, and hence constructing the triangulations of the space, in such a way that the musical relations between adjacent pitches (both harmonic and melodic) produce the most compact configuration within the given space. This clearly suggests that his Network technique is deeply rooted in a spatial approach to music analysis, which we can properly formalize in terms of simplicial complexes as presented in Sect. 3.3. Moreover, as Pousseur suggests, the music analyst can transform the underlying geometrical space and move from a given network to a different one by simply changing the generating axes, which modifies the hierarchy of intervallic relations as well as the structural proximity between the pitches (or pitch classes). The next two sections will show how to transform this original compositional and music-theoretical intuition into a computational analytical model.

3.2.2 Generalized Tonnetze and T/I Classes

The highlighting of particular chords (minor/major chords as triangles in the neo-Riemannian *Tonnetz* and dominant seventh/half diminished chords as tetrahedra in the three-dimensional *Tonnetz*) suggests the idea that the starting point of the construction of a *Tonnetz* could be a set of chords rather than a set of interval axes. In the two examples above, the represented chords in a *Tonnetz* are all transpositionally and inversionally equivalent—that is, they belong to the same *T/I class* (Forte, 1973). This property comes from the repetition and the invertibility of the intervals on the axes.

It is common to identify a T/I class by the intervallic structure which is shared by all the chords of the class. For instance, the 24 major and minor chords all share the intervallic structure $[3,4,5]$ because the row of intervals between the pitch classes they are resulting from is composed of a minor third (3 semitones), a major third (4 semitones) and a fourth (5 semitones). This notation of the intervallic structure is defined up to reflection and circular permutation. Intervals are ordered in the opposite direction (up to a cyclic permutation) for major ($[4,3,5]$) and minor chords ($[3,4,5]$). Intervallic structures can be diatonic as well. In this case, the intervals add up to 7 instead of 12. For example, the triads on the seven degrees of the diatonic scale belong to the class identified by the intervallic structure $[2,2,3]$. Even though T/I classes can be enumerated for any division of the octave (i.e., for any N), we focus in this work on the diatonic ($N = 7$) and chromatic ($N = 12$) systems.[2]

There exist 224 such classes in the chromatic system, also known as *Forte classes* (Forte, 1973). In the diatonic system, which divides the octave into seven (non-equal) parts, there exist 18 such classes. Following this line, we are interested in building the *generalized Tonnetze* associated with the 224 T/I chromatic classes and 18 T/I diatonic classes.

3.3 Generalized Tonnetze as Chord Complexes

This section presents a method to represent any arbitrary set of chords by a multi-dimensional structure called a *chord complex*. Figure 3.7 illustrates an example of a *chord complex* representing a set of four chords. A *chord complex* is a *simplicial complex* whose components, called *simplices*, are labelled by chords.[3] In a chord complex, the dimension of the simplices represents the size of the chords. Furthermore, the intersections of the simplices represent the common pitch classes of the chords. *Chord complexes* representing the chords of a T/I class are called *T/I complexes* and relate to *Generalized Tonnetze*.

---

[2] For enumeration and classification purpose, T/I classes can be associated with the orbits of the action of the dihedral group $\mathbb{D}_N$ on the subsets of $\mathbb{Z}_N$, as described by Andreatta and Agon (2003).

[3] *Simplicial complexes* belong to a more general family of spaces called *cellular complexes*, which have already proved to be useful in music theory (Bigo et al., 2011).

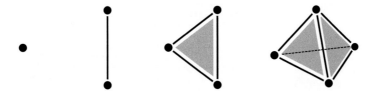

Fig. 3.4 From left to right: a 0-simplex, a 1-simplex, a 2-simplex and a 3-simplex represented with their closure

3.3.1 Simplicial Complexes

A *simplicial complex* is a multidimensional space built by gluing together more elementary spaces called *simplices*. A *simplex* (more precisely a *d-simplex*) is the abstraction of a space of dimension d. As illustrated in Fig. 3.4, a 0-simplex corresponds to a vertex, a 1-simplex corresponds to an edge, a 2-simplex to a triangle, a 3-simplex to a tetrahedron, etc. In a simplicial complex, a d-simplex is necessarily incident to $d+1$ simplices of dimension $d-1$. For instance, a 1-simplex (i.e., an edge) is incident to two 0-simplices (i.e., 2 vertices), a 2-simplex (i.e., a triangle) is incident to three 1-simplices (i.e., 3 edges), etc. This recursive property defines the *closure* of a simplex, consisting of all its incident simplices of lower dimension. In a simplicial complex, a subset of simplices that itself constitutes a simplicial complex is called a *sub-complex*.

A *simplicial d-complex* is a simplicial complex where the highest dimension of any simplex is d. A graph is a simplicial 1-complex. For any natural number n, the *n-skeleton* of a simplicial complex $\mathcal{K}$ is defined by the sub-complex $\mathcal{S}_n(\mathcal{K})$ of this complex formed by its simplices of dimension n or less. Figure 3.5 illustrates a simplicial 3-complex and its 1-skeleton.

The *f-vector* of a simplicial d-complex corresponds to the finite sequence $(f_1, \ldots, f_{d+1})$ where f_{p+1} is the number of p-simplices included in the complex. The *f*-vector of the complex in Fig. 3.5 is $(11, 17, 7, 1)$ because it includes 11 ver-

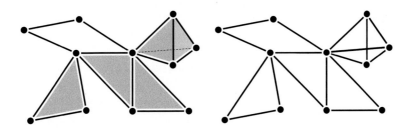

Fig. 3.5 A simplicial 3-complex (on the left) and its 1-skeleton (on the right)

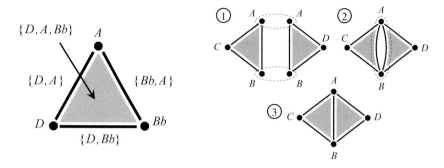

Fig. 3.6 On the left, the 2-simplex $\mathcal{S}(C)$ representing the chord $C = \{D,A,Bb\}$ and all sub-chords and notes included in it. On the right, the identification of boundaries illustrating the self-assembly process on the 2-simplices representing the chords $\{C,A,B\}$ and $\{D,A,B\}$

tices, 17 edges, 7 triangles and one tetrahedron. The term f_p of the f-vector of a complex $\mathcal{K}$ is denoted by $f_p(\mathcal{K})$.

Simplicial collections are simplicial complexes in which every simplex is labelled by an arbitrary value. The left side of Fig. 3.6 illustrates a simplicial collection of dimension 2. A simplicial collection can be built from a set of labelled simplices by applying a self-assembly process (Giavitto and Spicher, 2008). This process is based on the identification of the simplex boundaries that share the same labels. This topological operation holds in all dimensions. The right side of Fig. 3.6 illustrates the process on two 2-simplices. In step 1, nodes A and B are merged. Then, in step 2, the resulting edges $\{A,B\}$ are merged. The final structure is a connected, two-dimensional, simplicial collection in which every simplex is labelled with its own value (step 3).

3.3.2 Chord Complexes

We use a method described by Bigo et al. (2011) to represent a set of chords by a simplicial collection that we call a *chord complex*. In this representation, chords are reduced to pitch class sets. This requires some abstraction since some properties of chords as they actually occur within a musical context (e.g., the octave and duration of each note) are not represented. An n-pitch class set (i.e., a set of n pitch classes) is represented by an $(n-1)$-simplex. In particular, a 0-simplex represents a single pitch class, a 1-simplex a 2-pitch class set, etc. We denote by $\mathcal{S}(A)$ the simplex representing the pitch class set A. The simplices constituting the closure of $\mathcal{S}(A)$ represent all the sub-chords of A. The 2-simplex representing the pitch class set $\{D,A,Bb\}$ is illustrated on the left of Fig. 3.6. A chord complex is built by:

1. representing each chord of the collection by a simplex as described above,

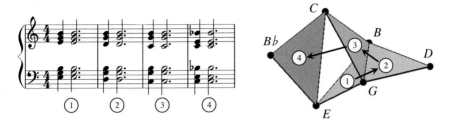

Fig. 3.7 First measures of *Metamorphosis* by Philip Glass (left) represented by a chord complex (right). The three arrows provide the order in which the four chords are played

2. applying the self-assembly process to the resulting collection of simplices.

This method ensures that a given chord cannot be represented more than once in the simplicial complex. As an example, on the right in Fig. 3.7 is shown the complex resulting from the assembly of the four introductory chords of the piano piece *Metamorphosis* by Philip Glass, shown on the left in the same figure. The four chords are respectively associated with the pitch class sets $\{E,G,B\}$, $\{D,G,B\}$, $\{C,G,B\}$ and $\{C,E,B\flat\}$. Each chord includes three pitch classes and is represented by a 2-simplex, that is, a triangle. The whole complex exhibits the intersections between the four pitch class sets.

This representation method provides a topological signature for any chord sequence. The musical interpretation of topological properties of chord complexes (dimension, size, connectedness, morphisms, etc.) is discussed by Bigo (2013). In the following, we will focus on chord complexes representing sets of chords related by some theoretic properties (for example chords belonging to the same T/I class) rather than sets of chords included in a given musical sequence as illustrated by the example in Fig. 3.7.

3.3.3 T/I Complexes

We represent a *generalized Tonnetz* as a chord complex composed of *n*-simplices representing the chords of a given T/I class. In the following, we consider in particular $\mathcal{K}_{TI}[a_1,\dots,a_i]$, the complex associated with the T/I class identified by the intervallic structure $[a_1,\dots,a_i]$. To build such a complex, we first enumerate all the chords belonging to the T/I class, we then build the corresponding complex, as explained in Sect. 3.3.2. As a consequence, the dimension of a T/I complex corresponds to the size of its intervallic structure minus one.

Figure 3.8 illustrates the diatonic complexes $\mathcal{K}_{TI}[2,5]$, $\mathcal{K}_{TI}[2,2,3]$ and $\mathcal{K}_{TI}[1,2,2,2]$ associated with the scale of C major. These complexes were described by Mazzola et al. (2002) as *interpretations* of the diatonic scale. They have the topology of a circle, a Möbius strip and a torus, respectively. An alternative represen-

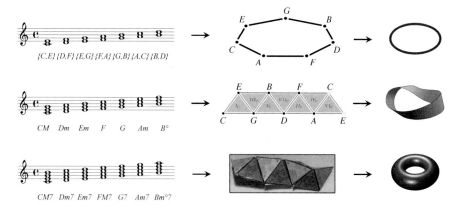

Fig. 3.8 Construction of the diatonic complexes $\mathcal{K}_{TI}[2,5]$, $\mathcal{K}_{TI}[2,2,3]$ and $\mathcal{K}_{TI}[1,2,2,2]$ by assembling degrees of the tonality of C major (Mazzola et al., 2002)

tation of the complex $\mathcal{K}_{TI}[1,2,4]$ in which all pitch classes of the diatonic scale are neighbours has been used for music analysis by Hook (2014).

Figure 3.9 illustrates the chromatic complexes $\mathcal{K}_{TI}[2,5,5]$ and $\mathcal{K}_{TI}[3,4,5]$ which result from the assembly of suspended chords (Sus4 chords) and major/minor chords respectively. The organization of pitch classes in $\mathcal{K}_{TI}[2,5,5]$ corresponds to the well-known *Wicki–Hayden note layout*, which is used for the key layout on some keyboard instruments, such as the bandoneon. The 1-skeleton of $\mathcal{K}_{TI}[3,4,5]$ corresponds to the *Tonnetz*. Topological properties of T/I chord complexes of dimension 2 were studied by Catanzaro (2011). Although the present study focuses on T/I complexes (i.e., $\mathcal{K}_{TI}[\cdot]$) due to their relation with *Generalized Tonnetze*, this approach can be generalized to enumerate chord complexes defined by any equivalence relation, not

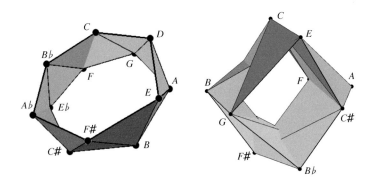

Fig. 3.9 On the left, the complex of the suspended chords ($\mathcal{K}_{TI}[2,5,5]$) of size 12. On the right, the complex of major and minor chords ($\mathcal{K}_{TI}[3,4,5]$) of size 24, whose 1-skeleton corresponds to the *Tonnetz*. The first complex is a strip and the second is a torus

just transposition and inversion. For example, complexes of chords equivalent up to transposition only ($\mathcal{K}_T[\cdot]$), up to transposition and interval permutation ($\mathcal{K}_{TP}[\cdot]$) and up to affine transformation ($\mathcal{K}_M[\cdot]$) have been enumerated and classified in a catalogue (Bigo, 2013).[4]

3.3.4 Unfolded Representations of T/I Complexes

The neo-Riemannian *Tonnetz* was originally designed as a triangular graph embedded within a two-dimensional Euclidean space, as illustrated on the left in Fig. 3.2. One may imagine the triangulation as being generated by the choice of three axes representing three privileged intervallic directions starting from a referential initial point. In the case of Fig. 3.2 (left), we start from the note C and we consider three axes corresponding to the minor third, perfect fifth and major third intervals. Note that two axes suffice to generate the triangulation of the plane, since the interval corresponding to one of the axes is simply the sum of the intervals corresponding to the two remaining axes. In our case, for example, the horizontal axis, going from left to right, represents a fifth interval which is the sum of a minor third and a major third, corresponding, respectively, to the two diagonal directions within the graph. This property is easily generalized to the case of the three-dimensional *Tonnetz*, as represented on the right side of Fig. 3.2. In this case, three axes are necessary to generate the three-dimensional model and they correspond to the minor third, major sixth and perfect fifth intervals. Note that, in this case, the reference point is G, as indicated on the right side of Fig. 3.2. In both representations, pitch classes are replicated infinitely along the axes by applying successive transpositions of the same interval.

These spaces can equivalently be thought of as the result of two T/I chord complexes which have been unfolded in a Euclidean space. Starting from a given n-note chord considered as belonging to a T/I class, one can first represent it by an $(n-1)$-simplex. The simplex is then embedded in an equilateral manner in the $(n-1)$-dimensional Euclidean space. For a 3-note chord, this space is the Euclidean plane and the chord is embedded as an equilateral triangle. The directions given to the 1-simplices (i.e., edges) define axes associated with particular intervals, as in the *Tonnetz*. Then, simplices are naturally replicated along these axes, in such a way that the represented chords respect the transpositions induced by the intervals of the axes. By starting with a major chord and a dominant seventh chord, one obtains the complexes $\mathcal{K}_{TI}[3,4,5]$ and $\mathcal{K}_{TI}[2,3,3,4]$ which are then unfolded as shown in Fig. 3.10. A consequence of this generic method of construction is that two complexes associated with chord classes of the same size are represented by identical structures (they are said to be isomorphic). Figure 3.10 shows the unfolding of the

---

[4] This "paradigmatic approach", where groups act as "paradigms" in the enumeration and classification of musical structures, corresponds to well-known catalogues of chords (respectively, the Vieru–Zalewsky catalogue of transpositional chord classes, Forte's pitch class sets catalogue, Estrada's permutohedron and Morris–Mazzola's affine orbits catalogue).

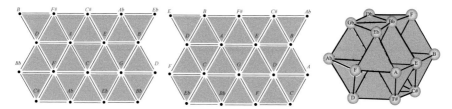

Fig. 3.10 Unfolded representations of 2-dimensional chord complexes $\mathcal{K}_{TI}[3,4,5]$ (left) and $\mathcal{K}_{TI}[2,3,7]$ (centre) as isomorphic structures. On the right, the unfolded representation of the 3-dimensional chord complex $\mathcal{K}_{TI}[2,3,3,4]$ composed of dominant seventh and half-diminished chords

complexes $\mathcal{K}_{TI}[3,4,5]$ and $\mathcal{K}_{TI}[2,3,7]$, both corresponding to a two-dimensional infinite triangular tessellation.

3.4 Analysis and Transformation of Trajectories in T/I Complexes

In this section, we represent musical sequences by *trajectories* in T/I complexes. We first perform a harmony-based analysis and classification by studying the shape of these trajectories. We then present a variety of spatial transformations on these trajectories which result in musical transformations on the represented sequences.

3.4.1 Representation of a Piece in a Chord Complex

In this work, a *trajectory* corresponds to a temporal sequence of regions in a chord complex. Each successive region represents a temporal segment of the piece. We use a very simple segmentation method, based on appearance and disappearance of pitch classes. Each time a pitch class enters or leaves the set of played notes, the current segment stops and a new one begins. This principle is illustrated in Fig. 3.11. Note that a musical sequence could be represented by a trajectory constructed using any other segmentation process, including more sophisticated algorithms involving automatic harmonic analysis. Each segment is characterized by its relative duration, compared to the other segments. A musical sequence P is thus reduced to a sequence of pitch class sets, each associated with a relative duration. We thus have $P = [(A_0, d_0), \ldots, (A_N, d_N)]$ where A_i is the set of *active* pitch classes during a duration d_i.

We represent the chord A in the chord complex $\mathcal{K}$ by the sub-complex $\mathcal{K}_A$ of $\mathcal{K}$ consisting of all the simplices in $\mathcal{K}$ which are labelled by a pitch class set included in A. A *trajectory* in a chord complex $\mathcal{K}$ is a sequence of sub-complexes of $\mathcal{K}$, each of

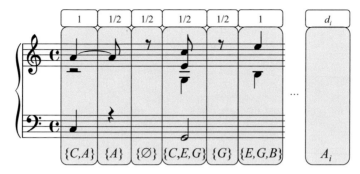

Fig. 3.11 Segmentation of a sequence depending on the set of played pitch classes. The duration of a segment (grey box) is calculated with respect to the quarter note taken as a unit

which is associated with a duration. The musical sequence $[(A_0, d_0), \ldots, (A_N, d_N)]$ is represented in a complex $\mathcal{K}$ by a trajectory $[(\mathcal{K}_0, d_0), \ldots, (\mathcal{K}_N, d_N)]$.

Figure 3.12 shows the sub-complexes constituting the trajectory of the sequence in Fig. 3.11 in $\mathcal{K}_{TI}[3,4,5]$. For more clarity, the trajectory is represented in the unfolded representation of the complex. Note that the 1-skeleton of this representation corresponds to the *Tonnetz* depicted on the left of Fig. 3.2.

Figure 3.13 shows the representation of the chorale, BWV 326, by J. S. Bach, by a trajectory in the T/I complexes $\mathcal{K}_{TI}[3,4,5]$ and $\mathcal{K}_{TI}[1,4,7]$. The trajectory on the left constitutes a shape that is more compact than the trajectory on the right. This observation suggests the idea that the different T/I complexes might not be equally

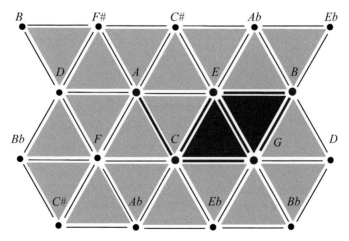

Fig. 3.12 Union (in dark grey) of the subcomplexes constituting a trajectory representing the sequence illustrated in Fig. 3.11 in $\mathcal{K}_{TI}[3,4,5]$. Note that the edge between A and C is also included in the union

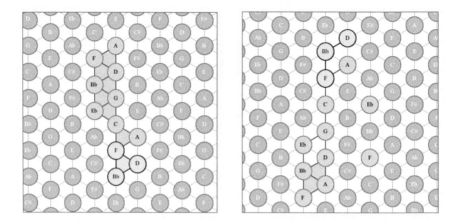

Fig. 3.13 First measures of the chorale, BWV 326, by J. S. Bach, represented as a trajectory in $\mathcal{K}_{TI}[3,4,5]$ (on the left) and in $\mathcal{K}_{TI}[1,4,7]$ (on the right)

well adapted to representing and analysing a particular musical sequence. In the next section, we propose a method for computing the compactness of a trajectory, in order to estimate how well a complex is adapted to representing a given musical sequence.

3.4.2 Computing Trajectory Compactness

In this section, we propose a method for computing the compactness of a trajectory representing a musical sequence in a chord complex.

3.4.2.1 Chord Compactness

Let $\mathcal{K}$ be a chord complex and $\mathcal{K}_A$ the sub-complex of $\mathcal{K}$ representing a pitch class set A. We define the *compactness at the dimension d* (or the *d-compactness*) of A in $\mathcal{K}$ to be

$$\mathcal{C}_d(\mathcal{K},A) = \frac{f_{d+1}(\mathcal{K}_A)}{f_{d+1}(\mathcal{S}(A))} .$$

In other words, the d-compactness corresponds to the number of d-simplices included in the representation of A in $\mathcal{K}$ divided by the number of d-simplices included in the simplicial representation of A.[5] Note that the value of the d-compactness varies between 0 and 1 whatever the dimension d is. The value chosen for the parameter

---

[5] This ratio recalls the *global clustering coefficient* (Holland and Leinhardt, 1971) in graph theory, which measures the degree to which nodes in a graph tend to cluster together. Our approach is more general because it applies to a set of arbitrary elements of the space (not necessarily neighbours of

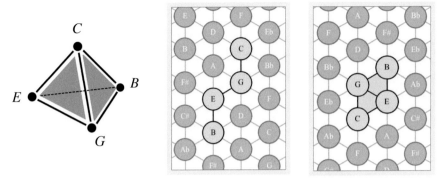

Fig. 3.14 The pitch class set $A = \{C,E,G,B\}$ represented by the 3-simplex $\mathcal{S}(A)$ (left), by a sub-complex of $\mathcal{K}_{TI}[2,3,7]$ (centre) and by a sub-complex of $\mathcal{K}_{TI}[3,4,5]$ (on the right)

d in the computation of the compactness depends on the type of study which is being performed. 1-compactness will be calculated for a study based on intervals. If the study relates to the inclusion of chords of size 3, one may prefer to work with 2-compactness.

As an example, let us compute the 1-compactness of the pitch class set $A = \{C,E,G,B\}$ in $\mathcal{K}_{TI}[2,3,7]$ and $\mathcal{K}_{TI}[3,4,5]$. As explained in Sect. 3.3.2, a 4-pitch class set is represented by a 3-simplex which includes six 1-simplices (i.e., $f_2(\mathcal{S}(A)) = 6$). As Fig. 3.14 shows, the representation of A in $\mathcal{K}_{TI}[2,3,7]$ includes three 1-simplices, whereas its representation in $\mathcal{K}_{TI}[3,4,5]$ includes five 1-simplices. We thus have $\mathcal{C}_1(\mathcal{K}_{TI}[2,3,7],A) = 3/6 = 0.5$ and $\mathcal{C}_1(\mathcal{K}_{TI}[3,4,5],A) = 5/6 = 0.83$. Analogously, by focusing on 2-simplices, we have $\mathcal{C}_2(\mathcal{K}_{TI}[2,3,7],A) = 0/4 = 0$ and $\mathcal{C}_2(\mathcal{K}_{TI}[3,4,5],A) = 2/4 = 0.5$. These results show that the representation of A in $\mathcal{K}_{TI}[3,4,5]$ is more compact than in $\mathcal{K}_{TI}[2,3,7]$ (as can be seen in Fig. 3.14).

Figure 3.15 illustrates the 2-compactness of four types of chords commonly used in tonal music: major, major seventh, dominant seventh and diminished seventh. This diagram shows that the compactness of a chord can be more or less equally distributed among a set of different complexes. For example, the equal compactness of the dominant seventh chord in $\mathcal{K}_{TI}[2,3,7]$, $\mathcal{K}_{TI}[2,4,6]$, $\mathcal{K}_{TI}[3,3,6]$ and $\mathcal{K}_{TI}[3,4,5]$ shows the harmonic diversity of this chord. On the other hand, the diminished seventh chord is represented with strong compactness in $\mathcal{K}_{TI}[3,3,6]$ only. This is due to the fact that the 3-note sub-chords included in this chord all belong to the T/I class $[3,3,6]$.

This type of diagram provides an original description of the constitution of a chord and can be exploited to represent *Z-relations* between chords (Mandereau et al., 2011).

---

the same element) and in a simplicial complex of any dimension (graphs are simplicial complexes of dimension 1).

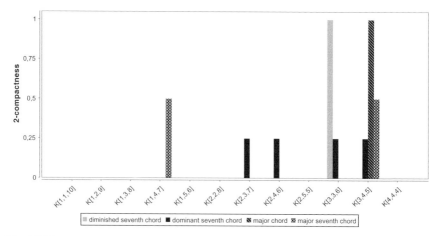

Fig. 3.15 2-compactness of diminished seventh, dominant seventh, major and major seventh chords in the twelve two-dimensional T/I complexes

Figure 3.16 illustrates the average 2-compactness of the set of all 3-pitch class sets. The compactness is computed in the twelve two-dimensional T/I complexes. The irregularity of the histogram shows that T/I complexes do not tend to represent arbitrary chords with the same compactness. This property depends on the size of the complex. For example, the probability of a random chord being represented compactly in $\mathcal{K}_{TI}[3,4,5]$ (which includes twenty-four 2-simplices) is six times higher than in $\mathcal{K}_{TI}[4,4,4]$ (which includes only four 2-simplices). The average value $E(\mathcal{C}_d(\mathcal{K},A))$ of the d-compactness $\mathcal{C}_d$ of chords of size greater than or equal to d in a complex $\mathcal{K}$ is equal to the number of $(d+1)$-simplices in $\mathcal{K}$ divided by the total number of chords of size $d+1$:

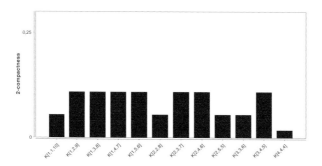

Fig. 3.16 Average 2-compactness of the set of all 3-pitch class sets in the twelve T/I complexes of dimension 2

$$E(\mathcal{C}_d(\mathcal{K},A)) = \frac{f_{d+1}(\mathcal{K})}{\binom{N}{d+1}} \, .$$

3.4.2.2 Trajectory Compactness

The global d-compactness of a trajectory T_P can be defined as the average of the d-compactness of its successive chords weighted by their duration d_i:

$$\mathcal{C}_d(\mathcal{K},T_P) = \frac{1}{D} \times \sum_{i=0}^{N} d_i \mathcal{C}_d(\mathcal{K},\mathcal{K}_i) \,,$$

where $D = \sum_{i=0}^{N} d_i$ represents the duration of the whole piece.

In the following, the compactness of the trajectory of a piece in a complex will systematically be displayed in comparison with the average compactness of chords in that same complex.

3.4.3 Computing the Compactness of Trajectories for Musical Analysis and Classification

We now analyse a number of pieces in terms of the compactness of their trajectories in different T/I complexes.

3.4.3.1 Comparing Spaces Regarding a Piece

The histograms in Fig. 3.17 illustrate the 2-compactness of the trajectories of three different pieces in the 12 chromatic T/I complexes of dimension 2. In each complex, the compactness of the trajectory of the piece (in black) is compared to the average compactness of its chords (in grey). The histograms have been generated with the software HexaChord which will be described in Sect. 3.5.

The first piece is the chorale, BWV 328, by J. S. Bach . The high compactness of the trajectory in $\mathcal{K}_{TI}[3,4,5]$ results from the strong use of major and minor chords which is typical of tonal music in general and Bach's chorales in particular. The high compactness of the trajectories in $\mathcal{K}_{TI}[2,3,7]$ and $\mathcal{K}_{TI}[2,5,5]$ is due to the use of dominant seventh and suspended chords which have particular functions in this style of music. The compactness in the complexes $\mathcal{K}_{TI}[2,2,8]$, $\mathcal{K}_{TI}[2,4,6]$ and $\mathcal{K}_{TI}[4,4,4]$ of Claude Debussy's prelude, *Voiles*, highlights the predominant use of the whole-tone scale in this piece. Finally, the piece *Parodie* from Schoenberg's *Pierrot Lunaire* illustrates for each complex a compactness relatively close to the average compactness of chords. This results from an almost equally distributed use

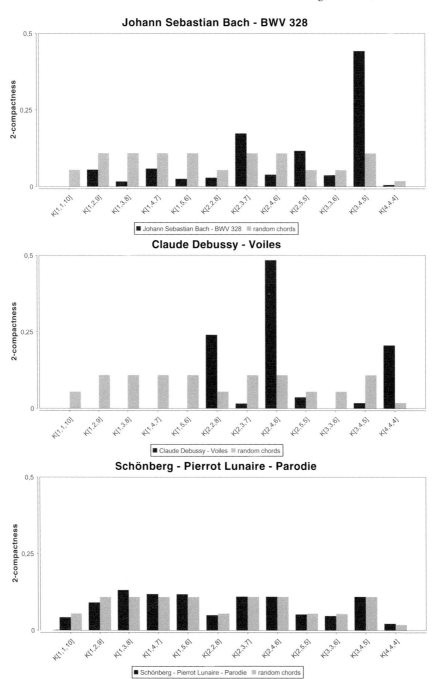

Fig. 3.17 2-compactness of the trajectories of three pieces in the 12 chromatic T/I complexes. In each complex, the compactness of the pieces (in black) is compared to the average compactness of chords (in grey)

of pitch class sets of size 3 or more throughout the piece, as one might expect in twelve-tone or atonal music.

Three drastically different pieces have been chosen in this example in order to illustrate how the compactness of trajectories can depend on the musical style in an illuminating and informative way. However, this method can also be used to reveal more refined nuances between pieces in the same style.

3.4.3.2 Distance and Classification

The previous examples show that calculating the compactness of a piece in a set of complexes provides an abstract description that can highlight certain aspects of its harmonic structure. This description can be used to compare pieces as well. We propose a notion of distance between musical sequences based on compactness regarding a set of complexes. For a set of complexes $E = \{\mathcal{K}_1, \mathcal{K}_2 \dots\}$, we define the d-distance between two pieces P and P' by the Euclidean distance:

$$D_{E,d}(P,P') = \sqrt{\sum_{\mathcal{K} \in E} \left(\mathcal{C}_d(\mathcal{K}, T_\mathcal{K}) - \mathcal{C}_d(\mathcal{K}, T'_\mathcal{K})\right)^2} \,,$$

where $T_\mathcal{K}$ and $T'_\mathcal{K}$ are the trajectories representing, respectively, P and P' in $\mathcal{K}$. The d-distance is computed by only taking into account chords whose size is greater than or equal to $d+1$.

The mean compactness of the pieces constituting a corpus allows us to calculate a distance between any piece and this corpus. This notion of harmonic distance has been used for music classification (Bigo, 2013).

3.4.4 Transformations on Trajectories

The method described above allows any musical sequence to be represented by a trajectory within a given chord complex. Thanks to the symmetry properties of some T/I complexes, it is sometimes easy to have an immediate intuition of the musical interpretation of some geometrical transformations on trajectories or their embedding in different support spaces. In the first case we can, for example, interpret a transposition or an inversion operation as a translation or a rotation, respectively, of a given trajectory.

Figure 3.18 displays the trajectory representing the first measures of Bach's chorale, BWV 332, which is rotated by 180°. This operation transforms major chords into minor chords (and vice versa). A second type of transformation consists of the embedding of a given trajectory in a new support space. This corresponds to a relabelling of the notes attached to a trajectory according to the pitch content of the new underlying space. Although the trajectory remains the same, its embedding in a new space dramatically changes the intervallic relations between the notes. As an

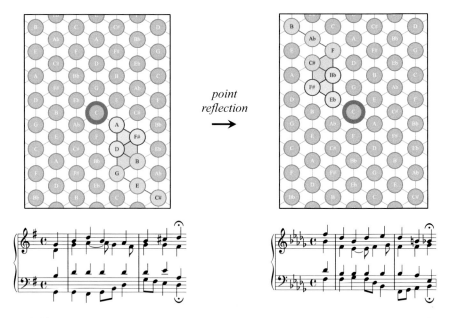

Fig. 3.18 On the left, a trajectory representing the first measures of the chorale, BWV 332, by J. S. Bach in $\mathcal{K}_{TI}[3,4,5]$. On the right, a point reflection is applied to this trajectory, producing a new sequence

example, Fig. 3.19 shows the result of embedding the trajectory in $\mathcal{K}_{TI}[3,4,5]$ of the first measures of the chorale, BWV 332, in the new support space, $\mathcal{K}_{TI}[2,3,7]$. This embedding produces a new musical sequence which will sound more exotic, due to the prominence of the pentatonic scale in the new support space. From a mathematical point of view, transformations of trajectories within chord complexes can be formalized as *morphisms* (Bigo et al., 2014).

3.5 The HexaChord Software

HexaChord is a freely available computer-aided music analysis software package based on the spatial representations presented in this chapter.[6] The software provides a 3-D visualization of the complex representing any arbitrary set of chords. To improve intelligibility, chromatic and diatonic T/I complexes of dimension 2 (i.e., constituted of 3-note chords) can be unfolded as infinite two-dimensional triangular tessellations, in the same style as the planar representation of the *Tonnetz* (see Figs. 3.2 and 3.12). The 12 chromatic T/I complexes together with the four diatonic T/I complexes, each

---

[6] http://www.lacl.fr/ lbigo/hexachord

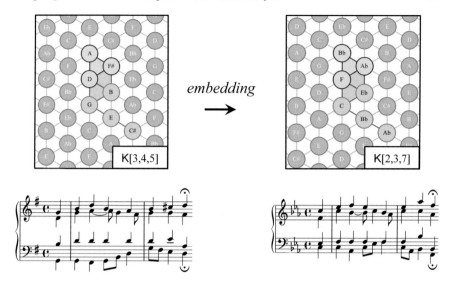

Fig. 3.19 On the left, the first measures of Bach's chorale, BWV 332, represented by a trajectory in $\mathcal{K}_{TI}[3,4,5]$. On the right, the transformation of the sequence resulting from the embedding of the trajectory in $\mathcal{K}_{TI}[2,3,7]$

available in the 12 diatonic scale, result in a total of 60 available planar organizations of pitch classes.

In the unfolded representation, pitch-classes and chords are repeated multiple times along interval axes in the complex. As a consequence, a piece can be represented by an infinite number of trajectories. Different strategies can then be applied to build a satisfying trajectory from a musical sequence (Bigo, 2013). An algorithm that minimizes the distance between every pair of successive chords in the complex will be more efficient for analysing chord progressions in time. On the other hand, an algorithm maximizing the compactness of each chord (independently of the other chords) will be more efficient for analysing the harmonic content of a piece.

Musical pieces are imported as MIDI files. A trajectory is automatically computed for any given piece–complex pair. The trajectory is represented as a path which evolves in real time within its complex while the piece is being played. The compactness of the trajectory over time (and on average) is automatically computed for any T/I complex and in any dimension. The calculation of compactness reveals the complexes which are the most harmonically related to the piece. Following this hypothesis, this functionality should suggest to the user which spaces can be used in order to reveal some interesting harmonic properties of a piece via its visualization.

HexaChord also allows the geometrical transformations described in Sect. 3.4.4 to be carried out on trajectories. A trajectory in a complex $\mathcal{K}$ can be translated, rotated, or even embedded in an other chord complex $\mathcal{K}'$. Every spatial transformation causes the values labelling the sub-complexes constituting the trajectory to be refreshed. The harmonic and melodic content of the original piece can be transformed according to the new labels of the selected trajectory, thus leading to a new musical piece which can be exported in MIDI format or analysed and transformed using the spatial techniques described in this chapter.

3.6 Conclusion

In this chapter, we have presented a method for identifying any set of chords by a labelled simplicial complex. The family of T/I complexes relate to *Generalized Tonnetze* and can be used as support spaces to represent musical pieces for analysis and classification purposes.

The analysis method proposed here relates to the instantaneous verticality of chords. However, studying harmonic properties within a piece requires a horizontal approach as well (i.e., to study transitions between successive chords). In future work, we intend to address this issue by investigating methods for computing distances between sub-complexes within a complex.

We believe that the visual and intuitive aspects of this spatial approach constitute a strong pedagogical advantage for the understanding of harmony. For example, T/I complexes offer an original and intuitive reformulation of the notion of inversionally/transpositionally related chord classes. Moreover, we believe that the spatial reformulation of musical problems has a heuristic advantage. Thanks to its intuitive

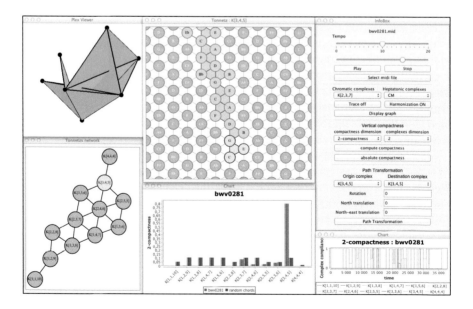

Fig. 3.20 Graphical user interface of HexaChord

aspects, spatial structures frequently suggest unexpected questions, thus opening new research areas.

Finally, methods for automatically computing space-related descriptors (compactness of sub-complexes, distances within complexes, etc.) should allow for the construction of statistical models given a corpus of a particular style. Such models, based so far on *viewpoints* without spatial considerations, have been shown to be useful in various areas including music prediction and classification (Conklin and Witten, 1995). In future work we therefore intend to carry out an in-depth investigation of some statistical models built from spatial descriptions of musical pieces.

Acknowledgements The authors are very grateful to Antoine Spicher and Olivier Michel from LACL - Université Paris-Est, Jean-Louis Giavitto from IRCAM - Université Pierre et Marie Curie, Jean-Marc Chouvel from Université de Reims, and Darrell Conklin from Universidad del Pais Vasco for numerous fruitful discussions. This research is partially supported by the project "Learning to create" (Lrn2Cre8). The project Lrn2Cre8 acknowledges the financial support of the Future and Emerging Technologies (FET) programme within the Seventh Framework Programme for Research of the European Commission, under FET grant number 610859.

References

Andreatta, M. (2008). Calcul algébrique et calcul catégoriel en musique: Aspects théoriques et informatiques. In Pottier, L., editor, *Le calcul de la musique*, pages 429–477. Publications de l'Université de Saint-Etienne.

Andreatta, M. and Agon, C. (2003). Implementing algebraic methods in OpenMusic. In *Proceedings of the International Computer Music Conference*, Singapore.

Bigo, L. (2013). *Représentations symboliques musicales et calcul spatial*. PhD thesis, LACL/IRCAM, Université Paris-Est.

Bigo, L. and Andreatta, M. (2014). A geometrical model for the analysis of pop music. *Sonus*, 35(1):36–48.

Bigo, L., Ghisi, D., Spicher, A., and Andreatta, M. (2014). Spatial transformations in simplicial chord spaces. In *Proceedings of the Fortieth International Computer Music Conference and Eleventh Sound and Music Computing Conference (ICMC/SMC 2014)*, pages 1112–1119, Athens, Greece.

Bigo, L., Giavitto, J.-L., and Spicher, A. (2011). Building topological spaces for musical objects. In *Mathematics and Computation in Music: Third International Conference, MCM 2011, Paris, France, June 2011, Proceedings*, volume 6726 of *Lecture Notes in Artificial Intelligence*, pages 13–28. Springer.

Callender, C., Quinn, I., and Tymoczko, D. (2008). Generalized voice-leading spaces. *Science*, 320(5874):346.

Catanzaro, M. (2011). Generalized *Tonnetze*. *Journal of Mathematics and Music*, 5(2):117–139.

Chew, E. (2002). The spiral array: An algorithm for determining key boundaries. In *Music and Artificial Intelligence: Second International Conference, ICMAI 2002, Edinburgh, Scotland, UK, September 2002, Proceedings*, pages 18–31. Springer.

Chouvel, J.-M. (2009). Traversée du vent et de la lumière. Six remarques pour une phénoménologie de la création musicale. Available online at http://jeanmarc.chouvel.3.free.fr/textes/Traversee0.0.pdf.

Cohn, R. (1997). Neo-Riemannian operations, parsimonious trichords, and their "Tonnetz" representations. *Journal of Music Theory*, 41(1):1–66.

Cohn, R. (2012). *Audacious Euphony: Chromatic Harmony and the Triad's Second Nature*. Oxford University Press.

Conklin, D. and Witten, I. H. (1995). Multiple viewpoint systems for music prediction. *Journal of New Music Research*, 24(1):51–73.

Euler, L. (1739). *Tentamen novae theoriae musicae ex certissismis harmoniae principiis dilucide expositae*. Saint Petersburg Academy.

Forte, A. (1973). *The Structure of Atonal Music*. Yale University Press.

Giavitto, J.-L. and Michel, O. (2001). MGS: a rule-based programming language for complex objects and collections. In van den Brand, M. and Verma, R., editors, *Electronic Notes in Theoretical Computer Science*, volume 59, pages 286–304. Elsevier Science Publishers.

Giavitto, J.-L. and Spicher, A. (2008). Simulation of self-assembly processes using abstract reduction systems. In Krasnogor, N., Gustafson, S., Pelta, D., and Verdegay, J. L., editors, *Systems Self-Assembly: Multidisciplinary Snapshots*, pages 199–223. Elsevier.

Gollin, E. (1998). Some aspects of three-dimensional "Tonnetze". *Journal of Music Theory*, 42(2):195–206.

Holland, P. W. and Leinhardt, S. (1971). Transitivity in structural models of small groups. *Small Group Research*, 2:107–124.

Hook, J. (2014). *Generic sequences and the generic* Tonnetz. Oxford Handbooks Online.

Mandereau, J., Ghisi, D., Amiot, E., Andreatta, M., and Agon, C. (2011). Z-relation and homometry in musical distributions. *Journal of Mathematics and Music*, 5(2):83–98.

Mazzola, G. et al. (2002). *The Topos of Music: Geometric Logic of Concepts, Theory, and Performance*. Birkhäuser.

Pousseur, H. (1968). L'apothéose de Rameau. Essai sur la question harmonique. *Musiques Nouvelles. Revue d'esthétique, 21*, pages 105–172.

Pousseur, H. (1998). Applications analytiques de la technique des réseaux. *Revue belge de Musicologie, 52*, pages 247–298.

Rameau, J.-P. (1722). *Traité de l'harmonie, reduite à ses principes naturels*. Jean-Baptiste-Christophe Ballard.

Tymoczko, D. (2012). The generalized *Tonnetz*. *Journal of Music Theory*, 56(1):1–52.

Chapter 4
Contextual Set-Class Analysis

Agustín Martorell and Emilia Gómez

Abstract In this chapter, we review and elaborate a methodology for contextual multi-scale set-class analysis of pieces of music. The proposed method provides a systematic approach to segmentation, description and representation in the analysis of the musical surface. The introduction of a set-class description domain provides a systematic, mid-level, and standard analytical lexicon, which allows for the description of any notated music based on a fixed temperament. The method benefits from representation completeness, a balance between generalization and discrimination of the set-class spaces, and access to hierarchical inclusion relations over time. Three new data structures are derived from the method: *class-scapes*, *class-matrices* and *class-vectors*. A *class-scape* represents, in a visual way, the set-class content of each possible segment in a piece of music. The *class-matrix* represents the presence of each possible set class over time, and is invariant to time scale and to several transformations of analytical interest. The *class-vector* summarizes a piece by quantifying the temporal presence of each possible set class. The balance between dimensionality and informativeness provided by these descriptors is discussed in relation to standard content-based tonal descriptors and music information retrieval applications. The interfacing possibilities of the method are also discussed.

4.1 Introduction

The representation of the musical surface is a fundamental element for analysis, as it constitutes the raw material to be explained by the analyst. As for any information representation problem, favouring the observation of some specific musical parameters comes at the price of misrepresenting others. The choice of an appropriate surface characterization is not only a critical step that conditions the whole analysis,

Agustín Martorell · Emilia Gómez
Universitat Pompeu Fabra, Barcelona, Spain
e-mail: {agustin.martorell, emilia.gomez}@upf.edu

© Springer International Publishing Switzerland 2016
D. Meredith (ed.), *Computational Music Analysis*,
DOI 10.1007/978-3-319-25931-4_4

but it also often requires considerable effort from the analyst. Proper music information representations and interfacing techniques can free analysts from the most systematic, time-consuming and error-prone tasks, and assist them in finding and testing material of analytical relevance. Human analysts can then exploit the preprocessed data using their perception, intuition and inference abilities, in order to make appropriate analytical decisions. The best processing capabilities of computers (good systematization, poor inference) and humans (good inference, poor systematization) can then complement each other in a constructive way.

In this chapter, we propose an approach to the musical surface, in terms of generalized *contextual* pitch-wise information. This way of conceiving of the surface extends the usual application domain of analysis in terms of *events* (e.g., chords), giving access to richer, multi-scale, hierarchical information about the music. We propose that three aspects of the analytical process are particularly relevant for such an endeavour: first, the segmentation of the music into analysable units; second, the description of these units in adequate terms; and, third, the representation of the results in ways that are manageable and provide insight. We consider each of these three aspects from a systematic point of view. First, we present a comprehensive segmentation policy that extracts every possible (different) segment of music. Second, we propose that these segments be described in terms of pitch-class set theory. Third, we propose usable data structures for representing the resulting data.

The remainder of this chapter is organized as follows. In Sect. 4.2, we present the problems of segmentation, description and representation in the context of surface analysis, and introduce basic set-theoretical concepts. In Sect. 4.3, we describe the proposed computational approach. In Sect. 4.4, we introduce the basic set of data structures, while in Sects. 4.5 and 4.6, we discuss these data structures in the context of several music information retrieval (MIR) applications. Finally, in Sect. 4.7, we consider the interfacing possibilities of the descriptors.

4.2 Background and Motivation

4.2.1 On Segmentation

A main concern for analysis is the grouping of musical elements into units of analytical pertinence, a complex process that we refer to here by the term *segmentation*. According to Forte (1973, p. 83),

> by segmentation is meant the procedure of determining which musical units of a composition are to be regarded as analytical objects.

In the context of pitch-class set analysis, Cook (1987, p. 146) observes that

> no set-theoretical analysis can be more objective, or more well-founded musically, than its initial segmentation.

Considering the joint problem of finding appropriate segments and assessing their pertinence, a pursuit of systematization and *neutrality* in the surface characterization arises as a convenient preprocessing stage.[1] On the other hand, there is no such thing as a truly neutral representation, as pointed out by Huron (1992, p. 38):

> a representation system as a whole may be viewed as a signifier for a particular assumed or explicit explanation...

In our work, we aim for neutral representations in order to allow for a wide range of musical idioms to be analysed using only a limited set of assumptions. Our method assumes the concept of a *musical note*, temporally limited between its onset and offset. We also assume octave equivalence in a twelve-tone equal-tempered pitch system. The general framework, however, can be adapted for any discrete pitch organization of the octave. We do not, of course, claim that systematization and neutrality suffice for analysis. Indeed, one could distinguish between a *systematic* segmentation (as a preprocessing step), and an *analytic* (i.e., meaningful) segmentation

> not as something imposed upon the work, but rather... as something to be discovered.

> (Hasty, 1981, p. 59)

In our approach, the term *segment* is used formally to mean a temporal interval (i.e., chunk) of music, irrespective of its actual musical content. This content may be analysed by subsequent processing stages.

Systematization can, of course, be conceived of in various ways. Conventional segmentation strategies, such as those applied by human analysts working on scores, rely on some prior rhythmic or metric knowledge of the music. For instance, the analysis of chords benefits from a temporal segmentation into beats or bars. This information, however, may not be explicitly available in computer-based music encodings, such as a MIDI file generated from a live performances or automatically transcribed from an audio file. Moreover, this kind of segmentation may not be meaningful or appropriate for certain types of music (e.g., free rhythm, melismatic or *ad-libitum* passages).

A useful, general-purpose, segmentation approach is to apply a *sliding window* with an appropriate *resolution*. In this context, a *window* is a temporal *frame*, which isolates a segment of music to be analysed. A window which is gradually *displaced* over time is referred to as a *sliding window*, and allows sequential discrete observations. The *resolution* of a sliding window is given by its duration (time scale or window size) and the amount of time displaced between consecutive frames (the *hop size*). This resolution is obviously a critical parameter. It depends on the musical parameter under inspection, as well as on the music itself, so adaptive methods may be required in general. In this sense, a systematic segmentation may be thought of as the problem of inspecting *every* possible (different) segment in the music, no matter its position in time or its duration. By adopting the concept of *note*, it is possible to reduce these infinitely many segments to a finite set of segments capturing every distinct pitch aggregate in the piece.

---

[1] For a discussion about neutrality and the risks of circular reasoning in the context of set-theoretical analysis, see Deliège (1989), Forte (1989) and Nattiez (2003).

Forte claimed that this kind of systematic segmentation (which he called 'imbrication') would be impractical for analysis, as it would result in an unmanageable number of overlapping segments, most of which would not be musically significant (see Cook (1987, p. 147) for a discussion). Forte thus claims a need for 'editing' these segments according to criteria which would depend on the specific music, a process unlikely to be systematized in any useful way (Forte, 1973, pp. 90–91). These observations were made with the conventional methods and goals of (academic) musical analysis in mind. For more general (and modest) analysis-related applications, however, one can take advantage of computational methods. In our work, we adopt some interface-design strategies and filtering techniques that can handle such a cumbersome amount of information, and we then apply them to specific music information retrieval tasks.

Among the most systematic approaches to general pitch-class set analysis, Huovinen and Tenkanen (2007) propose a segmentation algorithm based on a 'tail-segment array', in which each note in a composition is associated with all the possible segments of a given cardinality that contain it.[2] This segmentation is combined with certain 'detector functions' to obtain summarized information from the piece. This segmentation method has a number of shortcomings (see Martorell and Gómez, 2015). First, the note-based indexing in terms of 'tail segments' can result in many segments that only contain some of the notes in a vertical chord. Second, considering only segments of a specified cardinality undermines systematization by defining a content-dependent segmentation. Moreover, it undermines neutrality, by defining cardinality to be an analytical parameter, resulting in most of the possible segments being ignored and, in some cases, absurd segmentations. Third, the non-uniqueness of the tail-segment arrays associated with a given time point can result in an ill-defined temporal continuity. For example, in their analysis of Bach's *Es ist genug* (BWV 60), Huovinen and Tenkanen (2007, p. 163) order the notes lexicographically, sorting first by time and then by pitch height. This means that two 'successive' notes may either have different onset times or they may be from the same chord and thus have the same onset time. In such cases, the temporal ordering of the notes is therefore ill-defined.

4.2.2 On Description

In our work, the description stage consists of associating each segment with some content-based property of analytical interest. The descriptive value of such information depends on both the property of the segment that we are interested in (e.g., pitch, rhythm or timbre), and on the way in which the retrieved information is represented (e.g., different ways of encoding or summarizing pitch information). The design of a proper feature space requires some considerations and compromises, among which we identify the following.

---

[2] See Sect. 4.2.2.1 for a formal definition of *cardinality*.

1. *The trade-off between discrimination and generalization*   On the one hand, the descriptive *lexicon* should be able to identify distinct musical realities. On the other hand, such a lexicon should be able to connect segments related by some analytical and/or perceptual criteria. A description *for analysis* should facilitate the observation of relationships.
2. *The trade-off between dimensionality and informativeness*   Related to the previous point, this involves maximizing the overall informativeness, using a reasonable (i.e., manageable) lexicon of musical objects.
3. *Completeness*   We want a system that is capable of describing *any* possible segment in meaningful ways, covering a wide range of musical idioms.
4. *Communicability*   The descriptive lexicon should not only be meaningful, but, ideally, readily understandable by humans, so that analytical conclusions can be derived and explained. This implies that some standard musical terminology is desirable.

4.2.2.1 Pitch-Class Set Concepts

In this section, we will review some basic concepts from pitch-class set theory, as they constitute the descriptive basis of our method. The *pitch class* (Babbitt, 1955) is defined, for the twelve-tone equal-tempered (TET) system, as an integer representing the residue class modulo 12 of some continuous integer representation of pitch, that is, any pitch (represented as a single integer) is mapped to a pitch-class by removing its octave information. A *pitch-class set* (henceforth *pc-set*) is an unordered set of pitch classes (i.e., without repetitions). In the twelve-tone equal-tempered system, there exist $2^{12} = 4096$ distinct pc-sets, so a vocabulary of 4096 symbols is required for describing any possible segment of music. Any pc-set can also be represented by its intervallic content (Hanson, 1960). Intervals considered regardless of their direction are referred to as *interval classes*. There exist 6 different interval classes, corresponding to 1, 2, 3, 4, 5 and 6 semitones respectively. The remaining intervals in the octave are mapped to these 6 classes by inversion. For instance, the perfect fifth (7 semitones up) is mapped to the perfect fourth (5 semitones down), and represented by the interval class 5. The total count of interval classes in a pc-set can be arranged as a 6-dimensional data structure called an *interval vector* (Forte, 1964). For instance, the diatonic set $\{0,2,4,5,7,9,11\}$ is represented by the interval vector $\langle 254361 \rangle$, as the set contains 2 semitones, 5 whole-tones, 4 minor thirds, 3 major thirds, 6 perfect fourths and 1 tritone.

Relevant relational concepts for analysis are the *set-class equivalences*, whereby two pc-sets are considered equivalent if and only if they belong to the same *set class* (defined below). Put differently, set-class spaces result from applying certain equivalence relations among all the possible pc-sets. As pointed out by Straus (1990), equivalence is not the same thing as identity, rather it is a link between musical entities that have something in common.[3] This commonality underlying the surface

---

[3] In this sense, a class equivalence can be conceived of as an all-or-nothing *similarity measure* between two pc-sets. Later on in this chapter, we will discuss similarity measures between different

can potentially lend unity and/or coherence to musical works (Straus, 1990, pp. 1–2). In the context of pc-sets, the number of pitch classes in a set is referred to as its *cardinality*. This provides the basis for perhaps the coarsest measure of similarity (Rahn, 1980). Despite its theoretical relevance, comparing pitch class sets on the basis of their cardinalities provides too general a notion of similarity to be of use in most analytical situations. Among the many kinds of similarity in the set-theoretical literature, three are particularly useful:[4]

1. *Interval vector equivalence* (henceforth *iv-equivalence*), which groups all the pc-sets sharing the same interval vector. There exist 197 different iv-types.
2. *Transpositional equivalence* (henceforth T_n-*equivalence*), which groups all the pc-sets related to each other by transposition. There exist 348 distinct T_n-types.
3. *Inversional and transpositional equivalence* (henceforth T_nI-*equivalence*), which groups all the pc-sets related by transposition and/or inversion. There exist 220 different T_nI-types (also referred to as T_n/T_nI-types).

The compromise between discrimination and generalization of these equivalence relations fits a wide range of descriptive needs, hence their extensive use in general-purpose music analysis. Of these relations, iv-equivalence is the most general (197 classes). It shares most of its classes with T_nI-equivalence (220 classes), with some exceptions, known as *Z-relations* (Forte, 1964), for which the same interval vector groups pitch-class sets which are not T_nI-equivalent (Lewin, 1959). The most specific of these three relations is T_n-equivalence (348 classes). T_n-equivalence satisfies two of the most basic types of perceptual similarity between pitch configurations: octave and transposition invariance. Two pc-sets related to each other by transposition only belong to the same transpositional set class, and they share a similar sonority in many musical contexts. For instance, it is clear that a pentatonic melody would sound very similar to any of its transpositions. The set-class counterpart to this, under T_n-equivalence, states that all pentatonic music, based on the same set or any transposition of the set, would sound pentatonic.

More general class equivalences have also been proposed in the set-theoretical and analysis literature, such as the *K complexes* and *Kh sub-complexes* (Forte, 1964), or *set genera* (Forte, 1988). Despite their theoretical importance, their resulting classes group together too distinct musical realities to be of practical use for our general purposes. More specific class equivalences, such as pitch (invariant to timbral transformations) or pitch-class (invariant to octave transformations), constitute the usual descriptive lexicon in score-based descriptions and MIR applications alike. However, despite their descriptive power, they cannot encode even basic analytical relations or perceptual implications, without further processing.

We thus propose iv-, T_nI- and T_n-equivalences as a convenient mid-level descriptive domain, bridging the gap between (too specific) pitches or pitch-classes and (too

---

classes, which are used to quantify the distances between pc-sets beyond mere class-belonging relations. In order to avoid misconceptions with the usage of the term 'similarity' in this work, the reader is encouraged to attend to the proper contextualization.

[4] See Forte (1964) for a comprehensive formalization or Straus (1990) for a pedagogical approach. A worked example is given in Sect. 4.3.2.

generic) higher-level concepts. Set-classes do not refer *explicitly* to other mid-level musical objects, such as chords or keys. However, they encode an analytically important property of such pitch collections, with the additional benefit of covering the complete set of possible pitch aggregates.

4.2.3 On Representation

Here, we use the term *representation* to mean the data structures serving as a substrate of the descriptions—that is, the final descriptors as they will be processed, whether by human analysts or by automatic algorithms. As discussed above in relation to Huovinen and Tenkanen's (2007) approach, the enormous number of overlapping segments, together with the somewhat large lexicon of classes, gives rise to problems of practical indexing and summarization of the data.

Summarization, in general, implies a loss of information. The time dimension is usually the first parameter to be sacrificed when summarizing pitch information. Some methods based on statistical averaging rarely retain usable time-related information. For instance, Huovinen and Tenkanen (2007) characterize the interval content of a given tail-segment array as a *mean interval-class vector (MICV)*, by computing the dimension-wise mean from the interval vectors of each segment belonging to the array. A more compact summary computes the mean from all the MICVs in a piece (Huovinen and Tenkanen, 2007, p. 172). This results in a single six-dimensional vector, which is an indicator of the relative *prevalence* of the different intervals in the music, but it is not straightforwardly interpretable—to a large extent, because most of the intervals are accounted for several times in the tail-segment arrays, and this number varies according to the polyphonic writing.

Another common method of summarization consists of quantifying the number of occurrences of each class from some given lexicon of classes (e.g., the number of instances of each chord type). While histograms from these *event counting* methods may provide useful indicators of the relative importance of each class, they present an inherent conceptual problem: they assume that the pitch content is to be understood in terms of *events*, as instances that can be unambiguously segmented and counted (for instance, beat-wise chords). Aside from requiring prior knowledge about how to segment the music, this approach fails to take into consideration the description of tonal contexts in a wider sense. For instance, a diatonic passage usually embeds several overlapped diatonic subsegments, so *counting* the number of diatonic instances in a piece may not be very informative. An alternative to this may be to quantify the diatonicism by *measuring* its overall temporal existence in the piece.

Here, we propose alternative summarization and quantification strategies. We avoid thinking in terms of *events*, by conceptualizing every segment as a *context*. Each segment (context) can thus be embedded in larger contexts, and can embed shorter ones. Quantification is not conceived of as the number of instances of the different classes, but as the amount of time these classes are *active* in the music.[5] Deviating from other systematic approaches, this allows for the preservation of a great deal of class-wise and temporal information through each reduction stage. An additional goal is that the various scaled representations should complement each other, in order to maximize overall informativeness when it comes to interface design (see Sect. 4.7).

4.2.3.1 Visualization

In representation design, the final *user* of the information constitutes a major factor. As humans have tremendous, innate capabilities for inferring useful information from images, visualizing information effectively is often the best way of communicating it to humans. Musical information is not an exception. When talking about music, the use of terms related to space is ubiquitous (e.g., references to the *height* of a pitch, a harmonic *attraction*, a modulation to a *distant* key, a *vertical* chord or a *horizontal* interval between notes in a melody). Even time is often conceived of as a spatial dimension, as reflected in many musical notations. Spatial representations and associations seem to be an inherent part of human thinking, presumably related to the fact that we live in a physical (three-dimensional) world with which we interact through our senses (Leman, 2008).

Many visual representations have been proposed for capturing and revealing pitch-related concepts, usually relying on mid-level musical concepts, such as chords or keys.[6] A variety of spaces, based on set-theoretical concepts, are at the core of many mathematical music theories (see Chap. 3, this volume). Tymoczko (2011), for instance, represents voice-leading relations between a given set of chord types in geometric spaces. In those spaces, it is possible to represent somewhat abstract relations as *pictorial* patterns, reinforcing the auditory phenomena with intuitive visual cues.

The analysis of complete pieces of music in these spaces is challenging, however. The time dimension in these representations can be conveniently introduced by movement-in-space metaphors.[7] When it comes to representing long passages, these methods present visual problems relating to leaving traces of the past, compromising any practical temporal indexing of the music. For instance, it may be difficult to distinguish among different instances of the same recurring pattern, as they can appear superimposed on each other in the space. However, it is often of interest to analyse long segments of music, in order to observe far-reaching relationships over time. The temporal dimension, thus, arises as a convenient (explicit) dimension to be considered in the design of visual representations of music (Martorell, 2013).

---

[5] A large number of event instances does not imply prevalence, as the events themselves can be very short in duration, e.g., in *tremolo* passages.

[6] See Lerdahl (2001, pp. 42–47) for a review.

[7] In Tymoczko's chordal spaces, this is more than a metaphor: while a *sequence of states* can represent chord progressions, the representation of their voice-leading relations needs the actual (continuous) *paths* followed by each individual voice (Tymoczko, 2011, pp. 43–44).

4.2.3.2 Temporal Multi-scale Representation Methods

Sapp (2005) proposes a systematic, user-oriented approach to tonal analysis and representation. After a comprehensive multi-scale (temporal multiresolution) segmentation of the music, the tonal centre is estimated for each segment. The different estimations are coded through a colourmap, and all the segments are plotted as a two-dimensional image, called a *keyscape*, whose dimensions represent time on the horizontal axis and, on the vertical axis, time-scale (i.e., time-scale of observation, or window size, corresponding to the durations of the analysis segments). The method, which gives access to hierarchical descriptions of tonality, has been adapted by Martorell (2013) to form the basis of a general framework for *tonal context* analysis. This method can operate in both the symbolic and audio domains, and extends the concept of keyscape to tonal systems other than the major–minor system.

4.3 Hierarchical Multi-scale Set-Class Analysis

The method proposed here takes as its starting point the concept of a keyscape and extends its systematization (with respect to segmentation and representation) to the description stage. For that, the key estimation is substituted with a set-class description. Figure 4.1 sketches the general framework proposed by Martorell (2013, p. 26), here adapted for set-class analysis. A detailed description of each stage (segmentation, description and representation) follows.[8]

4.3.1 Segmentation

The input to the system is a sequence of MIDI events, which can be of any rhythmic or polyphonic complexity. Segmentation is implemented by two different algorithms: a) an approximate technique, non-comprehensive but practical for interacting with the data; and b) a fully systematic method, which exhausts all the segmentation possibilities. Figure 4.2 illustrates both cases.

The approximate method consists of applying many overlapping sliding windows, each of them scanning the music at a different time-scale (duration of observation). The minimum window size and the number of time-scales are user parameters, and can be fine tuned as a trade-off between resolution and computational cost. The actual time-scales are defined by applying a logarithmic law covering the range between the minimum window size and the whole duration of the piece.[9] In order to provide a regular grid for indexing, visualization and interfacing purposes, the same hop size

---

[8] The method is explained following the same blocks of Sect. 4.2: segmentation, description and representation. For computational convenience, the actual implementation differs slightly, as depicted in Fig. 4.1.

[9] Motivated by the fact that larger time-scales usually yield coarser changing information.

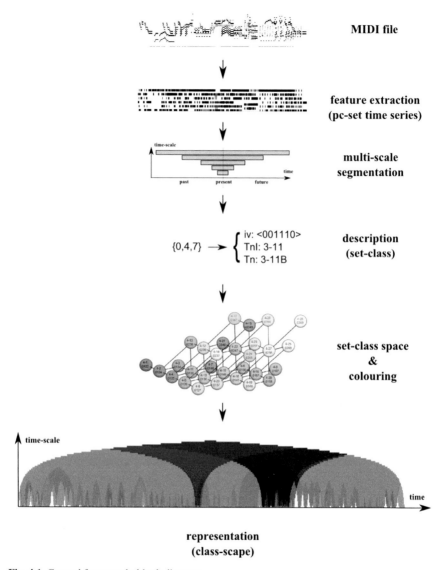

MIDI file

**feature extraction
(pc-set time series)**

**multi-scale
segmentation**

$\{0,4,7\} \longrightarrow \begin{cases} \text{iv: <001110>} \\ \text{TnI: 3-11} \\ \text{Tn: 3-11B} \end{cases}$ **description
(set-class)**

**set-class space
&
colouring**

**representation
(class-scape)**

Fig. 4.1 General framework: block diagram

is applied for all the time-scales. Each segment is thus indexed by its centre location
(time) and its duration (time-scale).

The fully systematic method is required for the quantitative descriptors in which
completeness of representation is necessary (see Sect. 4.4.2.2). The algorithm first
finds every change in the pc-set content over time, regardless of whether the change is
produced by the onset or the offset of a note. The piece is then segmented according
to every pairwise combination among these boundaries.

4.3.2 Description

Denoting pitch-classes by the ordinal convention (C=0, C♯=1, ..., B=11), each segment is analysed as follows. Let $b_i = 1$ if the pitch-class i is contained (totally or partially) in the segment, or 0 otherwise. The pc-set of a segment is encoded as an integer $p = \sum_{i=0}^{11} b_i \cdot 2^{11-i} \in [0,4095]$. This integer serves as an index for a precomputed table of set classes,[10] including the iv-, T_nI- and T_n-equivalences (defined in Sect. 4.2.2.1). For systematization completeness, the three class spaces are extended to include the so-called *trivial forms*.[11] With this, the total number of interval vectors rises to 200, while the T_nI- and T_n-equivalence classes sum to 223 and 351 categories respectively. In this work, we use Forte's cardinality-ordinal convention to name the classes, as well as the usual A/B suffix for referring to the prime/inverted forms under T_n-equivalence. We also follow the conventional notation to name the Z-related classes, by inserting a 'Z' between the hyphen and the ordinal.

As an example, a segment containing the pitches {G5,C3,E4,C4} is mapped to the pc-set {0,4,7} and coded as $p = 2192$ (100010010000 in binary). The precomputed table is indexed by p, resulting in the interval vector $\langle 001110 \rangle$ (iv-equivalence, grouping all the sets containing exactly 1 minor third, 1 major third, and 1 fourth), the class 3-11 (T_nI-equivalence, grouping all the major and minor trichords), and the class 3-11B (T_n-equivalence, grouping all the major trichords). The discrimination between major and minor trichords is thus possible under T_n-equivalence (no major trichord can be transformed into any minor trichord by transposition only), but not under iv- or T_nI-equivalences (any major trichord can be transformed into any minor trichord by transposition and inversion).

The beginning of Bach's chorale *Christus, der ist mein Leben* (BWV 281), shown in Fig. 4.2(a), illustrates the segmentation and description stages. Figure 4.2(b) (bottom) depicts the pitch-class set content of the excerpt over time. Figure 4.2(b) (top) sketches the approximate segmentation method at three different time scales, using window sizes of 1, 3 and 7 quarter notes, respectively. The same hop size (1 quarter note) is used in all three cases, providing a regular indexing grid. Three sample points (in light grey) show the relation between the indexing and the actual segments.

The set-class description of the corresponding segments under T_n-equivalence is also provided. For example, the lowest sample segment contains the pitch classes {C,F,A}={0,5,9} which belongs to the class 3-11B under T_n-equivalence: transposing (mod$_{12}$) the set {0,5,9} by 7 semitones up gives {0+7,5+7,9+7}={0,4,7},[12] which is

---

[10] As formalized by Forte (1964). See http://agustin-martorell.weebly.com/set-class-analysis.html for a comprehensive table of set classes.

[11] The *null set* and *single pitches* (cardinalities 0 and 1, containing no intervals), the *undecachords* (cardinality 11) and the *universal set* (cardinality 12, also referred to as the *aggregate*). These classes were not included in Forte's formalization. However, any truly systematic formalization of the set-class space should include them, as segments expressing these sets do occur in real music.

[12] Pitch-class sets are, by definition, *unordered* sets, meaning that the ordering of the elements is not of importance.

(a)

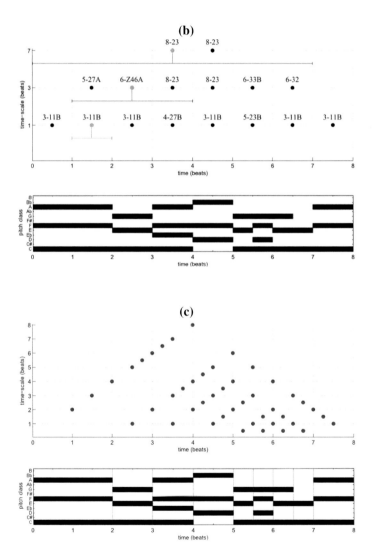

Fig. 4.2 J. S. Bach's *Christus, der ist mein Leben* (BWV 281) (excerpt). (a) Score. (b) Approximate segmentation and description. (c) Fully systematic segmentation

the standard form for all the major trichords under T_n-equivalence, and named 3-11B in Forte's convention.

This particular segmentation is only approximate, as it does not capture the pitch-class-set content of every different segment. For that, the fully systematic segmentation approach is required. The music is first segmented by finding every change in the pitch-class set (vertical) content over time, as in Fig. 4.2(c) (bottom). Then, a segment is defined for every pairwise combination of boundaries. As depicted in Fig. 4.2(c) (top), this exhausts every possible (different) pitch-class aggregate in the piece. In general, as for this example, this results in non-regular indexing grids.

4.3.3 Representation

The representation stage relies upon the general framework depicted in Fig. 4.1. The substitution of the inter-key space used by Martorell (2013, p. 26) by a set-class space is followed by a convenient colouring of the set-class space. The set-class content (description) of each segment is thus mapped to position in the class space, and associated with a colour. All the segments are then represented as coloured pixels in a two-dimensional plot, called a *class-scape*, and indexed by time (x-axis) and time-scale (y-axis). The designs of the class-space and the colouring strategy are application specific, depending on the pitch-related properties of interest. Sections 4.4.1 and 4.4.1.1 describe the method for two application scenarios.

4.4 Basic Set-Class Multi-scale Descriptors

This section presents the basic set of data structures (henceforth, *descriptors*) obtained by the proposed method. Each descriptor is explained and interpreted in the context of analytical examples.

4.4.1 The Class-Scape

A simple but useful task is to localize all the segments in the music belonging to a given class. This is illustrated in Fig. 4.3, where the main features of the multi-scale representation are also introduced. The top figure shows the class-scape computed for Debussy's *Voiles*,[13] filtered by the class 6-35 (pixels in black), which corresponds to the predominant hexatonic (whole-tone) scale in the composition. As a visual

---

[13] The example has been chosen for illustrative purposes. It has clearly distinctive sonorities and is 'easy' to listen to, however, it is barely describable using conventional tonal description methods. As with any music not based on the major–minor paradigm, its description in terms of standard (non-systematic) dictionaries of chords or keys is nonsensical.

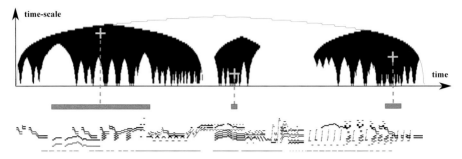

Fig. 4.3 Debussy's *Voiles*. Class-scape filtered by 6-35, piano roll, and 3 sample segments

reference, a thin blue line delineates the boundary in time and time-scale of the complete, non-filtered, class-scape information. At the bottom of Fig. 4.3 is shown an aligned piano-roll representation of the score for visual indexing of the composition, as used in our interactive analysis tool (see Sect. 4.7).

Each pixel in the class-scape, visible or not after the class filtering, represents a unique segment of music. Its *x*-coordinate corresponds to the temporal position of the segment's centre, and its *y*-coordinate represents its duration in a logarithmic scale. The higher a pixel is in the class-scape, the longer the duration of the represented segment. Three sample points (+ signs) and their corresponding segments are sketched as an example. In the figure, three large-scale structural hexatonic contexts are clearly revealed.

4.4.1.1 Multi-class Representation and Inter-class Distances

An alternative representation, allowing for the inspection of all segments and classes simultaneously, consists of assigning colours to classes. Given the relatively large number of classes, an absolute mapping of classes to colours is unlikely to be informative in general, so a relative solution is adopted. The method is a set-class adaptation of the concept of 'distance-scape', introduced by Martorell (2013, pp. 48–49). A distance-scape is a keyscape, in which each pixel (segment) is coloured according to its distance in pitch-space to a chosen tonal centre (e.g., the tonic of the home key of the piece).

The adaptation of the method to our set-class domain requires the definition of a systematic inter-class measure, able to relate every possible segment with any chosen reference. Among the many set-class distances proposed in the literature, a number of them can handle any pair of classes.[14] Lewin's *REL* (Lewin, 1979), Rahn's *ATMEMB* (Rahn, 1979), and Castrén's *RECREL* (Castrén, 1994) are among

---

[14] Most measures require pairwise cardinality equality. Some very informative measures, such as Tymoczko's voice-leading spaces (Tymoczko, 2011), could operate with different cardinalities. However, the class equivalences for capturing such sophistications are more specific than our set classes (iv, T_n and T_nI), and they even require the use of *multisets* (pc-sets *with* repetitions).

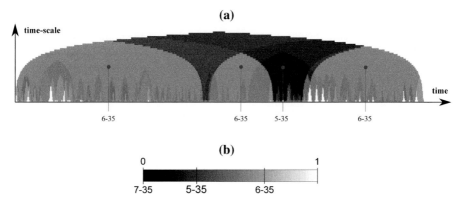

Fig. 4.4 Debussy's *Voiles*. (a) Class-scape relative (*REL*) to 7-35. (b) *REL* distances from 7-35

the so-called *total measures*. They are based on vector analysis, considering the complete subset content of the classes under comparison, and exhausting all the possible pc-set inclusion relations. For systematization completeness, these measures are adapted in our method, in order to accommodate the trivial forms.[15]

Each pixel in the class-scape is coloured according to the distance between the class it represents and any chosen reference class. Figure 4.4(a) shows the class-scape computed for Debussy's *Voiles*, in which the diatonic class 7-35 has been chosen as the reference class,[16] and *REL* as the inter-class measure. This piece does not have a single diatonic segment, so it is clear that the basic all-or-nothing filtering would result in a completely white image. We denote by *REL*(7-35,*) the *REL* distance from any class (asterisk) to the reference class 7-35, and encode its value with a greyscale (from black = 0 to white = 1), as depicted in Fig. 4.4(b). This way, every segment of the music (every pixel in the class-scape) is represented according to its *REL*-closeness to 7-35.

In Fig. 4.4, it is straightforward to visualize the darkest areas in the class-scape, corresponding to a brief pentatonic (5-35) passage, and its closest vicinity. It is also clear that the large whole-tone (6-35) passages depicted in Fig. 4.3, as well as their component subsets, are represented as being far from 7-35. Figure 4.4 clearly reveals the overall structure, while evidencing the radical analytical and perceptual differences between symmetric (whole-tone) and asymmetric (diatonic-based, here the pentatonic subset) scalar contexts.[17] Incidentally, there exist some

---

[15] See Harley (2014) for a comprehensive survey of set-class measures, formalized according to their suitability for tonal analysis. Harley also discusses the accommodation of the trivial forms.

[16] The diatonic class has been chosen for illustration purposes, as a common and well-known set.

[17] By *symmetric*, in this work we refer to maximally even sets (Clough and Douthett, 1991) featuring a reduced number of distinct transpositions, often known as Messiaen's *modes of limited transposition*. These sets present highly symmetric distributions in the chromatic circle. For instance, the whole-tone-scale set (6-35) has 2 different transpositions and 6 symmetry axes in the chromatic circle, in contrast with the anhemitonic pentatonic set (5-35), which features 12 distinct transpositions and 1 symmetry axis.

isolated segments (just two pixels in the class-scape) belonging to the scalar formation set 6-33B,[18] which are the closest ones to 7-35 in the composition.

This points to an interpretative aspect of the class-scapes: the analytical relevance of what is shown is often related to the accumulation of evidence in time and time-scale. A significantly large area of the class-scape showing the same material is probably representative of a section of music in which such evidence is of analytical and/or perceptual relevance, in the sense that it accounts for a passage in which the inspected properties are stable (i.e., a stable context). Smaller patches, even single isolated pixels, capture the class content of their corresponding segments as well. However, they could just be pitch-aggregate by-products lacking analytical interest, such as the spurious 6-33B in *Voiles*. Human cognitive (visual) abilities play an important role here in focusing the viewer's attention on the areas where homogeneous evidence accumulates, an important feature of multi-scale representations for assisting pattern recognition tasks.[19] On the other hand, localized spots of residual evidence may be worth closer inspection, and so interaction with the class-scape is facilitated.

A relevant benefit of pc-set-based spaces, as opposed to continuous ones,[20] is that music can be analysed in terms of different class systems at no extra computational cost. Being finite and discrete spaces (4096 classes at most for the TET system), the whole equivalence systems, including their inner metrics, can be precomputed. The mapping from pc-sets to set-classes, as well as the distances between any pair of music segments, can thus be implemented by table indexing. Once the pc-set of each possible segment has been computed (which constitutes the actual bottleneck of the method), the rest of the process is inexpensive, and multiple *set-class lenses* can be changed in real time, allowing fast interactive explorations of the massive data. This alleviates part of Forte's concerns about the unfeasibility of systematic segmentation and filtering decisions (Sect. 4.2.1). This feature, along with a variety of filtering options for visual exploration, can be tested with our proof-of-concept set-class analysis tool (see Sect. 4.7).

4.4.2 Piecewise Summarization: Class-Matrix and Class-Vector

The class-scape provides a comprehensive bird's-eye view of the piece, well adapted for visual exploration. However, other applications would require more compact and manageable, yet informative, data structures. As discussed in Sect. 4.2.3, it is of interest to preserve the class integrity and as much temporal information as possible. In this subsection, we present two such dimensional reductions, derived from the class-scape: the *class-matrix* and the *class-vector*.

---

[18] The class 6-33B results from removing the third degree from a major diatonic set.

[19] In his classic work on visualization, Tufte (2001, pp. 16–20) discusses similar cognitive implications to demonstrate the usefulness of his massive 'data maps' as instruments for reasoning about quantitative information.

[20] Such as those accommodating the so-called *chroma features*, which are finite but continuous.

(a)

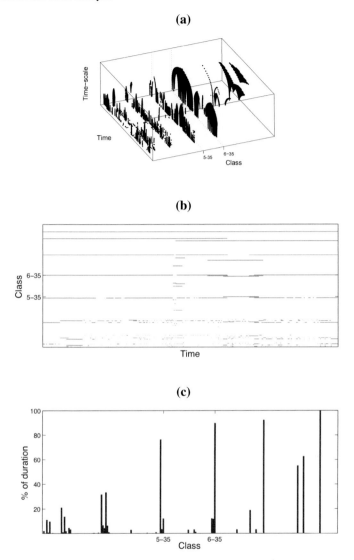

(b)

(c)

Fig. 4.5 Debussy's *Voiles*. (a) Class-scape as a sparse 3-D matrix. (b) Class-matrix. (c) Class-vector

4.4.2.1 The Class-Matrix

As a data structure, the 2-dimensional class-scape presented above can be thought of
as a sparse 3-dimensional binary matrix, in which each segment is indexed by the
temporal location of its centre (*x*-axis), its duration (*y*-axis), and its class content
(*z*-axis). In Fig. 4.5(a), such an arrangement is shown for Debussy's *Voiles*, with
the classes 5-35 (pentatonic) and 6-35 (whole-tone) annotated as reference. The
first reduction process consists of projecting this information into the time–class

plane. Given the special meaning of the lost dimension (time-scale), this implies growing each point to the actual duration of the segment it represents. The resulting data structure, referred to as a *class-matrix*, is a multi-dimensional time series of a special kind, which requires a proper interpretation. It represents the N classes as N rows, arranged from bottom to top according to Forte's cardinality-ordinal convention (Forte, 1964). An *activated* position (t, c) in the class matrix (black pixels) means that at least one segment belonging to the class c includes the time position t. A position on the time axis of the class-matrix is not associated with a unique segment, but with all the segments containing that time point. The class-matrix, thus, summarizes information from all the time-scales simultaneously. Unlike the approach of Huovinen and Tenkanen (2007), which also accounts for several time-scales in a single tail-segment array, the class-matrix preserves a strict separation of classes. This feature can be exploited in more subtle descriptive tasks, as discussed in Sect. 4.5.2.

Figure 4.5(b) shows the class-matrix for Debussy's *Voiles* under iv-equivalence, revealing the prelude's economy of sonorities, characteristic of works mostly based upon symmetric scalar formations. Even with the loss of information, it helps to visualize the contribution of each individual class, since colouring is no longer required. The individual duration of each frame from the initial segmentation may not be appreciated in the class-matrix, since overlapped segments belonging to the same class are projected as their union in the time domain, which has interpretative consequences when looking at individual classes. However, the strict separation of classes allows one to capture relational details of certain structural relevance, by analysing the inclusion relations down the hierarchy of classes, as will be discussed below in Sect. 4.5.2.

4.4.2.2 The Class-Vector

An even more compact representation provides a means for quantification. For each row in the class-matrix, the activated positions are accumulated and expressed as a percentage of the total duration of the piece. This data structure, henceforth *class-vector*, has a dimension equal to the number of classes, and quantifies the temporal presence of each possible class in a piece. Figure 4.5(c) shows the class-vector computed for Debussy's *Voiles*. The potential of class-vectors for comparing different pieces of music, however, raises the problem of resolution. The segmentation used so far was convenient for visualization and fast interaction with the data, but it is clear that the same segmentation parameters may not resolve equally the class content of different pieces, compromising any quantitative comparison. However, class-vectors can be computed with absolute precision, by substituting the multi-scale policy by a truly systematic approach, which captures all the possible different segments, as described in Sect. 4.3.1 (see also the worked example in Sect. 4.3.2). Such exhaustive computation is thus performed for any application involving quantification.[21]

---

[21] Class-matrices are also suitable for precise quantitative applications. Our method relies upon lists of temporal segments for each class.

4.5 Mining Class-Matrices

This section presents two applications of the information conveyed by the class-matrices.

4.5.1 Case Study: Structural Analysis

Self-similarity matrices (SSMs) are simple tools commonly used for finding recurrences in time series (Foote, 1999). In music-related applications, the typical inputs to an SSM are spectral or chroma feature time series. Some of the SSM-based methods can handle different time-scales, and some of the chroma methods allow for transpositional invariance (Müller, 2007). These functionalities are usually implemented at the SSM computation stage,[22] or as a post-processing step. In the class-matrices, both the equivalence mappings (including their inherent hierarchies) and the multi-scale nature of the information are *already* embedded in the feature time-series, so a plain SSM can be used for finding sophisticated recurrences. For instance, a passage comprised of a chord sequence can be recognized as similar to a restatement of the passage with different arpeggiations and/or inversions of the chord intervals (e.g., from major to minor triads). A *vertical* chord and its arpeggiated version may not be recognized as very similar at the lowest cardinalities, but their common T_nI-sonority will certainly emerge at their corresponding time-scales. Moreover, any sonority containing the chords (i.e., *supersets*) will also be captured at their proper time-scales, climbing up the hierarchy until we reach the whole-piece segment, everything indexed by a common temporal axis. A quantification of similarity between variations may thus be possible at the level of embedded sonorities.

We now consider the application of the above method to the analysis of large-scale recurrence in Webern's *Variations for piano* op.27/I, as an example of a challenging musical work, barely describable by standard tonal features (such as chroma, chords or keys). This dodecaphonic (early serialism) piece presents an A–B–A' structure, built upon several instantiations of the main twelve-tone row under different transformations, involving transpositions, inversions and distinct harmonizations. Figure 4.6 (top) depicts the class-scape of the piece, filtered by the prominent hexachordal iv-sonority $\langle 332232 \rangle$, and Fig. 4.6 (bottom) shows the well-known structure of the row instantiations (extensively analysed in the literature), annotated according to Cook (1987).[23] The large-scale A–B–A' structure can be observed with the naked eye in Fig. 4.6 (top).

---

[22] For instance, transpositional invariance is often achieved by computing twelve SSMs, accounting for each of the twelve ring-shifted versions of the chroma features.

[23] The standard terminology in row analysis is followed: P stands for the prime form of a row, R for a row's retrograde, I for its inversion, and the ordinal number indicates the transposition. For instance, RI-6 refers to a row instantiation, which appears transposed 6 semitones above the original row, with all its intervals inverted, and retrograded. The double labelling stands for the simultaneous occurrence of each row instantiation with its own retrograde version throughout the piece. For a

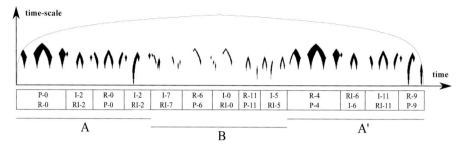

Fig. 4.6 Webern's op.27/I. Top: class-scape filtered by $\langle 332232 \rangle$; Bottom: structure

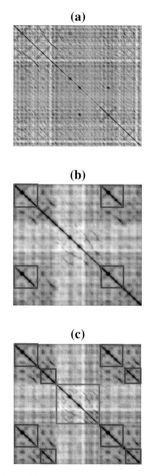

Fig. 4.7 SSMs for Webern's op.27/I. (a) pc-equivalence. (b) T_n-equivalence. (c) T_nI-equivalence

Finding this large-scale A–B–A' form thus requires us to look for transformed repetitions. This can be done with an SSM, fed with an input time-series that is invariant to those transformations. Figure 4.7 depicts the output of a plain SSM, computed from three different inputs: a) the pc-set time series;[24] b) the class-matrix under T_n; and c) the class-matrix under $T_n I$. The pc-equivalence does not capture any large-scale recurrence. The restatement of the first two phrases in A is captured by the T_n-equivalence, as these phrases are mainly related by transposition in A'. Finally, the $T_n I$-equivalence reveals the complete recapitulation, including the last two phrases of A, which are restated in A' in both transposed and inverted transformations.

It is worth noting that the method is agnostic with respect to the general sonority, the ubiquitous $\langle 332232 \rangle$ that reveals the large-scale structure (as in Fig. 4.6). Moreover, it is not necessary for the recurrences to be *exact* transformations (e.g., exact transpositions). This is because, by using class-matrices as input to the SSM, similarity is conceived of as a construction down the subclass (hierarchical) inclusion relations.[25] This allows for the discrimination of the B section, built upon the same iv-hexachordal sonority and the same kind of row instantiations as A and A', but presented in distinct harmonizations.

4.5.2 Case Study: Hierarchical Subclass Analysis

Class-matrices can also be exploited to describe the subclass content *under* any class, revealing the building blocks of particular class instantiations. The next case study analyses two corpora in terms of pure diatonicism, by characterizing the subset content of only the diatonic segments.

The computation process for the Agnus Dei from Victoria's *Ascendens Christus* mass is depicted in Fig. 4.8. The diatonic-related subclass content is isolated by considering only the information *below* the activated 7-35 positions in the class-matrix, as shown in Fig. 4.8(a). The result of this process is a *subclass-matrix*, in Fig. 4.8(b), with a number of rows equal to the number of subset classes (up to cardinality 6 here). Partially overlapped classes which are not a subset of 7-35 are then removed from the subclass-matrix. Following the same method as for class-vectors, a *subclass-vector* is then computed from the subclass-matrix. The subclass-vector, in Fig. 4.8(c), quantifies the total subclass content contributing to the reference class, describing what (and how much of it) the particular diatonicism consists of. The most prominent subclasses at 3-11, 5-27 and 6-Z25 stand out in the subclass-vector, which also reveals other common scalar formation classes of cardinalities 4 to 6.

The method can be extended for characterizing a corpus, according to some specific sonorities, by taking a class-wise average across the subclass-vectors extracted

---

detailed analytical discussion of the piece, in terms of this hexachordal sonority under different equivalences, see Martorell and Gómez (2015).

[24] In a sense, the discrete *equivalent* of the chroma features.

[25] The SSM compares multi-dimensional (*vertical*) views of the class-matrix, each of them accounting for all the embedded contexts around its corresponding temporal location.

(a)

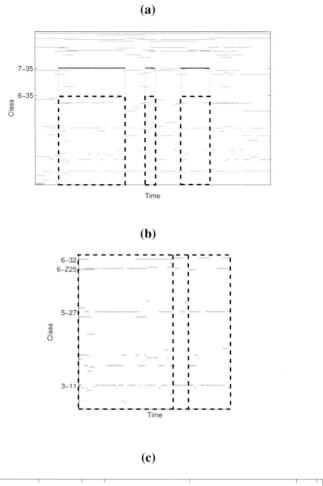

(b)

(c)

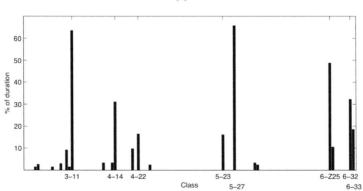

Fig. 4.8 Victoria's *Ascendens Christus*, Agnus Dei. (a) Filtering under 7-35. (b) Subclass-matrix. (c) Subclass-vector

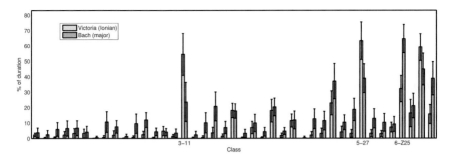

Fig. 4.9 Diatonicism in Victoria and Bach. Mean subclass-vectors under 7-35

from all the pieces. Figure 4.9 depicts the mean subclass-vector under 7-35 computed for two contrasting corpora: a) Victoria's parody masses in Ionian mode;[26] and b) the preludes and fugues in major mode from Bach's Well-Tempered Clavier. The selection of the corpora is based on the close relationship between the major and the Ionian modes, the comparable number of voices and movements in both corpora, and the (loose) assumption of homogeneity in the usage of contrapuntal resources by each composer. For clarity of comparison including standard deviations, only the actual subclasses of 7-35 are represented. The prominent use of major and minor triads (3-11) in Victoria's diatonicism relative to Bach's stands out. Similarly predominant is the class 5-27, a far more recurrent cadential resource in Victoria.[27] On the other hand, the Locrian hexachord 6-Z25 is far more prevalent in Bach. Apart from its instantiations as perfect cadences[28] in both corpora, 6-Z25 appears consistently in many motivic progressions in Bach, which are not idiomatic in Victoria's contrapuntal writing.[29]

4.6 Mining Class-Vectors

This section elaborates upon the information conveyed by the class-vectors. As mentioned, a class-vector quantifies the temporal presence of every class sonority, relative to the duration of the piece. Finding specific sonorities in large datasets can be combined with the extraction of the actual segments from the MIDI files. This can be exploited in various applications, ranging from the analysis of corpora to music

---

[26] Including *Alma Redemptoris Mater, Ave Regina Caelorum, Laetatus Sum, Pro Victoria, Quam Pulchri Sunt*, and *Trahe Me Post Te*. See Rive (1969) for a modal classification.

[27] The class 5-27 results from the combination of the dominant and tonic major triads.

[28] The class 6-Z25 results from the combination of a major triad and its dominant seventh chord.

[29] By interfacing class-vectors with class-scapes, the content of particular class instantiations can be easily explored and listened to with our interactive analysis tool (see Sect. 4.7).

education. For this work, a dataset of class-vectors was computed from more than 16000 MIDI tracks.[30]

4.6.1 Case Study: Query by Set-Class

A simple but useful application is querying a database of pieces for a given set-class. It can be used for finding pieces with a relevant presence of any chordal or scalar sonority, such as *exotic* scales. This kind of task is problematic using standard tonal features, which (usually) support neither contextual descriptions nor tonal systems other than the common-practice harmonic idioms. Table 4.1 shows 10 retrieved pieces with a notable presence (relative duration) of the sonority 7-22, usually referred to as the Hungarian minor set-class.[31] Both monophonic and polyphonic pieces are retrieved, ranging over different styles and historic periods, as the unique requisite for capturing a given sonority was its existence as a temporal segment. The instantiations of 7-22 in the retrieved pieces are also varied, ranging from passages using an actual Hungarian minor modality, to short but frequent (colouring) deviations from the minor mode, including some non-relevant pitch concatenation by-products.

Table 4.1 Retrieved pieces: 7-22

Retrieved piece	7-22 (%)
Scriabin - Prelude op.33 n.3	68.61
Busoni - 6 etudes op.16 n.4	63.22
Essen - 6478	62.50
Liszt - Nuages gris	42.41
Essen - 531	36.67
Scriabin - Prelude op.51 n.2	31.74
Lully - Persee act-iv-scene-iv-28	29.73
Alkan - Esquisses op.63 n.19	28.87
Satie - Gnossienne n.1	28.15
Scriabin - Mazurka op.3 n.9	24.61

---

[30] Including works by: Albeniz, Albinoni, Alkan, Bach, Bartók, Beethoven, Berlioz, Bizet, Brahms, Bruckner, Busoni, Buxtehude, Byrd, Chopin, Clementi, Corelli, Couperin, Debussy, Dowland, Dufay, Dvořák, Fauré, Franck, Frescobaldi, Gesualdo, Guerrero, Handel, Haydn, Josquin, Lasso, Liszt, Lully, Mahler, Mendelssohn, Messiaen, Monteverdi, Morales, Mozart, Mussorgsky, Pachelbel, Paganini, Palestrina, Prokofiev, Rachmaninoff, Rameau, Ravel, Reger, Saint-Saëns, Satie, Scarlatti, Schoenberg, Schubert, Schütz, Schumann, Scriabin, Shostakovich, Soler, Stravinsky, Tchaikovsky, Telemann, Victoria and Vivaldi. It also includes anonymous medieval pieces, church hymns, and the Essen folksong collection.

[31] Sometimes also called Persian, major gypsy, or double harmonic scale, among other denominations. Its prime form is $\{0,1,2,5,6,8,9\}$.

4.6.2 Case Study: Query by Combined Set-Classes

The strict separation of classes in the class-vectors allows for the exploration of any class combination, whether common or unusual. For instance, the first movement of Stravinsky's *Symphony of Psalms* is retrieved by querying for music containing substantial diatonic (7-35) and octatonic (8-28) material, certainly an uncommon musical combination. The class-vector also reveals the balance between both sonorities, as 30.18 % and 29.25 % of the piece duration, respectively.

As discussed in Sect. 4.5.2, the class-matrices allow for the hierarchical analysis of specific sonorities. The class-vectors, on the other hand, summarize the information in a way that does not, in general, elucidate the subclass content under a given class. However, if the queried sonorities have a substantial presence (or absence) in the piece, the class-vectors alone can often account for some hierarchical evidence. One can, for instance, query the dataset for pieces with a notable presence of the so-called *suspended* trichord (3-9),[32] constrained to cases of mostly diatonic contexts (7-35). This situation is likely to be found in folk songs, medieval melodies, early counterpoint, or works composed as reminiscent of them. It is worth noting that the 3-9 instantiations may appear as a result of a variety of pitch aggregates, such as in monophonic melodies, as a combination of melody and tonic-dominant drones, as a combination of tenor and parallel motion in fifths and octaves, and as actual (voiced) suspensions.

Similarly, as non-existing sonorities may also reveal important characteristics of music, the dataset can be queried for combinations of present and absent classes. For instance, the sonority of purely diatonic (7-35) pieces depends on whether they contain major or minor trichords (3-11) or not. If we constrain the query to polyphonic music, the retrieved pieces in the latter case (diatonic, not triadic) belong mostly to early polyphony, prior to the establishment of the triad as a common sonority.

These results point to interesting applications related to music similarity, such as music education or recommendation systems. Music similarity is, to a great extent, a human construct, as it depends upon cultural factors and musical background. Of particular interest is the possibility of retrieving pieces sharing relevant tonal-related properties, but pertaining to different styles, composers, or historical periods. Music discovery or recommendation systems could thus serve as music appreciation or ear-training tools, by suggesting pieces across standard taxonomies (e.g., composer or style) subjected to musically relevant similarity criteria. This would help to reinforce listening skills for specific sonorities, while enriching the contextual situations in which they appear in real music. Recommender systems able to *explain* the basis of their recommendations, using some standard musicological lexicon (e.g., as provided by the set-classes), would be a particularly useful application for such purposes.

---

[32] A major or minor trichord with the third degree substituted by the fourth or the second.

4.6.3 On Dimensionality and Informativeness

As pointed out in Sect. 4.2.2, the compromise between the dimensionality of the feature space and the informativeness of a description is a relevant factor in feature design. The class content of a piece, as described by its class-vector, has 200, 223 or 351 dimensions, depending on the chosen equivalence (iv, T_nI or T_n). Compared with other tonal feature spaces, these dimensions may seem quite large. However, the benefits of class vectors are the systematicity, specificity and precision of the description. Several relevant differences with respect to other tonal-related features are to be noticed. A single class-vector, computed after a fully systematic segmentation,

1. accounts for every distinct segment in a piece, regardless of its time position or duration;
2. accounts for every possible sonority in the set-class space, which is *complete*;
3. provides an objective and precise description of the *set-class sonority*;
4. provides a description in music-theoretical terms, readable and interpretable by humans;
5. provides an objective quantification of every possible sonority in terms of time;
6. provides a content-based, model-free, description of the piece; and,
7. in some cases, provides an approximation to the hierarchical inclusion relations.

In contrast, the most common tonal piecewise and labelwise feature (global key estimation) provides

1. a single label for the whole piece;
2. 24 different labels, but only two different sonorities (major and minor);
3. an *estimation* of the key, which is often misleading;
4. a description in music-theoretical terms, but of little compositional relevance;
5. quantification (sometimes) by key strength, but with no temporal information at all;
6. a description based on specific and biased models (e.g., profiling methods); and
7. no access to the hierarchical relations of the piece's tonality.

With this in mind, it seems to us that a piecewise description in 200 dimensions provides a reasonable trade-off between size and informativeness. Considering the somewhat sophisticated tonal information conveyed by the class-vectors, they may constitute a useful complementary feature for existing content-based descriptors.

4.7 Interfacing Representations

As pointed out in Sect. 4.2.3, the design of the proposed descriptors aims to maximize the *overall* informativeness of the method. This is proposed through interaction with the user, in our proof-of-concept set-class analysis tool. In this section, we briefly describe the basic functionalities of the tool.[33]

Figure 4.10 depicts a screenshot of the interface, in which the basic descriptors (class-scape, class-matrix and class-vector) are readily accessible. Debussy's *Voiles* serves again as an analytical example. Both the class-scape and the class-vector can be navigated with a cursor. Any class can be chosen from the class-vector, establishing a reference sonority which affects the visualization of the class-scape. The class-scape has two visualization modalities (*single-class* and *multi-class*), corresponding to those described in Sects. 4.4.1 and 4.4.1.1, both controlled by the reference class chosen from the class-vector. The equivalence system as a whole can be changed (iv, T_n and T_nI are supported), as well as the inter-class measure (*REL, RECREL* and *ATMEMB* are supported). The class-scape can also be filtered by any set of cardinalities. Any segment can be selected from the class-scape, in order to inspect its properties, and it can be played for auditory testing. All the information is interactively updated according to the user actions, allowing a fast exploration of different filtering possibilities. This facilitates the *analysis loop*, understood as the process whereby an analyst refines the observation parameters according to his or her findings and intuitions.

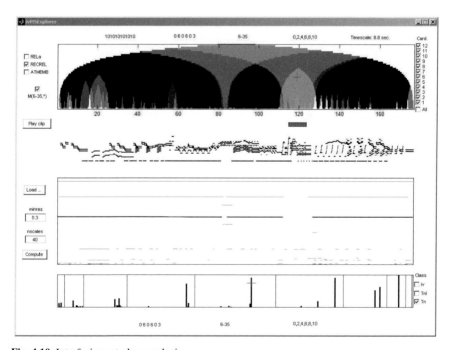

Fig. 4.10 Interfacing set-class analysis

---

[33] See http://agustin-martorell.weebly.com/set-class-analysis.html for details.

4.8 Conclusions

This work presents a systematic approach to segmentation, description and representation of pieces of music. The methodology is designed for analysing the musical surface in terms of embedded contexts, as an alternative to the usual event-based approaches. A set-class description domain provides a mid-level lexicon, which encodes useful tonal properties of pitch aggregates of any kind, allowing the description of any chordal or scalar sonority. The class-scapes provide a bird's-eye view of a complete piece of music, furnishing information about the class content of every possible segment, whether in absolute terms or relative to any reference class. The class-matrices are multi-dimensional time series, invariant to time-scale and to several transformations, representing the existence of every possible class over time. They can be combined with the simplest pattern finding methods for capturing complex tonal recurrences, and they can provide information about the hierarchical construction of any class sonority. The class-vectors are piecewise tonal summaries, quantifying the temporal presence of every possible class in a piece. They can be exploited in querying tasks of certain sophistication, beyond the possibilities of standard tonal features, while providing a means for describing (and explaining) similarity in alternative and insightful ways. The compromise between dimensionality and informativeness of the class-vectors may constitute a useful complement to existing content-based features. The insights provided by the class-scape visualizations can be interfaced with class-vectors, different class-spaces, inter-class measures, and standard pitchwise filters, in order to provide fast interactive assistance to the analyst. The examples in this chapter show that these descriptors can provide information about very different musical idioms, ranging from monophonic folk tunes and early polyphony to pieces that use exotic scales as well as atonal music.

Acknowledgements This work was supported by the EU 7th Framework Programme FP7/2007-2013 through PHENICX project [grant no. 601166].

Supplementary Material The interactive potential of the methods discussed in this work can be tested with our multi-scale set-class analysis prototype for Matlab, freely available from http://agustin-martorell.weebly.com/set-class-analysis.html. A detailed manual of the tool, a comprehensive table of set-classes, and a (growing) dataset of class-vectors, are also available at this site.

References

Babbitt, M. (1955). Some aspects of twelve-tone composition. *The Score and I.M.A. Magazine*, 12:53–61.

Castrén, M. (1994). *RECREL. A similarity measure for set-classes*. PhD thesis, Sibelius Academy, Helsinki.

Clough, J. and Douthett, J. (1991). Maximally even sets. *Journal of Music Theory*, 35(1/2):93–173.

Cook, N. (1987). *A Guide to Musical Analysis*. J. M. Dent and Sons.

Deliège, C. (1989). La set-theory ou les enjeux du pléonasme. *Analyse Musicale*, 17:64–79.

Foote, J. (1999). Visualizing music and audio using self-similarity. In *Proceedings of the Seventh ACM International Conference on Multimedia (MM99)*, pages 77–80, Orlando, FL.

Forte, A. (1964). A theory of set-complexes for music. *Journal of Music Theory*, 8(2):136–183.

Forte, A. (1973). *The Structure of Atonal Music*. Yale University Press.

Forte, A. (1988). Pitch-class set genera and the origin of modern harmonic species. *Journal of Music Theory*, 32(2):187–270.

Forte, A. (1989). La set-complex theory: Elevons les enjeux! *Analyse Musicale*, 17:80–86.

Hanson, H. (1960). *The Harmonic Materials of Modern Music: Resources of the Tempered Scale*. Appleton-Century-Crofts.

Harley, N. (2014). Evaluation of set class similarity measures for tonal analysis. Master's thesis, Universitat Pompeu Fabra.

Hasty, C. (1981). Segmentation and process in post-tonal music. *Music Theory Spectrum*, 3:54–73.

Huovinen, E. and Tenkanen, A. (2007). Bird's-eye views of the musical surface: Methods for systematic pitch-class set analysis. *Music Analysis*, 26(1–2):159–214.

Huron, D. (1992). Design principles in computer-based music representations. In Mardsen, A. and Pople, A., editors, *Computer Representations and Models in Music*, pages 5–39. Academic Press.

Leman, M. (2008). *Embodied Music: Cognition and Mediation Technology*. MIT Press.

Lerdahl, F. (2001). *Tonal Pitch Space*. Oxford University Press.

Lewin, D. (1959). Re : Intervallic relations between two collections of notes. *Journal of Music Theory*, 3(2):298–301.

Lewin, D. (1979). Some new constructs involving abstract pcsets and probabilistic applications. *Perspectives of New Music*, 18(1–2):433–444.

Martorell, A. (2013). *Modelling tonal context dynamics by temporal multi-scale analysis*. PhD thesis, Universitat Pompeu Fabra.

Martorell, A. and Gómez, E. (2015). Hierarchical multi-scale set-class analysis. *Journal of Mathematics and Music*, 9(1):95–108.

Müller, M. (2007). *Information Retrieval for Music and Motion*. Springer.

Nattiez, J. J. (2003). Allen Forte's set theory, neutral level analysis and poietics. In Andreatta, M., Bardez, J. M., and Rahn, J., editors, *Around Set Theory*. Delatour / Ircam.

Rahn, J. (1979). Relating sets. *Perspectives of New Music*, 18(1):483–498.

Rahn, J. (1980). *Basic Atonal Theory*. Schirmer.

Rive, T. N. (1969). An examination of Victoria's technique of adaptation and re-working in his parody masses - with particular attention to harmonic and cadential procedure. *Anuario Musical*, 24:133–152.

Sapp, C. S. (2005). Visual hierarchical key analysis. *ACM Computers in Entertainment*, 4(4):1–19.

Straus, J. N. (1990). *Introduction to Post-Tonal Theory*. Prentice-Hall.

Tufte, E. R. (2001). *The Visual Display of Quantitative Information*. Graphics Press.

Tymoczko, D. (2011). *A Geometry of Music: Harmony and Counterpoint in the Extended Common Practice*. Oxford University Press.

Part III
Parsing Large-Scale Structure: Form and Voice-Separation

Chapter 5
Computational Analysis of Musical Form

Mathieu Giraud, Richard Groult, and Florence Levé

Abstract Can a computer understand *musical forms*? Musical forms describe how a piece of music is structured. They explain how the sections work together through repetition, contrast, and variation: repetition brings unity, and variation brings interest. Learning how to hear, to analyse, to play, or even to write music in various forms is part of music education. In this chapter, we briefly review some theories of musical form, and discuss the challenges of computational analysis of musical form. We discuss two sets of problems, *segmentation* and *form analysis*. We present studies in music information retrieval (MIR) related to both problems. Thinking about codification and automatic analysis of musical forms will help the development of better MIR algorithms.

5.1 Introduction

Can a computer understand *musical forms*? Musical forms structure the musical discourse through repetitions and contrasts. The forms of the Western common practice era (e.g., binary, ternary, rondo, sonata form, fugue, variations) have been studied in depth by music theorists, and often formalized and codified centuries after their emergence in practice. Musical forms are used for pedagogical purposes, in composition as in music analysis, and some of these forms (such as variations or fugues) are also principles of composition that can be found inside large-scale works.

Mathieu Giraud
CNRS, France
Centre de Recherche en Informatique, Signal et Automatique de Lille (CRIStAL), Université de Lille 1, Villeneuve d'Ascq, France
e-mail: mathieu@algomus.fr

Richard Groult · Florence Levé
Laboratoire Modélisation, Information et Systèmes, Université Picardie Jules Verne, Amiens, France
e-mail: {richard, florence}@algomus.fr

© Springer International Publishing Switzerland 2016   113
D. Meredith (ed.), *Computational Music Analysis*,
DOI 10.1007/978-3-319-25931-4_5

For computer scientists working in music information retrieval (MIR) on symbolic scores, computational analysis of musical forms is challenging. On the one hand, very constrained music structures or forms can have rather consensual analyses, such as in an ABA form, and can therefore constitute good benchmarks for MIR algorithms. On the other hand, even if it seems difficult to automatically analyse more elaborate forms, where musicological or aesthetic considerations would seem to demand human expertise, an MIR analysis could provide a valuable time or computation gain towards systematic study and comparison of big musical data sets. More generally, symbolic MIR methods on musical forms are in their infancy and are a long way from the analysis done by performers, listeners, or music theorists: research into the codification and automatic analysis of musical forms will help the development of better MIR algorithms.

We begin this chapter by briefly reviewing some theories of musical form (Sect. 5.2). Two sets of MIR problems arise from these notions of musical structure: *segmentation*, which may be studied in all genres of music, and *form analysis*. We then present studies in MIR related to both problems (Sect. 5.3) as well as evaluation datasets and methods (Sect. 5.4). We conclude by discussing some perspectives as well as the usefulness of form analysis in MIR.

5.2 Musicological Motivation and MIR Challenges

5.2.1 Theories of Form

Musical forms describe how pieces of music are structured. Such forms explain how the sections work together through repetition, contrast, and variation: repetition brings unity, and variation brings interest. The study of musical forms is fundamental in musical education as, among other benefits, the comprehension of musical structures leads to a better knowledge of composition rules, and is the essential first approach for a good interpretation of musical pieces. Not every musical piece can be put into a formal restrictive scheme. However, forms do exist and are often an important aspect of what one expects when listening to music (Cook, 1987).

Even if musical forms have been discussed for several centuries, there are still debates between musicologists on their exact nature. The formalization of many musical forms was done in nineteenth century textbooks aimed at teaching composition to music students (Czerny, 1848; Marx, 1847; Reicha, 1824). Many theories of musical form and how to analyse form have arisen since (Nattiez, 1987; Ratner, 1980; Ratz, 1973; Schoenberg, 1967). Systematic methods for music analysis generally include some formalization of large-scale structure or form, such as the fundamental structure and more superficial structural levels (*Schichten*) of Schenkerian analysis (Schenker, 1935), the growth category of LaRue (1970), or the grouping structures and reductions of Lerdahl and Jackendoff's (1983) *Generative Theory of Tonal Music* (see also Chaps. 9 and 10, this volume).

Table 5.1 Musical forms from a thematic point of view. Letters designate contrasting sections

Form	Structure	Further details
Fugue	Contrapuntal form	
Variations	A A′ A″ A‴	
Binary	AA′, AB, AAB, ABB, AA′BB′	
Ternary	ABA, ABA′	
Rondo	ABACADA...	A: 'chorus', B, C, D: 'verse'
Sonata form	AB–Dev–AB	A: 'principal' theme/zone
Rondo-Sonata form	AB–AC–AB	B: 'secondary' theme/zone
Cyclic form		
Free forms		

Musical form is still an active field of research in musicology. Contemporary approaches to musical form include the "theory of formal functions", describing the role played by each section and formal processes inside and between them; "dialogic form", that is, form in dialogue with historically conditioned compositional options; and "multivalent analysis", which consists of form analysis along several independent elements (Caplin, 2000; Caplin et al., 2009).

5.2.2 Usual Forms

Table 5.1 lists the most common forms, taking the usual *segmentation* point of view: forms are here given as a succession of sections denoted by labels. Binary form consists of two sections, where one or both sections can be repeated, usually with some variation (as for the Bar form, AAB). The sections can use the same or different thematic material. They usually have a comparable length, but the second section can sometimes be longer. In ternary forms, a contrasting section comes between the two statements of the first section. A ternary form can be simple (as in the aria da capo or lied form), or compounded of binary forms (as in trio forms, such as Minuet/Scherzo) or even of ternary forms. Sonata form consists of an exposition, a development, and a recapitulation, and is generally built on two thematic areas.

One should note that the segmentation is only an element of the form analysis. The proper understanding of a ternary form often requires that one explains in which aspects (tonality, texture, rhythm, etc.) the contrasting section B differs from, or complements, the initial section A. Many forms also include high-level tension and dynamics that should be explained. Sonata forms combine these principles, including a tonal path: the piece goes to a secondary key, often the dominant, and then comes back to the tonic. A segmentation is thus a very partial view on a form.

More generally, there are many *free forms* that are more difficult to classify according to a section-based view. Baroque preludes and inventions are often viewed as free forms. However, this does not mean that they are not structured, but rather that their organization depends on other components, such as texture or tension. An extreme case is some *open forms*, where the order of execution of the sections is not fixed by the composer, but where some components can still be conceived of in terms of form.

A full musical analysis that reveals a musical form should thus include consideration of *all organizational principles*, not just a simple segmentation. Note that there are typically many possible analyses, focusing on different aspects of a score. One may even start from different musicological hypotheses. For example, the conception of sonata form has evolved over time. Originally defined in two parts from a thematic perspective (Reicha, 1824), it was then theorized as a ternary form by A. B. Marx, who first named it, and C. Czerny (Czerny, 1848; Marx, 1847). Then Rosen returned to the view that this form derived from *binary* form, and that the most critical feature is the tonal and harmonic path followed (Rosen, 1980). The recent theory of Hepokoski and Darcy (2006) further emphasizes the importance of the medial caesura and rotations. Depending on the underlying musicological assumptions, an analysis of such a form will thus focus on different organizational principles.

5.2.3 Challenges for MIR

Based on these conceptions of musical form, we see two sets of challenges related to structure and form in MIR:

- *Segmentation* consists of taking a piece—either a score, or an audio file—and chunking it into sections, possibly labelled, as in Table 5.1. There are several MIR challenges involved in segmentation, such as identifying correct phrase or section boundaries and assessing the similarity between sections.
- *Form analysis* consists of predicting a segmentation together with *semantics* on this segmentation and on the global layout of the piece. The provided semantics can be both *internal*, indicating the formal function of a section and how the sections relate to each other and to the global layout ("B is a variation of A"); or *external*, explaining how the sections are organized with respect to some historical corpus or analytical practice ("A is in dialogic form", "A and B are the two thematic zones of a sonata form"). Finally, it has to build upon several elements (multivalent analysis): a thematic segmentation is one of these elements, but not the only one. For example, evolution of tension and tonal path are elements that should be included in a complete form analysis.

Even if the term "musical form" is often applied to baroque, classical and romantic music analysed within traditional musicology, form analysis can be carried out on any genre of music, and many of the studies that will be discussed in this chapter focused on popular music.

Of course, segmentation and form analysis are related: segmentation is an essential component of an analysis of a musical form; and to assign labels to segments (A, A_1, A′, B, etc.) requires knowledge about the relations between sections and their semantics. Segmentation problems can (partially) be formalized and evaluated against reference analyses (see Sect. 5.4.2), and are an important set of challenges for the MIR community.

Nevertheless, we believe that the computational music analysis (CMA) community should aim at solving full "form analysis" problems, trying to have a better understanding of musical structure, beyond mere segmentation. Unfortunately, formalization of these tasks—and thus of their evaluation—is even more challenging than it is for segmentation. One may believe that some tasks inevitably resist computer formalization, as research in CMA should be linked to musicological practice, including subjectivity in the description of forms. However, this subjectivity might be modelled in some ways. Ideally, a model should be able to predict where there might be a disagreement about the form of a piece, and even predict several different formal analyses of the same piece where ambiguity exists.

5.3 Methods for Segmentation and Form Analysis

In this section, we review existing algorithmic methods for segmentation and form analysis.

5.3.1 Musical Structure and Segmentation

5.3.1.1 Phrase-Structure Analysis and Melodic Segmentation

Even if the aim of melodic segmentation is not to give a large-scale structure for a musical piece, it allows us to chunk music into phrases, which can provide clues about boundaries between structural sections.

A common way to handle *monophonic* data is to observe the differences between successive intervals or durations. It is not simply a large interval or a large duration that marks the end of a phrase, but the variation in these quantities. One reference algorithm here is Cambouropoulos' (2001, 2006) *local boundary detection model* (LBDM) which is a simple algorithm that achieves good results. This algorithm considers both melodic intervals, durations and rests, and detects points of segmentation as the maxima of some profile function. More recent work on melodic segmentation includes that of Muellensiefen et al. (2008), Wiering et al. (2009) and Rodríguez-López et al. (2014). Phrase segmentation can also be done on *polyphonic* data: for example, Rafailidis et al. (2008) proposed a method to infer *stream segments*, based on an *n*-nearest-neighbour clustering from grouping criteria.

Note that *pattern inference and matching* algorithms (see Chaps. 11–17, this volume) can also be used to detect repeating sections and predict their boundaries.

5.3.1.2 Global Segmentation

We focus here on algorithms that aim to provide a high-level segmentation of a musical piece. Structural music segmentation consists of dividing a musical piece into several parts or sections and then assigning to those parts identical or distinct labels according to their similarity. The founding principles of structural segmentation, whether it be from audio or symbolic sources, are homogeneity, novelty, and/or repetition.

Audio Sources Many methods for segmenting audio files are based on auto-correlation matrices (Foote, 1999). Some methods focus on the detection of repeated sections (Chai, 2006; Dannenberg and Goto, 2009; Dannenberg and Hu, 2002) possibly after the extraction of features from a signal (Peeters, 2007). Other methods are based on probabilistic approaches (Paulus and Klapuri, 2008), or on timbre characteristics (Levy et al., 2007). Maddage et al. (2009), Paulus et al. (2010) and Klapuri (2011) provide recent surveys. Some systems and algorithms can be applied to both audio and symbolic sources, such as that of Sargent et al. (2011), where a Viterbi algorithm predicts the segments, taking into account both a content-based cost, based on similarity between segments, and a "regularity cost" favouring segments of similar lengths. This regularity cost improves the segmentation on Western popular songs.

Symbolic Sources There is less work to date that focuses on segmentation of symbolic scores. On monophonic data, Chen et al. (2004) segments the musical piece into sections called "sentences". The phrases predicted by the LBDM algorithm are compared (using their first pitch and the subsequent contour) and clustered. The score is then processed another time to obtain a sequence of labels and to predict the actual starts of each section. For track-separated polyphonic data, Rafael and Oertl (2010) propose combining segmentations from different tracks into a global fragmentation. In each track, a set of repeated patterns is computed by a modified version of the algorithm proposed by Hsu et al. (1998) allowing transpositions. Then these sets are cleaned and further processed to obtain non-overlapping patterns. The segmentations are then clustered into a global segmentation by maximizing a score function that favours compatible segments from several tracks. However, besides some examples, the authors do not report any evaluation of this method.

Several authors have proposed systems for generating analyses at larger scales in accordance with well-established theories of tonal musical structure, such as Schenkerian analysis (Schenker, 1935) or Lerdahl and Jackendoff's (1983) *Generative Theory of Tonal Music* (GTTM) (e.g., Hamanaka and Tojo, 2009; Hirata and Matsuda, 2002; Kirlin and Jensen, 2011; Marsden, 2010; see also Chaps. 9 and 10, this volume). This is very challenging and still an open problem: in both Schenkerian analysis and GTTM theory, carrying out a musically relevant analysis requires the making of analytical choices that rely on a great deal of musical information. Other work has also tried to model specific large-scale features, such as tonal tension (Farbood, 2010; Lerdahl and Krumhansl, 2007), that may also result in a global segmentation of a piece.

5.3.1.3 Discussion

Are such methods able to analyse classical musical forms? As discussed earlier, segmentation is an important step towards the analysis of a musical structure, but to be satisfactory, a musical analysis cannot just provide a segmentation into similar or distinct parts. It is also necessary to identify the *formal function* of each segment of the piece, and ideally to indicate the evolution of the compositional material when it is used differently in several segments. Indeed, a segmentation ABABCAB could just as well correspond to a popular song with verses and chorus with a transition (a bridge), as to a classical sonata form where A and B are the principal and secondary themes, played twice, followed by a development and a recapitulation.

5.3.2 Systems for Analysing Specific Musical Forms

In this chapter, we present *computational systems tailored for the analysis of classical musical forms*, focusing on two particular cases: fugues and sonata form. In both cases, we start from a score in which all voices are separated, and we compute some local features using discrete tools (based on string comparison) and statistical approaches. These local features can be gathered into a global analysis.

Note that other methods have been designed to check whether a piece follows a given structure. For example, Weng and Chen (2005) built a tool to decide whether a piece is a fugue, a rondo, or none of these, with a method to find occurrences of thematic materials.

5.3.2.1 Fugue

Elements of Fugal Structure A fugue is a contrapuntal polyphonic piece built on several melodic themes, including a *subject* (S) and, in most cases, one or several *countersubjects* (CS1, CS2). A fugue is structured as a set of *voices*, where each voice is mostly a monophonic sequence of notes. In the first section, the *exposition*, the patterns are played by each voice in turn. First, the subject is stated in one voice until a second voice enters. The subject is then repeated in the second voice, generally transposed, while the first voice continues with the first countersubject, combining with the subject. Bruhn (1993, p. 43) states that

> the perfect little musical entity we call subject is in fact at the origin of the fugue. [...] The subject is responsible for the feelings of density and relaxation in the fugue, and it is the main force in creating structure.

The fugue alternates between other instances of the subject and the countersubjects (either in their initial form, altered or transposed), and developments on these patterns called *episodes* (E). The episodes can contain *cadential passages*, and are often composed with *harmonic sequences*, which are passages where a pattern is consecutively repeated starting on a different pitch, possibly modulating from one tonality to another. At the end of the fugue, one often finds *stretti* (shorter and narrower statements of the head of the subject) and *bass pedals*.

Algorithms for Fugue Analysis   Many MIR studies take examples from corpora of fugues, for pattern extraction or grammar inference (e.g., Sidorov et al., 2014), but few studies have been specifically devoted to fugue analysis. Browles (2005) proposed several heuristics to aid in the selection of candidate fugue subjects using the repeated pattern extraction algorithms of Hsu et al. (1998). These algorithms maximize the number of occurrences of repeating patterns.

   We have proposed several tools in a system for automated fugue analysis (Giraud et al., 2015, 2012). Starting from a symbolic score that is separated into voices, we compute the end of the subject and its occurrences (including augmentations or inversions), and then retrieve CS1 and possibly CS2. Harmonic sequences, cadences, and pedals are detected. Some of these elements are then combined to sketch the global structure of the fugue. Figure 5.1 shows an example of the output of the system on a fugue in B♭ major by J. S. Bach.

S/CS1/CS2 Patterns   All the occurrences of S/CS1/CS2, as well as the patterns that form harmonic sequences in episodes, are not necessarily identical, but can be transposed or altered. The similarity score between a pattern and the rest of the fugue can be computed via dynamic programming using equations similar to the ones proposed by Mongeau and Sankoff (1990), and the alignment is retrieved through backtracking in the dynamic programming table. A threshold determines whether an occurrence is retained or discarded. Various methods have been proposed for measuring similarity between pitch intervals. These include directly computing intervals between *diatonic* pitches, strict pitch equality, "up/down" classes (Ghias et al., 1995), "step/leap intervals" (Cambouropoulos et al., 2005) and "quantized partially overlapping intervals" (QPI) (Lemström and Laine, 1998). We use very conservative substitution functions: repeated patterns are detected using a substitution function by considering the diatonic similarity of pitch intervals, and forcing the duration of all except the first and the last notes to take the same value.

   The subject is first heard alone by a unique voice until the second voice enters, but the end of the subject is generally not exactly at the start of the second voice—in all but one of 36 fugues by Bach or Shostakovich, the opening statement of the subject ends between eight notes before and six notes after the start of the second entry. In the first voice, we thus test patterns that finish between eight notes before and six notes after the start of the second voice: each of these candidates is matched against all the voices, and the candidate having the best total score on all its occurrences is then selected. The subject can appear augmented (all durations are doubled) or inverted (all pitch intervals are reversed), and once the subject is known, the same matching algorithm retrieves the inversions or the augmentations of the subject.

   The countersubject starts right after the subject (or very infrequently, after some additional notes), and ends (in the majority of cases) exactly at the same position as the subject. The second countersubject (when it exists) starts and ends approximately at the start and end, respectively, of the third occurrence of the subject. We use the same matching algorithm to retrieve CS1/CS2. We allow a CS1 only when there is a concurrent S, and a CS2 only when there is a CS1 in a "compatible" position.

Other Analytical Elements and Global Structure Using the substitution function, we look for partial harmonic sequences—that is, consecutive transposed occurrences of the same pattern across at least two voices (Giraud et al., 2012). Every bass note that lasts strictly more than four beats (for binary metres) is labelled "bass pedal" (or six beats for ternary metres). We try to identify a perfect authentic cadence (V–I in root position) by detecting a dominant chord followed by a complete or partial tonic chord with the root in the bass.

Finally, we use a hidden Markov model to combine previous elements to discover the sequence of states that structure the fugue (exposition, codetta, further exposition, further episodes). The observed symbols are the elements output by the preceding analysis steps (entries of subjects and countersubjects, harmonic sequences).

Results Our aim with this system was to provide *algorithms with high precision* rather than high recall. As all the content of a fugue is somewhat derived from the base patterns, what is interesting is not to locate as many approximate occurrences as possible or to infer very short patterns, but to provide an analysis with some *semantics*: the occurrences of the patterns and of other analytical elements should be organized into a meaningful analysis. The system has been tested on 36 fugues of Bach and Shostakovich, and was successful in finding the main patterns and the global structure in at least half of the fugues (Giraud et al., 2015). In both the Bach and Shostakovich corpora, the precision of pattern detection is more than 85% for S, CS1, and CS2. For example, false positive subjects were found in only three of Bach's fugues and four of Shostakovich's fugues. Most of the time, false positive subjects detected by the system are in fact relevant to the analysis, because they correspond to incomplete thematic patterns. Finally, the analysis of some fugues yielded poor results, especially when the subject detection failed. Some noteworthy cases were the double and triple fugues, where additional subjects have their own expositions in the middle of a fugue, as in Bach's Fugue in C♯ minor (BWV 849). Because the detection of subjects is done at the beginning of a fugue, our system was not able to detect these other subjects and their occurrences.

5.3.2.2 Sonata Form

A movement in sonata form is built on a *tonal progression* and on two thematic zones (primary, P, and secondary, S) (Hepokoski and Darcy, 2006). A first step towards computing an analysis of such a movement is to be able to detect the global structure (exposition–development–recapitulation).

A study on audio signals managed to find these approximate boundaries (Jiang and Müller, 2013). We presented preliminary results on identifying such global structure in symbolic signals (David et al., 2014). After detecting putative phrase endings, we try to locate a P zone, from the start to a phrase ending, that is repeated in the recapitulation. Then we try to locate, after P, an S zone, under the constraint

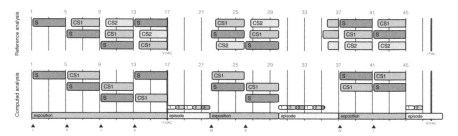

Fig. 5.1 Reference annotations on Fugue in B♭ major (BWV 866) from the first book of the Well-Tempered Clavier by J. S. Bach (top), and computed analysis (bottom). The computed analysis detects thematic patterns (S/CS1) with scale degrees, harmonic sequences (1/2/3), and the two cadences (rIAC and PAC). Here the algorithms find a good structure, even if the second countersubject (CS2) and some incomplete patterns at measures 35 and 36 are undetected

of a transposition from the dominant in the recapitulation. In a corpus of eleven first movements from string quartets by Mozart, Haydn or Schubert, this method allows for the retrieval of the majority of exposition/recapitulation pairs. The starting boundary of P in the recapitulation is often precise, but not the P/S separation. The predicted S zone can be detected before the start of the actual S, because the end of the transition is often already transposed in the recapitulation. An objective could be to precisely locate the *medial caesura*, when it exists, marking the end of the P zone and the beginning of the S zone (Hepokoski and Darcy, 2006).

5.4 Benchmark Data and Evaluation

In this section, we discuss how to evaluate and compare algorithms for segmentation and form analysis. As computer scientists, we would like to have computer-readable reference datasets that may be used as a "ground truth" to evaluate algorithms. But as music theorists, we know that there is rarely one correct analysis of a given piece: listeners, players, or analysts often disagree or at least propose several points of view.

We now discuss the possibility of having reference datasets, present datasets for segmentation and form analysis, and finally discuss evaluation methods.

5.4.1 Can We Have a Reference Segmentation or a Reference Music Form Analysis?

A music theorist performing an analysis focuses on particular aspects of a score with respect to what she wants to reveal. The relevant observations are not necessarily the same as the ones perceived by a listener or by a player. When one wants to evaluate computational analysis methods, one thus needs to ask *which specific task one needs to evaluate*, and one has to use an adapted ground truth. Which analytical points to consider is not so straightforward and depends on the studied piece and on some musicological assumptions.

Different opinions exist regarding the definition of basic analytical elements, the placement of section boundaries, and the functional labelling of sections. In the following, we will see how different datasets encode the same popular song (Figs. 5.3 and 5.4). In classical music, there are also many points where different people may have different answers. Considering different analyses of fugues from the first book of Bach's Well-Tempered Clavier, for 8 out of 24 fugues, at least two musicological sources disagree on defining the *end* of the subject, that is the main theme of a fugue (Fig. 5.2). Indeed, in fugues, whereas the starting points of subjects are notable cognitive events, their endings are not always important and may be constructs arising from music theory. More radically, considering that the ambiguity can be part of the music, Tovey (1924) writes about J. S. Bach's Fugue in E major (BWV 854) from the first book of the Well-Tempered Clavier: "It is not worthwhile settling where the subject ends and where the countersubject begins".

On the other hand, there is consensus among many music theorists, players and listeners about some analytical elements. The fact that reaching consensus may be difficult on some points should not prevent us from trying to formalize some elements. Ideally we should have a collection of reference analyses highlighting different points of view on the same piece by different musicologists. This could be achieved either by having several annotators agree on a reference annotation, or, even better, by having analyses or alternative solutions by several annotators. Finally, dealing with ambiguities does not exclude the possibility of having an "exact" symbolic approach: one can indicate in the dataset that one may consider two or more boundaries for a section, but the precise position of each boundary can be specified.

5.4.2 Datasets on Music Segmentation

Several reference datasets exist for segmentation/structuration purposes, trying to take into account multiple dimensions of music (Peeters and Deruty, 2009). The four datasets presented below are plain-text files describing the structure of audio files as annotations at some offsets (measured in seconds). These datasets consist mostly of popular music, although some "classical" works can be found in them too. Annotations have been produced manually, often using a platform such as Sonic Visualiser.[1]

SALAMI The SALAMI dataset (Structural Analysis of Large Amounts of Music Information) (Smith et al., 2011), version 2.0 (March 2015), contains the structure of 1164 audio files, each one analysed by *one or two listeners*, totalling 1933 annotation files, and 75191 segments.[2] The annotation format can describe "musical similar-

---

[1] http://www.sonicvisualiser.org/

[2] http://ddmal.music.mcgill.ca/research/salami/annotations

Fig. 5.2 The eight subjects in the first book of Bach's *Well-Tempered Clavier* where at least two sources disagree on the end of the subject (Giraud et al., 2015). Circled notes show the proposed endings of the subjects. For example, in Fugue number 7, Prout (1910) and Bruhn (1993) state that the subject ends on the B♭ (tonic), with a cadential move that is strengthened by the trill. Keller (1965) states that the subject ends after the sixteenth notes, favouring a longer subject that ends on the start of the countersubject. Charlier (2009) has a motivic approach, resulting in shorter subjects in some fugues

ity, function, and instrumentation". Musical similarity is described on two levels: lowercase letters indicate small-scale similar segments, whereas uppercase letters indicate sections. Functions are described by a controlled vocabulary of 20 labels ("intro", "verse", etc.). Some of these labels are specific to a genre or a form ("head", "main theme", "exposition", "development", etc.). The leading instruments are also described—instruments are delimited by opening and closing parentheses (Fig. 5.3, right, and Fig. 5.4, right). The fact that some files are encoded by *two* listeners allows for some ambiguities to be included, coming from different annotators.

IRISA Semiotic Annotations The Semiotic Annotations dataset (Bimbot et al., 2012, 2014), version 2012, describes the structure of 383 audio files in 6725 segments, produced and cross-checked by two annotators.[3] Authors identified *segments* respecting a "System-and-Contrast" model, a segment being usually a sequel of four elements where the last element has some contrast within a logical progression. This enables traditional antecedent/consequent *abac* periods to be modelled. Further extensions can model shorter or longer periods such as *ab* or *abaac*. Segments are clustered according to the similarity of their logical progression and are labelled according to some functional properties (for instance I for an introduction and C for a central part, often the chorus). Composite labels are also used, such as A_B for an overlap between two segments. The method usually requires a limited number of symbols to model a piece, providing a high-level view of its structure (Fig. 5.3, left). These annotations rely on a methodology that is well-defined in the guidelines for this dataset—ideally, they should be independent of the annotator.

AIST Annotations AIST Annotations (Goto, 2006) (National Institute of Advanced Industrial Science and Technology) describe the structure of 276 files of the RWC database (Goto, 2004),[4] in 4485 segments (Fig. 5.3, middle). Some annotations also include other elements such as beats or melody line. Synchronized MIDI files, obtained by the procedure described by Ewert et al. (2009), are available for the Popular Music database and Classical Music database, allowing this dataset to be used for symbolic MIR studies.

Isophonics The C4DM (Centre for Digital Music) provides segmentation for 301 files (Mauch et al., 2010) (Fig. 5.4, left). Some of these files also have other annotations (chords, keys, and beats).[5]

Do These Datasets Agree? Figures 5.3 and 5.4 show examples of these annotations on the same files. Staying at the *segmentation* level, one can observe that the boundaries of these manual annotations generally coincide (with slight differences in the offsets) and that the clustering of labels is also generally done in the same way. However, several differences are found when one goes to functional labelling, getting closer to what could be a form analysis. Even in popular songs, identifying the formal function of a chorus, a verse or a bridge is sometimes ambiguous.

5.4.3 Datasets with Reference Analyses of Musical Forms

The datasets described above are well adapted to popular music. On the other hand, large musical forms, such as sonata form, feature complex relationships between parts that cannot be satisfactorily modelled simply by labelled sections. Moreover, the musical score, when it exists, contains many details that can be analysed beyond a raw segmentation. We argue for the need for *specific reference datasets for musical forms* adapted to computational music analysis.

---

[3] http://metissannotation.irisa.fr/

[4] https://staff.aist.go.jp/m.goto/RWC-MDB/AIST-Annotation/

[5] http://www.isophonics.net/content/reference-annotations

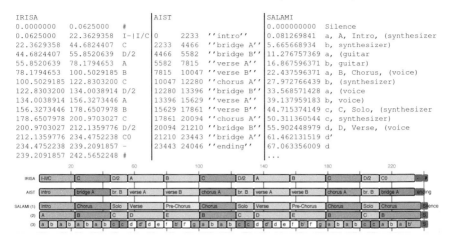

```
IRISA                              AIST                          SALAMI
0.0000000   0.0625000   #                                       0.000000000  Silence
0.0625000   22.3629358  I-|I/C|0     2233   ''intro''           0.081269841  a, A, Intro, (synthesizer
22.3629358  44.6824407  C      2233  4466   ''bridge A''        5.665668934  b, synthesizer)
44.6824407  55.8520639  D/2    4466  5582   ''bridge B''        11.276757369 a, (guitar
55.8520639  78.1794653  A      5582  7815   ''verse A''         16.867596371 b, guitar)
78.1794653  100.5029185 B      7815  10047  ''verse B''         22.437596371 a, B, Chorus, (voice)
100.5029185 122.8303200 C      10047 12280  ''chorus A''        27.972766439 b, (synthesizer)
122.8303200 134.0038914 D/2    12280 13396  ''bridge B''        33.568571428 a, (voice
134.0038914 156.3273446 A      13396 15629  ''verse A''         39.137959183 b, voice)
156.3273446 178.6507978 B      15629 17861  ''verse B''         44.715374149 c, C, Solo, (synthesizer
178.6507978 200.9703027 C      17861 20094  ''chorus A''        50.311360544 c, synthesizer)
200.9703027 212.1359776 D/2    20094 21210  ''bridge B''        55.902448979 d, D, Verse, (voice
212.1359776 234.4752238 C      21210 23443  ''bridge A''        61.462131519 d'
234.4752238 239.2091857 -      23443 24046  ''ending''          67.063356009 d
239.2091857 242.5652248 #                                       ...
```

Fig. 5.3 Reference annotations from IRISA, AIST and SALAMI for "Spice of Life", sung by Hisayoshi Kazato (track 4 of RWC-MDB-P-2001). The three annotations generally agree on the segmentation even though their onsets differ slightly. Note that the four sections labelled B, Chorus by SALAMI are labelled C, C, C, and C0 by IRISA and bridge A, chorus A, chorus A, and bridge A by AIST. The SALAMI annotation has several levels, giving both functions (1), sections (2) and small-scale segments (3)

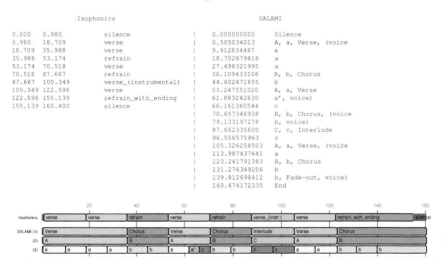

```
             Isophonics                          SALAMI
0.000   0.980     silence                |   0.000000000   Silence
0.980   18.709    verse                  |   0.505034013   A, a, Verse, (voice
18.709  35.988    verse                  |   9.912834467   a
35.988  53.174    refrain                |   18.702879818  a
53.174  70.518    verse                  |   27.498321995  a
70.518  87.667    refrain                |   36.109433106  B, b, Chorus
87.667  105.349   verse_(instrumental)   |   44.602471655  b
105.349 122.596   verse                  |   53.247551020  A, a, Verse
122.596 155.139   refrain_with_ending    |   61.883242630  a', voice)
155.139 160.400   silence                |   66.161360544  c
                                         |   70.657346938  B, b, Chorus, (voice
                                         |   79.133197278  b, voice)
                                         |   87.652335600  C, c, Interlude
                                         |   96.556575963  c
                                         |   105.326258503 A, a, Verse, (voice
                                         |   113.987437641 a
                                         |   123.241791383 B, b, Chorus
                                         |   131.276349206 b
                                         |   139.812698412 b, Fade-out, voice)
                                         |   160.474172335 End
```

Fig. 5.4 Reference annotations from Isophonics and SALAMI on the Beatles song "Yellow Submarine". The annotations mainly agree on the segmentation even if the onsets differ slightly, and the segments are different: the first two segments labelled verse by Isophonics correspond to only one segment, labelled A (aaaa) by SALAMI: verse corresponds to the sub-segments aa or aa' c, with a' and c having half the length of the other sub-segments. The last Chorus (refrain_with_ending for Isophonics) has three small-scale segments, bbb, instead of only two

```
== S [length 4 start +1/8]        == CS1 [length 3 start -1/4]
     S   1, 13, 37                      S   6, 23, 42
     A   5, 22, 41                      A  10, 27, 38
     T   9, 26                          T  14

== S-inc [base S length 2]        == CS1-inc [base CS1 length 1]
     A  35                              S  36


== cadences                       == CS2 [length 3 start -3/16]
     *  17 (V:rIAC)                     S  10, 27
     *  48 (I:PAC)                      A  14
                                        T  23, 38, 42

                                  == CS2-inc [base CS2 length 1]
                                        T  36
```

Fig. 5.5 Reference annotations from the Algomus group on Fugue in B♭ major (BWV 866) by J. S. Bach, obtained from several sources including the books by Bruhn (1993) and Prout (1910). These annotations show the entries of the subject (S), countersubjects (CS1 and CS2) in soprano (S), alto (A), and tenor (T) voices, as well as incomplete entries (S-inc, CS1-inc, CS2-inc). The position of each occurrence is denoted by measure numbers (1 is the first beat of measure 1), but the actual start is shifted from this logical position (one eighth note forward for S, one quarter note backward for CS1, three sixteenth notes backward for CS2). This fugue also contains perfect and root position imperfect authentic cadences (PAC and rIAC) in the tonic (I) and dominant (V) keys. A graphical representation of this annotation can be found at the top of Fig. 5.1

As we saw in the introduction, there are different conceptions of musical forms. So the nature of a specific "musical form analysis" depends on the musicological assumptions on which it is based. There are many "correct" or at least "pertinent" ways to analyse musical forms. The points of view will not be the same when one focuses on a particular piece, on the evolution of the techniques used by a composer, or on a corpus including works of other composers.

In any case, one needs to annotate both features occurring in all parts or voices (cadences, sequences, texture, global segmentation) and at the voice or instrument level (e.g., melodic themes). This latter level is still valid when the voices are not explicitly separated, such as in piano or guitar music. The annotations should rely on one or several musicological reference analyses indicating the locations and the durations of precise elements (e.g., for sonata form, the thematic zones in the exposition and recapitulation or thematic elements in the development). Offsets can be exact symbolic values (measure numbers and positions within the measure).

For annotators, a problem is that even a detailed musicological analysis does not always provide the level of precision required in a formalized dataset. For example, the books of Bruhn (1993) on Bach's fugues detail the list of occurrences of the S and CS patterns, including complementary details for the strongly varied occurrences. However, very slight variations are not always described, and an annotator transcribing this analysis has to encode the precise location to report the exact offset value in the reference dataset. Moreover, since human language itself can be ambiguous, the encoder of the reference analysis may sometimes have to make some interpretations, even if the intended meaning is obvious most of the time. Such interpretations should be recorded in the formalized dataset.

Finally, to provide subtle analyses of musical pieces closer to human interpretations, algorithms should also model ambiguities, ideally by predicting several solutions with their associated likelihoods.

Algomus Fugue Reference Analysis We released a reference analysis for the 24 fugues of the first book of Bach's Well-Tempered Clavier and the first 12 fugues of Shostakovich (Op. 87) (Giraud et al., 2015), totalling about 1,000 segments.[6] The dataset is built on several musicological references, such as the analysis of Bruhn (1993), and was produced and cross-checked by several annotators. The annotations give the symbolic positions of the occurrences of subjects and countersubjects, as well as cadences and pedals (Fig. 5.5). Slight modifications of the thematic patterns, such as varied start or ending or delayed resolutions, are also reported. Our dataset differs from the ones presented in Sect. 5.4.2: the length and the position of each pattern in each voice are given, in terms of the number of measures and beats, and several analytical elements beyond patterns are specified.

The purpose of this dataset is to give "correct" analytical elements for evaluable tasks, that should be part of a more complete analysis. In most of the fugues, there is consensus between theorists on some very technical points. Indeed, considering again Fig. 5.2, all our sources perfectly agree on the definition of the subject in 16 out of the 24 fugues. There may be also agreements on modulations, some cadences, and so on. The algorithms can thus be evaluated on all these points. We also reported ambiguous definitions of the subject. Further work should be done to encode even more ambiguities concerning the exact boundaries of other elements constituting the analysis.

5.4.4 Evaluating Segmentation and Form Analysis Algorithms

Even once a reference dataset is established, there are several ways to assess the efficiency of a segmentation algorithm or of a form analysis system against this dataset taken as a "ground truth": one can focus on a segmentation, on some precise borders, on a more semantic segmentation with relations between the sections, or on a subjective assessment of the quality of the algorithm.

Frame-Based Evaluation—How Often Does the Algorithm Predict the Right Section? On audio files, segmentation can be seen as a prediction of a label for every audio "frame", for example with a prediction every 40 milliseconds. On symbolic data, algorithms may also predict sections at the resolution of the smallest symbolic duration, or at another resolution, such as one quarter note or one measure. The most simple evaluation is then to consider frames one by one and to compute the ratio

---

[6] http://www.algomus.fr/datasets

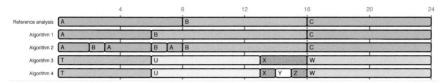

Fig. 5.6 Comparing segmentation labels from a reference analysis (top) against several algorithm predictions on a piece with 24 measures

of correctly predicted frames over the total number of frames. This is equivalent to comparing the *length* of the predicted sections in the computed analysis and in the ground truth: what is the proportion of section A that is found by the algorithm? For example, in Fig. 5.6, considering the measures as frames, 22 out of 24 frames are "correctly" predicted by both algorithms 1 and 2.

However, these evaluations need to assert which label in one analysis is equivalent to another label in the other analysis. When the predicted labels are different from those of the ground truth (such as for algorithms 3 and 4 in Fig. 5.6), one solution can be to link each computed segment with the largest overlapping segment in the ground truth (T with A, U with B and W with C), giving here 21 out of 24 frames for both algorithms 3 and 4. These evaluations may not behave correctly when a ground truth section is mapped to several predicted sections. Here algorithm 3 can be considered to have a better result than algorithm 4, because section B is segmented into only two sections, U and X. A solution is to measure the *mutual information* between the algorithm output and the ground truth. Extending the ideas of Abdallah et al. (2005), Lukashevich (2008) defines scores reporting how an algorithm may over-segment (S_o) or under-segment (S_u) a piece compared to the ground truth. These scores are based on normalized entropies.

On algorithms segmenting audio signals, all these evaluation measures, and other ones, were compared in a meta-analysis of the MIREX 2012 structural segmentation task results (Smith and Chew, 2013). On symbolic data, one can also consider the *number of notes* in each section—"How many notes are correctly put into section A?"—thus preventing biases that might arise from assigning greater weight to long notes than to short notes.

Boundary-Based Evaluation—How Many Section Boundaries Are Correctly Predicted? Frame-based evaluations ignore the actual boundaries of the segmentation. In particular, they do not take into account the fact that an algorithm may make too many transitions between sections. In Fig. 5.6, all the methods presented above give the same evaluation for algorithms 1 and 2, but algorithm 1 may be preferable because it predicts longer sections.

An evaluation can thus focus on *section boundaries*. One can compute the usual *precision* (ratio of correct predictions to all predictions) and *recall* (ratio of correct predictions to all ground-truth annotations). For example, in Fig. 5.6, there are 2 boundaries in the ground truth (A/B, B/C). Algorithm 1 successfully predicts the B/C boundary; it thus has a recall of 1/2 and a precision 1/2 (2 predicted boundaries, including the false boundary A/B). Algorithm 2 successfully predicts the two ground truth boundaries: it has a perfect 2/2 recall. However, as it predicts 4 other false boundaries, its precision is only 2/6.

These evaluations are well adapted to melodic segmentation. Again, one has to decide which boundary in one analysis is equivalent to another boundary in the other analysis. In symbolic data, one can require that the boundaries *exactly* coincide: most of the time, a phrase, a section, or even some events such as a modulation, starts on a precise note or chord, and the goal of segmentation could be to retrieve this exact point. One can also allow some flexibility with a tolerance window, either in audio time (0.5 seconds, 3 seconds) (Sargent et al., 2011), or, for symbolic data, in terms of notated duration ("two quarter notes", "one measure") or in number of notes in a monophonic sequence ("one note", "two notes").

Section-Based Evaluation—How Many Sections Are Correctly Predicted? One can also choose to focus on whole sections, evaluating the proportion of sections correctly predicted. Again, thresholds can be added to this detection; should the start and the end exactly coincide? In Fig. 5.6, depending on the threshold, the performance of algorithm 1 will be evaluated to either 1/3 (only section C) or 3/3 (all sections).

Evaluating Form Analysis—Is My Computer a Good Music Analyst? Implementing frame-based, boundary-based and section-based evaluations allow us to quantify different aspects of the *segmentation* task. But these procedures do not evaluate other elements such as structural labelling. As we mentioned in Sect. 5.2.3, the challenge of *form analysis* needs to go beyond segmentation. In Fig. 5.6, are the A/B/C and T/U/W labels only symbols, or do they have some semantics? To evaluate an algorithm aiming to analyse a pop song, a fugue, or a sonata form movement, an evaluation should be conducted on the segmentation elements but also on the global output, including the semantics of the proposed analysis.

The results given by the computer should be compared to a reference analysis, when it exists, or, better, evaluated by musicologists, asserting how close a particular analysis is to a "musically pertinent" analysis, keeping in mind that there may be several pertinent analyses. Along with specific comments, some subjective notations such as "bad", "correct" or "good" can be used. Such an evaluation can pinpoint the strengths and the weaknesses of an algorithm on different pieces in the same corpus. Ideally, such an evaluation should be done by several experts.

Of course, as there is no absolute "musicologically correct" analysis, even this expert evaluation cannot be considered final and only evaluates what is expected according to a particular analysis model. Nevertheless, students in music analysis are evaluated on their homework, both on technical formal points (harmonic progressions, cadences, segmentations, etc.) and even on the aesthetic aspects of their work. Algorithms need to be evaluated too, and the difficulty of developing sound methodologies for carrying out such evaluation should not deter us from attempting to do so.

5.5 Discussion and Perspectives

There are many MIR and CMA challenges in segmentation and form analysis, in designing new algorithms, establishing reference datasets and conducting evaluations. Segmentation has been studied more extensively on audio signals than it has on symbolic representations, and some evaluation datasets are already available. Some studies have now begun to specifically address form analysis challenges, but more work is needed in this field of research.

One should remember that musical forms evolved (and perhaps were even designed) for *pedagogical purposes* in composition, as well as in music analysis and performance. The student who follows a lecture on music analysis learns to take a score and to recognize and analyse a fugue, a variation, or a sonata form. The student in harmony or composition learns how to write something that should sound like a fugue by Bach, respecting some rules or not. This is also true of performers: the artist playing a fugue has in some way to play with this special form, choosing between several plausible interpretations.

All these forms are also *building blocks* or *techniques* that one can find inside large-scale works. If you know how to hear, how to analyse, how to perform, or perhaps how to write a fugue, you will be able to hear, to analyse, to perform, or to write a fugato passage in some larger work. A further MIR/CMA challenge is to detect fragments of forms inside large works, or, more generally, to describe an unknown score with more elements than a segmentation. A solution is to test several known forms and take the best matched form, but further research should be done to propose better pipelines that predict the musical form on-the-fly.

Returning to the original question, "Can a computer understand musical forms?", we are not even sure that, as casual or experienced listeners, or even as music theorists, we ourselves hear and *understand* a fugue or a sonata form correctly. However, we all know that there is not a unique way to hear or to understand any musical piece—and it is not the relation to the form that makes a piece a pleasure to listen to. What we do know is that the process of learning to hear, to analyse, to play, and even to write such forms is important in musical education. Knowledge of these forms is one of the key ingredients for a better understanding of repertoires and genres.

We believe that algorithms in computational musical analysis are in their infancy: they are like students in a first-year music analysis classroom. They learn or they infer rules. They need to be evaluated—even if there are many different analyses that can be done, some are definitely more correct than others. Perhaps these student algorithms do not understand the big picture with respect to musical form, but they are learning how to handle some analytical concepts—thematic analysis, segmentation, and other musical parameters—that can also be useful for other MIR applications. One day, algorithms may perhaps manage to do more complete analyses, breaking the rules and including aesthetic and comparative elements.

Acknowledgements This work was supported by a grant from the French Research Agency (ANR-11-EQPX-0023 IRDIVE).

References

Abdallah, S., Noland, K., and Sandler, M. (2005). Theory and evaluation of a Bayesian music structure extractor. In *Proceedings of the 6th International Conference on Music Information Retrieval (ISMIR 2005)*, pages 420–425, London, UK.

Bimbot, F., Deruty, E., Sargent, G., and Vincent, E. (2012). Semiotic structure labeling of music pieces: Concepts, methods and annotation conventions. In *Proceedings of the 13th International Society for Music Information Retrieval Conference (ISMIR 2012)*, pages 235–240, Porto, Portugal.

Bimbot, F., Sargent, G., Deruty, E., Guichaoua, C., and Vincent, E. (2014). Semiotic description of music structure: an introduction to the quaero/metiss structural annotations. In *Proceedings of the AES 53rd International Conference on Semantic Audio*, pages P1–1, London, UK.

Browles, L. (2005). Creating a tool to analyse contrapuntal music. Bachelor Dissertation, University of Bristol, UK.

Bruhn, S. (1993). *J. S. Bach's Well-Tempered Clavier. In-Depth Analysis and Interpretation.* Mainer International.

Cambouropoulos, E. (2001). The local boundary detection model (LBDM) and its application in the study of expressive timing. In *Proceedings of the International Computer Music Conference (ICMC 2001)*, La Habana, Cuba.

Cambouropoulos, E. (2006). Musical parallelism and melodic segmentation. *Music Perception*, 23(3):249–268.

Cambouropoulos, E., Crochemore, M., Iliopoulos, C. S., Mohamed, M., and Sagot, M.-F. (2005). A pattern extraction algorithm for abstract melodic representations that allow partial overlapping of intervallic categories. In *Proceedings of the 6th International Conference on Music Information Retrieval (ISMIR 2005)*, pages 167–174, London, UK.

Caplin, W. E. (2000). *Classical Form: A Theory of Formal Functions for the Instrumental Music of Haydn, Mozart, and Beethoven.* Oxford University Press.

Caplin, W. E., Hepokoski, J., and Webster, J. (2009). *Musical Form, Forms & Formenlehre—Three Methodological Reflections.* Leuven University Press.

Chai, W. (2006). Semantic segmentation and summarization of music: Methods based on tonality and recurrent structure. *IEEE Signal Processing Magazine*, 23(2):124–132.

Charlier, C. (2009). *Pour une lecture alternative du Clavier Bien Tempéré.* Jacquart.

Chen, H.-C., Lin, C.-H., and Chen, A. L. P. (2004). Music segmentation by rhythmic features and melodic shapes. In *IEEE International Conference on Multimedia and Expo (ICME 2004)*, pages 1643–1646.

Cook, N. (1987). *A Guide to Musical Analysis.* Oxford University Press.

Czerny, C. (1848). *School of Practical Composition.* R. Cocks & Co.

Dannenberg, R. B. and Goto, M. (2009). Music structure analysis from acoustic signals. In Havelock, D., Kuwano, S., and Vorländer, M., editors, *Handbook of Signal Processing in Acoustics*, pages 305–331. Springer.

Dannenberg, R. B. and Hu, N. (2002). Pattern discovery techniques for music audio. In *Proceedings of the 3rd International Conference on Music Information Retrieval (ISMIR 2002)*, pages 63–70, Paris, France.

David, L., Giraud, M., Groult, R., Louboutin, C., and Levé, F. (2014). Vers une analyse automatique des formes sonates. In *Journées d'Informatique Musicale (JIM 2014)*.

Ewert, S., Müller, M., and Grosche, P. (2009). High resolution audio synchronization using chroma onset features. In *IEEE International Conference on Acoustics, Speech and Signal Processing (ICASSP 2009)*, pages 1869–1872.

Farbood, M. (2010). A global model of musical tension. In *Proceedings of the 11th International Conference on Music Perception and Cognition (ICMPC 11)*.

Foote, J. (1999). Visualizing music and audio using self-similarity. In *Proceedings of the 7th ACM International Conference on Multimedia (MM99)*, pages 77–80, Orlando, FL.

Ghias, A., Logan, J., Chamberlin, D., and Smith, B. C. (1995). Query by humming: Musical information retrieval in an audio database. In *Proceedings of the 3rd ACM International Conference on Multimedia*, pages 231–236, San Francisco, CA.

Giraud, M., Groult, R., Leguy, E., and Levé, F. (2015). Computational fugue analysis. *Computer Music Journal*, 39(2):77–96.

Giraud, M., Groult, R., and Levé, F. (2012). Detecting episodes with harmonic sequences for fugue analysis. In *Proceedings of the 13th International Society for Music Information Retrieval Conference (ISMIR 2012)*, Porto, Portugal.

Goto, M. (2004). Development of the RWC music database. In *International Congress on Acoustics (ICA 2004)*, pages I–553–556.

Goto, M. (2006). AIST annotation for the RWC music database. In *Proceedings of the 7th International Conference on Music Information Retrieval (ISMIR 2006)*, pages 359–360, Victoria, Canada.

Hamanaka, M. and Tojo, S. (2009). Interactive GTTM analyzer. In *Proceedings of the 10th International Society for Music Information Retrieval Conference (ISMIR 2009)*, pages 291–296, Kobe, Japan.

Hepokoski, J. and Darcy, W. (2006). *Elements of Sonata Theory: Norms, Types, and Deformations in the Late-Eighteenth-Century Sonata*. Oxford University Press.

Hirata, K. and Matsuda, S. (2002). Interactive music summarization based on GTTM. In *Proceedings of the 3rd International Conference on Music Information Retrieval (ISMIR 2002)*, Paris, France.

Hsu, J. L., Liu, C. C., and Chen, A. (1998). Efficient repeating pattern finding in music databases. In *Proceedings of the 7th International Conference on Information and Knowledge Management (CIKM 1998)*, pages 281–288, Bethesda, MD.

Jiang, N. and Müller, M. (2013). Automated methods for analyzing music recordings in sonata form. In *Proceedings of the 14th International Society for Music Information Retrieval Conference (ISMIR 2013)*, Curitiba, Brazil.

Keller, H. (1965). *Das Wohltemperierte Klavier von Johann Sebastian Bach*. Bärenreiter.

Kirlin, P. B. and Jensen, D. D. (2011). Probabilistic modeling of hierarchical music analysis. In *Proceedings of the 12th International Society for Music Information Retrieval Conference (ISMIR 2011)*, pages 393–398, Miami, FL.

Klapuri, A. (2011). Pattern induction and matching in music signals. In Ystad, S., Aramaki, M., Kronland-Martinet, R., and Jensen, K., editors, *Exploring Music Contents: 7th International Symposium, CMMR 2010, Málaga, Spain, June 21–24, 2010. Revised Papers*, volume 6684 of *Lecture Notes in Computer Science*, pages 188–204. Springer.

LaRue, J. (1970). *Guidelines for Style Analysis*. Harmonie Park Press.

Lemström, K. and Laine, P. (1998). Musical information retrieval using musical parameters. In *Proceedings of the International Computer Music Conference (ICMC 1998)*, pages 341–348, Ann Arbor, MI.

Lerdahl, F. and Jackendoff, R. S. (1983). *A Generative Theory of Tonal Music*. MIT Press.

Lerdahl, F. and Krumhansl, C. L. (2007). Modeling tonal tension. *Music Perception*, 24(4):329–366.

Levy, M., Noland, K., and Sandler, M. (2007). A comparison of timbral and harmonic music segmentation algorithms. In *IEEE International Conference on Acoustics, Speech, and Signal Processing (ICASSP 2007)*, pages 1433–1436, Honolulu, HI.

Lukashevich, H. M. (2008). Towards quantitative measures of evaluating song segmentation. In *Proceedings of the 9th International Conference on Music Information Retrieval (ISMIR 2008)*, pages 375–380, Philadelphia, PA.

Maddage, N., Li, H., and Kankanhalli, M. (2009). A survey of music structure analysis techniques for music applications. In Grgic, M., Delac, K., and Ghanbari, M., editors, *Recent Advances in Multimedia Signal Processing and Communications*, volume 231 of *Studies in Computational Intelligence*, pages 551–577. Springer.

Marsden, A. (2010). Schenkerian analysis by computer. *Journal of New Music Research*, 39(3):269–289.

Marx, A. B. (1837–1847). *Die Lehre von der musikalischen Komposition, praktisch theoretisch*. Breitkopf und Härtel.

Mauch, M., Cannam, C., Davies, M., Dixon, S., Harte, C., Kolozali, S., Tidhar, D., and Sandler, M. (2010). OMRAS2 metadata project 2009. In *Proceedings of the 11th International Society for Music Information Retrieval Conference (ISMIR 2010)*, Utrecht, The Netherlands.

Mongeau, M. and Sankoff, D. (1990). Comparison of musical sequences. *Computers and the Humanities*, 24(3):161–175.

Muellensiefen, D., Pearce, M., and Wiggins, G. (2008). A comparison of statistical and rule-based models of melodic segmentation. In *Proceedings of the 9th International Conference on Music Information Retrieval (ISMIR 2008)*, pages 89–94, Philadelphia, PA.

Nattiez, J.-J. (1987). *Musicologie générale et sémiologie*. Christian Bourgeois.

Paulus, J. and Klapuri, A. (2008). Music structure analysis using a probabilistic fitness measure and an integrated musicological model. In *International Conference on Music Information Retrieval (ISMIR 2008)*, pages 369–374.

Paulus, J., Müller, M., and Klapuri, A. (2010). Audio-based music structure analysis. In *Proceedings of the 11th International Society for Music Information Retrieval Conference (ISMIR 2010)*, pages 625–636, Utrecht, The Netherlands.

Peeters, G. (2007). Sequence representation of music structure using higher-order similarity matrix and maximum-likelihood approach. In *Proceedings of the 8th International Conference on Music Information Retrieval (ISMIR 2007)*, Vienna, Austria.

Peeters, G. and Deruty, E. (2009). Is music structure annotation multi-dimensional? A proposal for robust local music annotation. In *International Workshop on Learning the Semantics of Audio Signals*, pages 75–90.

Prout, E. (1910). *Analysis of J. S. Bach's Forty-Eight Fugues (Das Wohltemperirte Clavier)*. E. Ashdown.

Rafael, B. and Oertl, S. M. (2010). MTSSM – A framework for multi-track segmentation of symbolic music. In *World Academy of Science, Engineering and Technology Conference*, Turkey.

Rafailidis, D., Nanopoulos, A., Manolopoulos, Y., and Cambouropoulos, E. (2008). Detection of stream segments in symbolic musical data. In *Proceedings of the 9th International Conference on Music Information Retrieval (ISMIR 2008)*, Philadelphia, PA.

Ratner, L. (1980). *Classical Music: Expression, Form, and Style*. Schirmer.

Ratz, E. (1973). *Einführung in die musikalische Formenlehre*. Universal Edition. Second edition.

Reicha, A. (1824). *Traité de haute composition musicale*. A. Diabelli.

Rodríguez-López, M. E., Volk, A., and Bountouridis, D. (2014). Multi-strategy segmentation of melodies. In *Proceedings of the 15th International Society for Music Information Retrieval Conference (ISMIR 2014)*, pages 207–212, Taipei, Taiwan.

Rosen, C. (1980). *Sonata Forms*. W. W. Norton.

Sargent, G., Bimbot, F., and Vincent, E. (2011). A regularity-constrained Viterbi algorithm and its application to the structural segmentation of songs. In *Proceedings of the 12th International Society for Music Information Retrieval Conference (ISMIR 2011)*, Miami, FL.

Schenker, H. (1935). *Der freie Satz*. Universal Edition.

Schoenberg, A. (1967). *Fundamentals of Musical Composition*. Faber & Faber.

Sidorov, K., Jones, A., and Marshall, D. (2014). Music analysis as a smallest grammar problem. In *Proceedings of the 15th International Society for Music Information Retrieval Conference (ISMIR 2014)*, pages 301–3016, Taipei, Taiwan.

Smith, J. B. L., Burgoyne, J. A., Fujinaga, I., De Roure, D., and Downie, J. S. (2011). Design and creation of a large-scale database of structural annotations. In *Proceedings of the 12th International Society for Music Information Retrieval Conference (ISMIR 2011)*, Miami, FL.

Smith, J. B. L. and Chew, E. (2013). A meta-analysis of the MIREX structural segmentation task. In *Proceedings of the 14th International Society for Music Information Retrieval Conference (ISMIR 2013)*, pages 251–6, Curitiba, Brazil.

Tovey, D. F., editor (1924). *Forty-Eight Preludes and Fugues by J. S. Bach*. Associated Board of the Royal Schools of Music.

Weng, P.-H. and Chen, A. L. P. (2005). Automatic musical form analysis. In *Proceedings of the International Conference on Digital Archive Technologies (ICDAT 2005)*, Taipei, Taiwan.

Wiering, F., Nooijer, J. D., Volk, A., and Tabachneck-Schijf, H. J. M. (2009). Cognition-based segmentation for music information retrieval systems. *Journal of New Music Research*, 38(2):139–154.

Chapter 6
Chord- and Note-Based Approaches to Voice Separation

Tillman Weyde and Reinier de Valk

Abstract Voice separation is the process of assigning notes to musical voices. A fundamental question when applying machine learning to this task is the architecture of the learning model. Most existing approaches make decisions in note-to-note steps (N2N) and use heuristics to resolve conflicts arising in the process. We present here a new approach of processing in chord-to-chord steps (C2C), where a solution for a complete chord is calculated. The C2C approach has the advantage of being cognitively more plausible but it leads to feature modelling problems, while the N2N approach is computationally more efficient.

We evaluate a new C2C model in comparison to an N2N model using all 19 four-voice fugues from J. S. Bach's *Well-Tempered Clavier*. The overall accuracy for the C2C model turned out slightly higher but without statistical significance in our experiment. From a musical as well as a perceptual and cognitive perspective, this result indicates that feature design that makes use of the additional information available in the C2C approach is a worthwhile topic for further research.

6.1 Introduction

Voice separation is the process of assigning notes to a musical voice. This is not only an important feature of our auditory and specifically musical perception and cognition, but also a practical problem when working with semi-structured musical data, such as tablature, MIDI recordings, or automatically transcribed audio. When using any of these forms of input data, automatic voice separation (AVS) is an important part of creating musical scores together with pitch estimation and beat tracking. AVS has not achieved as much attention as some other tasks in music information retrieval, such as genre classification or melodic similarity estimation. This is possibly because

Tillman Weyde · Reinier de Valk
Department of Computer Science, City University London, London, UK
e-mail: {t.e.weyde, r.f.de.valk}@city.ac.uk

© Springer International Publishing Switzerland 2016   137
D. Meredith (ed.), *Computational Music Analysis*,
DOI 10.1007/978-3-319-25931-4_6

polyphonic transcription from audio has not reached the level of accuracy needed for practical software applications. However, in applications with MIDI and tablature AVS can be useful immediately.

Several algorithmic methods have been developed, using different approaches. Almost all existing voice separation models are based on the Gestalt principle of proximity in pitch and time. This leads to a well-defined solution for simple cases, but in practice the complexity of real music requires trade-offs between many different factors such as time and pitch proximity. This creates two challenges. First, it is not obvious how to weight different features to achieve decisions in situations with conflicting cues. This problem can be addressed with machine learning by adapting the weights to fit the data, e.g., using a neural network as in the work presented in this chapter. Second, there are many possible assignments of notes to voices, so that the implementation of an exhaustive search of all possible combinations of note-to-voice assignments across all notes in a piece is computationally intractable. Therefore, a localized modelling of the decision process is necessary. We describe here a new chord-to-chord (C2C) approach to voice assignment, with two different feature extraction methods, and compare it to the previously introduced note-to-note (N2N) approach. From a computational perspective, the C2C approach has the advantage over existing note-based models that notes can be assigned to voices even where the individual assignment is not optimal (e.g., in terms of pitch distance), if it leads to a better fit for the whole chord. The different approaches exhibit differences in terms of their runtime complexity and performance and entail different trade-offs.

From a perceptual and cognitive perspective, the separation and integration processes in forming multiple voices or streams of auditory events are an example of the binding problem, i.e., the integration of stimuli, like notes, to percepts, like voices (cf. Wrigley and Brown, 2004). These binding mechanisms in general and for music in particular are not yet well understood, but it is clear that parallel processing is involved. The C2C approach includes that aspect in the model, increasing its power and cognitive plausibility. However, the C2C approach poses the problem of how to model the relation between the notes and the voices and their combinations, both from a perceptual and cognitive as well as from a machine learning perspective.

In the N2N approach, the concepts of pitch and time proximity can be modelled directly, because only one note is treated per decision, so that the time and pitch distance to notes in previous voices can be directly used as feature values. In the C2C approach, however, the modelling of variable chord sizes with a vector of fixed dimension is an open problem. Conversely, in the C2C approach the interaction between notes in the same chord is naturally modelled in the voice assignment and learning process, while the N2N approach requires the use of additional rules and heuristics and cannot guarantee optimal results on the chord level. We have performed experiments on the four-voice fugues in J. S. Bach's Well-Tempered Clavier, testing implementations of the N2N and C2C approaches in different variants.

In Sect. 6.2, we give an introduction to AVS and related work in this area. In Sect. 6.3, the application of machine learning to voice separation, feature design, and the implications of the C2C and N2N model are discussed. The experiments we conducted are described in Sect. 6.4 and the results are discussed in Sect. 6.5. The final conclusions and directions for further work are presented in Sect. 6.6.

6.2 Voice Separation

Voice separation has been approached both from the perspective of music perception and cognition, in particular with respect to the underlying neural mechanisms, as well as from a computational perspective, with a focus on practical problem solving.

6.2.1 Perception and Cognition of Polyphony

Several methods for voice separation in symbolic music formats have been suggested in recent decades. Earlier work in the 1980s and 1990s focused on modelling cognitive and perceptual phenomena relating to polyphonic structure. Specifically the work of Huron (1989, 1991b) addressed the perception of polyphony, prevalence of voice crossings, and inner-voice entries in corpora (Huron, 1991a; Huron and Fantini, 1989), presenting a model for measuring pseudo-polyphony; Marsden (1992) developed rule-based models for the perception of voices in polyphonic music. Gjerdingen (1994) used a neural network to model the perception of 'apparent motion'.

Auditory streaming, and more generally *auditory scene analysis* as defined by (Bregman, 1994), i.e., the integration and separation of auditory stimuli into separate streams, representing environmental properties (sounds originating from the same source), is generally assumed to be the perceptual and cognitive basis for the development of musical polyphony (e.g., Huron, 1991a; Wright and Bregman, 1987). McCabe and Denham (1997) presented a model of the early stages of the process of auditory streaming on the acoustic level, which is not directly applicable to symbolic voice separation. Perception of separate voices has been shown to take place in musically trained and untrained subjects, and to depend on sensory-driven and attention-driven processes (Fujioka et al., 2008, 2005). Both the temporal processes and concurrent stimulus processing in chord perception interact, and this interaction is not fully understood (McDermott and Oxenham, 2008; Turgeon and Bregman, 2001). The neural mechanisms underlying these functions are the topic of current research in auditory neuroscience (see, e.g., Ragert et al., 2014; Shamma et al., 2011).

Modelling the perception of multiple voices in polyphonic music poses an instance of the binding problem, i.e., the segregation and combination of different stimuli into a perceptual entity, and it is not fully understood how this is represented or processed in the brain. In particular the combinatorial representation of auditory features and objects (voices) poses modelling questions: assuming specific neurons representing possible combinations would require many representation units, which would have very sparse activations, and thus be ecologically implausible. Many researchers assume that temporal synchronization mechanisms play a role (Brown et al., 1996; Shamma et al., 2011).

6.2.2 Automatic Voice Separation

Apart from being of importance for understanding underlying musical principles and perceptual and cognitive aspects of polyphony, AVS is necessary for music transcription and music information retrieval tasks on recorded MIDI data or automatically transcribed audio, where no score is available. Therefore several practical approaches have been proposed.

Over the past 15 years, several computational methods for voice separation have been developed, most of them rule-based like the earlier work by Marsden (1992). Temperley (2001) adopted an approach based on four 'preference rules', i.e., criteria for evaluating a possible analysis. Two of these match the Pitch Proximity Principle and the Principle of Temporal Continuity (Huron, 2001), which dictate that the closer two notes are to one another in terms of pitch and time, the more likely they are perceived as belonging to the same voice; the other two aim to minimize the number of voices (New Stream Rule) and to avoid shared notes (Collision Rule). Cambouropoulos (2000) briefly described an elementary version of a voice separation algorithm based on path length minimization. Chew and Wu (2004), and an extended method by Ishigaki et al. (2011), used a *contig* approach, in which the music is divided into segments where a constant number of voices is active (the contigs). The voice fragments in the segments are then connected on the basis of pitch proximity, disallowing voice crossings. Szeto and Wong (2006) considered voices to be clusters containing events proximal in the pitch and time dimensions, and model voice separation as a clustering problem. The aim of their research, however, was to design a system for pattern matching, not voice separation. In their method, voice separation is only a preprocessing step that prevents "perceptually insignificant" (p. 111) stream-crossing patterns from being returned by the system. Kilian and Hoos (2002) presented an algorithm that is not intended primarily for correct voice separation, but rather for creating "reasonable and flexible score-notation" (p. 2), so that their method allows for complete chords in a single voice. Similarly, in the method presented by Karydis et al. (2007), a voice is also not necessarily a monophonic sequence of notes. Rather, they preferred to use the term 'stream' (see Cambouropoulos, 2008) as a perceptually independent sequence of notes or multi-note sonorities. Hence, in addition to the 'horizontal' pitch and time proximity principles, they included two 'vertical integration' principles, based on principles suggested by Huron (2001), into their method: the Synchronous Note Principle (based on Huron's Onset Synchrony Principle) and the Principle of Tonal Fusion (based on Huron's Tonal Fusion Principle). A related algorithm is described by Rafailidis et al. (2009). Madsen and Widmer (2006) present an algorithm based fundamentally on the pitch proximity principle, which combines rules, optimization, and heuristics.

Both the rule-based and the machine learning algorithms that are described below treat the music as a set of events in a two-dimensional pitch-time grid. To search the full space of all possible voice assignments on this view would mean to explore all possible combinations of assignments of notes to voices. Thus the total number of combinations is V^n, where V is the number of voices and n is the number of notes. For example, for a relatively short piece with $V = 4$ and $n = 150$ this yields $4^{150} = 2^{300} \approx 2 \times 10^{90}$, making a complete search intractable. One principled approach to addressing this issue is the use of dynamic programming, which reduces the search space to a series of individual decisions, such that the overall result is optimal. However, in order to apply dynamic programming, the problem formulation must conform to Bellman's *principle of optimality* (Bellman, 2003) and decompose into *overlapping subproblems* (Cormen et al., 2009). Dynamic programming is used, for example, in Temperley's voice separation system (Temperley, 2001). The Viterbi algorithm is also based on dynamic programming and is used with hidden Markov models, which we have applied to AVS in earlier work (De Valk et al., 2013). However, the use of dynamic programming limits the modelling flexibility. Therefore the rule-based methods listed above reduce the complexity by applying specifically designed techniques that are based on decisions made per note or per note-pair within a limited context. They use heuristics and conflict resolution techniques to make sure that constraints are respected and some interaction between the note-level decisions is realized.

Machine learning approaches, in contrast, normally use a reduced representation, typically vectors of real numbers, that fits the requirements of the chosen learning technique. Kirlin and Utgoff (2005) consider only pairs of notes within a window, and use decision tree learning to determine whether or not they belong to the same voice. Assigning notes to voices in order of their onsets, they use pitch proximity to disambiguate between multiple voices. Within a chord (notes with common onset time), only one note is considered at a time and all possible next notes within the voice are evaluated. The complexity is further reduced by limiting the window size and using the pitch proximity heuristic.

Jordanous (2008) also adopts a machine-learning approach. In her method, within windows based on instances of the maximal number of voices present, every note is compared to every possible next or previous note (the method starts from a marker, which defines the middle of the window). Using learned pitch transition probabilities and voice probabilities given a pitch, the most probable voice for each note is determined. As in Kirlin and Utgoff's algorithm, for each note within a chord, all pairs that it forms with possible next and previous notes are considered, with conflict resolution based on the highest probabilities.

In neither Kirlin and Utgoff's (2005) nor Jordanous' (2008) machine learning approaches is there any optimization of the assignment of notes to voices for a chord as a whole.

6.3 Method

We approach the problem of AVS in a standard machine learning set-up. AVS on symbolic music representations operates on a complex input consisting of a stream of often synchronous note events, and machine learning offers the possibility for a system to adapt its behaviour to data. By using given voice information, e.g., as given by the composer or a human transcriber, the assignment of the events to voices can be seen as a supervised machine learning problem. The given voice information, the so-called *ground-truth*, defines the target output of the system.

Most machine learning models use a vector of numbers as input and output a vector of numbers or symbols. An important question is how the properties of the musical decision context can be encoded in a vector, so that the relevant aspects of time and pitch structure are reflected and usable for the learning model (dynamics, timbre and expressive timing are not included in the model at this point). In the case of voice separation, a straightforward approach is the N2N model, where the context is modelled for each note using a vector of features such as the pitch distances to the previous notes in the voices (a detailed description follows in the next section). Based on this feature vector, a decision to assign the current note to a voice is made and the following steps are based on this decision—that is, we follow a greedy approach. The advantage is that the system is conceptually straightforward and has a computational complexity that is linear in the number of notes processed. The disadvantage is that the solution may be sub-optimal, because decisions are not revised. For example, in some cases, it may be better *not* to minimize the proximity of the current note within its voice, but rather go for another option if that enables a better fit for the remaining notes in the chord. In the N2N approach such a solution cannot be found. The N2N approach has nevertheless been applied using neural networks with good results, but also with potential for improvement by supporting chord-level optimization.

We therefore propose our new C2C approach for modelling voice separation as a machine learning problem on the level of chords rather than notes, where a non-linear rating function that maps notes to voices per chord is learned. The C2C approach is still local in time but global in the vertical dimension—that is, we evaluate all possible assignments of notes to voices. This approach is cognitively and perceptually more plausible, as it addresses the concurrent processing that takes place in the human auditory system. The binding problem, however, also applies in this context, as the machine learning process requires a compact representation, which also helps to keep the model plausible. This approach requires the design of features representing complete chords rather than just notes, for which we use two approaches.

The first is to represent each voice separately with a set of features, raising the problem of how to represent voices without notes with a fixed-size vector. The second is to average the feature values over the notes in the chord, avoiding the problem of missing notes and leading to a compact representation with fixed dimensions, but also to a loss of information. Within this framework we are not aware of a solution that would avoid these problems.

6.3.1 Representation

As discussed above, most methods for voice separation focus on features of the music that represent the proximity of notes in pitch and time. This can be measured, for example, as the pitch difference from the note to be assigned to the previous note in each voice. Similarly we can measure the time from the end of the previous note in each voice to the beginning of the current note. We can then choose the voice that minimizes one of these distances or a combined distance, but that may not be the optimal solution for a whole chord, which requires the definition of a global measure. Before we discuss the question of how to determine the best trade-off for a given chord and mapping, we present the feature definitions that we use in the C2C and the N2N approaches.

6.3.1.1 Features

We define an n-dimensional feature vector as a numerical representation of the notes in a chord in their polyphonic context. n is fixed within a learning and application model, but depends on the maximum number of voices V the model supports. Pitches are represented as MIDI note numbers, pitch intervals as semitones, and durations as whole notes. When using a model designed for V voices, a chord can contain 1 to V notes.

The feature vector has three parts:

1. *note-specific features* are different for the individual notes in the chord. Each of these gets a default value of -1 for each note the chord is short of V, that is, for notes c to $V-1$, where c is the number of notes in the chord (using zero-based indexing);
2. *chord-level features* are calculated per chord;
3. *polyphonic embedding features* depend on the mapping of notes to voices for the chord; each mapping results in a different polyphonic embedding.

Let n_t^v be the chord note mapped to voice v under the current mapping, n_{t-1}^v the previous note in v, $\mathrm{p}(n)$ a note's pitch, $\mathrm{on}(n)$ its onset time, and $\mathrm{off}(n)$ its offset time. For each voice v we calculate

- the pitch proximity of n_t^v to n_{t-1}^v:

$$\mathtt{pitchProx}(v) = \frac{1}{|\mathrm{p}(n_t^v) - \mathrm{p}(n_{t-1}^v)| + 1} ; \tag{6.1}$$

- the inter-onset time proximity of n_t^v to n_{t-1}^v:

$$\mathtt{intOnProx}(v) = \frac{1}{(\mathrm{on}(n_t^v) - \mathrm{on}(n_{t-1}^v)) + 1} ; \tag{6.2}$$

- the offset-onset time proximity n_t^v to n_{t-1}^v:

$$\text{offOnProx}(v) = \begin{cases} \frac{1}{(\text{on}(n_t^v)-\text{off}(n_{t-1}^v))+1}, & \text{if off}(n_{t-1}^v) \le \text{on}(n_t^v), \\ \frac{1}{(\text{on}(n_t^v)-\text{off}(n_{t-1}^v))-1}, & \text{if off}(n_{t-1}^v) > \text{on}(n_t^v); \end{cases} \quad (6.3)$$

- the pitch movements—that is, for each voice v, the difference $p(n_t^v) - p(n_{t-1}^v)$, in semitones;
- the pitch–voice correlation ρ between the chord's pitch ordering and voice ordering, as measured by the Pearson correlation coefficient:

$$\rho_{pv}(C) = \frac{\sum p_i v_i - c\bar{p}\bar{v}}{s_p s_v} = \frac{\sum p_i v_i - \sum p_i \sum v_i}{\sqrt{\sum p_i^2 - (\sum p_i)^2}\sqrt{\sum v_i^2 - (\sum v_i)^2}}, \quad (6.4)$$

where c is the number of notes in the chord C, p_i the pitch of note i, and v_i the voice assigned to note i. If there is only one note, 0 is returned.

The decision to model proximity as $1/\text{distance}$ rather than using distance was taken in order to emphasize differences between smaller distances.

The whole feature vector is described in Table 6.1 for the C2C model and in Table 6.2 for the N2N model. Features marked with an asterisk (*) are assigned a value of -1 for every note the chord is short of V.

6.3.1.2 Variable Chord Sizes

A central problem in the C2C approach is that chords are of variable size, and standard neural networks, like most machine learning algorithms, use fixed-size vectors. We consider two approaches here for pitch and time proximity:

1) representing each voice separately, using default values when there are no notes in a voice;
2) averaging values over notes.

Approach 1 has the advantage of capturing all information in the voice assignment. However, when not all voices are present, the voice features are filled with default values. These values are outside the regular range of values, but this information is not explicit to the neural network (or any other vector-based learning system used). Therefore the learning system needs to learn the relation between the appearance of the default values and the rating of the mapping in context.

6.3.2 Learning Model

We have previously addressed the task of AVS with the N2N approach. The N2N approach models the task as a classification problem, where each note is assigned to a voice (a class). For each note in the dataset, a training example is created consisting of a feature vector and a ground-truth label (a one-of-n representation of the note's

Table 6.1 The feature vector for the C2C model, assuming $V = 4$

Position	Name	Description
Note-specific features		
1, 5, 9, 13	indexInMapping*	index (based on pitch) in the chord, excluding sustained previous notes
2, 6, 10, 14	indexInChord*	index (based on pitch) in the chord; including any sustained previous notes
3, 7, 11, 15	pitch*	pitch
4, 8, 12, 16	duration*	duration
Chord-level features		
17	chordSize	number of notes in the chord; including any sustained previous notes
18	isOrnamentation	true (1) if a sixteenth note or smaller and the only new note in the chord
19	metricPosition	metric position within the bar
20–22	intervals*	intervals in the chord; including any sustained previous notes
Polyphonic embedding features		
23–26	pitchProx	for each voice v: the pitch proximity of n_t^v to n_{t-1}^v
27–30	intOnProx	for each voice v: the inter-onset time proximity of n_t^v to n_{t-1}^v
31–34	offOnProx	for each voice v: the offset-onset time proximity of n_t^v to n_{t-1}^v
35–38	pitchMovements	for each voice v: the pitch movement of n_t^v with respect to n_{t-1}^v
39–42	voicesAlreadyOccupied	binary vector encoding all voices already occupied in the chord
43	pitchVoiceRelation	correlation coefficient between pitches and voices; including any sustained previous notes
44	numberOfVoiceCrossingPairs	number of voice crossing pairs; including any sustained previous notes
45	summedDistOfVoiceCrossingPairs	total distance of all voice crossing pairs; including any sustained previous notes
46	avgDistOfVoiceCrossingPairs	average distance of all voice crossing pairs; including any sustained previous notes
47–50	mapping	vectorial representation of the mapping of notes to voices

voice). Given the feature vectors as input, the network is trained so that its output approximates the labels. The trained network is then applied to unseen data to predict voices; the predictions are determined by the output neuron with the highest activation. More details on this approach are provided by De Valk and Weyde (2015).

In the C2C approach, the task is modelled as a regression problem, where the ratings for the mappings of notes to voices are learned with the aim of giving the ground-truth mapping the highest rating. Each chord in the dataset is represented as a set of *m* *n*-dimensional feature vectors, where *n* depends on the selected feature set, voice number and use of averaging. Each vector encodes properties of that chord in its polyphonic context under one of *m* possible mappings of the chord notes to voices. The goal is to have a model that, for each chord in a piece, takes as input a set of feature vectors representing that chord in its context for all possible mappings of notes to voices, and that rates the correct mapping highest. We use a three-layer

Table 6.2 The feature vector for the N2N model, assuming $V = 5$

Position	Name	Description
Note-specific features		
0	pitch	pitch
1	duration	duration
2	isOrnamentation	true (1) if a sixteenth note or smaller and the only new note in the chord
3	metricPosition	metric position within the bar
Chord-level features		
4	chordSize	number of notes in the chord; including any sustained previous notes
5	indexInChord	index (based on pitch) in the chord; including any sustained previous notes
6	pitchDistTo NoteBelow	pitch distance to the note below in the chord; including any sustained previous notes
7	pitchDistTo NoteAbove	pitch distance to the note above in the chord; including any sustained previous notes
8–12	intervals	intervals in the chord; including any sustained previous notes
Polyphonic embedding features		
13–17	pitchProx	proximities in pitch to the previous note in each voice
18–22	intOnProx	proximities in time (inter-onset) to the previous note in each voice
23–27	offOnProx	proximities in time (offset-onset) to the previous note in each voice
28–32	voicesAlready Occupied	binary vector encoding all voices already occupied in the chord

feed-forward neural network model with an output layer containing only a single neuron. The activation value of this neuron ranges between 0 and 1, and represents the rating for a mapping given a chord and context. We use a sigmoid activation function and resilient backpropagation (RPROP) as the learning algorithm (Igel and Hüsken, 2003; Riedmiller and Braun, 1993).

6.3.3 Mappings: Enumeration and Pruning

In the C2C approach, the input to the neural network depends on the mapping of the chord notes to the voices. For each chord, given the number of notes in the chord and the number of voices in the dataset, all possible mappings of notes to voices are enumerated. A mapping is encoded as a V-dimensional vector, where V is the maximum number of voices and the ith element is an integer from -1 to $(N-1)$, where N is the maximum number of concurrent notes, which is normally equal to V. The element indicating the (zero-based) index into the chord of the note assigned to the ith voice (with the voices ordered from top to bottom and sustained previous notes excluded). A value of -1 at the ith position indicates that no note in the chord is mapped to the ith voice. Note that the vectorial representation used does not allow for more than one note to be mapped to one voice (in which case the voice would no longer be monophonic). Thus there are initially V^{N+1} possible mappings of notes to voices.

The enumeration of mappings per chord is restricted according to the following constraints:

1. all chord notes are mapped to a voice;
2. each chord note is mapped to only one voice;
3. no chord note is mapped to a voice that is already taken by a sustained note from a previous chord.

We then prune the enumerations, both to avoid the method becoming computationally too expensive and to improve the model's performance. All mappings that contain more than two voice crossing pairs are removed, where voice crossing pairs are instances of voice crossings within a chord. If, for example, the tenor voice (T) moves above both the soprano (S) and the alto (A) in a chord (and the soprano is above the alto), this chord contains two voice crossing pairs: TS and TA. When counting voice crossing pairs, sustained notes from previous chords (if applicable) are included, and unisons are not considered to be voice crossings. The limit of two was chosen as this is the maximum number of voice crossing pairs encountered in our dataset. This is an ad hoc choice which matches the difficulty that listeners experience in perceiving voice crossings. However, whether this can be generalized and whether a more flexible solution can be found are questions that are worth exploring more thoroughly. Pruning can be very effective in reducing the number of mapping possibilities, as shown in Table 6.3, which gives the number of possibilities for a chord of c notes in a context of V voices before and after pruning (all numbers provided are for the case where there are no sustained notes from a previous chord). The table shows that the effect increases as the number of notes in a chord grows, and that it is stronger when there are more voices. When the number of notes approaches the number of voices, there are fewer options left within the given limit of voice crossings, leading to lower numbers of mappings (e.g., in the case $V = 5, c = 5$). In our experiments we used values of 4 and 5 for V, and we can read from the table the relative increase of computation compared to the N2N model. In the N2N model, c feature vectors need to be calculated and evaluated with the neural network. For the C2C model, the number in column P describes the number of feature vector calculations and neural network evaluations per chord after pruning. We can see that the increase for chords with more notes (i.e., P/c) is bounded by a constant factor of 7 for $V = 4$ and of 17 for $V = 5$. The feature vectors are larger for the C2C model, which adds additional processing, but in practice the overall increase was lower than predicted and below 11 (see Table 6.4), which is substantial but not prohibitive on modern computers.

As mentioned above, we used a neural network to calculate the gain function for each mapping, i.e., a rating of the quality of the mapping in the context. For learning from data we train the neural network to rate the mapping output (as in the ground-truth) better than any other mapping. For this we use relative training as used

Table 6.3 Number of mapping possibilities for a chord of c notes in a context of V voices, with no restrictions (N), meeting enumeration constraints (C) and after pruning (P) of mappings containing more than two voice crossing pairs

	$V = 3$			$V = 4$			$V = 5$		
	N	C	P	N	C	P	N	C	P
$c = 1$	3	3	3	4	4	4	5	5	5
$c = 2$	9	6	6	16	12	12	25	20	20
$c = 3$	27	6	5	64	24	20	125	60	50
$c = 4$				256	24	9	625	120	45
$c = 5$							3125	120	20

by Weyde and Dalinghaus (2003), which is based on Braun et al. (1991). Unlike a standard regression approach, where desired outputs—i.e., the ratings—are given directly, we train the model by comparing the output for the ground-truth mapping with the outputs for all other mappings, the goal being that, for each chord, the ground-truth mapping should lead to higher network output than the other mappings.

6.3.4 Relative Training

The relative training technique can be thought of as instantiating the network twice, sharing the structure and the weight values, with the ground-truth mapping input to one network and a generated mapping to the other. For training, both networks feed into a single *comparator* neuron through connections with fixed weights, -1 and $+1$, as shown in Fig. 6.1. In this structure, the feature vector of the ground-truth data is applied to 'net 1' and the feature vector of the other examples to 'net 2'. If net 1 with the ground-truth input has a higher output than net 2 (i.e., the relative rating is correct), then the input to the comparator becomes negative, otherwise the input value is positive, or zero if the networks produce equal outputs.

We used a rectified linear unit for the comparator neuron—that is, we used $\max(x, 0)$ as the activation function and set the target output of the comparator to 0, so that for all correct relative ratings (where $\text{out}(\text{net } 1) > \text{out}(\text{net } 2)$) the comparator output error $(actual - target)^2$ is 0. This network can be trained with standard backpropagation or any other gradient descent algorithm to avoid or reduce incorrect relative ratings. It is helpful for new data to aim for an output difference that is not just negative, but below some threshold $-\varepsilon$. In neural network terminology, this means setting a bias for the comparator neuron. This introduces some robustness against variations in the input data and improves the performance on new data. An alternative, that was used by Hörnel (2004), is to use a logistic activation function $\frac{1}{1+e^{-x}}$, which leads to a positive error signal of varying size for all inputs. We did preliminary experiments with both approaches, and found that both approaches lead

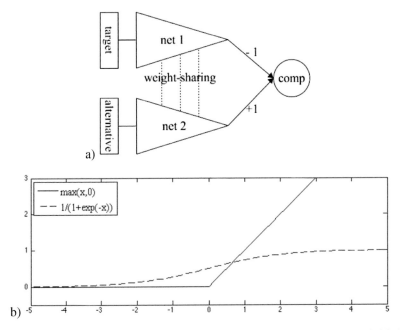

Fig. 6.1 (a) The neural network structure for relative learning, the comparator neuron is labelled 'comp'. (b) Activation functions for the comparator neuron: rectified linear ($\max(x,0)$) and logistic ($\frac{1}{1+e^{-x}}$)

to similar results. We chose the rectified linear units for the final experiments as they are computationally more efficient and lead to slightly better results on the test data.

6.4 Experiments

We evaluated the performance of the C2C model with the proximity features represented per-voice (C2C) and averaged (C2CA). We also evaluated the effect of additional—unused—voice features, by testing a five-voice version. For evaluation of the two approaches, the 19 four-voice fugues of J. S. Bach's *Well-Tempered Clavier* (BWV 846–893) were used. The MIDI encodings for the pieces from www.musedata.org were used and all notes beyond four simultaneous voices were removed (this is typically the final chord and a few notes just before the final chord). This decision was taken to enable comparison with the N2N model, which in its current implementation does not allow more than one note per voice at any given time. The models were trained and evaluated using 19-fold cross-validation, where each piece is one fold. We did not use random division of training samples, as samples from the same piece would contain regularities, possibly verbatim repetitions, which would make the results unrepresentative for new music. By using piece-wise cross-validation we can use the results as estimates for results on unseen data of the same style.

Two modes of evaluation were used:

1. *test mode*, where the context features are calculated on the basis of the ground truth. This mode is useful for assessing the effectiveness of learning and generalization of the neural network to new data, without the effect of propagating errors; and
2. *application mode*, where the context features are calculated on the basis of the predicted voice assignments. This mode is like the intended use case, where no ground truth, i.e., no score, exists.

We used preliminary experiments to determine the values of the rating margin ε as 0.05 and weight decay λ as 0.00001 (C2C) and 0.00003 (N2N). The method showed little sensitivity to variations in these parameters, as long as ε was not much smaller and λ not much larger than the chosen values.

Five models were tested overall. The N2N model (see De Valk and Weyde, 2015), the C2C4 and C2C5 models without averaging of the proximity features, which have four and five voices, respectively, and the C2CA4 and C2CA5 with averaging and four and five voices, respectively.

6.5 Results and Discussion

Accuracy (number of notes correctly assigned, divided by total number of notes) was chosen as the evaluation metric. The accuracy of the C2C, N2N and C2CA models is shown in Table 6.4. The differences between the models' accuracies are not vast, but several differences are statistically significant. We used the Wilcoxon signed-rank test, a non-parametric test for different medians, to calculate significance. The test was applied to the accuracies per piece, thus with 19 samples per condition. As opposed to the frequently used Student's t-test, the signed-rank test does not assume the values to be normally distributed, and for the majority of the combinations in Table 6.4 the values' distributions are significantly non-normal according to a Jarque–Bera test.

Overall, the results are similar to previously reported results for the N2N model (De Valk et al., 2013), although somewhat lower, as this dataset contains no three-voice fugues. The test results are in a similar range to the training results, indicating no overfitting. The results in application mode are substantially lower than those in test mode, which is due to error propagation.

In the application mode, which represents the intended use case, the C2CA4 model is most accurate, improving over the N2N model by over 2 percentage points, but, as the standard deviation is high, the difference is not significant ($p = 0.11$). A general observation in the results is that the four- and five-voice versions of the C2C models perform similarly (as expected) and the differences between corresponding four- and five-voice models are not significant in the test and application modes.

Table 6.4 Voice assignment accuracy per model (columns) and mode (rows) with averages and standard deviations over 19 folds in cross-validation. The best average accuracies per mode are shown in bold. The running times on a four-core system are shown in the lower part of the table

		N2N	C2C4	C2C5	C2CA4	C2CA5
Training	Mean	**97.89%**	96.51%	96.20%	97.17%	97.03%
	Std-Dev	0.13	0.24	0.42	0.15	0.16
Test	Mean	**97.54%**	96.19%	96.17%	96.90%	96.79%
	Std-Dev	0.79	1.52	1.06	1.16	1.24
Application	Mean	77.70%	78.50%	76.91%	**80.24%**	78.31%
	Std-Dev	7.74	10.09	9.86	9.55	11.22
Running times (sec)	Training	1,498	11,579	12,608	11,005	11,777
	Test	48	485	503	493	507
	Application	55	306	313	308	320

The N2N model shows the highest accuracy in the training and test modes, which is significantly higher than the values for the C2C models. In test mode, the results are similar to training mode, but the standard deviation is greater and the difference between the N2N and C2CA models is not significant.

The averaging of the proximity features has a positive effect on the accuracy of the C2CA models compared to the standard C2C models. The difference between the different C2C and C2CA models is mostly significant for training and test mode, while in application mode only the difference between C2CA4 and C2C5 is significant.

Overall, the C2CA models perform slightly better than the N2N model in the application mode. In the training and test mode, the accuracy of the C2CA models is slightly lower than that of the N2N model, indicating that these models are not as flexible. This could be related to the loss of information due to averaging the proximity values, but the default values used in the C2C4 and C2C5 models seem to have an even worse effect and lead to lower accuracy in all cases.

Table 6.5 The significance p-values of differences between models according to a Wilcoxon signed-rank test. Above the diagonal is the test mode and below the application mode. Values shown in bold indicate significance at the 5% level. In the training mode, all models are significantly different from each other

	N2N	C2C4	C2C5	C2CA4	C2CA5
N2N		**.0001**	**.0000**	**.0008**	**.0004**
C2C4	.8596		.5412	**.0082**	**.0258**
C2C5	.4413	.1819		**.0003**	**.0039**
C2CA4	.1134	.4653	**.0062**		0.2753
C2CA5	.6507	.3736	.1336	.4180	

6.6 Conclusions

We introduced a new chord-to-chord (C2C) approach to automatic voice separation (AVS) in symbolic music representations. The C2C approach is based on processing the voice assignments for one chord as a whole, and calculating all possible assignments. This approach has the advantage of modelling interactions between notes in a chord and being perceptually and cognitively more plausible. Its disadvantage is that it is difficult to define the features effectively, where there is a trade-off between the problematic use of default values and the loss of information by averaging. In the presented evaluation, the differences in performance are small and vary between modes. The C2C model performs better than the N2N model when averaging the proximity features in application mode, which represents the use case. However, due to high variability, this result is not significant in our experiment. Given that the C2C model is clearly slower than the N2N model, the latter may be preferable for practical applications at the moment.

However, the results show that a C2C approach to voice separation can be successful. There is a need to understand better how to design effective chord-wise features for AVS. The temporal dynamics of the auditory scene analysis are only rudimentarily modelled here, and there may be better solutions to the representation and processing problem, for example using a time-based modelling approach (e.g., one based on synchronous activation of neurons). The development of better feature representations and effective global optimization techniques are thus relevant research topics for musical voice separation, which could help realize the potential of the C2C approach more fully in the future.

Acknowledgements Reinier de Valk is supported by a funded studentship from City University London and by a grant from Semantic Media Network/EPSRC.

References

Bellman, R. (2003). *Dynamic Programming*. Dover.

Braun, H., Feulner, J., and Ullrich, V. (1991). Learning strategies for solving the problem of planning using backpropagation. In *Proceedings of the Fourth International Conference on Neural Networks*, Nimes, France.

Bregman, A. S. (1994). *Auditory Scene Analysis: The Perceptual Organization of Sound*. MIT Press.

Brown, G. J., Cooke, M., and Mousset, E. (1996). Are neural oscillations the substrate of auditory grouping. In *ESCA Tutorial and Workshop on the Auditory Basis of Speech Perception, Keele University, July*, pages 15–19.

Cambouropoulos, E. (2000). From MIDI to traditional musical notation. In *Proceedings of the AAAI Workshop on Artificial Intelligence and Music: Towards Formal Models for Composition, Performance and Analysis*, Austin, TX.

Cambouropoulos, E. (2008). Voice and stream: Perceptual and computational modeling of voice separation. *Music Perception*, 26(1):75–94.

Chew, E. and Wu, X. (2004). Separating voices in polyphonic music: A contig
mapping approach. In Wiil, U. K., editor, *Computer Music Modeling and Retrieval*,
volume 3310 of *Lecture Notes in Computer Science*, pages 1–20. Springer.

Cormen, T. H., Leiserson, C. E., Rivest, R. L., and Stein, C. (2009). *Introduction to
Algorithms*. MIT Press, 3rd edition.

De Valk, R. and Weyde, T. (2015). Bringing 'musicque into the tableture': machine
learning models for polyphonic transcription of 16th-century lute tablature. *Early
Music*, in press.

De Valk, R., Weyde, T., and Benetos, E. (2013). A machine learning approach to
voice separation in lute tablature. In *Proceedings of the Fourteenth International
Society for Music Information Retrieval Conference (ISMIR 2013)*, pages 555–560,
Curitiba, Brazil.

Fujioka, T., Trainor, L. J., and Ross, B. (2008). Simultaneous pitches are encoded
separately in auditory cortex: an MMNm study. *Neuroreport*, 19(3):361–366.

Fujioka, T., Trainor, L. J., Ross, B., Kakigi, R., and Pantev, C. (2005). Automatic
encoding of polyphonic melodies in musicians and nonmusicians. *Journal of
Cognitive Neuroscience*, 17(10):1578–1592.

Gjerdingen, R. (1994). Apparent motion in music? *Music Perception*, 11(4):335–370.

Hörnel, D. (2004). Chordnet: Learning and producing voice leading with neural
networks and dynamic programming. *Journal of New Music Research*, 33(4):387–
397.

Huron, D. (1989). Voice denumerability in polyphonic music of homogeneous
timbres. *Music Perception*, 6(4):361–382.

Huron, D. (1991a). The avoidance of part-crossing in polyphonic music: perceptual
evidence and musical practice. *Music Perception*, 9(1):93–103.

Huron, D. (1991b). Tonal consonance versus tonal fusion in polyphonic sonorities.
Music Perception, 9(2):135–154.

Huron, D. (2001). Tone and voice: A derivation of the rules of voice-leading from
perceptual principles. *Music Perception*, 19(1):1–64.

Huron, D. and Fantini, D. (1989). The avoidance of inner-voice entries: Perceptual
evidence and musical practice. *Music Perception*, 7(1):43–48.

Igel, C. and Hüsken, M. (2003). Empirical evaluation of the improved RPROP
learning algorithms. *Neurocomputing*, 50:105–123.

Ishigaki, A., Matsubara, M., and Saito, H. (2011). Prioritized contig combining to
segregate voices in polyphonic music. In *Proceedings of the Sound and Music
Computing Conference*. Università di Padova.

Jordanous, A. (2008). Voice separation in polyphonic music: A data-driven approach.
In *Proceedings of the International Computer Music Conference 2008*, Belfast,
UK.

Karydis, I., Nanopoulos, A., Papadopoulos, A., Cambouropoulos, E., and Manolopoulos, Y. (2007). Horizontal and vertical integration/segregation in auditory streaming: a voice separation algorithm for symbolic musical data. In *Proceedings of the
4th Sound and Music Computing Conference (SMC '07)*, Lefkada, Greece.

Kilian, J. and Hoos, H. H. (2002). Voice separation—A local optimization approach. In *Proceedings of the Third International Conference on Music Information Retrieval (ISMIR 2002)*, Paris, France.

Kirlin, P. B. and Utgoff, P. E. (2005). VoiSe: Learning to segregate voices in explicit and implicit polyphony. In *Proceedings of the Sixth International Conference on Music Information Retrieval (ISMIR 2005)*, pages 552–557, London, UK.

Madsen, S. T. and Widmer, G. (2006). Separating voices in MIDI. In *Proceedings of the Seventh International Conference on Music Information Retrieval (ISMIR 2006)*, pages 57–60, Victoria, Canada.

Marsden, A. (1992). Modelling the perception of musical voices: a case study in rule-based systems. In Marsden, A. and Pople, A., editors, *Computer representations and models in music*, pages 239–263. Academic Press.

McCabe, S. L. and Denham, M. J. (1997). A model of auditory streaming. *The Journal of the Acoustical Society of America*, 101(3):1611–1621.

McDermott, J. H. and Oxenham, A. J. (2008). Music perception, pitch, and the auditory system. *Current opinion in neurobiology*, 18(4):452–463.

Rafailidis, D., Cambouropoulos, E., and Manolopoulos, Y. (2009). Musical voice integration/segregation: Visa revisited. In *Proceedings of the 6th Sound and Music Computing Conference*, Porto, Portugal.

Ragert, M., Fairhurst, M. T., and Keller, P. E. (2014). Segregation and integration of auditory streams when listening to multi-part music. *PLoS one*, 9(1):e84085.

Riedmiller, M. and Braun, H. (1993). A direct adaptive method for faster backpropagation learning: The RPROP algorithm. In *IEEE International Conference on Neural Networks*, pages 586–591.

Shamma, S. A., Elhilali, M., and Micheyl, C. (2011). Temporal coherence and attention in auditory scene analysis. *Trends in neurosciences*, 34(3):114–123.

Szeto, W. M. and Wong, M. H. (2006). Stream segregation algorithm for pattern matching in polyphonic music databases. *Multimedia Tools and Applications*, 30(1):109–127.

Temperley, D. (2001). *The Cognition of Basic Musical Structures*. MIT Press.

Turgeon, M. and Bregman, A. S. (2001). Ambiguous musical figures. *Annals of the New York Academy of Sciences*, 930(1):375–381.

Weyde, T. and Dalinghaus, K. (2003). Design and optimization of neuro-fuzzy-based recognition of musical rhythm patterns. *International Journal of Smart Engineering System Design*, 5(2):67–79.

Wright, J. K. and Bregman, A. S. (1987). Auditory stream segregation and the control of dissonance in polyphonic music. *Contemporary Music Review*, 2(1):63–92.

Wrigley, S. N. and Brown, G. J. (2004). A computational model of auditory selective attention. *IEEE Transactions on Neural Networks*, 15(5):1151–1163.

Part IV
Grammars and Hierarchical Structure

Chapter 7
Analysing Symbolic Music with Probabilistic Grammars

Samer Abdallah, Nicolas Gold, and Alan Marsden

Abstract Recent developments in computational linguistics offer ways to approach the analysis of musical structure by inducing probabilistic models (in the form of grammars) over a corpus of music. These can produce idiomatic sentences from a probabilistic model of the musical language and thus offer explanations of the musical structures they model. This chapter surveys historical and current work in musical analysis using grammars, based on computational linguistic approaches. We outline the theory of probabilistic grammars and illustrate their implementation in Prolog using PRISM. Our experiments on learning the probabilities for simple grammars from pitch sequences in two kinds of symbolic musical corpora are summarized. The results support our claim that probabilistic grammars are a promising framework for computational music analysis, but also indicate that further work is required to establish their superiority over Markov models.

7.1 Introduction

Music is, arguably and amongst other things, *structured* sound. *Music analysis* is that branch of musicology which aims to explain the structure of pieces of music, in the sense of giving an account both of the relationships between different parts of the same piece, and the relationships between the piece and patterns common to other pieces of music. Theories of music analysis thus typically identify, classify, and relate musically meaningful parts of a work or works. These structural aspects of a piece of music, on the small and large scales, are crucial to its impact.

Samer Abdallah · Nicolas Gold
Department of Computer Science, University College London, London, UK,
e-mail: {s.abdallah, n.gold}@ucl.ac.uk

Alan Marsden
Lancaster Institute for the Contemporary Arts, Lancaster University, Lancaster, UK,
e-mail: a.marsden@lancaster.ac.uk

© Springer International Publishing Switzerland 2016
D. Meredith (ed.), *Computational Music Analysis*,
DOI 10.1007/978-3-319-25931-4_7

Music analysis, whether formal or informal, thus relies on "data": this includes the piece itself in sonic and/or symbolic form, but also, in most cases, a wealth of background knowledge and experience to make both the structure of a piece of music and the derivation of that structure explicit and so open to scrutiny.

We observe that listeners come to be able to perceive structure in pieces of music through mere exposure, though they might not be able to give an account of *how* they have come to perceive this structure, nor might they be able to justify it. In both these respects, music resembles language: speakers are able to understand and construct grammatical sentences, but they often require training to be able to explain what makes a sentence grammatical.

Shannon's (1948) work on information theory perhaps offers some explanation for this, in short, indicating that structure exists in any *departure from complete randomness* (this is explored further in the next section). Humans learn probabilities implicitly from exposure, and so effectively learn to perceive structure. This suggests that probabilistic modelling may offer a fruitful approach to music analysis (and one that likely demands a computational approach).

The field of computational linguistics has recently developed techniques that can be applied in the analysis of musical structure. These can induce models over a corpus of music. Such models take the form of probabilistic grammars from which idiomatic sentences can be produced. The derivation and application of the grammar rules thus offers an explanation of the musical structures modelled by them.

This chapter surveys historical and current research in computational linguistics applied to symbolic music analysis (by which we mean analysis of music in the form of symbolic, score-like data). The principles and operation of key developments are discussed, and we summarize our recent feasibility studies in using probabilistic programming techniques to provide tractable computation in this framework.

7.2 Information and Structure

Information theory provides a number of concepts that can help us to understand and quantify what we mean by 'structure'. Shannon's (1948) information theory is, to a large degree, concerned with the notion of *uncertainty*, quantified as *entropy*, and how the reduction of uncertainty can be considered a gain in information. Entropy is a function of probability distributions, and probability distributions can represent *subjective* beliefs, that is, the degrees of belief that an intelligent agent (whether biological like ourselves or artificial like our computers) places in a set of mutually exclusive propositions.[1] These degrees of belief can be based on any knowledge currently possessed by the agent in combination with any prior or innate dispositions it may have.

---

[1] Indeed, this *subjectivist* view of probability was espoused by, among others, de Finetti (1975), while Cox (1946) showed that, given certain reasonable assumptions, any system for reasoning consistently with numerical degrees of belief must be equivalent to probability theory.

Psychologists such as Attneave (1954) and Barlow (1961) proposed that perceptual systems in animals are attuned to the detection of *redundancy* in sensory signals, which means, essentially, the ability to predict one part of the sensory field from another. Often, the reason for such sensory regularities is the presence of coherent objects and processes in the outside world, so detecting and accounting for redundancy can enable the mind to see beyond the mass of sensory signals to relevant phenomena in the world. Redundancy of this sort ensues whenever different parts of the sensory field depart from complete statistical independence. This can be taken as a definition of what 'structure' is, and perceptual learning can be seen as a process of detecting statistical regularities on exposure to structured objects, and thereby making inferences about events in the world. This idea has successfully accounted for many features of perceptual processing (Knill and Pouget, 2004).

Thus, the use of probabilistic models, an approach on which we shall elaborate further in Sect. 7.4, is not merely a computational device: it is at the heart of our current understanding of human perception and cognition (Knill and Richards, 1996) and also addresses ideas about the role of uncertainty and expectation in music (Meyer, 1956).

A distinct, but related branch of information theory is *algorithmic information theory*, which is built on the idea that any object which can be represented as a sequence of symbols can also be represented by a computer program which outputs those symbols when run. Sometimes, a very short computer program can output a very long sequence of symbols, and hence, an ostensibly large object may be specified by a much smaller program. The *Kolmogorov complexity* (Li and Vitányi, 2009) of such an object is defined as the length of the smallest program that outputs the object when run, and can be considered a measure of the amount of information in the original object. As such, it is related to the *minimum description length* principle (Rissanen, 1978). Kolmogorov complexity also forms the basis of Martin-Löf's (1966) definition of a random object as one which does not admit of any smaller description and therefore cannot be compressed; this corresponds loosely with the notion of redundancy described above.

Given the close connection between predictability and compressibility (Cover and Thomas, 1991), and the probabilistic basis of optimal compression algorithms, we observe that in both theoretical frameworks (Shannon's information theory and algorithmic information theory), *structure* can be defined as that which enables an apparently large object to be represented more efficiently by a smaller description. The probabilistic approach and its subjectivist interpretation also emphasize that predictability (and hence compressibility) depend on the expectations of the observer, and thus can accommodate the subjectivity of perception in a natural manner. In addition, while the Kolmogorov complexity of an object is claimed to be an *objective* measure, in practice, it must be approximated by using compression programs that encode implicit or explicit assumptions about the data to be compressed and that are usually based on probabilistic models.

7.3 Theories of Structural Music Analysis

There are various established approaches to structure in music analysis, each of which
gives quite a different account of what a musical structure is. A Schenkerian analysis
(Schenker, 1935), for example, reveals the structure of a piece of music in hierarchical
layers of reduction, resulting in something like a tree or some other kind of restricted
directed graph (Fig. 7.1).[2] A paradigmatic and syntagmatic analysis in the manner of
Nattiez (1975), on the other hand, divides the piece into units (syntagms) and groups
those units by recurrence or resemblance into paradigms. At a higher level, then, the
structure of the piece can be shown as a sequence of syntagms, each of which is an
instance of a particular paradigm (Fig. 7.2). Theories of form, dating back to the
nineteenth century, identified themes and other kinds of segments of music, assigning
each to a role within one of a number of established formal patterns such as Sonata
Form, Rondo or Binary.

Each of these analytical approaches has three common factors:

Segmentation   The music is divided into meaningful units.
Classification   Segments are assigned to classes.
Relation   Segments are related to each other according to their role in forming
                    patterns of significance with other segments.

In the case of syntagmatic and paradigmatic analysis, the first two factors are clear,
and the third often follows in a later stage of the analysis where patterns in sequences
of instances of paradigms are identified, or a pattern in the occurrence of particular
paradigms, or in their evolution. In the case of Schenkerian analysis, the first two
factors work together, as groups of notes are identified as prolongations of notes at a

Fig. 7.1 An example Schenkerian analysis of the opening of Mozart's piano sonata in A major,
K. 331. Notes on lower staves are considered to elaborate the structural notes with which they
align or between which they occur on the staff above. Notes on the upper two staves with smaller
noteheads are considered to elaborate notes with larger noteheads, and ones with solid noteheads
to elaborate ones with open noteheads. The beam links the three notes forming the *Urlinie* which
Schenker considered to constitute the fundamental line of every proper piece of tonal music

---

[2] For an explanation of the relation of Schenkerian analyses to trees and graphs, see Marsden (2005).

Fig. 7.2 An example syntagmatic and paradigmatic analysis of the opening of Mozart's piano sonata in A major, K. 331. The melody is divided into six syntagms, identified as 1–6, and organized into two paradigms, a and b

higher level. The patterns of those higher-level notes in turn govern the relations of the lower-level units. Even such an apparently different approach to musical structure as *set theory* (Forte, 1973) employs these three factors: groups of adjacent notes are separated from other notes (segmentation); the pitch-class set of each group is identified (classification); and the structure of the piece is considered to be determined in part by the relations between the pitch-class sets.

These three are also factors in language, and grammars exist to explain how a sentence falls into a relational structure of words (segments) according to the parts of speech (classes). We therefore consider the idea of grammar to be applicable to the analysis of musical structure not only because of the oft-remarked correspondence between Schenkerian reduction and parsing a sentence, but also because of a deeper correspondence between the factors determining structure in both music and language.

This is not to deny that there are also obvious and significant differences between language and music, in particular the often multidimensional (in the sense that a musical event can usually be characterized in multiple ways, such as pitch, duration, loudness, timbre, etc.) and polyphonic nature of music. These characteristics may necessitate the development of grammars that go beyond those commonly used in linguistics, though we note that even natural language can sometimes be described in a multidimensional way (Bilmes and Kirchhoff, 2003).

Furthermore, we find grammars particularly suited to computational analysis of music because (a) they are liable to implementation in computer software, and (b) they can be learned or derived from examples of sentences or pieces of music. The latter consideration is important, first, because it is evident that most people come to be able to perceive structure in music simply by exposure to it,[3] and second, because crafting a grammar 'by hand' is not always practical for music (as we discuss below).

---

[3] We do not claim, however, that people will necessarily come to be able to *produce* musical structures simply by exposure.

7.3.1 Links to Linguistics

It is in the field of computational linguistics that grammars have been best developed, and so we will briefly review some of the important developments in linguistics before narrowing our focus to grammars in music later in this section.

Languages and Grammars A *language* is, in theoretical terms, defined as follows: given a well-defined set of symbols, or *alphabet*, a *sentence* is a finite sequence of such symbols, and a language is a set of sentences. This set may be finite or infinite; for example, if we take as our alphabet the set of lower-case latin letters a, b, c etc., then

$$\{pat, pet, pit, pot, put\} \tag{L1}$$

is a finite language, while the languages

$$\{ab, abab, ababab, abababab, \ldots\} \tag{L2}$$
$$\{ab, aabb, aaabbb, aaaabbbb, \ldots\}\,, \tag{L3}$$

continued in the obvious way, are both infinite. A grammar specifies, by means of rewrite or production rules, a recursive generative process which produces such sentences and therefore defines a language. More formally, a grammar consists of a set of *terminal* symbols that will form the alphabet of the language, a disjoint set of *non-terminal* symbols, a set of production rules describing how certain sequences of symbols may be re-written, and a distinguished non-terminal called the start symbol (conventionally S). For example the language (L1) results from the following rules for non-terminals S and V:

$$\begin{aligned} S &\to pVt, \\ V &\to a \mid e \mid i \mid o \mid u\,, \end{aligned} \tag{G1}$$

where $V \to a \mid e \mid \ldots$ is shorthand for the multiple rules $V \to a, V \to e$, etc. Similarly, language (L2), sometimes referred to as $(ab)^n$, results from

$$S \to ab \mid abS \tag{G2}$$

and (L3) (or $a^n b^n$) from

$$S \to ab \mid aSb\,. \tag{G3}$$

Note that the two infinite languages involve *recursive* production rules, that is, non-terminals that can expand to a sequence containing themselves.

As well as providing a recipe for *generating* strings from the language, a grammar also defines a way to *analyse* a given sentence in terms of the sequence of rule applications that could have been used to generate it, a process known as *parsing*. Thus, parsing seeks an *explanation* of the observed sequence in terms of possible generative structures and their semantic implications.

A particularly important class of grammars is that of the *context-free grammars*. A context-free grammar (or CFG) is a grammar in which only single non-terminal symbols appear on the left-hand side of production rules. All of the examples above are context-free grammars. Parsing a sequence using a CFG results in a *syntax tree*; for example, the sentences *abab* and *aabb* can be parsed using grammars (G2) and (G3) respectively as follows:

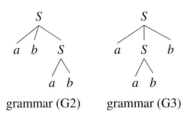

grammar (G2)   grammar (G3)

Hierarchy of Grammars Chomsky (1957) classified grammars on the basis of their production rules into a hierarchy, with simple "regular" grammars at the bottom, followed by "context-free", "context-sensitive", and finally "unrestricted" grammars at the top. Each level up is more general than the level below. For example, grammars (G1) and (G2), as well as being context-free, are also members of the more restricted class of regular grammars. There is an intimate relationship between the levels of the hierarchy and the complexity of the computing machine, or *automaton*, that is required to judge whether or not a given sequence is grammatical. Grammars higher in the hierarchy can produce languages with more complex structures, but require more computational resources (time and memory) to process. For example, regular grammars require only a *finite state automaton* for recognition of grammatical sequences; CFGs require a *push-down* automaton, which essentially means an automaton with an arbitrarily deep stack in order to keep track of arbitrarily deep recursive structures; while unrestricted grammars require a Turing tape for recognition, or a Turing machine, which is the most general type of computing machine, for further processing. Given that natural languages are for human consumption, this places limits on the complexity of the grammars that might describe them, especially when the situation demands real-time production or understanding (e.g., during conversation). For this reason, the consensus seems to be that natural languages are "mildly" context-sensitive. Whether or not the same applies to music is an interesting question. Johnson-Laird (1991) suggests that, during jazz improvisation, limitations on working memory demand that improvised structures can be described by at most a regular grammar, whereas precomposed structures, like the chord sequence, may be described by a context-free grammar (CFG) or higher. Similarly, we might posit that, on a first listening, only structures describable by a regular grammar are accessible, but repeated listening (and analysis) might reveal more complex structures, the utility of which is to explain surface features which may have seemed surprising or arbitrary when analysed using the simpler grammar.

Formalisms A variety of grammar formalisms have been proposed in order to deal with linguistic structures that cannot be described simply in a context-free way; these include tree adjoining grammars (Joshi et al., 1975), definite clause grammars or

DCGs (Pereira and Warren, 1980), extraposition grammars (Pereira, 1981), a variety
of unification based grammars (Shieber, 1985), and type-theoretical grammars such
as Lambek calculus (Lambek, 1958) and combinatory categorical grammars or CCGs
(Steedman, 2001; Steedman and Baldridge, 2011). A unifying idea behind all these
grammar formalisms is that they attempt to provide a system, or meta-language, for
specifying grammars, that is just powerful enough to describe linguistic structures in
the domain of interest, but not so powerful that it leads to intractable computations.
In the case of both natural languages and music, this seems to require something
more than a (finite) CFG, but less than an unrestricted grammar. With the exception
of the DCG formalism, which is Turing complete (i.e., capable of performing any
computation performable by a Turing machine), the carefully limited complexity of
these meta-languages means that generation and parsing is computationally tractable
and so practically usable. Thus we may think of the grammar formalism as a kind of
special purpose programming language, which is, in the terminology of programming
language design, a *high-level*, *declarative*, *domain specific language* (DSL) designed
to make sentence structure easy to describe.

Parsing A wide variety of parsing technologies have been studied. DCGs written in
Prolog can be translated directly into an executable program that can both generate
and recognize sentences from the language: Prolog's execution strategy results in top
down (recursive descent) parsing; however, this can be inefficient for very ambiguous grammars. More efficient parsers can be written using dynamic programming
techniques to avoid redundant computations; these *chart parsers* include the bottom-
up CKY algorithm (Younger, 1967) and Earley's top-down parser (Earley, 1970).
The close relationship between Earley's algorithm and tabling or memoization in
general purpose logic programming (also known as Earley deduction) is well-known
(Pereira and Warren, 1983; Porter, 1986), and can be carried over very elegantly to
functional programming languages such as Scheme and Haskell using *memoizing
parser combinators* (Frost and Hafiz, 2006; Johnson, 1995; Norvig, 1991).

Probabilistic Grammars When a grammar is extended to cover a wide corpus,
then the number of production rules and/or the size of the lexical database means that
parsing can become very expensive due to the resulting high degree of ambiguity. It
was recognized that a majority of these alternative parses would be nonsensical, and
that this notion could be characterized by noticing that certain words or constructs
are much more likely to occur than others. Thus, though it is conceivable that "[the
man] [saw [the dog with a telescope]]", it is much more likely that "[the man] [[saw
[the dog]] [with a telescope]]". A grammar augmented with probabilities becomes a
probabilistic language model, capable of being used in either direction: assigning
probabilities to sentences and their syntax trees, or generating idiomatic as opposed
to merely grammatical sentences.

Perhaps the simplest examples are probabilistic context-free grammars (PCFGs),
which consist of a CFG supplemented with, for each non-terminal, a probability distribution over the possible expansions of that non-terminal. The *inside-out algorithm*
(Baker, 1979) can compute the probabilities of alternative parses. Efficient algorithms
for probabilistic parsing were developed during the 1990s (Abney, 1997; Collins,

1999; Goodman, 1998; Stolcke, 1995) and have gone on to revolutionize computational linguistics, resulting in the current state-of-the-art in parsing and natural language understanding.

Probabilistic grammars can support *grammar induction*, which is a form of inductive learning where the grammar rules are not given, but must be inferred from a collection of sample sentences. This is analogous to the situation in which a child finds itself in the first few years of life: beginning with no knowledge of nouns, verbs, etc., the child gains enough implicit grammar to produce (more or less) grammatical utterances simply from hearing spoken language. This process has been modelled in several ways; for example, Kurihara and Sato (2006) used rule splitting to explore the space of grammar rules and Bayesian model selection criteria to choose from the resulting grammars; Bod (2006) applied his *data oriented parsing* method, which builds a collection of commonly occurring syntactic sub-trees, to both language and music; and O'Donnell et al. (2009) used Bayesian nonparametric models to achieve a similar goal.

One family of probabilistic grammars is based on so-called 'log-linear' or 'undirected' models, which involve assigning numerical likelihoods to grammatical features in such a way that they need not sum to one, as probabilities are required to do (Abney, 1997; Charniak, 2000; Collins, 1997, 2003). These can yield flexible probability models, but, due to this lack of normalization, suffer from some technical difficulties in learning their parameters from a corpus. Goodman's (1998) *probabilistic feature grammars* retain much of the flexibility but avoid these problems by using directed dependencies to obtain a properly normalized probability model. Probabilistic extensions of CCG have been developed (Hockenmaier, 2001; Hockenmaier and Steedman, 2002), also using log-linear models, with statistical parsing and parameter learning algorithms (Clark and Curran, 2003, 2007).

7.3.2 Grammars in Musicology

While the parallels between music and linguistics go back much further (Powers, 1980), the application of formal grammars in music began in the 1960s. Winograd (1968) used a grammar formalism called "systemic grammar" to define a grammar for music, covering cadential and harmonic progression, chord voicing and voice leading, and presented a LISP implementation to parse a given fragment. Despite the use of heuristics to guide the search, high computational complexity meant that the system was limited to analysing relatively small fragments.

Kassler (1967) made steps toward formalizing Schenker's theory , encoding recursive functions to describe the process of elaboration from *Ursatz* to middleground for the top and bass voices in a polyphonic score, showing that the resulting grammar was decidable, meaning there exists an algorithm (given in the paper) which can determine in a finite number of steps whether or not a given musical sequence is a member of the language defined by the grammar. Software, using backtracking search and written in APL, was presented in later work (Kassler, 1976, 1987).

Another system notable for its wide scope and technological sophistication was Ebcioğlu's (1987) CHORAL, which was implemented in a custom logic programming language and included nondeterminism and heuristically-guided "best-first" backtracking search. It was applied to harmonizing chorales in the style of J. S. Bach.

Other researchers have focused on narrower goals, such as melody analysis (Baroni et al., 1983; Lindblom and Sundberg, 1970), jazz chord analysis (Pachet, 2000; Pachet et al., 1996; Steedman, 1984; Ulrich, 1977) and grammars for melodic improvisation (Johnson-Laird, 1991). Smoliar's (1980) system was notable in that it did not attempt to do Schenkerian analysis *automatically*, but instead provided the analyst with a collection of tools to facilitate the process.

The *Generative Theory of Tonal Music* (GTTM) of Lerdahl and Jackendoff (1983) was perhaps one of the more complete attempts to account for structure in music, including melodic phrase structure, metrical structure, and hierarchical reduction similar to that described by Schenker. Lerdahl and Jackendoff expressed their theory in generative rules, but their approach was not computational. Subsequent attempts to implement the theory (e.g., Hamanaka et al., 2006, 2007, see also Chaps. 9 and 10, this volume) have encountered difficulty with their 'preference rule' concept.

More recent years have seen developments in computational linguistics, especially probabilistic grammars, filtering back into musicological work. For example, Steedman's chord grammar has inspired a number of researchers to apply more sophisticated grammar formalisms to more general harmonic models (Granroth-Wilding, 2013; Granroth-Wilding and Steedman, 2012; Rohrmeier, 2006, 2011; Steedman, 2003).

On the melodic side, Mavromatis and Brown (2004) reported that they had been able to design a grammar for Schenkerian analysis as a Prolog DCG. Schenker's melodic elaborations are similar to grammar production rules but because some of them, such as the introduction of neighbour notes or passing notes, depend on *two* adjacent notes, they cannot be written as a *context-free* grammar if the melody is represented as a sequence of pitches. Instead, Mavromatis and Brown represented melodic sequences as sequences of pitch *intervals* and were thus able to devise a CFG to embody melodic elaborations. However, practical obstacles to a working implementation were encountered, due to the large number of rules required.

Gilbert and Conklin (2007) also adopted this approach and designed a PCFG to model both melodic and rhythmic elaborations. Their grammar included five basic melodic elaborations (including the repeat, neighbour, passing, and escape types of ornamentation used in our experiments, described in Sect. 7.5). Figure 7.3 shows how a short melodic sequence can be represented as a sequence of pitch intervals and described in terms of a syntax tree using two of the elaboration rules (the *term* rule simply emits a terminal symbol). We will build on this grammar later in Sect. 7.5.

Issues of how to represent tree-like elaboration structures to enable a grammar-based analysis were examined by Marsden (2005), who showed that adopting an interval-based encoding, though sufficient to allow a context-free description for some types of melodic elaboration, is not sufficient in general to cope with other musical structures such as suspensions and anticipations which are (locally) context-dependent in a fundamental way. He went on to develop software for the analysis of

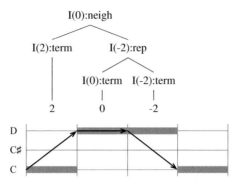

Fig. 7.3 An example of a syntax tree for a short sequence of melodic intervals. The grid below is a piano-roll representation of the notes with the arrows showing the pitch (in semitones) and time intervals between successive notes

short fragments based on bottom-up chart parsing, heuristics for ranking the quality of analyses, and pruning (similar to beam search) to limit the search space (Marsden, 2007, 2010, 2011).

Kirlin and Jensen (2011) and Kirlin (2014) also base their probabilistic model of musical hierarchies on the elaboration of intervals, adopting Yust's (2009) triangulated graphs as their structured representation, rather than the trees of conventional grammatical analysis. Another recent grammar-based approach to music analysis is that of Sidorov et al. (2014), who implement a non-probabilistic form of grammar induction.

In the literature on music theory, Temperley (2007) is the most prominent application of a probabilistic approach. Most of the book is concerned with recognition of high-level features such as metre and key rather than structures at the level of phrases and notes, but it does include a discussion of a possible approach to modelling Schenkerian analysis through a probabilistic grammar (pp. 172–179). This chapter could be seen in part as a response to Temperley's challenge to Schenkerian theorists to demonstrate how the theory 'reduces the uncertainty of tonal music' (p. 179).

7.4 Probabilistic Models

A probabilistic model (henceforth, simply 'model') of a domain is essentially an assignment of probabilities to things in that domain. It is these probabilities which determine how surprising a thing is and, in the case of a partially observed temporally unfolding object such as a piece of music, how it might continue.

Although models and data may seem rather abstracted from issues of music, if one considers 'data' to be one or many musical works in symbolic form and a 'model' as, for example, a structural analysis of a single piece, or a music theory for a large corpus of works, the application of these concepts becomes clearer.

7.4.1 Model Selection Criteria

The most effective models are adaptable to new situations (such as new musical styles) on the basis of observations. Even when listening to an individual piece, our expectations are fluid and adaptable: a theme or motif is less surprising when heard a second time or in some subsequent variation.

In all practical cases, the data is finite. Unless we have very specific information about how the data was generated, it will not be possible to determine a single 'correct' probabilistic model. For one thing, it is not possible to extract the infinite amount of information required to determine real-valued parameters from data that contains only a finite amount of information about them; for example, neither the mean and variance of a Gaussian distribution, nor the probability of a biased die rolling a six can be determined with certainty from a finite sequence of observations. In another, deeper sense, if the amount if data is limited in an essential way, such that there *cannot be* any more data (for example, the set of pieces composed by Ravel) then it can be argued that an objective probability distribution describing this set does not exist. To give another example, in a certain literal sense, the only pieces in the style of Mozart are the ones he actually wrote. However, musicians regularly use this concept, and broadly mean 'if Mozart had written another piece, then it might have been like this'. This of course is contrafactual, making clear why an objectively 'correct' model is not possible. Thus candidate models must be evaluated to determine which is the most plausible given the data available.

A number of familiar machine-learning issues arise in this problem of 'model selection'. One is *over-fitting*, where an overly complex model becomes too tightly coupled to incidental rather than essential features of the data, leading to poor *generalization*. Conversely, an overly simple model may *under-fit*, and not capture enough of the regularities that are in the data.

Bayesian model selection criteria offer a theoretically and philosophically appealing approach to addressing these issues (Dowe et al., 2007; Kass and Raftery, 1995). Bayesian inference is underpinned by the consistent use of probability to capture the inferrer's uncertainty about everything under consideration, including the models themselves (and their parameters). An inferring agent with model $\mathcal{M}$ with parameters $\theta \in \Theta$ (where Θ is the parameter space) can initially only set those parameters as an uncertain probability distribution (the *prior* distribution $P(\theta|\mathcal{M})$). After observing some data $\mathcal{D}$, the agent will update the state of its belief, giving a *posterior* distribution:

$$P(\theta|\mathcal{D},\mathcal{M}) = \frac{P(\mathcal{D}|\theta,\mathcal{M})P(\theta|\mathcal{M})}{P(\mathcal{D}|\mathcal{M})} , \tag{7.1}$$

This accounts for the prior and the likelihood that the model with parameters θ could have produced the data. To best predict a new item of data d, given the model and observations so far, the agent needs to compute

$$P(d|\mathcal{D},\mathcal{M}) = \int_{\Theta} P(d|\theta,\mathcal{M})P(\theta|\mathcal{D},\mathcal{M}) \, d\theta \,.$$

As long as the agent remembers the posterior distribution $P(\theta|\mathcal{D},\mathcal{M})$, the data is no longer needed. The *evidence* (the denominator in (7.1)) is computed thus

$$P(\mathcal{D}|\mathcal{M}) = \int_{\Theta} P(\mathcal{D}|\theta,\mathcal{M})P(\theta|\mathcal{M}) \, d\theta \,. \tag{7.2}$$

With multiple candidate models, inference takes place on distributions over those models (rather than parameters) with prior $P(\mathcal{M}_i)$ and posterior

$$P(\mathcal{M}_i|\mathcal{D}) = \frac{P(\mathcal{D}|\mathcal{M}_i)P(\mathcal{M}_i)}{P(\mathcal{D})} \,. \tag{7.3}$$

If the prior over models $P(\mathcal{M}_i)$ is relatively flat (i.e., no model is distinctly more probable than others), then the evidence is the key determinant of the relative plausibility of each model after data observation. The posterior distribution can be used to make predictions and decisions (*model averaging*) and if a decision is required, the model with the greatest evidence can be selected. While it is clear that the evidence $P(\mathcal{D}|\mathcal{M})$ rewards models that are able to fit the data well in some part of their parameter space—since $P(\mathcal{D}|\theta,\mathcal{M})$ will be large in this region—it also penalizes models that are more complex than the data can support.

To see why this is so, consider that, for a given size of dataset, $P(\mathcal{D}|\mathcal{M})$ is a probability distribution over the space of complete datasets and therefore only has a finite amount of probability mass to spread out over that space. Simple models are only able to assign significant probability mass to a small set of datasets, while complex models betray their complexity by being able to assign probability mass to a much larger space of datasets. Figure 7.4 shows how this results in trade-off when we wish to choose a model for a particular observed dataset $\mathcal{D}_1$. In short, model $\mathcal{M}_1$ is too inflexible and a poor fit, while $\mathcal{M}_3$ is flexible enough but unnecessarily complex. Model $\mathcal{M}_2$ out-performs both.

This automatic penalty for overly-complex models gives us a formal expression of Ockham's razor, the philosophical principle that, other things being equal, we should choose the *simplest* explanation for observations.

Simplicity can also be expressed in terms of the *minimum message length* principle (Wallace and Boulton, 1968) and the related *minimum description length* principle (Rissanen, 1978). These state that models that produce the shortest possible description of the data (including the description of any necessary model parameters) should be selected. The close relationship between compression and probabilistic structure means that this is essentially the same as the Bayesian approach (MacKay, 2003), with some minor differences (Baxter and Oliver, 1994).

The relationship between message length, the Bayesian evidence, and model complexity can be illuminated further by recalling that, for optimal compression, an object x should be encoded by a message of length $\lceil -\log P(x) \rceil$ bits (assuming logarithms to the base 2), where $P(x)$ is the probability that both sender and receiver assign to x and $\lceil \cdot \rceil$ is the operation of rounding-up to an integer value. If the ob-

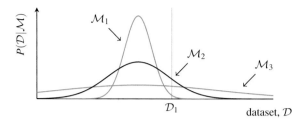

Fig. 7.4 An illustration of how model complexity and data-fit interact to determine the Bayesian evidence. The x-axis represents the space of all possible datasets of a given size (in most cases this will be a very high-dimensional space, but one dimension is sufficient to illustrate the principle). The curves are the probability distributions over datasets assigned by each of three models, so the total area under each curve is the same. $\mathcal{M}_1$ is not flexible enough to assign much probability to the observed dataset $\mathcal{D}_1$, while $\mathcal{M}_3$ is flexible enough to assign probability to a great variety of datasets, including $\mathcal{D}_1$. In doing so, however, it must spread out its probability mass more thinly. By being just flexible enough, $\mathcal{M}_2$ receives greater evidence than either $\mathcal{M}_1$ or $\mathcal{M}_3$

ject to be transmitted is a dataset $\mathcal{D}$, then clearly, the model $\mathcal{M}_i$ with the greatest evidence $P(\mathcal{D}|\mathcal{M}_i)$ will yield the shortest message, encoding the entire dataset in approximately $-\log P(\mathcal{D}|\mathcal{M}_i)$ bits.

Looking more closely at how the evidence relates to the model parameters θ, we can reason that a well-fitting model would assign a high probability to the data for a certain optimal value of θ, say $\hat{\theta}$. Given that $P(\mathcal{D}|\hat{\theta},\mathcal{M})$ is relatively high, a relatively short message of length approximately $-\log P(\mathcal{D}|\hat{\theta},\mathcal{M})$ bits could be sent to describe the dataset, but only if sender and receiver had agreed on $\hat{\theta}$ beforehand. Since $\hat{\theta}$ depends on the data that only the sender has access to, this is not possible, so the sender must send a message approximately $-\log P(\hat{\theta}|\mathcal{M})$ bits long describing $\hat{\theta}$ first. If the model is complex in the sense of having a large parameter space, this message may be large enough to offset any gains obtained from using a complex model to increase $P(\mathcal{D}|\hat{\theta},\mathcal{M})$.

The above considerations mean that the length of the message describing a dataset $\mathcal{D}$ will be approximately

$$-\log P(\mathcal{D}|\hat{\theta},\mathcal{M}) - \log P(\hat{\theta}|\mathcal{M}) = -\log P(\mathcal{D},\hat{\theta}|\mathcal{M}) . \qquad (7.4)$$

This is not the same as the $-\log P(\mathcal{D}|\mathcal{M})$ bits we estimated before considering the parameters. How can we resolve this discrepancy?

Bits Back Coding Let us look again at the length of the message required to send $\mathcal{D}$ and θ: this depends on $P(\mathcal{D},\theta|\mathcal{M})$ which, for a fixed dataset, is proportional to $P(\theta|\mathcal{D},\mathcal{M})$, the posterior distribution over the parameters given the data. If this distribution is relatively broad, it defines a *region* of Θ over which the total coding cost is approximately minimal. If, instead of sending the optimal value $\hat{\theta}$, the sender sends a value chosen *at random* from the posterior distribution, the coding cost will remain about the same, but this extra freedom of choice can allow an additional message to be sent at no extra cost. This is the basis of the 'bits back' coding scheme, first described by Wallace (1990), but so named by Hinton and van Camp (1993). We can see how this accounts for the discrepancy noted above as follows:

$$
\begin{aligned}
P(\mathcal{D}, \theta | \mathcal{M}) &= P(\theta | \mathcal{D}, \mathcal{M}) P(\mathcal{D} | \mathcal{M}) , \\
\log P(\mathcal{D}, \theta | \mathcal{M}) &= \log P(\theta | \mathcal{D}, \mathcal{M}) + \log P(\mathcal{D} | \mathcal{M}) , \\
\log P(\mathcal{D} | \mathcal{M}) &= \langle \log P(\mathcal{D}, \theta | \mathcal{M}) \rangle - \langle \log P(\theta | \mathcal{D}, \mathcal{M}) \rangle , \\
-\log P(\mathcal{D} | \mathcal{M}) &= \langle -\log P(\mathcal{D}, \theta | \mathcal{M}) \rangle - H(P_{\theta | \mathcal{D}, \mathcal{M}}) ,
\end{aligned}
\tag{7.5}
$$

where $\langle \cdot \rangle$ denotes an expectation with respect to the posterior $P(\theta | \mathcal{D}, \mathcal{M})$, and $H(\cdot)$ is the entropy of the given probability distribution. Thus, the difference between the theoretical message length $-\log P(\mathcal{D} | \mathcal{M})$ and the average message length for sending both $\mathcal{D}$ and θ when θ is chosen randomly from the posterior $P(\theta | \mathcal{D}, \mathcal{M})$ is the entropy of the posterior.

Variational Free Energy Representing uncertainty about model parameters, computing the evidence and doing model averaging can be expensive operations computationally and approximations are often needed. For some models, *variational Bayesian learning* (Jordan et al., 1998; MacKay, 1997) can be a good solution, combining an efficient representation of uncertainty about parameters with a tractable learning algorithm, delivering an estimate of the evidence as a function of the *variational free energy* F. As with the bits back coding scheme, it too is defined by focusing on the posterior distribution $P(\theta | \mathcal{D}, \mathcal{M})$. However, instead of trying to work with the exact posterior, we choose to approximate it with a distribution $Q(\theta)$ chosen from a more tractable class of distributions. The free energy is then defined as a function of this variational distribution Q:

$$
F(Q) = -\langle \log P(\mathcal{D}, \theta | \mathcal{M}) \rangle_Q + \langle \log Q(\theta) \rangle_Q
\tag{7.6}
$$

where $\langle \cdot \rangle_Q$ denotes an expectation with respect to θ drawn from the variational distribution $Q(\theta)$. Note that this is the same, except for the reversal of sign, as the third line of (7.5) with Q replacing the true posterior $P_{\theta | \mathcal{D}, \mathcal{M}}$. This tells us that $F(Q)$ is the effective number of bits required to transmit the dataset after using the bits back coding scheme to recover an extra $H(Q)$ bits encoded in a random choice of θ from $Q(\theta)$. It can be shown that F is an upper bound on $-\log P(\mathcal{D} | \mathcal{M})$, minimized when Q is as close as possible to the true posterior in a certain sense:

$$
F(Q) = -\log P(\mathcal{D} | \mathcal{M}) + D(Q || P_{\theta | \mathcal{D}, \mathcal{M}}),
\tag{7.7}
$$

where $D(\cdot || \cdot)$ is the Kullback–Leibler divergence, a measure of distance between two probability distributions, and non-negative. Variational Bayesian methods search the chosen space of variational distributions to find a Q that minimizes the free energy, and so, after the procedure is complete, we can use $F(Q)$ instead of the true evidence for model comparisons.

Thus, we come to the methodology we adopt for our subsequent modelling experiments: given a dataset and a number of candidate models, we fit each model using variational Bayesian learning and use the variational free energy to compare them—the lower the free energy, the better the model. The variational free energy itself indicates how much information is needed to transmit the dataset using the bits back coding scheme with the optimal variational distribution Q.

7.4.2 Probabilistic Programming

While probabilistic modelling is a powerful technique for solving problems involving uncertainty, the translation of a model into a working computer program can become laborious if all the mathematical machinery has to be implemented from scratch. The development of *graphical models* or *Bayesian networks* (Pearl, 1988) made it possible to provide software libraries that require only a high level description of the model as a network of nodes and edges. However, the graph notation has limitations when it comes to models with an unknown or unbounded number of objects in the domain of interest. This motivated the development of more flexible languages for specifying and working with a broad class of probabilistic models, including grammars, Bayesian networks and probabilistic process models. The differences between language and music suggest that we will need such flexibility to go beyond the capabilities of linguistic grammar formalisms to model musical structure.

The idea behind probabilistic programming is to simplify this process by combining the flexibility of general purpose programming constructs (such as structured data types, recursion, functions, etc.) with probabilistic primitives in a high-level programming language, allowing the description of probabilistic models at a high level of abstraction and having the underlying framework provide the appropriate inference and learning functions *automatically*.

This is ideal for problems where some unobserved underlying structure is thought to give rise to observable consequences and an estimate of the underlying structure is desired. The probabilistic expression of the problem implies a resulting 'posterior' probability distribution over underlying structures and well-known general methods such as Markov chain Monte Carlo algorithms can be used to direct and give structure to the search over the solution space. It also means there is a clear separation between the exact statement of the problem and any approximations invoked to solve it.

Probabilistic programming is currently an active research topic in both artificial intelligence and cognitive modelling and marries the power of Bayesian methods with the flexibility and computational completeness of general programming languages.

Many probabilistic programming languages have been proposed and developed, including probabilistic Horn abduction (Poole, 1991, 1993), stochastic logic programming (Muggleton, 1996), PRISM (Sato and Kameya, 1997), Markov logic (Domingos and Richardson, 2007), IBAL (Pfeffer, 2001), Church (Goodman et al., 2008), and Hansei (Kiselyov and Shan, 2009).

PRISM (Sato and Kameya, 1997) supports efficient exact inference for a wide class of discrete-valued models, with PRISM equivalents of standard models such as hidden Markov models and PCFGs resulting in the equivalent of efficient standard inference and learning algorithms for these models. PRISM also supports a limited form of Bayesian learning for a wide class of discrete-valued models including hidden Markov models and probabilistic context-free grammars (PCFGs), resulting in the equivalent of efficient standard inference and learning algorithms for these models. PRISM has been used to implement probabilistic grammars for natural languages and estimate their parameters (Sato et al., 2001) and for grammar induction using Variational Bayes for model selection (Kurihara and Sato, 2006). It has already been used for music modelling (Sneyers et al., 2006), and as the basis for a probabilistic constraint logic programming (CLP) system which was also used for music modelling (Sneyers et al., 2009).

MIT Church (Goodman et al., 2008) on the other hand, uses approximate, random-sampling based inference mechanisms and can support a wider class of models, at the expense of greater computational requirements as compared with exact inference algorithms when these exist. Alternative implementations of Church have also been developed that address exact inference for some programs (Stuhlmüller and Goodman, 2012; Wingate et al., 2011a,b).

Hansei (Kiselyov and Shan, 2009) is an example of the embedded DSL approach, where an existing language (OCaml) is augmented with probabilistic primitives. It inherits from the host language a sophisticated type system, higher order programming facilities, a module system and libraries, all of which aid in the development of robust and flexible models.

7.4.3 Building Probabilistic Grammars in PRISM

PRISM (PRogramming In Statistical Modelling) (Sato and Kameya, 1997) is an attractive approach for the development of probabilistic grammars for several reasons: grammars and interpreters can be encoded very simply by virtue of its inheritance of Prolog's definite clause grammar (DCG) notation and meta-programming facilities, it can mimic Earley's efficient chart parsing without work from the programmer (using tabling provided by the underlying B-Prolog implementation), and it includes an efficient implementation of variational Bayesian inference (Kurihara and Sato, 2006; Sato et al., 2008).

To give a flavour of how PRISM can be used to encode probabilistic grammars, we will implement the grammar (G3) from Sect. 7.3.1. The non-probabilistic form of the grammar can be implemented trivially in Prolog using the DCG notation as:

$ab \longrightarrow [a,b]$.
$ab \longrightarrow [a], ab, [b]$.

The non-terminal S is represented by the DCG goal named ab with zero arguments, referred to as $ab//0$. (Some notes about Prolog syntax are provided in the appendix.) Given this program, Prolog environments are capable of answering queries about whether or not a given string is grammatical, and of generating strings from the language:

```
?- phrase(ab,[a,a,b,b]).
yes
?- phrase(ab,[a,a,a,b]).
no
?- phrase(ab,X).
X = [a,b] ?;
X = [a,a,b,b] ?;
% etc...
```

To develop this into a PCFG, we must use a PRISM 'switch' to encode probability distributions over the alternative expansions of each non-terminal. This can be done in more than one way, but in this example, we will assign a label to each expansion rule. Then we will define a switch with the same name as the associated non-terminal and ranging over the labels of the expansion rules of that non-terminal. Finally, we modify the definition of *ab* to include an explicit random choice using the *msw*/2 PRISM primitive, followed by a call to DCG goal (::)//2 (written without parentheses using :: as a binary operator) which takes two parameters: the name of the non-terminal and the name of the chosen rule. The complete program is

:− **op**(500,*xfx*,::).
values(*ab*, [*stop*,   *recurse*]).

ab ⟶ {*msw*(*ab*,*Label*)}, *ab*::*Label*.
ab :: *stop*   ⟶ [*a*, *b*].
ab :: *recurse* ⟶ [*a*], *ab*, [*b*].

Once loaded, the grammar can be used in several ways: (a) for generatively sampling from the implied probability distribution over sentences; (b) for analytically computing the probability of observing a given sentence; and (c) for estimating the parameters from a list of samples using variational Bayesian learning (note that the variational free energy quoted by PRISM is the negative of the free energy as usually defined):

```
?- sample(ab(X)).
X = [a,a,b,b]
yes
?- prob(ab([a,a,b,b]),P).
P = 0.25
yes
?- set_prism_flag(learn_model,vb).
yes
?- get_samples(50,ab(X),Data), learn(Data).
   % ...various statistics about learning...
   Final variational free energy: −78.533991360
   % ...more statistics about learning...
Data = [ab([a,a,b,b]),ab([a,b]),ab([a,a,b,b])|...]
yes
```

Now that the grammar is embedded in a Turing complete probabilistic programming language, extending it beyond what is possible using a CFG is relatively straightforward. For example, we can write a probabilistic DCG for the language $a^n b^n c^n$ by using a parameterized non-terminal *ab//1* similar to *ab//0*, but returning the number[4] of repeats of *a* and *b*, and then adding a parameterized recursive non-terminal *c//1* to produce that many copies of *c*:

values(ab, [stop,   recurse]).

$abc \quad \longrightarrow ab(N), c(N).$
$ab(N) \longrightarrow \{msw(ab,Label)\}, ab(N) :: \ Label.$
$ab(zero) :: \quad stop \quad \longrightarrow [].$
$ab(succ(N)) :: \ recurse \ \longrightarrow [a], \ ab(N), \ [b].$
$c(zero) \qquad \longrightarrow [].$
$c(succ(N)) \ \longrightarrow [c].$

This example demonstrates the 'bidirectional' nature of Prolog logic variables: the argument to *ab//1* is an *output* value, while the argument to *c//1* is an *input*. However, if an output argument is partially or fully instantiated on input (representing a constraint on its value) sampling execution of the program may fail, resulting in a form of rejection sampling: the sequence of random choices involved in sampling a sentence from the grammar can result in the violation of a constraint, requiring that that sample be thrown away and a new one started. This example was written carefully to avoid such an eventuality, but in general, when creating a probabilistic version of a DCG, the possibility of failure results in a significant complication of the algorithms required for learning and inference (Sato et al., 2005).

For our purposes, failure can be avoided by structuring the process of rule expansion to prevent any probabilistic choice resulting in failure. Instead of using B-Prolog's built-in DCG compiler, we wrote a DCG meta-interpreter (in PRISM) taking production rules written in one of two forms:

Head :: *Label* ⟹ *Body.*
Head :: *Label* ⟹ *Guard* |*Body.*

Guard is an ordinary Prolog goal, which, combined with pattern matching against arguments in *Head*, determines the rule's applicability given a particular *Head. Body* is not allowed to fail if the rule is selected, meaning that during non-terminal expansion a label (from the collection of applicable rules) is sampled from its associated switch (defined automatically by the interpreter). The body of the selected rule is interpreted as an ordinary DCG (with the exception of using +*X* instead of [*X*] for the emission of terminal symbols and *nil* instead of [] for empty productions). Non-failing Prolog/PRISM goals can be included in braces and $X \sim S$ (equivalent to $\{msw(S,X)\}$) can be used to sample a PRISM switch *S*.

Consider the program in Fig. 7.7. *neigh* denotes the neighbour note rule which expands a non-terminal *i(P)* (where *P* is a pitch interval in semitones, but only when *P*=0). The random switch *step* provides a sample (between −4 and 4) resulting in the deviation *P1* to the neighbour note. *term* defines how the non-terminal *i(P)* produces the integer *P*: a terminal symbol.

---

[4] Represented algebraically where zero is *zero*, one is *succ(zero)*, two is *succ(succ(zero))*, etc.

7.5 Experiments with Probabilistic Music Models

The techniques described above can be used to develop a range of probabilistic models on various corpora of music. We summarize our experiments (Abdallah and Gold, 2014a,b) to compare the performance of several models on a corpus of monophonic melodies in Humdrum/Kern format. This comprised four datasets from the KernScores website at http://kern.humdrum.org: 185 Bach chorales (BWV 253–438 excluding BWV 279), which is the same dataset used by Gilbert and Conklin (2007), a larger set of 370 Bach chorales, and two 1000-element random subsets of the Essen folk song collection. In the description below, these datasets are referred to as *chorales*, *chorales371*, *essen1000a* and *essen1000b* respectively.

Several probabilistic models were implemented as PDCGs, of which six are described here. The models, with their short names, are:

p1gram	0th order Markov model over pitches
p2gram	1st order Markov model over pitches
phmm	1st order hidden Markov model over pitches
i1gram	0th order Markov model over intervals
i2gram	1st order Markov model over intervals
gilbert2	Modified Gilbert and Conklin grammar

DCG rules for these models are presented in Fig. 7.5 (*p1gram*, *p2gram* and *phmm*), Fig. 7.6 (*i1gram* and *i2gram*), and Fig. 7.7 (*gilbert2*).

---

values(*nnum*, *X*) :− *numlist*(40,100,*X*).
values(*mc*(_),   *X*) :− *values*(*nnum*,*X*).
values(*hmc*(_),   *X*) :− *num_states*(*N*),   *numlist*(1,*N*,*X*).
values(*obs*(_),   *X*) :− *values*(*nnum*,*X*).

% **start symbol for p1gram**
s0 ::   *tail* $\Longrightarrow$ *nil*.
s0 ::   *cons* $\Longrightarrow$ *X*∼ *nnum*, +*X*, *s0*.

% **start symbol for p2gram**
s1(_) ::   *tail* $\Longrightarrow$ *nil*.
s1(*Y*) ::   *cons* $\Longrightarrow$ *X*∼ *mc*(*Y*), +*X*, *s1*(*X*).

% **start symbol for phmm**
sh(_) ::   *tail* $\Longrightarrow$ *nil*.
sh(*Y*) ::   *cons* $\Longrightarrow$ *X*∼ *hmc*(*Y*), *Z*∼ *obs*(*X*), +*Z*, *sh*(*X*).

Fig. 7.5 PDCGs for zeroth- and first-order Markov chains and first-order HMMs over pitch (encoded as MIDI note number). The number of states in the HMM is a parameter of the model

values(*ival*,   *X*) :− *numlist*(−20,20,*X*).
values(*mc*(_), *X*) :− *get_values*(*ival*,*X*).

% **start symbol for i1gram**
s0 :: *tail*   ⟹ +*end*.
s0 :: *cons* ⟹ *X*∼ *ival*, +*X*, *s0*.

% **start symbol for i2gram**
s1(_) :: *tail*   ⟹ +*end*.
s1(*Y*) :: *cons* ⟹ *X*∼ *mc*(*Y*), +*X*, *s1*(*X*).

Fig. 7.6 PDCG for zeroth- and first-order Markov chains over pitch interval to next note in semitones

We encode pitch using MIDI note numbers and intervals as integers, in a sequence terminated by a Prolog *end* atom (notes are represented as a pitch interval in semitones to the following note, but the final note element has no subsequent pitch to encode). In richer models including other musical attributes such as duration or metrical stress, the attributes of the final note could be associated with the terminating symbol.

We modify Gilbert and Conklin's (2007) original grammar in two ways. Firstly, a different mechanism is used for introducing new intervals not captured by the elaboration rules: the *s* non-terminal, instead of being parameterized by the interval covered by the entire sequence, simply expands into a sequence of *i*(*P*) non-terminals with the *P* sampled independently from the *leap* distribution. Secondly, because a note is represented by the pitch interval to the *following* note, the *i*(*P*) :: *rep* rule has *i*(0), *i*(*P*) on the right-hand side instead of *i*(*P*), *i*(0) as in Gilbert and Conklin's grammar (see Fig. 7.3 for an illustration of this). Additionally, we chose the numerical ranges of the various operations (steps, leaps, and limits for passing and escape note introduction) as these were not specified by Gilbert and Conklin.

7.5.1 Results

The models obtained in the first part of the experiment can be used to obtain probabilistic parses of melodic sequences. Examples of these are shown in Figs. 7.8 and 7.9, illustrating two analyses of individual phrases from one of the Bach chorales (BWV 270) in the *chorales* dataset. In the first example, note that the high values of relative probability (RP) on the first two parses show that this is a relatively unambiguous parse. Note also that all four parses share the same first and last subtrees below the *s* non-terminal. In the second example, the lower values of RP indicate that this parse is much more ambiguous than that of the first phrase. Still, there is much common structure between these parses, so we may conclude that this grammar is fairly confident in its analysis of, for example, the final repeated note.

values(step,   X) :− numlist(−4,4,X).
values(leap,   X) :− numlist(−16,16,X).
values(passing(N),   Vals) :−
   ($N>0 → M$ is $N−1$, *numlist(1,M,I1)*
   ; $N<0 → M$ is $N+1$, *numlist(M,−1,I1)*
   ),
   maplist(N1, (N1,N2),N2 is $N−N1,I1$,*Vals).*

values(escape(N),   Vals) :−
   ($N<0 → I1$ = [1,2,3,4]
   ; $N>0 → I1$ = [−1,−2,−3,−4]
   ),
   maplist(N1,(N1,N2),N2 is $N−N1,I1$,*Vals).*

% **start symbol**
s :: last   ⟹ i(end).
s :: grow ⟹ P∼ leap, i(P), s.

i(P) :: term   ⟹ +P.
i(P) :: rep   ⟹ i(0), i(P).
i(P) :: neigh ⟹ P=0 |
                      P1∼ step, {P2 is −P1}, i(P1), i(P2).
i(P) :: pass   ⟹ abs_between(2,5,P) |
                    (P1,P2)∼ passing(P), i(P1), i(P2).
i(P) :: esc   ⟹ abs_between(1,16,P) |
                    (P1,P2)∼ escape(P), i(P1), i(P2).
abs_between(L,U,X) :− Y is *abs(X), between(L,U,Y).*

Fig. 7.7 Extract from a grammar (Abdallah and Gold, 2014b) modelled on Gilbert and Conklin's (Gilbert and Conklin, 2007), written in a DCG language defined in PRISM. *maplist/5* and *between/3* are standard B-Prolog predicates and *numlist(L,U,X)* is true when *X* is a list of consecutive integers from *L* to *U*. Code to initialize the switch probabilities and perform ancillary tasks is omitted

Figure 7.10 summarizes the performance of all the models per dataset over a range of parameter values. To normalize the comparison of differently-sized datasets, the variational free energy was divided by the total number of notes in the dataset to give the 'bits per note' (bpn), offering a sense of the amount of information required to encode each note under that model using the 'bits back' coding scheme (Honkela and Valpola, 2004)—the lower this is, the better the model. Data for *p1gram* (the zeroth-order Markov model over pitches) is not shown as its best-case performance (3.7 bpn on the chorales) was consistently lower than all the other models.

We observe that the relative performance of *i1gram* and *p2gram* is what we would expect, since a pair of consecutive pitches (a 2-gram) contains information about both pitch interval *and* absolute pitch, while the latter is not available to *i1gram*.

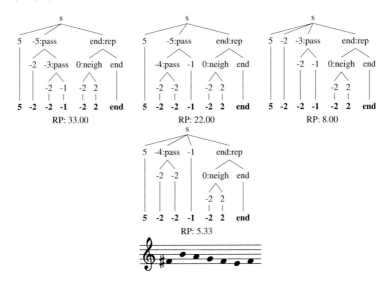

Fig. 7.8 Bach chorale BWV 270 ('Befiehl du deine Wege'), phrase #1, top 4 parses. Nodes representing non-terminals of the form *i(N)* are labelled with *N* and name of the rule used to expand them, while the terminal symbols are written in boldface aligned on the bottom row. Also, the top level sequence of *i(_)* non-terminals produced by recursive expansion of *s* using the *grow* rule have been collapsed into a single level below the *s* node, as suggested by Gilbert and Conklin (2007). The values labelled 'RP' are the posterior probabilities of each of the parses relative to that of the most likely parse not displayed, in this case, the 5th one

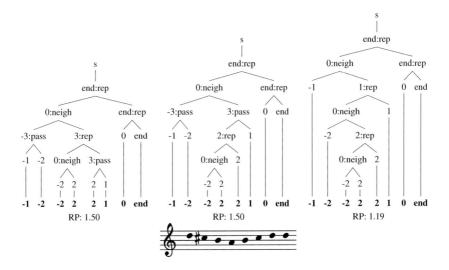

Fig. 7.9 Bach chorale BWV 270, phrase #3, top 3 parses. See Fig. 7.8 for an explanation of the RP values—here, the values are relative to the probability of the 4th most probable parse

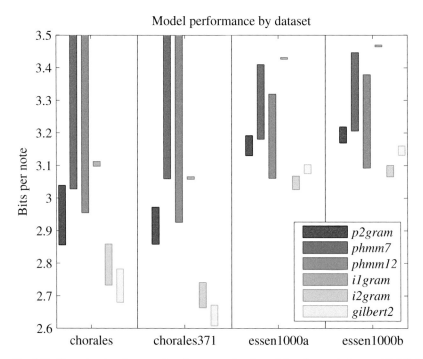

Fig. 7.10 Chart showing the overall performance of each model against each dataset (Abdallah and Gold, 2014b), measured in bits per note (lower bpn means better performance). For each model and dataset pair, the bar shows the range of values obtained using various parameter combinations. The chorales data extends beyond the top of the chart. Bars labelled as *phmmN* represent the HMMs with *N* states

We also note that the HMMs have the widest range of results, most likely due to the learning algorithm getting stuck in local optima (if this is the case, standard techniques (multiple restarts, simulated annealing) available within PRISM might be used to alleviate the problem).

Across all the datasets, the *gilbert2* and *i2gram* models perform consistently well, with the larger HMMs also performing competitively on the Essen collection. The *i2gram* model achieves approximately 2.68 bpn on the *chorales* dataset with its best parameter settings, comparable with the 2.67 bpn reported by Gilbert and Conklin (2007).

The grammar-based model gives the best fit on both chorales datasets, although it is beaten by the Markov model on the larger Essen datasets. The causes of this are unclear from the current data but investigation of the learned parameters would likely offer some explanation (some of these are illustrated in Fig. 7.11). One possibility is that the Essen dataset is relying proportionately more on the *s::grow* rule of the grammar to introduce new intervals. In the limit, this would reduce to a zeroth-order Markov model equivalent to *i1gram*, which, as we have seen, performs much worse than *i2gram*. Considering that higher-order Markov models would be likely to

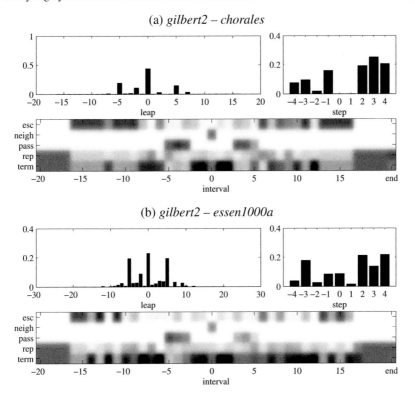

Fig. 7.11 Some of the switch distributions learned by fitting the *gilbert2* model to the *chorales* and *essen1000a* datasets. The *leap* distribution is used when introducing a new interval with the *s::grow* rule. The *step* distribution is used when introducing a neighbour note. The *intervals* greyscale images show the probability distributions over expansions of the non-terminal $i(N)$ for different values of N, bearing in mind that some rules are inapplicable for certain values. The Essen-fitted model appears to have a higher entropy *leap* distribution, makes less use of the *neigh* and *pass* rules, and has some curious structure in the *term* and *esc* probabilities for large intervals, all of which suggest that the grammar as designed is not such a good fit for it

perform better still, we might also conclude that designing *by hand* a probabilistic grammar (that is, the structure of the rules rather than the numerical probabilities which have been optimized in this experiment) capable of out-performing variable order Markov models would be a non-trivial task. Inducing grammar models over a corpus of works using probabilistic methods like those explored here is likely to make this more tractable and is desirable since variable-order Markov models cannot offer the explanatory power of a grammatical analysis.

7.6 Conclusions

This chapter has reviewed the principles, implementation, and application of grammar-based models in structural music analysis. It presented relevant aspects of the underpinning principles of information theory and probabilistic inference, showing how these can be applied to music.

The chapter concluded by showing that various probabilistic models of symbolic music can be implemented and applied to collections of Bach chorales and the Essen folk song collection (Abdallah and Gold, 2014b). A probabilistic grammar based on that of Gilbert and Conklin (2007) performed best (in the sense of allowing efficient representation of the collections) on the Bach chorales, but a more parsimonious parameterization of the same grammar performed worse than a first-order Markov model over pitch intervals.

In contrast to Markov models, however, grammars effect in a simple fashion the three factors identified above as common in music analysis: segmentation, classification and relation. Segmentation is embodied in the sequences of symbols on the right-hand side of rules, classification in the left-hand sides, and relation in the structure of the resultant parse tree. Putting this with the results of our experiments leads us to conclude that probabilistic grammars are a promising foundation for further developments in computational music analysis.

Acknowledgements This work was partially supported by the EPSRC CREST Platform grant [grant number EP/G060525/2] and the AHRC Digital Music Lab and ASyMMuS projects [grant numbers AH/L01016X/1 and AH/M002454/1]. Parts of this chapter (in particular, Fig. 7.5, Fig. 7.6, Fig. 7.7, Fig. 7.10 and the text of the Appendix) have previously appeared in Abdallah and Gold (2014a) and Abdallah and Gold (2014b), in the latter case used under the terms of the Creative Commons Attribution 3.0 Unported License (http://creativecommons.org/licenses/by/3.0/).

Supplementary Material Source code and data are available on request from Samer Abdallah (subject to copyright restrictions).

Appendix

Notes on Prolog Syntax Prolog code and data consist of *terms* built from a *functor* and a number of arguments; e.g., $a(10,b,X)$ is a term with a head functor $a/3$ (because it has three arguments), and arguments 10 (an integer), b (an atom or symbol), and X (a logic variable). Atoms and functor names start with a lower-case letter, while variable names start with an upper-case letter or underscore. A solitary underscore (_) stands for a variable whose value is not needed. Functors can be declared as prefix, infix, or suffix operators, for example, we declare $\sim$ to be an infix operator, so the head functor of $P \sim leap$ is $\sim /2$. The definite clause grammar (DCG) notation allows grammar rules to be defined using clauses of the form *Head* $\longrightarrow$ *Body*, where *Head* is a term and *Body* is a list of one or more comma separated DCG goals. Within the body, a list [*X,Y*,...] represents a sequence of terminals, while a term enclosed in braces {*Goal*} is interpreted as an ordinary Prolog goal.

References

Abdallah, S. A. and Gold, N. E. (2014a). Exploring probabilistic grammars of symbolic music using PRISM. In *Proceedings of the First Workshop on Probabilistic Logic Programming*, Vienna, Austria.

Abdallah, S. A. and Gold, N. E. (2014b). Comparing models of symbolic music using probabilistic grammars and probabilistic programming. In *Proceedings of the 2014 International Computer Music Conference (ICMC/SMC 2014)*, pages 1524–1531, Athens, Greece.

Abney, S. P. (1997). Stochastic attribute-value grammars. *Computational Linguistics*, 23(4):597–618.

Attneave, F. (1954). Some informational aspects of visual perception. *Pyschological Review*, 61(3):183–193.

Baker, J. K. (1979). Trainable grammars for speech recognition. *The Journal of the Acoustical Society of America*, 65(S1):S132.

Barlow, H. B. (1961). Possible principles underlying the transformation of sensory messages. In Rosenblith, W. A., editor, *Sensory Communication*, pages 217–234. MIT Press.

Baroni, M., Maguire, S., and Drabkin, W. (1983). The concept of musical grammar. *Music Analysis*, 2(2):175–208.

Baxter, R. A. and Oliver, J. J. (1994). MDL and MML: Similarities and differences. Technical Report 207, Department of Computer Science, Monash University.

Bilmes, J. A. and Kirchhoff, K. (2003). Factored language models and generalized parallel backoff. In *Proceedings of the 2003 Conference of the North American Chapter of the Association for Computational Linguistics on Human Language Technology: Companion Volume of the Proceedings of HLT-NAACL 2003, Short Papers, Volume 2*, pages 4–6. Association for Computational Linguistics.

Bod, R. (2006). An all-subtrees approach to unsupervised parsing. In *Proc. 21st Intl. Conf. on Computational Linguistics and the 44th Annual Meeting of the Association for Computational Linguistics*, pages 865–872. Association for Computational Linguistics.

Charniak, E. (2000). A maximum-entropy-inspired parser. In *Proceedings of the First North American Chapter of the Association for Computational Linguistics Conference*, pages 132–139. Association for Computational Linguistics.

Chomsky, N. (1957). *Syntactic Structures*. Mouton de Gruyter.

Clark, S. and Curran, J. R. (2003). Log-linear models for wide-coverage CCG parsing. In *Proceedings of the 2003 Conference on Empirical Methods in Natural Language Processing*, pages 97–104.

Clark, S. and Curran, J. R. (2007). Wide-coverage efficient statistical parsing with CCG and log-linear models. *Computational Linguistics*, 33(4):493–552.

Collins, M. (1997). Three generative, lexicalised models for statistical parsing. In *Proceedings of the 35th Annual Meeting of the Association for Computational Linguistics and Eighth Conference of the European Chapter of the Association for Computational Linguistics*, pages 16–23.

Collins, M. (1999). *Head-driven statistical models for natural language parsing*. PhD thesis, University of Pennsylvania.

Collins, M. (2003). Head-driven statistical models for natural language parsing. *Computational Linguistics*, 29(4):589–637.

Cover, T. M. and Thomas, J. A. (1991). *Elements of Information Theory*. Wiley.

Cox, R. T. (1946). Probability, frequency and reasonable expectation. *American Journal of Physics*, 14(1):1–13.

de Finetti, B. (1975). *Theory of Probability*. Wiley.

Domingos, P. and Richardson, M. (2007). Markov logic: A unifying framework for statistical relational learning. In Getoor, L. and Taskar, B., editors, *Introduction to statistical relational learning*, chapter 12, pages 339–372. MIT Press.

Dowe, D. L., Gardner, S., and Oppy, G. (2007). Bayes not bust! Why simplicity is no problem for Bayesians. *The British Journal for the Philosophy of Science*, 58(4):709–754.

Earley, J. (1970). An efficient context-free parsing algorithm. *Communications of the ACM*, 13(2):94–102.

Ebcioğlu, K. (1987). Report on the CHORAL project: An expert system for chorale harmonization. Technical Report RC 12628, IBM, Thomas J. Watson Research Center, Yorktown Heights, NY.

Forte, A. (1973). *The Structure of Atonal Music*. Yale University Press.

Frost, R. A. and Hafiz, R. (2006). A new top-down parsing algorithm to accommodate ambiguity and left recursion in polynomial time. *ACM SIGPLAN Notices*, 41(5):46–54.

Gilbert, É. and Conklin, D. (2007). A probabilistic context-free grammar for melodic reduction. In *International Joint Conference on Artificial Intelligence (Workshop on Artificial Intelligence and Music) (IJCAI-07)*, Hyderabad, India.

Goodman, J. (1998). *Parsing inside-out*. PhD thesis, Division of Engineering and Applied Sciences, Harvard University.

Goodman, N., Mansinghka, V., Roy, D., Bonawitz, K., and Tenenbaum, J. (2008). Church: a language for generative models. In *Proceedings of the Twenty-Fourth Annual Conference on Uncertainty in Artificial Intelligence (UAI-08)*, pages 220–229, Corvallis, Oregon. AUAI Press.

Granroth-Wilding, M. (2013). *Harmonic analysis of music using combinatory categorial grammar*. PhD thesis, School of Informatics, University of Edinburgh.

Granroth-Wilding, M. and Steedman, M. (2012). Harmonic analysis of jazz MIDI files using statistical parsing. In *Fifth International Workshop on Machine Learning and Music*, Edinburgh, UK.

Hamanaka, M., Hirata, K., and Tojo, S. (2006). Implementing "A Generative Theory of Tonal music". *Journal of New Music Research*, 35(4):249–277.

Hamanaka, M., Hirata, K., and Tojo, S. (2007). FATTA: Full automatic time-span tree analyzer. In *Proc. Intl. Computer Music Conference (ICMC2007), Copenhagen*, volume 1, pages 153–156.

Hinton, G. E. and van Camp, D. (1993). Keeping the neural networks simple by minimizing the description length of the weights. In *Proceedings of the Sixth Annual Conference on Computational Learning theory*, pages 5–13.

Hockenmaier, J. (2001). Statistical parsing for CCG with simple generative models. In *Association for Computational Linguistics, 39th Annual Meeting and 10th Conference of the European Chapter, Companion Volume to the Proceedings of the Conference: Proceedings of the Student Research Workshop and Tutorial Abstracts*, pages 7–12, Toulouse, France.

Hockenmaier, J. and Steedman, M. (2002). Generative models for statistical parsing with combinatory categorial grammar. In *Proceedings of the 40th Annual Meeting of the Association for Computational Linguistics*, pages 335–342.

Honkela, A. and Valpola, H. (2004). Variational learning and bits-back coding: An information-theoretic view to Bayesian learning. *IEEE Transactions on Neural Networks*, 15(4):800–810.

Johnson, M. (1995). Memoization in top-down parsing. *Computational Linguistics*, 21(3):405–417.

Johnson-Laird, P. N. (1991). Jazz improvisation: a theory at the computational level. In Howell, P., West, R., and Cross, I., editors, *Representing Musical Structure*, pages 291–325. Academic Press.

Jordan, M. I., Ghahramani, Z., Jaakkola, T. S., and Saul, L. K. (1998). An introduction to variational methods for graphical models. In Jordan, M. I., editor, *Learning in Graphical Models*, pages 105–161. MIT Press.

Joshi, A. K., Levy, L. S., and Takahashi, M. (1975). Tree adjunct grammars. *Journal of Computer and System Sciences*, 10(1):136–163.

Kass, R. E. and Raftery, A. E. (1995). Bayes factors. *Journal of the American Statistical Association*, 90(430):773–795.

Kassler, M. (1967). *A trinity of essays*. PhD thesis, Princeton University.

Kassler, M. (1976). The decidability of languages that assert music. *Perspectives of New Music*, 14/15:249–251.

Kassler, M. (1987). APL applied in music theory. *ACM SIGAPL APL Quote Quad*, 18(2):209–214.

Kirlin, P. B. (2014). *A probabilistic model of hierarchical music analysis*. PhD thesis, University of Massachusetts Amherst.

Kirlin, P. B. and Jensen, D. D. (2011). Probabilistic modeling of hierarchical music analysis. In *12th International Society for Music Information Retrieval Conference (ISMIR 2011)*, pages 393–398.

Kiselyov, O. and Shan, C.-C. (2009). Embedded probabilistic programming. In Taha, W. M., editor, *Domain-Specific Languages*, pages 360–384. Springer.

Knill, D. C. and Pouget, A. (2004). The Bayesian brain: the role of uncertainty in neural coding and computation. *TRENDS in Neurosciences*, 27(12):712–719.

Knill, D. C. and Richards, W., editors (1996). *Perception as Bayesian inference*. Cambridge University Press.

Kurihara, K. and Sato, T. (2006). Variational Bayesian grammar induction for natural language. In *Grammatical Inference: Algorithms and Applications*, volume 4201 of *Lecture Notes in Artificial Intelligence*, pages 84–96. Springer.

Lambek, J. (1958). The mathematics of sentence structure. *The American Mathematical Monthly*, 65(3):154–170.

Lerdahl, F. and Jackendoff, R. (1983). *A Generative Theory of Tonal Music*. MIT Press.

Li, M. and Vitányi, P. M. B. (2009). *An Introduction to Kolmogorov Complexity and its Applications*. Springer.

Lindblom, B. and Sundberg, J. (1970). *Towards a generative theory of melody*. Department of Phonetics, Institute of Linguistics, University of Stockholm.

MacKay, D. J. C. (1997). Ensemble learning for hidden Markov models. Technical report, Cavendish Laboratory, Cambridge University.

MacKay, D. J. C. (2003). *Information Theory, Inference, and Learning Algorithms*. Cambridge University Press.

Marsden, A. (2005). Generative structural representation of tonal music. *Journal of New Music Research*, 34(4):409–428.

Marsden, A. (2007). Automatic derivation of musical structure: A tool for research on Schenkerian analysis. In *International Conference on Music Information Retrieval (ISMIR 2007)*, pages 55–58, Vienna, Austria.

Marsden, A. (2010). Schenkerian analysis by computer: A proof of concept. *Journal of New Music Research*, 39(3):269–289.

Marsden, A. (2011). Software for Schenkerian analysis. In *Proceedings of the 2011 International Computer Music Conference (ICMC2011)*, pages 673–676, Huddersfield, UK.

Martin-Löf, P. (1966). The definition of random sequences. *Information and Control*, 9(6):602–619.

Mavromatis, P. and Brown, M. (2004). Parsing context-free grammars for music: A computational model of Schenkerian analysis. In *Proceedings of the Eighth International Conference on Music Perception and Cognition*, pages 414–415, Evanston, IL.

Meyer, L. B. (1956). *Emotion and Meaning in Music*. University of Chicago Press.

Muggleton, S. (1996). Stochastic logic programs. In de Raedt, L., editor, *Advances in Inductive Logic Programming*, volume 32, pages 254–264. IOS Press.

Nattiez, J.-J. (1975). *Fondements d'une sémiologie de la musique*. Union Générale d'Editions.

Norvig, P. (1991). Techniques for automatic memoization with applications to context-free parsing. *Computational Linguistics*, 17(1):91–98.

O'Donnell, T. J., Tenenbaum, J. B., and Goodman, N. D. (2009). Fragment grammars: Exploring computation and reuse in language. Technical Report MIT-CSAIL-TR-2009-013, MIT.

Pachet, F. (2000). Computer analysis of jazz chord sequence: Is *Solar* a blues? In Miranda, E. R., editor, *Readings in Music and Artificial Intelligence*, pages 85–114. Routledge.

Pachet, F., Ramalho, G., and Carrive, J. (1996). Representing temporal musical objects and reasoning in the MusES system. *Journal of New Music Research*, 25(3):252–275.

Pearl, J. (1988). *Probabilistic Reasoning in Intelligent Systems: Networks of Plausible Inference*. Morgan Kaufmann.

Pereira, F. (1981). Extraposition grammars. *Computational Linguistics*, 7(4):243–256.

Pereira, F. C. and Warren, D. H. (1980). Definite clause grammars for language analysis—a survey of the formalism and a comparison with augmented transition networks. *Artificial Intelligence*, 13(3):231–278.

Pereira, F. C. and Warren, D. H. (1983). Parsing as deduction. In *Proceedings of the 21st Annual Meeting of the Association for Computational Linguistics*, pages 137–144.

Pfeffer, A. (2001). IBAL: A probabilistic rational programming language. In *Proceedings of the Seventeenth International Joint Conference on Artificial Intelligence (IJCAI-01)*, pages 733–740, Seattle, WA.

Poole, D. (1991). Representing Bayesian networks within probabilistic Horn abduction. In *Proceedings of the Seventh conference on Uncertainty in Artificial Intelligence*, pages 271–278, Los Angeles, CA.

Poole, D. (1993). Probabilistic Horn abduction and Bayesian networks. *Artificial Intelligence*, 64(1):81–129.

Porter, H. H. (1986). Earley deduction. Technical report, Oregon Graduate Center.

Powers, H. S. (1980). Language models and musical analysis. *Ethnomusicology*, 24(1):1–60.

Rissanen, J. (1978). Modeling by shortest data description. *Automatica*, 14(5):465–471.

Rohrmeier, M. (2006). Towards modelling harmonic movement in music: Analysing properties and dynamic aspects of pc set sequences in Bach's chorales. Technical Report DCRR-004, Darwin College, University of Cambridge.

Rohrmeier, M. (2011). Towards a generative syntax of tonal harmony. *Journal of Mathematics and Music*, 5(1):35–53.

Sato, T., Abe, S., Kameya, Y., and Shirai, K. (2001). A separate-and-learn approach to EM learning of PCFGs. In *Proceedings of the Sixth Natural Language Processing Pacific Rim Symposium*, pages 255–262, Tokyo, Japan.

Sato, T. and Kameya, Y. (1997). PRISM: a language for symbolic-statistical modeling. In *Proceedings of the Fifteenth International Joint Conference on Artificial Intelligence (IJCAI-97)*, volume 2, pages 1330–1335, Nagoya, Aichi, Japan.

Sato, T., Kameya, Y., and Kurihara, K. (2008). Variational Bayes via propositionalized probability computation in PRISM. *Annals of Mathematics and Artificial Intelligence*, 54(1–3):135–158.

Sato, T., Kameya, Y., and Zhou, N.-F. (2005). Generative modeling with failure in PRISM. In *Proceedings of the International Joint Conference on Artificial Intelligence*, pages 847–852, Edinburgh, UK.

Schenker, H. (1935). *Der freie Satz*. Universal Edition. (Published in English as E. Oster (trans., ed.) *Free Composition*, Longman, New York, 1979.).

Shannon, C. E. (1948). A mathematical theory of communication. *The Bell System Technical Journal*, 27(3–4):379–423,623–656.

Shieber, S. M. (1985). Criteria for designing computer facilities for linguistic analysis. *Linguistics*, 23(2):189–212.

Sidorov, K., Jones, A., and Marshall, D. (2014). Music analysis as a smallest grammar problem. In *Proceedings of the Fifteenth International Society for Music Information Retrieval Conference (ISMIR)*, pages 301–306, Taipei, Taiwan.

Smoliar, S. W. (1980). A computer aid for Schenkerian analysis. *Computer Music Journal*, 4(2):41–59.

Sneyers, J., Meert, W., and Vennekens, J. (2009). CHRiSM: Chance rules induce statistical models. In *Proceedings of the Sixth International Workshop on Constraint Handling Rules (CHR'09)*, pages 62–76, Pasadena, CA.

Sneyers, J., Vennekens, J., and De Schreye, D. (2006). Probabilistic-logical modeling of music. In van Hentenryck, P., editor, *Practical Aspects of Declarative Languages: 8th International Symposium, PADL 2006, Charleston, SC, USA, January 9–10, 2006, Proceedings*, volume 3819 of *Lecture Notes in Computer Science*, pages 60–72. Springer.

Steedman, M. (2001). *The Syntactic Process*. MIT Press.

Steedman, M. (2003). Formal grammars for computational musical analysis. In *INFORMS Annual Meeting*, Atlanta, GA.

Steedman, M. and Baldridge, J. (2011). Combinatory categorial grammar. In Borsley, R. D. and Börjars, K., editors, *Non-Transformational Syntax: Formal and explicit models of grammar*, pages 181–224. Wiley-Blackwell.

Steedman, M. J. (1984). A generative grammar for jazz chord sequences. *Music Perception*, 2(1):52–77.

Stolcke, A. (1995). An efficient probabilistic context-free parsing algorithm that computes prefix probabilities. *Computational Linguistics*, 21(2):165–201.

Stuhlmüller, A. and Goodman, N. D. (2012). A dynamic programming algorithm for inference in recursive probabilistic programs. *arXiv preprint arXiv:1206.3555*.

Temperley, D. (2007). *Music and Probability*. MIT Press.

Ulrich, J. W. (1977). The analysis and synthesis of jazz by computer. In *Proceedings of the Fifth International Joint Conference on Artificial Intelligence (IJCAI-77)*, pages 865–872, Cambridge, MA.

Wallace, C. S. (1990). Classification by minimum-message-length inference. In Akl, S. G., Fiala, F., and Koczkodaj, W. W., editors, *Advances in Computing and Information—ICCI'90*, volume 468 of *Lecture Notes in Computer Science*, pages 72–81. Springer.

Wallace, C. S. and Boulton, D. M. (1968). An information measure for classification. *The Computer Journal*, 11(2):185–194.

Wingate, D., Goodman, N., Stuhlmueller, A., and Siskind, J. M. (2011a). Nonstandard interpretations of probabilistic programs for efficient inference. In Shawe-Taylor, J., Zemel, R. S., Bartlett, P. L., Pereira, F., and Weinberger, K. Q., editors, *Advances in Neural Information Processing Systems 24 (NIPS 2011)*, pages 1152–1160, Granada, Spain.

Wingate, D., Stuhlmüller, A., and Goodman, N. D. (2011b). Lightweight implementations of probabilistic programming languages via transformational compilation. In *Proceedings of the Fourteenth International Conference on Artificial Intelligence and Statistics (AISTATS 2011)*, pages 770–778, Ft. Lauderdale, FL.

Winograd, T. (1968). Linguistics and the computer analysis of tonal harmony. *Journal of Music Theory*, 12(1):2–49.

Younger, D. H. (1967). Recognition and parsing of context-free languages in time n^3. *Information and Control*, 10(2):189–208.

Yust, J. (2009). The geometry of melodic, harmonic, and metrical hierarchy. In Chew, E., Childs, A., and Chuan, C.-H., editors, *Mathematics and Computation in Music: Second International Conference, MCM 2009, New Haven, CT, USA, June 19–22, 2009. Proceedings*, volume 38 of *Communications in Computer and Information Science*, pages 180–192. Springer.

Chapter 8
Interactive Melodic Analysis

David Rizo, Plácido R. Illescas, and José M. Iñesta

Abstract In a harmonic analysis task, melodic analysis determines the importance and role of each note in a particular harmonic context. Thus, a note is classified as a harmonic tone when it belongs to the underlying chord, and as a non-harmonic tone otherwise, with a number of categories in this latter case. Automatic systems for fully solving this task without errors are still far from being available, so it must be assumed that, in a practical scenario in which the melodic analysis is the system's final output, the human expert must make corrections to the output in order to achieve the final result. Interactive systems allow for turning the user into a source of high-quality and high-confidence ground-truth data, so online machine learning and interactive pattern recognition provide tools that have proven to be very convenient in this context. Experimental evidence will be presented showing that this seems to be a suitable way to approach melodic analysis.

David Rizo
Universidad de Alicante, Alicante, Spain
Instituto Superior de Enseñanzas Artísticas de la Comunidad Valenciana (ISEA.CV), EASD Alicante, Alicante, Spain
e-mail: drizo@dlsi.ua.es

Plácido R. Illescas
Universidad de Alicante, Alicante, Spain
e-mail: placidoroman@gmail.com

José M. Iñesta
Universidad de Alicante, Alicante, Spain
e-mail: inesta@dlsi.ua.es

© Springer International Publishing Switzerland 2016
D. Meredith (ed.), *Computational Music Analysis*,
DOI 10.1007/978-3-319-25931-4_8

8.1 Introduction

Musical analysis is the means to go into depth and truly understand a musical work. A correct musical analysis is a proper tool to enable a musician to perform a rigorous and reliable interpretation of a musical composition.

It is also very important for music teaching. In addition, the outcome of computer music analysis algorithms is very relevant as a first step for a number of music information retrieval (MIR) applications, including similarity computation (de Haas, 2012; Raphael and Stoddard, 2004), reduction of songs to an intermediate representation (Raphael and Stoddard, 2004), music summarization (Rizo, 2010), genre classification (Pérez-Sancho et al., 2009), automatic accompaniment (Chuan and Chew, 2007; Simon et al., 2008), pitch spelling in symbolic formats (Meredith, 2007), algorithmic composition (Ulrich, 1977), harmonization (Ebcioğlu, 1986; Feng et al., 2011; Kaliakatsos-Papakostas, 2014; Pachet and Roy, 2000; Raczyński et al., 2013; Suzuki and Kitahara, 2014), performance rendering (Ramírez et al., 2010), preparing data for Schenkerian analysis (Kirlin, 2009; Marsden, 2010), key finding (Temperley, 2004), metre analysis (Temperley and Sleator, 1999), and others.

From the artificial intelligence perspective, the interest in studying how a machine is able to perform an intrinsically human activity is a motivation by itself (Raphael and Stoddard, 2004). Furthermore, from a psychological point of view, the comparison of analyses by a computer with those made by a human expert may yield interesting insights into the process of listening to musical works (Temperley and Sleator, 1999).

The first written evidence of a musical analysis dates from 1563 and appears in a manuscript entitled 'Praecepta Musicae Poeticae' by Dressler (Forgács, 2007). In 1722, Jean-Philippe Rameau, in his 'Traité de l'harmonie réduite à ses principes naturels', established the basis of harmonic analysis (Rameau, 1722). However, music analysis enjoyed a significant growth in the 19th century.

From the computational point of view, the various aspects of musical analysis have all been addressed since the 1960s (Forte, 1967; Rothgeb, 1968; Winograd, 1968), and there has been a sustained interest in the area up to the present day. In the last few years, several theses (bachelor, master and Ph.D.) have been published from this point of view (de Haas, 2012; Granroth-Wilding, 2013; Mearns, 2013; Sapp, 2011; Tracy, 2013; Willingham, 2013), which underlines the importance of this area of study.

The relevance of a melodic analysis depends on its ultimate purpose: in composition it helps the author to study the different harmonization options, or in the reverse direction, given a chord sequence, to create melodic lines. In the case of analysing a work for playing or conducting, it helps to establish the role each note plays regarding stability or instability. For teaching, it is an indispensable tool for the student and the teacher.

The analysis of a composition involves several interrelated aspects: aesthetic analysis related to the environment of the composer that influences him or her when creating the work, formal analysis to suitably identify the structure of the composition and its constituent elements, and finally tonal analysis, which can be divided into harmonic and melodic analysis. Harmonic analysis studies chords and tonal functions, to shed light on the tensions and relaxations throughout a work, while melodic analysis establishes the importance and role of each note and its particular harmonic context.

This chapter is focused on melodic analysis, specifically using a symbolic format as input. Thus, as output, every note in a musical work is classified as a *harmonic tone* when it belongs to the underlying chord, and as a *non-harmonic tone* otherwise, in which case it should be further assigned to a category, such as *passing tone*, *neighbour tone*, *suspension*, *anticipation*, *echappée*, *appoggiatura* and so on (see Willingham (2013, p. 34) for a full description).

There is still no objective benchmark or standardized way of comparing results between methods. Even if such a benchmark existed, very different analyses can be correctly obtained from most musical works, a fact that reflects different analysts' preferences (Hoffman and Birmingham, 2000).

Nonetheless, it is widely accepted that none of the computerized systems proposed to date is able to make an analysis that totally satisfies the musicologist or musician; and what is worse, it seems that no system can be built to totally solve the problem. The case of melodic analysis is a good example of the variability between the different interpretations that can be extracted from a piece of music, due to the fact that it depends on harmony, which in turn is derived from parts (such as accompaniment voices) that may not be available or that may not even exist when making the analysis.

Maxwell (1984) differentiated between "computer-implemented" analysis, where the output of the system is the final analysis, and "computer-assisted" analysis, where the output must be interpreted by the user. All systems found in the literature[1] choose the "computer-implemented" analysis approach. In order to overcome the limitation exposed above, we introduce a system that follows the "computer-assisted" approach—that is, an interactive melodic analysis, integrating automatic methods and interactions from the user. This is accomplished in the present work by using the "Interactive Pattern Recognition" (IPR) framework, which has proven successful in other similar tasks from the human action point of view, like the transcription of hand-written text images, speech signals, machine translation or image retrieval (see Toselli et al. (2011) for a review of IPR techniques and application domains). We will present experimental evidence that shows that IPR seems to be a suitable way to approach melodic analysis.

This chapter is structured as follows. First the main trends in harmonic analysis, along with ways of dealing with melodic analysis, and the introduction of interactivity, are reviewed in Sect. 8.2. The classical pattern matching classification paradigm, most commonly used so far, is formulated in Sect. 8.3. The interactive pattern recognition approach will then be introduced in Sect. 8.4.

Our proposal to solve the problem of melodic analysis using various approaches based on manual, classical pattern matching and IPR methods will be described in Sect. 8.5. A graphical user interface (GUI) has been developed to assert the expectations presented theoretically, and it is described in Sect. 8.6. The experimental

---

[1] Except the study by Taube and Burnson (2008), but that work focuses on the correction of analyses rather than on assisting the analyst's task.

results are then presented in Sect. 8.7, and finally, some conclusions are drawn in Sect. 8.8.

8.2 State of the Art

Several non-comprehensive reviews of computational harmonic analysis can be found in the recent literature (de Haas, 2012; Kröger et al., 2010; Mearns, 2013).

Two main tasks in harmonic analysis are recurrent in most of the approaches: first the partition of the piece into segments with harmonic significance, then the assignment of each segment to a chord in a key context using either a Roman numeral academic approach (e.g., V7 dominant chord) or a modern notation (e.g., a chord like GMaj7). From a human perspective, an analysis cannot be made as a sequence of independent tasks (e.g., first a key analysis, then a chordal analysis, then a melodic analysis and so on). However, the simultaneity in the execution of these phases may depend on the particular musical work. In some cases all the tasks are computed simultaneously, while in others, for each phase, several possibilities are generated and the best solution has to be selected using an optimization technique. For example, melodic analysis conditions the other tasks, helping in discarding ornamental notes that do not belong to the harmonic structure, in order to make decisions on segmentation and chord identification.

8.2.1 Segmentation

The partition of a piece of music into segments with different harmonic properties (i.e., key, chord, tonal function), referred to as "one of the most daunting problems of harmonic detection" by Sapp (2007, p. 102), has been tackled so far using two related approaches: one that may be named *blind*, because it does not use any prior tonal information, and another that takes into account some computed tonal information from the beginning, that Mouton and Pachet (1995) have called *island growing*. The *blind* approach is based only on timing information and involves chopping the input into short slices (Barthélemy and Bonardi, 2001; Illescas et al., 2007; Pardo and Birmingham, 2000), using either points of note onset and offset, a given fixed duration, or the duration of the shortest note in a bar or in the whole piece. Then, once the key and chord information are available after the initial segmentation, these slices are combined, if they are contiguous and share the same chord and key, to build meaningful segments (usually in a left-to-right manner).

The *island-growing* method finds tonal centres based on evident chords, cadences or any clue that allows a chord to be attached to a given segment in a key context. Once these tonal centres are obtained, they are grown in a similar way to the *blind* approach. This is a more usual approach in the literature (Meredith, 1993; Sapp, 2007; Scholz et al., 2005; Ulrich, 1977). Note that this method also needs to split the work horizontally in order to assign these tonal centres, so distinguishing between *blind* and *island growing* in some cases is difficult or not totally clear.

Finally, as Pardo and Birmingham (2002) state, there are approaches that receive an already segmented input (e.g., Winograd, 1968) or where it is not clear how the segmentation is obtained.

8.2.2 Knowledge-Based and Statistical Approaches

The identification of chords and keys alone, given the already computed segments or simultaneously with the calculation of these segments, has been performed using two very different approaches: one based on rules established by experts, sometimes referred to as *knowledge-based*, and the other built on top of statistical machine learning systems, which Chuan and Chew (2011) properly refer to as *data-driven*.

There is no sound experimental evidence on which approach yields the best analysis results, but currently it seems to be assumed that machine learning systems are more adequate than knowledge-based systems (Chuan and Chew, 2011). Some systems use a hybrid solution. Nevertheless, even the less knowledge-based systems incorporate at least some a priori information in the intermediate music representation itself or in the learning strategy designed from a preconceived guided solution. Some of them even include some rules that restrict or direct the statistical methods (Raphael and Stoddard, 2004).

Of the two approaches, knowledge-based systems were the first to be used to tackle the problem. They were formulated using preference-rule systems (Temperley, 1997, 2001; Temperley and Sleator, 1999), using a classical forward-chaining approach or other typical solutions in expert systems (Maxwell, 1984; Pachet, 1991; Scholz et al., 2005), as constraint-satisfaction problems (Hoffman and Birmingham, 2000), embedded in the form of grammars (de Haas, 2012; Rohrmeier, 2007; Tojo et al., 2006; Winograd, 1968) or using numerical methods based on template matching. The latter methods work by matching the input set of pitches that comes from the segmentation process to a list of possible chord templates. By using a similarity measure between chords, the list of templates is ordered, and the algorithm either selects the most similar template or passes the list to a later process that uses either some kind of algorithm (Prather, 1996; Taube, 1999) or an optimization technique to find the best sequence of chords by means of a graph (Barthélemy and Bonardi, 2001; Choi, 2011; Illescas et al., 2007; Kirlin, 2009; Pardo and Birmingham, 2002). Passos et al. (2009) use a k-nearest neighbours technique to perform the matching process.

The main advantage of statistical machine learning systems is their ability to learn from examples, either supervised from tagged corpora or unsupervised, thus, theoretically overcoming the problem of the variability of the myriad of applicable rules. There are in the literature almost as many proposals for this approach as there are machine learning techniques: *HMPerceptron* to solve a supervised sequential learning (SSL) problem, like those used in part-of-speech tagging (Radicioni and

Esposito, 2007), hidden Markov models (Mearns, 2013; Passos et al., 2009; Raphael and Stoddard, 2004) or neural networks (Scarborough et al., 1989; Tsui, 2002).

Both approaches have advantages and disadvantages, as noted in various studies (Mouton and Pachet, 1995). The main disadvantage of rule-based systems is the impossibility for any system to include rules for every possible situation, able to cope, for example, with any genre or composer. In fact, in many situations, composers try to break established rules in a creative manner. Another disadvantage of rule-based approaches is the fact that, in many cases, two different rules may conflict. This situation has often been solved by using preference rules (*meta-rules*) that solve those conflicts. Raphael and Stoddard (2004) highlight another problem, namely, that, as the rule systems work by ordering a sequence of decisions, the propagation of errors from an early decision may compromise the final result. The main advantage of rule-based systems is their capacity for explanation, which may be used to guide the user action in an interactive approach or educational environment. In the case of numerically based methods, Raphael and Stoddard (2004) point out that the numerical values returned by their chord similarity algorithm are difficult to justify and must be found just by empirically tuning the system. To overcome this problem, statistical procedures have been applied that automatically optimize parameter values by methods like linear dynamic programming (Raphael and Nichols, 2008) or genetic algorithms (Illescas et al., 2011).

Besides segmentation and chord identification, there are important details that differentiate the depth of the different studies reported in the literature. One is the handling of modulations and tonicizations. Modulation is the process by which one tonal centre is substituted by another. Usually, the tonality may change throughout a piece. In many cases, it starts with a key, modulates to other keys and eventually returns to the initial tonality. The concept of tonicization (Piston, 1987) is used to describe the cadence of a secondary dominant onto its tonic, in such a way that, in a given tonality, when there is a perfect cadence onto any degree, this degree acts as the tonic of the secondary dominant that precedes it. More detailed explanations are provided by Tsui (2002, pp. 7–8) and Mearns (2013, pp. 20–22). Some methods consider tonicization to be just a key change, ignoring this temporal key context change (Illescas et al., 2007), others reinterpret the result in a post-process to adapt it to the correct interpretation (Kirlin, 2009). There are, however, plenty of approaches that explicitly include this concept in their models (Hoffman and Birmingham, 2000; Rohrmeier, 2011; Sapp, 2011; Scholz et al., 2005; Taube, 1999).

8.2.3 Melodic Analysis

The other aspect that is central to the present work is melodic analysis. No work has focused in depth just on melodic tagging in a harmonic analysis task from a computational point of view. A first attempt was made by Illescas et al. (2011) and a musicological study was presented by Willingham (2013). Nevertheless, in many studies, melodic analysis has received the attention it deserves (e.g., Chuan and

Chew, 2011; Mearns, 2013; Sapp, 2007) or, at least, it has been acknowledged that a better understanding of melodic analysis would improve the chord identification process (Pardo and Birmingham, 2002; Raphael and Stoddard, 2004). In some methods, ornamental notes are removed in an a priori manual preprocess, in order to avoid the melodic analysis task (Winograd, 1968). In many studies, notes are chosen just using their metrical position: that is, strong notes, or using a regular span (Yi and Goldsmith, 2007). Others use very simple rules: for example, Barthélemy and Bonardi (2001) and Kirlin (2009) assume that non-chord notes are followed by a joint movement. In rule-based systems, there are usually rules that deal specifically with melodic analysis, e.g., Temperley's (2001) "Ornamental Dissonance Rule" or rules 10 to 20 in Maxwell's (1984) model. Template matching was used by Taube (1999).

From a machine learning perspective, two contemporary approaches have been proposed that work in virtually the same way: one proposed by the authors of the current work (Illescas et al., 2011) that will be extended here, and Chuan and Chew's (2011) "Chord-Tone Determination" module. In both cases, notes are passed as a vector of features (up to 73 in Chuan and Chew's (2011) model; whereas Illescas et al. (2011) use a smaller but similar set) to a decision tree learner that learns rules to classify either harmonic tones vs. non-harmonic tones (Chuan and Chew, 2011) or harmonic tones vs. each different kind of non-harmonic tone (Illescas et al., 2011).

8.2.4 Interactivity

One of the aspects of this work that has received less attention in the literature is the opportunity for interaction between potential users and such a system. Some authors have expressed in some cases the need for interactivity (Scholz et al., 2005) that is implicit in the concept of "computer-assisted" analysis suggested by Maxwell (1984). Sapp (2011) reviews errors generated by his algorithm, finding that sometimes the obtained key was wrong but closely related to the actual tonic key. From a classical standpoint, this is an error, but maybe it could be considered a minor mistake. In an interactive approach, this could easily be solved by presenting a ranking of keys to the user. Phon-Amnuaisuk et al. (2006) present their system as a "platform for music knowledge representation including harmonization rules to enable the user to control the system's harmonization behaviour". This "user control" is indeed an interactive process. Something similar is asserted by Taube (1999): "The user may directly control many aspects of the analytical process".

Some authors have expressed their intention to add an interactive user interface; for example, Chuan and Chew (2010) present a preliminary design. For a harmonization task, Simon et al. (2008) add some possible interaction that allows the user to choose the kind of chords generated. In the teaching environment, the system "Choral Composer" (Taube and Burnson, 2008) allows the students to see their mistakes as they do each exercise (guided completion).

Other software tools for visualizing musical analyses include Chew and François' (2003) "MuSA.RT, Opus 1", which represents a work using the Spiral Array model; and the graphical user interface tool, "T2G", cited by Choi (2011).[2]

There is also the "Impro-Visor" software,[3] which is a music notation program designed to help jazz musicians compose and hear solos similar to ones that might be improvised. The system, built on top of grammars learned from transcriptions, shows improvisation advice in the form of visual hints.

Finally, though not interactive, the "Rameau" system (Passos et al., 2009) allows users to experiment with musicological ideas in a graphical visualization interface, and Sapp's (2011) "keyscapes" also provide visual analyses of works.

The interactive pattern recognition paradigm has not been applied to the tonal analysis task so far. However, many of the problems uncovered when analysing the analyses performed by computer tools (see for example the manual analysis of errors by Pardo and Birmingham (2002)) could be addressed in an interactive model. Any data-driven approach can directly benefit from the IPR approach as well. It would not be straightforward, but adding user decisions as specific rules to a model, in a similar manner to that used in a case-based-reasoning system (Sabater et al., 1998), could be a way to take advantage of user feedback.

The lack of standardized ground truth or evaluation techniques has been mentioned above. Some methods compare their results using very isolated works. Nevertheless, it seems that J. S. Bach's harmonized chorales have been frequently used as a corpus (Illescas et al., 2007, 2008, 2011; Maxwell, 1984; Radicioni and Esposito, 2007; Tsui, 2002), perhaps because they form the most scholastic corpus available and because most analysts agree upon how these pieces should be analysed.

Regarding evaluation techniques, there is no agreement on a quantitative evaluation measure to use in order to compare the performance of different proposals. In any case, as will be detailed below, under the interactive pattern recognition approach introduced here, systems are not assumed to be fully automatic but rather to require user supervision. Here, quantitative evaluation is therefore less oriented to performance accuracy and more to the workload (e.g., number of user interactions) that is required in order to achieve the correct output.

8.3 Classical Pattern Recognition Approach

The computational methods utilized in the present work for solving the problem of melodic analysis are related to the application of pattern recognition and matching techniques to the classification of the notes in a score into seven categories: harmonic and six classes of non-harmonic tone. This way, we can consider this task as a classical seven-class classification problem in pattern recognition. For that, we can consider that every note is an input sample, x_i. From the sample and its context

---

[2] http://members.shaw.ca/akochoi-T2/jazz-harmonic-analysis/index.html

[3] http://www.cs.hmc.edu/ keller/jazz/improvisor/

(x_{i-1}, x_i, x_{i+1}), a number of features can be computed that are expressed as a feature vector, $\mathbf{x}_i$, that can be regarded as evidence for categorizing the note i. From this information, the system's underlying model $\mathcal{M}$ should be able to output a hypothesis $\hat{h}_i$, classifying the input sample into one of the seven classes.

Usually, $\mathcal{M}$ is inferred from example pairs $(\mathbf{x}, h) \in \mathcal{X}$ provided to the system in the training phase. For learning, a strategy for minimizing the error due to incorrect h is followed. Once the system is trained by achieving an acceptable error measure, the model is applied to new, previously unseen, samples. In this operation phase, the decision on each sample is the hypothesis $\hat{h}_i$ that maximizes the posterior probability value estimated $\Pr(h_i \mid \mathbf{x}_i)$, considering that this value is provided by the model learnt:

$$\hat{h}_i = \arg\max_{h \in \mathcal{H}} \Pr(h \mid \mathbf{x}_i) \approx \arg\max_{h \in \mathcal{H}} P_{\mathcal{M}}(h \mid \mathbf{x}_i) . \qquad (8.1)$$

The input to the classification system is a series of vectors $\mathbf{x} = \mathbf{x}_1, ..., \mathbf{x}_{|M|}$, where $|M|$ is the number of notes of the melody. The output is a sequence of decisions $\mathbf{h} = h_1, ..., h_{|M|} \in \mathcal{H} = \{\text{H,P,N,S,AP,AN,ES}\}$ (see Sect. 8.5 for a definition of these classes).

8.4 Interactive Pattern Recognition Approach

Multimodal human interaction has become an increasingly important field that aims at solving challenging application problems in multiple domains. Computer music systems have all the potential features for this kind of technique to be applied: multimodal nature of the information (Lidy et al., 2007), need for cognitive models (Temperley, 2001), time dependency (Iñesta and Pérez-Sancho, 2013), adaptation from human interaction (Pérez-García et al., 2011) and so on.

Assuming that state-of-the-art systems are still far from being perfect, not only in terms of accuracy, but also with respect to their applicability to any kind of music data, it seems necessary to assume that human intervention is required, at least for a correction stage after the automatic system output. It could also be interesting to take advantage of this expert knowledge during the correction process and to work on techniques for efficiently exploiting the information provided (that relies on the user's expertise) in the context of adaptive systems. Therefore, the pattern recognition (PR) system accuracy is just a starting point, but not the main issue to assess. In IPR systems, evaluation tries to measure how efficiently the system is taking advantage of this human feedback and to work on techniques towards better adaptive schemes able to reduce the user's workload.

Placing the human in the IPR framework requires changes in the way we look at problems in these areas. Classical PR is intrinsically grounded on error-minimization algorithms, so they need to be revised and adapted to the new, minimum-human-effort performance criterion (Toselli et al., 2011). This new paradigm entails important research opportunities involving issues related to managing the feedback information provided by the user in each interaction step to improve raw performance, and the use of feedback-derived data to adaptively re-train the system and tune it to the user behaviour and the specific data at hand.

We shall now analyse these aspects of research in IPR in more detail in the context of our research.

8.4.1 Exploiting Feedback

We have described the solution to our problem as a hypothesis $\hat{\mathbf{h}}$ coding the classes of every note in our problem score. These hypotheses were those that maximize the posterior probabilities among all possible hypotheses for every note. Now, in the interactive scheme, the user observes the input $\mathbf{x}$ and the hypothesis $\hat{\mathbf{h}}$ and provides a feedback signal, f, in the form of a local hypothesis that constrains the hypothesis domain $\mathcal{H}$, so we can straightforwardly say that $f \in \mathcal{H}$. Therefore, by including this new information in the system, the best system hypothesis now corresponds to the one that maximizes the posterior probability, but given the data and the feedback:

$$\hat{\mathbf{h}} = \arg\max_{h \in \mathcal{H}} P_{\mathcal{M}}(\mathbf{h} \mid \mathbf{x}, f) , \qquad (8.2)$$

and this can be done with or without varying the model $\mathcal{M}$. After the new hypothesis is computed, the system may prompt the user to provide further feedback information in a new interaction step, k. This process continues until the system output, $\hat{\mathbf{h}}$, is acceptable to the user.

Constructing the new probability distribution and solving the corresponding maximization, may be more difficult than the corresponding problems with feedback-free posterior distributions. The idea is to perform the analysis again after each feedback input, f_k, taking this information as a constraint on the new hypothesis in such a way that the new $\hat{\mathbf{h}}^{(k+1)} \in \mathcal{H}^{(k+1)} = \mathcal{H}^{(k)} - \hat{\mathbf{h}} \subset \mathcal{H}^{(k)}$.[4] This way, the space of possible solutions is restricted by the user's corrections, because the user is telling the system that the hypothesis $\hat{\mathbf{h}}$ is not valid. Clearly, the more feedback-derived constraints can be added, the greater the opportunity to obtain better hypotheses.

This iterative procedure can make available a history of hypotheses, $h' = \hat{\mathbf{h}}^{(0)}, \hat{\mathbf{h}}^{(1)}$, ..., $\hat{\mathbf{h}}^{(k)}$, from previous interaction steps that lead eventually to a solution that is acceptable to the user. Taking this into account explicitly as

$$\hat{\mathbf{h}}^{k+1} = \arg\max_{h \in \mathcal{H}} P_{\mathcal{M}}(\mathbf{h} \mid \mathbf{x}, h', f) , \qquad (8.3)$$

may improve the prediction accuracy gradually throughout the correction process.

---

[4] In order to simplify the notation we have omitted that vector $\hat{\mathbf{h}}$ is actually a member of the Cartesian product $\mathcal{H}^{|M|}$.

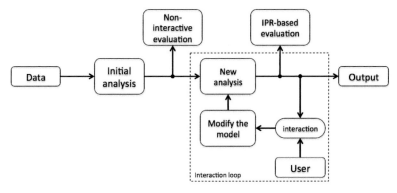

Fig. 8.1 Performance and evaluation based on an interactive pattern recognition (IPR) approach

8.4.2 System's Adaptation from Feedback

Human interaction offers a unique opportunity to improve a system's behaviour by tuning the underlying model. Everything discussed in the preceding section can be applied without varying the model $\mathcal{M}$, restricting the solution space through the feedback and thus approximating the solution.

We can go one step further using the feedback data obtained in each step of the interaction process f_k, which can be converted into new, valid training information, $(\mathbf{x}_i, h = f_k)$. This way, after each correction we get a new training set $\mathcal{X}^{(k+1)} = \mathcal{X}^{(k)} \cup \{(\mathbf{x}_i, h = f_k)\}$, allowing for the model to be re-trained or adapted. After a number of iterations the initial training set $\mathcal{X}^{(0)}$ has been completed with ground-truth training pairs.

The application of these ideas in our musical analysis framework will require establishing adequate evaluation criteria. These criteria should allow the assessment of how adaptive training algorithms are taking the maximum advantage of the interaction-derived data to ultimately minimize the overall human effort.

The evaluation issue in this interactive framework is different from classical PR algorithms (see Fig 8.1). In those systems, performance is typically assessed in terms of elementary hypothesis errors; i.e., by counting how many local hypotheses h_i differ from the vector of correct labels (non-interactive evaluation in Fig. 8.1). For that, the assessment is based on labelled training and test corpora that can be easily, objectively, and automatically tested and compared, without requiring human intervention in the assessment procedures.

Nevertheless, in an interactive framework, a human expert is embedded "in the loop", and system performance has to be gauged mainly in terms of how much human effort is required to achieve the goals. Although the evaluation of the system performance in this new scenario apparently requires human work and judgement, by carefully specifying goals and ground truth, the corpus-based assessment paradigm is still applicable in the music analysis task, just by counting how many interaction

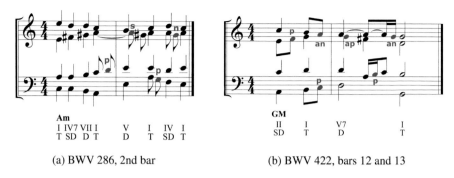

(a) BWV 286, 2nd bar   (b) BWV 422, bars 12 and 13

Fig. 8.2 Examples of non-harmonic notes in a melodic analysis. Only non-harmonic notes are tagged

steps are needed to produce a fully correct hypothesis (see IPR-based evaluation in Fig. 8.1).

8.5 Method

The problem we address here is the melodic analysis of a work in a tonal context—in particular, to tag all notes as harmonic tone (H), passing tone (P), neighbour tone (N), suspension (S), appoggiatura (AP), anticipation (AN), or echappée (ES) (see Fig. 8.2). As described in Sect. 8.2, this process, embedded in a more general tonal analysis problem, has been tackled so far using knowledge-based systems and machine learning techniques. In previous work, using the classical pattern recognition paradigm (Illescas et al., 2011), similar success rates for both approaches were obtained using some of Bach's harmonized chorales, with better results using statistical methods. The IPR paradigm will be applied to improve that result.

The model in IPR systems can be built using any of the classifiers employed in classical PR approaches. In order to assess the improvement of IPR over PR, the same classifier will be used in the experiments for both paradigms.

Machine learning systems are those that can benefit the most from the IPR improvements highlighted above. In order to choose among the variety of machine learning algorithms, only those capable of providing a full explanation of the decisions taken are considered here, with the aim of offering the user a full and understandable interactive experience. This is why a decision-tree learner has been chosen. Illescas et al. (2011) used a RIPPER algorithm (Cohen, 1995) to overcome the imbalance in the data (around 89% of the notes are harmonic tones). However, in agreement with the results of Chuan and Chew (2011), a C4.5 decision tree algorithm (Quinlan, 2014) gave better results using a leave-one-out scheme on a training corpus of 10 Bach chorales (previously used by (Illescas et al., 2011)). We extend and provide details of this corpus in Sect. 8.7.2.1.

8.5.1 Features

The classifier receives as input a note x_i represented by a vector of features, $\mathbf{x}_i$, and yields as output a probability for each tag: $P(h_i \mid \mathbf{x}_i)$, $h_i \in \mathcal{H} = \{H, P, N, S, AP, AN, ES\}$ on which the classification decision will be made. We shall now define these features.

Definition *previousIntervalName*$(x_i) \in \mathbb{N}$

The absolute interval of a note with its predecessor as defined in music theory, i.e., unison, minor 2nd, major 2nd, 3rd, etc.

Definition *previousIntervalDir*$(x_i) = \begin{cases} undefined, & i = 1 \\ ascending, & pitch(x_i) > pitch(x_{i-1}) \\ descending, & pitch(x_i) < pitch(x_{i-1}) \\ equal, & pitch(x_i) = pitch(x_{i-1}) \end{cases}$

Definition *previousIntervalMode*$(x_i) \in \{major, minor, perfect, augmented,$ *diminished, double augmented, double diminished*$\}$

This is computed using the music theory rules from the *previousIntervalName* and the absolute semitones from x_{i-1} to x_i.

Definition *nextIntervalName, nextIntervalMode* and *nextIntervalDir* are defined similarly using the interval of the note x_{i+1} with respect to x_i.

Definition *tied*$(x_i) \in \mathbb{B}$ is true if the note x_i is tied from the note x_{i-1}.

Definition $rd(x_i) = duration(x_i)/duration(beat)$

The relative duration function determines the ratio between the duration of x_i and the duration of a beat.

Definition $ratio(x_i) = \frac{rd(x_i)}{rd(x_{i-1})} \times \frac{rd(x_i)}{rd(x_{i+1})}$

The ratio function is used to compare the relative duration of x_i to its next and previous notes.

Definition *meterNumerator*(x_i) is the numerator of the active metre at *onset*(x_i). The value of *onset*$(\cdot)$ is defined locally for each measure, depending on the metre, as the position in the measure in terms of sixteenth notes, counted from 0 to (16 $\times$ numerator / denominator) $-$ 1.

Definition *instability*(x_i): given *onset*(x_i), and *meterNumerator*(x_i), it returns a value relative to the metrical weakness of x_i.

The stronger the beat in which the onset of a note is, the lower its instability value will be. See Table 8.1 for the list of values used.[5]

---

[5] The instability values for the binary metres can be obtained directly using the method described by Martin (1972). Ternary and compound metres need a straightforward extension of the method.

Table 8.1 Instability values as a function of the onset position for the different metres used. The resolution is one sixteenth note

Metre	Instability values indexed by $onset(x_i)$
4/4	(1, 9, 5, 13, 3, 11, 7, 15, 2, 10, 6, 14, 4, 12, 8, 16)
2/4	(1, 5, 3, 7, 2, 6, 4, 8)
3/4	(1, 7, 4, 10, 2, 8, 5, 11, 3, 9, 6, 12)
6/8	(1, 5, 9, 3, 7, 11, 2, 6, 10, 4, 8, 12)
9/8	(1, 7, 13, 4, 10, 16, 2, 8, 14, 5, 11, 17, 3, 9, 15, 6, 12, 18)
12/8	(1, 9, 17, 5, 13, 21, 3, 11, 19, 7, 15, 23, 2, 10, 18, 6, 14, 22, 4, 12, 20, 8, 16, 24)

Definition $nextInstability(x_i) = instability(x_{i+1})$; refers to the instability of the next note.

Definition $belongsToChord(x_i) \in \mathbb{B}$ is true if, given the pitch class of the note $pc(x_i)$, at $onset(x_i)$ there is an active chord made up of a set of notes **C**, and $pc(x_i) \in$ **C**.

Definition $belongsToKey(x_i) \in \mathbb{B}$ is true if, given the pitch class $pc(x_i)$, at $onset(x_i)$ there is a key using the scale made up of a series of notes **S**, and $pc(x_i) \in$ **S**.

The scale is the major diatonic for major keys, and the union of ascending, descending, and harmonic scales for minor keys.

Definition $prevNoteMelodicTag(x_i) \in \mathcal{H}$ is the melodic tag of the previous note, h_{i-1}, if already analysed.

Definition $nextNoteMelodicTag(x_i)$ is equivalent to the previous definition but referred to the next note, h_{i+1}.

The information about key and chord needed in the definitions above depends on the order in which the user carries out the different analysis stages. If, at a given stage, any of this information is not available, a feature will remain undefined, and the classifier will not yet be able to use it. During the interaction stage, this information becomes increasingly available.

Note that this feature-extraction scheme is using a window size of 3 notes. In some studies (e.g., Meredith, 2007) a wider window is used for determining the pitch spelling of notes. However, in our case, our system is able to explain the decision using the predecessor and successor notes, based on the underlying harmony, as explained in most music theory books.

8.5.2 Constraint Rules

As we are just focusing on the baroque period, some rules have been manually added that constrain the set of possible outputs by removing those that are invalid (e.g., two consecutive anticipations). Moreover, these rules allow the system to take advantage of some additional information the user provides by using the system, as will be seen below.

As introduced above, the system avoids invalid outputs by checking the following conditions. Let x_i be the note to be analysed, $pc(x_i)$ its pitch class, c the active chord at $onset(x_i)$, and $\mathbf{C}$ the pitches in chord c:

1. x_i cannot be tagged as H (harmonic tone) if its onset occurs on a weak beat, i.e., $instability(x_i) > meterNumerator(x_i)$, and $pc(x_i) \notin \mathbf{C}$.
2. $h_i = H$ always if $pc(x_i) \in \mathbf{C}$.
3. x_i cannot be tagged as passing tone (P) if $h_{i-1} \in \{AP, S, AN, N\}$ (appoggiatura, suspension, anticipation or neighbour tone).
4. x_i cannot be tagged as N if $h_{i-1} \in \{AP, S, AN, P\}$.
5. x_i cannot be tagged as $\{A, AP, S\}$ if $h_{i-1} \in \{AP, S, AN, N, P\}$.

These rules involving key and chord information, as well as the tagging of surrounding notes, are only available to the system through the interactive action of the user. The computing of key and chord information would imply the full tonal analysis process, and this work focuses only the melodic analysis task, the rest of the process is performed manually by the user.

8.5.3 IPR Feedback and Propagation

The underlying classification model was required to provide a readable explanation of the decision mechanism, so we focus on decision trees, as discussed at the beginning of Sect. 8.5. The C4.5 decision tree algorithm, using the same features both for the classical PR approach and the IPR system, was utilized. The C4.5 algorithm provides the a posteriori probability $P(h_i \mid \mathbf{x}_i)$ as the proportion of samples in the leaf that belongs to each class (Margineantu and Dietterich, 2003) using a Laplacian correction to smooth the probability estimations. Although it cannot be incrementally updated, it trains in a very short time. In this way, in our case, it is fully re-trained after each interaction using the new information provided by the user. This fact does not limit its usability for melodic analysis, since the re-training is perceived as a real-time update by the user. Moreover, the size of the data set will never be too large, because analysis rules are specific to each genre, so the need for scalability is not an issue.

As introduced in Sect. 8.4.1, each time the user provides a feedback $f \in \mathcal{H}$, the model is rebuilt as if the pair $(\mathbf{x}_i, h'_i = f)$ was in the training set. Furthermore, this means that, if the user amends the analysis of a note x_i with features $\mathbf{x}_i$ to be $h'_i \neq \hat{h}_i$, the analysis $\hat{h}_j$ of further notes x_j with features $\mathbf{x}_j = \mathbf{x}_i$ should be the same, i.e., the analysis of them will be modified accordingly as $h'_j = h'_i$. This is called *propagation* and it is performed for the rest of notes $x_j, \forall j \neq i$ after each user interaction on note x_i.

8.6 Application Prototype

In order to prove the validity of the IPR approach for the melodic analysis task in a real user scenario and in order to study how it leverages users' effort using the assistant system, an interactive prototype has been developed in JavaFX 8,[6] a graphical user interface developer framework built on top of the Java language.

The application allows not only the melodic analysis, but also helps in the task of key and chord analysis, because chord identification and melodic analysis cannot be done as isolated tasks, but need to be done in a coordinated fashion. The reason is that the decision as to which notes have to be included to form a chord depends on which ones have been tagged as harmonic; but in order to tag a note as harmonic, one has to predict which chord will be formed (as well as other considerations).

In order to perform the analysis, the prototype has the following features:

- It reads and writes from and to MusicXML. Chords are encoded using the corresponding schema elements, the remaining analyses, such as tonal functions, tonicizations, and so on, are encoded/decoded using lyrics.
- It reads from **kern format including the harmonic spines.
- It renders the score visually allowing for the selection of individual elements.
- It helps the user select the most probable chord and key at each moment.
- It permits the introduction and editing by the user of all the tonal analysis: melodic tags, chords, key changes, tonicizations, and secondary dominants.
- It logs all the user actions for later study.

In order to compare the user's actions using the three approaches considered (manual, automatic PR-based automatic, and IPR-assisted), the user can select the operation mode in the application.

8.6.1 Manual Mode

Not too different from employing a sheet of paper and a pencil, one computer-aided way of doing an analysis is to use any kind of score editor like Finale or Musescore, adding the melodic tags as lyrics under each note. This approach, which was adopted by the authors in their creation of the first ground truth (Illescas et al., 2007), is tedious, and the effort required to analyse a work, measured as number of interactions, is at least equal to the number of notes. That method is not taken into account in this experimentation.

The use of the prototype in manual mode allows the user to manually introduce the melodic tag of each note. It acts as a helping tool to annotate the key and chord of the selected sonority in an assisted way. The only logged user actions will be those related to the melodic tagging, with those referring to chord and key being discarded.

In a typical scenario, the user proceeds as follows:

[6] http://www.oracle.com/technetwork/es/java/javafx/overview/index.html

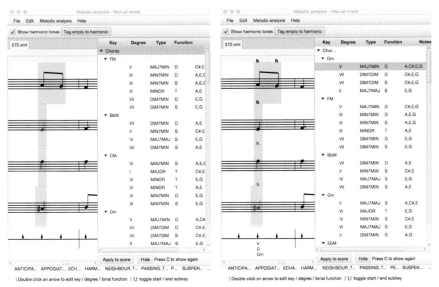

(a) After selecting alto note E, sonority is high-lighted. Last key was FM

(b) Apply selected chord. All notes belonging to chord are tagged as 'H'

Fig. 8.3 Highlight of sonority and application of selected key and chord

1. A note is selected. The corresponding sonority is highlighted accordingly by including all the notes that are simultaneously active at any time during the selected note (Fig. 8.3(a)). For them, a list of possible keys and chords in each key is displayed hierarchically. The details of how this list is constructed are given below.

2. A chord is selected from the list of valid keys and chords and is applied to the current sonority (Fig. 8.3(b)). If the user prefers to apply another chord and key not present in the proposed list (such as tonicizations or secondary dominants, not included in it), it can be done using a dialogue as shown in Fig. 8.4. Once the context is established, as a help to the user, notes not belonging to the active chord are highlighted.

3. Finally, using a set of predefined keyboard keys, the user selects the suitable melodic tag for each note. The system just logs this last action, because it is the only one that corresponds strictly to the melodic analysis task.

This process is repeated for each note in the musical work. Note that the user may backtrack on a decision and the same note could be tagged several times.

In most musical works, at least in the baroque period, almost all notes are harmonic tones, not ornamental. This implies that the note tags follow a highly imbalanced distribution in favour of class H. In order to avoid the user having to carry out unnecessary actions, the prototype includes a button that tags all previously untagged notes as harmonic (see Fig. 8.5). This allows the user to tag only non-harmonic tones, reducing considerably the number of interactions.

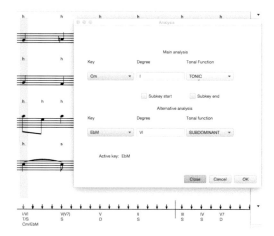

Fig. 8.4 Dialogue box that allows the user to apply a chord not present in the proposed chords list. Used for assigning tonicizations and secondary dominants

8.6.1.1 Chord and Key List Construction

The valid keys added to the list are those whose associated scale includes all the notes in the selected sonority.

The chords are chosen using a template-based approach: given the set of notes, all possible combinations of groups of at least two notes are matched with the list of chord types shown in Table 8.2. Finally, the list of keys is ranked using the following ordering: the current key first (or the major mode of the key present in the key signature if no previous key was found), then the next key up and down in the circle of fifths and the relative minor or major. The rest of the keys are ordered inversely, proportional to the distance along the circle of fifths. In the minor key, the relative major key is located at the second position of the list.

Inside each key, the chords with more notes in the sonority are ordered first. When having the same number of notes, those containing the root are located in upper positions, and when comparing chords containing the root and having the same number of notes, the tonal functions are ordered this way: tonal, dominant, and subdominant. Figure 8.3(b) shows an example.

Fig. 8.5 Button that tags all non previously tagged notes as "harmonic tone"

Table 8.2 Chord templates. The semitones of the first pitch correspond to the semitones from the tonic of the chord

Chord type	Semitones from previous pitch
Major triad	(4,3)
Minor triad	(3,4)
Augmented triad	(4,4)
Diminished triad	(3,3)
Major with minor seventh	(4,3,3)
Augmented with major seventh	(4,4,3)
Diminished with minor seventh	(3,3,4)
Diminished with diminished seventh	(3,3,3)
Major seventh with major seventh	(4,3,4)
Minor seventh with minor seventh	(3,4,3)

8.6.2 Automatic Mode

In automatic mode, previously introduced as "computer-implemented" by Maxwell (1984) and described under the classical pattern recognition paradigm (Sect. 8.3), the user proceeds using this protocol:

1. First, the system analyses the score automatically. The Weka (Hall et al., 2009) implementation of the C4.5 algorithm (Quinlan, 2014) has been embedded in the prototype and it is fed using the features described in Sect. 8.5.1, excluding the chord- and key-related features (*belongsToChord* and *belongsToKey*) because they are not available when the work is analysed automatically the first and only time.
2. All notes have now an analysis tag, that may be correct or not. Now, the user proceeds just like the manual mode explained above, by choosing chords and keys, and, instead of setting the melodic tag for each note, just changing those tags that the C4.5 classifier has misclassified (see Fig. 8.6).

The system has been trained using a bootstrap set of 10 Bach chorales manually tagged (see list of works below in Sect. 8.7.2.1).

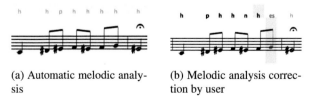

(a) Automatic melodic analysis

(b) Melodic analysis correction by user

Fig. 8.6 Highlight of sonority and application of selected key and chord

8.6.3 Assisted Mode

The assisted mode corresponds to the introduced IPR approach, named by Maxwell (1984) as "computer-assisted" analysis. Here the system reacts against all the user actions. The loop of actions is described next:

1. As in the manual mode, the user selects a note and a sonority is highlighted, for which the user identifies and assigns key and chord.
2. The prototype performs a melodic analysis of the work using the C4.5 classifier. Now the features *belongsToChord* and *belongsToKey* already have a value for all the notes located from the selected sonority and forwards. Moreover, all the constraint rules (Sect. 8.5.2) can now be applied.
3. As in the automatic mode, the user may amend (feedback) any melodic analysis tag, which fires the propagation of that decision to all notes with the same features, and runs again the C4.5 classifier, now re-trained with the new corrected sample. A user-amended tag is never modified by the new classifier decision.
4. The process is repeated until all notes are melodically tagged.

This process is not a mere repetition of the automatic mode process for each note, it has several important implications:

- In order to show the valid chords in the help list, notes tagged as any of the non-harmonic tones are not used. This method narrows the search of the desired chord, but also forces the user to tag as harmonic the notes the system had tagged incorrectly as non-harmonic. It may seem that the correct chord and key identification can slow down the melodic tagging. However, as the *belongsToChord* and *belongsToKey* features use the key information, the classifier has more information about the harmonic context after each interaction, which boosts the melodic tagging.
- The change of a melodic tag affects the surrounding notes, that may be modified by the constraining rules after a user interaction, leading to a correction of a possibly incorrect tagging.

This process may not be done sequentially from left to right because the user could proceed in an "island-growing" way, by first locating tonal centres and then browsing back and forth.

8.6.4 User Interaction Analysis

The prototype logs each action carried out by the user. In this study, only the actions relating to the melodic analysis itself have been taken into account. So, in order not to block the user interaction at any moment, the Java logging framework has been customized to export the kind of information shown in Table 8.3, printing the user actions to a file, using a separate thread. This file has been parsed in order to extract

Table 8.3 Example of log entries

Action time stamp	Session time stamp	Action type	Action
		...	
1417009922812	1417009922796	actionloggersystem	started
1417010341734	1417009922796	MELODICANALYSIS.CHANGE	PASSING_TONE
1417010390390	1417009922796	MELODICANALYSIS.CHANGE	PASSING_TONE
1417010550375	1417009922796	MELODICANALYSIS.CHANGE	SUSPENSION
1417010665140	1417009922796	MELODICANALYSIS.CHANGE	HARMONIC
		...	

times and number of user interactions. The system records session information in order that the user may close the prototype and continue the analysis task in a later session.

8.7 Experiments

8.7.1 Proof of Concept: Ability to Learn Interactively

In order to assess the ability of the interactive system to learn online from the interaction of the user, a simulation has been built in which the system receives a musical work whose notes have been manually tagged with their corresponding melodic analysis labels. It simulates the user actions as follows:

1. The work is automatically analysed using a (possibly untrained) classifier. After this step, both the correct tag for each note obtained from the manual analysis and the tag assigned by the classifier are available for every note.
2. The interaction system now proceeds as a human would: it looks for an error in the analysis (at random to simulate the back-and-forth action by a real user), then it replaces the incorrect label (assigned by the classifier) with the correct tag (obtained from the previous manual analysis).
3. This interaction fires the interactive pattern-matching loop, i.e., the feedback decision is propagated to all notes not previously corrected, and the classifier model is updated including this new sample.
4. The process is repeated until no errors remain. The number of changes performed (equal to the number of times the process has been carried out) is the actual system performance evaluation value.

Using this setup, the complete collection of Bach's harmonized chorales (see Sect. 8.7.2.1) has been used. The system has been fed sequentially with the set of chorales, starting with an untrained C4.5 classifier that learns after each user action

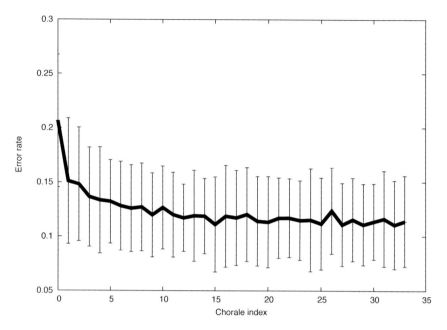

Fig. 8.7 Evolution of the error rate as the user analyses works. The x axis represents the order in which a work is analysed. The plot shows the average (thick line) of the results of 100 different orderings of the input corpus. The standard deviations are also shown. The error rate is measured as the number of interactions required to correct a piece divided by the number of notes it contains

on each musical piece. Not all chorales have the same level of complexity, so the presentation order may affect the evolution of the error rate. In order to avoid any bias, the process has been repeated 100 times in different random orderings of the pieces. Figure 8.7 shows how the error rate becomes lower as the system analyses more and more works. This provides evidence that the system is able to learn from the interaction of the user.

Considering the possibility of using a decision-tree classifier able to update the model online without having to train it for each new feedback sample, the simulation has also been carried out using a Hoeffding tree (VFDT) (Hulten et al., 2001). However, the results obtained, both with the classical PR approach and with the setup just described were worse than those using the C4.5 classifier. Moreover, there was no perceptible improvement in the training speed for the online VFDT learning compared to the full re-training of the C4.5.

8.7.2 Experimental Setup and Data

In order to test the prototype, the following process has been followed:

1. A musicologist[7] has manually tagged the training set.
2. Students of the final course of a music degree analysed the test set using the three modes of the prototype: manual, automatic, and interactive. The analysis of the same work using different modes by the same user was avoided.
3. In all analyses, the system was bootstrapped using the same trained model.

8.7.2.1 Corpora

The system was assessed using some of Bach's chorales, encoded using MusicXML files. These pieces are widely accepted as a scholastic tonal harmony ground truth, as mentioned in Sect. 8.2 above. Furthermore, they contain monodic lines for each voice that help in the construction of features for the classifier.

For the training phase, the following chorales were used: catalogue BWV numbers 89/6, 148/6, 253, 272, 274, 275, 280, 437, 438.

For the test, the following were used: catalogue BWV numbers 255, 256, 257, 259, 260, 281, 282, 285, 286, 287, 288, 290, 292, 293, 294, 295, 296, 420, 421, 423, 424, 426, 427, 429, 431.

BWV 257, 260, 420 were analysed by several students, thus, a total of 30 pieces were utilized for test.

8.7.3 Results

Figure 8.8 shows the results of the melodic analysis using the test set described above. The percentage of less than 15% of non-harmonic tones (NHT) on average, gives an indication of the minimum number of interactions the user has to complete when using the "Tag all as harmonic tones" button first, and then tagging just the non-harmonic tones. This assumes that no note is tagged twice due to a user changing his or her mind.

The results show that the best performance is obtained using the proposed IPR approach. The graph demonstrates what could be expected. The results for the manual approach are worse than the theoretical minimum number of interactions (i.e., ≈ 15%), expected to be equal to the number of non-harmonic tones plus one for the action of pushing the "tag all as harmonic" button. This is caused by the fact that the user, solving the problem heuristically, provides several possible solutions leading to different taggings of the same note. The automatic, classical PR approach, leverages the user's effort, who takes advantage of some of the correctly classified melodic tags that, in turn, help with the correct selection of keys and chords, thus narrowing the user's heuristic search for the solution. Finally, in the proposed IPR system the advantages found in the PR approach are used, and they are improved in two ways by the use of the feedback from the user. First, this feedback enriches the

---

[7] The author Plácido R. Illescas.

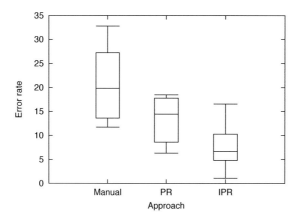

Fig. 8.8 Results in terms of number of user interactions required to solve the melodic analysis. The percentages are obtained as the number of interactions divided by the number of notes

input features to the classifier after each interaction. Second, the feedback re-trains the model, incorporating the corrected analyses as new examples in the training set. Moreover, these examples are very probably found in the same work several times, reducing in this way the number of interactions required to get a correct final analysis.

It is important to stress the fact that the IPR approach in this task has a competitive advantage over a single PR one, due to the fact that the harmonic information (key context and chords) cannot be analysed before doing the melodic analysis. This is because each of the three aspects depends on the other two. Thus, the PR approach cannot use the harmonic information that the user provides with his or her interactive use of the tool.

In the current setup of the experiment, the most important improvement from the user feedback comes from the use of contextual information added after each user interaction, which is not available for the classical PR paradigm. The propagation, which is the same as incorporating new samples in the model, that can be used to solve similar situations in the future, constitutes a second enhancement. Finally, the experiments have not really taken full advantage of the on-line training and tuning of the model, as the model is not incrementally maintained from analysis to analysis. Indeed, it is reset for each experiment in order to be compared with the manual and PR approaches under similar conditions.

8.8 Conclusions

The tonal analysis of musical works in a computational environment is a problem that has been addressed since the 1960s. Many different approaches have been proposed since that time that roughly fall into two categories belonging to the pattern recognition discipline: knowledge-based and machine learning methods. Although interesting results have been obtained in several studies, a full solution to the problem has still not been found.

In this work, a different approach, called Interactive Pattern Recognition (IPR), has been applied, that focuses on trying to reduce the final effort made by the user, rather than minimizing the errors initially made by the system in an automatic analysis.

Using well-known techniques from the classical Pattern Recognition paradigm, IPR improves their performance by incorporating user feedback into the model after each interaction, which helps the system to be refined as the user works with it.

In order to explore the suitability of the method, this IPR approach has been applied to one part of the tonal analysis task: melodic analysis, leaving aside the key and chord computation to be done manually. The proposal has been assessed by means of a prototype software application that, besides performing this melodic analysis using IPR, helps the user to annotate the tonal context of the work.

Using a widely-used corpus, a subset of Bach's harmonized chorales, the IPR paradigm has been proven to provide a suitable approach for finally obtaining a satisfactory solution to the problem of tonal analysis, assisted by computer from the user's point of view.

Acknowledgements This work has been funded by the Spanish Ministry project TIMuL (TIN2013-48152-C2-1-R). Additional support was provided by European FEDER funds. Thanks to Craig Sapp and David Meredith for their valuable aid and advice.

References

Barthélemy, J. and Bonardi, A. (2001). Figured bass and tonality recognition. In *Proceedings of the Second International Symposium on Music Information Retrieval (ISMIR 2001)*, pages 129–136, Bloomington, IN.

Chew, E. and François, A. (2003). MuSA.RT: Music on the spiral array. Real-time. In *Proceedings of the Eleventh ACM International Conference on Multimedia*, pages 448–449, New York, NY.

Choi, A. (2011). Jazz harmonic analysis as optimal tonality segmentation. *Computer Music Journal*, 35(2):49–66.

Chuan, C.-H. and Chew, E. (2007). A hybrid system for automatic generation of style-specific accompaniment. In *Proceedings of the 4th International Joint Workshop on Computational Creativity*, pages 57–64, London, UK.

Chuan, C.-H. and Chew, E. (2010). Quantifying the benefits of using an interactive decision support tool for creating musical accompaniment in a particular style. In *Proceedings of the Eleventh International Society for Music Information Retrieval Conference (ISMIR 2010)*, pages 471–476, Utrecht, The Netherlands.

Chuan, C.-H. and Chew, E. (2011). Generating and evaluating musical harmonizations that emulate style. *Computer Music Journal*, 35(4):64–82.

Cohen, W. W. (1995). Fast effective rule induction. In *Proceedings of the 12th International Conference on Machine Learning (ICML)*, pages 115–123.

de Haas, W. B. (2012). *Music information retrieval based on tonal harmony*. PhD thesis, Utrecht University.

Ebcioğlu, K. (1986). An expert system for chorale harmonization. In *Proceedings of the American Association for Artificial Intelligence, AAAI*, pages 784–788.

Feng, Y., Chen, K., and Liu, X.-B. (2011). Harmonizing melody with meta-structure of piano accompaniment figure. *Journal of Computer Science and Technology*, 26(6):1041–1060.

Forgács, R. (2007). *Gallus Dressler's Praecepta Musicae Poeticae*. University of Illinois Press.

Forte, A. (1967). Music and computing: The present situation. In *AFIPS Proceedings of the Fall Joint Computer Conference*, pages 327–329, Anaheim, CA.

Granroth-Wilding, M. (2013). *Harmonic analysis of music using combinatory categorial grammar*. PhD thesis, University of Edinburgh, UK.

Hall, M., Frank, E., Holmes, G., Pfahringer, B., Reutemann, P., and Witten, I. (2009). The WEKA data mining software: an update. *SIGKDD Explorations*, 11(1):10–18.

Hoffman, T. and Birmingham, W. (2000). A constraint satisfaction approach to tonal harmonic analysis. Technical report, Electrical Engineering and Computer Science Department, University of Michigan.

Hulten, G., Spencer, L., and Domingos, P. (2001). Mining time-changing data streams. In *ACM SIGKDD International Conference on Knowledge Discovery and Data Mining*, pages 97–106. ACM Press.

Illescas, P. R., Rizo, D., and Iñesta, J. M. (2007). Harmonic, melodic, and functional automatic analysis. In *Proceedings of the 2007 International Computer Music Conference (ICMC)*, pages 165–168, Copenhagen, Denmark.

Illescas, P. R., Rizo, D., and Iñesta, J. M. (2008). Learning to analyse tonal music. In *Proceedings of the International Workshop on Machine Learning and Music (MML 2008)*, pages 25–26, Helsinki, Finland.

Illescas, P. R., Rizo, D., Iñesta, J. M., and Ramírez, R. (2011). Learning melodic analysis rules. In *Proceedings of the International Workshop on Music and Machine Learning (MML 2011)*.

Iñesta, J. and Pérez-Sancho, C. (2013). Interactive multimodal music transcription. In *Proceedings of the IEEE International Conference on Acoustics, Speech and Signal Processing (ICASSP 2013)*, pages 211–215, Vancouver, Canada.

Kaliakatsos-Papakostas, M. (2014). Probabilistic harmonisation with fixed intermediate chord constraints. In *Proceedings of the 11th Sound and Music Computing Conference (SMC) and 40th International Computer Music Conference (ICMC)*, Athens, Greece.

Kirlin, P. B. (2009). Using harmonic and melodic analyses to automate the initial stages of Schenkerian analysis. In *Proceedings of the 10th International Conference on Music Information Retrieval (ISMIR 2009)*, pages 423–428, Kobe, Japan.

Kröger, P., Passos, A., and Sampaio, M. (2010). A survey of automated harmonic analysis techniques. Technical Report 1, Universidade Federal da Bahia.

Lidy, T., Rauber, A., Pertusa, A., and Iñesta, J. M. (2007). Improving genre classi-fication by combination of audio and symbolic descriptors using a transcription system. In *Proceedings of the 8th International Conference on Music Information Retrieval (ISMIR 2007)*, pages 61–66, Vienna, Austria.

Margineantu, D. D. and Dietterich, T. G. (2003). Improved class probability estimates from decision tree models. In *Nonlinear Estimation and Classification*, pages 173–188. Springer.

Marsden, A. (2010). Schenkerian analysis by computer: A proof of concept. *Journal of New Music Research*, 39(3):269–289.

Martin, J. G. (1972). Rhythmic (hierarchical) versus serial structure in speech and other behavior. *Psychological Review*, 79(6):487–509.

Maxwell, H. J. (1984). *An artificial intelligence approach to computer-implemented analysis of harmony in tonal music*. PhD thesis, Indiana University.

Mearns, L. (2013). *The computational analysis of harmony in Western art music*. PhD thesis, School of Electronic Engineering and Computer Science, Queen Mary University of London.

Meredith, D. (1993). Computer-aided comparison of syntax systems in three piano pieces by Debussy. *Contemporary Music Review*, 9(1-2):285–304.

Meredith, D. (2007). *Computing pitch names in tonal music: A comparative analysis of pitch spelling algorithms*. PhD thesis, Oxford University.

Mouton, R. and Pachet, F. (1995). The symbolic vs. numeric controversy in automatic analysis of music. In *Proceedings of the Workshop on Artificial Intelligence and Music (IJCAI 1995)*, pages 32–39.

Pachet, F. (1991). A meta-level architecture applied to the analysis of jazz chord sequences. In *Proceedings of the International Computer Music Conference*, pages 1–4, Montreal, Canada.

Pachet, F. and Roy, P. (2000). Musical harmonization with constraints: A survey. *Constraints*, 6(1):7–19.

Pardo, B. and Birmingham, W. (2002). Algorithms for chordal analysis. *Computer Music Journal*, 26(2):27–49.

Pardo, B. and Birmingham, W. P. (2000). Automated partitioning of tonal music. *FLAIRS Conference*, pages 23–27.

Passos, A., Sampaio, M., Kröger, P., and de Cidra, G. (2009). Functional harmonic analysis and computational musicology in Rameau. In *Proceedings of the 12th Brazilian Symposium on Computer Music (SBMC)*.

Pérez-García, T., Iñesta, J. M., Ponce de León, P. J., and Pertusa, A. (2011). A multimodal music transcription prototype. In *Proceedings of ACM International Conference on Multimodal Interaction (ICMI 2011)*, pages 315–318, Alicante, Spain.

Pérez-Sancho, C., Rizo, D., and Iñesta, J. M. (2009). Genre classification using chords and stochastic language models. *Connection Science*, 21(2,3):145–159.

Phon-Amnuaisuk, S., Smaill, A., and Wiggins, G. (2006). Chorale harmonization: A view from a search control perspective. *Journal of New Music Research*, 35(4):279–305.

Piston, W. (1987). *Harmony*. W. W. Norton & Company. Revised and expanded by Mark DeVoto.

Prather, R. (1996). Harmonic analysis from the computer representation of a musical score. *Communications of the ACM*, 39(12es):239–255.

Quinlan, J. R. (2014). *C4.5: Programs for Machine Learning*. Elsevier.

Raczyński, S., Fukayama, S., and Vincent, E. (2013). Melody harmonization with interpolated probabilistic models. *Journal of New Music Research*, 42(3):223–235.

Radicioni, D. and Esposito, R. (2007). Tonal harmony analysis: A supervised sequential learning approach. In Basili, R. and Pazienza, M. T., editors, *AI*IA 2007: Artificial Intelligence and Human-Oriented Computing*, volume 4733 of *Lecture Notes in Artificial Intelligence*, pages 638–649. Springer.

Rameau, J.-P. (1722). *Traité de l'harmonie, reduite à ses principes naturels*. Jean-Baptiste-Christophe Ballard.

Ramírez, R., Perez, A., Kersten, S., Rizo, D., Roman, P., and Iñesta, J. M. (2010). Modeling violin performances using inductive logic programming. *Intelligent Data Analysis*, 14(5):573–585.

Raphael, C. and Nichols, E. (2008). Training music sequence recognizers with linear dynamic programming. In *Proceedings of the International Workshop on Machine Learning and Music (MML)*, Helsinki, Finland.

Raphael, C. and Stoddard, J. (2004). Functional harmonic analysis using probabilistic models. *Computer Music Journal*, 28(3):45–52.

Rizo, D. (2010). *Symbolic music comparison with tree data structures*. PhD thesis, Universidad de Alicante.

Rohrmeier, M. (2007). A generative grammar approach to diatonic harmonic structure. In *Proceedings of the 4th Sound and Music Computing Conference*, pages 97–100.

Rohrmeier, M. (2011). Towards a generative syntax of tonal harmony. *Journal of Mathematics and Music*, 5(1):35–53.

Rothgeb, J. E. (1968). *Harmonizing the unfigured bass: A computational study*. PhD thesis, Yale University.

Sabater, J., Arcos, J., and López de Mántaras, R. (1998). Using rules to support case-based reasoning for harmonizing melodies. In Freuder, E., editor, *Multimodal Reasoning: Papers from the 1998 AAAI Spring Symposium (Technical Report, SS-98-04)*, pages 147–151, Menlo Park, CA. AAAI Press.

Sapp, C. (2007). Computational chord-root identification in symbolic musical data: Rationale, methods, and applications. *Computing in Musicology*, 15:99–119.

Sapp, C. (2011). *Computational methods for the analysis of musical structure*. PhD thesis, Stanford University.

Scarborough, D. L., Miller, B. O., and Jones, J. A. (1989). Connectionist models for tonal analysis. *Computer Music Journal*, 13(3):49.

Scholz, R., Dantas, V., and Ramalho, G. (2005). Automating functional harmonic analysis: The Funchal system. In *Seventh IEEE International Symposium on Multimedia*, Irvine, CA.

Simon, I., Morris, D., and Basu, S. (2008). MySong: Automatic accompaniment generation for vocal melodies. In *CHI '08: Proceedings of the SIGCHI Conference on Human Factors in Computing Systems*, pages 725–734, New York, NY.

Suzuki, S. and Kitahara, T. (2014). Four-part harmonization using Bayesian networks: Pros and cons of introducing chord nodes. *Journal of New Music Research*, 43(3):331–353.

Taube, H. (1999). Automatic tonal analysis: Toward the implementation of a music theory workbench. *Computer Music Journal*, 23(4):18–32.

Taube, H. and Burnson, W. A. (2008). Software for teaching music theory. Technical report, University of Illinois at Urbana-Champaign.

Temperley, D. (1997). An algorithm for harmonic analysis. *Music Perception*, 15(1):31–68.

Temperley, D. (2001). *The Cognition of Basic Musical Structures*. The MIT Press.

Temperley, D. (2004). Bayesian models of musical structure and cognition. *Musicae Scientiae*, 8(2):175–205.

Temperley, D. and Sleator, D. (1999). Modeling meter and harmony: A preference-rule approach. *Computer Music Journal*, 23(1):10–27.

Tojo, S., Oka, Y., and Nishida, M. (2006). Analysis of chord progression by HPSG. In *AIA'06: Proceedings of the 24th IASTED international conference on Artificial intelligence and applications*.

Toselli, A. H., Vidal, E., and Casacuberta, F. (2011). *Multimodal Interactive Pattern Recognition and Applications*. Springer.

Tracy, M. S. (2013). *Bach in Beta: Modeling Bach chorales with Markov Chains*. PhD thesis, Harvard University.

Tsui, W. (2002). Harmonic analysis using neural networks. Master's thesis, University of Toronto.

Ulrich, J. W. (1977). The analysis and synthesis of jazz by computer. In *Proceedings of the 5th International Joint Conference on Artificial intelligence (IJCAI)*.

Willingham, T. J. (2013). *The harmonic implications of the non-harmonic tones in the four-part chorales of Johann Sebastian Bach*. PhD thesis, Liberty University.

Winograd, T. (1968). Linguistics and the computer analysis of tonal harmony. *Journal of Music Theory*, 12(1):2–49.

Yi, L. and Goldsmith, J. (2007). Automatic generation of four-part harmony. In *Proceedings of the Fifth UAI Bayesian Modeling Applications Workshop (UAI-AW 2007, BMA'07*, Vancouver, Canada.

Chapter 9
Implementing Methods for Analysing Music Based on Lerdahl and Jackendoff's *Generative Theory of Tonal Music*

Masatoshi Hamanaka, Keiji Hirata, and Satoshi Tojo

Abstract We describe and discuss our computer implementations of Lerdahl and Jackendoff's (1983) *Generative Theory of Tonal Music* (GTTM). We consider this theory to be one of the most relevant music theories with regard to formalization because it captures aspects of musical phenomena based on the Gestalts perceived in music and presents these aspects with relatively rigid rules. However, the theory has several problems in terms of computer implementation. To overcome these problems, we have proposed four different kinds of analyser: an automatic time-span tree analyser (ATTA); a fully automatic time-span tree analyser (FATTA); the σGTTM analyser, which detects local grouping boundaries by combining GTTM with statistical learning using a decision tree; and the σGTTM-II analyser, with which we introduce full parameterization and statistical learning.

9.1 Introduction

Over the past ten years, we have developed several music analysers, based on Lerdahl and Jackendoff's (1983) *Generative Theory of Tonal Music* (GTTM), which provide us with abstracted structures from scores (Hamanaka et al., 2006, 2007; Kanamori and Hamanaka, 2014; Miura et al., 2009). When implementing music-theory-based methods for analysing music on a computer, we have to consider several problems,

Masatoshi Hamanaka
Clinical Research Center, Kyoto University, Kyoto, Japan
e-mail: masatosh@kuhp.kyoto-u.ac.jp

Keiji Hirata
Future University Hakodate, Hakodate, Hokkaido, Japan
e-mail: hirata@fun.ac.jp

Satoshi Tojo
Japan Advanced Institute of Science and Technology (JAIST), Nomi, Ishikawa, Japan
e-mail: tojo@jaist.ac.jp

© Springer International Publishing Switzerland 2016   221
D. Meredith (ed.), *Computational Music Analysis*,
DOI 10.1007/978-3-319-25931-4_9

including ambiguity, dependence on context and the trade-off between automation and variation in analysis results. Each of these problems will now be briefly introduced.

Ambiguity in music analysis A piece of music will typically have more than one interpretation, and dealing with such ambiguity is a major obstacle when implementing a music theory on a computer. We have to consider two types of ambiguity in music analysis, one involving human understanding of music and the other concerning the representation of music theory. The former stems from subjective interpretation and the latter from the incompleteness of formal theory. GTTM is no exception. Therefore, due to the presence of ambiguity, we assume that there is always more than one correct result.

Context dependence in music analysis Even if the same musicologist analyses the same note sequence, the analysis results will not always be the same. This is because the results depend on so many different factors, such as rhythm, chord progression, melody of the other parts, and the historical period in which the piece of music was composed. Moreover, a musicologist might take into account other unknown factors.

Trade-off relationship in music analysis There is a trade-off relationship between the automation of the analysis process and variation in the analysis results. Since an analysis program outputs only one interpretation for a given score, different ways of interpreting that score are ignored.

These problems are not specific to music analysis but arise whenever we try to build a computer model of an ability that, in a human, would require intelligence. This includes most abilities that involve recognition or understanding. Therefore, implementing a music theory on a computer can be considered an artificial intelligence problem.

The rest of this chapter is organized as follows. In Sects. 9.2 and 9.3, we give a brief overview of GTTM and present related work. In Sect. 9.4, we discuss the difficulty of implementing the theory on a computer. In Sects. 9.5 to 9.8, we go into depth about the four proposed analysers: the automatic time-span tree analyser (ATTA), the fully automatic time-span tree analyser (FATTA), the σGTTM analyser, and the σGTTM-II analyser. In Sect. 9.9, we propose our interactive analyser for the theory, and in Sect. 9.10, we describe a GTTM database we have constructed. Some experimental results are presented in Sect. 9.11.

9.2 Lerdahl and Jackendoff's (1983) *Generative Theory of Tonal Music*

Lerdahl and Jackendoff's (1983) *Generative Theory of Tonal Music* (henceforth, GTTM) generates four different types of structural description for a piece of music, each one intended to represent a separate aspect of the way that a listener understands

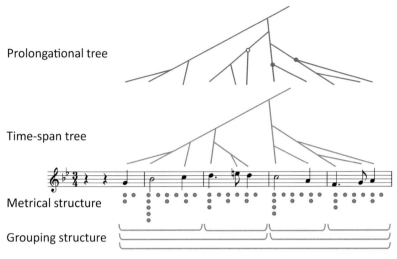

Fig. 9.1 Grouping structure, metrical structure, time-span tree, and prolongational tree

the piece. The respective outputs are a grouping structure, a metrical structure, a time-span tree, and a prolongational tree (see Fig. 9.1).

The grouping structure is intended to formalize the intuition that tonal music is organized into groups composed of subgroups (see bottom row in Fig. 9.1). The metrical structure describes the rhythmic hierarchy of a piece by identifying the positions of beats at different metrical levels. Metrical levels are represented as rows of dots below the staff. For example, in Fig. 9.1, the strongest beats occur at the beginning of every second bar, the next strongest at the beginning of each bar, the next strongest at the quarter note level and so on. The time-span tree is a binary tree having a hierarchical structure that describes the relative structural importance of notes that differentiate the essential parts of the melody from the ornamentation. The prolongational tree is a binary tree that expresses the structure of tension and relaxation in a piece of music.

A GTTM analysis has four processes: grouping structure analysis, metrical struc-ture analysis, time-span reduction analysis, and prolongational reduction analysis. Each process has two types of rule: *well-formedness rules* (WFRs) and *preference rules* (PRs). Well-formedness rules are necessary conditions on assigning the struc-ture and restrictions on these structures. For example, the GWFRs (grouping WFRs) are defined as follows (Lerdahl and Jackendoff, 1983, p. 345):

GWFR1: Any contiguous sequence of pitch events, drum beats, or the like can constitute a group, and only contiguous sequences can constitute a group.

GWFR2: A piece constitutes a group.

GWFR3: A group may contain smaller groups.

GWFR4: If group G_1 contains part of group G_2, it must contain all of G_2.

GWFR5: If group G_1 contains a smaller group G_2, then G_1 must be exhaustively partitioned into smaller groups.

Fig. 9.2 Examples of GWFRs
being satisfied or violated

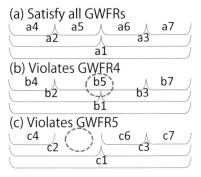

The grouping structure in Fig. 9.2(a) satisfies all the GWFRs. In contrast, the grouping structure in Fig. 9.2(b) violates GWFR4 because a segment boundary at the second level of the grouping structure occurs in the middle of a group at the lowest level. The grouping structure in Fig. 9.2(c) violates GWFR5 because group c2 is not exhaustively partitioned into smaller groups.

When more than one structure can satisfy the WFRs, the PRs indicate the superiority of one structure over another. In the PRs, some rules are for the local level and others for the hierarchical level. For example, GPR2 is a local rule that is applied to four consecutive notes n_1, n_2, n_3, n_4 as follows (Lerdahl and Jackendoff, 1983, p. 345):

> **GPR 2 (Proximity)** Consider a sequence of four notes n_1, n_2, n_3, n_4. All else being equal, the transition n_2–n_3 may be heard as a group boundary if
>
> a. (Slur/Rest) the interval of time from the end of n_2 to the beginning of n_3 is greater than that from the end of n_1 to the beginning of n_2 and that from the end of n_3 to the beginning of n_4, or if
> b. (Attack-point) the interval of time between the attack points of n_2 and n_3 is greater than that between the attack points of n_1 and n_2 and that between the attack points of n_3 and n_4.

GPR2b is applied after a note that has a long duration (Fig. 9.3(a)), while GPR2a is applied after a note that has a long gap, even if the inter-onset interval (IOI) of each note is equal (Fig. 9.3(b)).

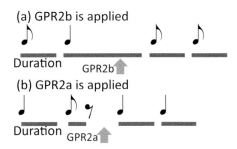

Fig. 9.3 Application of
GPR2b and GPR2a

9.3 Related Work

Here, we briefly take a look at the history of cognitive music theory. The implication–realization model (IRM) proposed by Eugene Narmour abstracts and represents music according to changes in a melody, expressed symbolically (Narmour, 1990, 1992). The IRM has recently been implemented on computers, which can acquire the chain structures of IRM from a score (Yazawa et al., 2014). *Schenkerian* analysis acquires a deeper structure, called the *Urlinie* and *Ursatz*, from the musical surface (Schenker, 1935). Short segments of music can be analysed through Schenkerian analysis on a computer (Marsden, 2011). Other examples of music theories that lend themselves to computer implementation include that of Lerdahl (2001). The preference rule approach, pioneered by Lerdahl and Jackendoff (1983), was also adopted by Temperley (2001) and Daniel Sleator in their *Melisma Music Analyzer*.[1]

The main advantage of analysis by GTTM is that it can acquire tree structures (specifically, time-span and prolongational trees). These trees provide a summarization of a piece of music, which can then be used as the representation of an abstraction, resulting in a music retrieval system (Hirata and Matsuda, 2003). It can also be used for performance rendering to generate expressive musical performances (Hirata and Hiraga, 2003) and to reproduce music (Hirata and Matsuda, 2004). Moreover, the time-span tree can be used for melody prediction (Hamanaka et al., 2008a) and melody morphing (Hamanaka et al., 2008b). Figure 9.4 shows an iOS application that implements this melody morphing method and changes the degree of morphing of each half bar by using the values from the device's accelerometer (Hamanaka et al., 2011). When the user stops moving the device, the unit plays the backing melody of "The Other Day, I Met a Bear (The Bear Song)". When the user shakes it vigorously, it plays heavy soloing. When the user shakes it slowly, it plays a morphed melody ranging in morphing degree from copying the backing to heavy soloing.

The grouping structure analysis generated by GTTM is a type of melody segmentation. Previous segmentation methods have been unable to construct hierarchical grouping structures because they have been focused on detecting the local bound-

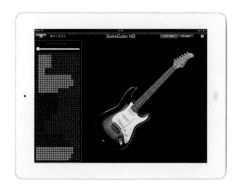

Fig. 9.4 ShakeGuitar

---

[1] Available at http://www.link.cs.cmu.edu/melisma/

aries of a melody (Cambouropoulos, 2006; Rodriguez-Lopez et al., 2014; Stammen and Pennycook, 1994; Temperley, 2001). A metrical structure analysis generated by GTTM, in contrast, is a kind of beat tracking. Current methods based on beat tracking (Davies and Bock, 2014; Dixon, 2001; Goto, 2001; Rosenthal, 1992) are only able to acquire the hierarchical metrical structure up to the bar level but not above that (e.g., at the two- and four-bar level).

9.4 Problems with Implementing GTTM

There are a number of features of GTTM that make it difficult to implement as a computer program. The main problems with implementation are discussed in this section.

9.4.1 Ambiguous Rule Definition

Some rules in GTTM are expressed ambiguously. For example, GPR4 is defined as follows (Lerdahl and Jackendoff, 1983, p. 346):

> **GPR4 (Intensification)** Where the effects picked out by GPRs 2 and 3 are relatively more pronounced, a larger-level group boundary may be placed.

The words "relatively" and "may be" in this sentence are ambiguous. The sentence also contains the phrase "more pronounced", but the comparison is unclear. Another example is that GTTM has rules for selecting proper structures when discovering similar melodies (called parallelism), but does not define similarity. To implement such ambiguous rules on a computer, we have to formalize the criteria for deciding whether each rule is applicable.

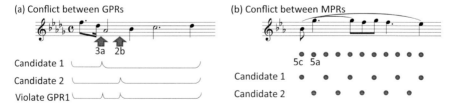

Fig. 9.5 Example of conflict between PRs

9.4.2 Conflict Among Preference Rules

Because there is no strict order for applying the GTTM rules, conflict between rules often occurs when applying them, resulting in ambiguities in analysis. Figure 9.5(a) shows a simple example of a conflict between GPR2b (Attack-Point) and GPR3a (Register). GPR2b states that a relatively greater interval of time between attack points initiates a grouping boundary, while GPR3a states that relatively greater pitch differences between smaller neighbouring intervals initiates a grouping boundary. Because GPR1 (alternative form) strongly prefers that note 3 in Fig. 9.5(a) should not form a group on its own, placing boundaries between notes 2 and 3 *and* between notes 3 and 4 is discouraged.

Figure 9.5(b) shows an example of conflict between MPRs 5c and 5a. MPR5c states that a relatively long slur results in a strong beat, and MPR5a states that a relatively long pitch event results in a strong beat. Because metrical well-formedness rule 3 (MWFR3) states that strong beats are spaced either two or three beats apart, a strong beat cannot be perceived at the onset of both the first and second notes.

To solve these problems, we have introduced the notion of *parameterization* in Sect. 9.5. Each rule in the theory should be given a weight, allowing the strength of its effect to be compared with that of other rules; this weight can be regarded as a parameter of the analysis process. In addition, we have externalized the hidden alternatives in the theory. This externalization in mechanizing GTTM includes introducing an algorithm for generating a hierarchical structure of the time-span tree. We call such weighting and externalization *full parameterization*. Employing these parameters together with statistical learning, we obtain a methodology to control the strength of each rule (described in Sect. 9.7).

9.4.3 Lack of Working Algorithm

Lerdahl and Jackendoff (1983) do not specify an algorithm for constructing a hierarchical structure because the preference rules only indicate preferred structures. For example, no algorithm is provided for acquiring a hierarchical grouping structure after acquiring local grouping boundaries in the grouping structure analysis. Also, there are many time-span reduction preference rules (TSRPRs) for selecting the head of a time-span, and there are various examples of analysis. However, no algorithm is presented for acquiring the hierarchical time-span tree. It is not realistic to first generate every structure that satisfies the WFRs and then select the optimal structure. For example, even for a musical fragment containing just 10 notes, there are 185,794,560 $(= 9^2 * 9!)$ possible time-span trees.

To solve this problem, in Sect. 9.5 we present an algorithm for acquiring the hierarchical structure, taking into consideration some of the examples in GTTM (Hamanaka et al., 2006).

9.4.4 Less Precise Explanation of Feedback Link

GTTM has various feedback links from higher-level structures to lower-level ones, e.g., GPR7 (time-span and prolongational stability) requires a grouping structure that results in a more stable time-span and/or prolongational reduction. However, no detailed description and only a few examples are given.

Other feedback links in the GTTM rules are not explicit. For example, analysing the results of a time-span tree strongly affects the interpretation of chord progression, and various rules are related to chord progression, e.g., MPR7 (Cadence) requires a metrical structure in which cadences are metrically stable.

To solve this problem, in Sect. 9.9, we propose a tool that allows a user to modify the automatic analysis process and manually edit the structures generated. A user can thus acquire a target analysis that reflects his or her interpretation of a piece of music by iterating the automatic and manual processes interactively and easily.

9.5 ATTA: Automatic Time-Span Tree Analyser

We extended the original theory of GTTM with full externalization and parameterization and proposed a machine-executable extension of GTTM called exGTTM (Hamanaka et al., 2006). The externalization includes introducing an algorithm to generate the hierarchical structure of a time-span tree using a combination of top-down and bottom-up processes. The parameterization includes introducing a parameter for controlling the priorities of rules, in order to avoid conflict among rules, as well as parameters for controlling the shape of the hierarchical time-span tree. We developed an automatic time-span tree analyser (ATTA) to implement exGTTM. The user can manually configure parameters and thus alter the analysis results generated by the program. An example of constructing a time-span tree is given in the following subsections.

9.5.1 Time-Span Segmentation

In the procedure of time-span reduction, we divide the entire piece into hierarchical time-spans. The division procedure, shown in Fig. 9.6, is as follows.

1. Regard all of the resultant groups in a grouping analysis as time-spans.
2. Divide a time-span into two at the strongest beat when a time-span in the lowest level includes more than one note.
3. Repeat 2 recursively.

Steps 1 and 2 correspond, respectively, to Lerdahl and Jackendoff's (1983, pp. 146–147) time-span reduction Segmentation Rules 1 and 2.

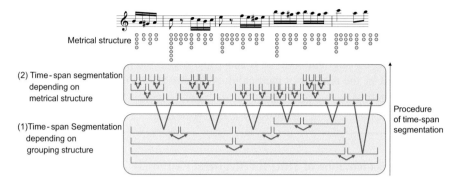

Metrical structure

(2) Time-span segmentation depending on metrical structure

(1) Time-span Segmentation depending on grouping structure

Procedure of time-span segmentation

Fig. 9.6 Time-span segmentation

9.5.2 Implementation of Time-Span Reduction Preference Rules

A piece of music is formed into a binary tree where, at each node, the more important branch extends upward as a head node. The selection of a head at each node is hierarchically computed from the lower level. Therefore, heads are selected from leaves to root branches. At the lowest level, every note is selected as a head for its time-span and the next level head is selected repetitively. In this section, we explain our implementations of time-span reduction preference rules (TSRPRs) 1, 3, 4, 8 and 9.

9.5.2.1 Calculation of Basic Parameters

For each level in the hierarchy, we provide the following basic parameters and rule-application principles.

We calculate four basic parameters:

ϕ_i Offset-to-onset interval (OOI) of ith gap between heads
ψ_i Inter-onset interval (IOI) of ith gap between heads
ξ_i Difference in pitch in semitones of ith gap between heads
μ_i Number of metrical levels in which ith head is a beat

The term i indicates the order of heads at the current level of time-span. For example, at the lowest level, the head order is the same as the note order. In the first three parameters, i represents the ith gap between heads, that is, the gap between the ith and $(i+1)$th head, while μ_i is the number of metrical dots for the ith head (i.e., the number of metrical levels in which the ith head is a beat). The probability that the ith head becomes a next-level head by the kth rule is denoted by $D_{\text{TSRPR}k}(i)$ where $0 \leq D_{\text{TSRPR}k}(i) \leq 1$ and $k \in \{1,3,4,8,9\}$. The basic parameters and $D_{\text{TSRPR}k}(i)$ are renewed at each level in the time-span tree, because the number of heads changes as a result of selecting heads at each hierarchical level.

9.5.2.2 Implementation of TSRPR1 (Metrical Position)

TSRPR1 prefers heads of time-spans to occur in relatively strong metrical positions. We normalize the strength between 0 and 1 and define the likelihood of an event being a head by the number of metrical dots divided by the maximum number of metrical dots, thus

$$D_{\text{TSRPR1}}(i) = \mu_i / \max_j \mu_j \, . \tag{9.1}$$

9.5.2.3 Implementation of TSRPR3 (Registral Extremes)

TSRPR3 is concerned with the pitch of a head. TSRPR3a weakly prefers an event to be a head if its melodic pitch is higher; while TSRPR3b weakly prefers an event to be a head if its bass pitch is lower. Thus, $D_{\text{TSRPR3a}}(i)$ returns a higher value if ξ_i is higher:[2]

$$D_{\text{TSRPR3a}}(i) = \xi_i / \max_j \xi_j \, . \tag{9.2}$$

Conversely, $D_{\text{TSRPR3b}}(i)$ returns a higher value if ξ_i is lower:

$$D_{\text{TSRPR3b}}(i) = 1 - \xi_i / \max_j \xi_j \, . \tag{9.3}$$

9.5.2.4 Implementation of TSRPR4 (Parallelism)

TSRPR4 involves parallelism and prefers heads to be in parallel positions in time-spans that are construed to be parallel. The parallelism between heads in the current hierarchical level's time-spans is evaluated using the same method as is used in the grouping and metrical analysis.

$D_{\text{TSRPR4}}(i)$ is calculated as follows. First, we calculate the similarity between the interval from head i with length r and the one from j with the same length. Next, for each i, we calculate the similarity for all js with the same length r. As Lerdahl and Jackendoff (1983) do not define an effective melodic similarity measure, we define our own. This similarity measure does not affect any other parts of the system, so we can substitute other methods such as that proposed by Hewlett and Selfridge-Field (1998).

Let us first consider the example in Fig. 9.7. In the figure, three notes out of four coincide with respect to onset time. Two notes out of the three also coincide with respect to pitch. In our implementation, we regard a greater number of notes having the same onset time as indicating greater similarity of melodies. Furthermore, the greater the number of instances where notes with the same onset time have the same pitch, the more similar the melodies are considered to be. In the example in

---

[2] There are several ways in which registral extremity could be explicated. We define $D_{\text{TSRPRk}}(i)$ as simply as possible in order to allow the user who is manipulating the parameters of ATTA to understand it easily.

Fig. 9.7 Similarity of parallel
phrases

Fig. 9.7, we use *notes* and their *durations* for explanation. However, when calculating
similarity of time-spans, we use *heads* and the *lengths of their time-spans*.

We formalize the above discussion as follows. We assume that the beginning and
ending heads possess beats and that the length of an interval r is a multiple of a
beat. Also, we assume that parallelism cannot occur between time-spans separated
by distances less than, say, a quarter note of a beat. Given a beat number m (≥ 1),
we write the interval of r beats from m as $[m, m+r)$, which does not include the
$(m+r)$th beat. We define the basic parameters as follows:

$N(m,r)$ the number of heads in $[m, m+r)$.
$O(m,n,r)$ the number of heads with the same time-span onset in
            $[m, m+r)$ and $[n, n+r)$.
$P(m,n,r)$ the number of heads with the same pitch, as well as the same
            time-span onset.

We define the similarity between intervals $[m, m+r)$ and $[n, n+r)$ with these parameters:

$$G(m,n,r) = \left\{ \frac{O(m,n,r)}{N(m,r)+N(n,r)} \times (1-W_m) + \frac{P(m,n,r)}{O(m,n,r)} \times W_m \right\} \times r^{W_l}, \quad (9.4)$$

where

W_m ($0 \leq W_m \leq 1$)   For each head, gives more weight to similarity of time-span
                    onset than similarity of pitch.
W_l ($0 \leq W_l \leq 1$)   Gives more weight to longer intervals, r, than shorter ones,
                    when parallel intervals overlap each other.

In the above expressions, $1 \leq m, n \leq L-r+1$ and $1 \leq r \leq L$, where L is the total
number of beats. Beyond this domain, we regard $G(m,n,r) = 0$. Note that r^{W_l} becomes 1 when $W_l = 0$, and as r increases, r^{W_l} also increases provided $W_l > 0$. Thus,
as W_l approaches 1, the similarity of longer intervals becomes more significant.

The similarity of head i in $[m, m+r)$ and j in $[m, m+s)$ is expressed by

$$A(i,j) = G(timespan_s(i), timespan_s(j), timespansize(i)), \quad (9.5)$$

where $timespan_s(i)$ is the first beat of the time-span including i, and $timespansize(i)$ is
the length (the number of beats) of the time-span including i. We define $D_{\text{TSRPR4}}(i,j)$,
by normalizing $A(i,j)$, as

$$D_{\text{TSRPR4}}(i,j) = \begin{cases} A(i,j)/A_{\max}, & \text{if } timespanpos(i) = timespanpos(j); \\ 0, & \text{otherwise.} \end{cases} \quad (9.6)$$

where $A_{max} = \max(A(i,1), A(i,2), \ldots, A(i,L))$ and $timespanpos(i)$ is the interval from the beginning of the time-span to i. Note that i indicates the order of heads at the current time-span level, after which $D_{TSRPR4}(i,j)$ renews at each level of time-span.

9.5.2.5 Implementation of TSRPR8 (Structural Beginning)

TSRPR8 prefers heads to be nearer the beginnings of their time spans. $D_{TSRPR8}(i)$ returns 1 if the head is at the beginning position; otherwise, 0:

$$D_{TSRPR8}(i) = \begin{cases} 1, & \text{if } i = i_{start}, \\ 0, & \text{otherwise,} \end{cases} \tag{9.7}$$

where i_{start} is the head at the beginning of the time-span.

9.5.2.6 Implementation of TSRPR9 (Structural Ending)

TSRPR9 prefers heads to be nearer the tails of their time-spans. $D_{TSRPR9}(i)$ returns 1 if the head is at the tail position, otherwise, 0:

$$D_{TSRPR9}(i) = \begin{cases} 1, & \text{if } i = i_{end}, \\ 0, & \text{otherwise,} \end{cases} \tag{9.8}$$

where i_{end} is the head at the tail of the time-span.

9.5.3 Generation of Time-Span Tree

We calculate the plausibility of head $D^{timespan}(i)$ using $D_{TSRPRk}(i)$ where $k \in \{1, 3a, 3b, 4, 8, 9\}$, as follows:

$$D^{timespan}(i) = B^{timespan}(i) + \sum_k \begin{cases} B^{timespan}(k) \times S_{TSRPR4}, & \text{if } D_{TSRPR4}(i,k) = 1, \\ 0, & \text{if } D_{TSRPR4}(i,k) = 0, \end{cases} \tag{9.9}$$

where

$$B^{timespan}(i) = \sum_k D_{TSRPRk}(i) \times S_{TSRPRk} \tag{9.10}$$

where $k \in \{1, 3a, 3b, 8, 9\}$. S_{TSRPRk} indicates the relative weighting associated with each rule. The larger this value is, the more strongly the rule acts. $B^{timespan}(i)$ represents the weighted summation of S_{TSRPRk} and $D_{TSRPRk}(i)$ where k is the rule number and $D^{timespan}(i)$ represents the sum of $B^{timespan}(i)$ and the summation of $B^{timespan}(k)$, where the ith head and kth head are parallel and consequently $D_{TSRPR4}(i,k) = 1$. A

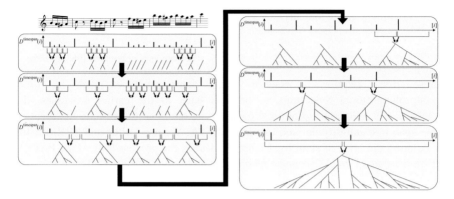

Fig. 9.8 Selecting next-level heads

hierarchical time-span tree is constructed by iterating the calculation of the plausibility of head $D^{\text{timespan}}(i)$ for the current heads and choosing the next-level heads (Fig. 9.8). If there are two candidate heads in the current hierarchical level, we choose the next-level head $\hat{h}$, as expressed by

$$
\hat{h} = \begin{cases} i, & \text{if } D^{\text{timespan}}(i) \leq D^{\text{timespan}}(j); \\ j, & \text{otherwise.} \end{cases}
\tag{9.11}
$$

The order of choosing the next-level head is the reverse of that of constructing time-spans in the time-span segmentation, as described in Sect. 9.5.2. $D_{\text{TSRPR}k}(i)$ and $D^{\text{timespan}}(i)$ are renewed at each level of the hierarchy, since i indicates the order of heads in the current level and changes at each level of time-spans.

9.6 FATTA: Fully Automatic Time-Span Tree Analyser

Although the ATTA has adjustable parameters for controlling the weight or priority of each rule, these parameters have to be set manually (Hamanaka et al., 2006). This takes a long time, because finding the optimal values of the settings themselves takes a long time. Therefore, we also developed a fully automatic time-span tree analyser (FATTA), which can automatically estimate the optimal parameters by introducing a feedback loop from higher-level structures to lower-level structures on the basis of the stability defined in GPR7 and TSRPR5 (Hamanaka et al., 2007):

GPR7 (Time-Span and Prolongational Stability) Prefer a grouping structure that results in more stable time-span and/or prolongational reductions.

(Lerdahl and Jackendoff, 1983, p. 52)

and

TSRPR5 (Metrical Stability): In choosing the head of a time-span T, prefer a choice
that results in more stable choice of metrical structure

(Lerdahl and Jackendoff, 1983, p. 165)

These rules require information from later processes, such as time-span/prolongational reductions, to be sent back to the earlier processes. To automatically estimate the optimal parameters, we have to evaluate the level of time-span tree stability derived using the ATTA. We use GPR7 and TSRPR5 for calculating the level of stability. Figure 9.9 shows the process flow of the FATTA, which consists of the ATTA and a feedback loop by the GPR7 and TSRPR5.

9.6.1 Implementation of GPR7 with Tonal Pitch Space

GPR7 is the rule applied to the feedback loop between the time-span/prolongational reduction and grouping structure analysis. This rule leads to a preference for a grouping structure that results in more stable time-span and/or prolongational reductions. The term D_{GPR7} indicates the degree of being a head by GPR7, which varies continuously between 0 and 1. We define D_{GPR7} as

$$D_{\mathrm{GPR7}} = \sum_i distance(p(i), s(i)) \times size(i)^2 / \sum_i size(i)^2 , \qquad (9.12)$$

where i indicates the head of the time-span, which has primary and secondary branches denoted by $p(i)$ and $s(i)$, respectively. The $distance(x, y)$ indicates the distance between notes x and y in the tonality of the piece, which is defined according to Lerdahl's (2001) theory of tonal pitch space. We normalized the distance from 0 to 1. The $size(i)$ indicates the length of the time-span that has head i. When calculating D_{GPR7}, we use the square of $size(i)$ for weightings for empirical reasons.

9.6.2 Implementation of TSRPR5

TSRPR5 is the rule applied to the feedback loop between the time-span reduction and the metrical structure analyser. This rule leads to a preference that results in a more stable choice of metrical structure in choosing the head of a time-span. The term D_{TSRPR5} indicates the strength of the rule in a given instance, which varies continuously between 0 and 1. We define D_{TSRPR5} as

$$D_{\mathrm{TSRPR5}} = \frac{1}{\sum_i size(i)^2} \begin{cases} size(i)^2, & \text{if } dot(p(i)) \geq dot(s(i)) , \\ 0, & \text{otherwise} , \end{cases} \qquad (9.13)$$

where $dot(x)$ indicates the number of metrical dots for note x.

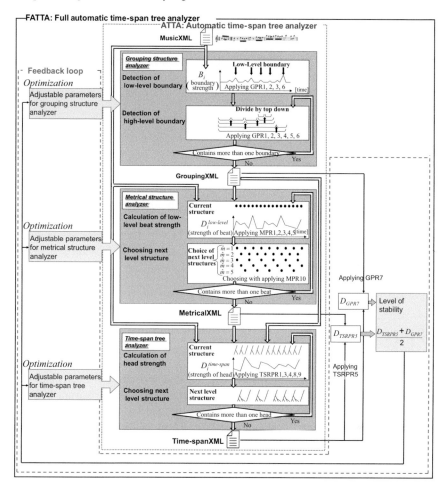

Fig. 9.9 Processing flow of fully automatic time-span tree analyser

9.6.3 Optimization of Adjustable Parameters

The optimal parameter sets of the ATTA can be obtained by maximizing the average of $D_{\mathrm{GPR7}}(0 \leq D_{\mathrm{GPR7}} \leq 1)$ and $D_{\mathrm{TSRPR5}}(0 \leq D_{\mathrm{TSRPR5}} \leq 1)$. Because there are 46 adjustable parameters, e.g., S_{rules} or W_m, it takes a long time to calculate all the combinations of parameter sets. To decrease the calculation time, we constructed the following algorithm:

1. Maximize the average of D_{GPR7} and D_{TSRPR5} by changing a parameter from minimum to maximum.
2. Repeat 1 for all parameters.

3. Iterate 1 and 2, as long as the average of D_{GPR7} and D_{TSRPR5} is increased from the previous iteration.

Finally, the FATTA can output only one analysis result without manual configuration. The computation time depends on the piece. In our experiment, described in Sect. 9.11, the shortest piece took about 5 minutes to analyse and the longest took about one week.

9.7 σGTTM Analyser

Our σGTTM system can detect the local grouping boundaries in a GTTM analysis by combining GTTM and statistical learning with a decision tree (Miura et al., 2009). A decision tree is a statistical learning method in which decisions are made by considering the value of each ramification. When learning the decision tree, bigger ramifications have a greater influence on the decision-making process, which causes it to be closer to the root position.

9.7.1 Abstraction of Training Data

As training data, we selected 100 MusicXML files that were then manually analysed by a musicologist and checked by GTTM experts. The value we want to know is the existence of a local grouping boundary (denoted as b), so that the value can be represented as 1 or 0 (boundary exists or not). A local GPR such as GPR 2 or 3 should also be abstracted because whether there is a boundary or not is determined by the local GPR. Considering that there is a local GPR for avoiding groups consisting of single notes, not only interval n (between note n and note $n+1$) but also the neighbouring intervals (interval $n-1$ and interval $n+1$) should be checked. Therefore, the data were abstracted in the form, B_{GPR}^{n}, where the superscript n refers to the nth interval and the subscript GPR means the type of local GPR, of which there are six (2a, 2b, 3a, 3b, 3c, 3d). The abstracted data for interval n can thus be denoted by $B_{2a}^{n}, B_{2b}^{n}, B_{3a}^{n}, B_{3b}^{n}, B_{3c}^{n}, B_{3d}^{n}$. Considering the neighbouring intervals, the total abstracted data can be represented by 18 ($= 6$ *rules* $\times 3$ $(n-1, n, n+1)$) elements. Each element has a value of 1 or 0 (rules exist or not). The existence of a local grouping boundary (b) is determined on the basis of these 18 elements.

9.7.2 Detecting the Priority of Local GPRs Using a Decision Tree

We chose C4.5, an algorithm developed by Quinlan (1993), to construct the decision tree. Figure 9.10 shows an example of the constructed decision tree. From the training data, we can obtain the conditional probability of local grouping boundaries for each

Fig. 9.10 Example of constructed decision tree

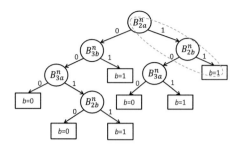

combination of local GPRs. When this conditional probability is 0.5 or more, GTTM detects the existence of a local grouping boundary ($b = 1$), and when it is less than 0.5, no boundary is detected ($b = 0$). For the example in Fig. 9.10, we detect a local grouping boundary when $B_{2a}^n = 1$ and $B_{2b}^n = 1$.

Unfortunately, the performance of the σGTTM analyser is not good enough because it can construct only one decision tree from 100 fragments of a piece and grouping analysis data, and it sometimes outputs irrelevant results.

9.8 σGTTM-II Analyser

We therefore developed the σGTTM-II analyser, based on the assumption that a piece of music has multiple interpretations; thus, it constructs multiple decision trees (each corresponding to a different interpretation) (Kanamori and Hamanaka, 2014).

The main idea with the σGTTM-II analyser is to reiterate clustering and statistical learning to classify each piece of music on the basis of the priority of the local GPR and to detect the local grouping structure more appropriately and easily. This analyser classifies a set of piece of music into clusters and outputs one detector of local grouping structure per cluster. We can detect a local grouping boundary more easily by choosing the most favourable detector from among various candidates.

First, we randomly classify training data into clusters. The training data of each cluster is then trained by a decision tree. After this training, a decision tree of GPR priority is constructed. We refer to this constructed decision tree as the "detector". In Fig. 9.11, clusters and detectors A and B mean that detector A is constructed in cluster A, detector B is constructed in cluster B, and so on. However, this part is problematic because an irrelevant analysed music structure might exist in a cluster. This is due to the detectors of each cluster representing the features of the entire music structure as the same for each cluster.

To solve this problem, the analyser evaluates the performance of each detector as it is constructed and then reclassifies the training data into clusters that generate the best performing detector. In Fig. 9.11, the clusters after reclassification are represented as A', B', and so on. The analyser then compares the training data of each cluster before $(A, B, \ldots)$ and after $(A', B', \ldots)$ reclassification. The less the training data in

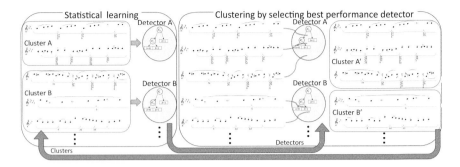

Fig. 9.11 Iterations of clustering and statistical learning

the cluster change, the more the constructed detectors cover the features such as priority of the local GPRs of all training data in the cluster.

After this comparison between clusters, if the total difference of training data in clusters before and after reclassification is more than two, the analyser returns to constructing detectors again, and if the total difference is less than one, or if reclassification has been performed 150 times, it outputs the training data and detectors of each cluster. Finally, we construct the most appropriate detector on the basis of the priority of the local GPRs of the entire training data in a cluster.

In our experiment in Sect. 9.11, we changed the initial number of clusters from 1 to 100 in order to compare the performance.

9.9 Interactive GTTM Analyser

We propose an interactive GTTM analyser that can use either the ATTA or σGTTM-II analyser (Fig. 9.12). We should point out that there is a trade-off relationship between the automation of the analysis process and variation in the analysis results (Fig. 9.13). Figure 9.14 shows an overview of our interactive GTTM analyser consisting of the ATTA/σGTTM-II analyser, GTTM manual editor, and GTTM process editor.

9.9.1 Manual Editor for GTTM

In some cases, ATTA may produce an acceptable result that reflects the user's interpretation, but in other cases it may not. A user who wants to change the analysis result according to his or her interpretation can use the GTTM manual editor. This editor has numerous functions including loading and saving the analysis results, calling the ATTA or σGTTM-II analyser, recording the editing history, undoing the editing, and autocorrecting incorrect structures.

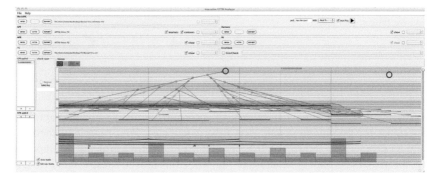

Fig. 9.12 Interactive GTTM analyser

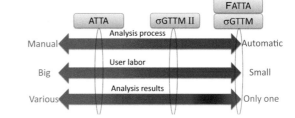

Fig. 9.13 Trade-off between automation of analysis process and variation of analysis results

9.9.2 Process Editor for GTTM

The analysing process with the ATTA and GTTM manual editor is complicated, and sometimes a user may become confused as to what he or she should do next, since there are three analysing processes in the ATTA and five editing processes in the GTTM manual editor. A user may iterate the ATTA and manual edit processes multiple times.

To solve this problem, we propose a GTTM process editor that presents candidates for the next process of analysis. A user can change the process simply by selecting the next process. The process editor enables seamless change in the analysis process by using the ATTA and, in the manual edit process, by using the GTTM manual editor, representing candidates for the next process of analysis. The representation method differs depending on the number of candidates for the next process.

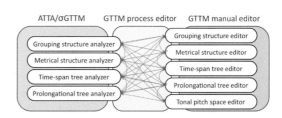

Fig. 9.14 Overview of interactive GTTM analyser

Fig. 9.15 Two types of solution for broken grouping structure

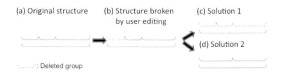

When there are multiple candidates, the process controlling function automatically opens the popup menu and shows the candidates. For example, if there is a grouping structure, as shown Fig. 9.15(a), and a user deletes a group at the upper left (Fig. 9.15(b)), the grouping structure of Fig. 9.15(b) is broken because GWFR3 does not hold. The GWFR3 has the constraint that a group must contain smaller groups. There are only two processes for solving this problem:

- Delete all the groups at the same level of the deleted group (Fig. 9.15(c)).
- Extend the group following the deleted group to the left (Fig. 9.15(d)).

The next process can then be executed depending on which of the two processes displayed in the popup menu the user selects.

9.9.3 Implementation on Client-Server System

The ATTA and σGTTM-II are updated frequently, and sometimes it is a little difficult for users to download an updated program. We therefore implement our interactive GTTM analyser on a client-server system. The graphic user interface on the client side runs as a Web application written in Java, while the analyser on the server side runs as a program written in Perl. This enables us to update the analyser frequently while allowing users to access the most recent version automatically.

9.10 GTTM Database

In constructing a musical analyser, test data from musical databases are useful for evaluating and improving the performance of the analyser. At present, we have a database of 300 analyses that are being used for researching music structural analysis (Hamanaka et al., 2014). At this stage, several rules in the theory allow only monophony, so we restrict the target analysis data to monophonic music in the GTTM database.

9.10.1 XML-Based Data Structure

We use an XML format for all analysis data. MusicXML was chosen as the primary input format because it provides a common exchange format for music notation, analysis, retrieval, and other applications (Recordare, 2011). We designed GroupingXML (XML format for grouping structure), MetricalXML (XML format for metrical structure), TimespanXML (XML format for time-span tree), and ProlongationalXML (XML format for prolongational tree) as the export formats for our four proposed analysers. We also designed HarmonicXML to express the chord progressions. The XML format is suitable for expressing the hierarchical grouping structures, metrical structures, time-span trees, and prolongational trees.

9.10.2 Score Data

The database should contain a variety of different musical pieces. When constructing it, we used 8-bar excerpts from whole pieces of music because the time required for analysing and editing by a musicology expert would be too long if whole pieces had to be analysed. We collected 300 monophonic 8-bar excerpts from classical music that included notes, rests, slurs, accents, and articulations entered manually with the *Finale* music notation software (MakeMusic, 2015). We exported the MusicXML using the *Dolet* plug-in.[3] The 300 whole pieces and the 8-bar segments were selected by a musicologist.

9.10.3 Analysis Data

We asked an expert musicologist to analyse manually the score data in a way that was faithful to GTTM by using the manual editor in the GTTM analysis tool to assist in editing the grouping structure, metrical structure, time-span tree, and prolongational tree. She also analysed the chord progression. Three other experts cross-checked these manually produced results.

9.11 Experimental Results

In this section, we compare the performance of our four analysers and show examples of the analysis results.

---

[3] http://www.musicxml.com/dolet-plugin/dolet-6-plugin-for-finale/

Fig. 9.16 Analysis of
Mozart's Sonata K 331

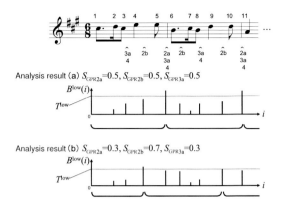

9.11.1 Analysis by ATTA

There are at least two plausible grouping structures for the main theme from Mozart's
Sonata K 331: a structure that has a boundary between notes 4 and 5 (Fig. 9.16(a));
or one in which there is a boundary between notes 5 and 6 (Fig. 9.16(b)). The
analyser can output either of these grouping structures by using exGTTM with
appropriate values for the strengths of grouping preference rules such as S_{GPR2a},
S_{GPR2b}, and S_{GPR3a}. In Fig. 9.16, T^{low}, where $0 \leq T^{\text{low}} \leq 1$, is an adjustable parameter
for the threshold in the low-level grouping boundary and $B^{\text{low}}(i)$ is a local strength,
represented by a real number between 0 and 1, defined so that the larger this value is,
the more likely the boundary is.

Figure 9.17 shows the analyses of two pieces, Beethoven's "Turkish March"
and the traditional English folk song "Greensleeves", that were set with the same
parameters. The numbers at the nodes in the tree in Fig. 9.17 indicate the applicable
rules. The parameters of ATTA are configured by hand, because the optimal values
of the parameters depend on a piece of music.

9.11.2 Comparison of ATTA and FATTA

We evaluated the performance of ATTA and FATTA using an F-measure given by the
weighted harmonic mean of precision P (proportion of selected groupings/dots/heads
that are correct) and recall R (proportion of correct groupings/dots/heads that are
identified). In calculating the F-measure of the grouping analyser and time-span tree
analyser, we did not consider the possibility that a low-level error is propagated up
to a higher level; we counted wrong answers without regard to the differences in
grouping levels and time-span levels.

The grouping, metrical, and time-span tree structures will change depending on
the adjustable parameters. To evaluate the baseline performance of ATTA, we used
the following default parameters: $S_{rules} = 0.5$, $T_{rules} = 0.5$, $W_s = 0.5$, $W_r = 0.5$, $W_l =$

0.5, and σ = 0.05. The parameter range of T_{rules}, W_s, W_r, and W_l was 0 to 1.0 and the resolution was 0.1. The parameter range of σ was 0 to 0.1 and the resolution was 0.01 (see Table 9.1).

On average, it took about 10 minutes per piece to find a tuning for the set of parameters (Table 9.1). As a result of configuring the parameters, each F-measure of ATTA outperformed the baseline. After automatic parameter optimization, FATTA achieved average F-measures of 0.48 for grouping structure, 0.89 for metrical structure and 0.49 for time-span tree (see Table 9.2). FATTA thus outperformed the baseline of ATTA, but did not perform as well as ATTA when the latter's parameter values were configured by hand.

9.11.3 Number of Clusters in σGTTM-II Analyser

When we first classify each piece of music into clusters, we do not know the optimum number of clusters for producing the best performance of the σGTTM-II analyser.

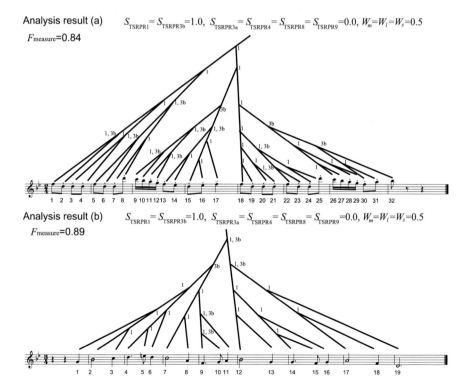

Fig. 9.17 Analysis of two pieces having same parameter sets: (a) Beethoven, "Turkish March", (b) English Traditional, "Greensleeves"

Table 9.1 Adjustable parameters

Structure	Parameter	Description
Grouping structure	$S_{\mathrm{GPR}j}$	The strength of each grouping preference rule. $j \in \{2a, 2b, 3a, 3b, 3c, 3d, 4, 5, 6\}$
	σ	The standard deviation of a normal distribution for GPR5.
	W_s	Preference weighting for end of a parallel segment in favour of the start of a parallel segment.
	W_r	Preference weighting of same rhythm in favour of the same register in parallel segments.
	W_l	Preference weighting for larger parallel segments.
	T^{GPR4}	The value of the threshold that decides whether GPRs 2 and 3 are relatively pronounced or not.
	$T^{low-level}$	The value of the threshold that decides whether transition i is a low-level boundary or not.
Metrical structure	$S_{\mathrm{MPR}j}$	The strength of each metrical preference rule. $j \in \{1, 2, 3, 4, 5a, 5b, 5c, 5d, 5e, 10\}$
	W_r	Preference weighting for same rhythm in favour of same register in parallel groups.
	$T^{\mathrm{MPR}j}$	The value of the threshold that decides whether or not each rule is applicable. $j \in \{4, 5a, 5b, 5c\}$
Time-span tree	$S_{\mathrm{TSRPR}j}$	The strength of each time-span tree preference rule. $j \in \{1, 3a, 3b, 4, 8, 9\}$

Therefore, we first tested the system with the number of clusters ranging from 1 to 100. This means the number of input clusters of the σGTTM-II analyser is one and the analyser outputs one detector, and then the number of input clusters is two and the analyser outputs two detectors, and so on. Thus, the analyser runs 100 times through the input and output. On each run, the analyser reiterates clustering and statistical learning multiple times until it is ready to output detectors. The results of this experiment are shown in Fig. 9.18.

Table 9.2 F-measures of ATTA and FATTA

	Baseline of ATTA	ATTA	FATTA
Grouping structure	0.46	0.77	0.48
Metrical structure	0.84	0.90	0.89
Time-span tree	0.44	0.60	0.49

Fig. 9.18 Performance of
σGTTM-II analyser

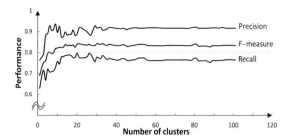

9.11.4 Comparison of ATTA, σGTTM Analyser, and σGTTM-II Analyser

We compared σGTTM-II with the ATTA and σGTTM analysers. The performance
of the σGTTM-II analyser was highest when the number of clusters was 10. The
σGTTM-II analyser outperformed the ATTA with adjusted parameters and the
σGTTM analyser when it came to selecting the optimum detector (Table 9.3).

9.11.5 Comparison of Analysis Results from Two Musicologists with GTTM Database

Another musicologist who had not been involved in the construction of the GTTM
database was asked to manually analyse the 300 scores in the database in a way that
was faithful to GTTM. We provided her with only the 8-bar-long monophonic pieces
but allowed her to refer to the original score as needed. When analysing pieces of
music, she could not see the analysis results already in the GTTM database. She was
told to take as much time as she needed. The time needed for analysing one song
ranged from fifteen minutes to six hours.

The analysis results for 267 of the 300 pieces were the same as the original results
in the GTTM database. The remaining 33 pieces had different interpretations, so we
added 33 new analysis results to the GTTM database after they were cross-checked
by three other experts.

For those 33 pieces with different interpretations, we found the grouping structure
in the database to be the same as that obtained by the musicologist. For all 33 pieces,
in the time-span tree, the root branch and branches directly connected to the root

Table 9.3 Performance comparison of ATTA, σGTTM
analyser, and σGTTM-II
analyser

	Precision	Recall	F-measure
ATTA	0.78	0.79	0.77
σGTTM	0.76	0.63	0.69
σGTTM-II	0.91	0.73	0.81

branch in the database were the same as those in the musicologist's results. In other words, only some branches were different in both analyses.

Of the pieces analysed, one of Johann Pachelbel's fugues in C major had the most unmatched time-spans when the analysis results in the GTTM database (Fig. 9.19(a)) were compared with those from the musicologist (Fig. 9.19(b)). From yet another musicologist, we obtained the following comments about different analysis results for this piece of music.

> **Analysis results from GTTM database** In analysis result (a), note 2 was interpreted as the start of the subject of the fugue (Fig. 9.19(a)). Note 3 is more salient than note 2 because note 2 is a non-chord tone. Note 5 is the most salient note in the time-span tree of the first bar because notes 4 to 7 are a fifth chord and note 5 is a tonic of the chord. The reason that note 2 was interpreted as the start of the subject of the fugue is uncertain, but a musicologist who is familiar with music before the Baroque era should be able to see that note 2 is the start of the subject of the fugue.
>
> **Analysis results from musicologist** Analysis result (b) was a more simple interpretation than result (a), in which note 1 is the start of the subject of the fuga. However, it is interesting that the trees of the second and third beats of the third bar are separated because both are the fifth chord.

The musicologist who made this comment said that it is difficult to analyse a monophonic piece of music from a contrapuntal piece of music without seeing the other parts. Chord information is necessary for a GTTM analysis, and a musicologist who is using only a monophonic piece of music has to imagine the other parts, which can result in multiple interpretations.

9.12 Conclusion

We have described our efforts to develop computer implementations of analytical methods based on music theory. By introducing full parameterization and statistical learning, we were able to improve the performance of our analysers. However, a few problems still remain. For example, none of our analysers can automatically analyse polyphonic music, which consists of several independent parts (Hamanaka et al., 2013). We plan to address this problem in future versions of the analyser.

The GTTM database contains analysis data for 300 monophonic pieces. However, the manual editor in our interactive GTTM analyser is designed to deal with polyphonic pieces. Although the analyser works only on monophonic pieces, a user can analyse polyphonic pieces by using the analyser's manual editor to divide polyphonic pieces into monophonic parts. We also attempted to extend the GTTM framework to enable the analysis of polyphonic pieces. We plan to publicize 100 pairs of polyphonic scores and the analysis results of the musicologists consulted in this study. Although the 300 pieces in the current GTTM database are only eight bars long, we

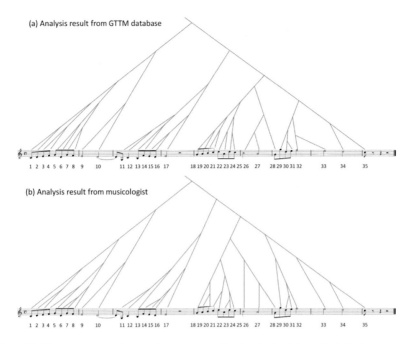

Fig. 9.19 Time-span trees of one part from a fugue in C major by Johann Pachelbel

plan to also analyse whole pieces of music by using the interactive GTTM analyser's slide bar for zooming piano-roll scores and GTTM structures.

Supplementary Material The interactive GTTM analyser and GTTM database are available online at http://www.gttm.jp/.

References

Cambouropoulos, E. (2006). Musical parallelism and melodic segmentation. *Music Perception*, 23(3):249–267.

Davies, M. and Bock, S. (2014). Evaluating the evaluation measures for beat tracking. In *Proceedings of the 15th International Society for Music Information Retrieval Conference (ISMIR 2014)*, pages 637–642, Taipei, Taiwan.

Dixon, S. (2001). Automatic extraction of tempo and beat from expressive performances. *Journal of New Music Research*, 30(1):39–58.

Goto, M. (2001). An audio-based real-time beat tracking system for music with or without drum-sounds. *Journal of New Music Research*, 30(2):159–171.

Hamanaka, M., Hirata, K., and Tojo, S. (2006). Implementing "A Generative Theory of Tonal Music". *Journal of New Music Research*, 35(4):249–277.

Hamanaka, M., Hirata, K., and Tojo, S. (2007). FATTA: Full automatic time-span tree analyzer. In *Proceedings of the 2007 International Computer Music Conference (ICMC 2007)*, pages 153–156, Copenhagen, Denmark.

Hamanaka, M., Hirata, K., and Tojo, S. (2008a). Melody expectation method based on GTTM and TPS. In *Proceedings of the 9th International Conference on Music Information Retrieval (ISMIR 2008)*, pages 107–112, Philadelphia, PA.

Hamanaka, M., Hirata, K., and Tojo, S. (2008b). Melody morphing method based on GTTM. In *Proceedings of the 2008 International Computer Music Conference (ICMC 2008)*, pages 155–158, Belfast, UK.

Hamanaka, M., Hirata, K., and Tojo, S. (2013). Time-span tree analyzer for polyphonic music. In *10th International Symposium on Computer Music Multidisciplinary Research (CMMR 2013)*, pages 886–893, Marseille, France.

Hamanaka, M., Hirata, K., and Tojo, S. (2014). Music structural analysis database based on GTTM. In *Proceedings of the 15th International Society for Music Information Retrieval Conference (ISMIR 2014)*, pages 325–330, Taipei, Taiwan.

Hamanaka, M., Yoshiya, M., and Yoshida, S. (2011). Constructing music applications for smartphones. In *Proceedings of the 2011 International Computer Music Conference (ICMC 2011)*, pages 308–311, Huddersfield, UK.

Hewlett, W. and Selfridge-Field, E. (1998). *Melodic Similarity: Concepts, Procedures, and Applications*, volume 11 of *Computing in Musicology*. MIT Press.

Hirata, K. and Hiraga, R. (2003). Ha-Hi-Hun plays Chopin's Etude. In *Working Notes of IJCAI-03 Workshop on Methods for Automatic Music Performance and their Applications in a Public Rendering Contest*, pages 72–73.

Hirata, K. and Matsuda, S. (2003). Interactive music summarization based on generative theory of tonal music. *Journal of New Music Research*, 5(2):165–177.

Hirata, K. and Matsuda, S. (2004). Annotated music for retrieval, reproduction. In *Proceedings of the 2004 International Computer Music Conference (ICMC 2004)*, pages 584–587, Miami, FL.

Kanamori, K. and Hamanaka, M. (2014). Method to detect GTTM local grouping boundaries based on clustering and statistical learning. In *Proceedings of the 2014 International Computer Music Conference (ICMC 2014)*, pages 1193–1197, Athens, Greece.

Lerdahl, F. (2001). *Tonal Pitch Space*. Oxford University Press.

Lerdahl, F. and Jackendoff, R. S. (1983). *A Generative Theory of Tonal Music*. MIT Press.

MakeMusic (2015). Finale. http://www.finalemusic.com/.

Marsden, A. (2011). Software for Schenkerian analysis. In *Proceedings of the 2011 International Computer Music Conference (ICMC2011)*, pages 673–676, Huddersfield, UK.

Miura, Y., Hamanaka, M., Hirata, K., and Tojo, S. (2009). Decision tree to detect GTTM group boundaries. In *Proceedings of the 2009 International Computer Music Conference (ICMC 2009)*, pages 125–128, Montreal, Canada.

Narmour, E. (1990). *The Analysis and Cognition of Basic Melodic Structures: The Implication–Realization Model*. University of Chicago Press.

Narmour, E. (1992). *The Analysis and Cognition of Melodic Complexity: The Implication–Realization Model*. University of Chicago Press.

Quinlan, J. (1993). *C4.5: Programs for Machine Learning*. Morgan Kaufmann.

Recordare (2011). MusicXML 3.0 tutorial. http://www.musicxml.com/wp-content/uploads/2012/12/musicxml-tutorial.pdf.

Rodriguez-Lopez, M., Volk, A., and Bountouridis, D. (2014). Multi-strategy segmentation of melodies. In *Proceedings of the 15th International Society for Music Information Retrieval Conference (ISMIR 2014)*, pages 207–212, Taipei, Taiwan.

Rosenthal, D. (1992). Emulation of human rhythm perception. *Computer Music Journal*, 16(1):64–76.

Schenker, H. (1935). *Der freie Satz*. Universal Edition. (Published in English as E. Oster (trans., ed.) *Free Composition*, Longman, New York, 1979.).

Stammen, D. R. and Pennycook, B. (1994). Real-time segmentation of music using an adaptation of Lerdahl and Jackendoff's grouping principles. In *Proceedings of the 3rd International Conference on Music Perception and Cognition (ICMPC 1994)*, pages 269–270, Liège, Belgium.

Temperley, D. (2001). *The Cognition of Basic Musical Structures*. MIT Press.

Yazawa, S., Hamanaka, M., and Utsuro, T. (2014). Melody generation system based on a theory of melody sequences. In *Proceedings of the International Conference on Advanced Informatics: Concepts, Theory and Applications*, pages 347–352.

Chapter 10
An Algebraic Approach to Time-Span Reduction

Keiji Hirata, Satoshi Tojo, and Masatoshi Hamanaka

Abstract In this chapter, we present an algebraic framework in which a set of simple, intuitive operations applicable to music can be flexibly combined to realize a target application and generate music. We formalize the concept of time-span tree introduced by Lerdahl and Jackendoff (1983) in their *Generative Theory of Tonal Music* (GTTM) and define the distance between time-span trees, on the hypothesis that this might coincide with the psychological resemblance between melodies heard by human listeners. To confirm the feasibility of the proposed framework, we conduct an experiment to determine whether the distance calculated on the basis of the framework reflects cognitive distance in human listeners. To demonstrate that the algebraic framework is computationally tractable, we present the implementation of a musical morphing system that, given two original melodies, generates an intermediate melody at any internally dividing point between them (i.e., at any ratio).

10.1 Introduction

The analogy between music and natural language has long been discussed (Aiello, 1994; Cook, 1994; Jackendoff, 2009; Molino, 2000; Sloboda, 1985). Our short-term memory plays an important role in understanding music as well as language (Baroni et al., 2011). Since short-term memory is used to realize a push-down stack, it can

Keiji Hirata
Future University Hakodate, Hakodate, Hokkaido, Japan
e-mail: hirata@fun.ac.jp

Satoshi Tojo
Japan Advanced Institute of Science and Technology (JAIST), Nomi, Ishikawa, Japan
e-mail: tojo@jaist.ac.jp

Masatoshi Hamanaka
Kyoto University, Clinical Research Center, Kyoto University Hospital, Kyoto, Japan
e-mail: masatosh@kuhp.kyoto-u.ac.jp

© Springer International Publishing Switzerland 2016   251
D. Meredith (ed.), *Computational Music Analysis*,
DOI 10.1007/978-3-319-25931-4_10

accept a context-free grammar (CFG) language. It is commonly accepted that human language is mostly generated by a CFG in Chomsky's hierarchy; at the same time, we often encounter linguistic phenomena that are context-sensitive (Stabler, 2004). Most sentences can be generated by CFGs, which have long distance dependency and a *tree* structure. Thus, we may assume that music is also governed by a CFG-like grammar. Many natural language researchers have tried to implement music parsers with CFG-like grammars (Steedman, 1996; Tojo et al., 2006; Winograd, 1968). For another example of the importance of short-term memory in music, we consider melodic recognition. In a piece of music, the identical *motif* or *phrase* appears repeatedly in time and/or in other voices. When we recognize such a motif/phrase, this suggests that we possess an ability to group consecutive notes or parallel phrases together with the help of short-term memory; this psychological phenomenon is called *Gestalt*.

Influenced by Noam Chomsky's framework of transformational generative grammar (Chomsky, 1957, 1965), Lerdahl and Jackendoff (1983) proposed their *Generative Theory of Tonal Music* (GTTM). GTTM consists of modules for grouping-structure analysis, metrical-structure analysis, time-span reduction, and prolongational reduction. The grouping structure analysis segments a piece of music into nested groups of varying sizes. The metrical structure analysis identifies the positions of strong and weak beats at the levels of a quarter note, half note, whole note, and so on.

The time-span tree is constructed on the basis of the results of the grouping structure and metrical structure analyses in a bottom-up manner: parts come together to form wholes, in accordance with the Gestalt principle. Time-span reduction represents the intuitive idea, originating from Schenkerian analysis, that, if we remove ornamental notes from a long melody, we obtain a simple melody that sounds similar. By time-span reduction, an entire piece of music can eventually be reduced to an important note or a tonic triad. Hence, the time-span tree stands for the progression of this time-span reduction.

Prolongational reduction represents musical intuitions relating to both the harmonic and melodic aspects of the global structure of a piece. In contrast to the time-span reduction, a prolongational tree is constructed in a top-down manner, by recognizing that parts of a piece—or even entire pieces—exhibit patterns of tension and relaxation. That is, given a homophonic (i.e., homorhythmic) sequence, an important note or chord is first selected, and the sequence is then split at that note or chord.

The rules of GTTM comprise well-formedness rules for specifying all the possible tree structures on the basis of analyses, along with preference rules for designating which of the possible tree structures to adopt. As described above, the time-span and prolongational trees represent aspects of the underlying structure of a piece. The theory attempts to look for a unique underlying structure by applying the preference rules. However, a piece can be interpreted in various ways, and, of course, the analysis occasionally derives more than one time-span tree and prolongational tree.

To understand the relationships between GTTM and Chomsky's generative grammar more precisely, let us compare the analysis process of GTTM with the derivation of a sentence using a generative grammar. In Fig. 10.1(a), the meaning of an utter-

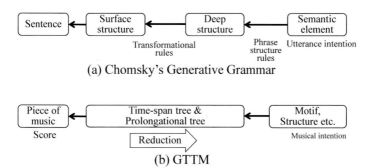

Fig. 10.1 Framework for giving meaning to a sentence and a piece of music

ance is represented by its semantic content, which is transformed into deep and then surface structures by applying the phrase structure rules and the transformational grammar. These grammar rules give meaning to a transformed tree structure. The direction of giving meaning is the same as that of producing a sentence.

The time-span tree and prolongational tree are generated from a motif and a global structure by an elaboration that is the opposite of reduction (Fig. 10.1(b)). The rules and the roles of tree structures in GTTM are different from those they have in linguistic generative grammars. Thus, Lerdahl and Jackendoff (1983, p. 9) state that

> we have found that a generative theory, unlike a generative linguistic theory, must not only assign structural descriptions to a piece, but must also differentiate them along a scale of coherence, weighting them as more or less "preferred" interpretations... The preference rules, which do the major portion of the work of developing analyses within our theory, have no counterpart in linguistic theory; their presence is a prominent difference between the forms of the two theories...

Thus, a generative grammar usually assigns different derivational trees to different sentences, mostly in a one-to-one manner (of course, there are exceptions). Accordingly, in language, the surface structure (a sentence) typically carries enough information to allow direct manipulation and/or calculation of a derivational tree. In contrast, in music, the relationship between the surface structure (a score) and a time-span tree/prolongational tree is more ambiguous due to the preference rules. The time-span/prolongational tree conveys more precise information of musical meaning than the surface structure.

This chapter is structured as follows. In Sect. 10.2, we describe an algebraic framework that formalizes the concept of a time-span tree. We introduce the concepts of reduction and maximal time-span, define the time-span tree operations *join* and *meet*, and provide a theoretical distance between time-span trees. On the basis of this development, in Sect. 10.3, we conduct an experiment to confirm the feasibility of the proposed framework. We compare the cognitive distances of human listeners, measured experimentally, with those calculated by the framework, and determine whether the theoretical distances correctly reflect our cognitive reality. Next, in Sect. 10.4, to illustrate that the combination of primitive operators straightforwardly

realizes a more complicated operation, we implement a musical morphing system.
As in the previous section, we employ human listeners to determine whether the
morphed melodies generated by the system properly correspond to internally dividing
points between the two original melodies given.

10.2 Formal Treatment of Time-Span Trees

In this section, we will explain our approach and introduce some fundamental definitions and properties relating to time-span trees.

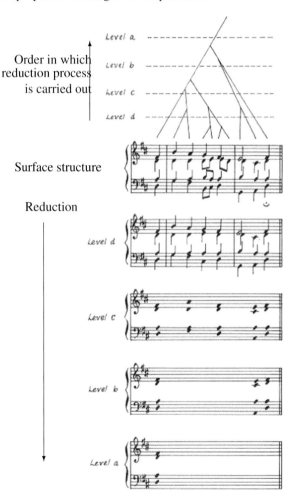

Fig. 10.2 Reduction hierarchy of the chorale, 'O Haupt voll Blut und Wunden' from the St. Matthew
Passion by J. S. Bach (from Lerdahl and Jackendoff, 1983, p. 115)

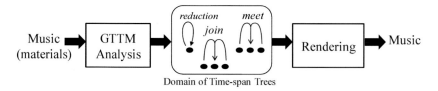

Fig. 10.3 Proposed framework for composition and creation

10.2.1 The Time-Span Tree as a Domain for Modification

We consider that in computational composition or arrangement, it is more promising to modify the time-span tree than the score itself for the following two reasons. First, the tree is more *meaningful*. The time-span tree is organized on the basis of the *reduction hypothesis* so that neighbouring pitch events[1] are compared in a bottom-up way in terms of importance, and the less important notes are absorbed into more significant ones in a hierarchical manner. As a result, we can obtain the fundamental skeleton of the music (Marsden, 2005). We illustrate this process in Fig. 10.2.[2] We can also use the reduction process to obtain a hypothesis regarding the original intent of the music, on an analogy with a Chomskyan analysis of natural language (Fig. 10.1(b)). This relates to the Schenkerian notion that we can retrieve the underlying structure of a piece by selecting pitch events that represent its tonality (Cadwallader and Gagné, 1998). This selection process exactly corresponds to the reduction hypothesis. In both theories, as each note is classified according to its rhythmic and/or tonal significance, it contributes to the formation of a specific *interpretation* of the music, and, for this reason, we claim that a hierarchical tree is more meaningful than a raw score.

Second, we can distinguish the realm of formal modification (i.e., composition and arrangement) from that of listening. In the former, we need to introduce a *rendering* process which is the reverse of music analysis. In a time-span reduction analysis, a tree is constructed on the basis of the reduction hypothesis; whereas, in the rendering process, a concrete piece of music is created—that is, a musical score is externalized and made performable and audible (Fig. 10.3). Rendering can be viewed as playing the role of resolving ambiguity in the musical surface, which relates to the raw score being less meaningful.

In general, the mapping from musical surfaces to time-span reductions is many-to-many: for a given piece, there is typically more than one possible time-span tree; and for a given time-span tree, there is typically more than one possible surface that has that tree (Marsden et al., 2013). Fig. 10.4(a) shows that two possible time-span

---

[1] A pitch event originally means a single note or a chord. In this work, we restrict our interest to homophonic analysis as the method of polyphonic recognition is not included in the original theory.

[2] Once a piece of music is reduced, each note with onset-offset and duration becomes a virtual note; it is only meant to be a pitch event that is salient during the corresponding time-span. Therefore, to listen to a reduced piece of music, we need a rendering process that compensates for this onset-offset/duration information.

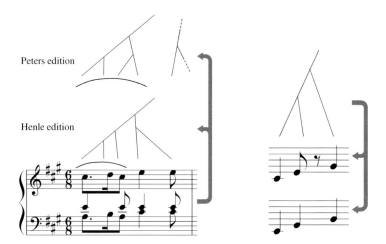

(a) 1-to-many mapping in time-span reduction analysis (from score to time-span trees)

(b) 1-to-many mapping in rendering (from a time-span tree to scores)

Fig. 10.4 Samples of ambiguity in time-span reduction analysis and rendering. In (a), the time-span reduction depends on slurring, which is different in different editions of the piece. In (b), two different surfaces have the same time-span reduction analysis

trees may exist, depending on the edition of a score that is used. Conversely, in Fig. 10.4(b), we show that one time-span tree can be rendered in multiple ways, as the time-span tree does not include rests and the occurrences of a rest in a score have various realizations.

10.2.2 Maximal Time-Span

The *head* pitch event of a tree is the most salient event in the tree—i.e., the salient event dominates the whole tree. As the situation is the same in each subtree, we consider that each pitch event has its maximal length of saliency, called its *maximal time-span*. For example, let us think of two maximal time-spans such that one's temporal interval is subsumed by the other's. Since the longer maximal time-span dominates a longer interval, we assume that the longer maximal time-span conveys more information and that the amount of information is proportional to the length of the maximal time-span. Then, we hypothesize that, if a branch with a single pitch event is reduced, the amount of information corresponding to the length of its maximal time-span is lost.

Figure 10.5(a) contains four contiguous pitch events: e1, e2, e3 and e4. Each has its own temporal span (duration on the surface score) denoted by thin lines: s1, s2, s3

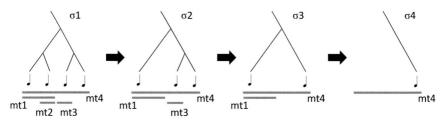

(b) Reduction proceeds by removing reducible maximal time-spans

Fig. 10.5 Reduction of time-span tree and maximal time-span hierarchy; thick grey lines denote maximal time-spans while thin ones denote pitch durations

and s4. Figure 10.5(b) depicts time-span trees and corresponding maximal time-span hierarchies, denoted by thick grey lines. The relationship between spans in (a) and maximal time-spans in (b) is as follows: at the lowest level in the hierarchy, a span is the same length as a maximal time-span: $mt2 = s2$, $mt3 = s3$; at the other levels, $mt1 = s1 + mt2$, and $mt4 = mt1 + mt3 + s4 = s1 + s2 + s3 + s4$. In the figure, if the duration of a quarter note is 12 ticks, then $s1 = s2 = s3 = s4 = 12$, $mt2 = mt3 = 12$, $mt1 = 24$, and $mt4 = 48$. That is, every span extends itself by concatenating the span at a higher level along the configuration of a time-span tree. When all subordinate spans are concatenated into one span, the span reaches the maximal time-span.

10.2.3 Lattice and Join/Meet

Here we consider a sequence of reductions from a tree. First, the relation between two trees on the sequence becomes the *subsumption relation*, which is the most fundamental mereological relation among real-world objects in knowledge representation. Since the reduction is generally made in a different order, the sequence bifurcates, and the set of reduced time-span trees becomes a partially ordered set (*poset*).[3] Moreover, if we can define *join* and *meet* in the set, the set becomes a *lattice*.

For the base case, we define *join* and *meet* of two time-spans (Fig. 10.6). If τ_A and τ_B are separated from each other (that is, they do not temporally overlap), *join* does not exist, while *meet* becomes empty, denoted by $\bot$. Next, we consider the inductive case for a time-span tree. Let σ_1 and σ_2 be time-span trees. σ_1 is subsumed by σ_2,

---

[3] Reflexive, anti-symmetric, and transitive set.

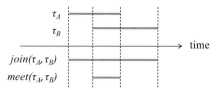

Fig. 10.6 *join* and *meet* operators applied to maximal time-spans

denoted by $\sigma_1 \sqsubseteq \sigma_2$, if and only if for any branch in σ_1 there is a corresponding branch in σ_2.[4] Now let σ_A and σ_B be time-span trees for pieces A and B, respectively.

> *join*: If there is a smallest unique y such that $\sigma_A \sqsubseteq y$ and $\sigma_B \sqsubseteq y$, we call such y the *join* of σ_A and σ_B, denoted by $\sigma_A \sqcup \sigma_B$.
> *meet*: If there is a largest unique x such that $x \sqsubseteq \sigma_A$ and $x \sqsubseteq \sigma_B$, we call such x the *meet* of σ_A and σ_B, denoted by $\sigma_A \sqcap \sigma_B$.

We illustrate *join* and *meet* in a simple example in Fig. 10.7. The '$\sqcup$' (*join*) operation takes eighth notes in the scores to fill sub-time-span trees so that a missing note in one side is complemented. On the other hand, the '$\sqcap$' (*meet*) operation takes $\bot$ for possibly mismatching sub-time-span trees, and thus only the common notes appear as a result.

In the process of unification between σ_A and σ_B, when a single branch is unifiable with a tree, $\sigma_A \sqcup \sigma_B$ chooses the tree while $\sigma_A \sqcap \sigma_B$ chooses the branch recursively. Because there is no alternative action in these procedures, $\sigma_A \sqcup \sigma_B$ and $\sigma_A \sqcap \sigma_B$ exist uniquely. Then, the partially ordered set of time-span trees becomes a lattice, as mentioned above, where $\sigma_A \sqcup x = \sigma_A$ and $\sigma_A \sqcap x = x$ if $x \sqsubseteq \sigma_A$. Moreover, if $\sigma_A \sqsubseteq \sigma_B$, then $x \sqcup \sigma_A \sqsubseteq x \sqcup \sigma_B$ and $x \sqcap \sigma_A \sqsubseteq x \sqcap \sigma_B$ for any x. In an algebraic lattice where

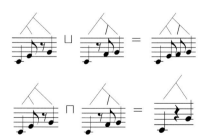

Fig. 10.7 Samples of *join* and *meet*

---

[4] Currently, we are concentrating on the theory for handling the configurations of trees and the time-spans based on the subsumption relation introduced above, ignoring pitch events. When we become able to define the proper subsumption relation between pitch events and integrate both subsumption relations into a coherent framework, the total theory for handling melodies will be realized. We consider Lerdahl's (2001) tonal pitch space theory to be a valid starting point for developing the subsumption relation between pitch events.

meet and *join* exist uniquely, we can easily confirm the absorption law as follows: $(\sigma_A \sqcup \sigma_B) \sqcap \sigma_A = \sigma_A$ and $(\sigma_A \sqcap \sigma_B) \sqcup \sigma_A = \sigma_A$.

Tojo and Hirata (2012) provided the data representation of a time-span tree in a feature structure and mentioned the algorithms for *join* and *meet*. The framework we propose can be considered algebraic because the set of time-span trees works as a domain and *join* and *meet* are operators defined on this set. Moreover, we consider this algebraic approach to be an implementation of Donald Norman's (1999, p. 67) design principle of 'Simplicity':

> Simplicity: The complexity of the information appliance is that of the task, not the tool. The technology is invisible.

That is, Norman argued that a user should be provided with a framework in which a set of simple, intuitive primitives can be flexibly combined to realize an intended function.

10.2.4 Reduction Distance

We call a sequence of reductions of a piece of music a *reduction path*. We regard the sum of the lengths of maximal time-spans lost in going from one tree to another in the reduction path as the distance between the two trees. We generalize the notion to be applicable not only between trees in the same reduction path, but also in any direction in the lattice. We presuppose that branches are reduced only one-by-one, for convenience in summing up distances. A branch is *reducible* only in the bottom-up direction, i.e., a reducible branch possesses no other sub-branches except a single pitch event as a leaf of a tree.

Let $\varsigma(\sigma)$ be a set of pitch events in a time-span tree σ and let $\#\varsigma(\sigma)$ be its cardinality. We denote by s_e the maximal time-span of event e. The distance $d_\sqsubseteq$ of two time-span trees such that $\sigma_A \sqsubseteq \sigma_B$ in a reduction path is defined as follows

$$d_\sqsubseteq(\sigma_A, \sigma_B) = \sum_{e \in \varsigma(\sigma_B) \backslash \varsigma(\sigma_A)} s_e.$$

For example in Fig. 10.5(b), the distance between $\sigma 1$ and $\sigma 4$ becomes $mt1 + mt2 + mt3$. Note that, if e3 is first reduced and e2 is subsequently reduced, the distance is the same. Although the distance appears at a glance to be a simple summation of maximal time-spans, there is a latent order in the addition, because the reducible branches are different in each reduction step. To give a constructive procedure to this summation, we introduce the notion of total sum of maximal time-spans as:

$$tmts(\sigma) = \sum_{e \in \varsigma(\sigma)} s_e \ ,$$

which we call the *total maximal time-span*. When $\sigma_A \sqsubseteq \sigma_B$, $d_\sqsubseteq(\sigma_A, \sigma_B) = tmts(\sigma_B) - tmts(\sigma_A)$. As a special case of the above, $d_\sqsubseteq(\perp, \sigma) = tmts(\sigma)$.

We now consider the requirements for the distance between two trees to be a true metric. As there is a reduction path between $\sigma_A \sqcap \sigma_B$ and $\sigma_A \sqcup \sigma_B$, it follows that

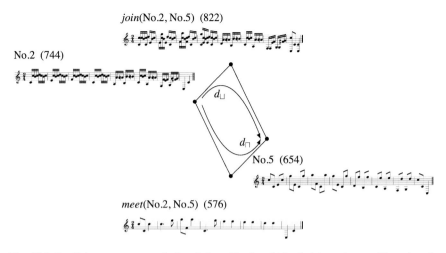

Fig. 10.8 Parallelogram composed of variations No. 2 and No. 5, *join* and *meet*. The values in parentheses are total maximal time-spans

$\sigma_A \sqcap \sigma_B \sqsubseteq \sigma_A \sqcup \sigma_B$ and that $d_\sqsubseteq(\sigma_A \sqcap \sigma_B, \sigma_A \sqcup \sigma_B)$ is unique. Suppose we define the following two distance metrics:

$$d_\sqcap(\sigma_A, \sigma_B) \equiv d_\sqsubseteq(\sigma_A \sqcap \sigma_B, \sigma_A) + d_\sqsubseteq(\sigma_A \sqcap \sigma_B, \sigma_B) \,,$$
$$d_\sqcup(\sigma_A, \sigma_B) \equiv d_\sqsubseteq(\sigma_A, \sigma_A \sqcup \sigma_B) + d_\sqsubseteq(\sigma_B, \sigma_A \sqcup \sigma_B) \,.$$

We immediately obtain the lemma, $d_\sqcup(\sigma_A, \sigma_B) = d_\sqcap(\sigma_A, \sigma_B)$, by the uniqueness of reduction distance (see Tojo and Hirata (2012) for the outline of a proof). From here on, we therefore omit $\{\sqcap, \sqcup\}$ from $d_{\{\sqcap, \sqcup\}}$, and simply express it as 'd'. Here, $d(\sigma_A, \sigma_B)$ is unique among the shortest paths between σ_A and σ_B. Finally, we obtain the triangle inequality:

$$d(\sigma_A, \sigma_B) + d(\sigma_B, \sigma_C) \geq d(\sigma_A, \sigma_C) \,.$$

For more details on the theoretical background, see Tojo and Hirata (2012).

We show an example in which, given two pieces, the *join* and *meet* are calculated (Fig. 10.8). The two pieces are taken from Mozart's variations K.265/300e '*Ah, vous dirai-je, maman*', variations No. 2 and No. 5. The value in parentheses shows the total maximal time-span of each time-span tree, as defined above. In Fig. 10.8, if we let the duration of a quarter note be 12 ticks, the total maximal time-span of variation No. 2 amounts to 744 ticks, which is the sum of the maximal time-spans of all notes contained in variation No. 2. Similarly, the total maximal time-span of variation No. 5 is 654 ticks. According to the definition of distance, we obtain $d_\sqcap = (744 - 576) + (654 - 576) = 246$, and $d_\sqcup = (822 - 744) + (822 - 654) = 246$. Notice that the four time-span trees form a parallelogram because the lengths of the opposite sides are equal. Then, we have confirmed the lemma on uniqueness of reduction distance in the proposed framework.

In general, *join* and *meet* of the time-span trees in Fig. 10.8 are possible as long as the left-/right-branching coincides in every subtree. However, we have enhanced the algorithm to tolerate the matching between two different directions of branching. In the current implementation, the *join* and *meet* operations have already been improved to handle unmatched-branching trees so that they preserve the results of *join* and *meet* in the matched-branching trees and satisfy the absorption law, $(\sigma_A \sqcup \sigma_B) \sqcap \sigma_A = \sigma_A$ and $(\sigma_A \sqcap \sigma_B) \sqcup \sigma_A = \sigma_A$, and the lemma, $d_{\sqcup}(\sigma_A, \sigma_B) = d_{\sqcap}(\sigma_A, \sigma_B)$, even for the unmatched-branching trees. For more details, see Hirata et al. (2014).

As described in footnote 4, since the subsumption relation between pitch events is not given, at present, the distance between pitch events is not calculated. Thus, we suppose that every pitch event occurring in a time-span tree is identical. Therefore, within the calculation of the distance between time-span trees, *join* and *meet* neither generate a homophonic pitch event nor a chord; that is, let e be such a pitch event, so we have $join(e, e) = meet(e, e) = e$.

10.3 Verification: Distance and Cognitive Similarity

In this section, we investigate whether the definition of distance correctly reflects cognitive reality. For this purpose, we employ human listeners to compare the distance with intuitive similarity.

The target set of pieces was Mozart's variations K.265/300e '*Ah, vous dirai-je, maman*' (known in English as 'Twinkle, twinkle little star'). The piece consists of the theme and 12 variations. In our experiment, we used the first eight bars of the theme and each variation (Fig. 10.9). Although the original piece includes multiple voices, our framework can only handle monophony; therefore, the original pieces were reduced to monophonic melodies. We did this by extracting salient pitch events from each of two voices, choosing a prominent note from a chord, and disregarding the difference in octave so that the resultant melody sounded fluid. In total, we used 8-bar excerpts from the theme and 12 variations and thus obtained 78 pairs to be compared ($_{13}C_2 = 78$).

For the similarity assessment by human listeners, 11 university students participated in our study, seven of whom had some experience in playing musical instruments. Each participant listened to all pairs of excerpts, $\langle m_1, m_2 \rangle$, in a random order without duplication, and ranked each pair for similarity on a 5-point scale, ranging from -2 (very different) through to 2 (very similar). To counteract a potential cold start bias, each participant first heard all 8-bar excerpts without ranking them. To avoid order effects, each pair of excerpts was presented in both possible orders on separate trials The average rankings were calculated for each participant and then for all participants. Finally, we computed a distance matrix based on the participants' responses.

For the theoretical estimation by the proposed theory, we used the reduction distance introduced in Sect. 10.2.4. In order to calculate the reduction distance, a unit of duration must be defined. We set this unit to be one-third of a sixteenth note so

Fig. 10.9 Monophonic melodies used in the experiment

that pieces in both duple and triple time could be represented (this is the same unit as used in the examples in Figs. 10.5 and 10.8). The correct time-span trees of the theme and 12 variations were first created by the authors and cross-checked against each other.

It was not easy to examine the correspondence between the results calculated by $d(\sigma_A, \sigma_B)$ and the psychological resemblance obtained by participants in the distance matrix. We thus employed multidimensional scaling (MDS) to visualize the correspondence. MDS takes a distance matrix containing dissimilarity values or distances among items, identifies the axes to discriminate items most prominently, and plots items on the coordinate system of these axes. Therefore, the more similar items are, the closer together they are in the resulting MDS solution.

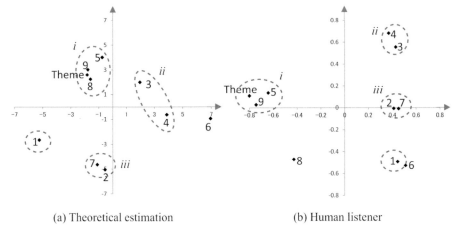

(a) Theoretical estimation   (b) Human listener

Fig. 10.10 Relative distances among melodies in multidimensional scaling

First, we used Torgerson's (1952) traditional method of scaling in MDS to plot the proximity among the 13 melodies. However, it was still difficult to find a clear correspondence between the results calculated by the reduction distance and the psychological resemblance obtained by participants. We then removed the results for variations 10–12 (Fig. 10.10). The contributions in MDS are as follows: (a) Theoretical estimation: the first axis (horizontal) = 0.21 and the second = 0.17; (b) Human listeners: the first axis (horizontal) = 0.32 and the second = 0.17.

In Fig. 10.10, we can see an interesting correspondence between (a) and (b) in terms of positional relationships among the 10 melodies. In both (a) and (b), we find that the Theme and variations 5 and 9 are clustered together (cluster *i*), that variations 3 and 4 form a cluster (*ii*) and that variations 2 and 7 form a cluster (*iii*). The positional relationships among clusters *i*, *ii* and *iii* resemble each other. The positional relationships between variation 1 and the others in (a) and (b) (except for variation 6) show a similar tendency. Since the contribution in the first axis of (a) is considered close to the second, by rotating the axes of (a) by 90 degrees anticlockwise, a more intuitive correspondence between (a) and (b) emerges. On the other hand, the discrepancy between them is quite apparent; the positional relationship between No.6 and the others is significantly different.

These results suggest a correspondence between our calculated reduction distance and intuitive similarity, if we focus on the rhythmic structure (Hirata et al., 2013). However, in order to claim that our methodology was adequate, we would need to include pitch similarity (see footnote 4). In addition, we need to carry out further comparisons with other distance measures, such as Levenshtein (edit) distance and Earth mover's distance.

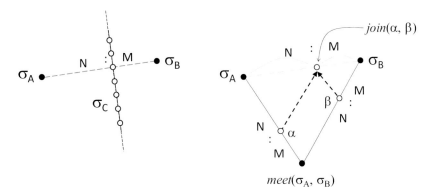

Fig. 10.11 There are infinitely many σ_Cs (left). On the right, the proposed morphing algorithm

10.4 Application: Melodic Morphing

In image processing, a morphing algorithm takes two images and finds an intermediate image. In a similar way, we now propose a new method for composing an intermediate piece of music, given two existing variations with a common theme. Let σ_A and σ_B be two time-span trees of music, and σ_C be the expected result of morphing; we require σ_C to reside at a point between σ_A and σ_B that internally divides the distance between these two in the ratio $M : N$, calculated in terms of the total sum of maximal time-spans (denoted as *tmts* in Sect. 10.2.4). Note that there are uncountably many σ_Cs such that the ratio of the distance between σ_A and σ_C to that between σ_C and σ_B is $M : N$. This is because σ_C resides at any point on the straight line that crosses at such an internally dividing point of $M : N$ and forms an angle of 90 degree with the line segment between σ_A and σ_B (the left-hand side of Fig. 10.11). Thus, we should restrict σ_C to the one that resides on the line segment between σ_A and σ_B, respectively.

Our morphing algorithm, shown on the right-hand side of Fig. 10.11 (Hirata et al., 2014), consists of the following steps:

1. Given the time-span trees of two melodies σ_A and σ_B, calculate $meet(\sigma_A, \sigma_B)$.
2. Find a time-span tree α that divides the line between σ_A and $meet(\sigma_A, \sigma_B)$ in the ratio of $N : M$ by removing pitch events in order from σ_A.
3. Similarly, find β that divides the line between σ_B and $meet(\sigma_A, \sigma_B)$ in the ratio of $M : N$.
4. Calculate $join(\alpha, \beta)$.
5. Obtain a real piece of music by rendering the result of $join(\alpha, \beta)$.

We see that the four time-span trees, $\{\alpha, \beta, meet(\sigma_A, \sigma_B), join(\alpha, \beta)\}$, form a parallelogram, as in Fig. 10.8. Clearly, in terms of the distance between σ_A and σ_B, we have $d(\sigma_A, \sigma_B) = d(\sigma_A, join(\alpha, \beta)) + d(join(\alpha, \beta), \sigma_B)$. Moreover, $tmts(\sigma_A) \leq tmts(join(\sigma_A, \sigma_B)) \leq tmts(\sigma_B)$ holds if $tmts(\sigma_A) \leq tmts(\sigma_B)$.[5]

Here, we add two more comments on the morphing algorithm. The first concerns the unmatched-branching in *join*, i.e., the unification of left- and right-branching trees. In the current implementation, we interpret the value of *join* as the superimposition of the differently branching nodes of two time-span trees. Thus, the result of *join* simply becomes a chord of two notes sounding simultaneously. Otherwise, for instance, it could be rendered as a transformation of the superimposed time-spans.[6]

The second issue concerns the rendering algorithm itself. The current rendering algorithm works in a top-down manner so that a maximal time-span is basically regarded as a horizontal line segment in a piano-roll representation, and the time-spans at lower levels (closer to the leaves) overwrite those at higher levels. Thus, the entirety of the maximal time-span may be overwritten by the lower-level time-spans; that is, even though a pitch event is quite salient, it may become inaudible, or its assigned duration in a real score may become very short. Consequently, there are cases where the simple top-down algorithm does not generate a proper melody. Thus, we are considering algorithms that, for example, integrate some bottom-up process with the current top-down one; alternatively, we may employ a new process, based on GTTM, for determining whether the rendering process generates a correct melody.

The morphing algorithm is implemented in SWI-Prolog (SWI, 1987). The target set of pieces was again Mozart's variations K.265/300e 'Ah, vous dirai-je, maman'. In this experiment, we took the first 8 bars of each of the variations 1, 2, and 5 as the sources for morphing (Fig. 10.12). We have chosen these three variations because, for every pair of these three variations, we can calculate *join*—that is, the maximal time-spans are all correctly concatenated. The morphed melodies are shown in Fig. 10.12 between the scores of the variations. For example, "No.2&No5 1:1" means the morphed melody at the midpoint of variations 2 and 5. Ratio "1:3" indicates the position of the internally dividing point, e.g., "No.2&No5 1:3" means the internally dividing point is closer to variation 2 than it is to variation 5. Thus, the bottom three melodies in Fig. 10.12 are formed by morphing variations 1 and 5, with different ratios of internal division. We see that the melodic patterns are gradually changed in accordance with the ratio in distance.

Next, taking "No.2&No.5 1:1" as an example, we examine the morphing calculation in more detail. For convenience of explanation, we show only the first bars of variations 2 and 5 and intermediate time-span trees α and β (Fig. 10.13). In the figure, the intermediate time-span trees are shown in the rendered melodies. Time-span tree α is generated by dividing σ_A (variation 2) and $meet(\sigma_A, \sigma_B)$ in the ratio of $1:1$. Then, α is generated by removing some reducible branches in σ_A one-by-one so that $tmts(\alpha) = (tmts(\sigma_A) + tmts(meet(\sigma_A, \sigma_B)))/2$. This condition means that $tmts(\alpha)$ is positioned at the centre of $tmts(\sigma_A)$ and $tmts(meet(\sigma_A, \sigma_B))$. Similarly, β is generated by removing some reducible pitch events in σ_B. Finally, by *joining* α and β, we obtain the first bar of "No.2&No.5 1:1" in Fig. 10.12.

---

[5] *tmts* means total maximal time-span, as introduced in Sect. 10.2.4.

[6] This resembles the notion of a transformation head (Lerdahl and Jackendoff, 1983, p. 155).

Fig. 10.12 Variations 1, 2, and 5, and morphed melodies between them

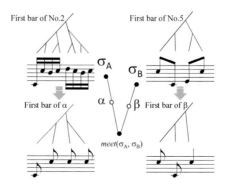

Fig. 10.13 Detailed morphing calculation of first bars of No.2&No.5 1:1

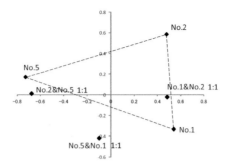

Fig. 10.14 Relative distance among variations and morphed melodies according to the impression of human listeners

For the similarity assessment of the morphed melodies by human listeners, six university students participated in our study, four of whom had played musical instruments for five years or more. We used the same experimental method as described in Sect. 10.3. A participant listened to all pairs $\langle m_1, m_2 \rangle$ in a random order without duplication, where m_i ($i \in \{1,2\}$) were either variations 1, 2 or 5 or the morphed melodies between them, such as "No.2&No.5 $M : N$". The experimental results were used to construct a distance matrix between these three variations and the morphed melodies between them. We then visualized the results using multidimensional scaling (MDS) (Fig. 10.14).

As can be seen in Fig. 10.14, for variation pairs, $\langle 1,2 \rangle$ and $\langle 1,5 \rangle$, the morphed melodies lie near the midpoints between the original variations, as expected. On the other hand, the position of "No.2&No.5 1:1" is problematic. As can be seen in Fig. 10.12, the number of notes in "No.2&No.5 1:1", which is supposed to be at the midpoint between variations 2 and 5, seems to be the average of the numbers of notes in variations 2 and 5. However, "No.2&No.5 1:1" is almost entirely made of eighth notes, and, as a result, many notes co-occur temporally. This may help to explain why this intermediate melody was perceived by participants as being more similar to variation 5 than variation 2.

10.5 Conclusions

In this chapter, we began by focusing on the structural information provided by a time-span reduction tree produced in accordance with Lerdahl and Jackendoff's (1983) *Generative Theory of Tonal Music* (GTTM), where the process of reduction reflects the hierarchical abstraction of the music. Then, we introduced the concept of *maximal time-span* and formalized the time-span tree; thus, as the subsumption relation exists between trees, the set of trees is a partially ordered set (*poset*) and is qualified as a domain for computational processing and modification. Next, we defined such primitive operations as *join/meet* on this domain, thus generating a *distributive lattice* from this poset. We are then able to define more complicated algebraic operations, combining *join/meet* operations. As we can numerically measure the length of a maximal time-span, we can define the notion of a distance between trees on a reduction path as being the sum of reduced time-spans. Extending this idea, we were able to define the distance between any two arbitrarily chosen trees in the lattice.

To assess the feasibility of the proposed framework, we conducted two experiments. In the first, we focused on the similarity between variations, and compared the reduction distance of our framework with the psychological distance of human intuition. As we discussed in Sect. 10.3, we found a correspondence between the computed reduction distance and experimentally determined intuitions of similarity, when we focused on rhythmic structure. However, further experiments need to be carried out on distance measures that take pitch structure into account, and these measures need to be compared with other metrics that have been proposed in the literature. Next, we implemented a music morphing system in order to illustrate that a combination of primitive operators realizes a more complicated operation. Since the distance between time-span trees defined in our framework satisfies the proper geometric properties, we could locate the internally dividing point on a line segment with a simple ratio. We also found that such geometric positioning coincides to some extent with the cognitive intuition of human listeners.

In order to develop and deploy our proposed framework, we need to consider the following issues. The first concerns *music rendering*, which is the process of realizing a musical score from a time-span tree as we discussed in Sect. 10.2.1. In fact, the applicability of our framework seems to depend strongly on the quality of the rendering. There are many possible algorithms for the rendering process besides the one described in Sect. 10.4. Ideally, a rendering algorithm would restore the original pitch and duration of each note, since the algorithm can be viewed as the reverse of the analysis process shown in Fig. 10.3. However, this is rarely the case in practice. One practical strategy might be to employ machine learning on a large database of pieces paired with their time-span trees. Here, we considered the "round-trip" scenario in which a time-span tree, obtained by carrying out a time-span reduction analysis, can be rendered as a real score which can then be re-analysed to generate a time-span tree. Conversely, we could first have considered the process of generating a tree from a musical surface, and then rendering the tree again to produce a (possibly different) piece of real music. In this way, we would be able to assess the fidelity of the analysis and rendering processes.

Thus far, we have provided only *meet* and *join* as primitive operators and shown an example of music morphing by the combination of these operations. Indeed, if we can extend the notion of such simple arithmetic operations in the domain of time-span trees, we will be able to benefit from richer music manipulation systems. An even more expressive algebra might be achieved by introducing a complement or inverse element to make the set a *group*. As *join* behaves intuitively as addition and *meet* as multiplication, introducing a complement could enhance the algebra by allowing operations analogous to subtraction and division. As the current lattice we have obtained is distributive, in our future work, we intend to employ the *relative pseudo-complement* for each tree and apply it to a new arithmetic operation in a pseudo-Boolean (Heyting) algebra. This would provide us with much more expressive methods for arranging time-span trees.

Although we have selected time-span trees as the semantic domain in our framework, there are other possibilities. For example, we could incorporate the concept of reduction into the implication–realization theory (Narmour, 1990). This is another direction that we intend to explore in our future work.

Acknowledgements The authors thank the anonymous reviewers for their valuable and essential comments and suggestions, which greatly contributed to improving the quality of this chapter. This work was supported by JSPS KAKENHI Grant Numbers 20300035, 23500145, 25330434 and 26280089.

References

Aiello, R. (1994). Music and language: Parallels and contrasts. In Aiello, R. and Sloboda, J., editors, *Musical Perceptions*, pages 40–63. Oxford University Press.

Baroni, M., Dalmonte, R., and Caterina, R. (2011). Salience of melodic tones in short-term memory: Dependence on phrasing, metre, duration, register tonal hierarchy. In Deliège, I. and Davidson, J., editors, *Music and the Mind: Essays in honour of John Sloboda*, pages 139–160. Oxford University Press.

Cadwallader, A. and Gagné, D. (1998). *Analysis of Tonal Music: A Schenkerian Approach*. Oxford University Press.

Chomsky, N. (1957). *Syntactic Structures*. Mouton de Gruyter.

Chomsky, N. (1965). *Aspects of the Theory of Syntax*. MIT Press.

Cook, N. (1994). Perception—A perspective from music theory. In Aiello, R. and Sloboda, J., editors, *Musical Perceptions*, pages 64–95. Oxford University Press.

Hirata, K., Tojo, S., and Hamanaka, M. (2013). Cognitive similarity grounded by tree distance from the analysis of K.265/300e. In Aramaki, M., e. a., editor, *Music and Motion: Proceedings of the 10th International Symposium on Computer Music Multidisciplinary Research (CMMR 2013)*, volume 8905 of *Lecture Notes in Computer Science*, pages 589–605, Marseille, France.

Hirata, K., Tojo, S., and Hamanaka, M. (2014). Algebraic Mozart by tree synthesis. In *Proceedings of the Joint 40th International Computer Music Conference and 11th Sound and Music Computing Conference (ICMC/SMC 2014)*, pages 991–997, Athens, Greece.

Jackendoff, R. (2009). Parallels and nonparallels between language and music. *Music Perception*, 26(3):195–204.

Lerdahl, F. (2001). *Tonal Pitch Space*. Oxford University Press.

Lerdahl, F. and Jackendoff, R. S. (1983). *A Generative Theory of Tonal Music*. MIT Press.

Marsden, A. (2005). Generative structural representation of tonal music. *Journal of New Music Research*, 34(4):409–428.

Marsden, A., Hirata, K., and Tojo, S. (2013). Towards computable procedures for deriving tree structures in music: Context dependency in GTTM and Schenkerian theory. In *Proceedings of the 10th Sound and Music Computing Conference (SMC 2013)*, pages 360–367, Stockholm, Sweden.

Molino, J. (2000). Toward an evolutionary theory of music and language. In Wallin, N. L., Merker, B., and Brown, S., editors, *The Origins of Music*, pages 165–176. MIT Press.

Narmour, E. (1990). *The Analysis and Cognition of Basic Melodic Structure: The Implication–Realization Model*. University of Chicago Press.

Norman, D. (1999). *The Invisible Computer*. MIT Press.

Sloboda, J. (1985). *The Musical Mind: The Cognitive Psychology of Music*. Oxford University Press.

Stabler, E. P. (2004). Varieties of crossing dependencies: Structure dependence and mild context sensitivity. *Cognitive Science*, 28(4):699–720.

Steedman, M. (1996). The blues and the abstract truth: Music and mental models. In Garnham, A. and Oakhill, J., editors, *Mental Models In Cognitive Science*, pages 305–318. Psychology Press.

SWI (1987). SWI-Prolog. `http://www.swi-prolog.org/` Accessed on 20 December 2014.

Tojo, S. and Hirata, K. (2012). Structural similarity based on time-span tree. In *Proceedings of the 9th International Symposium on Computer Music Modeling and Retrieval (CMMR 2012)*, pages 645–660, London, UK.

Tojo, S., Oka, Y., and Nishida, M. (2006). Analysis of chord progression by HPSG. In *Proceedings of the IASTED International Conference on Artificial Intelligence and Applications (AIA 2006)*, Innsbruck, Austria.

Torgerson, W. S. (1952). Multidimensional scaling: I. Theory and method. *Psychometrika*, 17(4):401–419.

Winograd, T. (1968). Linguistics and the computer analysis of tonal harmony. *Journal of Music Theory*, 12(1):2–49.

Part V
Motivic and Thematic Analysis

Chapter 11
Automated Motivic Analysis: An Exhaustive Approach Based on Closed and Cyclic Pattern Mining in Multidimensional Parametric Spaces

Olivier Lartillot

Abstract Motivic analysis provides very detailed understanding of musical compositions, but is also particularly difficult to formalize and systematize. A computational automation of the discovery of motivic patterns cannot be reduced to a mere extraction of all possible sequences of descriptions. The systematic approach inexorably leads to a proliferation of redundant structures that needs to be addressed properly. Global filtering techniques cause a drastic elimination of interesting structures that damages the quality of the analysis. On the other hand, a selection of closed patterns allows for lossless compression. The structural complexity resulting from successive repetitions of patterns can be controlled through a simple modelling of cycles. Generally, motivic patterns cannot always be defined solely as sequences of descriptions in a fixed set of dimensions: throughout the descriptions of the successive notes and intervals, various sets of musical parameters may be invoked. In this chapter, a method is presented that allows for these *heterogeneous* patterns to be discovered. Motivic repetition with local ornamentation is detected by reconstructing, on top of "surface-level" monodic voices, longer-term relations between non-adjacent notes related to deeper structures, and by tracking motives on the resulting syntagmatic network. These principles are integrated into a computational framework, the *MiningSuite*, developed in Matlab.

11.1 Systematic and Automated Motivic Analysis

One main dimension of music analysis is related to the repetition of particular sequences and their development throughout pieces of music. These sequential repetitions form core theoretical aspects of music, whose actual denomination (motive, theme, cell, etc.) depends on their specificity within genres, the way they repeat within pieces and their sizes (cells and motives typically correspond to very short patterns,

Olivier Lartillot
Department of Architecture, Design and Media Technology, Aalborg University, Aalborg, Denmark
e-mail: ol@create.aau.dk

© Springer International Publishing Switzerland 2016   273
D. Meredith (ed.), *Computational Music Analysis*,
DOI 10.1007/978-3-319-25931-4_11

whereas themes are typically several bars in length). Studying these repetitions is an important part of the analytical characterization of particular pieces of music, as well as a means of deciphering the stylistic particularities of pieces in the context of other related works (e.g., other works by the same composer or in the same genre or from the same period).

Throughout the long tradition of motivic analysis (understood in a broad sense to include thematic analysis), one can appreciate the value but also the possible limitations of analyses carried out entirely by hand by musicologists, essentially driven by musical intuition. Music reveals itself as a hugely rich and complex structure, that cannot be easily grasped by human endeavour, no matter how expert it might be. Twentieth-century musicology, nurtured by the advent of linguistics, structural anthropology, semiology and cognitive science (Nattiez, 1990; Ruwet, 1987), proclaimed the need for more formalized and systematic analytical processes. Yet no working methodology towards that aim has yet been initiated, due to the huge structural complexity underlying this issue. Systematic attempts have been hampered by the underlying complexity of possible strategies and structures. Formalized descriptions of segmentation strategies offered by psychological and cognitive studies might be utilized as a means of guiding and making discovery processes explicit.

Computational modelling seems to be the most natural way of formalizing and automating thematic and motivic analysis, allowing for exhaustive analyses of sizeable pieces of music to be carried out. Yet, it is still a struggle to control the combinatorial explosion of structures and to offer musically relevant analyses. The main question of how to model such analytical processes remains open. This chapter presents a model that may offer an answer to these problems. Section 11.2 introduces the general principles of the approach that can discover motives defined along multiple parametric dimensions, such that each successive note of the motivic pattern can be defined on different parameters. Section 11.3 explains the issues related to structural proliferation of redundant structures. We show how these questions have been addressed in previous work and how a solution based on closed and cyclic patterns allows for a compact, but detailed structural analysis. Section 11.4 generalizes the model to the study of ornamented patterns.

11.2 Heterogeneous Multiparametric Pattern Mining

11.2.1 Why Heterogeneous Patterns?

What is a *motive*? At first sight, it could be considered a sequence of notes that is repeated throughout a piece or a corpus of pieces of music. However, motives can be transformed in various ways (e.g., transposed), so that what is repeated are not the notes themselves, but more generally musical *descriptions*. So a motive is a *pattern* representing a sequence of descriptions that is repeated at least once in a piece of music.[1] Each successive description represented by a pattern will be called the *pattern's individual description*. Each sequence of notes in the score whose sequence of descriptions is compatible with the sequence of descriptions defined by a pattern forms an *occurrence* of that pattern.

Music is a complex signal that conveys a lot of information:

1. Scores contain many notes, and, at each instant, several of them can sound together to form chords along multiple instrumental voices.
2. Each note conveys data along several parameters, related to diverse musical dimensions (pitch, rhythm, accentuation, etc.) and to the musical context: a metrical grid determines metrical positions, tonal/modal scales govern diatonic representations of pitches, pitch intervals and gross contours can be defined in particular with the previous note, rhythmic values are defined with respect to the next note and so on.
3. A large range of structures can be inferred from those configurations, based on motivic repetition, local (dis)continuities along the various parametric dimensions and so on.

In this chapter, the focus is on monodic music, consisting of a succession of notes without superpositions. Hence we ignore point 1 above, but still have to consider points 2 and 3. Concerning point 3, this chapter will mainly address the question of motivic repetition. However, in Sect. 11.4.2, local (dis)continuities are discussed, particularly with respect to how they interact with motivic repetition.

According to point 2, the successive descriptions that form a motive can be defined along various musical dimensions. In previous studies this has been addressed either by the notion of "viewpoints" (Conklin and Anagnostopoulou, 2001) (see also Chap. 15, this volume) or through representing pieces of music as sets of points in multi-dimensional spaces (Meredith et al., 2002) (see also Chaps. 13 and 17, this volume). These previous studies do not encompass the entire set of possible motivic descriptions: often motives can be characterized by particular parametric descriptions that are applied to particular notes and intervals of the motives, but not all (Conklin and Bergeron, 2008; Lartillot, 2005). In the following sections, some concrete examples of what can be called *heterogeneous patterns* will be developed.

11.2.2 Musical Parameters

Figure 11.1 shows the hierarchical parametric space presented in this chapter. Additional parameters can be integrated if required. This figure should be read as follows:

- Parameters indicated in bold letters indicate the detailed information composing each note description: for instance for the second note in Fig. 11.2 (pitch F♯4 at

---

[1] In this chapter, a "*pattern*" represents a sequence of descriptions that is repeated at least once. If a sequence is not repeated, it is not considered to be a pattern.

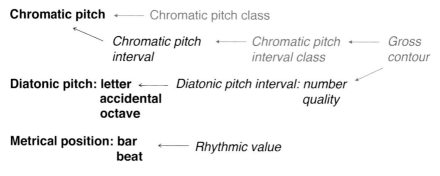

Fig. 11.1 Dimensions of the hierarchical parametric space currently used in the proposed model. See the text for an explanation of the schema

note 1-2),[2] the chromatic pitch value is the MIDI pitch value 66, the diatonic pitch letter is F, accidental is sharp, octave is 4, metrical position is bar #1, beat #2. Other information could be considered as well, such as articulation (e.g., staccato, marcato).

- Parameters shown in grey are directly deduced from more *specific* information: for our previous example, chromatic pitch class is 6 and is obtained from the chromatic pitch information, by simply performing a modulo 12 operation.
- Parameters written in italics describe intervals between successive notes, and are therefore obtained directly as a difference of the parameters associated with each note. To continue our previous example, the second note is preceded by the first note 1-1 (pitch D4 and a rhythmic value of quarter note): the interval between the two notes has chromatic pitch interval +4 semi-tones, diatonic pitch interval number +2 (an increasing third interval, i.e., 2 degrees upwards) and quality 'major', and rhythmic value 1 (a quarter note being the unit in 3/4 metre).
- Interval descriptions can themselves accept more *general* information also indicated in grey: here, chromatic pitch interval class, which is chromatic pitch interval modulo 12, is 4 and gross-contour is 'increasing'.

11.2.3 Pattern Prefix Tree

Following a common straightforward convention, all the motives (i.e., patterns) extracted in the analysis are stored in a single prefix-tree (or *trie*), such as the one shown in Fig. 11.3. Each pattern is represented by a chain from the root, $\emptyset$, of the tree to one particular node N_L. This chain $\emptyset \rightarrow N_1 \rightarrow \ldots \rightarrow N_L$ represents the successive

---

[2] Throughout this chapter, each note is identified with a label of the form i-j, where i is the bar number and j the beat index in the bar.

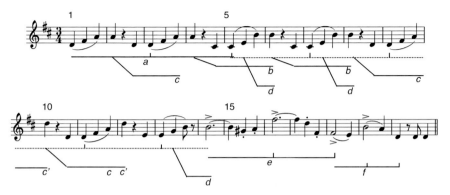

Fig. 11.2 Reduced and simplified version of the beginning of the first waltz theme in Johann Strauss' op. 314: "*An der schöne blauen Donau*". Pattern occurrences are shown below each stave. Patterns are described in Fig. 11.3. The figure is further discussed in Sect. 11.2.4. The horizontal lines with graduation notches correspond to cyclic patterns, as described in Sects. 11.3.3. Patterns branching out from cyclic patterns, such as pattern d, are figure against cyclic background, as further explained in Sect. 11.3.4

prefixes of the pattern. The whole pattern can therefore be identified with the final node N_L. The length of pattern N_L is the number of nodes in that chain, root excluded, i.e., L. In our illustration, pattern d is of length 2, pattern f of length 3, and pattern a is of length 6.

Patterns are commonly constructed incrementally, by progressively adding new nodes in the pattern tree, which initially is represented by only one node, i.e., the root of the tree. Two cases should be considered:

- Adding a node as a direct child of the root of the tree corresponds to the discovery of the repetition of a single note description.
- In other cases, the parent of that node already corresponds to a given pattern, so the new node indicates that several occurrences of that pattern are immediately followed by the same description. Notes that immediately follow occurrences of a pattern are called the *continuations* of that pattern.

Each occurrence of a pattern in the musical sequence is a structure connected to particular notes of the sequence and, at the same time, aligned with the corresponding pattern. Such a structure interconnecting the concrete score with the abstract pattern dictionary will be called a *construct*.

11.2.4 Illustration

The concepts developed in this section are illustrated on a particular example: a reduced and simplified version of the beginning of the first waltz theme in Johann Strauss' op. 314: "*An der schöne blauen Donau*", shown in Fig. 11.2. The prefix-tree is shown in Fig. 11.3. Motive e, for instance, is shown on the sixth branch

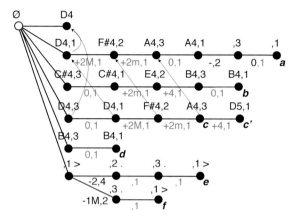

Fig. 11.3 Pattern trie related to the motivic analysis of the score shown in Fig. 11.2. The white disk represents the root, ∅, of the tree, while other nodes are shown with black disks. Each note description is written next to its node; interval descriptions are shown along the edges between nodes. See the text for further explanation. Arrows link more specific to less specific patterns, as explained in Sect. 11.3.1

starting from the top, ending at the node labelled '*e*'. The successive descriptions of the notes composing the motive are shown on each successive node in the branch: '‚1 >' represents a note on the first beat of a bar (1) that is accented (>); '‚2.' represents a note on the second beat that is staccato (.), and so on for '‚3.' and '‚1 >'. Further description of the motive is also associated with the intervals between successive notes, and represented on the edge between successive notes. In the example, there is an interval description between the two first nodes, indicated '$\overrightarrow{-2,4}$'‚[3] which represents a decreasing third interval ('−2' indicating two degrees down) and a 4-beat rhythmic value ('4'). The whole pattern can thus be described as "‚1 > $\overrightarrow{-2,4}$‚2. ,$\overrightarrow{1}$‚3. ,$\overrightarrow{1}$‚1 >".[4]

We can see that the descriptions of the successive notes and intervals of these motives do not always use the same types of musical parameter. Heterogeneous patterns cannot be defined solely as sequences of descriptions in a fixed set of dimensions.

---

[3] Parameters related to the interval between successive notes are indicated with an arrow above the parameter descriptions.

[4] The interval descriptions related to the two subsequent intervals, both "−1", do not convey additional information: they directly result from the difference of the parametric description of the corresponding pair of notes. For that reason, this information is shown in grey in Fig. 11.3.

11.2.5 Heterogeneous Pattern Construction

The method presented in this section is capable of discovering heterogeneous patterns. Instead of first decomposing the music into a superposition of viewpoints on which motivic analysis is performed, each note is associated with its entire set of related descriptions, and the analysis is performed on the whole set of descriptions at once. The description of a given note consists not only of the descriptions associated specifically with that note, but also includes the descriptions of the interval with its previous note.

Focus on particular dimensions is made adaptively for each successive step of the incremental construction of patterns. If, for instance, two notes share the same pitch value, D4, but have different other parameters, they become an occurrence of the pattern described solely by the pitch parameter "D4", shown as the upper child of the root in Fig. 11.3. If both notes are also on beat 1 of a bar, that beat representation is indicated as well in the pattern ("D4,1"). If what is repeated is just an accented note on the first beat of a bar, we obtain the pattern ",1>".

A given pattern can be extended by a new description in the same way. To continue our example, notes 1-1 and 3-1 are occurrences of the pattern "D4,1". Each occurrence is continued with the same pitch F♯4 on notes 1-2 and 3-2. Hence pattern "D4,1" can be extended with a new node related to the note-description "D4, 1 $\overrightarrow{+2M, 1}$ F♯4, 2". The interval-description "$\overrightarrow{+2M, 1}$" indicates the pitch interval of an ascending major third (two degrees upwards, in major mode) and the rhythmic value of one quarter note.

11.2.6 One-Pass Approach

The classical method for pattern construction (Cambouropoulos, 2006; Pasquier et al., 1999; Wang et al., 2007) would be to first find all patterns of length 1, then all patterns of length 2, and so on. To extend a given pattern, all its continuations are compared: any repetition of a given parameter in at least two of these continuations leads to the inference of a new hypothetical pattern extension.

In contrast, the pattern mining approach adopted here is based on an entirely chronological approach, where, for each successive note in the score, all possible patterns are inferred. This *one-pass* approach allows for redundant information to be discarded more easily, as explained in Sect. 11.3.2.

11.2.6.1 Pattern Continuation Memory and Its Use

In the one-pass approach, the detection of new patterns is made possible through the use of *associative tables*, one table for each parameter, that store, for each parameter value, the set of notes in the score that share that particular value. For instance, the associative table in the top left-hand corner of Fig. 11.4 is related to pitch, and stores, for each pitch value (D4, F♯4, etc.), the set of notes where this pitch occurs.

For each pattern, P, all its possible continuations are stored in a set of dedicated associative tables called *continuation memory*, associated with pattern P. In Fig. 11.4, continuation memories related to patterns in the pattern tree introduced in Fig. 11.3 are shown.

- The root of the tree ∅ stores the descriptions of all the notes in the score in a dedicated continuation memory. In the example in Fig. 11.4, it is composed solely of one associative table storing notes according to their pitches. This is precisely the aforementioned table in the top left-hand corner of the figure.
- Each child of ∅ corresponds to patterns made of one single note. For instance, the topmost child of ∅ in Fig. 11.4 is related to pattern "D4". Its continuation memory stores all the notes that immediately follow occurrences of "D4". This continuation memory is made of four different associative tables. From left to right, they are related, respectively, to pitch, inter-pitch interval, beat and rhythm. For instance, the pitch table shows occurrences of "D4" continued by either F♯4 or D4.
- This associative table allows us to detect that several occurrences of "D4" are followed by F♯4. This triggers the detection of a new pattern, that we could describe simply for the moment as "D4 F♯4". It is a child of the node related to pattern "D4" and is displayed with a grey disk in Fig. 11.4. We will see in Sect. 11.2.6.2 that the pattern would be described more precisely as "D4 $\overrightarrow{+2M, 1}$ F♯4, 2". We will see in Sect. 11.3 that this pattern is actually not interesting, because it is already described by another more specific pattern, "D4, 1 $\overrightarrow{+2M, 1}$ F♯4, 2", shown also in the figure.
- That more specific pattern "D4, 1 $\overrightarrow{+2M, 1}$ F♯4, 2" also features a continuation memory, decomposed into associative tables related to parameters pitch ("P."), inter-pitch interval ("I.p.") and beat ("Bt"). The tables show that several occurrences of the pattern are followed by the same description, leading to an extension of the pattern into "D4, 1 $\overrightarrow{+2M, 1}$ F♯4, 2 $\overrightarrow{+2m, 1}$ A4, 3".

11.2.6.2 Description of the One-Pass Approach

The one-pass approach ensures an exhaustive heterogeneous pattern mining by proceeding as follows: for each successive note n_i in the piece of music to be analysed, the previous note n_{i-1} has already been linked to its corresponding patterns, forming a certain number of constructs ended by that note. Constructs attached to the previous note n_{i-1} are considered one after each other. Each construct is related to a particular pattern p.

For instance, in Fig. 11.5, let us consider note 5-2. The previous note, 5-1, ends two constructs: one occurrence of pattern "D4", and one occurrence of pattern "D4,1". Since the first construct is more general than the second construct, it is redundant and therefore indicated in grey.

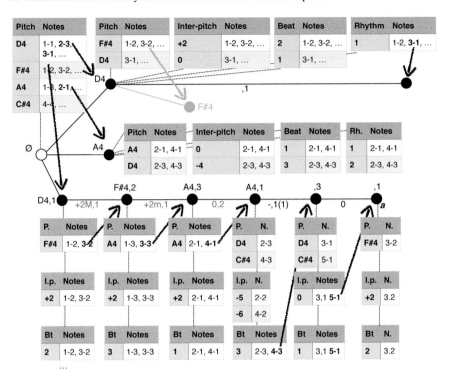

Fig. 11.4 Part of the pattern trie shown and described in Fig. 11.3. Associative tables are connected to their corresponding pattern nodes with dotted lines. In each table are stored the notes (right column) associated with each parameter value (left column). Notes memorized in the associative tables that trigger the inference of new patterns are shown in bold and arrows point to the new nodes. The node shown in grey is an example of a non-closed pattern that is actually not inferred by the model, as mentioned in Sect. 11.2.6.1 and further explained in Sect. 11.3.2

For each of these constructs, three tests are carried out:

1. **Pattern recognition** If the description of the new note n_i and of the interval between the two notes n_{i-1} and n_i is *entirely compatible*[5] with the description of one possible child c of pattern p, the construct is extended accordingly.
   For instance, in Fig. 11.5, the description of 5-2 and the interval between 5-1 and 5-2 corresponds exactly to the child "D4, 1 $\overrightarrow{+2M}$, 1 F♯4, 2" of pattern "D4, 1". This pattern already exists because it was discovered while analysing note 3-2 (cf. below). Consequently, the construct is extended into an occurrence of that child.

2. **Pattern generalization** Else if that description is *partially compatible*, the *common description between the child's description and the description of the current note n_i and its interval with n_{i-1}* is computed. If it does not exist already,

---

[5] Expressions in italics are explained in more detail in Sect. 11.2.7.

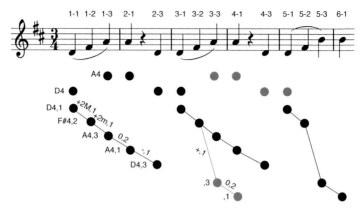

Fig. 11.5 Analysis of a variant of the beginning of the waltz melody in Fig. 11.2 (the pitches of the notes at 4-3 and 5-1 have been changed from C♯4 to D4). Constructs are shown by disks below the notes. In each line, all constructs are occurrences of the same pattern. The first 3 lines are related respectively to the elementary patterns "A4", "D4" and "D4,1". Other lines below correspond to successive prefixes of the two branches of a simple pattern tree

a new child of pattern p is created, related to the common description. The construct is extended accordingly.

For instance, in Fig. 11.5, the description of 5-3 and the interval between 5-2 and 5-3 corresponds only partially to the child "D4,1 $\overrightarrow{+2M,1}$ F♯4,2 $\overrightarrow{+2m,1}$ A4,2" of pattern "D4,1 $\overrightarrow{+2M,1}$ F♯4,2". The common description between the child and the current context defined by the succession 5-2 and 5-3 is an interval of ascending pitch in the same rhythmical description, i.e., "$\overrightarrow{+,1}$,3". This leads therefore to the next pattern "D4,1 $\overrightarrow{+2M,1}$ F♯4,2 $\overrightarrow{+,1}$,3".

3. **Pattern discovery** The current context (i.e., the construct and the new note's description) is stored in the continuation memory of pattern p. If there already exists a previous context with identical value along a particular parameter (i.e., if a previous context is already stored for the same parameter value as key on one or several parametric dimensions), then the *common description between these two contexts*, d, is computed. If there does not exist a child of pattern p with that description d, then

 a. a new child c of pattern p is created, related to that description d;
 b. the current construct is extended into a new construct that is an occurrence of c; and
 c. the retrieved construct[6] is also extended into a new construct. Apart from this, the note that follows that extended retrieved construct is also stored in the continuation memory of the new pattern c.

---

[6] In the context of closed pattern mining, as developed in Sect. 11.3, there can actually be several retrieved constructs. Each construct is extended accordingly.

For instance, let us return to note 3-2 in the analysis in Fig. 11.5. The previous note is 3-1, with two associated constructs, which are occurrences of elementary patterns "D4" and "D4,1". The new note 3-2 is stored in the continuation memory of pattern "D4,1" (as in Fig. 11.4). In these associative tables, we detect that a previous context, the occurrence of "D4,1" at note 1-1 followed by note 1-2, already shares same description along at least one parameter (pitch, but also inter-pitch interval, beat and rhythm). The common description between these two contexts is "$\overrightarrow{+2M, 1}$ F♯4, 2". This leads to the inference of a new child of pattern "D4,1", of description "D4, 1 $\overrightarrow{+2M, 1}$ F♯4, 2". Its two occurrences at notes 1-2 and 3-2 are also created.

The three tests described above are also carried out in exactly the same way for the root, $\emptyset$, of the pattern tree:

1. **Pattern recognition** If the description of the new note n_i is *entirely compatible* with the description of one possible child c of the root, a new construct indicates that n_i is an occurrence of c. For instance, let us return to note 3-1 in the analysis in Fig. 11.5. Note 3-1 can be recognized as forming an occurrence of the elementary pattern "D4" that was created at an earlier stage (for note 2-3).

2. **Pattern generalization** Else if that description is *partially compatible*, the *common description between the child's description and the description of the current note n_i* is computed. If it does not exist already, a new child c of the root is created, related to the common description. A new construct indicates that n_i is an occurrence of c.

3. **Pattern discovery** The new note's description is stored in the root's continuation memory. If there exists already a previous note with identical value along a particular parameter (i.e., if a previous note is already stored for the same parameter value as key on one or several parametric dimensions), the *common description between these two notes*, d, is computed. If there does not exist a child of the root with that description d, then

   a. a new child c of the root is created, related to that description d;
   b. a new construct indicates that n_i is an occurrence of c; and
   c. another construct indicates that the retrieved note[7] is also an occurrence of c. Besides, the note that follows that construct is stored in the continuation memory of the new pattern c.

For instance, let us return to note 2-3 in the analysis in Fig. 11.5. This note is stored in all the different associative tables (each one related to a different musical dimension) that form the continuation memory of the root ($\emptyset$) pattern (as in Fig. 11.4). In particular, the associative table related to pitch shows that there is already a previous context with the same pitch value D4 at note 1-1. The common description between these two contexts is "D4". The elementary pattern "D4" is created and its two occurrences at notes 1-1 and 2-3 are constructed.

---

[7] Here also, in the context of closed pattern mining, there can actually be several retrieved notes. Each of them forms a construct accordingly.

11.2.7 Comparing Musical Descriptions

To understand more precisely how musical descriptions are compared, it is important to distinguish between two types of description:

- The description *of a given note* (and its previous interval) in the score is specified entirely by the most specific parameters represented in bold letters in Fig. 11.1. All other parameters can be deduced directly from the most specific parameters.
- In contrast, a *pattern's individual description* is defined on particular parameters in that space, not necessarily the most specific ones.

For instance, as we saw in the previous example, pattern "D4" only specifies note pitch information. In motive *e* (see Figs. 11.2 and 11.3), ",1 >" only indicates beat and articulation; whereas, "$\overrightarrow{-2,4}$,2." specifies diatonic interval number, rhythmic value, beat position and articulation.

Recognizing a new occurrence of an already-discovered pattern requires testing whether or not the description of a given note (and its previous interval) in the score is *totally compatible* with a pattern's individual description. This implies the following.

- If the pattern description contains any specific note- or interval-related parametric description (along parametric dimensions indicated in black in Fig. 11.1: chromatic and diatonic pitch and pitch interval, metrical position and rhythmic value, articulation), the given note (with its previous interval) should feature the same parametric description.
- If the pattern description contains any more general parametric description (along parametric dimensions indicated in grey in Fig. 11.1: chromatic pitch class and pitch interval class, gross contour), the description of the given note (with its previous interval) should be congruent. For instance, if the pattern contains an ascending pitch contour, the interval description should also contain an ascending pitch contour.

Detecting a new pattern more general than another pre-existing pattern requires testing whether or not the description of a given note (and its previous interval) in the score is *partially compatible* with a pattern's individual description. This means that the two descriptions are compared along all the different individual parameters, and if there is any identity between the two descriptions along any parameter, they are partially compatible. In such cases, the *common description* between these two descriptions is the set of all these common parametric descriptions.

Finally, detecting a new pattern extension requires detecting an identity between two different contexts (notes and their previous intervals) in the score. Once any identity along any parameter is detected using the continuation memories, the *common description* between these two contexts is the set of all common parametric descriptions.

11.3 Richness and Concision of Pattern Description

At first sight, finding motivic patterns consists simply of extracting all possible sequence of descriptions in the piece of music. But it turns out that the problem is more complex, due to the proliferation of a large number of redundant structures (Cambouropoulos, 1998).

In order to reduce that structural proliferation at the pattern extraction phase, filtering heuristics are generally added that select a sub-class of the result based on global criteria such as pattern length, pattern frequency (within a piece or among different pieces), etc. (Cambouropoulos, 2006). Similarly, Conklin and Anagnostopoulou (2001) base the search for patterns on general statistical characteristics.

One limitation of these methods comes from the lack of selectivity of global criteria. Hence, by selecting longest patterns, one may discard short motives that listeners may nevertheless consider as highly relevant. Even more problematic is the fact that particular structural configurations (that will be studied in Sect. 11.3.3 and 11.3.4) lead to the generation of very long artefacts that do not necessarily correspond to the types of structure that were looked for in the first place.

The design of the model presented in this chapter was motivated by the aim of discovering the origins of the combinatorial explosion hampering the efficiency of computational models. The objective was to build a model as simple as possible, founded on heuristics ensuring a compact representation of the pattern configurations without significant loss of information, thanks to an adaptive and lossless selection of most specific descriptions. We found that pattern redundancy is based on two core issues: *closed patterns* (Sect. 11.3.1) and *cyclic patterns* (Sects. 11.3.3 and 11.3.4).

Another class of methods consists of cataloguing all possible pairs of sequential repetitions, and in clustering these pairs into pattern classes (Rolland, 1999) (see also Chap. 12, this volume). This paradigm allows for compact description, akin to the closed patterns selection that will be presented in Sect. 11.3.1, but no method in this category has yet been conceived of that performs exhaustive mining of heterogeneous patterns.

11.3.1 Closed Pattern Mining

When a pattern is repeated, all *more general* pattern representations it encompasses are repeated as well. A sequence of descriptions S_1 is *more general* than another sequence of descriptions S_2 if the sequence S_1 features less information than the sequence S_2, so that S_1 can be directly inferred from the description given by S_2. In such cases, we can also say that S_2 is *more specific* than S_1. More *general* patterns correspond to substrings[8] (prefixes, suffixes, prefixes of suffixes) of the pattern, but also to more general representations of such substrings where individual descriptions are replaced by more general ones as defined in Sect. 11.2.7. Figure 11.6 shows an

_____

[8] More generally, subsequences can be considered as well. This will be studied in Sect. 11.4.

example of proliferation of general patterns. Examples of multiparametric pattern comparison in music are shown by arrows in Fig. 11.3.

Restricting the search to the most specific (or "maximal") patterns is excessively selective as it filters out potentially interesting patterns (such as CDE in Fig. 11.6), and would solely focus on large sequence repetitions.[9] Pattern redundancy can be filtered out without loss of information by taking into account both patterns' descriptions and the ways in which these patterns repeat in the sequences: the set of repetitions of a given pattern provides relevant structural information that should not be excluded from the analysis, unless that set of repetitions is *equivalent* to the set of repetitions of another more specific pattern. In our example, the set of two repetitions of pattern ABCDE is equivalent to the set of two repetitions of ABCDECDE: each occurrence of ABCDE is a construct that can be further extended to become an occurrence of ABCDECDE. On the other hand, the set of four repetitions of pattern CDE is not equivalent to the set of two repetitions of ABCDECDE, as there are more occurrences of CDE.

In order to obtain a compact lossless description, each possible set of pattern repetitions is subject to a *closure* operation that assigns its most specific pattern description, which is hence called a *closed pattern* (Pasquier et al., 1999). In our example, the most specific description of the set of two repetitions is ABCDECDE, and the most specific description of the pattern repeated four times is CDE.

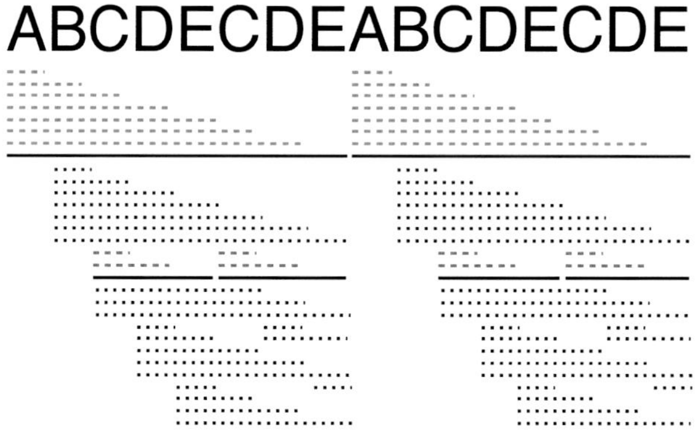

Fig. 11.6 Patterns found in a sequence of symbols. Below the sequence, each row represents a different pattern class with the occurrences aligned to the sequence. Solid lines correspond to closed patterns (the upper one is the maximal pattern), grey dashed lines to prefixes of closed patterns, and dotted lines to other non-closed patterns

---

[9] Note that the term "maximal" is used here in the way that it is commonly used in the data-mining literature to mean a pattern that is not included in any other patterns (see, e.g., Bayardo, 1998). This differs from the way "maximal'" is used in Meredith et al.'s (2002) concept of a "maximal translatable pattern", of which the pattern CDE is actually an example. See Chap. 13, this volume, for a definition of the latter concept.

Closed patterns are usually considered as preliminary information that is further processed for maximal or frequent pattern mining (Conklin and Bergeron, 2008; Pasquier et al., 1999). However, such global filtering results, once again, in the patterns that are finally produced as output being of limited practical use. On the other hand, by keeping the whole closed pattern lattice without further filtering, a detailed motivic analysis can be produced without combinatorial explosion. We call such an approach *exhaustive closed pattern mining*.

11.3.2 One-Pass Closed Pattern Mining

In previous studies on closed pattern mining in computer science (e.g., Pasquier et al., 1999; Wang et al., 2007), the pattern dictionary is constructed in a breadth-first fashion, while considering the whole document to be analysed (in our case, the piece of music). First, all closed patterns of length 1 are constructed, then all closed patterns of length 2, and so on. But such methods create a large number of hypothetical patterns that turn out to be non-closed once the pattern tree is further extended.

By adopting a one-pass approach, as presented in Sect. 11.2.6, there is no useless inference of non-closed patterns, and the closure test is far simpler. Indeed, in the one-pass approach, each pattern inference is made for a particular pattern occurrence candidate, for which we can infer the most specific description. This ensures that the obtained pattern is either closed, or is a prefix that will subsequently be extended into a longer closed pattern. Indeed, there cannot be more specific patterns that would contain that particular occurrence, apart from the possible extension of that occurrence into an occurrence of a longer pattern. Prefixes of closed patterns are the only type of possible non-closed pattern retained in the pattern tree. This is to ensure that the latter is a complete pattern prefix tree, which is easier to use for tracking patterns during the one-pass approach. It can also be shown that the one-pass approach uncovers the whole set of closed patterns.

When considering a given pattern candidate at a given point in the piece of music, we need to be already informed about the possible existence of more specific pattern occurrences at the same place. Hence, for a given note, patterns need to be extended *in decreasing order of specificity*, so that constructs[10] are built also in decreasing order of specificity.

For instance, in Fig. 11.7, when analysing the last note, E, there are two candidate patterns for extension, ABCD and CD. We first extend the most specific pattern to obtain ABCDE; then, when considering the more general pattern, CD, extension CDE is found as non-closed and is thus not inferred.

---

[10] A construct is an occurrence of a pattern (cf. Sect. 11.2.3).

CDABCDEABCDE

Fig. 11.7 Closed patterns found in a sequence of symbols. The occurrence during which a pattern is discovered is shown in black. Dashed extensions indicate two possible pattern extensions when integrating the last note

11.3.2.1 Comparing Constructs

As has already been mentioned, the specificity of the one-pass approach for closed pattern mining is that general/specific comparisons are not made between patterns in general, but only between constructs that are aligned on a particular note in a musical sequence. We need to define more precisely this notion of comparing constructs. A construct A is more general than another construct B, if the set of notes connected to A is included in the set of notes connected to B, and if, for each of those notes, the underlying pattern's individual description in A is equal to or more general than the corresponding individual description in B.

For instance, in Fig. 11.5, a construct indicated with a grey disk is more general than another construct in black vertically aligned on the same note. For note 3-3, for instance, occurrences of "A4" and "D4, 1 $\overrightarrow{+2\text{M}, 1}$ F♯4, 2 $\overrightarrow{+, 1}$, 3" are both more general than the occurrence of "D4, 1 $\overrightarrow{+2\text{M}, 1}$ F♯4, 2 $\overrightarrow{+2\text{m}, 1}$ A4, 3".

We can notice that it is possible to compare the extension of a construct to other constructs already inferred even if that construct extension is not actually inferred yet. More precisely, a construct A extended with a new individual description d is more general than another construct C already inferred if the two conditions below are verified:

- the construct A is more general than a prefix B of the construct C,
- the new description d is more general than the description of the extension from B to C.

This will be considered in the next paragraph as the comparison of a *candidate construct extension* with actual constructs.

11.3.2.2 Integration in the One-Pass Approach

The closed pattern filtering constraint can simply be integrated in step number 3 of the description of the one-pass approach given in Sect. 11.2.6.2, by replacing the condition "If there does not exist a child of pattern p with that description d" by the following condition: "If the candidate construct extension is not more general than another construct already inferred".

11.3.2.3 Motivic/Thematic Classes

Extending the exhaustive method developed in the previous section to the hetero-geneous pattern paradigm allows us to describe all possible sequential repetitions along all parametric dimensions. This leads to very detailed pattern characterization, describing all common sequential descriptions between any pair of similar motives. However, a more synthetic analysis requires structuring the set of discovered patterns into motivic or thematic classes. Manual motivic taxonomy of these discovered pat-terns was demonstrated by Lartillot (2009). Lartillot (2014a) devised a method for the collection of all patterns belonging to the same motivic or thematic class into what is called a *paradigmatic sheaf.*

11.3.3 Cyclic Pattern Mining

When repetitions of a pattern are immediately successive, another combinatorial set of possible sequential repetitions can be logically inferred, as shown in Fig. 11.8. As each occurrence is followed by the beginning of a new occurrence, each pattern can be extended by a description that is identical to the first description of the pattern. This extension can be prolonged recursively, leading to a proliferation of patterns in an intertwined network (Cambouropoulos, 1998), which is detrimental to the effectiveness of the computation and the clarity of the results.

Avoiding overlapping between pattern occurrences (Cambouropoulos, 1998) al-lows for some of these patterns to be filtered out. But the effect of this heuristic is limited: as soon as the cyclicity is prolonged further, by repeating even further the periodic motive, those patterns that were filtered out will reappear.

This redundancy can be avoided by explicitly modelling the cyclic loop in the pattern representation. Once a successive repetition of a pattern has been detected, such as the 3-note pattern starting the musical example in Fig. 11.9, the two occur-rences are *fused into one single construct*, and all the subsequent notes in the cyclic sequence are progressively added to that construct. This *cyclic construct* is first used to track the development of the new cycle (i.e., the third cycle, since there were already two cycles). The tracking of each new cycle is guided by a model describing

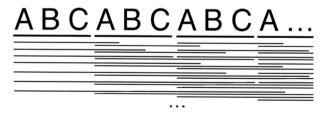

Fig. 11.8 Closed patterns found in a cyclic sequence of symbols. The occurrences of the pattern shown in thick lines do not overlap, whereas those shown in thin lines do

the expected sequence of musical parameters, i.e., the whole pattern *P* that is being
repeated. Initially, for the third cycle, this model corresponds to the pattern that was
repeated twice in the two first cycles.

- Every time a new cycle is being constructed, the growing cyclic construct keeps
  in memory the cycle model that describes a complete cycle, as well as a *cycle
  state* that indicates the current position of the last cycle of the cyclic construct.
- Every time the cycle state reaches the whole cycle model, a cycle has been
  completed, so that the cycle state points back to the beginning of the cycle model,
  which remains unchanged.
- If the current candidate extension is actually more general than the expected
  continuation given by the cycle state (such as the modification, at the beginning
  of bar 2 in Fig. 11.9, of the decreasing sixth interval, replaced by a more general decreasing contour), the cycle state is generalized accordingly. The cycle
  model, although now more specific than the actual cycle, is kept for the moment
  unchanged as it can still be used as a guiding point. When the cycle is completed,
  the cycle model can now be replaced by the new generalized cycle model given
  by the complete generalized cycle state.
- If at some point, the new note does not match at all the corresponding description
  in the model, the cyclic sequence is terminated.

This method allows us to track the cyclic development of repeated patterns, while
avoiding the proliferation of patterns that was discussed above. Indeed, each of these
problematic structures is detected as a candidate construct extension that is more

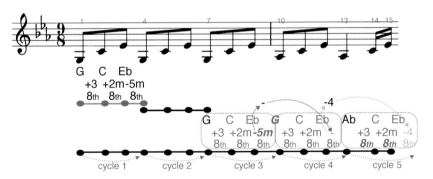

Fig. 11.9 Two successive repetitions of the three-note pattern that begins this sequence, characterized by a pitch sequence (G, C, Eb, and back to G), a pitch interval sequence (ascending perfect
fourth (+3), ascending minor third (+2m) and descending minor sixth (−5m)), and a rhythmical
sequence made of a succession of eighth notes. This successive repetition leads to the inference of
a cyclic chain, indicated at the bottom of the figure. When this cycle is initially inferred, at note
7, the model of the cycle, labelled "cycle 3", corresponds to the initial pattern description. At note
10, some descriptions expected by the model (indicated in bold italics) are not fulfilled, but a more
general description is inferred (descending gross contour (−)). Consequently, the model for the next
cycle (i.e., cycle 4) is generalized accordingly. At note 13, a new regularity is detected, due to the
repetition of pitch Ab and of descending perfect fifth (−4). Consequently, the model for cycle 5 is
specialized accordingly

general than another construct already inferred. As such, following the closed pattern constraint defined in Sect. 11.3.2.2, the redundant structure is not inferred at all.

In the waltz melody in Fig. 11.2, the successive repetition of pattern *a* at the beginning of the piece leads to the creation of a cyclic construct related to that pattern. That is why the occurrences of the pattern are shown in a single horizontal line with tick marks showing the start of each new cycle.[11] From bar 5 on, this cycle is progressively altered: the initial specific pattern is not repeated exactly anymore, but a more general pattern continues to be repeated. The generalization of the initial cycle is indicated by a dotted line in Fig. 11.2.

11.3.4 Pattern Figure—Cyclic Background

Cyclic patterns engender further structural issues to be considered. A cyclic pattern can be extended into a non-cyclic pattern: this would happen when a cyclic pattern is repeated several times, and for several of those occurrences, the cycle at a specific phase is followed by the same description *d*. Consider, for example, 'ABCABCABD...ABCABCABCABD'.

Without the addition of particular mechanisms to handle this phenomenon, the acyclic pattern corresponding to that particular cycle phase is extended with that description *d*. In the example, D extends the acyclic patterns AB, or CAB, etc. But this information is insufficient, as it fails to represent the fact that the description *d* extends not only that particular acyclic pattern, but also a cyclic pattern. In our example, D can be considered as an extension of the cyclic pattern ABCA...at phase AB.

We can account for this type of situation by defining a new type of pattern extension related to cyclic contexts. In the example, as shown in Fig. 11.10, AB is extended by D in the particular cyclic context where AB is a phase of the cycle ABCA.... In this way, if a new cyclic repetition of ABCA...occurs with the same ending, it will be immediately recognized as a new occurrence of that extension of the phase AB.

Another difficulty arises when the description *d* that extends one particular phase of the cycle is compatible with its next phase. In other words, *d* does not lead to an interruption of the cycle, as in the previous case, but rather to a continuation of the cycle with the addition of new information. For instance, in the waltz melody in Fig. 11.2, patterns *b*, *c* and *d* could, in fact, be considered extensions of the cyclic pattern initiated by the successive repetitions of pattern *a*. The problem in this case is that this extended pattern could theoretically be further extended by the cyclical pattern, leading to a chaotic proliferation of patterns. For instance, pattern *d*, which simply represents the repetition of pitch B4, could in principle be extended by the next descriptions in the cycle: decreasing interval, unison, ascending interval, and

---

[11] We should note that the tick marks do not necessarily correspond to segmentation points, but are used here only as a way to represent the locations of an arbitrarily chosen phase in each cycle. Hypothetical segmentation points can be inferred based on other strategies, such as local grouping, as discussed in Sect. 11.4.2.

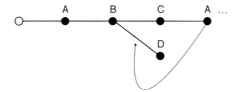

Fig. 11.10 Pattern tree with cyclic extension: AB is extended by D in the context where AB is in fact a phase of the cycle ABCA...

so on, without any clear limit in this pattern extension. If the cycle is repeated many times, this would engender very long and uninformative patterns.

This difficulty can be solved by using a heuristic, inspired by the 'figure-ground' principle: the additional information given by the description *d* can be considered as an extra layer on top of the cyclic pattern description. Further extensions of the pattern by descriptions richer than the cycle description lead to an extension of the extra layer, while keeping track of the background cycle. Whenever the next description corresponds merely to the cyclical description without additional information, this can be considered as a return of the background information without the extra-layer structure. Hence this would be perceived as a termination of the specific pattern on top of the cyclical background: in other words, the figure is not extended any more. The integration of this heuristic in the model allows us to suppress the chaotic proliferation of redundant structures.

11.4 Ornamented Pattern Mining

11.4.1 Ornamentation and Reduction

An ornamentation of a motive generally consists of the addition of one or several notes—the ornament—between some of the notes of the initial motive. Each repetition of a given motive can be ornamented in its own way, or not ornamented at all. In order to be able to detect the pattern repetition corresponding to the reduced motive, it is necessary to go beyond the "*surface*" of the actual music representation, i.e., beyond the mere succession of notes forming a single "*syntagmatic chain*" (de Saussure, 1916).

The detection of pattern repetition with tolerance for the addition, suppression or modification of individual descriptions has been previously addressed with the use of edit distance and dynamic programming (Rolland, 1999). This technique allows for a similarity distance to be computed between specific pattern occurrences, based on their local transformations. This leads to a network of numerical distances between occurrences, which cannot easily be turned into a clear categorization of pattern occurrences into pattern classes with precise descriptions. Moreover, the use of numerical distances requires a choice of similarity threshold, leading to a non-exhaustive search that is dependent on parametric choices. Another way to detect pattern repetition despite ornamentation is the "geometric approach", with patterns made of notes scattered anywhere in the score without constraint of sequentiality between the successive notes (Meredith et al., 2002). As mentioned in Sect. 11.3, similarity-based and geometric approaches have not yet been used for exhaustive mining of heterogeneous patterns.

We propose a solution to the problem of ornamentation reduction that is compatible with our vision of pattern discovery as an exhaustive search for exact identification along multiple parametric dimensions. The approach stems from the idea that, in a motive formed of notes that are not immediately successive in the syntagmatic surface, there is already implicitly a syntagmatic chaining between these successive notes in the motive that could be perceived as such. We see that beyond the initial syntagmatic chain at the "surface" emerges a more complex syntagmatic network. In the most complex case, we could theoretically imagine that all pairs of notes could be syntagmatically connected, but, perceptually speaking, we can understand that there should be constraints on the establishment of such syntagmatic connections.

It is then possible to find the whole set of closed patterns along all possible branches using the algorithm presented in the previous sections, appropriately generalized to the new framework. This will be shown in Sect. 11.4.3. But before that, we present one way to construct the syntagmatic network: first, a hierarchical local grouping structure is derived, then the resulting structures are used to determine the structurally more important notes and construct syntagmatic connections between them.

11.4.2 Syntagmatic Network Based on Local Grouping

There has been significant research around the concept of local segmentation, studying the emergence of structure related to the mere variability in the succession of musical parameters. These studies (Cambouropoulos, 2006; Lerdahl and Jackendoff, 1983; Tenney and Polansky, 1980) focus on the analysis of monodies, and model this structural phenomenon as a segmentation of the monody, which cuts the temporal span at particular instants, resulting in a linear succession of segments. In these approaches, the heuristics for segmentation are based on a mixture of several constraints related to what happens both before and after each candidate segmentation point, which leads to approximate and incomplete segmentation results. Here we present a simple approach that reveals a clear structural description and that can be explained with simple principles. The approach focuses on grouping instead of segmentation. In other words, what needs to be characterized is not the segmentation boundaries between notes, but rather the groups of notes that are progressively constructed. In this study, so far, this clustering mechanism has been applied only to the time domain, for grouping based on temporal proximity, following the second Grouping Preference Rule (GPR2) from Lerdahl and Jackendoff's (1983) *Generative Theory of Tonal*

Fig. 11.11 Beginning of the right-hand part of the theme of Mozart's Variations on "*Ah, vous dirai-je maman*", K. 265/300e. Repeated notes are shown with ellipses. Local groups are represented with rectangles. The last note, playing the role of group head, is circled. Syntagmatic connections that are drawn between non-successive notes are shown with straight and curved lines. By traversing the syntagmatic chain represented by the dotted lines, we can recognize the successive notes of the underlying theme (in English: "*Twinkle, Twinkle, Little Star*")

Music (GTTM). Another type of grouping, based on change (GPR3) is currently under study.

In the time domain, local grouping can aggregate in a purely hierarchical fashion. For any succession of two notes n_1 and n_2, with inter-onset-interval (IOI) I, a local group is formed by taking all successive notes before n_1 and after n_2 as long as the IOI between successive notes does not exceed I. Smaller groups are related to short IOIs while larger groups that contain other groups are related to longer IOIs. For instance, the excerpt in Fig. 11.11 consists of a succession of quarter notes, except for the last three notes. The shortest note (a sixteenth note) induces a local group, joining that note with the final note. On a slightly larger scale, the last three notes are grouped together, because the longer internal IOI, a dotted eighth note, is shorter than the IOIs between the preceding quarter notes.

In Fig. 11.12, notes 2 and 3 form a local group because note 2 is a sixteenth note, which is shorter than the rhythmic values that precede and follow it. The same applies for notes 4 and 5. On a larger scale, because the quarter note (note 6) is longer than all the notes before, these first 6 notes also form a local group. Notes 7 to 9 are grouped together for the same reason: their successive IOIs do not exceed an eighth note while the IOIs before and after that group are larger (one quarter note).

By definition, a time-based local group terminates with a note that is followed by an IOI (before the next note) that is significantly longer than the IOIs between notes within the group. As such, the local group can be perceived as a phrase that terminates with a concluding note that has a higher structural importance. This hypothesis seems to offer some general interest, even though it might not be always valid—in particular, if notes within the group are accentuated. Following this observation, we formalize this hierarchy of notes in local groups by associating with each local group a main note, or "head", following Lerdahl and Jackendoff's (1983) Time-Span Reduction terminology, which would in the simple case be the last note of the group. Heads are circled in Fig. 11.12.

Based on this local grouping, two rules for inferring syntagmatic connections between distant notes are proposed as follows:

- Any local group head is connected to the note preceding the group.
  Thus, in Fig. 11.12, note 3, head of the local group starting with note 2, is connected to the note immediately before that group (note 1).

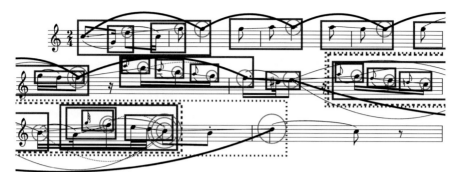

Fig. 11.12 Beginning of the right-hand part of Mozart's Variation XI on "*Ah, vous dirai-je maman*", K. 265/300e. Local groups are represented by rectangles, notes that play the role of group heads are circled. Syntagmatic connections that are drawn between non-successive notes are shown with straight and curved lines. By traversing the syntagmatic chain represented by bold lines, we can recognize the successive notes of the underlying theme (in English: "*Twinkle, Twinkle, Little Star*")

- Any local group head is connected to the first element in the group. If the first note of the group is not included in another internal local group, that first element is the first note of the group. Otherwise, it is the head of the largest first local group included in the local group.

  Thus, in Fig. 11.12, note 6 is connected to note 1, because note 1 is not part of any other local group. At the beginning of the second bar in stave 2, the note F is the head of a local group. The first note of that group, note 4 in stave 2, is included in another smaller local group whose head is the next note (note 5 in stave 2). Hence note F is connected to that note 5, as shown by the dotted curved line above the two notes.

A syntagmatic chain of notes with the same pitch forms a single *meta-note* whose time onset is defined to be that of the first note. This meta-note can be syntagmatically connected to the note that follows the meta-note. For instance, in Fig. 11.11, repetitions of the same pitch form a single meta-note, and successive meta-notes are syntagmatically connected, forming one syntagmatic chain with successive pitches C, G, A, G, F, E, D and C.

11.4.3 Closed Pattern Mining in a Syntagmatic Network

We can observe that a motive is a construct that is more general than an ornamentation of that motive. If a motive is always ornamented in the same way, the actual closed pattern is the ornamented motive, while the reduced motive is a non-closed pattern. If and only if the motive appears at least once without ornament, or with an ornamentation that does not share any commonality with the other ornamentations, does the motive become a closed pattern.

As before, closed pattern mining requires that constructs be inferred in decreasing order of specificity: a hypothetical construct extension should be compared to more specific constructs already inferred. In this more general context, this means that ornamented constructs should be discovered before their corresponding reduced constructs.

This implies the following ordering of operations. As before, the score is analysed chronologically, note by note. But for each note, n_i, there exist one or more syntagmatic connections from one or more previous notes $p_{i,j}$ to that note n_i. We consider these previous notes in reverse order, starting with the most recent note and working backwards in time. For each previous note, $p_{i,j}$, we try to extend the constructs it terminates with the syntagmatic connection between $p_{i,j}$ and n_i.

For each candidate construct extension, we need, as before, to consider all more specific constructs already inferred. The comparison between constructs is the same as in Sect. 11.3.2.1, because the proposed formalism can immediately be adapted to a syntagmatic network: the prefix B of the more specific construct C is not necessarily the immediate prefix of C, so that the description of the extension of B into C corresponds to a syntagmatic connection that is above the surface. This syntagmatic connection is therefore a chaining of several syntagmatic connections from the surface. The parametric description of that connection is hence a summation of the individual descriptions.

These rules allow for the detection of closed patterns along the different paths of the syntagmatic network. For instance, it allows for the identification of the repetition of the pitch sequence C, G, A, G, F, E, D, C that appears in the theme and variation XI shown in Figs. 11.11 and 11.12 (and similarly in other variations in the piece). To be more precise, a more detailed pattern C, G, G, A, A, G, G, F, E, D, C can be detected.

11.5 Evaluation

The system described above has been implemented in Matlab and is publicly available as part of the *MiningSuite* (Lartillot, 2015).

11.5.1 MIREX Task on Discovery of Repeated Themes & Sections

One version of the algorithm (*PatMinr* in *MiningSuite* 0.7.1) has been tested in the MIREX task on Discovery of Repeated Themes & Sections (Collins, 2014). The ground truth, called the Johannes Kepler University Patterns Test Database (JKUPTD), is based on motives and themes in analyses by Barlow and Morgenstern, Schoenberg and Bruhn, repeated sections marked explicitly in the score and supplementary annotations by Tom Collins. The ground truth is not made available in order to prevent developers from overfitting their algorithms to the test data.

Because *PatMinr* did not produce an analysis of one of the pieces in the test database for technical reasons,[12] the algorithms participating in this MIREX competition in 2014 were compared on the 4 remaining pieces of the test database. *PatMinr*'s results using the establishment metric are not particularly high: its establishment precision is .62 while Velarde and Meredith's (2014) method obtains better values for both versions they submitted: .67 for VM1 and .63 for VM2. *PatMinr*'s establishment recall is .56 and F1 is .5, which are both lower than for most of the other algorithms. *PatMinr* gives better results with the occurrence metric: occurrence precision ($c = .75$) is .88 whereas other algorithms' measures are between .48 to .75; occurrence recall is .76 whereas Velarde and Meredith's (2014) VM1 method gives a better result of .82; occurrence F1 is .81 whereas other algorithms' measures are between .34 and .6. This superiority in the occurrence metric means that the algorithm can find a large number of the occurrences of a given pattern, despite their transformations. This capability is related to the heterogeneous pattern representation that was presented in Sect. 11.2. Three-layer precision is .51, which is the highest value, also met by VM1; three-layer recall is also the best one at .494, which is very slightly better than 2 other algorithms: VM2 and Meredith's (2013) SIATECCOM-PRESSSegment; three-layer F1 is .43, which is lower than Velarde and Meredith's (2014) method, with value .49 for VM1 and .45 for VM2.

11.5.2 Example on the MIREX Development Database

The JKU Patterns Development Database (JKUPDD) allows developers to try out and train algorithms to be used on the JKUPTD. Details of the analysis of one particular piece of music included in the JKUPDD, the Fugue in A minor from Book II of J. S. Bach's *Well-Tempered Clavier* (BWV 889) are presented by Lartillot (2014a). The ground truth consists of the first two bars of the third entry in the exposition, along with the other two voices that constitute this fugue (Bruhn, 1993). The third entry is chosen because it is the first entry where the subject and the two countersubjects are stated together. The fugue's subject is detected by *PatMinr* as one single motivic/thematic class, i.e., one complete paradigmatic sheaf, resulting from the bundling method presented in Sect. 11.3.2.3. All occurrences indicated in the ground truth are retrieved. The patterns forming this thematic class are longer than the two-bar motive indicated in the ground truth. The limitation of all subjects and counter-subjects in the musicological analysis to two bars stems from a theoretical understanding of fugue structure that cannot be automatically inferred from a direct analysis of the score.

The model used in this analysis did not integrate mechanisms for the reduction of ornamentation, as discussed in Sect. 11.4. The only melodic ornamentation appearing amid the occurrences of the fugue's subject is the addition of a passing note after

---

[12] The piece was not analysed entirely, because the version of the algorithm was producing redundant patterns in such a way that the computation took an excessive amount of time and had to be interrupted.

the first notes of some occurrences. This leads to a small error in the model's results, where the first actual note is not detected.

The thematic class related to the first countersubject is extracted in the same way, forming a paradigmatic sheaf. The pattern class given by the model corresponds mostly to the ground truth. Here again, some occurrences present similar extensions that are inventoried by the model, although they are ignored in the ground truth. One occurrence is not properly detected, once again due to the addition of passing notes.

The second countersubject is more problematic, because it is only 7 notes long. Several other longer patterns are found by the model, and the specificity of this countersubject is not grounded on characteristics purely related to pattern repetition. As mentioned above, the ground-truth selection of these three patterns is based on principles related to fugue rules, namely the synchronized iteration of the three patterns along the separate voices. It seems questionable to expect a general pattern mining algorithm non-specialized to a particular type of music to be able to infer this type of configuration.

The analysis offered by the computational model offers richer information than simply listing the occurrences of the subjects and countersubjects. It shows what musical descriptions characterize them, and details particular commonalities shared by occurrences of these subjects and countersubjects.

Various versions of the presented computational model have been used to analyse pieces of music of different genres: among others, an 18th-century French folk song "*Au clair de la lune*", or the beginning of the upper voice of the theme of the *Andante grazioso* of Wolfgang Amadeus Mozart's Piano Sonata No. 11 in A major, K. 331 (Lartillot, 2014b).

11.6 Discussion

11.6.1 About Complexity

The determination of the computational costs of the method in time and space is a complex question that is currently under investigation. The objective of the approach was to achieve an exhaustive analysis, while keeping the representation compact and the computation realistic. When evaluating the behaviour of the successive versions of the model, there has been an implicit concern that the number of structural inferences for each successive note analysed should not grow asymptotically. In other words, a linear complexity in input to output size relationship is desired. Closed pattern mining and elementary principles of cyclic pattern mining allow the output size to be reduced significantly without loss of structural information. Still, further reduction in time complexity would require enhancing the cyclic pattern mining mechanisms as well as adding long-term memory limitations, so that a certain type of structural complexity is discarded. Core hypotheses here are that the human cognitive system also carries out some kind of selection process in order to reduce the number of inferred structures, and that a similar type of selection might be modelled computationally. Assessing the validity of these claims will require significant further work.

11.6.2 Connection With Serial Pattern Learning

According to Restle's (1970) theory of serial pattern learning, learning a patterned sequence involves dividing it into subparts, where some subparts are generated by applying simple rules on other subparts. A pattern representation such as the one developed in this chapter allows a more general understanding of structure, in which sequential repetitions are not necessarily repeated successively: they can start anywhere in the sequence. Moreover, the proposed pattern representation models not only the final structure, but also the incremental perspective taking place while observing (i.e., listening to) a sequence.

When pattern occurrences do occur successively, this corresponds to cyclic patterns as studied in Sect. 11.3.3, and this corresponds to the "repeat" operation R in Restle's theory (or equivalently to the "same" operation S in Simon's (1972) model). In Restle's and Simon's theories this is represented by a mere succession of a given pattern. For the example shown in Fig. 11.8, this would be represented as $R^n(A + B + C) + A$ using Restle's formalism.[13] The cyclic pattern representation shows that each occurrence of the pattern is immediately followed by another occurrence, by showing that each occurrence is followed by the first note of a new occurrence. But this first note is not only the first note of an occurrence of that pattern, it is also the note that follows a previous complete occurrence. This is what is represented by the cyclic pattern: at each step in each occurrence of the pattern, we know that the occurrence being constructed actually follows a previous occurrence of the periodic pattern. Moreover, whereas Restle's and Simon's representations impose one single understanding of the structure as the successive repetition of one given period, the cyclic pattern representation, due to its symmetry, implicitly encompasses all possible rotations of that period—for example, ABCABCA can be understood not only as (ABC)(ABC)A, but also as A(BCA)(BCA).

11.6.3 Future Work

By controlling the factors of combinatorial redundancy, the approach proposed in this chapter allows for the generation of a detailed description of pattern repetitions. The approach is incremental, progressively analysing the musical sequence through one single pass. This allows the structural complexity to be controlled using simple heuristics. Besides the chronological approach, other techniques introduced in the model include the concept of motivic cyclicity as a way to filter out the proliferation of

---

[13] We note that prefixes, such as the final A which is a prefix of ABC, are not represented as such in Restle's representation.

redundant patterns, and the integration of heuristics based on the figure-ground Gestalt principle. We might hypothesize that the proposed model offers some explanation concerning the ways listeners actually perceive and understand music; however, further experiments need to be carried out in order to test this claim. The cognitive validation of the principles underlying the model presented in this chapter could form a topic for future work.

Gross contour needs to be constrained by factors related to local saliency and short-term memory (Lartillot, 2009). The integration of beat positions and articulation information, as shown in the examples developed in Sect. 11.2, is currently under development. The study of ornamentation based on a syntagmatic network needs further investigation: the solutions proposed in Sect. 11.4 only partially solve this problem—further mechanisms need to be taken into account.

The model presented in this chapter is restricted to the analysis of monodies, which is evidently a major limitation on the scope of application of the analytic method. Polyphonic scores could be analysed if they are decomposed into a set of monodies, which is possible for pieces like fugues that are in a contrapuntal style. Of course, the automation of voice extraction from polyphony remains a challenging problem. We are currently working on extending the model towards the detection of repeated monodic patterns within a general polyphony without prior specification of monodic lines. We also plan to generalize the model to the detection of patterns in chord sequences.

We are also currently investigating the modelling of patterns of patterns, where the meta-pattern consists of, for instance, various occurrences of the same pattern. Motivic analysis can also provide useful input for the analysis of metrical structure, leading to an interesting interdependency between these two types of analysis.

Acknowledgements This chapter benefited from valuable comments and suggestions from David Meredith and two anonymous reviewers. The work reported in this chapter was carried out within the European project, "Learning to Create" (Lrn2Cre8). The project Lrn2Cre8 acknowledges the financial support of the Future and Emerging Technologies (FET) programme within the Seventh Framework Programme for Research of the European Commission, under FET grant number 610859.

References

Bayardo, R. J. (1998). Efficiently mining long patterns from databases. In *Proceedings of the 1998 ACM SIGMOD International Conference on Management of data (SIGMOD '98)*, pages 85–93.

Bruhn, S. (1993). *J. S. Bach's Well-Tempered Clavier: In-Depth Analysis and Interpretation*. Mainer International.

Cambouropoulos, E. (1998). *Towards a general computational theory of musical structure*. PhD thesis, University of Edinburgh.

Cambouropoulos, E. (2006). Musical parallelism and melodic segmentation: A computational approach. *Music Perception*, 23(3):249–268.

Collins, T. (2014). MIREX 2014: Discovery of repeated themes and sections. http://www.music-ir.org/mirex.

Conklin, D. and Anagnostopoulou, C. (2001). Representation and discovery of multiple viewpoint patterns. In *Proceedings of the International Computer Music Conference (ICMC 2001)*, pages 479–485, Havana, Cuba.

Conklin, D. and Bergeron, M. (2008). Feature set patterns in music. *Computer Music Journal*, 32(1):60–70.

de Saussure, F. (1916). *Cours de linguistique générale*. Payot.

Lartillot, O. (2005). Multi-dimensional motivic pattern extraction founded on adaptive redundancy filtering. *Journal of New Music Research*, 34(4):375–393.

Lartillot, O. (2009). Taxonomic categorisation of motivic patterns. *Musicae Scientiae*, Discussion Forum 4(B):25–46.

Lartillot, O. (2014a). In-depth motivic analysis based on multiparametric closed pattern and cyclic sequence mining. In *Proceedings of the International Society for Music Information Retrieval Conference (ISMIR 2014)*, pages 361–366, Taipei, Taiwan.

Lartillot, O. (2014b). An integrative computational modelling of music structure apprehension. In *Proceedings of the International Conference on Music Perception and Cognition (ICMPC 2014)*, pages 80–86, Seoul, South Korea.

Lartillot, O. (2015). Miningsuite. https://code.google.com/p/miningsuite.

Lerdahl, F. and Jackendoff, R. (1983). *A Generative Theory of Tonal Music*. MIT Press.

Meredith, D. (2013). COSIATEC and SIATECCompress: Pattern discovery by geometric compression. In *MIREX 2013 (Competition on Discovery of Repeated Themes & Sections)*. Available online at http://www.titanmusic.com/papers/public/MeredithMIREX2013.pdf.

Meredith, D., Lemström, K., and Wiggins, G. A. (2002). Algorithms for discovering repeated patterns in multidimensional representations of polyphonic music. *Journal of New Music Research*, 31(4):321–345.

Nattiez, J.-J. (1990). *Music and discourse: Toward a semiology of music*. Princeton University Press.

Pasquier, N., Bastide, Y., Taouil, R., and Lakhal, L. (1999). Efficient mining of associative rules using closed itemset lattices. *Information Systems*, 24(1):25–46.

Restle, F. (1970). Theory of serial pattern learning: structural trees. *Psychological Review*, 77(6):481–495.

Rolland, P.-Y. (1999). Discovering patterns in musical sequences. *Journal of New Music Research*, 28(4):334–350.

Ruwet, N. (1987). Methods of analysis in musicology. *Music Analysis*, 6(1-2):11–36.

Simon, H. A. (1972). Complexity and the representation of patterned sequences of symbols. *Psychological Review*, 79(5):369–382.

Tenney, J. and Polansky, L. (1980). Temporal gestalt perception in music. *Journal of Music Theory*, 24(2):205–241.

Velarde, G. and Meredith, D. (2014). A wavelet-based approach to the discovery of themes and sections in monophonic melodies. In *Music Information Retrieval*

Evaluation Exchange (MIREX 2014), Competition on Discovery of Repeated Themes and Sections, Taipei, Taiwan.

Wang, J., Han, J., and Li., C. (2007). Frequent closed sequence mining without candidate maintenance. *IEEE Transactions on Knowledge and Data Engineering*, 19(8):1042–1056.

Chapter 12
A Wavelet-Based Approach to Pattern Discovery in Melodies

Gissel Velarde, David Meredith, and Tillman Weyde

Abstract We present a computational method for pattern discovery based on the application of the wavelet transform to symbolic representations of melodies or monophonic voices. We model the importance of a discovered pattern in terms of the compression ratio that can be achieved by using it to describe that part of the melody covered by its occurrences. The proposed method resembles that of paradigmatic analysis developed by Ruwet (1966) and Nattiez (1975). In our approach, melodies are represented either as 'raw' 1-dimensional pitch signals or as these signals filtered with the *continuous wavelet transform* (CWT) at a single scale using the Haar wavelet. These representations are segmented using various approaches and the segments are then concatenated based on their similarity. The concatenated segments are compared, clustered and ranked. The method was evaluated on two musicological tasks: discovering themes and sections in the JKU Patterns Development Database and determining the parent compositions of excerpts from J. S. Bach's Two-Part Inventions (BWV 772–786). The results indicate that the new approach performs well at finding noticeable and/or important patterns in melodies and that filtering makes the method robust to melodic variation.

12.1 Introduction

Since the 19th century, music theorists have placed great importance on the analysis of motivic repetition and variation (Marx, 1837; Reicha, 1814; Riemann, 1912;

Gissel Velarde · David Meredith
Department of Architecture, Design and Media Technology, Aalborg University, Aalborg, Denmark
e-mail: {gv, dave}@create.aau.dk

Tillman Weyde
Department of Computer Science, City University London, London, UK
e-mail: t.e.weyde@city.ac.uk

© Springer International Publishing Switzerland 2016
D. Meredith (ed.), *Computational Music Analysis*,
DOI 10.1007/978-3-319-25931-4_12

Schoenberg, 1967), leading to the development of *paradigmatic analysis* by Ruwet (1966) and Nattiez (1986) during the latter half of the 20th century. Ruwet's method consists of an exhaustive similarity comparison of small units or segments in order to generate a structural description (see Monelle, 1992). Paradigmatic analysis focuses on clustering similar segments in a melody into "paradigms", regardless of where these segments might occur. It is typically carried out in parallel with *syntagmatic analysis* which focuses on identifying sequential relationships between consecutive segments. Syntagmatic and paradigmatic analysis can be seen as complementary tools for exploring the *semiotic* structure of a melody.

Almost three decades after the work by Ruwet, the first computational models to automate paradigmatic analysis of music appeared (Adiloglu et al., 2006; Anagnostopoulou and Westermann, 1997; Cambouropoulos, 1998; Cambouropoulos and Widmer, 2000; Conklin, 2006; Conklin and Anagnostopoulou, 2006; Grilo et al., 2001; Höthker et al., 2001; Weyde, 2001). However, it is difficult to evaluate these models, as some are not fully automated (e.g., require a user-supplied segmentation), the implementations are generally not public and they have not been tested on a common ground truth. Although the notion of defining a ground truth at all for a musical analysis is controversial, the MIREX task on discovery of repeated themes and sections (Collins, 2014) offers a practical opportunity to evaluate thematic analysis algorithms. However, it should be noted that the 'ground truth' analyses used in this task do not include any analyses by experts in paradigmatic analysis.

In this chapter, we focus on describing a fully automated method of musical analysis that closely resembles paradigmatic analysis. It has been implemented in Matlab and it is publicly available.[1] The method is based on segmenting melodies, clustering the resulting segments by similarity and then ranking the clusters obtained. In Sect. 12.3 we present the results obtained when our method was used for discovering repeating themes and sections in the Johannes Kepler University Patterns Development Database (JKU PDD).[2] We also compare these results with those obtained using other methods. In order to test the generalizability of the proposed method, we also evaluated it on a second musicological task, namely, that of identifying the parent compositions of excerpts from J. S. Bach's Two-Part Inventions (BWV 772–786).[3]

---

[1] Available at http://www.create.aau.dk/music/software/. It is implemented in MATLAB (R2014a, The Mathworks, Inc), using the following toolboxes: Signal Processing, Statistics, Symbolic Math, Wavelet, and the MIDI Toolbox (Eerola and Toiviainen, 2004). We also used an implementation of the dynamic time warping algorithm (DTW) by Paul Micó, accessed on 30-April-2013 from http://www.mathworks.com/matlabcentral/fileexchange/16350-continuous-dynamic-time-warping.

[2] https://dl.dropbox.com/u/11997856/JKU/JKUPDD-Aug2013.zip. Accessed on 12-May-2014.

[3] MIDI encodings edited by Steve Rasmussen, http://www.musedata.org/encodings/bach/rasmuss/inventio/. Accessed April 2011

12.1.1 Melodic Structure and Wavelet Analysis

Our understanding of melodic structure has benefited from work that has been carried out in a number of fields, including music theory, psychology neuroscience and computer science. For example, melodic contour has been studied by Huron (1996), who classified melodies into 9 types according to their shapes (e.g., ascending, descending, arc-like, etc.) by considering the first, last and average pitches of a melody. In contrast, Schenkerian analysis aims to recursively reduce the musical surface or *foreground* to a *fundamental structure (Urzatz)* via one or more *middleground* levels *(Schichten)* (Schenker, 1935). Furthermore, listeners typically hear melodies to be "chunked" into *segments* or, more generally, *groups* (Cambouropoulos, 1997; Lerdahl and Jackendoff, 1983; Tenney and Polansky, 1980). Neuroscientific evidence from fMRI studies suggests that brain activity increases when subjects perceive boundaries between musical movements, and, indeed, boundaries between events in other, non-musical domains (Kurby and Zacks, 2008). Such evidence strongly supports the notion that segmentation is an essential component of perception, occurring simultaneously at multiple timescales. Psychological approaches focus on perception and memory and have tried to determine relevant melodic structures empirically (see, e.g., Lamont and Dibben, 2001; Müllensiefen and Wiggins, 2011b).

Computational approaches to the analysis of melodic structure include geometric approaches to pattern discovery, grammars, statistical descriptors, Gestalt features and data mining (see, e.g., Conklin, 2006; Mazzola et al., 2002; Meredith et al., 2002; Weyde, 2002). Wavelet analysis is a relatively new approach that has been widely used in audio signal processing. However, to our knowledge, it has been scarcely used on symbolic music representations, except by Smith and Honing (2008), who used wavelets to elicit rhythmic content from sparse sequences of impulses of a piece, and Pinto (2009), who used wavelets for melodic indexing as a compression technique.

As mentioned above, the wavelet-based method that we present below is closely related to paradigmatic analysis. It is based on the assumption that, if a melody is segmented appropriately, then it should be possible to produce a high-quality analysis by gathering together similar segments into clusters and then ranking these clusters by their importance or salience. In our study, we were particularly interested in exploring the effectiveness of the *wavelet transform* (WT) (Antoine, 1999; Farge, 1992; Mallat, 2009; Torrence and Compo, 1998) for representing relevant properties of melodies in segmentation, classification and pattern detection.

Wavelet analysis is a mathematical tool that compares a time-series with a wavelet at different positions and time scales, returning similarity coefficients. There are two main forms of the WT, the *continuous wavelet transform* (CWT) and the *discrete wavelet transform* (DWT). The CWT is mostly used for pattern analysis or feature detection in signal analysis (e.g., Smith and Honing, 2008), while the DWT is used for compression and reconstruction (e.g., Antoine, 1999; Mallat, 2009; Pinto, 2009). In our method, we sample symbolic representations of melodies or monophonic voices to produce one-dimensional (1D) *pitch signals*. We then apply the continuous wavelet transform (CWT) to these pitch signals, filtering with the Haar wavelet (Haar, 1910). Filtering with wavelets at different scales resembles the mechanism by

Fig. 12.1 A schematic overview of the main stages of the proposed method

which neurons, such as orientation-selective simple cells in the primary visual cortex, gather information from their receptive fields (Hubel and Wiesel, 1962). Indeed, more recently, Gabor wavelet pyramids have been used to model the perception of visual features in natural scenes (Kay et al., 2008).

Wavelet coefficient encodings seem to be particularly appropriate for melodic analysis as they provide a transposition-invariant representation. We also use wavelet coefficient representations to determine local segment boundaries at different time scales, which accords well with the notion that listeners automatically organize the musical surface into coherent segments, or groups, at various time scales (Lerdahl and Jackendoff, 1983).

12.2 Method

The method presented in this chapter extends our previously reported approach to melodic segmentation and classification based on filtering with the Haar wavelet (Velarde et al., 2013), and also incorporates an approach to segment construction similar to that developed by Aucouturier and Sandler (2002) for discovering patterns in audio data. A schematic overview of the method is shown in Fig. 12.1. In the following sub-sections we explain the method in detail.

12.2.1 Representation

A wide variety of different strategies have been adopted in music informatics for representing melodies, including (among others) viewpoints (Conklin, 2006), strings (McGettrick, 1997), contours (Huron, 1996), polynomial functions (Müllensiefen and Wiggins, 2011a), point sets (Meredith et al., 2002), spline curves (Urbano, 2013), Fourier coefficients (Schmuckler, 1999) and global features (van Kranenburg et al., 2013).

The representations used in this study are illustrated in Fig. 12.2. The top graph in this figure shows what we call a *raw pitch signal*. This is a discrete pitch signal, v, with length, L, constructed by sampling from MIDI files at a rate, r, in samples per quarter note (qn). MIDI files encode pitches as MIDI Note Numbers (MIDI NN). We denote the pitch value at time point t by $v[t]$. This representation is not used for

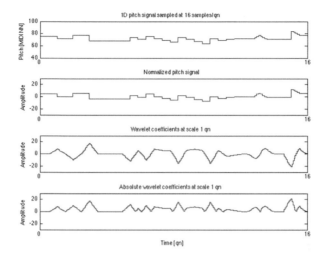

Fig. 12.2 Representations used in the method. From top to bottom: a raw pitch signal, a normalized pitch signal, a wavelet coefficient representation and an absolute wavelet coefficient representation

segment comparison directly. It is either filtered by the Haar wavelet or transformed into what we call a *normalized pitch signal* in order to obtain a transposition-invariant representation which is then segmented.

The second graph in Fig. 12.2 shows a *normalized pitch signal*, obtained by subtracting the average pitch of a segment from the pitch values in that segment. This process is applied to each segment individually after segmentation. It serves to reduce the measured dissimilarity between segments that have very similar contour but occur at different pitch heights (i.e., have different transpositions).

The third graph in Fig. 12.2 shows a *wavelet coefficient representation* resulting from carrying out a continuous wavelet transform (CWT) on the pitch signal with the Haar wavelet at a single time scale. This process tends to highlight structural features at the scale of the wavelet. The Haar wavelet (Haar, 1910) is used because it measures the movement direction of the melody and because its shape reflects the step-wise nature of symbolic pitch signals. Figure 12.3 shows an example of a Haar wavelet.

The CWT computed at a single time scale acts as a *filter* by the convolution of v, the pitch signal, with the scaled and flipped real-valued wavelet for each translation, u, and scale, s:

$$w_s[u] = \sum_{\ell=1}^{L} \psi_{s,u}[\ell]v[\ell] \ . \tag{12.1}$$

To avoid edge effects due to finite-length sequences (Torrence and Compo, 1998), we pad on both ends with a mirror image of v (Woody and Brown, 2007). To maintain

Fig. 12.3 The Haar wavelet

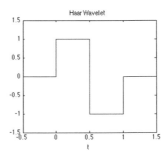

the signal's original length, the segments that correspond to the padding on both ends
are removed after convolution.

The bottom graph in Fig. 12.2 shows an *absolute wavelet coefficient* representation.
The value at each time point in this representation is the absolute value of the wavelet
coefficient at that time point.

The type of wavelet to use depends on the kind of information one wishes to
extract from the signal, since the wavelet coefficients combine information about
the signal and the analysing function (Farge, 1992). We use the Haar wavelet (Haar,
1910) as the analysing function, as defined by Mallat (2009):

$$\psi_t = \begin{cases} 1, & \text{if } 0 \le t < 0.5, \\ -1, & \text{if } 0.5 \le t < 1, \\ 0, & \text{otherwise.} \end{cases} \tag{12.2}$$

The choice of time scale depends on the scale of structure in which one is interested.
Local structure is best analysed using short time scales, while longer-term structure
can be revealed by using wavelets at longer time scales. When features of the wavelet-
based representations are used for segmentation (as will be described in Sect. 12.2.2),
using a shorter wavelet leads to smaller segments in general. We therefore expect
shorter wavelets to be more appropriate for finding smaller melodic structural units
such as motives, while longer wavelets might be expected to produce segments at
longer time scales such as the phrase level and above. In the experiments reported
below, we used a variety of different scales in order to explore the effect of time scale
on performance.

12.2.2 Segmentation

Segmentation is a central component of music perception, occurring simultaneously
at multiple timescales as an adaptive mechanism of the brain. It has been shown
that brain activity increases transiently at musical movement boundaries, as well as
other non-musical event boundaries (Kurby and Zacks, 2008). In agreement with the
neuroscientific evidence, most theories of music perception and cognition note the

importance of segmentation, or grouping at various different time scales. Typically, such theories concentrate on the perceived associations of events, relating visual Gestalt principles to the musical domain. Examples of such theories include Tenney and Polansky's theory of temporal Gestalt-units (Tenney and Polansky, 1980), Lerdahl and Jackendoff's theory of grouping structure (Lerdahl and Jackendoff, 1983) and Cambouropoulos' Local Boundary Detection Model (LBDM) (Cambouropoulos, 1997, 2001). The rules in these models address changes in both local parameters and longer-term averages. Similarly, wavelet filters could be used to represent melodic movements at different scales, leading to different levels of localization on the time-axis for deriving group boundaries. Conklin (2006) also stresses the importance of melodic analysis on segmentation. He additionally demonstrates the effect of different symbolic melodic representations called *viewpoints* at different time scales (note, beat, bar, phrase and piece level) in the context of style discrimination.

As shown in Fig. 12.1, the *Segmentation* phase of our method is split into three subphases: *Preliminary segmentation*, *Comparison* and *Concatenation*. Each of these subphases will now be described.

12.2.2.1 Preliminary Segmentation

In this study, we explored three strategies for producing a preliminary segmentation: constant-duration segmentation; segmentation at zero crossings in the wavelet coefficient and absolute wavelet coefficient representations; and segmentation at local maxima in the absolute wavelet coefficient representation. The lower three graphs in Fig. 12.4 show three of the possible combinations of representation and segmentation.

The simplest segmentation strategy that we explore is *constant-duration segmentation* in which the signal is chunked into segments of constant duration (with the possible exception of the final segment which could be shorter than the other segments). The second graph in Fig. 12.4 shows an example of this type of segmentation combined with a normalized pitch signal representation.

We also experiment with *zero-crossings* segmentation in the wavelet-based representations, where segment boundaries are set at time points with value zero in the representation. Zero-crossings occur when the inner product between the melody and the Haar wavelet is zero. This means that the average pitch in the first half of the scale period is equal to the average pitch in the second half of the scale period.

The third segmentation strategy we use is *absolute maxima* segmentation, where segment boundaries are set at time points corresponding to local maxima in the absolute wavelet coefficient representation. These maxima occur when the inner product of the wavelet and the signal is locally maximal. In our case, this corresponds to time points when there is a maximal positive or negative correlation between the shape of the melody and the Haar wavelet. These points occur when there is a locally maximal fall or rise in average pitch content at the scale of the wavelet used. The absolute maxima of a real wavelet such as the Haar wavelet are a special case of the *modulus maxima* of a wavelet transform in general. The latter were used by Muzy

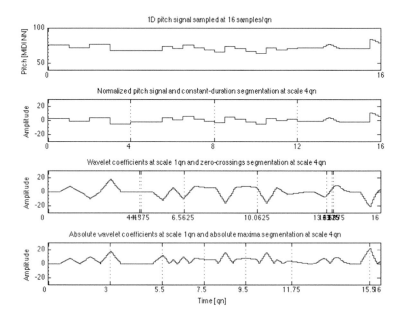

Fig. 12.4 Segmentation approaches used in the method, from top to bottom: a raw pitch signal without segmentation; normalized pitch signal and constant-duration segmentation at a scale of 4 qn; wavelet coefficient representation filtered with the Haar wavelet at a scale of 1 qn and segmented at zero-crossings at a scale of 4 qn; absolute wavelet coefficient representation filtered at a scale of 1 qn and segmented at absolute maxima at a scale of 4 qn. Note that the wavelet scales used to generate the *representations* shown in the third and fourth graphs are different from those used to produce the *segmentations*. The segmentation points therefore do not necessarily coincide with zero-crossings or maxima in the wavelet coefficient representations shown

et al. (1991) to show the structure of fractal signals and by Mallat and Hwang (1992) to indicate the location of edges in images. The bottom graph in Fig. 12.4 shows an example of absolute maxima segmentation of an absolute wavelet coefficient representation.

The segments obtained using these three strategies generally have different durations. However, in order to measure similarity between them using standard metrics such as *city block* or *Euclidean distance*, it is necessary for the segments to be the same length. We achieve this by defining a maximal length for all segments and padding shorter segments as necessary with zeros at the end.

12.2.2.2 Comparison

Segments are compared by building an $m \times m$ distance matrix, H, giving all pair-wise distances between segments in terms of normalized distance. m is the number of segments. We use three different distance measures: *Euclidean distance*, *city block distance* and *dynamic time warping* (DTW). For city block and Euclidean distances, the segments compared must be of equal length and in these cases the normalization consists of dividing the pairwise distance by the length of the smallest segment before segment-length equalization by zero padding. When using DTW, which is an alignment-based method, it is not necessary to equalize the lengths of the segments being compared. In this case, therefore, the normalization consists of dividing the distance by the length of the aligned segments.

We use the *Euclidean distance* $d_E(x,y)$ between two segments, x and y, which is defined as follows:

$$d_E(x,y) = \sqrt{\sum_{j=1}^{n} (x[j] - y[j])^2} \,, \tag{12.3}$$

and the *city block distance* $d_C(x,y)$ between x and y:

$$d_C(x,y) = \sum_{j=1}^{n} |x[j] - y[j]| \,. \tag{12.4}$$

The *dynamic time warping distance* (DTW), $d_D(x,y)$, is the minimal cost of a *warping path* between sequences x and y. A warping path of length, L, is a sequence of pairs $p = ((n_1,m_1),...,(n_L,m_L))$, where n_i is an index into x and m_i is an index into y. p needs to satisfy several conditions which ensure that it can be interpreted as an alignment between x and y that allows skipping elements in either sequence (see Müller, 2007, p. 70). The DTW distance, $d_D(x,y)$, is then defined to be the total cost of a warping path, defined to be the sum of a local cost measure, $c(x[n_i],y[m_i])$, along the path:

$$d_D(x,y) = \sum_{i=1}^{L} c(x[n_i],y[m_i]) \,, \tag{12.5}$$

where, here, $c(x[n_i],y[m_i])$ is defined to be simply the absolute difference, $|x[n_i] - y[m_i]|$.

Having computed all the pairwise distances in the matrix, H, these values are then normalized in the range $[0,1]$ by dividing each pairwise distance by the largest distance in the matrix for that distance type.

12.2.2.3 Concatenation of Segments

The final subphase of the segmentation phase is to concatenate consecutive segments found in the preliminary segmentation to form larger units that are then compared, clustered and ranked in the subsequent phases of the method.

The first subphase of the segmentation phase gives a preliminary segmentation of the melody. It is preliminary, as it may be the case that a repeated (or approximately repeated) segment discovered in the preliminary segmentation only occurs as part of a longer repeated segment, such that a paradigmatic relation is found. In such cases, one would generally only be interested in the longer repeated segment (this relates to the concept of "closed patterns" (see Lartillot, 2005, and Chap. 11, this volume) and Meredith et al.'s (2002) concept of "maximal translatable patterns" (see also Chap. 13, this volume). One would only want to report the shorter segment if it also occurred independently of the longer segment. In the third subphase of the segmentation phase, we therefore concatenate, or merge locally, the preliminary segments derived in the preliminary segmentation into generally longer units, that are then passed on to the later phases of the method.

Segments are concatenated based on their similarity. We therefore set a threshold, τ, that defines the level of similarity between preliminary segments required to allow concatenation. The $m \times m$ distance matrix, H, is therefore binarized as follows:

$$H(i,j) = \begin{cases} 1, & \text{if } H(i,j) \leq \tau, \\ 0, & \text{otherwise,} \end{cases} \qquad (12.6)$$

for $1 \leq i \leq m$ and $i \leq j \leq m$ (note that we use 1-based indexing in this chapter).

Segments are concatenated to form units based on the information contained in the upper triangle including the leading diagonal in the binarized similarity matrix, H, scanning the matrix horizontally and diagonally. A *unit*, $\overline{(i,j)}$, $i \leq j$, consists of the concatenated segments $i, \ldots, j$, and we use two concatenation processes to generate units.

A process of *horizontal concatenation* generates units that consist of consecutive occurrences of the "same" segment (i.e., corresponding to horizontal sequences of consecutive 1s in the binarized similarity matrix, H). The units, $\overline{(i,k)}$, generated by this process are those for which $hor(i,k)$ is true, where

$$hor(i,k) \iff (hor(i,k-1) \wedge H(k-1,k) = 1) \vee (i=k). \qquad (12.7)$$

A process of *diagonal concatenation* generates units that are repeated in the piece, and $dia(i,j)$ must be true, where

$$dia(i,j) \iff (dia(i,j-1) \wedge \exists \ell, k \mid \ell - k = j - i \wedge dia(k,\ell-1) \wedge H(j-1,\ell-1) = H(j,\ell) = 1)$$
$$\vee (j-i=1 \wedge \exists \ell \mid H(i,\ell-1) = H(j,\ell) = 1). \qquad (12.8)$$

Any $hor(i,j)$ or $dia(i,j)$ that is not a strict subset of another generates a unit $\overline{(i,j)}$. Subsets will be identified as *trivial units*.

When these two concatenation processes are carried out on the matrix in Fig. 12.5, horizontal concatenation generates the unit $\overline{(9,10)}$ and diagonal concatenation generates the units $\overline{(1,2)}$, $\overline{(4,5)}$ and $\overline{(7,8)}$.

The concatenation method presented here is similar to the one described by Aucouturier and Sandler (2002).

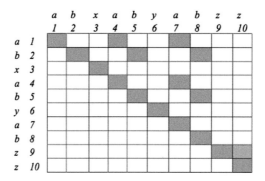

Fig. 12.5 Upper triangular matrix, grey means 1 and white 0. It corresponds to the binarized distance matrix H of the sequence $v_1 = abxabyabzz$

12.2.3 Comparison and Clustering of Units

In this second comparison, the units constructed in the previous concatenation step (Sect. 12.2.2.3) are compared using the same process of similarity measurement as that described in Sect. 12.2.2.2. Any two units $\overline{(\ell, j)}$ and $\overline{(p, r)}$ obtained by concatenation, will then be units x and y respectively, to be compared in this second comparison.

Having obtained values for the pairwise similarity between units, these similarity values are then used to cluster the units into classes. To achieve this, we use a simple hierarchical agglomerative clustering method called *single linkage*, or *nearest-neighbour*, which produces a series of successive fusions of the data, starting from N single-member clusters that fuse together to form larger clusters (Everitt et al., 2011; Florek et al., 1951; Johnson, 1967; Sneath, 1957). Here, the distance matrix obtained from the comparison as described in Sect. 12.2.3 is used for clustering. *Single linkage* takes the smallest distance between any two units, one from each group or cluster. The distance $D(X,Y)$ between clusters X and Y is described as

$$D(X,Y) = \min_{x \in X, y \in Y} d(x,y) \,, \tag{12.9}$$

where clusters X and Y are formed by the fusion of two clusters, x and y, and $d(x,y)$ denotes the distance between the two units x and y (Everitt et al., 2011). Consider the case of five units or clusters v, w, x, y and z, as shown on the left in Fig. 12.6 as points in a Euclidean space. The minimal distance occurs for x and y, and for z and w. Then, two new clusters are formed, a cluster s consisting of x and y and a cluster t consisting of z and w. The next minimal distance occurs for v and t, forming a new cluster u consisting of v and t. Finally, clusters s and u are grouped together into a cluster c. The right plot in Fig. 12.6 shows a dendrogram of the formed clusters. The y-axis corresponds to the distances between clusters; for instance, clusters x and y

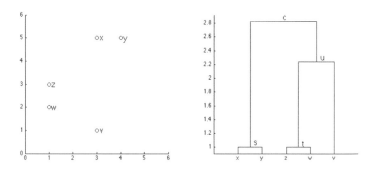

Fig. 12.6 Example of the hierarchical clustering of units or clusters v, w, x, y and z. Left plot shows the units in a Euclidean space. Right plot shows a dendrogram of the formed clusters

have a distance of 1, and clusters t and u have a distance of 2.2. In this example, the number of clusters ranges from 1, where all units form a single cluster, to 5, where each cluster contains just one unit. The number of clusters can be set to be three, having clusters s, t and u or it can be set to two, giving clusters s and u. Finally, the number of clusters is set to yield the best classification results.[4]

12.2.4 Ranking

In general, if X and Y are two parts of some object, then one can describe $X \cup Y$ in an *in extenso* fashion simply by specifying the properties of each atomic component in X and Y. Alternatively, if there exists a sufficiently simple transformation, T, that maps X onto Y, then it may be possible to provide a compact description of $X \cup Y$ by providing an in extenso description of X along with a description of T.[5]

In the current context, each cluster generated by the previous stage of the method contains units (i.e., parts of a melody) that are similar to each other. If every member of a cluster can be generated by a simple transformation of one member (e.g., if all the units within a cluster are exact repeats of the first occurrence), then the portion of the melody *covered* by the cluster (i.e., the union of the units in the cluster) can be represented by giving an explicit description of the first occurrence along with the positions of the other occurrences. If the members of the cluster do not overlap, then such a representation can be compact because the starting position of a unit can usually be specified using fewer bits than explicitly describing the content of the unit. This would give a losslessly compressed encoding of the part of the melody

---

[4] When preliminary experiments were performed on the JKU PDD, using between 3 and 10 clusters, the best classification results were obtained using 7 clusters. We therefore used 7 clusters in the experiments reported in Sect. 12.3 below.

[5] This idea is discussed in more detail in Chap. 13, this volume.

covered by the union of the units in the cluster. This is the essential idea behind the compression-driven geometric pattern discovery algorithms described by Meredith (2006, 2013) and Forth (2012). If we represent the music to be analysed as a set of points in pitch-time space and if a cluster (or 'paradigm'), C, only contains the *exact* occurrences of a pattern, p, then the compression ratio achieved is

$$CR(C) = \frac{|\bigcup_{q \in C} \{q\}|}{|p| + |C| - 1},$$ (12.10)

where $|\cdot|$ denotes the cardinality of a set. Here, however, the units within a cluster are not necessarily exact repetitions of some single pattern. This means that the degree of compression achievable with one of the clusters generated in the previous sections will not, in general, be as high as in (12.10).

Collins et al. (2011) have provided empirical evidence that the compression ratio achievable in this way by a set of occurrences of a pattern can be used to help predict which patterns in a piece of music are heard to be noticeable and/or important. In the method presented in this chapter, we therefore adapt (12.10) to serve as a measure of importance or noticeability for the clusters generated in the previous phase of the method. Here, we define the "compression ratio", CR_k, of cluster k as follows:

$$CR_k = \frac{\sum_{i=1}^{n_k} S_i}{(n_k + \bar{S}_k)},$$ (12.11)

where n_k is the number of units in cluster k, S_i is the length in sample points of unit i in cluster k, and $\bar{S}_k$ is the mean length of a unit in cluster k. Clusters are ranked into descending order by this value of "compression ratio". All clusters are kept in the final output.

12.3 Experiments

The method described above was evaluated on two tasks: discovering repeated themes and sections in monophonic music; and identifying the parent works of excerpts from J. S. Bach's Two-Part Inventions (BWV 772–786). The methods used and results obtained in these experiments will now be presented.

12.3.1 Experiment 1: Discovering Repeated Themes and Sections in Monophonic Music

Various computational methods for discovering patterns in music have been developed over the past two decades (see Janssen et al., 2013, for a recent review), but only recently have attempts been made to compare their outputs in a rigorous way.

Notable among such attempts are the two tasks on discovering repeated themes and sections that have been held at the Music Information Retrieval Evaluation eXchange (MIREX) in 2013 and 2014 (Collins, 2014). In these tasks, algorithms have been run on a set of five pieces and the analyses generated by the algorithms have been compared with ground truth analyses by expert analysts. A number of measures were devised for evaluating the performance of pattern discovery algorithms in this competition and comparing the output of an algorithm with a ground truth analysis (Collins, 2014). Collins has also provided a training database, the JKU PDD, which exists in both monophonic and polyphonic versions. The JKU PDD consists of the following five pieces along with ground truth analyses:

• Orlando Gibbons' madrigal, "Silver Swan" (1612);
• the fugue from J. S. Bach's Prelude and Fugue in A minor (BWV 889) from Book 2 of *Das wohltemperirte Clavier* (1742);
• the second movement of Mozart's Piano Sonata in E flat major (K. 282) (1774);
• the third movement of Beethoven's Piano Sonata in F minor, Op. 2, No. 1 (1795); and
• Chopin's Mazurka in B flat minor, Op. 24, No. 4 (1836).

The monophonic versions of the pieces by Beethoven, Mozart and Chopin were produced by selecting the notes in the most salient part (usually the top part) at each point in the music. For the contrapuntal pieces by Bach and Gibbons, the monophonic encodings were produced by concatenating the voices (Collins, 2014).

We used the JKU PDD as a training set for determining optimal values for the parameters of the analysis method described above. Heuristics based on knowledge gained from previous experiments (Velarde et al., 2013) were used to start tuning the parameters. Then, in an attempt to approach optimal values, all parameters were kept fixed, except one which was varied along a defined range to find an optimal adjustment. This process was repeated for all parameters. Finally, the method was run on the JKU PDD with 162 different parameter value combinations, consisting of all possible combinations of the following:

• 1 sampling rate: 16 samples per qn
• 3 representations: normalized pitch signal, wavelet coefficients filtered at the scale of 1 qn, absolute wavelet coefficients filtered at the scale of 1 qn
• 3 segmentation strategies: constant-duration segmentation, segmentation at zero-crossings, segmentation at absolute maxima
• 2 scales for segmentation: 1 qn and 4 qn
• 1 threshold for binarizing the similarity matrix: 0.001
• 3 distances for measuring similarity between segments on the first comparison: city block (CB), Euclidean (Eu) and dynamic time warping (DTW)
• 3 distances for measuring similarity between segments on the second comparison: city block (CB), Euclidean (Eu) and dynamic time warping (DTW)
• 1 strategy for equalizing the lengths of segments for comparison: segment length normalization by zero padding
• 1 clustering method: Single linkage (nearest neighbour)
• 1 value for the number of clusters: 7

- 1 criterion for ranking clusters: compression ratio

12.3.1.1 Results

We used the monophonic version of the JKU PDD with the evaluation metrics defined by Collins (2014) and Meredith (2015), which we computed using Collins' Matlab implementation.[6] The evaluation metrics consist of a number of variants on standard precision, recall and F_1 score, designed to allow algorithms to gain credit for generating sets of occurrences of patterns that are similar but not identical to those in the ground truth. The standard versions of the metrics are not adequate for evaluating pattern discovery algorithms because they return 0 for a computed pattern even if it differs from a ground truth pattern by only one note.

The more robust versions of the precision, recall and F_1 score are designed to measure (1) the extent to which an algorithm finds at least one occurrence of a pattern (*establishment recall/precision/F_1 score*); (2) the extent to which an algorithm finds all the occurrences of a pattern (*occurrence recall/precision/F_1 score*); and (3) the overall similarity between the set of occurrence sets generated by an algorithm and the set of occurrence sets in a ground truth analysis (*three-layer precision/recall/F_1 score*). As these different metrics reveal different aspects of the method's strengths or weaknesses, we decided to evaluate our method based on the standard F_1 score, where P is precision and R is recall

$$F_1 = \frac{2PR}{P+R} \tag{12.12}$$

and on the mean of establishment F_1 ($F1\_est$), occurrence F_1 at (c=.75) ($F1\_occ_{(c=.75)}$), occurrence F_1 at (c=.5) ($F1\_occ_{(c=.5)}$) (Collins, 2014), and three-layer F_1 ($F1\_TL$) (Meredith, 2015):

$$F1\_mean = \frac{F1\_est + F1\_occ_{(c=.75)} + F1\_occ_{(c=.5)}) + F1\_TL}{4}. \tag{12.13}$$

Figure 12.7 shows the highest mean F_1 scores ($F1\_mean$) for each combination, considering segmentation scale, representation type and segmentation type. The left plot shows nine combinations where the segmentation scale was 1 qn, while the right plot shows the scores of nine combinations where the segmentation scale was 4 qn. For each plot in Fig. 12.7, there are 3 bars grouped for each segmentation method, where the grey tones (dark grey, light grey and white) indicate the three representation types, and finally, the distance measures associated with the first and second comparison (e.g., "EU,EU", "CB,CB", etc.). Figure 12.8 shows the corresponding standard F_1 scores for the same combinations. Finally, Fig. 12.9 shows the runtimes in seconds obtained with our implementations of the method, associated with each combination.

---

[6] https://dl.dropbox.com/u/11997856/JKU/JKUPDD-Aug2013.zip. Accessed on 12-May-2014.

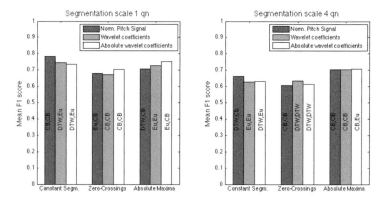

Fig. 12.7 Mean F_1 score ($F1\_mean$)

We ran the experiment twice, the first time keeping trivial units and the second time discarding trivial units. Figures 12.7, 12.8 and 12.9 show the results when keeping trivial units. A Wilcoxon signed rank test indicated that keeping or discarding trivial units did not significantly affect the results of mean F_1 scores ($Z = -1.2439$, $p = 0.2135$), standard F_1 scores ($Z = -1.633$, $p = 0.1025$), or runtimes ($Z = -0.8885$, $p = 0.3743$), for a segmentation scale of 1 qn. Similarly, no difference was found in the results when keeping or discarding trivial units for a scale of 4 qn for mean F_1 scores ($Z = 1.007$, $p = 0.3139$), standard F_1 scores ($Z = 0$, $p = 1$), or runtimes ($Z = -0.53331$, $p = 0.5940$). Therefore, only the results of the first run are shown and explained in the following paragraphs.

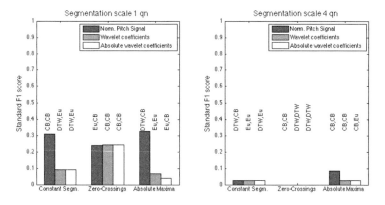

Fig. 12.8 Standard F_1 score

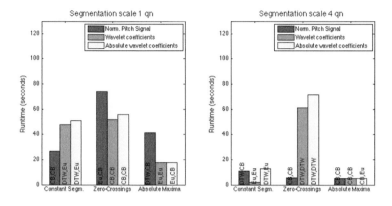

Fig. 12.9 Runtimes in seconds obtained using our implementation of the method. The implementation was programmed using Matlab 2014a and run on a MacBook Pro using MAC OS X with a 2.3 GHz, Intel Core i7 processor and 8 GB 1600 MHz DDR3 RAM

According to the parameters tested, we observe that the segmentation scale used in the preliminary segmentation phase has a greater effect on the results. Figures 12.8 and 12.9 show that using a smaller segmentation scale of 1 qn as opposed to 4 qn was in general slower but produced better results. A Wilcoxon signed rank test indicated there is a statistically significant difference between the use of a smaller and larger scale ($Z = 2.6656$, $p = 0.007$), suggesting that a scale of 1 qn should be used in the preliminary segmentation phase, for higher (mean or standard) F_1 scores.

In terms of mean F_1 score (Fig. 12.7), the normalized pitch signal representation worked slightly better than the wavelet representations when constant-duration segmentation was used. We speculate that only with additional pattern data containing greater variation between occurrences would the benefit of wavelet over normalized pitch representations emerge (see Sect. 12.3.2.1 for more discussion on this point). DTW was used less frequently than Euclidean or city block distance in the best-performing combinations. It seems possible that DTW might have proved more useful if the input representations had included temporal deviations such as *ritardando* or *accelerando* such as might occur in an encoding generated from a live performance.

From Figs. 12.7, 12.8 and 12.9 it is not possible to determine whether the running time is more dependent on the segmentation approach or on the distance measure used. Tables 12.1 and 12.2, show the highest mean F_1 scores of combinations using the same distance measure for both comparison phases, averaged by representation approach. From Table 12.1, it is possible to observe that when using a scale of 1 qn for the preliminary segmentation phase, Euclidean and city-block distances have similar performance, and their F_1 scores are higher than the ones delivered when using DTW distance. However, this gap becomes smaller when the scale is 4 qn. The results in Table 12.2 show that the running times using DTW are more than 8 times slower than those obtained using Euclidean or city-block distances. Evaluating runtimes according to segmentation approaches, it is possible to observe that for the smaller

Table 12.1 Mean F_1 scores averaged over representations, combinations of same distance measure for both comparisons. The rows correspond to the different combinations of distances (CB = city-block, Eu = Euclidean and DTW = dynamic time warping), while the columns correspond to the segmentation approaches (CS = constant-duration segmentation, ZC = zero-crossings segmentation, and AM = absolute maxima segmentation). Mean and standard deviation values are shown per row and per column

	Segmentation scale 1 qn					Segmentation scale 4 qn				
	CS	ZC	AM	**Mean**	SD	CS	ZC	AM	**Mean**	SD
CB-CB	0.74	0.69	0.75	**0.73**	0.03	0.65	0.60	0.70	**0.65**	0.05
Eu-Eu	0.73	0.68	0.72	**0.71**	0.03	0.63	0.59	0.70	**0.64**	0.05
DTW-DTW	0.57	0.64	0.60	**0.60**	0.04	0.59	0.61	0.66	**0.62**	0.03
Mean	**0.68**	**0.67**	**0.60**			**0.62**	**0.60**	**0.69**		
SD	0.10	0.03	0.08			0.03	0.01	0.03		

Table 12.2 Corresponding mean running times in seconds of the combinations in Table 12.1

	Segmentation scale 1 qn					Segmentation scale 4 qn				
	CS	ZC	AM	Mean	SD	CS	ZC	AM	Mean	SD
CB-CB	24.3	60.8	17.9	**34.32**	23.17	2.2	5.4	5.2	**4.23**	1.80
Eu-Eu	24.4	57.1	17.8	**33.10**	21.02	2.1	5.3	5.1	**4.16**	1.79
DTW-DTW	664.4	2248.2	720.1	**1210.91**	898.77	21.5	61.5	67.4	**50.14**	25.01
Mean	237.69	788.70	251.93			8.58	24.04	25.92		
SD	369.56	1263.98	405.44			11.17	32.44	35.97		

Table 12.3 Mean F_1 scores averaged over representations, when the concatenation phase is not performed. The rows of the Table indicate the distances used for comparison (CB = city-block, Eu = Euclidean and DTW = dynamic time warping), while the columns correspond to the segmentation approaches (CS = constant-duration segmentation, ZC = zero-crossings segmentation, and AM = absolute maxima segmentation). Mean and standard deviation values are shown per rows and per columns

	Segmentation scale 1 qn					Segmentation scale 4 qn				
	CS	ZC	AM	**Mean**	SD	CS	ZC	AM	**Mean**	SD
CB	0.10	0.18	0.11	**0.13**	0.04	0.22	0.23	0.18	**0.21**	0.03
Eu	0.10	0.14	0.10	**0.11**	0.02	0.22	0.21	0.16	**0.20**	0.03
DTW	0.10	0.09	0.11	**0.10**	0.01	0.22	0.20	0.18	**0.20**	0.02
Mean	**0.10**	**0.14**	**0.11**			**0.22**	**0.21**	**0.18**		
SD	0.00	0.04	0.01			0.00	0.02	0.01		

scale of 1 qn in the preliminary segmentation phase, the runtimes of constant-duration segmentation and wavelet absolute maxima segmentation are similar and about twice as fast as the runtimes of the zero-crossings segmentation. On the other hand, for a larger scale of 4 qn in the preliminary segmentation phase, constant-duration segmentation is three times faster than wavelet segmentation approaches.

Table 12.3 shows the effect of not using the concatenation phase: melodies undergo the preliminary segmentation phase, but skip the first comparison and the concatenation phases, such that all preliminary segments are used for the comparison, clustering and ranking phases. The results in Table 12.3 show that omitting the concatenation phase severely reduces the performance of the method on this task. In this case, when segments are not concatenated, a segmentation scale of 4 qn is, in almost all combinations, twice as good as a segmentation scale of 1 qn. On the other hand, as seen in Table 12.1, a preliminary segmentation phase with a finer segmentation scale, helps to improve the identification of patterns in this dataset.

12.3.1.2 Comparison with Other Computational Methods

The other computational methods addressing the MIREX task on Discovery of repeated themes and sections, included geometric approaches (Meredith, 2013), incremental mining methods (Lartillot, 2014) and methods based on audio techniques (Nieto and Farbood, 2013, 2014).[7] For comparison, we selected our submission VM1, as this configuration was also selected for comparison in the published results of the task. The details of the parameters settings of VM1 are described by Velarde and Meredith (2014).

Table 12.4 shows the results obtained by the different algorithms in the 2014 MIREX task on the monophonic version of the JKU Patterns Test Database (PTD). As can be seen in this table, our method ranked highest at discovering at least one occurrence of each ground truth pattern ($F1\_est$) as well as being the fastest method. Lartillot's method (OL1) performed better at finding inexact occurrences of patterns ($F1\_occ_{(c=.75)}$) but is considerably slower. VM1 and OL1 performed at a similar level with respect to finding exact occurrences of the patterns, and, in both cases, the standard deviation was high. The addition of more pieces to training and test databases over time will enable researchers to investigate the generalizability of their methods.

Table 12.4 Results on the JKU test set. NF1 (Nieto and Farbood, 2014), OL1 (Lartillot, 2014), VM1 (Velarde and Meredith, 2014) and DM10 (Meredith, 2013)

		$F1\_est$	$F1\_occ_{(c=.75)}$	TL_F1	$F1$	*Runtime*
NF1	Mean	0.50	0.41	0.33	0.02	480.80
	SD	0.14	0.27	0.12	0.05	558.43
OL1	Mean	0.50	**0.81**	0.43	0.12	35508.82
	SD	0.17	0.12	0.13	0.13	52556.11
VM1	Mean	**0.73**	0.60	**0.49**	**0.16**	**100.80**
	SD	0.14	0.09	0.14	0.15	119.18
DM10	Mean	0.55	0.62	0.43	0.03	161.40
	SD	0.06	0.09	0.08	0.04	194.87

---

[7] Results of the annual MIREX competitions on Discovery of Repeated Themes and Sections can be found on the MIREX website at at http://www.music-ir.org/.

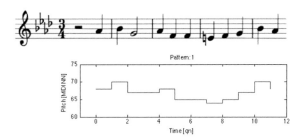

Fig. 12.10 Notation and pitch-signal representations of the first ground truth pattern for the third movement of Beethoven's Piano Sonata in F minor, Op. 2, No. 1 (1795)

12.3.1.3 Comparing Patterns Discovered Automatically with Patterns Identified by Experts

In this section, we present the output of the computational method compared to the JKU PDD ground truth analysis of the monophonic version of the third movement of Beethoven's Piano Sonata in F minor, Op. 2, No. 1 (1795). In order to visualize the ground truth and computationally discovered patterns and their occurrences, we will present them as pitch signals rather than in notation. To help with understanding the correspondence between the pitch signal representation and notation, Fig. 12.10 shows both representations of the first ground truth pattern.

The ground truth analysis for this piece identifies seven patterns and their occurrences as shown in Fig. 12.11. In this figure, plots on the left correspond to patterns, while plots on the right correspond to pattern occurrences. Each pattern occurrence is marked with vertical dotted lines in the graphs on the right side of the figure. All pitch signals have been shifted to start at time 0. The patterns are ordered, from top to bottom, in decreasing order of salience. The lengths of these seven ground truth patterns range from 12 to 119 qn. Some occurrences of the patterns overlap as is the case for the occurrences of pattern 1 and pattern 3, or pattern 2 and pattern 5.

The computational analysis of the piece can be seen in Fig. 12.12. The parameters used are the following:

- 1 sampling rate: 16 samples per qn
- representations: absolute wavelet coefficients filtered at the scale of 1 qn
- segmentation at absolute maxima
- scales for segmentation: 1 qn
- threshold for binarizing the similarity matrix: 0.001
- distance for measuring similarity between segments on the first comparison: city block (CB)
- distance for measuring similarity between segments on the second comparison: city block (CB)
- clustering method: Single linkage (nearest neighbour)
- value for the number of clusters: 7

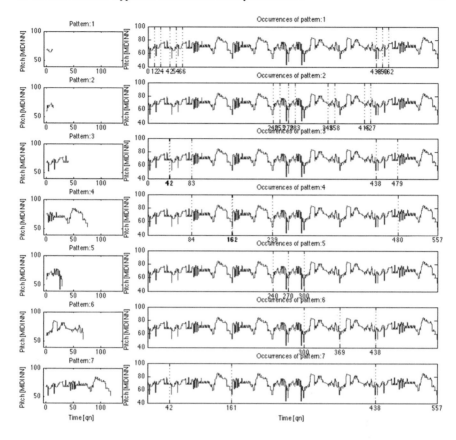

Fig. 12.11 JKU PDD Ground truth patterns for the third movement of Beethoven's Piano Sonata in F minor, Op. 2, No. 1 (1795). Pitch signal representation, with signals shifted to start at time 0. Plots on the left correspond to the patterns, while plots on the right correspond to the entire piece, with each pattern occurrence marked with a vertical dotted line at its starting and ending position

• criterion for ranking clusters: compression ratio

In this example, the number of clusters is the same as the number of patterns in the ground truth. Once again, the salience of patterns can be seen from top to bottom, where the most salient pattern is shown in the top plot. Six out of seven pattern shapes match approximately the ground truth pattern shapes (in some cases, some notes may be missing at the beginning or end of a pattern). The pattern that has been ranked as the most salient, corresponds to pattern 2 in the ground truth analysis, and all its four occurrences have been found. The shape of the second most salient computed pattern, does not resemble the shape of any of the patterns in the ground truth. Pattern 2 is a short-duration pattern, whose cluster contains several melodic units, including segments that approximate the occurrences of pattern 1 in the ground truth (this cannot be seen in Fig. 12.12). The remaining computed pattern shapes (patterns 3–7) can be found in the ground truth, each with the same number of occurrences. The ranking of salience is not exactly the same as in the ground truth, but it is similar in chunks, such that:

- the first two computed clusters correspond to the first two pattern occurrences in the ground truth;
- computed cluster 3 corresponds to the occurrences of ground truth pattern 3;
- computed clusters 4–6 correspond to the occurrences of ground truth patterns 4–6,
- and finally the last computed cluster corresponds to the occurrences of the last ground truth pattern.

The second cluster contains several melodic units. In future work, we would like to cluster such clusters until they satisfy a given condition and discard clusters that fail to satisfy the condition. We expect that the effect on such clusters of keeping or discarding trivial units may be more evident if we carry out this process.

12.3.2 Experiment 2: Classification of Segments from J. S. Bach's Two-Part Inventions

We also evaluated the method on a second task where the goal was to recognize the parent works of excerpts from J. S. Bach's 15 Two-Part Inventions (BWV 772–786). In contrast to the first experiment, in this task, all segments were used in the evaluation, not just concatenated units. Also, whereas in the first experiment there was room for disagreement about the validity of the ground truth, in this second task, the ground truth was not controversial—there was no doubt as to which parent Invention each test excerpt belonged to. The notion that the piece to which an excerpt belongs can be identified on the basis of the content of the excerpt is based on the premise that the musical material in the excerpt is motivically related to the rest of the piece. Specifically, in the case of Bach's Two-Part Inventions, it is well established that the opening exposition of each of these pieces presents the motivic material that is developed throughout the rest of the piece, which is typically divided into three sections (Dreyfus, 1996; Stein, 1979). In this experiment, we followed the experimental setup described by Velarde et al. (2013), building the classifier from the expositions of the pieces and the test set from the three following sections of each piece. More precisely, an initial, 16 qn segment from each piece was used to build the classifier, and the remainder of each piece was split into three sections of equal length which were used to build the test set. We could have attempted to determine the length of each exposition precisely, but we wanted to avoid making subjective analytical judgements. We therefore used a fixed length of 16 qn as the length of each "exposition" section despite the fact that the actual lengths of the expositions in the Inventions vary. This particular length was chosen because it was the length of the longest exposition in the pieces, thus ensuring that no exposition material would be included in the test set.

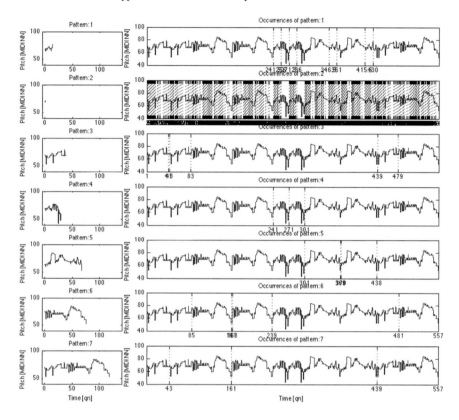

Fig. 12.12 Patterns discovered by the method for the third movement of Beethoven's Piano Sonata in F minor, Op. 2, No. 1 (1795), JKU PDD monophonic version. Pitch signal representation, with signals shifted to start at time 0. Plots on the left correspond to the patterns, while plots on the right correspond to the entire piece, with each pattern occurrence marked with a vertical dotted line at its starting and ending position

We were also interested in investigating the amount of initial expository material required to enable the parent works of excerpts to be accurately identified. We therefore constructed classifiers from the first 4, 8 and 16 qn of the pieces.

Figure 12.13 shows schematically how the classifiers and the test sets were constructed. The classifier set C was built from segments $sc_{i,j}$ from the expositions of the 15 *Inventions*, where each segment could be from either the upper or the lower voice. $sc_{i,j}$ is the jth segment in Invention i. Each test set T was built from segments st, where each st could be from either the upper or the lower voice. We denote the jth segment in Invention i by $st_{i,j}$. To classify a segment st to one of the 15 classes, we applied 1-nearest neighbour classification (Mitchell, 1997). That is, we computed the distances between st and all sc in C, and classified st to the class i of the $sc_{i,j}$ that had the smallest distance to st. Each test excerpt was assigned the class most frequently

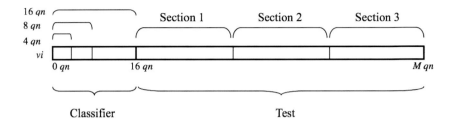

Fig. 12.13 Scheme of classifier and test construction based on signal v_i

predicted by its segments. In both cases we used the next nearest neighbour to break ties.

We expected higher classification rates with classifiers built from more exposition material, similar performance for the different combinations of wavelet-base classifiers, and higher classification rates in the first section compared to the following two, as the subject appears in the first section following the exposition at least once in each part (Stein, 1979).

The following parameters were used in the experiment:

- Sampling rate: 8 samples per qn[8]
- Representation: normalized pitch signal (WR), wavelet coefficients filtered at the scale of 1 qn (WR) and absolute wavelet coefficients filtered at the scale of 1 qn (WRA)
- Segmentation: constant-duration segmentation (CS), wavelet zero-crossing (ZC) and wavelet absolute maxima (AM)
- Scale segmentation at 1 qn
- Segment length normalization by zero padding
- Clustering: 1-nearest neighbour
- Distance measure: city block

12.3.2.1 Results

Figures 12.14 and 12.15 show the classification accuracy on each section, with the concatenation phase omitted and included, respectively. Both figures show the effect of segmentation and representation (columns vs. rows), and the number of qn used for the classifiers (asterisk, square, and circle markers). As expected, the amount of material used from the exposition (4, 8, or 16 qn) affects the classification success rates: the more material used, the higher the success rates. Moreover, segmentation has a stronger effect on the classification than representation. With respect to the results between sections, the classification rates for the first section are higher than

---

[8] The sampling rate was chosen to be the same as that used by Velarde et al. (2013).

those for the second and third sections. Representations associated with constant-duration segmentation are accurate in the first section after the exposition, where the subject is presented at least once in one of the voices (Stein, 1979), but far less accurate in the second and third sections where an increasing degree of variation of the original material occurs. Also, in sections 2 and 3, segment boundaries may not fall on whole-quarter-note time points, instead they may be shifted by a small amount, as an effect of the equal division of the sections. This may result in poor discriminatory information contained in segments when using constant-duration segmentation. The approach based on wavelet representation and segmentation is more robust to variation compared to constant-duration segmentation and the unfiltered pitch signal, resulting in similar classification rates for each classifier among all three sections.

A Wilcoxon signed rank test indicated that the concatenation phase did not significantly affect the results of accuracy per segmentation method (CS: $Z = 1.6036$, $p = 0.1088$, ZC: $Z = 0.4472$, $p = 0.6547$, AM: $Z = 1.6036$, $p = 0.1088$) or accuracy per representation type (VR: $Z = 1.4142$, $p = 0.1573$, WR: $Z = 1.6036$, $p = 0.1088$,

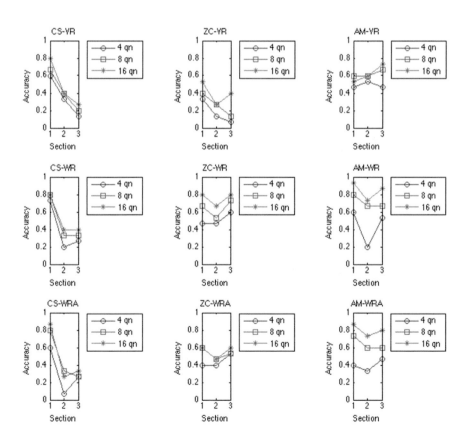

Fig. 12.14 Performance for each section with the classifier based on the exposition

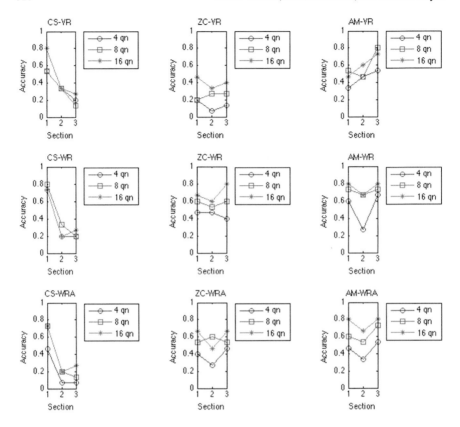

Fig. 12.15 Performance for each section with the classifier based on the exposition, and the concatenation phase included in the segmentation process

WA: $Z = 0.8165$, $p = 0.4142$) for classifiers built from the first 16 qn. However, while including the concatenation phase did not significantly affect the results, it slightly reduced the mean accuracy by 4%. We speculate that this may be a result of the concatenation phase causing some test-set segments to become much longer than the classifier segments, which would lead to segments of very unequal length being measured for similarity. This, in turn, could result in poorer classification accuracies.

12.4 Summary and Conclusions

We have presented a novel computational method for analysis and pattern discovery in melodies and monophonic voices. The method was evaluated on two musicological tasks. In the first task, the method was used to automatically discover themes and sections in the JKU Patterns Development Database. In the second task, the method was used to determine the parent composition of excerpts from J. S. Bach's Two-Part Inventions (BWV 772–786). We explored aspects of representation, segmentation, classification and ranking of melodic units. The results of the experiments led us to conclude that the combination of constant-duration segmentation and an unfiltered, "raw", pitch-signal representation is a powerful approach for pieces where motivic and thematic material is restated with only slight variation. However, when motivic material is more extensively varied, the wavelet-based approach proves more robust to melodic variation.

The method described in this chapter could be developed further, perhaps by evaluating the quality of clusters in order to discard clusters that are too heterogeneous. Other measures of pattern quality could also be explored for ranking patterns in the algorithm output, including measures that perhaps more precisely model human perception and cognition of musical patterns. Moreover, it would be interesting to study the method's performance on a corpus of human performances of the pieces in experiment 1, in order to test, in particular, the robustness of our distance measures.

Acknowledgements Gissel Velarde is supported by the Department of Architecture, Design and Media Technology at Aalborg University. The contribution of David Meredith to the work reported here was made as part of the "Learning to Create" project (Lrn2Cre8). The project Lrn2Cre8 acknowledges the financial support of the Future and Emerging Technologies (FET) programme within the Seventh Framework Programme for Research of the European Commission, under FET grant number 610859.

References

Adiloglu, K., Noll, T., and Obermayer, K. (2006). A paradigmatic approach to extract the melodic structure of a musical piece. *Journal of New Music Research*, 35(3):221–236.

Anagnostopoulou, C. and Westermann, G. (1997). Classification in music: A computational model for paradigmatic analysis. In *Proceedings of the International Computer Music Conference*, pages 125–128, Thessaloniki, Greece.

Antoine, J.-P. (1999). Wavelet analysis: a new tool in physics. In van den Berg, J. C., editor, *Wavelets in Physics*. Cambridge University Press.

Aucouturier, J.-J. and Sandler, M. (2002). Finding repeating patterns in acoustic musical signals: Applications for audio thumbnailing. In *Audio Engineering Society 22nd International Conference on Virtual, Synthetic, and Entertainment Audio (AES22)*, Espoo, Finland.

Cambouropoulos, E. (1997). Musical rhythm: A formal model for determining local boundaries, accents and metre in a melodic surface. In Leman, M., editor, *Music, Gestalt, and Computing*, volume 1317 of *Lecture Notes in Artificial Intelligence*, pages 277–293. Springer.

Cambouropoulos, E. (1998). *Towards a general computational theory of musical structure*. PhD thesis, University of Edinburgh.

Cambouropoulos, E. (2001). The local boundary detection model (LBDM) and its application in the study of expressive timing. In *Proceedings of the International Computer Music Conference (ICMC'2001)*, Havana, Cuba.

Cambouropoulos, E. and Widmer, G. (2000). Automated motivic analysis via melodic clustering. *Journal of New Music Research*, 29(4):303–317.

Collins, T. (2014). MIREX 2014 Competition: Discovery of Repeated Themes and Sections. http://tinyurl.com/krnqzn5. Accessed on 9 April 2015.

Collins, T., Laney, R., Willis, A., and Garthwaite, P. H. (2011). Modeling pattern importance in Chopin's Mazurkas. *Music Perception*, 28(4):387–414.

Conklin, D. (2006). Melodic analysis with segment classes. *Machine Learning*, 65(2-3):349–360.

Conklin, D. and Anagnostopoulou, C. (2006). Segmental pattern discovery in music. *INFORMS Journal on computing*, 18(3):285–293.

Dreyfus, L. (1996). *Bach and the Patterns of Invention*. Harvard University Press.

Eerola, T. and Toiviainen, P. (2004). MIDI Toolbox: MAT-LAB tools for music research. Available online at http://www.jyu.fi/hum/laitokset/musiikki/en/research/coe/materials/miditoolbox/.

Everitt, B., Landau, S., Leese, M., and Stahl, D. (2011). *Cluster Analysis*. Wiley Series in Probability and Statistics. Wiley.

Farge, M. (1992). Wavelet transforms and their applications to turbulence. *Annual Review of Fluid Mechanics*, 24(1):395–458.

Florek, K., Łukaszewicz, J., Perkal, J., Steinhaus, H., and Zubrzycki, S. (1951). Sur la liaison et la division des points d'un ensemble fini. *Colloquium Mathematicae*, 2(3–4):282–285.

Forth, J. (2012). *Cognitively-motivated geometric methods of pattern discovery and models of similarity in music*. PhD thesis, Goldsmiths College, University of London.

Grilo, C. F. A., Machado, F., and Cardoso, F. A. B. (2001). Paradigmatic analysis using genetic programming. In *Artificial Intelligence and Simulation of Behaviour (AISB 2001)*, York, UK.

Haar, A. (1910). Zur theorie der orthogonalen funktionensysteme. *Mathematische Annalen*, 69(3):331–371.

Höthker, K., Hörnel, D., and Anagnostopoulou, C. (2001). Investigating the influence of representations and algorithms in music classification. *Computers and the Humanities*, 35(1):65–79.

Hubel, D. H. and Wiesel, T. N. (1962). Receptive fields, binocular interaction and functional architecture in the cat's visual cortex. *The Journal of Physiology*, 160(1):106.

Huron, D. (1996). The melodic arch in Western folksongs. *Computing in Musicology*, 10:3–23.

Janssen, B., De Haas, W. B., Volk, A., and Van Kranenburg, P. (2013). Discovering repeated patterns in music: state of knowledge, challenges, perspectives. In *Proceedings of the 10th International Symposium on Computer Music Multidisciplinary Research (CMMR 2010)*, Marseille, France.

Johnson, S. C. (1967). Hierarchical clustering schemes. *Psychometrika*, 32(3):241–254.

Kay, K. N., Naselaris, T., Prenger, R. J., and Gallant, J. L. (2008). Identifying natural images from human brain activity. *Nature*, 452(7185):352–355.

Kurby, C. A. and Zacks, J. M. (2008). Segmentation in the perception and memory of events. *Trends in Cognitive Sciences*, 12(2):72–79.

Lamont, A. and Dibben, N. (2001). Motivic structure and the perception of similarity. *Music Perception*, 18(3):245–274.

Lartillot, O. (2005). Efficient extraction of closed motivic patterns in multi-dimensional symbolic representations of music. In *Proceedings of the 6th International Conference on Music Information Retrieval (ISMIR 2005)*, pages 191–198, London, UK. Available online at <http://ismir2005.ismir.net/proceedings/1082.pdf>.

Lartillot, O. (2014). PatMinr: In-depth motivic analysis of symbolic monophonic sequences. In *Music Information Retrieval Evaluation Exchange (MIREX 2014), Competition on Discovery of Repeated Themes and Sections*.

Lerdahl, F. and Jackendoff, R. (1983). *A Generative Theory of Tonal Music*. MIT Press.

Mallat, S. (2009). *A Wavelet Tour of Signal Processing: The Sparse Way*. Academic Press, 3rd edition.

Mallat, S. and Hwang, W. L. (1992). Singularity detection and processing with wavelets. *Information Theory, IEEE Transactions on*, 38(2):617–643.

Marx, A. B. (1837). *Die Lehre von der musikalischen Komposition: praktisch-theoretisch*, volume 1. Breitkopf and Härtel.

Mazzola, G. et al. (2002). *The Topos of Music*. Birkhäuser.

McGettrick, P. (1997). *MIDIMatch: Musical pattern matching in real time*. PhD thesis, MSc. Dissertation, York University, UK.

Meredith, D. (2006). Point-set algorithms for pattern discovery and pattern matching in music. In *Proceedings of the Dagstuhl Seminar on Content-based Retrieval (No. 06171, 23–28 April, 2006)*, Schloss Dagstuhl, Germany. Available online at http://drops.dagstuhl.de/opus/volltexte/2006/652.

Meredith, D. (2013). COSIATEC and SIATECCompress: Pattern discovery by geometric compression. In *Music Information Retrieval Evaluation Exchange (MIREX)*, Curitiba, Brazil.

Meredith, D. (2015). Music analysis and point-set compression. *Journal of New Music Research*, 44(3). In press.

Meredith, D., Lemström, K., and Wiggins, G. A. (2002). Algorithms for discovering repeated patterns in multidimensional representations of polyphonic music. *Journal of New Music Research*, 31(4):321–345.

Mitchell, T. (1997). *Machine Learning*. McGraw-Hill.

Monelle, R. (1992). *Linguistics and Semiotics in Music*. Harwood Academic.

Müllensiefen, D. and Wiggins, G. (2011a). Polynomial functions as a representation of melodic phrase contour. In Schneider, A. and von Ruschkowski, A., editors, *Systematic Musicology: Empirical and Theoretical Studies*, volume 28 of *Hamburger Jahrbuch für Musikwissenschaft*. Peter Lang.

Müllensiefen, D. and Wiggins, G. A. (2011b). Sloboda and Parker's recall paradigm for melodic memory: a new, computational perspective. In Deliége, I. and Davidson, J. W., editors, *Music and the Mind: Essays in Honour of John Sloboda*, pages 161–188. Oxford University Press.

Müller, M. (2007). *Information Retrieval for Music and Motion*, volume 2. Springer.

Muzy, J., Bacry, E., and Arneodo, A. (1991). Wavelets and multifractal formalism for singular signals: application to turbulence data. *Physical Review Letters*, 67(25):3515.

Nattiez, J.-J. (1975). *Fondements d'une sémiologie de la musique*. Union Générale d'Éditions.

Nattiez, J.-J. (1986). La sémiologie musicale dix ans après. *Analyse musicale*, 2:22–33.

Nieto, O. and Farbood, M. (2013). Mirex 2013: Discovering musical patterns using audio structural segmentation techniques. In *Music Information Retrieval Evaluation eXchange (MIREX 2013)*, Curitiba, Brazil.

Nieto, O. and Farbood, M. M. (2014). Mirex 2014 entry: Music segmentation techniques and greedy path finder algorithm to discover musical patterns. In *Music Information Retrieval Evaluation Exchange (MIREX 2014)*, Taipei, Taiwan.

Pinto, A. (2009). Indexing melodic sequences via wavelet transform. In *Multimedia and Expo, 2009. ICME 2009. IEEE International Conference on*, pages 882–885. IEEE.

Reicha, A. (1814). *Traité de mélodie*. Chez l'auteur.

Riemann, H. (1912). *Handbuch der Phrasierung*. Hesse.

Ruwet, N. (1966). Méthodes d'analyses en musicologie. *Revue belge de musicologie*, 20(1/4):65–90.

Schenker, H. (1935). *Der freie Satz*. Universal Edition. (Published in English as E. Oster (trans., ed.) *Free Composition*, Longman, New York, 1979.).

Schmuckler, M. A. (1999). Testing models of melodic contour similarity. *Music Perception*, 16(3):295–326.

Schoenberg, A. (1967). *Fundamentals of Musical Composition*. Faber.

Smith, L. M. and Honing, H. (2008). Time–frequency representation of musical rhythm by continuous wavelets. *Journal of Mathematics and Music*, 2(2):81–97.

Sneath, P. H. (1957). The application of computers to taxonomy. *Journal of General Microbiology*, 17(1):201–226.

Stein, L. (1979). *Structure & style: the study and analysis of musical forms*. Summy-Birchard Company.

Tenney, J. and Polansky, L. (1980). Temporal gestalt perception in music. *Journal of Music Theory*, 24(2):205–241.

Torrence, C. and Compo, G. P. (1998). A practical guide to wavelet analysis. *Bulletin of the American Meteorological society*, 79(1):61–78.

Urbano, J. (2013). Mirex 2013 symbolic melodic similarity: A geometric model supported with hybrid sequence alignment. In *Music Information Retrieval Evaluation Exchange (MIREX 2013)*, Curitiba, Brazil.

van Kranenburg, P., Volk, A., and Wiering, F. (2013). A comparison between global and local features for computational classification of folk song melodies. *Journal of New Music Research*, 42(1):1–18.

Velarde, G. and Meredith, D. (2014). A wavelet-based approach to the discovery of themes and sections in monophonic melodies. In *Music Information Retrieval Evaluation Exchange (MIREX 2014)*, Taipei, Taiwan.

Velarde, G., Weyde, T., and Meredith, D. (2013). An approach to melodic segmentation and classification based on filtering with the Haar-wavelet. *Journal of New Music Research*, 42(4):325–345.

Weyde, T. (2001). Grouping, similarity and the recognition of rhythmic structure. In *Proceedings of the International Computer Music Conference (ICMC)*, Havana, Cuba.

Weyde, T. (2002). Integrating segmentation and similarity in melodic analysis. In *Proceedings of the International Conference on Music Perception and Cognition*, pages 240–243, Sydney, Australia.

Woody, N. A. and Brown, S. D. (2007). Selecting wavelet transform scales for multivariate classification. *Journal of Chemometrics*, 21(7-9):357–363.

Chapter 13
Analysing Music with Point-Set Compression Algorithms

David Meredith

Abstract Several point-set pattern-discovery and compression algorithms designed for analysing music are reviewed and evaluated. Each algorithm takes as input a point-set representation of a score in which each note is represented as a point in pitch-time space. Each algorithm computes the *maximal translatable patterns* (MTPs) in this input and the *translational equivalence classes* (TECs) of these MTPs, where each TEC contains all the occurrences of a given MTP. Each TEC is encoded as a ⟨pattern, vector set⟩ pair, in which the vector set gives all the vectors by which the pattern can be translated in pitch-time space to give other patterns in the input dataset. Encoding TECs in this way leads, in general, to compression, since each occurrence of a pattern within a TEC (apart from one) is encoded by a single vector, that has the same information content as one point. The algorithms reviewed here adopt different strategies aimed at selecting a set of MTP TECs that collectively cover (or almost cover) the input dataset in a way that maximizes compression. The algorithms are evaluated on two musicological tasks: classifying folk song melodies into tune families and discovering repeated themes and sections in pieces of classical music. On the first task, the best-performing algorithms achieved success rates of around 84%. In the second task, the best algorithms achieved mean F_1 scores of around 0.49, with scores for individual pieces rising as high as 0.71.

13.1 Music Analysis and Data Compression

A *musical analysis* represents a particular way of understanding certain structural aspects of a *musical object*, where such an object may be any quantity of music, ranging from a motive, chord or even a single note through to a complete work or even an entire corpus of works (cf. Bent, 1987, p. 1). In the spirit of the theory of

David Meredith
Department of Architecture, Design and Media Technology, Aalborg University, Aalborg, Denmark
e-mail: dave@create.aau.dk

© Springer International Publishing Switzerland 2016
D. Meredith (ed.), *Computational Music Analysis*,
DOI 10.1007/978-3-319-25931-4_13

Kolmogorov complexity (Chaitin, 1966; Kolmogorov, 1965; Li and Vitányi, 2008; Solomonoff, 1964a,b) and the *minimum description length principle* (Rissanen, 1978), a musical analysis is conceived of here as being a compact or compressed encoding of an *in extenso description* of a musical object. An in extenso description is one in which the properties of each atomic component of the object are explicitly specified, without encoding any structural groupings of these components into higher-level constituents, and without encoding any relationships between atomic components (see Simon and Sumner (1968, 1993) for a similar use of the term, "in extenso"). Music theorists and analysts often refer to such in extenso descriptions as "musical surfaces" (Lerdahl and Jackendoff, 1983, pp. 3,10–11) (see also Chap. 2, this volume). The atomic components themselves might be, for example, notes in a score or events in a MIDI file or sample values in a PCM audio file. Their nature thus depends on both the nature of the object being described (e.g., a specification of what to play or a recording of an actual performance) and the level of detail or "granularity" of the description.

In contrast, while a musical analysis is itself a description of a musical object, it will typically differ from an in extenso description by representing the object as being constructed from *sets* of atomic components that form larger-scale constituents, such as motives, phrases, chords, voices and sections. An analysis will also typically encode *relationships* between such constituents (e.g., repetition, transposition, inversion, elaboration, augmentation and diminution).

The *Kolmogorov complexity* of an object is, roughly speaking, the length in bits of the shortest possible program that generates the object as its only output. In the spirit of Kolmogorov complexity, in this chapter, an analysis is thus conceived of as a program that outputs the in extenso description of a musical object that we want to analyse and explain. The precise way in which such a program generates the in extenso surface description of the object constitutes an hypothesis as to how that surface might have come about. Equivalently, we can thus consider an analysis to be a losslessly compressed encoding of an in extenso description of a musical object. In this way, an analysis is an *explanation for* or a *way of understanding* certain aspects of the structure of the musical object that it describes.

Suppose X and Y are two constituent sets of atomic components of a musical object (e.g., two sets of notes forming two occurrences of the subject in a fugue) and that the transformation, T, maps X onto Y (e.g., T could be "shift in time by x quarter notes and transpose by y semitones"). If T can be described more parsimoniously than Y, then the part of the musical surface consisting of X and Y (i.e., $X \cup Y$, or the union of the atomic components in X and Y) can be described more parsimoniously by giving an in extenso description of X together with a description of T, than it can by giving in extenso descriptions of both X and Y. In this way, by identifying structural relationships between constituents of a musical object, a musical analysis can convey at least as much information about that object as an in extenso description on the same level of detail, but may manage to do so more parsimoniously. A musical analysis can thus take the form of a compact description or compressed encoding of a musical object. Of course, a musical analysis usually conveys *more* information than an in extenso description on the same level of detail, since it also typically describes groupings of atomic components into larger constituents and structural relationships between these constituents.

Kolmogorov complexity (Chaitin, 1966; Kolmogorov, 1965; Li and Vitányi, 2008; Solomonoff, 1964a,b) (also known as *algorithmic information theory*, see also Chap. 7, this volume) suggests that the *length* of a program, whose output is an in extenso description of an object, can be used as a measure of the complexity of its corresponding explanation for the structure of that object: if we have two programs in the same programming language that generate the same output, then the shorter of the two will typically represent the simpler explanation for that output.

The level of structural detail on which an analysis (encoded as a program) explains the structure of a musical object is determined by the granularity of the in extenso description that it generates. Typically, much of the detailed structure of an object will not be encoded in the in extenso description generated by an analysis and this omitted structure will therefore go unexplained.

In the work presented in this chapter, I assume that the music analyst's goal is to find the *best possible* explanations for the structures of musical objects, which raises the question of how we are supposed to decide, given a pair of alternative explanations for the same musical object, which of these explanations is "better". In my view, we can only meaningfully claim that one analysis is "better than" another if it allows us to more successfully carry out some objectively evaluable task; and even then, we can only claim that the analysis is superior *for that task*. Such tasks might include, for example, detecting errors, memorizing pieces, identifying composers (or dates of composition, forms or genres), and predicting how incomplete pieces might be completed. It is possible that the best analysis for carrying out one such task might be different from the best analysis for carrying out another. However, the algorithms and experiments described in this chapter are founded on the hypothesis that the best possible explanations for a musical object (i.e., the best analyses for *all* objectively evaluable tasks) are those that are represented by that object's shortest possible descriptions—that is, the descriptions of the object whose lengths are equal to the Kolmogorov complexity of that object.

In general, the Kolmogorov complexity of an object is not computable.[1] This means that, if we have some in extenso description of an object and a compressed encoding of that description, then typically we cannot be sure that the compressed encoding is the shortest one possible. We can, of course, often prove that an encoding is *not* the shortest possible, simply by finding a shorter one. However, in the current context, the non-computability of Kolmogorov complexity does not pose a problem, as we will only use the relative lengths (i.e., information content) of analyses to predict which analyses will serve us better for carrying out musicological tasks. That is, in order to be able to evaluate whether we are making progress, we never really need to know if an analysis is the best possible (although, of course, that would be nice), we only need to be able to predict (at least some of the time) whether or not it will be better than another one.

---

[1] Actually prefix complexity, K, is upper semicomputable, but it cannot be approximated in general in a practically useful sense (Li and Vitányi, 2008, p. 216).

If we adopt the approach outlined above, then the music analyst's goal becomes that of finding the shortest possible "programs" (i.e., encodings, analyses) that generate the most detailed representations of as much music as possible. In other words, our ultimate goal may be considered to be to compress as detailed a description as possible of as much music as possible into as short an encoding as possible.

With this goal in mind, the main purpose of this chapter is to present, analyse and evaluate a number of compression algorithms that have been specifically designed for analysing music (see Sect. 13.3). Each of these algorithms takes an in extenso description of a musical object as input and generates a losslessly compressed encoding of this description as output. All of the algorithms examined in this study are based on Meredith et al.'s (2002) "Structure Induction Algorithm" (SIA) which takes as input a multidimensional point set (in this context, representing a musical object) and computes all the maximal repeated patterns in the point set.

The results of evaluating these compression algorithms on two musicological tasks will also be presented (see Sect. 13.4). In the first task, the algorithms were used as compressors to compute the *normalized compression distance* (NCD) (Li et al., 2004) between each pair of melodies in the *Annotated Corpus* of Dutch folk songs from the collection *Onder de groene linde* (Grijp, 2008; van Kranenburg et al., 2013; Volk and van Kranenburg, 2012). The NCD between two objects, x and y, is defined as follows:

$$\text{NCD}(x,y) = \frac{Z(xy) - \min\{Z(x), Z(y)\}}{\max\{Z(x), Z(y)\}} \, , \tag{13.1}$$

where $Z(x)$ is the length of a compressed encoding of x and $Z(xy)$ is the length of a compressed encoding of a concatenation of x and y. The NCD between two objects is designed to be a practical alternative to the *normalized information distance* (NID), a universal similarity metric based on Kolmogorov complexity. These calculated NCDs were then used to classify the melodies into tune families and the classifications generated were compared with "ground-truth" classifications provided by musicologists (van Kranenburg et al., 2013; Volk and van Kranenburg, 2012).

In the second task, the algorithms were used to find repeated themes and sections in five pieces of Western classical music in various genres and from various historical periods (Collins, 2013a). The analyses generated by the algorithms were, again, compared with "ground-truth" analyses provided by expert analysts (Collins, 2013b).

Before presenting the algorithms, however, it is first necessary to review some basic concepts and terminology relating to representing music with point sets.

13.2 Representing Music with Point Sets

In the algorithms considered in this chapter, it is assumed that the music to be analysed is represented in the form of a multi-dimensional point set called a *dataset*, as described by Meredith et al. (2002). Most of these algorithms work with datasets of any dimensionality. However, it will be assumed here that each dataset is a set of

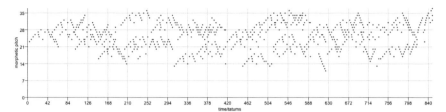

Fig. 13.1 An example of a dataset. A two-dimensional point-set representing the fugue from
J. S. Bach's Prelude and Fugue in C minor, BWV 846. The horizontal axis represents onset time in
tatums; the vertical axis represents morphetic pitch. Each point represents a note or a sequence of
tied notes

two-dimensional points, $\langle t, p \rangle$, where t and p are integers representing, respectively,
the onset time in *tatums* and the *chromatic* or *morphetic pitch* (Meredith, 2006b,
2007; Meredith et al., 2002) of a note or sequence of tied notes in a score. Assuming
the musical object to be analysed is the score of a single movement, then the tatum
for that score is defined to be the largest common divisor of every note onset and
duration in the score. The chromatic pitch of a note is an integer indicating the key on
a normal piano keyboard that would need to be pressed to play the note. For example,
if we define the chromatic pitch of A0 to be 0, then the chromatic pitches of B♯3, C4
and C♯4 are 39, 39 and 40, respectively. The morphetic pitch of a note is an integer
that depends on the position of the head of a note on the staff and the clef in operation
on that staff. It indicates pitch height while ignoring accidental. For example, if we
define the morphetic pitch of A0 to be 0, then the morphetic pitches of B♯3, C4 and
C♯4 are 22, 23 and 23, respectively. For a more extensive and in-depth discussion of
these and other pitch representations, see Meredith (2006b, pp. 126–130).

Figure 13.1 shows an example of such a dataset. When the music to be analysed is
modal or uses the major–minor tonal system, the output of the algorithms described
below is typically better when morphetic pitch is used. If morphetic pitch information
is not available (e.g., because the data is only available in MIDI format), then, for
modal or tonal music, it can be computed with usually very high accuracy from a
representation that provides the chromatic pitch (or MIDI note number) of each note,
by using an algorithm such as PS13s1 (Meredith, 2006b, 2007). For pieces of music
not based on the modal or major–minor tonal system, using chromatic pitch may give
better results than using morphetic pitch.

13.2.1 Maximal Translatable Patterns (MTPs)

If D is a dataset (as just defined), then any subset of D may be called a *pattern*. If
$P_1, P_2 \subseteq D$, then P_1, P_2, are said to be *translationally equivalent*, denoted by $P_1 \equiv_T P_2$,
if and only if there exists a vector v, such that P_1 translated by v is equal to P_2. That
is,

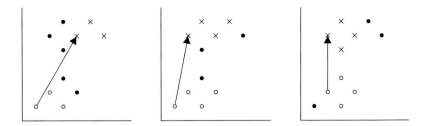

Fig. 13.2 Examples of maximal translatable patterns (MTPs). In each graph, the pattern of circles is the maximal translatable pattern (MTP) for the vector indicated by the arrow. The pattern of crosses in each graph is the pattern onto which the pattern of circles is mapped by the vector indicated by the arrow

$$P_1 \equiv_{\mathrm{T}} P_2 \iff (\exists v \mid P_2 = P_1 + v), \tag{13.2}$$

where $P_1 + v$ denotes the pattern that results when P_1 is translated by the vector v. For example, in each of the graphs in Fig. 13.2, the pattern of circles is translationally equivalent to the pattern of crosses. A pattern, $P \subseteq D$, is said to be *translatable* within a dataset, D, if and only if there exists a vector, v, such that $P + v \subseteq D$. Given a vector, v, then the *maximal translatable pattern* (MTP) for v in the dataset, D, is defined and denoted as follows:

$$\mathrm{MTP}(v, D) = \{p \mid p \in D \wedge p + v \in D\}, \tag{13.3}$$

where $p + v$ is the point that results when p is translated by the vector, v. In other words, the MTP for a vector, v, in a dataset, D, is the set of points in D that can be translated by v to give other points that are also in D. Figure 13.2 shows some examples of maximal translatable patterns.

13.2.2 Translational Equivalence Classes (TECs)

When analysing a piece of music, we typically want to find *all the occurrences* of an interesting pattern, not just one occurrence. Thus, if we believe that MTPs are related in some way to the patterns that listeners and analysts find interesting, then we want to be able to find all the occurrences of each MTP. Given a pattern, P, in a dataset, D, the *translational equivalence class* (TEC) of P in D is defined and denoted as follows:

$$\mathrm{TEC}(P, D) = \{Q \mid Q \equiv_{\mathrm{T}} P \wedge Q \subseteq D\}. \tag{13.4}$$

That is, the TEC of a pattern, P, in a dataset contains all and only those patterns in the dataset that are translationally equivalent to P. Note that $P \equiv_{\mathrm{T}} P$, so $P \in \mathrm{TEC}(P, D)$. Figure 13.3 shows some examples of TECs.

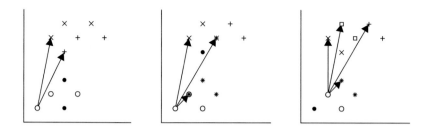

Fig. 13.3 Examples of translational equivalence classes (TECs). In each graph, the pattern of circles is translatable by the vectors indicated by the arrows. The TEC of each pattern of circles is the set of patterns containing the circle pattern itself along with the other patterns generated by translating the circle pattern by the vectors indicated. The covered set of each TEC is the set of points denoted by icons other than filled black dots

The *covered set* of a TEC, T, denoted by $\mathrm{COV}(T)$, is defined to be the union of the patterns in the TEC, T. That is,

$$\mathrm{COV}(T) = \bigcup_{P \in T} P . \qquad (13.5)$$

Here, we will be particularly concerned with *MTP TECs*—that is, the translational equivalence classes of the maximal translatable patterns in a dataset.

Suppose we have a TEC, $T = \mathrm{TEC}(P,D)$, in a k-dimensional dataset, D. T contains the patterns in D that are translationally equivalent to P. Suppose T contains n translationally equivalent occurrences of the pattern, P, and that P contains m points. There are at least two ways in which one can specify T. First, one can explicitly define each of the n patterns in T by listing the m points in each pattern. This requires one to write down mn, k-dimensional points or kmn numbers. Alternatively, one can explicitly list the m points in just one of the patterns in T (e.g., P) and then give the $n-1$ vectors required to translate this pattern onto its other occurrences in the dataset. This requires one to write down m, k-dimensional points and $n-1$, k-dimensional vectors—that is, $k(m+n-1)$ numbers. If n and m are both greater than one, then $k(m+n-1)$ is less than kmn, implying that the second method of specifying a TEC gives us a *compressed* encoding of the TEC. Thus, if a dataset contains at least two non-intersecting occurrences of a pattern containing at least two points, it will be possible to encode the dataset in a compact manner by representing it as the union of the covered sets of a set of TECs, where each TEC, T, is encoded as an ordered pair, $\langle P,V \rangle$, where P is a pattern in the dataset, and V is the set of vectors that translate P onto its other occurrences in the dataset. When a TEC, $T = \langle P,V \rangle$, is represented in this way, we call V the *set of translators* for the TEC and P the TEC's *pattern*. We also denote and define the *compression factor* of a TEC, $T = \langle P,V \rangle$, as follows:

$$\mathrm{CF}(T) = \frac{|\mathrm{COV}(T)|}{|P| + |V|} , \qquad (13.6)$$

where $|X|$ denotes the cardinality of set, X.[2] In this chapter, the pattern, P, of a TEC, used to encode it as a $\langle P, V \rangle$ pair, will be assumed to be the lexicographically earliest occurring member of the TEC (i.e., the one that contains the lexicographically earliest point).[3]

13.2.3 Approximate Versus Exact Matching

Each of the algorithms described in the next section takes a dataset as input, computes the MTPs in this dataset and may then go on to compute the TECs of these MTPs. Several of the algorithms generate compact encodings of the input dataset in the form of sets of selected TECs that collectively cover the input dataset. Two of these algorithms, COSIATEC (see Sect. 13.3.3) and SIATECCOMPRESS (see Sect. 13.3.7), generate *losslessly* compressed encodings from which the input dataset can be perfectly reconstructed. These encodings can therefore be interpreted as *explanations* for the input dataset that offer an account for *every note*, reflecting the assumption that, in a well-composed piece of music, notes will not be selected at random by the composer, but rather chosen carefully on the grounds of various aesthetic, expressive and structural reasons. Consequently, if one is interested in learning how to compose music in the style of some master composer, then one aims to understand the reasoning underlying the selection of *every note* in pieces in the form and style that one wishes to imitate. To do this, merely identifying instances in these pieces where patterns approximately resemble each other is not enough. One must also attempt to formulate precise explanations for the *differences* (however small) between these approximately matching patterns, so that one understands *exactly* how and why the patterns are transformed in the way they are. In other words, one needs to *exactly* characterize the transformations that map a pattern onto its various occurrences—even when the transformation is not simply a shift in time accompanied by a modal or chromatic transposition. This implies that, if one's goal is to achieve an understanding of a set of pieces that is complete and detailed enough to allow for high-quality novel pieces to be composed in the same style and form, then one requires *losslessly* compressed encodings of the existing pieces, based on *exact* matches (or, more generally, exactly characterized transformations) between pattern occurrences.

Nevertheless, if one's goal is only to produce an analysis that informs the listening process, or if one only needs to be able to classify existing pieces by genre, composer,

---

[2] In order to conform to standard usage in the data compression literature (see, e.g., Salomon and Motta, 2010, p. 12), in this chapter, the term "compression factor" is used to signify the quantity that I and other authors in this area have referred to as "compression ratio" in previous publications (e.g., Collins et al., 2011; Meredith et al., 2002).

[3] A collection of strings or tuples is sorted into *lexicographical* order, when the elements are sorted as they would be in a dictionary, with higher priority being given to elements occurring earlier. For example, if we lexicographically sort the set of points $\{\langle 1,0 \rangle, \langle 0,1 \rangle, \langle 1,1 \rangle, \langle 0,0 \rangle\}$, then we get the ordered set, $\langle \langle 0,0 \rangle, \langle 0,1 \rangle, \langle 1,0 \rangle, \langle 1,1 \rangle \rangle$.

period, etc., then approximate matching and lossily compressed encodings may suffice. In such cases, there are a number of ways in which the algorithms considered in this chapter can be adapted to account for occurrences of a pattern that are not exact transpositions in chromatic-pitch-time space. That is, there are a number of ways in which we might address what Collins et al. (2013) call the "inexactness problem" with the SIA-based algorithms. First, instead of using a chromatic-pitch vs. time representation as input, one can use some other point-set representation of a piece, such as morphetic-pitch vs. time, where translationally equivalent patterns correspond to sets of notes related by modal rather than chromatic transposition (e.g., C-D-E would match with D-E-F). Second, one can replace each occurrence of an MTP in the output of one of the algorithms described below with either the shortest segment in the music or bounding box in pitch-time space that contains the MTP (as was done in the experiment reported in Sect. 13.4.2 below). Third, Collins et al. (2013) address this "inexactness problem" in their SIARCT-CFP algorithm by combining their SIACT and SIAR algorithms (see Sects. 13.3.5 and 13.3.6, respectively) with a fingerprinting technique that computes a time-stamped hash key for each triple of notes in a dataset and then matches these keys (see Chap. 17, this volume).

13.3 The Algorithms

In this section, the algorithms evaluated in this study will be briefly described and reviewed.

13.3.1 SIA

SIA stands for "Structure Induction Algorithm" (Meredith, 2006a; Meredith et al., 2002, 2003, 2001). SIA finds all the maximal translatable patterns in a dataset containing n, k-dimensional points in $\Theta(kn^2 \lg n)$ time and $\Theta(kn^2)$ space.[4] SIA computes the vector from each point in the dataset to each lexicographically later point. Each of these vectors is stored in a list together with a pointer back to the origin point (see Fig. 13.4 (a) and (b)). This list of $\langle vector, point \rangle$ pairs is then sorted into lexicographical order, giving priority to the vector in each pair (see Fig. 13.4 (c)). The resulting sorted list is segmented at the points at which the vector changes (as indicated by the boxes in the column headed "Datapoint" in Fig. 13.4 (c)). The set of points in the entries within a segment in this list form the MTP for the vector for that segment. This means that all the MTPs can be obtained simply by scanning this list once (i.e., in $\Theta(kn^2)$ time, since the list has length $n(n-1)/2$).

---

[4] By using hashing instead of sorting to partition the inter-point vectors, the average running time can be reduced to $\Theta(kn^2)$. For an explanation of asymptotic notation, see Cormen et al. (2009, pp. 43–53)

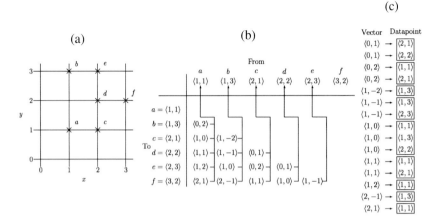

Fig. 13.4 The SIA algorithm. (a) A small dataset that could be provided as input to SIA. (b) The vector table computed by SIA for the dataset in (a). Each entry in the table gives the vector from a point to a lexicographically later point. Each entry has a pointer back to the origin point used to compute the vector. (c) The list of ⟨vector, point⟩ pairs that results when the entries in the vector table in (b) are sorted into lexicographical order. If this list is segmented at points at which the vector changes, then the set of points in the entries within a segment form the MTP for the vector for that segment. (Reproduced from Meredith et al. (2003))

Figure 13.5 gives pseudocode for a straightforward implementation of SIA. The pseudocode used in this chapter is based on that used by Meredith (2006b, 2007). In this pseudocode, unordered sets are denoted by italic upper-case letters (e.g., D in Fig. 13.5). Ordered sets are denoted by boldface upper-case letters (e.g., $\mathbf{V}$, $\mathbf{D}$ and $\mathbf{M}$ in Fig. 13.5). When written out in full, ordered sets are listed between angle brackets, "⟨⟩". Concatenation is denoted by "⊕" and the assignment operator is "←". $\mathbf{A}[i]$ denotes the $(i+1)$th element of the ordered set (or one-dimensional array), $\mathbf{A}$, (i.e., zero-based indexing is used). If $\mathbf{B}$ is an ordered set of ordered sets (or a two-dimensional array), then $\mathbf{B}[i][j]$ denotes the $(j+1)$th element in the $(i+1)$th element of $\mathbf{B}$. Elements in arrays of higher dimension are indexed analogously. Block structure is indicated by indentation alone.

The SIA algorithm in Fig. 13.5 takes a single argument, D, which is assumed to be an unordered set of n, k-dimensional points. The first step is to sort the points in D into lexicographical order (line 1) to give an ordered set of points, $\mathbf{D}$. This takes $\Theta(kn \lg n)$ time in the worst case using a comparison sort. In lines 2–5, the vector, $\mathbf{D}[j] - \mathbf{D}[i]$, from each point, $\mathbf{D}[i]$, to each lexicographically later point, $\mathbf{D}[j]$, is calculated and stored with the index, i, of the origin point in a pair, $\langle \mathbf{D}[j] - \mathbf{D}[i], i \rangle$. Each of these pairs is added to an ordered set, $\mathbf{V}$, in line 5. In line 6, the pairs in $\mathbf{V}$ are sorted lexicographically (i.e., by assigning higher priority to the vector in each pair, and by sorting the vectors themselves lexicographically). This produces a list, $\mathbf{V}'$, such as the one shown in Fig. 13.4 (c), in which all pairs with a given vector occur in a contiguous segment. Line 6 takes $\Theta(kn^2 \lg n)$ time and is asymptotically the most

```
SIA(D)
 1    D ← SORT_Lex(D)
 2    V ← ⟨⟩
 3    for i ← 0 to |D| − 2
 4        for j ← i + 1 to |D| − 1
 5            V ← V ⊕ ⟨⟨D[j] − D[i], i⟩⟩
 6    V' ← SORT_Lex(V)
 7    M ← ⟨⟩
 8    v ← V'[0][0]
 9    P ← ⟨D[V'[0][1]]⟩
10    for i ← 1 to |V'| − 1
11        if V'[i][0] = v
12            P ← P ⊕ ⟨D[V'[i][1]]⟩
13        else
14            M ← M ⊕ ⟨⟨P, v⟩⟩
15            v ← V'[i][0]
16            P ← ⟨D[V'[i][1]]⟩
17    M ← M ⊕ ⟨⟨P, v⟩⟩
18    return M
```

Fig. 13.5 The SIA algorithm

expensive step in the algorithm. In line 7, an empty ordered set, $\mathbf{M}$, is initialized. This ordered set will be used to hold the ⟨MTP, vector⟩ pairs computed in lines 8–17. As described above, the MTPs and their associated vectors are found simply by scanning $\mathbf{V}'$ once, starting a new MTP (stored in $\mathbf{P}$) each time the vector (stored in v) changes. This scan can be accomplished in $\Theta(kn^2)$ time.

The algorithm can easily be modified so that it only generates MTPs whose sizes lie within a particular user-specified range. It is also possible for the same pattern to be the MTP for more than one vector. If this is the case, there will be two or more ⟨pattern, vector⟩ pairs in the output of SIA that have the same pattern. This can be avoided and the output can be made more compact by generating instead a list of ⟨pattern, vector set⟩ pairs, such that the vector set in each pair contains all the vectors for which the pattern is an MTP. In order to accomplish this, the vectors for which a given pattern is the MTP are merged into a single vector set which is then paired with the pattern in the output.

Finally, it is possible to reduce the average running time of SIA to $\Theta(kn^2)$ by using hashing instead of sorting to partition the vector table into MTPs.

13.3.2 SIATEC

SIATEC (Meredith, 2006a; Meredith et al., 2002, 2003, 2001) computes all the MTP TECs in a k-dimensional dataset of size n in $O(kn^3)$ time and $\Theta(kn^2)$ space. In order to find the MTPs in a dataset, SIA only needs to compute the vectors from each point to each lexicographically later point. However, to compute *all occurrences* of the MTPs, it turns out to be beneficial in the SIATEC algorithm to compute the vectors between *all* pairs of points, resulting in a vector table like the one shown in Fig. 13.6. The SIATEC algorithm first finds all the MTPs using SIA. It then uses the vector table to find all the vectors by which each MTP is translatable within the dataset. The set of vectors by which a given pattern is translatable is equal to the intersection of the columns in the vector table headed by the points in the pattern (see Fig. 13.6). In a vector table computed by SIATEC each row descends lexicographically from left to right and each column increases lexicographically from top to bottom. SIATEC exploits these properties of the vector table to more efficiently find all the occurrences of each MTP (Meredith et al., 2002, pp. 335–338).

Figure 13.7 shows pseudocode for a straightforward implementation of SIATEC. The first step in the algorithm is to sort the points in the dataset, D, lexicographically, to produce the ordered point set, $\mathbf{D}$ (line 1). In line 2, an ordered set, $\mathbf{V}$ is initialized which serves the same purpose as it does in SIA (see Fig. 13.5). In line 3, the $|D| \times |D|$ array, $\mathbf{W}$, is initialized. This array will be used to hold a vector table like the one in Fig. 13.6. Lines 4–9 compute the inter-point vectors that are stored in $\mathbf{W}$ and $\mathbf{V}$ (cf. lines 3–5 in Fig. 13.5). Lines 10–24 compute the MTPs and closely resemble lines 6–17 in Fig. 13.5. The difference is that, in SIATEC, each MTP is stored with an ordered set, $\mathbf{C}$, containing the indices into the sorted dataset, $\mathbf{D}$, of the points in the MTP. This sequence of indices is used in lines 25–48 to compute the translator set of the TEC for each MTP. The ordered set of MTP TECs, $\mathbf{T}$, is computed in lines 25–48 and returned in line 49. The **for** loop starting in line 26 iterates over the list of MTPs, $\mathbf{M}$. For each MTP, $\mathbf{P}$ (line 27), and its associated index set, $\mathbf{C}$ (line 28), the **while** loop in lines 33–47 finds all the vectors by which $\mathbf{P}$ can be translated, by computing the intersection of the columns in the vector table $\mathbf{W}$ indexed by the values in $\mathbf{C}$. This is done by descending the columns in the table and starting and stopping these descents neither earlier nor later than necessary, respectively.

For a k-dimensional dataset of size n, the worst-case running time of line 1 of SIATEC is $\Theta(kn\lg n)$. Lines 2–9 run in $\Theta(kn^2)$ time. Line 10 takes $\Theta(kn^2\lg n)$ time and lines 11–24 take $\Theta(kn^2)$ time. Let m_i be the cardinality of the $(i+1)$th MTP in $\mathbf{M}$ at line 25. The $(i+1)$th iteration of the **for** loop that starts in line 26 computes the intersection of the columns in the vector table, $\mathbf{W}$, that are headed by the points in m_i. Each column has length n. Therefore the worst-case running time of lines 26–48

		From				
		$a = \langle 1,1 \rangle$	$b = \langle 1,3 \rangle$	$c = \langle 2,1 \rangle$	$d = \langle 2,2 \rangle$	$e = \langle 2,3 \rangle$	$f = \langle 3,2 \rangle$
	$a = \langle 1,1 \rangle$	$\langle 0,0 \rangle$	$\langle 0,-2 \rangle$	$\langle -1,0 \rangle$	$\langle -1,-1 \rangle$	$\langle -1,-2 \rangle$	$\langle -2,-1 \rangle$
	$b = \langle 1,3 \rangle$	$\langle 0,2 \rangle$	$\langle 0,0 \rangle$	$\langle -1,2 \rangle$	$\langle -1,1 \rangle$	$\langle -1,0 \rangle$	$\langle -2,1 \rangle$
	$c = \langle 2,1 \rangle$	$\langle 1,0 \rangle$	$\langle 1,-2 \rangle$	$\langle 0,0 \rangle$	$\langle 0,-1 \rangle$	$\langle 0,-2 \rangle$	$\langle -1,-1 \rangle$
To	$d = \langle 2,2 \rangle$	$\langle 1,1 \rangle$	$\langle 1,-1 \rangle$	$\langle 0,1 \rangle$	$\langle 0,0 \rangle$	$\langle 0,-1 \rangle$	$\langle -1,0 \rangle$
	$e = \langle 2,3 \rangle$	$\langle 1,2 \rangle$	$\langle 1,0 \rangle$	$\langle 0,2 \rangle$	$\langle 0,1 \rangle$	$\langle 0,0 \rangle$	$\langle -1,1 \rangle$
	$f = \langle 3,2 \rangle$	$\langle 2,1 \rangle$	$\langle 2,-1 \rangle$	$\langle 1,1 \rangle$	$\langle 1,0 \rangle$	$\langle 1,-1 \rangle$	$\langle 0,0 \rangle$

Fig. 13.6 The vector table computed by SIATEC for the dataset shown in Fig. 13.4 (a). (Reproduced from Meredith et al. (2003))

SIATEC(D)
1 $\mathbf{D} \leftarrow \text{SORT}_{\text{Lex}}(D)$
2 $\mathbf{V} \leftarrow \langle \rangle$
3 Allocate a $|D| \times |D|$ array, $\mathbf{W}$
4 **for** $i \leftarrow 0$ **to** $|D| - 1$
5   **for** $j \leftarrow 0$ **to** $|D| - 1$
6        $w \leftarrow \langle \mathbf{D}[j] - \mathbf{D}[i], i \rangle$
7   **if** $j > i$
8           $\mathbf{V} \leftarrow \mathbf{V} \oplus \langle w \rangle$
9        $\mathbf{W}[i][j] \leftarrow w$
10 $\mathbf{V}' \leftarrow \text{SORT}_{\text{Lex}}(\mathbf{V})$
11 $\mathbf{M} \leftarrow \langle \rangle$
12 $v \leftarrow \mathbf{V}'[0][0]$
13 $\mathbf{P} \leftarrow \langle \mathbf{D}[\mathbf{V}'[0][1]] \rangle$
14 $\mathbf{C} \leftarrow \langle \mathbf{V}'[0][1] \rangle$
15 **for** $i \leftarrow 1$ **to** $|\mathbf{V}'| - 1$
16   **if** $\mathbf{V}'[i][0] = v$
17       $\mathbf{P} \leftarrow \mathbf{P} \oplus \langle \mathbf{D}[\mathbf{V}'[i][1]] \rangle$
18       $\mathbf{C} \leftarrow \mathbf{C} \oplus \langle \mathbf{V}'[i][1] \rangle$
19   **else**
20       $\mathbf{M} \leftarrow \mathbf{M} \oplus \langle \langle \mathbf{P}, \mathbf{C}, v \rangle \rangle$
21       $v \leftarrow \mathbf{V}'[i][0]$
22       $\mathbf{P} \leftarrow \langle \mathbf{D}[\mathbf{V}'[i][1]] \rangle$
23       $\mathbf{C} \leftarrow \langle \mathbf{V}'[i][1] \rangle$
24 $\mathbf{M} \leftarrow \mathbf{M} \oplus \langle \langle \mathbf{P}, \mathbf{C}, v \rangle \rangle$
25 $\mathbf{T} \leftarrow \langle \rangle$
26 **for** $i \leftarrow 0$ **to** $|\mathbf{M}| - 1$
27    $\mathbf{P} \leftarrow \mathbf{M}[i][0]$
28    $\mathbf{C} \leftarrow \mathbf{M}[i][1]$
29    $\mathbf{R} \leftarrow \langle 0 \rangle$
30   **for** $j \leftarrow 1$ **to** $|\mathbf{P}| - 1$
31       $\mathbf{R} \leftarrow \mathbf{R} \oplus \langle 0 \rangle$
32    $\mathbf{X} \leftarrow \langle \rangle$
33   **while** $\mathbf{R}[0] \leq |D| - |\mathbf{P}|$
34   **for** $j \leftarrow 1$ **to** $|\mathbf{P}| - 1$
35          $\mathbf{R}[j] \leftarrow \mathbf{R}[0] + j$
36       $v_0 \leftarrow \mathbf{W}[\mathbf{C}[0]][\mathbf{R}[0]][0]$
37   *found* $\leftarrow$ false
38   **for** $c \leftarrow 1$ **to** $|\mathbf{P}| - 1$
39   **while** $\mathbf{R}[c] < |D| \wedge \mathbf{W}[\mathbf{C}[c]][\mathbf{R}[c]][0] < v_0$
40             $\mathbf{R}[c] \leftarrow \mathbf{R}[c] + 1$
41   **if** $\mathbf{R}[c] \geq |D| \vee v_0 \neq \mathbf{W}[\mathbf{C}[c]][\mathbf{R}[c]][0]$
42   **break**
43   **if** $c = |\mathbf{P}| - 1$
44   *found* $\leftarrow$ true
45   **if** *found* $\vee |\mathbf{P}| = 1$
46          $\mathbf{X} \leftarrow \mathbf{X} \oplus \langle v_0 \rangle$
47       $\mathbf{R}[0] \leftarrow \mathbf{R}[0] + 1$
48    $\mathbf{T} \leftarrow \mathbf{T} \oplus \langle \langle \mathbf{P}, \mathbf{X} \rangle \rangle$
49 **return** $\mathbf{T}$

Fig. 13.7 The SIATEC algorithm

is given by

$$\Theta\left(\sum_{i=0}^{|\mathbf{M}|-1} knm_i\right) = \Theta\left(kn\sum_{i=0}^{|\mathbf{M}|-1} m_i\right).$$

But we know that $\sum_{i=0}^{|\mathbf{M}|-1} m_i = n(n-1)/2$, since the MTPs are computed in lines 10–24 by scanning the sorted list, $\mathbf{V}'$. Therefore, the worst-case running time of lines 26–48 and the worst-case running time of SIATEC as a whole, is

$$\Theta\left(kn\sum_{i=0}^{|\mathbf{M}|-1} m_i\right) = \Theta\left(kn\frac{n(n-1)}{2}\right) = \Theta(kn^3).$$

It is easy to see that the algorithm uses $\Theta(kn^2)$ space.

13.3.3 COSIATEC

COSIATEC (Meredith, 2006a; Meredith et al., 2003) is a greedy point-set compression algorithm, based on SIATEC ("COSIATEC" stands for "COmpression with SIATEC"). COSIATEC takes a dataset, D, as input and computes a compressed encoding of D in the form of an ordered set of MTP TECs, $\mathbf{T}$, such that $D = \bigcup_{T\in\mathbf{T}} \mathrm{COV}(T)$ and $\mathrm{COV}(T_1)\cap\mathrm{COV}(T_2) = \emptyset$ for all $T_1, T_2 \in \mathbf{T}$ where $T_1 \neq T_2$. In other words, COSIATEC strictly partitions a dataset, D, into the covered sets of a set of MTP TECs. If each of these MTP TECs is represented as a $\langle$pattern, translator set$\rangle$ pair, then this description of the dataset as a set of TECs is typically shorter than an in extenso description in which the points in the dataset are listed explicitly.

Figure 13.8 shows pseudocode for COSIATEC. The first step in the algorithm is to make a copy of the input dataset which is stored in the variable D' (line 1). Then, on each iteration of the **while** loop (lines 3–6), the algorithm finds the "best" MTP TEC in D', stores this in T and adds T to $\mathbf{T}$. It then removes the set of points covered by T from D' (line 6). When D' is empty, the algorithm terminates, returning the list of MTP TECs, $\mathbf{T}$. The sum of the number of translators and the number of points in

```
COSIATEC(D)
1    D' ← COPY(D)
2    T ← ⟨⟩
3    while D' ≠ ∅
4        T ← GETBESTTEC(D',D)
5        T ← T ⊕ ⟨T⟩
6        D' ← D' \ COV(T)
7    return T
```

Fig. 13.8 The COSIATEC algorithm

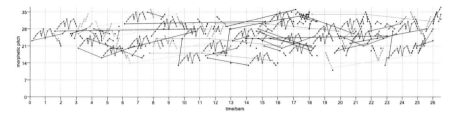

Fig. 13.9 A visualization of the output generated by COSIATEC for the fugue from J. S. Bach's Prelude and Fugue in C major (BWV 846) from the first book of *Das wohltemperirte Clavier*. Note that, for convenience, the time axis has been labelled in bars rather than tatums. See main text for details

this output encoding is never more than the number of points in the input dataset and can be much less than this, if there are many repeated patterns in the input dataset.

The GETBESTTEC function, called in line 4 of COSIATEC, computes the "best" TEC in D' by first finding all the MTPs using SIA, then iterating over these MTPs, finding the TEC for each MTP, and storing it if it is the best TEC so far. In this process, a TEC is considered "better" than another if it has a higher compression factor, as defined in (13.6). If two TECs have the same compression factor, then the better TEC is considered to be the one that has the higher *bounding-box compactness* (Meredith et al., 2002), defined as the ratio of the number of points in the TEC's pattern to the number of dataset points in the bounding box of this pattern. Collins et al. (2011) have provided empirical evidence that the compression factor and compactness of a TEC are important factors in determining its perceived "importance" or "noticeability". If two distinct TECs have the same compression factor and compactness, then the TEC with the larger covered set is considered superior.

Figure 13.9 shows a visualization of the output generated by COSIATEC for the fugue from J. S. Bach's Prelude and Fugue in C major (BWV 846) from the first book of *Das wohltemperirte Clavier*. In this figure, each TEC is drawn in a different colour. For example, occurrences of the subject (minus the first note) are shown in red. Points drawn in grey are elements of the *residual point set*. COSIATEC sometimes generates such a point set on the final iteration of its **while** loop (see Fig. 13.8) when it is left with a set of points that does not contain any MTPs of size greater than 1. In such cases, the final TEC in the encoding contains just the single occurrence of the residual point set. In the analysis shown in Fig. 13.9, the residual point set contains 26 notes (i.e., 3.57% of the notes in the piece). The overall compression factor achieved by COSIATEC on this piece is 2.90 (or 3.12, if we exclude the residual point set).

13.3.4 Forth's Algorithm

Forth (Forth and Wiggins, 2009; Forth, 2012) developed an algorithm, based on SIATEC, that, like COSIATEC, computes a set of TECs that collectively cover the

```
FORTHCOVER(D, C, W, c_min, σ_min)
S ← ⟨⟩
P ← ∅
found ← true
while P ≠ D ∧ found
    found ← false
    γ_max ← 0
    C_best ← nil
    i_best ← nil
    R ← ⟨⟩
    for i ← 0 to |C| − 1
        c ← |C[i] \ P|
        if c < c_min
            R ← R ⊕ ⟨i⟩
            continue
        γ ← cW[i]
        if γ > γ_max
            γ_max ← γ
            C_best ← C[i]
            i_best ← i
    if C_best ≠ nil
        R ← R ⊕ ⟨i_best⟩
        found ← true
        P ← P ∪ C_best
        i ← 0
        primaryFound ← false
        while ¬primaryFound ∧ i < |S|
            if (|S[i][0] ∩ C_best|)/|S[i][0]| > σ_min
                S[i] ← S[i] ⊕ ⟨C_best⟩
                primaryFound ← true
            i ← i + 1
        if ¬primaryFound
            S ← S ⊕ ⟨⟨C_best⟩⟩
    for each i ∈ R
        Remove W[i] from W and C[i] from C
return S
```

Fig. 13.10 An implementation of Forth's method for selecting a cover for the input dataset, D, from the set of TEC covered sets, $\mathbf{C}$

input dataset. However, unlike COSIATEC, Forth's algorithm runs SIATEC only once and the covers it generates are not, in general, strict partitions—the TECs in the list generated by Forth's algorithm may share covered points and, collectively, may not completely cover the input dataset. The first step in Forth's algorithm is to run SIATEC on the input dataset, D. This generates a sequence of MTP TECs, $\mathbf{T} = \langle T_1, T_2, \ldots T_n \rangle$. The algorithm then computes the covered set, $C_i = \bigcup_{P \in T_i} P$, for each TEC, T_i in $\mathbf{T}$, to produce a sequence of TEC covered sets, $\mathbf{C} = \langle C_1, C_2, \ldots C_n \rangle$. It then assigns a weight, W_i, to each covered set, C_i, to produce the sequence, $\mathbf{W} = \langle W_1, W_2, \ldots W_n \rangle$. W_i is intended to measure the "structural salience" (Forth, 2012,

p. 41) of the patterns in the TEC, T_i, and it is defined as follows:

$$W_i = w'_{cr,i} w'_{compV,i} \, , \tag{13.7}$$

where $w'_{cr,i}$ is a normalized value representing the compression factor of T_i and $w'_{compV,i}$ is a normalized value representing compactness. The algorithm then attempts to select a subset of $\mathbf{C}$ that covers the input dataset and maximizes the weights of the TECs in this cover.

Figure 13.10 gives pseudocode for Forth's cover selection algorithm. This algorithm takes five arguments: D, $\mathbf{C}$ and $\mathbf{W}$, as defined above, along with two numerical parameters, c_{min} and σ_{min}. On each iteration of the outer **while** loop (lines 4–34), the algorithm selects the "best" remaining TEC covered set in $\mathbf{C}$ and adds this to the cover, $\mathbf{S}$, which is ultimately returned in line 35. The point set, P, initialized in line 2, is used to store the set of points covered by the TEC covered sets selected. In order for a TEC covered set to be added to the cover, the number of *new* points that it covers, c, (i.e., that are not already in P) must be at least c_{min} (see line 12). The TEC covered set that is added on a particular iteration of the **while** loop is then the one for which cW_i is a maximum (lines 15–19). If no TEC covered set is selected on a particular iteration, then the algorithm terminates, even if the dataset has not been completely covered. In lines 20–32, the algorithm determines whether the selected TEC covered set, C_{best} should be added as a "primary" or a "secondary" pattern: a pattern C_s is defined to be secondary to another (primary) pattern, C_p, if the proportion of points in C_p that are also in C_s is greater than the parameter, σ_{min} (line 27) (Forth, 2012, p. 38). On each iteration of the **while** loop, the best pattern and patterns that fail to cover a sufficient number of new points are removed from $\mathbf{C}$ to improve efficiency (lines 33–34).

Figure 13.11 shows the analysis generated by Forth's algorithm for the fugue from the Prelude and Fugue in C major (BWV 846) from the first book of J. S. Bach's *Das wohltemperirte Clavier*. Again, each TEC is drawn in a different colour. This analysis was obtained with c_{min} set to 15 and σ_{min} set to 0.5, as recommended by Forth (2012, pp. 38, 42).

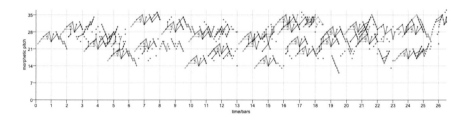

Fig. 13.11 A visualization of the output generated by Forth's algorithm for the fugue from J. S. Bach's Prelude and Fugue in C major (BWV 846) from the first book of *Das wohltemperirte Clavier*. For this analysis, c_{min} was set to 15 and σ_{min} was set to 0.5

13.3.5 SIACT

Collins et al. (2010) claim that all the algorithms described above can be affected by what they call the "problem of isolated membership". This 'problem' is defined to occur when "a musically important pattern is contained *within* an MTP, along with other temporally isolated members that may or may not be musically important" (Collins et al., 2010, p. 6). Collins et al. claim that "the larger the dataset, the more likely it is that the problem will occur" and that it could prevent the SIA-based algorithms from "discovering some translational patterns that a music analyst considers noticeable or important" (Collins et al., 2010, p. 6). Collins et al. propose that this problem can be solved by taking each MTP computed by SIA (sorted into lexicographical order) and "trawling" inside this MTP "from beginning to end, returning subsets that have a compactness greater than some threshold a and that contain at least b points" (Collins et al., 2010, p. 6). This method is implemented in an algorithm that they call SIACT, which first runs SIA on the dataset and then carries out "compactness trawling" (hence "SIA*CT*") on each of the MTPs found by SIA.

Suppose $\mathbf{P} = \langle p_1, p_2, \ldots p_m \rangle$ contains all and only the points in an MTP, sorted into lexicographical order. Suppose further that $i_L(p_i)$ is the index of p_i in the lexicographically sorted dataset and that $\mathbf{I}_L(\mathbf{P}) = \langle i_L(p_1), i_L(p_2), \ldots i_L(p_m) \rangle$. For each MTP discovered by SIA, SIACT 'trawls' the MTP for lexicographically compact subsets using the CT algorithm shown in Fig. 13.12. Given $\mathbf{P}$, $\mathbf{I}_L(\mathbf{P})$ and the thresholds, a and b, as just defined, CT first sets up two variables, X and Q (lines 1–2 in Fig. 13.12). X is used to store the compact subsets of $\mathbf{P}$ found by the algorithm and is eventually returned in line 18. Q is used to store each of these subsets as it is found. The algorithm then scans $\mathbf{P}$ in lexicographical order, considering a new point, $\mathbf{P}[i]$, with dataset index $\mathbf{I}_L(\mathbf{P})[i]$, on each iteration of the **for** loop in lines 3–15. On each iteration of this **for** loop, if Q is empty, then $\mathbf{P}[i]$ is added to Q and the dataset index of $\mathbf{P}[i]$ is stored in the variable $i_{L,0}$ (lines 4–6). Otherwise, the compactness of the pattern that would result if $\mathbf{P}[i]$ were added to Q is calculated and, if this compactness is not less than a, then $\mathbf{P}[i]$ is added to Q (lines 8–10). If the compactness of the resulting pattern would be less than a, then the algorithm checks whether Q holds at least b points and, if it does, Q is added to X and reset to the empty set (lines 11–13). If $|Q|$ is less than b, then it is discarded (lines 14–15). When the algorithm has finished scanning all the points in $\mathbf{P}$, it is possible that Q contains a pattern of at least b points. If this is the case, then it is also added to X (lines 16–17) before the latter is returned in line 18.

A problem with the CT algorithm is that the patterns found for a particular MTP depend on the order in which points in the MTP are scanned, and there seems to be no good musical or psychological reason why this should be so—why should the decision as to whether a given member point is considered 'isolated' depend on the order in which the points in the pattern are scanned? Suppose, for example, that $\mathbf{P} = \langle q_5, q_8, q_9, q_{10}, q_{11} \rangle$, where q_i is (lexicographically) the ith point in the dataset. Now suppose that $a = 2/3$ and $b = 3$, as Collins et al. (2010, p. 7) suggest. If $\mathbf{P}$ is scanned from left to right, as it would be by the CT algorithm, then the only compact pattern trawled is $\{q_8, q_9, q_{10}, q_{11}\}$, indicating that the first point, q_5 is an

$CT(\mathbf{P}, \mathbf{I}_L(\mathbf{P}), a, b)$
1   $X \leftarrow \emptyset$
2   $Q \leftarrow \emptyset$
3   **for** $i \leftarrow 0$ **to** $|\mathbf{P}| - 1$
4   **if** $Q = \emptyset$
5           $Q \leftarrow Q \cup \{\mathbf{P}[i]\}$
6           $i_{L,0} \leftarrow \mathbf{I}_L(\mathbf{P})[i]$
7   **else**
8           $s \leftarrow \mathbf{I}_L(\mathbf{P})[i] - i_{L,0} + 1$
9   **if** $(|Q| + 1)/s \geq a$
10              $Q \leftarrow Q \cup \{\mathbf{P}[i]\}$
11   **else if** $|Q| \geq b$
12              $X \leftarrow X \cup \{Q\}$
13              $Q \leftarrow \emptyset$
14   **else**
15              $Q \leftarrow \emptyset$
16 **if** $|Q| \geq b$
17      $X \leftarrow X \cup \{Q\}$
18 **return** X

Fig. 13.12 The SIACT compactness trawler

'isolated member'. However, if $\mathbf{P}$ were scanned from right to left, then the found pattern would be $\{q_5, q_8, q_9, q_{10}, q_{11}\}$—that is, $\mathbf{P}$ would not be considered to suffer from the 'problem of isolated membership'. Similarly, if the pattern to be trawled were $\mathbf{P}_2 = \langle q_8, q_9, q_{10}, q_{11}, q_{14} \rangle$, then clearly q_{14} in this pattern is no less 'isolated' (lexicographically) than q_5 in $\mathbf{P}$. However, the CT algorithm would remove q_5 from $\mathbf{P}$, but not q_{14} from $\mathbf{P}_2$. In other words, the CT algorithm would judge $\mathbf{P}$ but not $\mathbf{P}_2$ to suffer from the 'problem of isolated membership'.

Figure 13.13 shows the output obtained with COSIATEC for the fugue from BWV 846 when SIA is replaced by SIACT, with the parameters a and b set to 0.67 and 3, respectively, as suggested by Collins et al. (2010, p. 7). This modification

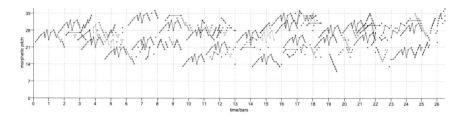

Fig. 13.13 A visualization of the output generated by the COSIATEC algorithm, with SIA replaced by SIACT, for the fugue from J. S. Bach's Prelude and Fugue in C major (BWV 846) from the first book of *Das wohltemperirte Clavier*. This analysis was obtained with parameter a set to 0.67 and parameter b set to 3

reduces the overall compression factor achieved from 2.90 to 2.53 and increases the size of the residual point set from 26 to 118 (16.19% of the dataset). With this residual point set excluded, the compression factor achieved over the remaining points is 3.59. Note that, when modified in this way, the encoding generated by COSIATEC includes the full subject, as opposed to the subject without the first note, discovered by the unmodified version of COSIATEC (see Fig. 13.9). On the other hand, this analysis using SIACT fails to find a pattern corresponding to the bass entry of the subject that starts $\frac{3}{4}$ of the way through bar 17.

13.3.6 SIAR

In an attempt to improve on the precision and running time of SIA, Collins (2011, pp. 282–283) defines an SIA-based algorithm called SIAR (which stands for "SIA for r superdiagonals"). Instead of computing the whole region below the leading diagonal in the vector table for a dataset (as in Fig. 13.4(b)), SIAR only computes the first r subdiagonals of this table. This is approximately equivalent to running SIA with a sliding window of size r (Collins, 2011; Collins et al., 2010). Pseudocode for SIAR is provided in Fig. 13.14, based on Collins's (2013c) own implementation.

The first step in SIAR is to calculate the first r subdiagonals of SIA's vector table (lines 1–7). This results in a list, $\mathbf{V}$, of $\langle v, i \rangle$ pairs, each representing the vector, v, from point p_i to p_j, where p_k is the $(k+1)$th point in $\mathbf{D}$, the lexicographically sorted input dataset. The next step in SIAR is to extract the (not necessarily maximal) translatable patterns discoverable from $\mathbf{V}$. This is done using the same technique as used in SIA: $\mathbf{V}$ is first sorted into lexicographical order and then segmented at points where the vector changes (lines 8–17). This produces an ordered set, $\mathbf{E}$, of patterns. SIA is then applied to each of the patterns in $\mathbf{E}$. However, the MTPs found by SIA are not required, so, for each pattern, $\mathbf{e} \in \mathbf{E}$, only the positive inter-point vectors for $\mathbf{e}$ are computed and these are stored in a list, $\mathbf{L}$ (lines 18–23). SIAR then produces a new list of vectors, $\mathbf{M}$, by removing duplicates in $\mathbf{L}$ and sorting the vectors into decreasing order by frequency of occurrence (lines 24–34). The final step in SIAR is to find the MTP for each of the vectors in $\mathbf{M}$, which, in Collins's (2013c) own implementation, is achieved using the method in lines 35–37 in Fig. 13.14. In line 37, the MTP for the vector $\mathbf{M}[i][0]$ is found by translating the input dataset, D, by the inverse of this vector and then finding the intersection between the resulting point set and the original dataset, D.

Figure 13.15 shows the analysis generated by COSIATEC for the fugue from BWV 846 when SIA is replaced by SIAR, with the parameter r set to 3. This modification reduces the overall compression factor from 2.90 to 2.41 and increases the size of the residual point set from 26 to 38 (5.21% of the dataset). If we exclude this residual point set, the compression factor over the remaining points is 2.61. Note that, if compactness trawling is enabled in this modified version of COSIATEC, then the output for this particular piece is identical to that shown in Fig. 13.13—that is, when SIA is replaced by SIACT.

SIAR(D,r)
 ▶ *Sort the dataset into lexicographical order*
1 **D** ← SORT$_{\text{Lex}}$(D)
 ▶ *Compute r subdiagonals of vector table and store in* **V**
2 **V** ← ⟨⟩
3 **for** i ← 0 **to** $|D| - 2$
4 j ← $i + 1$
5 **while** $j < |D| \wedge j \le i + r$
6   **V** ← **V** ⊕ ⟨⟨**D**[j] − **D**[i], i⟩⟩
7   j ← $j + 1$
 ▶ *Store patterns in* **E** *by sorting and segmenting* **V**
8 **V** ← SORT$_{\text{Lex}}$(**V**)
9 **E** ← ⟨⟩
10 v ← **V**[0][0]
11 **e** ← ⟨**D**[**V**[0][1]]⟩
12 **for** i ← 1 **to** $|\mathbf{V}| - 1$
13 **if** **V**[i][0] = v
14   **e** ← **e** ⊕ ⟨**D**[**V**[i][1]]⟩
15 **else**
16   **E** ← **E** ⊕ ⟨**e**⟩, **e** ← ⟨**D**[**V**[i][1]]⟩, v ← **V**[i][0]
17 **E** ← **E** ⊕ ⟨**e**⟩
 ▶ *For each pattern in* **E**, *find +ve inter-point vectors and store in* **L**
18 **L** ← ⟨⟩
19 **for** i ← 0 **to** $|\mathbf{E}| - 1$
20 **e** ← **E**[i]
21 **for** j ← 0 **to** $|\mathbf{e}| - 2$
22   **for** k ← $j + 1$ **to** $|\mathbf{e}| - 1$
23   **L** ← **L** ⊕ ⟨**e**[k] − **e**[j]⟩
 ▶ *Remove duplicates from* **L** *and order vectors by decreasing frequency of occurrence*
24 **L** ← SORT$_{\text{Lex}}$(**L**)
25 v ← **L**[0]
26 f ← 1
27 **M** ← ⟨⟩
28 **for** i ← 1 **to** $|\mathbf{L}| - 1$
29 **if** **L**[i] = v
30   f ← $f + 1$
31 **else**
32   **M** ← **M** ⊕ ⟨⟨v, f⟩⟩, f ← 1, v ← **L**[i]
33 **M** ← **M** ⊕ ⟨⟨v, f⟩⟩
34 **M** ← SORTDESCENDINGBYFREQ(**M**)
 ▶ *Find the MTP for each vector in* **M**, *store it in* **S** *and return* **S**
35 **S** ← ⟨⟩
36 **for** i ← 0 **to** $|\mathbf{M}| - 1$
37 **S** ← **S** ⊕ ⟨$D \cap (D - \mathbf{M}[i][0])$⟩
38 **return S**

Fig. 13.14 Pseudocode for SIAR, based on Collins's (2013c) own implementation

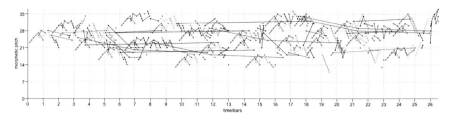

Fig. 13.15 A visualization of the output generated by the COSIATEC algorithm, with SIA replaced by SIAR, for the fugue from J. S. Bach's Prelude and Fugue in C major (BWV 846) from the first book of *Das wohltemperirte Clavier*. This analysis was obtained with the parameter *r* set to 3

13.3.7 SIATECCompress

One of the actions carried out by the GETBESTTEC function, called in line 4 of COSIATEC (see Fig. 13.8), is to run SIATEC on the set, D', which contains what remains of the input dataset, D, on each iteration of the **while** loop. Since SIATEC has worst-case running time $\Theta(n^3)$ where n is the number of points in the input dataset, running COSIATEC on large datasets can be time-consuming. On the other hand, because COSIATEC strictly partitions the dataset into non-overlapping MTP TEC covered sets, it tends to achieve high compression factors for many point-set representations of musical pieces (typically between 2 and 4 for a piece of classical or baroque music).

SIATECCOMPRESS(D)
1   $\mathbf{T} \leftarrow$ SIATEC(D)
2   $\mathbf{T} \leftarrow$ SORTTECSBYQUALITY($\mathbf{T}$)
3   $D' \leftarrow \emptyset$
4   $\mathbf{E} \leftarrow \langle \rangle$
5   **for** $i \leftarrow 0$ **to** $|\mathbf{T}| - 1$
6       $T \leftarrow \mathbf{T}[i]$
7       $S \leftarrow$ COV(T)
        ▶ *Recall that each TEC, T, is an ordered pair, ⟨pattern, translator set⟩*
8   **if** $|S \setminus D'| > |T[0]| + |T[1]|$
9           $\mathbf{E} \leftarrow \mathbf{E} \oplus \langle T \rangle$
10          $D' \leftarrow D' \cup S$
11   **if** $|D'| = |D|$
12   **break**
13 $R \leftarrow D \setminus D'$
14 **if** $|R| > 0$
15      $\mathbf{E} \leftarrow \mathbf{E} \oplus \langle$ASTEC($R$)$\rangle$
16 **return** $\mathbf{E}$

Fig. 13.16 The SIATECCOMPRESS algorithm

Like COSIATEC, the SIATECCOMPRESS algorithm shown in Fig. 13.16 is a greedy compression algorithm based on SIATEC that computes an encoding of a dataset in the form of a union of TEC covered sets. Like Forth's algorithm (but unlike COSIATEC), SIATECCOMPRESS runs SIATEC only *once* (line 1) to get a list of TECs. This list is then sorted into decreasing order by quality (line 2), where the decision as to which of any two TECs is superior is made in the same way as in COSIATEC (described above). The algorithm then finds a compact encoding, $\mathbf{E}$, of the dataset in the form of a set of TECs. It does this by iterating over the sorted list of TECs (lines 5–12), adding a new TEC, T, to $\mathbf{E}$ if the number of new points covered by T is greater than the size of its $\langle$pattern, translator set$\rangle$ representation (lines 8–12). Each time a TEC, T, is added to $\mathbf{E}$, its covered set is added to the set D', which therefore maintains the set of points covered so far after each iteration. When D' is equal to D or all the TECs have been scanned, the **for** loop terminates. Any remaining uncovered points are aggregated into a residual point set, R, (line 13) which is re-expressed as a TEC with an empty translator set (line 15) and added to the encoding, $\mathbf{E}$. SIATECCOMPRESS does not generally produce as compact an encoding as COSIATEC, since the TECs in its output may share points. However, it is faster than COSIATEC and can therefore be used practically on much larger datasets. Like COSIATEC, but unlike Forth's algorithm, SIATECCOMPRESS always produces a complete cover of the input dataset (although the last TEC in the encoding may consist of just a single residual point set).

Figure 13.17 shows the analysis generated by SIATECCOMPRESS for the fugue from BWV 846. The overall compression factor for this analysis is 1.94 compared with the value of 2.90 obtained using COSIATEC. The residual point set in this case contains 82 notes (11.25%) (cf. 26 notes, 3.57% for COSIATEC) and the compression factor excluding this residual point set is 2.20 (compared with 3.12 for COSIATEC).

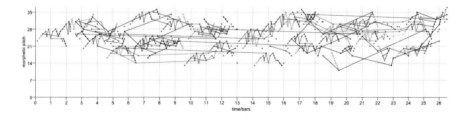

Fig. 13.17 A visualization of the output generated by the SIATECCOMPRESS algorithm, for the fugue from J. S. Bach's Prelude and Fugue in C major (BWV 846) from the first book of *Das wohltemperirte Clavier*

13.4 Evaluation

The algorithms described above were evaluated on two musicological tasks: classifying folk song melodies into tune families and discovering repeated themes and sections in polyphonic classical works. The results obtained will now be presented and discussed.

13.4.1 Task 1: Classifying Folk Song Melodies into Tune Families

For over a century, musicologists have been interested in measuring similarity between folk song melodies (Scheurleer, 1900; van Kranenburg et al., 2013), primarily with the purpose of classifying such melodies into *tune families* (Bayard, 1950), consisting of tunes that have a common ancestor in the tree of oral transmission. In the first evaluation task, COSIATEC, Forth's algorithm and SIATECCOMPRESS were used to classify a collection of folk song melodies into tune families. The collection used was the *Annotated Corpus* (van Kranenburg et al., 2013; Volk and van Kranenburg, 2012) of 360 melodies from the Dutch folk song collection, *Onder de groene linde* (Grijp, 2008), hosted by the Meertens Institute and accessible through the website of the Dutch Song Database (http://www.liederenbank.nl). The algorithms were used as compressors to calculate the *normalized compression distance* (NCD) (Li et al., 2004) between each pair of melodies in the collection (see (13.1)). Each melody was then classified using the 1-nearest-neighbour algorithm with leave-one-out cross-validation. The classifications obtained were compared with a ground-truth classification of the melodies provided by expert musicologists. Four versions of each algorithm were tested: the basic algorithm as described above, a version incorporating the CT algorithm (Fig. 13.12), a version using SIAR instead of SIA and a version using both SIAR and CT. As a baseline, one of the best general-purpose compression algorithms, BZIP2, was also used to calculate NCDs between the melodies.

Table 13.1 shows the results obtained in this task. In this table, algorithms with names containing "R" employed the SIAR algorithm with $r = 3$ in place of SIA. The value of 3 for r was chosen so as to be small, as the higher the value of r, the more SIAR approximates to SIA. Collins et al. (2013) ran SIAR with $r = 1$. Algorithms with names containing "CT" used Collins et al.'s (2010) compactness trawler, with parameters $a = 0.66$ and $b = 3$, chosen because these were the values suggested by Collins et al. (2010, p. 7). Forth's algorithm was run with $c_{min} = 15$ and $\sigma_{min} = 0.5$, as suggested by Forth (2012, pp. 38, 42). No attempt was made to find optimal values for these parameters, so overfitting is very unlikely. On the other hand, this also means that the chosen parameters are probably suboptimal. The column headed "SR" gives the classification success rate—i.e., the proportion of songs in the corpus correctly classified. The third and fourth columns give the mean compression factor achieved by each algorithm over, respectively, the corpus and the file-pairs used to compute the compression distances.

Table 13.1 Results on Task 1. *SR* is the classification success rate, CR_{AC} is the average compression factor over the melodies in the *Annotated Corpus*. CR_{pairs} is the average compression factor over the pairs of files used to obtain the NCD values

Algorithm	*SR*	CR_{AC}	CR_{pairs}
COSIATEC	0.8389	1.5791	1.6670
COSIARTEC	0.8361	1.5726	1.6569
COSIARCTTEC	0.7917	1.4547	1.5135
COSIACTTEC	0.7694	1.4556	1.5138
ForthCT	0.6417	1.1861	1.2428
ForthRCT	0.6417	1.1861	1.2428
Forth	0.6111	1.2643	1.2663
ForthR	0.6028	1.2555	1.2655
SIARCTTECCompress	0.5750	1.3213	1.3389
SIATECCompress	0.5694	1.3360	1.3256
SIACTTECCompress	0.5250	1.3197	1.3381
SIARTECCompress	0.5222	1.3283	1.3216
BZIP2	0.1250	2.7678	3.5061

The highest success rate of 84% was obtained using COSIATEC. Table 13.1 suggests that algorithms based on COSIATEC performed markedly better on this song classification task than those based on SIATECCOMPRESS or Forth's algorithm. Using SIAR instead of SIA and/or incorporating compactness trawling reduced the performance of COSIATEC. However, using both together, slightly improved the performance of SIATECCOMPRESS. Forth's algorithm performed slightly better than SIATECCOMPRESS. The performance of Forth's algorithm on this task was improved by incorporating compactness trawling; using SIAR instead of SIA in Forth's algorithm slightly reduced the performance of the basic algorithm and had no effect when compactness trawling was used. The results obtained using BZIP2 were much poorer than those obtained using the SIA-based algorithms, which may suggest that general-purpose compressors fail to capture certain musical structure that is important for this task. However, using an appropriate string-based input representation, where repeated substrings correspond to repeated segments of music, instead of a point set representation as was used here, may improve the performance of compressors such as BZIP2 that are designed primarily for text compression. Of the SIA-based algorithms, COSIATEC achieved the best compression on average, followed by SIATECCOMPRESS and then Forth's algorithm. COSIATEC also achieved the best success rate. However, since Forth's algorithm performed slightly better than SIATECCOMPRESS, it seems that compression factor alone was not a reliable indicator of classification accuracy on this task—indeed, the best compressor, BZIP2, produced the worst classifier. None of the algorithms achieved a success rate as high as the 99% obtained by van Kranenburg et al. (2013) on this corpus using several local features and an alignment-based approach. The success rate achieved by COSIATEC is within the 83–86% accuracy range obtained by Velarde et al.

(2013, p. 336) on this database using a wavelet-based representation, with similarity measured using Euclidean or city-block distance.

13.4.2 Task 2: Discovering Repeated Themes and Sections

In the second task, each of the SIA-based algorithms tested in Task 1 was used to discover repeated themes and sections in the five pieces in the JKU Patterns Development Database (JKU-PDD) (Collins, 2013a). This database contains Orlando Gibbons' madrigal, "Silver Swan" (1612); the fugue from J. S. Bach's Prelude and Fugue in A minor (BWV 889) from Book 2 of *Das wohltemperirte Clavier* (1742); the second movement of Mozart's Piano Sonata in E flat major (K. 282) (1774); the third movement of Beethoven's Piano Sonata in F minor, Op. 2, No. 1 (1795); and Chopin's Mazurka in B flat minor, Op. 24, No. 4 (1836). The database also contains encodings of ground-truth analyses by expert analysts that identify important patterns in the pieces. For each of these patterns, a ground-truth analysis encodes one or more occurrences, constituting an *occurrence set* for each of the ground-truth patterns. It is important to note, however, that each of these ground-truth occurrence sets does not necessarily contain *all* the occurrences within a piece of a particular pattern. For example, the ground-truth analyses fail to recognize that, in both of the minuet-and-trio movements by Beethoven and Mozart, the first section of the trio is recapitulated at the end of the second section in a slightly varied form. Why such occurrences have been omitted from the ground-truth is not clear.

It can also be argued that the ground-truth analyses in the JKU-PDD omit certain patterns that might reasonably be considered important or noticeable. For example, Figure 13.18 shows two patterns discovered by COSIATEC that help to account for the structure of the lyrical fourth section of the Chopin Mazurka, yet this section of the piece is completely ignored in the JKU-PDD ground truth. Again, why the

Fig. 13.18 Examples of noticeable and/or important patterns in Chopin's Mazurka in B flat minor, Op. 24, No. 4, that were discovered by COSIATEC, but are not recorded in the ground truth. Pattern (a) occurs independently of pattern (b) at bars 73 and 89

analysts whose work was used as a basis for the ground-truth should have ignored such patterns is not clear.

Each of the algorithms tested generates a set of TECs which is intended to contain all the occurrences of a particular pattern. That is, each TEC is intended to correspond to a ground-truth occurrence set. In general, in the ground-truth analyses, an "occurrence" of a pattern is not necessarily exactly translationally equivalent to it in pitch-time space. For example, it is common in the ground-truth analyses of the JKU-PDD for patterns to be specified by just the segments of the music that span them; or, if the pattern occurs entirely within a single voice, by the segment of that voice that spans the pattern. On the other hand, it is not uncommon for an MTP to contain only *some* of the notes within the shortest segment of the music or smallest rectangle in pitch-time space that contains it, resulting in it having a compactness less than 1. In such cases, a ground-truth pattern may be equal to the shortest segment containing an MTP or an MTP's bounding-box, rather than equal to the MTP itself. In this task, therefore, each of the 12 algorithms was tested on the JKU-PDD in three different "modes": "Raw" mode, "Segment" mode and "BB" mode. In "Raw" mode, the pattern occurrence sets generated are simply the "raw" TECs computed by the algorithm (see Fig. 13.19(a)). In "BB" mode, each raw pattern occurrence is replaced in the output with the pattern containing all the points in the bounding-box of the pattern (Fig. 13.19(b)). In "Segment" mode, each raw pattern occurrence is replaced with the pattern containing all the points in the temporal segment spanning the pattern (Fig. 13.19(c)). The results of this task are given in Table 13.2. The values in this table are *three-layer F_1 scores* (TLF1), as defined by Meredith (2013). Each value gives the harmonic mean of the precision and recall of the algorithm on a given piece. Three-layer F_1 score is a modification of the standard F_1 score that gives credit to an algorithm for discovering a pattern or an occurrence that is very similar but not identical to a ground-truth pattern. If the standard definition of F_1 score is used in this task, then an algorithm may score 0 even if each pattern that it generates differs from a ground-truth pattern by only one note. Three-layer F_1 score overcomes

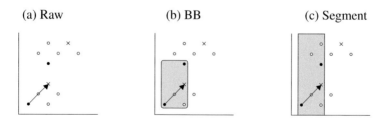

Fig. 13.19 (a) The pattern consisting of two black dots is a "raw" pattern, as might be output by one of the SIA-based algorithms. This pattern is the MTP for the vector indicated by the arrow. The pattern of crosses is the image of the black dot pattern after translation by this vector. (b) The shaded area indicates the corresponding bounding-box pattern output by the algorithm when operating in "BB" mode. (c) The shaded area indicates the corresponding segment pattern output when the algorithm operates in "Segment" mode

this problem by using F_1 score (or, equivalently, the Sørensen–Dice index (Dice, 1945; Sørensen, 1948)) to measure similarity on three levels of structure: between individual occurrences, between occurrence sets and between sets of occurrence sets. In Table 13.2, the highest values for each piece are in bold. The last column gives the mean TLF1 value over all the pieces for a given algorithm. The algorithms are named using the same convention as used in Table 13.1, except that, in addition, the mode (Raw, Segment or BB) is appended to the name.

Overall, the best performing algorithms on this task were COSIATEC and SIATE-CCOMPRESS in "Segment" mode. These were the best-performing algorithms on the Chopin, Gibbons and Beethoven pieces. Using SIAR instead of SIA in these algorithms in "Segment" mode did not change the overall mean performance, but

Table 13.2 Results on Task 2. Values are "three-layer F1" values, as defined by Meredith (2013)

Algorithm	Chopin	Gibbons	Beethoven	Mozart	Bach	Mean
COSIACTTEC	0.09	0.16	0.22	0.29	0.23	0.20
COSIACTTECBB	0.18	0.24	0.42	0.40	0.22	0.29
COSIACTTECSegment	0.25	0.31	0.56	0.45	0.19	0.35
COSIARCTTEC	0.09	0.16	0.22	0.29	0.23	0.20
COSIARCTTECBB	0.18	0.24	0.42	0.40	0.22	0.29
COSIARCTTECSegment	0.25	0.31	0.56	0.45	0.19	0.35
COSIARTEC	0.05	0.12	0.14	0.18	0.20	0.14
COSIARTECBB	0.22	0.31	0.49	0.38	0.22	0.32
COSIARTECSegment	**0.44**	**0.39**	**0.69**	0.55	0.19	**0.45**
COSIATEC	0.05	0.11	0.18	0.23	0.19	0.15
COSIATECBB	0.17	0.23	0.51	0.46	0.21	0.32
COSIATECSegment	0.37	0.37	**0.71**	**0.60**	0.18	**0.45**
Forth	0.12	0.33	0.32	0.21	0.17	0.23
ForthBB	0.18	0.27	0.32	0.27	0.17	0.24
ForthCT	0.23	0.35	0.56	0.56	**0.40**	0.42
ForthCTBB	0.27	0.34	0.57	0.58	**0.39**	0.43
ForthCTSegment	0.29	0.35	0.58	**0.59**	0.31	0.42
ForthR	0.12	0.30	0.20	0.25	0.30	0.23
ForthRBB	0.18	0.25	0.29	0.31	0.28	0.26
ForthRCT	0.23	0.35	0.56	0.56	**0.40**	0.42
ForthRCTBB	0.27	0.34	0.57	0.58	**0.39**	0.43
ForthRCTSegment	0.29	0.35	0.58	**0.59**	0.31	0.42
ForthRSegment	0.28	0.25	0.35	0.38	0.27	0.31
ForthSegment	0.33	0.26	0.35	0.33	0.19	0.29
SIACTTECCompress	0.12	0.20	0.23	0.30	0.27	0.22
SIACTTECCompressBB	0.17	0.27	0.30	0.35	0.27	0.27
SIACTTECCompressSegment	0.20	0.26	0.33	0.38	0.22	0.28
SIARCTTECCompress	0.12	0.20	0.23	0.30	0.27	0.22
SIARCTTECCompressBB	0.17	0.27	0.30	0.35	0.27	0.27
SIARCTTECCompressSegment	0.20	0.26	0.33	0.38	0.22	0.28
SIARTECCompress	0.10	0.18	0.19	0.18	0.25	0.18
SIARTECCompressBB	0.39	0.32	0.53	0.45	0.26	0.39
SIARTECCompressSegment	**0.60**	**0.39**	0.65	0.57	0.25	**0.49**
SIATECCompress	0.11	0.16	0.19	0.25	0.26	0.19
SIATECCompressBB	0.37	0.30	0.51	0.51	0.29	0.40
SIATECCompressSegment	**0.56**	**0.40**	0.63	**0.59**	0.29	**0.49**

did change the performance on individual pieces. The highest score obtained on any single piece was 0.71 by COSIATECSEGMENT on the Beethoven sonata movement. Interestingly, Forth's algorithm was the best-performing algorithm on the Bach fugue by a considerable margin. This suggests that there may be some feature of this algorithm that makes it particularly suited to analysing imitative contrapuntal music.

13.5 Conclusions

Each of the algorithms considered in this study takes a point-set representation of a piece of music as input and computes a set of TECs that collectively cover (or almost cover) this point set. All the algorithms attempt to select TECs in a way that maximizes compression factor and compactness. The results obtained on two quite different evaluation tasks suggest that this geometric, compression-based approach has the potential to lead to versatile algorithms that derive analyses from in extenso music representations that can profitably be used in a variety of musicological tasks. However, the results also indicate that certain variants of the algorithms may be more suited to some tasks than to others. The results do not unambiguously support the hypothesis that the best analyses of a piece correspond to the shortest possible descriptions of it. However, COSIATEC, the SIA-based algorithm that achieves the best compression in general, was the best-performing algorithm on Task 1 and achieved the second-best score overall on Task 2.

Acknowledgements The work reported in this chapter was partly carried out while working on a collaborative European project entitled "Learning to Create" (Lrn2Cre8). The project Lrn2Cre8 acknowledges the financial support of the Future and Emerging Technologies (FET) programme within the Seventh Framework Programme for Research of the European Commission, under FET grant number 610859.

The author would also like to thank Tom Collins and two anonymous reviewers for their helpful and constructive feedback on an earlier version of this chapter.

Supplementary Material The source code of the Java implementations of the algorithms described in this chapter that were used in the evaluation tasks are freely available at http://chromamorph.googlecode.com. For further information or advice on running or modifying these implementations, readers should contact the author.

References

Bayard, S. (1950). Prolegomena to a study of the principal melodic families of British-American folk song. *Journal of American Folklore*, 63(247):1–44.
Bent, I. (1987). *Analysis*. The New Grove Handbooks in Music. Macmillan. (Glossary by W. Drabkin).

Chaitin, G. J. (1966). On the length of programs for computing finite binary sequences. *Journal of the Association for Computing Machinery*, 13(4):547–569.

Collins, T. (2011). *Improved methods for pattern discovery in music, with applications in automated stylistic composition*. PhD thesis, Faculty of Mathematics, Computing and Technology, The Open University, Milton Keynes.

Collins, T. (2013a). JKU Patterns Development Database. Available at https://dl.dropbox.com/u/11997856/JKU/JKUPDD-Aug2013.zip.

Collins, T. (2013b). MIREX 2013 Competition: Discovery of Repeated Themes and Sections. http://tinyurl.com/o9227qg. Accessed on 5 January 2015.

Collins, T. (2013c). PattDisc-Jul2013. Available online at http://www.tomcollinsresearch.net/publications.html. Accessed 29 December 2013.

Collins, T., Arzt, A., Flossmann, S., and Widmer, G. (2013). SIARCT-CFP: Improving precision and the discovery of inexact musical patterns in point-set representations. In *Fourteenth International Society for Music Information Retrieval Conference (ISMIR 2013)*, Curitiba, Brazil.

Collins, T., Laney, R., Willis, A., and Garthwaite, P. H. (2011). Modeling pattern importance in Chopin's Mazurkas. *Music Perception*, 28(4):387–414.

Collins, T., Thurlow, J., Laney, R., Willis, A., and Garthwaite, P. H. (2010). A comparative evaluation of algorithms for discovering translational patterns in baroque keyboard works. In *Proceedings of the 11th International Society for Music Information Retrieval Conference (ISMIR 2010)*, pages 3–8, Utrecht, The Netherlands.

Cormen, T. H., Leiserson, C. E., Rivest, R. L., and Stein, C. (2009). *Introduction to Algorithms*. MIT Press, 3rd edition.

Dice, L. R. (1945). Measures of the amount of ecologic association between species. *Ecology*, 26(3):297–302.

Forth, J. and Wiggins, G. A. (2009). An approach for identifying salient repetition in multidimensional representations of polyphonic music. In Chan, J., Daykin, J. W., and Rahman, M. S., editors, *London Algorithmics 2008: Theory and Practice*, pages 44–58. College Publications.

Forth, J. C. (2012). *Cognitively-motivated geometric methods of pattern discovery and models of similarity in music*. PhD thesis, Department of Computing, Goldsmiths, University of London.

Grijp, L. P. (2008). Introduction. In Grijp, L. P. and van Beersum, I., editors, *Under the Green Linden—163 Dutch Ballads from the Oral Tradition*, pages 18–27. Meertens Institute/Music & Words.

Kolmogorov, A. N. (1965). Three approaches to the quantitative definition of information. *Problems of Information Transmission*, 1(1):1–7.

Lerdahl, F. and Jackendoff, R. S. (1983). *A Generative Theory of Tonal Music*. MIT Press.

Li, M., Chen, X., Li, X., Ma, B., and Vitányi, P. M. B. (2004). The similarity metric. *IEEE Transactions on Information Theory*, 50(12):3250–3264.

Li, M. and Vitányi, P. (2008). *An Introduction to Kolmogorov Complexity and Its Applications*. Springer, third edition.

Meredith, D. (2006a). Point-set algorithms for pattern discovery and pattern matching in music. In *Proceedings of the Dagstuhl Seminar on Content-based Retrieval (No. 06171, 23–28 April, 2006)*, Schloss Dagstuhl, Germany. Available online at http://drops.dagstuhl.de/opus/volltexte/2006/652.

Meredith, D. (2006b). The *ps13* pitch spelling algorithm. *Journal of New Music Research*, 35(2):121–159.

Meredith, D. (2007). *Computing pitch names in tonal music: A comparative analysis of pitch spelling algorithms*. PhD thesis, Faculty of Music, University of Oxford.

Meredith, D. (2013). Three-layer precision, three-layer recall, and three-layer F1 score. http://tinyurl.com/owtz79v.

Meredith, D., Lemström, K., and Wiggins, G. A. (2002). Algorithms for discovering repeated patterns in multidimensional representations of polyphonic music. *Journal of New Music Research*, 31(4):321–345.

Meredith, D., Lemström, K., and Wiggins, G. A. (2003). Algorithms for discovering repeated patterns in multidimensional representations of polyphonic music. In *Cambridge Music Processing Colloquium*, Department of Engineering, University of Cambridge. Available online at http://www.titanmusic.com/papers.php.

Meredith, D., Wiggins, G. A., and Lemström, K. (2001). Pattern induction and matching in polyphonic music and other multi-dimensional datasets. In Callaos, N., Zong, X., Verges, C., and Pelaez, J. R., editors, *Proceedings of the 5th World Multiconference on Systemics, Cybernetics and Informatics (SCI2001)*, volume X, pages 61–66.

Rissanen, J. (1978). Modeling by shortest data description. *Automatica*, 14(5):465–471.

Salomon, D. and Motta, G. (2010). *Handbook of Data Compression*. Springer, fifth edition.

Scheurleer, D. (1900). Preisfrage. *Zeitschrift der Internationalen Musikgesellschaft*, 1(7):219–220.

Simon, H. A. and Sumner, R. K. (1968). Pattern in music. In Kleinmuntz, B., editor, *Formal representation of human judgment*. Wiley.

Simon, H. A. and Sumner, R. K. (1993). Pattern in music. In Schwanauer, S. M. and Levitt, D. A., editors, *Machine Models of Music*, pages 83–110. MIT Press.

Solomonoff, R. J. (1964a). A formal theory of inductive inference (Part I). *Information and Control*, 7(1):1–22.

Solomonoff, R. J. (1964b). A formal theory of inductive inference (Part II). *Information and Control*, 7(2):224–254.

Sørensen, T. (1948). A method of establishing groups of equal amplitude in plant sociology based on similarity of species and its application to analyses of the vegetation on Danish commons. *Kongelige Danske Videnskabernes Selskab*, 5(4):1–34.

van Kranenburg, P., Volk, A., and Wiering, F. (2013). A comparison between global and local features for computational classification of folk song melodies. *Journal of New Music Research*, 42(1):1–18.

Velarde, G., Weyde, T., and Meredith, D. (2013). An approach to melodic segmentation and classification based on filtering with the Haar-wavelet. *Journal of New Music Research*, 42(4):325–345.

Volk, A. and van Kranenburg, P. (2012). Melodic similarity among folk songs: An annotation study on similarity-based categorization in music. *Musicae Scientiae*, 16(3):317–339.

Part VI
Classification and Distinctive Patterns

Chapter 14
Composer Classification Models for Music-Theory Building

Dorien Herremans, David Martens, and Kenneth Sörensen

Abstract The task of recognizing a composer by listening to a musical piece used to be reserved for experts in music theory. The problems we address here are, first, that of constructing an automatic system that is able to distinguish between music written by different composers; and, second, identifying the musical properties that are important for this task. We take a data-driven approach by scanning a large database of existing music and develop five types of classification model that can accurately discriminate between three composers (Bach, Haydn and Beethoven). More comprehensible models, such as decision trees and rulesets, are built, as well as black-box models such as support vector machines. Models of the first type offer important insights into the differences between composer styles, while those of the second type provide a performance benchmark.

14.1 Introduction

Automatic composer-identification is a complex task that remains a challenge in the field of music information retrieval (MIR). The problems we address here are, first, that of constructing an automatic system that is able to distinguish between music written by different composers; and, second, that of identifying the musical properties that are important for this task. The latter can offer interesting insights for music theorists.

A data-driven approach is taken in this research by extracting global features from a large database of existing music. Based on this data, five types of classification

Dorien Herremans · Kenneth Sörensen
ANT/OR, University of Antwerp Operations Research Group, Antwerp, Belgium
e-mail: {dorien.herremans, kenneth.sorensen}@uantwerpen.be

David Martens
Applied Data Mining Research Group, University of Antwerp, Antwerp, Belgium
e-mail: david.martens@uantwerpen.be

© Springer International Publishing Switzerland 2016   369
D. Meredith (ed.), *Computational Music Analysis*,
DOI 10.1007/978-3-319-25931-4_14

model (decision tree, ruleset, logistic regression, support vector machines and Naive Bayes) are developed that can accurately classify a musical piece between Bach, Haydn or Beethoven. Most of the developed models are comprehensible and offer insight into the styles of the composers. Yet, a few black-box models were also built as a performance benchmark.

14.2 Prior Work in Music Information Retrieval

The task of composer classification belongs to the domain of Music Information Retrieval (MIR), a multidisciplinary field concerned with retrieving and analysing multifaceted information from large music databases (Downie, 2003). The field of MIR has grown rapidly in recent years due to the digitization of the music industry. In 2011 alone, the European consumer expenditure on digital media exceeded 33 billion euros (Stenzel and Downes, 2012).

The first mention of the term MIR is due to Kassler (1966), who named the programming language he developed to extract information from music files "MIR". The early work done on the topic of computational music analysis is described in more detail by Mendel (1969).

Recently, many topics have been explored in the field of MIR. Examples of these are the content-based music search engine "query-by-humming", which allows a user to hum a tune in order to search for the original song in a large database (Ghias et al., 1995; Tseng, 1999). Pfeiffer et al. (1997) developed a system that can detect violence in video soundtracks. The techniques developed by Wold et al. (1996) are used to, for instance, identify different types of human speaker (e.g., female versus male). Music similarity research is another topic that has been explored by MIR scientists, in which the similarity of two musical pieces is measured (Berenzweig et al., 2004). For more detailed surveys of research done in the field of MIR, see Typke et al. (2005), Weihs et al. (2007) and Casey et al. (2008). In the current chapter, however, the focus will be on composer classification.

14.2.1 Classification Systems

The task of music classification can be seen as building models that assign one or more class labels to musical pieces based on their content. These models are often evaluated based on accuracy, i.e., the number of correctly classified instances versus the total number of instances. It should be noted however that accuracy is not always the best performance measure, for instance in the case of an unbalanced dataset. In this research, the area under the curve (AUC) of the receiver operating characteristic (ROC) is used to evaluate the performance of the models. This metric, which takes into account the true positives versus the false positives, is more suitable since the dataset is slightly skewed (see Fig. 14.1) (Fawcett, 2004). Most existing studies on music classification only evaluate their model based on the accuracy rate. When comparing the performance of previous studies, one should take into account that accuracy is not always comparable.

While the specific task of composer classification has not received a great deal of attention in the literature (Backer and van Kranenburg, 2005; Geertzen and van Zaanen, 2008; van Kranenburg, 2008), music classification has been applied to a plethora of other topics. Machine learning tools have been applied to classify pieces by, for example, cultural origin (Whitman and Smaragdis, 2002), geographic region (Hillewaere et al., 2009), timbre (Cosi et al., 1994), mood (Laurier et al., 2008), artist (Mandel and Ellis, 2005), hit ranking (Herremans et al., 2014) and genre (Chew et al., 2005; Tzanetakis and Cook, 2002).

There is an important difference between the data representation in classification models that work with *audio* data (e.g., WAV files) and *symbolic* data (e.g., MIDI files). The types of feature that can be extracted from a dataset and used to build models are vastly different for the two categories. Encouraging results have been obtained on classifying music audio data. For example, Whitman et al. (2001) built neural networks and support vector machine models for artist identification based on audio features. These models achieved classification accuracies of 91% in a one-in-five artist space over a small corpus (35 songs) and 70% correct over a larger corpus (50 songs) with ten artists. However, in this chapter, the focus will be on building *comprehensible* models, therefore we chose to work with symbolic features since they are generally more meaningful for music theorists.

In symbolic music classification, there are two main approaches. On the one hand, there are systems that use a language modelling approach, including n-grams and hidden Markov models. They take into account *local features* that change over the course of the musical fragment (Pérez-Sancho et al., 2008). On the other hand are systems that extract a finite vector of *global features* from each song (Steinbeck, 1982).

A study by Volk and van Kranenburg (2012) showed that recurring motifs are important when classifying songs into tune families. This suggests that locality, and thus local features, are important factors in classifying songs. This first approach, based on local features, was confronted by the challenge of efficiently representing data for machine learning. Techniques such as multiple viewpoints offer a possible solution to this problem (Conklin and Witten, 1995; Pearce et al., 2005). The problem of classifying folk songs by region was tackled with a language model by Li et al. (2006). They achieved an accuracy rate of 72.5% on a data set of European folk songs from six different regions. Pérez-Sancho et al. (2008) modelled chord progressions and melodies as n-grams and strings, and constructed genre classification models based on this representation. They were able to achieve an 86% accuracy rate for three broad genres. A success rate of 96.6% was obtained by Hontanilla et al. (2013) with an n-gram approach on discriminating between Shostakovich and Bach.

The second approach, based on global features, is the one that we focus on in this chapter. Other studies that have used this approach include that of Steinbeck (1982), who used global features to cluster melodies into meaningful groups such as hymns, children's songs and hunting songs. Eerola et al. (2001) used global features for assessing similarity. Ponce de León and Iñesta (2003) used global melodic, harmonic and rhythmic descriptors for style classification. The ensemble method based on a neural network and a k-nearest neighbour developed by McKay and Fujinaga (2004) for genre classification used 109 global features and achieved an accuracy of 98% for root genres and 90% for leaf genres. Moreno-Seco et al. (2006) also applied ensemble methods based on global features to a style classification problem. Bohak and Marolt (2009) used the same type of features to assess the similarity between Slovenian folk song melodies. Herlands et al. (2014) combined typical global features with a novel class of local features to detect nuanced stylistic elements. Their classification models obtained an accuracy of 80% when discriminating between Haydn's and Mozart's string quartets.

A small number of studies have compared both types of feature and compared their performance on the folk music classification problem. Jesser (1991) created classification models based on both features using the dataset from Steinbeck (1982). Her conclusion was that global features do not contribute much to the classification. A study by Hillewaere et al. (2009) found that event models outperform a global feature approach for classifying folk songs by their geographical origin (England, France, Ireland, Scotland, South East Europe and Scandinavia). In another study with European folk tunes, Hillewaere et al. (2012) compared string methods with n-gram models and global features for genre classification of 9 dance types. They concluded that features based on duration lead to better classification, no matter which method is used, although the n-gram method performed best overall. Van Kranenburg et al. (2013) obtained similar results for the classification of Dutch folk tunes into tune families. Their study showed that local features always obtain the best results, yet global features can be successful on a small corpus when the optimal subset of features is used. Similar results were obtained in a study to detect similarity between folk tunes (van Kranenburg, 2010).

Since the dataset used in our research was relatively small and global features were a relatively simple way of representing melodies that can be easily processed by different types of classifier, we opted to use a carefully selected set of global features in the research reported in this chapter.

14.2.2 Composer Classification

While a lot of research has been done on the task of automatic music classification (see Sect. 14.2.1), the subtask of composer classification remains relatively unexplored.

Wołkowicz et al. (2007) used n-grams to classify piano files into groups of five composers. Hillewaere et al. (2010) also used n-grams and compared them with global feature models to distinguish between string quartets by Haydn and Mozart. The classification accuracy of their trigram approach for recognizing composers for string quartets was 61% for violin and viola, and 75% for cello. Another system that classifies string quartet pieces by composer has been implemented by Kaliakatsos-Papakostas et al. (2011). They used a Markov chain to represent the four voices of the quartets as a monophonic melody. A classification success rate of 59 to 88% was achieved when classifying between two composers with their weighted Markov chain model. The study performed by Pollastri and Simoncelli (2001) had a lower accuracy rate than the previously discussed research. The Hidden Markov Models they designed for the classification of 605 monophonic themes by five composers had an accuracy of 42% on average. Backer and van Kranenburg (2005) have applied statistical pattern recognition to the problem of distinguishing Bach from Handel, Telemann, Haydn and Mozart using 20 features in different time slices throughout the pieces. They concluded that it is "very possible to isolate the style of J.S. Bach from Telemann, Handel, Haydn or Mozart".

Van Kranenburg and Backer (2004) used 20 global style markers based on properties of counterpoint. A decision tree (C4.5) (Quinlan, 1993) and nearest neighbour classification algorithm are built on a database of 320 pieces from the eighteenth and early nineteenth century. They are able to achieve a fairly low error rate. Although the features are described in the paper, a detailed description of the models is missing. Similar features based on counterpoint are used by Mearns et al. (2010) to develop a C4.5 decision tree and naive Bayes models. Their models correctly classified 44 out of 66 pieces with 7 groups of composers. The resulting decision tree could give music theorists insight into the differences between styles of composers; however, the tree is not shown in the paper.

In the following sections, the dataset used in this research is discussed together with the chosen features. These are then used to build accurate and comprehensible classification models (Sect. 14.4). The resulting models are described in detail in this chapter and give insight into the differences between the styles of Haydn, Beethoven and Bach.

14.3 Data Sources

The range of features that can be extracted from music depends heavily on the type of file they have to be extracted from. Computational music analysis is typically performed on two types of music file, those based on *audio signals* and *structured files*. The first category includes files representing audio signals (e.g., WAV and MP3) and files containing the values of features derived from audio signals (e.g., short-term Fourier spectra, MFCCs, etc.). While there is a large quantity of music available in such formats, the types of feature that result from analysing these files (e.g., spectral flux and zero-crossing rate (Tzanetakis et al., 2003)) are not the most comprehensible, especially for music theorists. For the purpose of our research, it was therefore more appropriate to work with files of the second type, i.e., structured files.

Structured, symbolic files, such as MIDI files, contain high-level structured information about music. MIDI files, in particular, describe a specific way of performing a piece and contain information such as the start, duration, velocity and instrument of each note. These files allow us to extract musically meaningful features.

Fig. 14.1 Class distribution
of the dataset for the different
composers

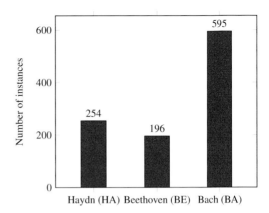

14.3.1 Dataset

We used MIDI files from the KernScores database, since they could be loaded into
jSymbolic, the software used to extract the features (see Sect. 14.3.2). This is a large
collection (7,866,496 notes in 108,703 files) of virtual music scores made available by
the Center for Computer Assisted Research in the Humanities at Stanford University
(CCARH) (CCARH, 2012). It must be pointed out that MIDI files are a performance
representation, often recorded by a human playing the score, and they therefore do
not guarantee an accurate representation of the score (van Kranenburg and Backer,
2004). However, the KernScore database contains MIDI files with correct timing and
pitch information, since they were derived from MuseData files that were produced
by manual encoding of printed scores (Sapp, 2005).

Three composers, Johann Sebastian Bach (BA), Ludwig van Beethoven (BE)
and Franz Joseph Haydn (HA), were chosen for this research since there are many
pieces by these composers in the KernScores database, allowing us to create more
accurate models. An overview of the composer class distribution of the selected 1045
movements is given in Fig. 14.1. Almost all available pieces by these composers
were included in our dataset, except for a few very short fragments.

14.3.2 Feature Extraction

There are a number of tools available for extracting musical features from symbolic
files, such as Humdrum (Huron, 2002) and MIDI toolbox for Matlab (Eerola and
Toiviainen, 2004). Due to its ease of use, compatibility with polyphonic music, good
support and the quality of the resulting features, the software package jSymbolic was
used to extract the features from the dataset (McKay and Fujinaga, 2007). jSymbolic
is contained within jMIR, the Java-based Open Source software toolbox designed for
automatic music classification (McKay and Fujinaga, 2009).

Table 14.1 Features extracted with jSymbolic

Variable	Feature description
x_1	Chromatic Motion Frequency - Fraction of chromatic intervals
x_2	Melodic Fifth Frequency
x_3	Melodic Octaves Frequency
x_4	Melodic Thirds Frequency
x_5	Most Common Melodic Interval Prevalence
x_6	Most Common Pitch Prevalence[a]
x_7	Most Common Pitch Class Prevalence[b]
x_8	Relative Strength of Most Common Intervals - fraction of intervals belonging to the second most common / most common melodic intervals
x_9	Relative Strength of Top Pitch Classes[c]
x_{10}	Relative Strength of Top Pitches[c]
x_{11}	Repeated Notes - fraction of notes that are repeated melodically
x_{12}	Stepwise Motion Frequency

[a] Pitch refers to MIDI pitch number.
[b] Pitch class refers to MIDI pitch number mod 12.
[c] Top pitch or top pitch class refers to the most common pitch or pitch class in the piece.

jSymbolic is able to extract 111 different features. However, for this research, not all of them are meaningful or computationally easy to implement in classification models. Multidimensional features, nominal features, features related to instrumentation or that depend upon the key were excluded from the dataset. This resulted in a selection of twelve one-dimensional features that output normalized frequency information related to intervals or pitches. All of these features are represented in Table 14.1. They are measured as normalized frequencies and offer information regarding *melodic* intervals and pitches.

A second reason, other than musical meaningfulness, for keeping the feature set small is to avoid overfitting the models (Gheyas and Smith, 2010). Having a limited number of features allows a thorough testing of a model, even with limited instances, and can thus enhance the quality of a classification model (McKay and Fujinaga, 2006). This way we avoid the "curse of dimensionality", where the number of labelled training and testing samples needed increases exponentially with the number of features.

In the following sections, five types of classification model are developed, based on the extracted features.

14.4 Classification Models

Predictive models can be used not only for classification, but also in theory-building
and testing (Shmueli and Koppius, 2011). Using powerful models, in combination
with high-level musical features enables us to construct models that give useful
insights into the characteristics of the style of a composer. The first models in this
section (i.e., rulesets and trees) are of a more linguistic nature and therefore fairly
easy to understand (Martens, 2008). Support vector machines and naive Bayes classifiers are more black-box, as they provide a complex non-linear output score. Using
pedagogical *rule extraction* techniques like Trepan and G-REX (Martens et al., 2007),
comprehensible rulesets can still be extracted from black-box models. However, this
falls outside the scope of this chapter. The ruleset described in Sect. 14.4.2 simply
induces the rules directly from the data. While this research focuses on building comprehensible models, some black-box models were included to provide performance
benchmarks.

The open source software, Weka, is used to create five different types of classification model, each with varying levels of comprehensibility, using supervised learning
techniques (Witten and Frank, 2005). This toolbox and framework for data mining
and machine learning is a landmark system in this field (Hall et al., 2009). jSymbolic,
used to extract features as described in Sect. 14.3.2 above, outputs the features of all
instances in ACE XML files. The jMIR toolbox offers a tool to convert these features
into Weka ARFF format (McKay and Fujinaga, 2008).

Table 14.2 shows the results of using each of these types of model for composer
classification on the dataset described in Sect. 14.3.1 above. For some types of
model, such as decision trees and rulesets, multiple models were built with different
levels of comprehensibility. In these cases, Table 14.2 shows the results for the best
performing model of that type. The results are based on a run with stratified 10-fold
cross validation (10CV), where the dataset is divided into 10 folds, with 9 used for
model building and 1 for testing. This procedure is repeated 10 times, so that each
fold is used once for testing. The AUC and accuracy values shown in Table 14.2
are the average results over the 10 test sets. The entire dataset is used to build the
resulting final model, which can be expected to have a performance at least as good as
the 10CV performance. In order to compare the performance of the different models,

Table 14.2 Performance of the models with 10-fold cross-validation

Method	Accuracy	AUC
C4.5 Decision tree	*80%*	*79%*
RIPPER ruleset	*81%*	*85%*
Logistic regression	*83%*	*92%*
Naive Bayes	*80%*	*90%*
Support vector machines	**86%**	**93%**

$p < 0.01$: italic, $p > 0.05$: bold, best: <u>bold</u>.

a Wilcoxon signed-rank test was conducted, the null hypothesis of this test being that there is no difference between the performance of a model and that of the best model.

14.4.1 C4.5 Tree

In this section we describe a decision tree classifier, which is a simple, yet widely used and comprehensible classification technique. Even though decision trees are not always the most competitive models in terms of accuracy, they are computationally efficient and offer a visual understanding of the classification process. A decision tree is a tree data structure that consists of decision nodes and leaves, where the leaves specify the class value (i.e., composer) and the nodes specify a test of one of the features. A predictive rule is found by following a path from the root to a leaf based on the feature values of a particular piece. The resulting leaf indicates the predicted composer for that particular piece (Ruggieri, 2002).

J48 (Witten and Frank, 2005), Weka's implementation of the C4.5 algorithm, is used to build decision trees (Quinlan, 1993). A "divide and conquer" approach is used by C4.5 to build trees recursively. This is a top-down approach, which repeatedly seeks a feature that best separates the classes, based on normalized information gain (i.e., difference in entropy). After this step, subtree raising is done by pruning the tree from the leaves to the root (Wu et al., 2008).

Three decision trees were built (T1, T2 and T3), each with a different setting for the confidence factor (confFactor) and the minimum number of instances per leaf (minNumObj). A low confidence factor will result in more pruning but a less accurate model. Requiring a greater minimum number of instances per leaf will also reduce the size of the tree, so that it becomes more easy to understand; on the other hand, it will also reduce accuracy. The settings for the three trees are shown in Table 14.3, together with their performance results and the sizes of the resulting trees (sizeTree), including the numbers of leaves (numLeaves).

The first model (T1) was heavily pruned, so that the resulting tree was compact. As expected, the accuracy and AUC values, respectively 73% and 72%, were lower than the less pruned models. Figure 14.2 shows the resulting classifier.

A second, slightly less pruned, model (T2) was built (see Fig. 14.3). As shown in Table 14.3, the accuracy and AUC values were slightly higher. The tree itself was slightly bigger (8 leaves), but still comprehensible.

Table 14.3 Performance and settings of the C4.5 decision trees (10CV)

ID	confFactor	minNumObj	numLeaves	sizeTree	Accuracy	AUC
T1	0.01	100	3	5	73%	72%
T2	0.01	50	8	15	76%	78%
T3	0.25	2	54	107	80%	79%

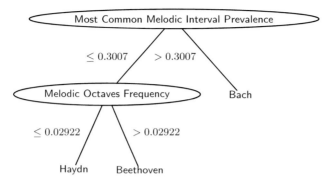

Fig. 14.2 C4.5 decision tree (T1)

We will not show the third tree (T3) here, as it is too large (54 leaves). With an accuracy of 80% and an AUC of 79%, it is the most accurate model; however, it is also the least easy to comprehend. The confusion matrix of this best model is displayed in Table 14.4. This matrix reveals that there is a relatively higher misclassification rate between Haydn and Beethoven and between Haydn and Bach. This could be due to the fact that the dataset was larger for Bach and Haydn. It might also be due to the fact that Haydn and Beethoven's styles are indeed more similar, as they had a greater amount of chronological and geographical overlap in their lives, just as Haydn and Bach had chronological overlap. Furthermore, Haydn was once Beethoven's teacher (DeNora, 1997). Bach and Beethoven on the other hand never lived in the same country, nor during the same time period (Greene, 1985). For more details on the musicological similarities and background of Haydn and Beethoven, the reader is referred to Rosen (1997).

When examining the three models, the importance of the 'Most common melodic interval prevalence' feature for composer recognition is clear, as it is the root node of

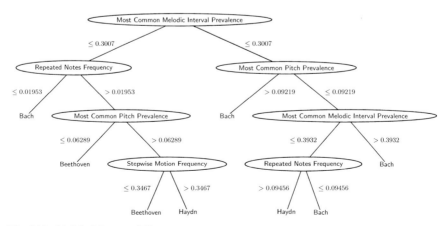

Fig. 14.3 C4.5 decision tree (T2)

all three models. It indicates that Bach focuses more on one particular interval than the other composers. Bach also seems to use fewer repeated notes than the other two composers. The 'Melodic octaves frequency' feature indicates that Beethoven uses more octaves in melodies than Haydn.

14.4.2 RIPPER

As with the decision trees just described, the rulesets presented in this section were built with an inductive rule-learning algorithm (as opposed to rule-extraction techniques such as Trepan and G-REX (Martens et al., 2007)). They are comprehensible models based on "if-then" rules, that are computationally efficient to implement.

JRip, Weka's implementation of the 'Repeated Incremental Pruning to Produce Error Reduction' (RIPPER) algorithm, was used to build a ruleset for composer classification (Cohen, 1995). RIPPER uses sequential covering to generate the ruleset. It consists of a building stage and an optimization stage. The building stage starts by growing one rule by greedily adding antecedents (or conditions) to the rule, until it is perfect (i.e., 100% accurate) based on an initial growing and pruning set (ratio 2:1). The algorithm tries every possible value for each attribute and selects the condition with the highest information gain. Then each condition is pruned in last-to-first order. This is repeated until either there are no more positive examples, or the description length (DL) is 64 bits greater than the smallest DL found so far, or the error rate is >50%. In the optimization phase, the instances covered by existing rules are removed from the pruning set. Based on this new pruning set, each rule is reconsidered and two variants are produced. If one of the variants offers a better description length, it replaces the rule. This process is repeated (Hall et al., 2009). The models below were created with 50 optimizations.

We again built three models (R1, R2 and R3), each with varying levels of complexity. This was achieved by varying the minimum total weight of the instances in a rule (minNo). Setting a higher level for this parameter forces the algorithm to have more instances for each rule, thus reducing the total number of rules in the model. The settings and performance results of the models are summarized in Table 14.5.

The first model (R1) was created by setting the minimum total weight of the instances in a rule very high. This resulted in an easy-to-understand ruleset (see Fig. 14.4). As can be seen in Table 14.5, its performance is slightly lower than the other models, yet comparable to the performance of the decision trees, described in the previous section.

Table 14.4 Confusion matrix for C4.5 (model T3)

a	b	c	classified as
175	39	40	a = HA
66	**110**	20	b = BE
24	21	**550**	c = BA

Table 14.5 Performance
and settings of the RIPPER
rulesets (10CV)

ID	minNo	Number of rules	Accuracy	AUC
R1	50	3	75%	75%
R2	25	5	78%	80%
R3	2	12	81%	85%

---

if (Most Common Melodic Interval Prevalence) ≤ 0.2678 and (Melodic Octaves
Frequency ≥ 0.03006) **then**
    Composer = BE
else if (Stepwise Motion Frequency ≤ 0.5464) and (Chromatic Motion Frequency
≥ 0.1726) and ($0.06466 \leq$ Most Common Pitch Prevalence ≤ 0.1164) **then**
    Composer = HA
else
    Composer = BA
end if

Fig. 14.4 RIPPER Ruleset (R1)

    The second model (R2) was created with a higher setting for the minimum total
weight of the instances in a rule. This resulted in the five "if-then" rules shown in
Fig. 14.5. The model is slightly more difficult to understand, but it also performed
better on the dataset used here (see Table 14.5).
    A final model (R3) was created by setting minNo very low. The resulting model,
consisting of 12 rules, is not shown here as it is too extensive. However, with an
accuracy of 81% and AUC of 87% it does outperform the previous two models. The

---

if (Most Common Melodic Interval Prevalence) ≤ 0.2688 and (Melodic Octaves
Frequency ≥ 0.04438) **then**
    Composer = BE
else if (Most Common Pitch Prevalence ≤ 0.07191) and (Most Common Melodic
Interval Prevalence ≤ 0.2956) and (Melodic Octaves Frequency ≥ 0.02489) **then**
    Composer = BE
else if (Most Common melodic Interval Prevalence ≤ 0.328) and (Melodic Thirds
Frequency ≥ 0.1119) and (Chromatic Motion Frequency ≥ 0.1692) and (Most
Common Pitch Prevalence ≤ 0.106) **then**
    Composer = HA
else if (Stepwise Motion Frequency ≤ 0.5245) and (Chromatic Motion Frequency
≥ 0.1166) and (Repeated Notes Frequency ≥ 0.1972) **then**
    Composer = HA
else
    Composer = BA
end if

Fig. 14.5 RIPPER Ruleset (R2)

Table 14.6 Confusion matrix
for RIPPER

a	b	c	classified as
189	32	33	a = HA
48	**124**	24	b = BE
37	21	**537**	c = BA

confusion matrix of the model is shown in Table 14.6. The misclassification rates are very similar to those of the decision trees in the previous section, with fewest misclassifications occurring between Beethoven and Bach.

It is noticeable that the first feature evaluated by the rulesets is the same as the root feature of the decision trees in Sect. 14.4.1 above, which confirms its importance. The rulesets and decision trees can be interpreted in a similar way. Like the decision trees, the rulesets suggest that Beethoven uses more melodic octaves than the other composers and that Haydn uses more repeated notes than Bach.

14.4.3 Logistic Regression

In the previous sections, two techniques were explored to build comprehensible models. Both trees and rulesets provide crisp classification. This means that they classify a musical piece as being either by a certain composer or not. The logistic regression model built in this section offers a continuous measure that indicates the probability that a piece is by each composer under consideration. These models are built for each composer and the one with the highest probability is chosen as the predicted class. Just like the previously discussed models, implementing logistic regression models is computationally efficient. They are also less prone to overfitting than other models such as neural networks (Tu, 1996).

A logistic regression model was built with Weka's SimpleLogistic function. This implementation uses LogitBoost, an algorithm that performs additive logistic regression (Witten and Frank, 2005). LogitBoost sequentially applies a simple regression function to re-weighted versions of the training data. The optimal number of LogitBoost iterations to perform is cross-validated, which leads to automatic attribute selection (Landwehr et al., 2005). This simple boosting strategy often results in dramatic performance improvements (Friedman et al., 2000).

The resulting model that we obtained outputs the probability, $P(L_y)$, that a piece is by a certain composer, y. $P(L_y)$ is defined as follows:

$$P(L_y) = \frac{1}{1 + e^{-L_y}}, \tag{14.1}$$

where

$$L_{HA} = -3.39 + 21.19 \cdot x_1 + 3.96 \cdot x_2 + 6.22 \cdot x_3 + 6.29 \cdot x_4 - 4.9 \cdot x_5$$
$$- 1.39 \cdot x_6 + 3.29 \cdot x_7 - 0.17 \cdot x_8 + 0 \cdot x_9 \qquad (14.2)$$
$$- 0.72 \cdot x_{10} + 8.35 \cdot x_{11} - 4.21 \cdot x_{12} ,$$

$$L_{BE} = 6.19 + 5.44 \cdot x_1 + 14.69 \cdot x_2 + 24.36 \cdot x_3 - 0.45 \cdot x_4 - 6.52 \cdot x_5$$
$$- 29.99 \cdot x_6 + 3.84 \cdot x_7 - 0.38 \cdot x_8 - 3.39 \cdot x_9 \qquad (14.3)$$
$$- 2.76 \cdot x_{10} + 2.04 \cdot x_{11} - 0.48 \cdot x_{12} ,$$

$$L_{BA} = -4.88 - 13.15 \cdot x_1 - 6.16 \cdot x_2 - 5.28 \cdot x_3 - 11.63 \cdot x_4 + 11.92 \cdot x_5$$
$$+ 34 \cdot x_6 - 13.21 \cdot x_7 + 3.1 \cdot x_8 + 2.37 \cdot x_9 \qquad (14.4)$$
$$+ 0.66 \cdot x_{10} - 5.05 \cdot x_{11} + 3.03 \cdot x_{12} .$$

In these expressions, x_i refers to the corresponding feature value from Table 14.1.

This type of continuous output score allows it to be included in an evaluation metric used by a music generation algorithm. In a previous study, the authors used a local search heuristic to generate music intended to have the characteristics of a certain composer. The amount of influence of a certain composer contained within a certain piece was measured by the probability of a logistic regression model (Herremans et al., 2015).

The logistic regression equations are not as straightforward to interpret as the previous two models. Yet they still offer a lot of information about the differences between the styles of the composers. When a feature has a high coefficient, it means that it is important for distinguishing a particular composer from other composers. For instance, x_5 ('Most Common Melodic Interval Frequency') has a high coefficient value, especially for BA. When looking at the previous models, this feature is also at the top of the decision trees (see Figs. 14.2 and 14.3) and occurs in almost all of the rules in the rulesets (see Figs. 14.4 and 14.5).

The logistic regression model that we obtained outperforms the two previous models with an AUC of 92% and accuracy of 83% and is the second best model overall (see Table 14.2). The confusion matrix, shown in Table 14.7, reflects this higher accuracy rate. When examining the misclassified pieces, we notice that their average probability is 64%. Examples of misclassified pieces include the fourth movement of Beethoven's String Quartet No. 9 in C major, Op. 59, No. 3 (Allegro molto), which is classified as Haydn with a probability of 4% and the first movement of Bach's Brandenburg Concerto No. 5 in D major (BWV 1050), which is classified as Haydn with a probability of 37%.

Table 14.7 Confusion matrix for logistic regression

a	b	c	classified as
190	30	34	a = HA
57	**119**	20	b = BE
25	15	**555**	c = BA

14.4.4 Naive Bayes

We also used Weka to build a naive Bayes classifier. Like the logistic regression model, a naive Bayes model outputs the probability that a piece is by a certain composer. This probability estimate is based on the assumption that the features are conditionally independent. Given class label (i.e., composer) y, this independence assumption can be represented as follows (Tan et al., 2007):

$$P(\mathbf{x} \mid Y = y) = \prod_{j=1}^{M} P(x_j \mid Y = y),$$ (14.5)

where each attribute set $\mathbf{x} = \{x_1, x_2, \ldots, x_M\}$ consists of M attributes.

Because of the independence assumption, we do not need to calculate the class-conditional probability for every combination of $\mathbf{x}$. Only the conditional probability of each x_i given that $Y = y$ has to be estimated. This offers a practical advantage, since a good estimate of the probability can be obtained without the need for a very large training set. Given a test piece, the posterior probability for each composer Y can be calculated by the following formula (Lewis, 1998):

$$P(Y \mid \mathbf{x}) = \frac{P(Y) \cdot \prod_{j=1}^{M} P(x_j \mid Y)}{P(\mathbf{x})}.$$ (14.6)

Since the attributes are continuous, a normal distribution is often chosen to represent the class-conditional probability. However, we found that better performance was achieved by using a kernel estimator instead of a normal distribution (John and Langley, 1995). However, unlike the previous models, the model produced is too extensive to show in this chapter and is not easily comprehensible. Its results are included as a benchmark value for the other models. The resulting model has an accuracy of 80% and an AUC value of 90%, which is less good than the logistic regression model described in the previous section. The confusion matrix is shown in Table 14.8. As can be seen in this table, many pieces by Haydn are misclassified as Beethoven. Other than that, the misclassification errors are comparable to those for the previous models (cf. Figs. 14.4, 14.6 and 14.7), with least confusion between Beethoven and Bach.

Table 14.8 Confusion matrix for naive Bayes

a	b	c	classified as
199	28	27	a = HA
69	**118**	9	b = BE
41	34	**520**	c = BA

14.4.5 Support Vector Machine

In order to provide a benchmark for the performance of the comprehensible models presented above, a support vector machine classifier was implemented. Support vector machines (SVMs) are black-box models, yet they outperform more traditional models in many areas including stock market prediction (Huang et al., 2005), text classification (Tong and Koller, 2002), Celtic violin performer identification (Ramirez et al., 2011), gene selection (Guyon et al., 2002) and others.

In this section, the library LibSVM (Chang and Lin, 2011) was used to build a support vector machine (SVM) classifier. This is a learning procedure based on statistical learning theory (Vapnik, 1995). Given a training set of N data points $\{(\mathbf{x}_i, y_i)\}_{i=1}^N$ where the features $\mathbf{x}_i \in \mathbb{R}^n$ and corresponding binary class labels $y_i \in \{-1, +1\}$, the SVM classifier should fulfil the following conditions (Cristianini and Shawe-Taylor, 2000; Vapnik, 1995):

$$\begin{cases} \mathbf{w}^T \varphi(\mathbf{x}_i) + b \geq +1, & \text{if } y_i = +1 \\ \mathbf{w}^T \varphi(\mathbf{x}_i) + b \leq -1, & \text{if } y_i = -1 \end{cases} \tag{14.7}$$

which is equivalent to

$$y_i \times (\mathbf{w}^T \varphi(\mathbf{x}_i) + b) \geq 1, \quad i = 1, ..., N . \tag{14.8}$$

The input space is mapped to a high (possibly infinite) dimensional feature space by the non-linear function $\varphi(\cdot)$. In this new feature space, the above inequalities construct a hyperplane $\mathbf{w}^T \varphi(\mathbf{x}) + b = 0$ discriminating between the two classes. The margin between the two classes is maximized by minimizing $\mathbf{w}^T \mathbf{w}$. Describing the inner workings of the SVM falls beyond the scope of this chapter. The interested reader is referred to Cristianini and Shawe-Taylor (2000), who describe the optimization problem that results in the following formula for the actual classifier:

$$y(\mathbf{x}) = \text{signum}(\textstyle\sum_{i=1}^N \alpha_i y_i K(\mathbf{x}_i, \mathbf{x}) + b) , \tag{14.9}$$

where $K(\mathbf{x}_i, \mathbf{x}) = \varphi(\mathbf{x}_i)^T \varphi(\mathbf{x})$ is taken with a positive definite kernel satisfying the Mercer theorem and α_i are the Lagrange multipliers, determined by optimizing the dual problem. Here, the Radial Basis Function (RBF) kernel was used to map the feature space to a hyperplane:

$$K(\mathbf{x}, \mathbf{x}_i) = \exp\{-\|\mathbf{x} - \mathbf{x}_i\|^2 / \sigma^2\}, \text{ (RBF kernel)}$$

where σ is a constant.

The GridSearch procedure in Weka was used to determine the optimal settings for the regularization parameter (see Cristianini and Shawe-Taylor (2000)) of the optimization problem and the σ for the RBF kernel (Weka, 2013).

Trying to comprehend the logic of the classifications made is quite difficult, if not impossible since the SVM classifier with non-linear kernel is a complex, non-linear function (Martens and Provost, 2014; Martens et al., 2009). It does however

Table 14.9 Confusion matrix
for support vector machines

a	b	c	classified as
204	26	24	a = HA
49	**127**	20	b = BE
22	10	**563**	c = BA

outperform the previous models. The resulting accuracy is 86% and the AUC-value is 93% for the SVM with RBF kernel (see Table 14.2). However, when testing for the difference in AUC performance between SVM and other models, the p-value remained > 0.01 for both logistic regression and naive Bayes. This indicates that these two models closely match the performance of the SVM. The confusion matrix (see Table 14.9) confirms that, of the types of model that we have considered, SVM provides the best model for discriminating between Haydn, Beethoven and Bach. Most misclassification occurs between Haydn and Beethoven, which might be correlated with the geographical and temporal overlap between the lives of these composers as mentioned in Sect. 14.4.1. When examining the misclassified pieces, they all seem to have a very low probability, with an average of 39%. Examples of misclassified pieces are the first movement of Haydn's String Quartet in C major, Op. 74, No. 1, which is misclassified as Bach with 38% probability; and the theme from Beethoven's Six Variations on a Swiss Song, WO 64, which is misclassified as Bach with a probability of 38%.

14.5 Summary of Results

The receiver operating characteristic (ROC) of the most accurate model for each of the different classifiers is shown in Fig. 14.6. The ROC curve displays the trade-off between true positive rate (TPR) and false negative rate (FNR). The logistic regression and the SVM classifiers score best, which is confirmed by their high AUC value in Table 14.2. The SVM classifier achieves the highest AUC value. Yet when testing for the difference in AUC performance between SVM and other models, the p-value remains > 0.01 for logistic regression, which makes this the best-performing comprehensible model. Although trees and rulesets are more intuitive to understand, their performance is slightly lower, which is reflected in their ROC curves.

All models clearly score better than a random classification, which is represented by the diagonal through the origin. While the SVM significantly outperforms the other models (except the AUC of logistic regression and naive Bayes), they can still be used to get a better understanding of the style characteristics of the three composers.

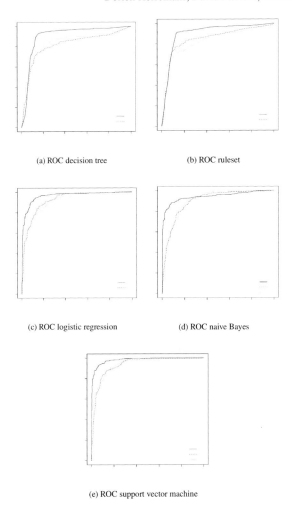

(a) ROC decision tree   (b) ROC ruleset

(c) ROC logistic regression   (d) ROC naive Bayes

(e) ROC support vector machine

Fig. 14.6 ROC curves of the models

14.6 Conclusions

In this study, a number of global musical features were extracted from a large database
of music consisting of pieces by three composers (Bach, Beethoven and Haydn).
Based on these features, five types of classification model were built. The first three
models are more comprehensible and thus offer more insight and understanding into
the characteristics of each composer's style and the differences between them. The
latter two models serve as a performance benchmark as they are too complex or
extensive to be easily understood. While black-box models (SVM) have the highest
performance (AUC 93% and accuracy 86%), comprehensible models such as the
RIPPER ruleset still perform well (AUC 85% and accuracy 81%).

The comprehensible models give us musical insights and can suggest directions for further musicological research. For example, the results of this study suggest that Beethoven typically does not focus on using one particular interval, in contrast to Haydn or Bach, who have a higher prevalence of the most common melodic interval. Clearly, this result is based on a limited corpus and cannot be generalized without further investigation.

It would be interesting to examine whether an approach based on local features could contribute to gaining even more insight into the styles of composers. Classification models with an even higher accuracy rate might also be developed. It could be interesting to extract comprehensible rules from SVM models with rule extraction techniques such as Trepan and G-REX (Martens et al., 2007). This might provide more accurate comprehensible models. According to Backer and van Kranenburg (2005), the composers examined in the study reported in this chapter are relatively easy to distinguish. It would therefore be interesting to apply the methods from this chapter to distinguishing between composers whose styles are more similar, such as Bach, Telemann and Handel.

References

Backer, E. and van Kranenburg, P. (2005). On musical stylometry—a pattern recognition approach. *Pattern Recognition Letters*, 26(3):299–309.

Berenzweig, A., Logan, B., Ellis, D., and Whitman, B. (2004). A large-scale evaluation of acoustic and subjective music-similarity measures. *Computer Music Journal*, 28(2):63–76.

Bohak, C. and Marolt, M. (2009). Calculating similarity of folk song variants with melody-based features. In *Proceedings of the 10th International Society for Music Information Retrieval Conference (ISMIR)*, pages 597–602, Kobe, Japan.

Casey, M., Veltkamp, R., Goto, M., Leman, M., Rhodes, C., and Slaney, M. (2008). Content-based music information retrieval: Current directions and future challenges. *Proceedings of the IEEE*, 96(4):668–696.

CCARH (2012). *KernScores, http://kern.ccarh.org*. Last accessed: November 2012.

Chang, C.-C. and Lin, C.-J. (2011). LIBSVM: A library for support vector machines. *ACM Transactions on Intelligent Systems and Technology (TIST)*, 2(3):27.

Chew, E., Volk, A., and Lee, C.-Y. (2005). Dance music classification using inner metric analysis. In Golden, B. L., Raghaven, S., and Wasil, E. A., editors, *The Next Wave in Computing, Optimization, and Decision Technologies*, pages 355–370. Springer.

Cohen, W. (1995). Fast effective rule induction. In *Proceedings of the 12th International Conference on Machine Learning*, pages 115–123, Tahoe City, CA.

Conklin, D. and Witten, I. H. (1995). Multiple viewpoint systems for music prediction. *Journal of New Music Research*, 24(1):51–73.

Cosi, P., De Poli, G., and Lauzzana, G. (1994). Auditory modelling and self-organizing neural networks for timbre classification. *Journal of New Music Research*, 23(1):71–98.

Cristianini, N. and Shawe-Taylor, J. (2000). *An Introduction to Support Vector Machines and Other Kernel-Based Learning Methods.* Cambridge University Press.

DeNora, T. (1997). *Beethoven and the Construction of Genius: Musical Politics in Vienna, 1792-1803.* University of California Press.

Downie, J. (2003). Music information retrieval. *Annual Review of Information Science and Technology*, 37(1):295–340.

Eerola, T., Järvinen, T., Louhivuori, J., and Toiviainen, P. (2001). Statistical features and perceived similarity of folk melodies. *Music Perception*, 18(3):275–296.

Eerola, T. and Toiviainen, P. (2004). MIR in Matlab: The Midi Toolbox. In *Proceedings of 6th International Conference on Music Information Retrieval (ISMIR 2005)*, pages 22–27, London, UK.

Fawcett, T. (2004). ROC graphs: Notes and practical considerations for data mining researchers. Technical Report HPL-2003-4, HP Laboratories, Palo Alto, CA.

Friedman, J., Hastie, T., and Tibshirani, R. (2000). Additive logistic regression: A statistical view of boosting (with discussion and a rejoinder by the authors). *The Annals Of Statistics*, 28(2):337–407.

Geertzen, J. and van Zaanen, M. (2008). Composer classification using grammatical inference. In *Proceedings of the International Workshop on Machine Learning and Music (MML 2008)*, pages 17–18, Helsinki, Finland.

Gheyas, I. and Smith, L. (2010). Feature subset selection in large dimensionality domains. *Pattern Recognition*, 43(1):5–13.

Ghias, A., Logan, J., Chamberlin, D., and Smith, B. (1995). Query by humming: Musical information retrieval in an audio database. In *Proceedings of the Third ACM International Conference on Multimedia*, pages 231–236, San Francisco, CA.

Greene, D. (1985). *Greene's Biographical Encyclopedia of Composers.* The Reproducing Piano Roll Foundation. Edited by Alberg M. Petrak.

Guyon, I., Weston, J., Barnhill, S., and Vapnik, V. (2002). Gene selection for cancer classification using support vector machines. *Machine Learning*, 46(1-3):389–422.

Hall, M., Frank, E., Holmes, G., Pfahringer, B., Reutemann, P., and Witten, I. (2009). The Weka data mining software: An update. *ACM SIGKDD Explorations Newsletter*, 11(1):10–18.

Herlands, W., Der, R., Greenberg, Y., and Levin, S. (2014). A machine learning approach to musically meaningful homogeneous style classification. In *Proceedings of the 28th AAAI Conference on Artificial Intelligence (AAAI-14)*, pages 276–282, Quebec, Canada.

Herremans, D., Martens, D., and Sörensen, K. (2014). Dance hit song prediction. *Journal of New Music Research*, 43(3):291–302.

Herremans, D., Sörensen, K., and Martens, D. (2015). Classification and generation of composer-specific music using global feature models and variable neighborhood search. *Computer Music Journal*, 39(3). In press.

Hillewaere, R., Manderick, B., and Conklin, D. (2009). Global feature versus event models for folk song classification. In *Proceedings of the 10th International Society for Music Information Retrieval Conference (ISMIR 2009)*, Kobe, Japan.

Hillewaere, R., Manderick, B., and Conklin, D. (2010). String quartet classification with monophonic models. In *Proceedings of the 11th International Society for Music Information Retrieval Conference (ISMIR 2010)*, Utrecht, The Netherlands.

Hillewaere, R., Manderick, B., and Conklin, D. (2012). String methods for folk tune genre classification. In *Proceedings of the 13th International Society for Music Information Retrieval Conference (ISMIR 2012)*, pages 217–222, Porto, Portugal.

Hontanilla, M., Pérez-Sancho, C., and Iñesta, J. (2013). Modeling musical style with language models for composer recognition. In Sanchez, J. M., Micó, L., and Cardoso, J., editors, *Pattern Recognition and Image Analysis: 6th Iberian Conference, IbPRIA 2013, Funchal, Madeira, Portugal, June 5–7. 2013, Proceedings*, volume 7887 of *Lecture Notes in Computer Science*, pages 740–748. Springer.

Huang, W., Nakamori, Y., and Wang, S.-Y. (2005). Forecasting stock market movement direction with support vector machine. *Computers & Operations Research*, 32(10):2513–2522.

Huron, D. (2002). Music information processing using the Humdrum Toolkit: Concepts, examples, and lessons. *Computer Music Journal*, 26(2):11–26.

Jesser, B. (1991). *Interaktive Melodieanalyse*. Peter Lang.

John, G. and Langley, P. (1995). Estimating continuous distributions in Bayesian classifiers. In *Proceedings of the Eleventh conference on Uncertainty in Artificial Intelligence*, pages 338–345, Montreal, Canada.

Kaliakatsos-Papakostas, M., Epitropakis, M., and Vrahatis, M. (2011). Weighted Markov chain model for musical composer identification. In Chio, C. D., Cagnoni, S., Cotta, C., Ebner, M., and et al., A. E., editors, *Applications of Evolutionary Computation*, volume 6625 of *Lecture Notes in Computer Science*, pages 334–343. Springer.

Kassler, M. (1966). Toward musical information retrieval. *Perspectives of New Music*, 4(2):59–67.

Landwehr, N., Hall, M., and Frank, E. (2005). Logistic model trees. *Machine Learning*, 59(1-2):161–205.

Laurier, C., Grivolla, J., and Herrera, P. (2008). Multimodal music mood classification using audio and lyrics. In *Seventh International Conference on Machine Learning and Applications (ICMLA'08)*, pages 688–693, La Jolla, CA.

Lewis, D. (1998). Naive (Bayes) at forty: The independence assumption in information retrieval. In Nedellec, C. and Rouveirol, C., editors, *Machine Learning: ECML-98*, volume 1398 of *Lecture Notes in Computer Science*, pages 4–15. Springer.

Li, X., Ji, G., and Bilmes, J. (2006). A factored language model of quantized pitch and duration. In *International Computer Music Conference (ICMC 2006)*, pages 556–563, New Orleans, LA.

Mandel, M. and Ellis, D. (2005). Song-level features and support vector machines for music classification. In *Proceedings of the 6th International Conference on Music Information Retrieval (ISMIR 2006)*, pages 594–599, London, UK.

Martens, D. (2008). Building acceptable classification models for financial engineering applications. *SIGKDD Explorations*, 10(2):30–31.

Martens, D., Baesens, B., Van Gestel, T., and Vanthienen, J. (2007). Comprehensible credit scoring models using rule extraction from support vector machines. *European Journal of Operational Research*, 183(3):1466–1476.

Martens, D. and Provost, F. (2014). Explaining data-driven document classifications. *MIS Quarterly*, 38(1):73–99.

Martens, D., Van Gestel, T., and Baesens, B. (2009). Decompositional rule extraction from support vector machines by active learning. *IEEE Transactions on Knowledge and Data Engineering*, 21(2):178–191.

McKay, C. and Fujinaga, I. (2004). Automatic genre classification using large high-level musical feature sets. In *Proceedings of the 5th International Conference on Music Information Retrieval (ISMIR 2004)*, Barcelona, Spain.

McKay, C. and Fujinaga, I. (2006). jSymbolic: A feature extractor for MIDI files. In *Proceedings of the International Computer Music Conference (ICMC 2006)*, pages 302–5, New Orleans, LA.

McKay, C. and Fujinaga, I. (2007). Style-independent computer-assisted exploratory analysis of large music collections. *Journal of Interdisciplinary Music Studies*, 1(1):63–85.

McKay, C. and Fujinaga, I. (2008). Combining features extracted from audio, symbolic and cultural sources. In *Proceedings of the 9th International Society for Music Information Retrieval Conference (ISMIR 2008)*, pages 597–602, Philadelphia, PA.

McKay, C. and Fujinaga, I. (2009). jMIR: Tools for automatic music classification. In *Proceedings of the International Computer Music Conference (ICMC 2009)*, pages 65–8, Montreal, Canada.

Mearns, L., Tidhar, D., and Dixon, S. (2010). Characterisation of composer style using high-level musical features. In *Proceedings of 3rd International Workshop on Machine Learning and Music*, pages 37–40, Florence, Italy.

Mendel, A. (1969). Some preliminary attempts at computer-assisted style analysis in music. *Computers and the Humanities*, 4(1):41–52.

Moreno-Seco, F., Inesta, J., Ponce de León, P. J., and Micó, L. (2006). Comparison of classifier fusion methods for classification in pattern recognition tasks. In Yeung, D.-Y., Kwok, J. T., Roli, A. F. F., and de Ridder, D., editors, *Structural, Syntactic, and Statistical Pattern Recognition: Joint IAPR International Workshops, SSPR 2006 and SPR 2006, Hong Kong, China, August 17–19, 2006. Proceedings*, volume 4109 of *LNCS*, pages 705–713. Springer.

Pearce, M., Conklin, D., and Wiggins, G. (2005). Methods for combining statistical models of music. In Kronland-Martinet, R., Voinier, T., and Ystad, S., editors, *Computer Music Modeling and Retrieval*, volume 3902 of *LNCS*, pages 295–312. Springer.

Pérez-Sancho, C., Rizo, D., and Inesta, J. M. (2008). Stochastic text models for music categorization. In da Vitoria Lobo, N. and others, editors, *Structural, Syntactic, and Statistical Pattern Recognition*, volume 5342 of *LNCS*, pages 55–64. Springer.

Pfeiffer, S., Fischer, S., and Effelsberg, W. (1997). Automatic audio content analysis. In *Proceedings of the 4th ACM International Conference on Multimedia*, pages 21–30, Boston, MA.

Pollastri, E. and Simoncelli, G. (2001). Classification of melodies by composer with hidden Markov models. In *Web Delivering of Music, 2001. Proceedings. First International Conference on*, pages 88–95. IEEE.

Ponce de León, P. J. and Iñesta, J. (2003). Feature-driven recognition of music styles. In Perales, F. J., Campilho, A. J. C., de la Blanca, N. P., and Sanfeliu, A., editors, *Pattern Recognition and Image Analysis: First Iberian Conference, IbPRIA 2003, Puerto de Andratx, Mallorca, Spain*, volume 2652 of *Lecture Notes in Computer Science*, pages 773–781. Springer.

Quinlan, J. (1993). *C4.5: Programs for Machine Learning*, volume 1. Morgan Kaufmann.

Ramirez, R., Maestre, E., Perez, A., and Serra, X. (2011). Automatic performer identification in Celtic violin audio recordings. *Journal of New Music Research*, 40(2):165–174.

Rosen, C. (1997). *The Classical Style: Haydn, Mozart, Beethoven*, volume 1. Norton.

Ruggieri, S. (2002). Efficient C4. 5 [classification algorithm]. *Knowledge and Data Engineering, IEEE Transactions on*, 14(2):438–444.

Sapp, C. (2005). Online database of scores in the Humdrum file format. In *Proceedings of the 6th International Conference on Music Information Retrieval (ISMIR 2005)*, pages 664–665, London, UK.

Shmueli, G. and Koppius, O. (2011). Predictive analytics in information systems research. *MIS Quarterly*, 35(3):553–572.

Steinbeck, W. (1982). Struktur und Ähnlichkeit. In *Methoden automatisierter Melodieanalyse*. Bärenreiter.

Stenzel, U. Lima, M. and Downes, J. . (2012). Study on Digital Content Products in the EU, Framework contract: Evaluation impact assessment and related services; Lot 2: Consumer's Policy. Technical report, EU, Brussels.

Tan, P. et al. (2007). *Introduction to Data Mining*. Pearson Education.

Tong, S. and Koller, D. (2002). Support vector machine active learning with applications to text classification. *The Journal of Machine Learning Research*, 2:45–66.

Tseng, Y.-H. (1999). Content-based retrieval for music collections. In *Proceedings of the 22nd Annual International ACM SIGIR Conference on Research and Development in Information Retrieval*, pages 176–182.

Tu, J. (1996). Advantages and disadvantages of using artificial neural networks versus logistic regression for predicting medical outcomes. *Journal of Clinical Epidemiology*, 49(11):1225–1231.

Typke, R., Wiering, F., and Veltkamp, R. (2005). A survey of music information retrieval systems. In *Proceedings of the 6th International Conference on Music Information Retrieval (ISMIR 2005)*, pages 153–160, London, UK.

Tzanetakis, G. and Cook, P. (2002). Musical genre classification of audio signals. *IEEE Transactions on Speech and Audio Processing*, 10(5):293–302.

Tzanetakis, G., Ermolinskyi, A., and Cook, P. (2003). Pitch histograms in audio and symbolic music information retrieval. *Journal of New Music Research*, 32(2):143–152.

van Kranenburg, P. (2008). On measuring musical style—The case of some disputed organ fugues in the J. S. Bach (BWV) catalogue. *Computing in Musicology*, 15:120–137.

van Kranenburg, P. (2010). *A computational approach to content-based retrieval of folk song melodies*. PhD thesis, Utrecht University.

van Kranenburg, P. and Backer, E. (2004). Musical style recognition—A quantitative approach. In *Proceedings of the Conference on Interdisciplinary Musicology (CIM04)*, pages 106–107, Graz, Austria.

van Kranenburg, P., Volk, A., and Wiering, F. (2013). A comparison between global and local features for computational classification of folk song melodies. *Journal of New Music Research*, 42(1):1–18.

Vapnik, V. (1995). *The Nature of Statistical Learning Theory*. Springer.

Volk, A. and van Kranenburg, P. (2012). Melodic similarity among folk songs: An annotation study on similarity-based categorization in music. *Musicae Scientiae*, 16(3):317–339.

Weihs, C., Ligges, U., Mörchen, F., and Müllensiefen, D. (2007). Classification in music research. *Advances in Data Analysis and Classification*, 1(3):255–291.

Weka (2013). Weka documentation, class GridSearch. Last accessed: October 2014.

Whitman, B., Flake, G., and Lawrence, S. (2001). Artist detection in music with Minnowmatch. In *Neural Networks for Signal Processing XI, 2001. Proceedings of the 2001 IEEE Signal Processing Society Workshop*, pages 559–568. IEEE.

Whitman, B. and Smaragdis, P. (2002). Combining musical and cultural features for intelligent style detection. In *Proceedings of the 3rd International Symposium on Music Information Retrieval (ISMIR 2002)*, pages 47–52, Paris, France.

Witten, I. and Frank, E. (2005). *Data Mining: Practical Machine Learning Tools and Techniques*. Morgan Kaufmann.

Wold, E., Blum, T., Keislar, D., and Wheaten, J. (1996). Content-based classification, search, and retrieval of audio. *MultiMedia, IEEE*, 3(3):27–36.

Wołkowicz, J., Kulka, Z., and Keselj, V. (2007). N-gram-based approach to composer recognition. Master's thesis, Warsaw University of Technology.

Wu, X., Kumar, V., Ross Quinlan, J., Ghosh, J., Yang, Q., Motoda, H., McLachlan, G., Ng, A., Liu, B., Yu, P., et al. (2008). Top 10 algorithms in data mining. *Knowledge and Information Systems*, 14(1):1–37.

Chapter 15
Contrast Pattern Mining in Folk Music Analysis

Kerstin Neubarth and Darrell Conklin

Abstract Comparing groups in data is a common theme in corpus-level music analysis and in exploratory data mining. Contrast patterns describe significant differences between groups. This chapter introduces the task and techniques of contrast pattern mining and reviews work in quantitative and computational folk music analysis as mining for contrast patterns. Three case studies are presented in detail to illustrate different pattern representations, datasets and groupings of folk music corpora, and pattern mining methods: subgroup discovery of global feature patterns in European folk music, emerging pattern mining of sequential patterns in Cretan folk tunes, and association rule mining of positive and negative patterns in Basque folk music. While this chapter focuses on examples in folk music analysis, the concept of contrast patterns offers opportunities for computational music analysis more generally, which can draw on both musicological traditions of quantitative comparative analysis and research in contrast data mining.

15.1 Introduction

In his introduction to computational and comparative musicology, Cook (2004) outlined the potential of computational approaches to analysing large repertoires of music, and proclaimed an opportunity for re-evaluating comparative analysis in musicology. For ethnomusicology, Nettl (2005, 2010) re-assessed comparative

Kerstin Neubarth
Canterbury Christ Church University, Canterbury, UK
e-mail: kerstin.neubarth@canterbury.ac.uk

Darrell Conklin
Department of Computer Science and Artificial Intelligence, University of the Basque Country UPV/EHU, San Sebastián, Spain
IKERBASQUE, Basque Foundation for Science, Bilbao, Spain
e-mail: darrell.conklin@ehu.eus

© Springer International Publishing Switzerland 2016
D. Meredith (ed.), *Computational Music Analysis*,
DOI 10.1007/978-3-319-25931-4_15

research, including quantified comparison (Nettl, 1973, 1975), as a methodological option among others rather than a defining feature of the discipline. Quantitative comparisons between groups or across time—based on music corpora, bibliographic data or compilations of context information—can support research on, for example, composers' and national styles (Trowbridge, 1986; VanHandel, 2009), a composer's choices (Lampert, 1982), a performer's repertoire selection (Kopiez et al., 2009), or changes in musical taste, music practice and its social, political, economic or technological context (Alessandri et al., 2014; Carter, 1987; Forrest and Heaney, 1991; Hess, 1953; Rose and Tuppen, 2014). In many cases, recent studies can draw on, and are confronted with, larger datasets than their forerunners (e.g., Forrest and Heaney, 1991; Rose and Tuppen, 2014). Data mining provides concepts and methods for organizing and analysing large datasets, discovering underlying relations in data and describing interesting patterns (Klösgen, 1999; Witten et al., 2011). *Contrast data mining* focuses on finding differentiating characteristics between groups in labelled data or trends in time-stamped data (Bay and Pazzani, 2001; Dong and Li, 1999; Webb et al., 2003). This chapter introduces concepts and methods of contrast data mining and illustrates their application to music with examples from folk music analysis.

Computational analysis of folk music has been referenced in the context of computational and empirical musicology (Cook, 2004; Lincoln, 1970, 1974), modern methods for musicology (Marsden, 2009) and digital humanities (Fujinaga and Weiss, 2004), and folk music corpora have attracted attention in music information retrieval (Cornelis et al., 2010; Tzanetakis et al., 2007; van Kranenburg et al., 2010). From a data mining point of view, folk music has proven a fruitful domain for exploring, developing and testing computational methods in corpus-level analysis thanks to the availability of relatively large, coherent, musicologically curated and annotated digital music collections. From a musicological point of view, ethnomusicologists have long explored computational approaches for organizing (Elscheková, 1966; Suchoff, 1967, 1968), indexing (Hoshovs'kyj, 1965; Járdányi, 1965), analysing (Elscheková, 1966, 1999; Suchoff, 1971) and better understanding (Elscheková, 1965, 1966) folk music collections and repertoires. The potential of computational methods is seen in facilitating the fast, accurate and reliable processing of large amounts of data (Csébfalvy et al., 1965; Elscheková, 1965, 1999; Járdányi, 1965; Rhodes, 1965; Steinbeck, 1976; Suchoff, 1968), supporting flexible search of folk music collections (Járdányi, 1965; Steinbeck, 1976; Suchoff, 1971), enhancing transparency of the analysis (Elscheková, 1999; Jesser, 1991), preserving analytical data (Elscheková, 1966) and enabling the discovery of hidden patterns in folk music corpora (Keller, 1984; Suchoff, 1970).

Comparative analysis of folk music has investigated acoustic, stylistic, functional or behavioural traits in folk music and their convergence, distribution or variation, both heuristically and speculatively (Bohlman, 1988; Nettl, 2005, 2010; Schneider, 2006). The analytical interest in finding differences between repertoires and practices within folk music corpora using statistical and computational methods is reflected in research questions such as those suggested by one of the pioneers of computational folk music analysis:

Historical Questions. [...] Are there different habits and preferences in melodic range and mode at different periods of history, and what is their relative strength?
Geographical Questions. What are the characteristic differentiae of specific regions? [...]
Typological Questions. What are the prevailing melodic forms within a given area of study?

(Bronson, 1959, p. 165)

Quantitative comparisons underlie observations on contrasting features such as:

A strange contrast [of songs by the Yuman and Yaqui] to all tribes previously analysed is shown in the relative proportion of songs ending on the third and fifth above the keynote [...]. The percentage ending on the keynote is smaller than in the total number of songs previously analysed. This is a peculiarity of this group of Indians [...].

(Densmore, 1932, p. 38)

We can conclude that organization and general war songs are low, rapid, and of wide range. By contrast the love songs tend to be high, slow, and of medium range.

(Gundlach, 1932, p. 138)

In contrast to German melodies, Chinese songs hardly ever start with an upbeat [...].

(Schaffrath, 1992, p. 108)

The average range of at least an eleventh [in Scottish melodies] is rather impressive. [...] In contrast to this, folksongs of the Shetlands seem to have less important [sic] ranges.

(Sagrillo, 2010, [p. 8])

Contrast data mining provides a coherent framework for relating early and more recent work in quantitative and computational folk music analysis.

More specifically, contrast data mining is the task of identifying significant differences between groups in data. In this chapter we focus on contrast data mining of folk music as a form of supervised descriptive pattern discovery (Herrera et al., 2011; Novak et al., 2009b). *Supervised* data mining is applied to labelled data instances: contrast data mining discovers contrasting characteristics of selected subpopulations in the data which are identified by group labels. In this respect supervised contrast mining differs from *unsupervised* techniques (e.g., clustering), in which groups are not predetermined but are identified during the mining. Supervised *descriptive* pattern discovery is primarily interested in finding individual rules which describe groups by characteristic local patterns: discovered contrast patterns make statements about parts of the data space (Hand et al., 2001), patterns tolerate some counter-examples (Lavrač et al., 2004), and patterns may overlap, describing different aspects of the same data instances (Klösgen, 1999; Lavrač et al., 2004). Exhaustive algorithms find all interesting patterns; heuristic algorithms apply strategies to reduce the search space, resulting in a subset of possible patterns (Herrera et al., 2011; Novak et al., 2009b). Descriptive patterns ideally are relatively simple and understandable (Herrera et al., 2011; Klösgen, 1996). In *predictive* data mining, on the other hand, induced models should be complete (i.e., cover all instances in the dataset) and ideally should be consistent (i.e., predict the correct group label for all instances) (Fürnkranz et al., 2012). Resulting models may be complex and possibly intransparent (Klösgen, 1996). Predictive methods generally infer one model out of a family of potential models

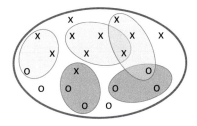 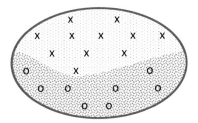

supervised descriptive

group labels
local patterns covering subsets of groups

patterns evaluated by interestingness
comprehensible patterns
exhaustive or heuristic search

supervised predictive

group labels
global models covering all examples of
groups
models evaluated by predictive accuracy
potentially intransparent models
heuristic search

Fig. 15.1 Schematic view and summary of supervised descriptive vs. predictive data mining

which best fits the complete dataset according to chosen heuristics (Hand et al., 2001).
Figure 15.1 summarizes the fundamental differences between supervised descriptive
and predictive data mining. The diagram constructs a small artificial data mining scenario, showing a dataset organized into two groups (labelled by x: 11 examples; and
o: 8 examples). For the descriptive schema, solidly shaded areas refer to individual
rules: three rules describing x examples (light regions) and two rules describing o
examples (dark shading). For the predictive task the hatched areas represent global
models constituted by sets of rules. Together the rules in a set provide a global
representation of a group (Witten et al., 2011); individual rules can be difficult to
interpret in isolation (Bay and Pazzani, 2001; Lavrač et al., 2004).

This chapter offers three main contributions to the area of computational music
analysis. First, it generalizes the concept of pattern in inter-opus and corpus-level
music analysis beyond melodic and polyphonic patterns: contrast patterns are primarily defined by their ability to distinguish groups of pieces within a music corpus.
Two possible representations of contrast patterns are considered in detail: sequential
patterns which capture succession relations between event features, and global feature
patterns which describe music pieces by unordered sets of global features. Second,
this chapter revisits existing research in quantitative folk music analysis spanning a
century—from early work, even predating computational methods, through to modern approaches—and shows how this work can be viewed as contrast pattern mining.
Contrast pattern mining provides a vocabulary which can highlight both shared analysis interests and approaches but also different choices in the methodological design.
Thus, current and future research in computational music analysis can draw on, possibly critically, both musicological experience and the substantial existing research
on theory, methods and algorithms for data mining. Third, this chapter shows how

Contrast pattern mining task
Contrast pattern mining is the task of discovering and describing patterns that differentiate groups in data.

Given:
- a dataset with N instances
- a target attribute which partitions the dataset into groups
- a pattern description language
- an evaluation measure and threshold

Discover: patterns which distinguish a group from other groups, returning patterns whose evaluation measure value is above some threshold, or a specified number of patterns ranked highly by the evaluation measure

Fig. 15.2 Definition of contrast pattern mining, adapting the definition of local pattern mining by Zimmermann and De Raedt (2009)

the concept of subsumption (Baader et al., 2003), the logical specialization relation between patterns, applies equally to global feature and sequential patterns. This provides a basis for navigating the search space during pattern discovery, and also for organizing and presenting the results of contrast pattern mining.

The task and terminology of contrast pattern mining are defined in Sect. 15.2. In the subsequent sections contrast pattern mining is applied to comparative analyses of folk music: Sect. 15.3 offers a systematic overview of existing work as contrast pattern mining; Sect. 15.4 presents three case studies illustrating different pattern representations, folk music corpora and contrast mining methods. Section 15.5 briefly looks beyond contrast pattern mining to other comparative approaches and looks ahead to possible directions for future work.

15.2 Contrast Pattern Mining

A recurring theme in exploratory data analysis is that of determining differences between groups. In inferential statistics, this is done by studying different samples and determining whether they significantly differ in their distribution of one or more variables. In contrast pattern mining (see Fig. 15.2 for a definition of the task) the aim is to find local patterns which capture differences between groups of data. This section introduces the contrast pattern mining task and particularly looks at how patterns are represented. The relevant notation and concepts of contrast pattern mining are introduced, and three contrast mining methods are reviewed. This theoretical background provides the context for rephrasing work in folk music analysis as contrast pattern mining in Sects. 15.3 and 15.4.

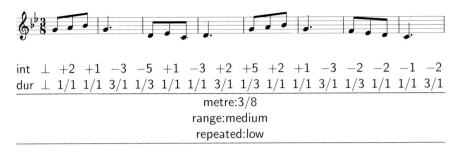

Fig. 15.3 Lullaby "Itsasoan laño dago" (excerpt) from the *Cancionero Vasco*. Top: score fragment. Middle: examples of event feature representation; viewpoints refer to melodic interval in semitones (int) and duration ratio (dur). These features are undefined ($\perp$) for the first event (Conklin and Witten, 1995). Bottom: examples of global features, numeric features discretized; the abbreviated attribute name repeated refers to the fraction of notes that are repeated melodically (McKay, 2010)

15.2.1 Patterns

In contrast pattern mining of music, *patterns* are predicates that map music pieces to boolean values. In this chapter, two types of pattern representation are considered: global feature patterns and sequential patterns based on event features. Here a *feature* is an attribute–value pair. A *global feature* represents a piece by a single value (see Fig. 15.3 bottom). A *global feature pattern* is a set of features, representing the logical conjunction of the features in the set. A pattern is *supported* by a piece of music in the corpus if all features in the feature set are true of the piece. Global features can be explicit in the metadata annotations of pieces (e.g., for attributes such as region, genre, tune family, collector), or can be derived directly from the score (e.g., for attributes such as average melodic interval, range). In classic contrast data mining, pattern descriptions are based on categorical attributes and continuous attributes are discretized, either in a pre-processing step (e.g., Bay, 2000; Kavšek and Lavrač, 2006) or dynamically during the data mining (e.g., Srikant and Agrawal, 1996). A *sequential pattern*, on the other hand, is a sequence of *event features* (see Fig. 15.3 middle): attribute–value pairs over contiguous events. Event features can be numeric (e.g., intervals, durations), categorical (e.g., contour, chord types) or binary (e.g., contour change, in scale/not in scale). Sequential patterns are by definition derived directly from the score. A piece *supports* a sequential pattern if the pattern occurs at least once within the piece. For both global feature patterns and sequential patterns, the absolute support or *support count* of a pattern X, denoted by $n(X)$, is the number of pieces in the dataset supporting the pattern.

	G	$\neg G$	
X	$n(X \wedge G)$	$n(X \wedge \neg G) = n(X) - n(X \wedge G)$	$n(X)$
$\neg X$	$n(\neg X \wedge G) = n(G) - n(X \wedge G)$	$n(\neg X \wedge \neg G) = n(\neg X) - n(\neg X \wedge G)$	$n(\neg X) = N - n(X)$
	$n(G)$	$n(\neg G) = N - n(G)$	N

Fig. 15.4 Contingency table describing all relationships between a pattern X and a group G

15.2.2 Contrast Patterns

As a supervised data mining technique, contrast pattern mining requires a dataset to be partitioned into labelled groups. Intuitively, groups arise from the values of a target attribute (see Fig. 15.2). For example, folk tunes may be grouped by their function into several genres, such as lullabies, wedding songs or laments. A piece in the dataset supports a group G if it is a member of group G. The number of pieces in the dataset supporting a group G gives the support count of the group, $n(G)$.

A pattern is a *contrast pattern* if its support differs significantly between groups in a dataset. The support count of pattern X in a group G, denoted by $n(X \wedge G)$, is the number of pieces in the dataset supporting both the pattern X and the group G. To assess whether or to what extent a pattern distinguishes a group from other groups, an evaluation measure compares the support of the pattern in the different groups. Many evaluation measures have been proposed, based on notions of, for example, generality, reliability, conciseness, peculiarity, surprisingness or utility (Geng and Hamilton, 2006). Contrast mining techniques commonly consider reliability (strength of the relation between a pattern and a group), generality (proportion of data instances supporting a pattern) and sometimes conciseness (simplicity of the description). Evaluation measures are used to prune the search space during the mining process, to filter or rank rules in a post-processing phase, or to provide additional information when presenting results.

Evaluation measures are usually computed from the 2×2 contingency table which summarizes the occurrence of a pattern in a specific group of interest G against other groups (see Fig. 15.4): the marginal counts $n(X)$ and $n(G)$ refer to the support counts of pattern X and group G. The variable N indicates the total number of pieces in the dataset. The notations $\neg X$ and $\neg G$ denote the complements of pattern X and group G: the pieces not supporting X and G respectively. The inner cells of the contingency table contain the support counts for pairwise conjunctions of X, $\neg X$, G and $\neg G$. If $n(X \wedge G)$, $n(X)$, $n(G)$ and N are known all other counts can be derived. From the absolute counts empirical probabilities are calculated as $P(X) = n(X)/N$, $P(G) = n(G)/N$ and $P(X \wedge G) = n(X \wedge G)/N$, and conditional probabilities are derived as $P(X|G) = P(X \wedge G)/P(G)$ and $P(G|X) = P(X \wedge G)/P(X)$. Statistical tests, such as Fisher's exact test, assess observed counts in the inner cells of the contingency table against expected counts based on the pattern and group distribution across the full corpus reflected in the marginal counts: the lower the p-value calculated by the test the less likely are the observed counts.

Relations between contrast patterns and the groups they characterize can be expressed as *rules*, directed relations between a pattern X and a group G: $X \rightarrow G$ (e.g., Novak et al., 2009b). The left-hand side of the rule is called the rule antecedent, the right-hand side of the rule is called the rule consequent. *Positive rules* describe patterns which are frequent or over-represented in a group: a rule $X \rightarrow G$ generally captures that pieces supporting pattern X tend to be members of group G and thus group G may be distinguished from other groups by a high proportion of pieces supporting pattern X. Patterns which are infrequent, under-represented or even absent in a group can be expressed as *negative rules*. Several formalizations of negative rules exist, depending on whether negation is applied to the rule antecedent or consequent as a whole, to attribute–value pairs within patterns or to the implication between antecedent and consequent (Cornelis et al., 2006; Savasere et al., 1998; Wong and Tseng, 2005). In this chapter only negative rules with negated consequent, $X \rightarrow \neg G$, are considered. An intuitive interpretation of a rule $X \rightarrow \neg G$ is that a pattern X tends to be found in pieces outside of group G and thus is rare or even absent in group G.

15.2.3 Methods for Contrast Pattern Mining

Specific methods of contrast pattern mining include subgroup discovery (Klösgen, 1996), emerging pattern mining (Dong and Li, 1999) and contrast set mining (Bay and Pazzani, 2001). At times, methods have been adapted from one contrast mining task to another, for example, subgroup discovery to perform contrast set mining (Novak et al., 2009a) or association rule mining to perform subgroup discovery (Kavšek and Lavrač, 2006). This section briefly summarizes three representative methods for discovering contrast patterns; examples of their application in folk music analysis will be presented in Sect. 15.4.

Subgroup Discovery The formulation of subgroup discovery is generally traced back to Klösgen (1996), although the term only appears in later publications (e.g., Klösgen, 1999; Wrobel, 1997). Here subgroup discovery is defined as the task of finding subgroups in a dataset which exhibit distributional unusualness with respect to a given target attribute. An additional condition requires subgroups to be sufficiently large. Several evaluation measures have been proposed, which trade off unusualness and generality of subgroups (Klösgen, 1996; Wrobel, 1997); the case study presented in Sect. 15.4.1 below uses *weighted relative accuracy*:

$$WRAcc(X \rightarrow G) = P(X) \times [P(G|X) - P(G)] . \qquad (15.1)$$

The first term, coverage $P(X)$, measures the generality of the pattern; the second term, relative accuracy or added value $P(G|X) - P(G)$, measures the reliability of the rule $X \rightarrow G$ as the gain between the probability of group G given pattern X and the default probability of group G. Subgroup discovery performs a one-vs-all comparison, in which data instances supporting a target group G are considered positive examples and all other instances are considered negative examples, corresponding to a 2×2 contingency table with columns indexed by G and its complement $\neg G$ (see Fig. 15.4).

Emerging Pattern Mining Emerging patterns are conjunctions of global features (Dong and Li, 1999) or sequential patterns (Chan et al., 2003), whose support increases significantly from one dataset (or group) to another. In its original formulation (Dong and Li, 1999), emerging pattern mining corresponds to a one-vs-one comparison and can be represented in a 2×2 contingency table with columns indexed by two groups G and G'. A contrast between the two groups is measured as the *growth rate* of a pattern X:

$$GrowthRate(X,G,G') = \frac{P(X \mid G)}{P(X \mid G')} \quad \text{with } P(X \mid G) > P(X \mid G') . \qquad (15.2)$$

A pattern X is considered an emerging pattern if its growth rate is above a user-defined threshold θ (with $\theta > 1$). Compared to weighted relative accuracy in subgroup discovery, growth rate in emerging pattern mining does not take into account the generality of a pattern: emerging pattern mining focuses on the change in relative support from group G' to group G, while the absolute support levels can be low (Dong and Li, 1999).

Association Rule Mining An association rule (Agrawal and Srikant, 1994) is a rule of the form $A \rightarrow B$, where A and B can be sets of attribute–value pairs. In *class association rule mining*, the consequent of the rule is restricted to a class or group in the dataset (Ali et al., 1997; Liu et al., 1998); then an association rule between a pattern X and a group G is of the form $X \rightarrow G$. The reliability of an association rule is generally evaluated by rule *confidence*:

$$c(X \rightarrow G) = P(G \mid X) . \qquad (15.3)$$

The generality of the rule is captured by its relative support, $s(X \rightarrow G) = P(X \wedge G)$. Support and confidence are computed from a 2×2 contingency table with columns indexed by G and $\neg G$ (see Fig. 15.4), thus comparing one group (G) against all other groups ($\neg G$). The task of association rule mining consists of finding all rules which meet user-defined support and confidence thresholds.

The methods summarized above differ mainly in their task or comparison strategy and in the evaluation measure used to assess candidate contrast patterns. Emerging pattern mining originally compares two groups by a one-vs-one strategy, while subgroup and class association rule discovery translate a multigroup mining task into a series of one-vs-all comparisons. In emerging pattern mining, growth rate builds on sensitivity $P(X \mid G)$ to evaluate the distribution of a pattern in the two groups; association rule mining uses confidence $P(G \mid X)$ to assess the relation between a pattern and a group, and weighted relative accuracy in subgroup discovery integrates added value $P(G \mid X) - P(G)$ to measure rule reliability. Relative support $P(X \wedge G)$ in association rule mining and pattern coverage $P(X)$ as part of weighted relative accuracy in subgroup discovery also consider the generality of potential contrast patterns. At an algorithmic level, implementations of these methods may differ in the search and pruning strategies employed to generate candidate contrast patterns and to filter redundant patterns, and in statistical techniques used to control false positives or false negatives (e.g., Atzmüller, 2015; Novak et al., 2009b; Webb et al., 2003).

15.3 Applications in Folk Music Analysis

Using the criteria and terminology introduced in the previous section, Table 15.1 summarizes 15 selected studies which analyse folk music corpora for contrasts between groups. The first nine of the listed studies use global feature representations; the remaining six studies mine for contrasting sequential patterns. The table includes both quantitative analyses which extract support counts of global feature or sequential patterns in different groups but do not explicitly quantify the contrast (Densmore, 1913, 1918, 1929; Edström, 1999; Grauer, 1965), and studies which directly adopt contrast data mining methods such as subgroup discovery (Taminau et al., 2009) and constrained association rule discovery (Neubarth et al., 2012, 2013a,b), or explicitly relate their method to emerging pattern mining or supervised descriptive rule discovery (Conklin, 2009, 2010a, 2013; Conklin and Anagnostopoulou, 2011).

Datasets The folk music corpora used by the cited studies range from regional repertoires through corpora covering larger areas to diverse styles across different continents: Cretan folk music (Conklin and Anagnostopoulou, 2011) and Basque folk music (Conklin, 2013; Neubarth et al., 2012, 2013a,b); European folk music (Neubarth et al., 2013b; Taminau et al., 2009) and North-American folk music (Densmore, 1913, 1918, 1929); or regional and cultural styles from around 250 areas across the world (Grauer, 1965; Lomax, 1962). Most regionally defined corpora represent a variety of folk music genres; on the other hand, Anagnostopoulou et al. (2013) focus on children's songs, and the European folk music corpus used in Taminau et al. (2009) and Neubarth et al. (2013b) is largely dominated by dance genres. The listed studies generally consider complete tunes, with two exceptions: Anagnostopoulou et al. (2013) take tune segments as data instances (505 segments derived from 110 tunes), and Edström (1999) extracts rhythmic patterns from the first four bars of refrains.

Groups Groupings in quantitative and computational folk music analyses often refer to geographical regions, ethnic groups and folk music genres or functions. The folk music styles suggested by Lomax (1959) and referenced in later analyses (Grauer, 1965; Lomax, 1962) are to some extent mapped onto geographical or cultural areas, such as Western European song style. Edström (1999) compares Swedish and German foxtrots in the context of constructing Swedishness. Regarding the analyses by Densmore, Table 15.1 includes both analyses of the song repertoires of different Native American tribes (Densmore, 1929) and of folk music genres among the songs of a tribe (Densmore, 1913). The third cited study by Densmore compares old and comparatively new songs within the music of the Teton–Sioux Indians (Densmore, 1918).

Table 15.1 Contrast analysis of folk music: example studies. Top: studies using global feature representations. Bottom: studies using event feature representations

Study	Dataset		Groups		Description		Contrast mining		
	Repertoire	No.	Target attr.	No.	Attributes	No.	Strategy	Measure	Rules
Densmore 1913	North American	340	genre	10	content	18^g		[narrative]	–
Densmore 1918	North American	600	style	2	content	18^g	one-vs-one	[narrative]	–
Densmore 1929	North American	1072	tribe	6	content	13^g	one-vs-one	[narrative]	–
Lomax 1962	cross-cultural	n.s.	style	5^e	perform.	37	one-vs-one	[visual]	–
Grauer 1965	cross-cultural	1700	style	4^e	perform.	37	one-vs-all	[narrative]	–
Taminau et al. 2009	European	3470	region	6	content	150	one-vs-all	WRAcc	pos
Neubarth et al. 2012	Basque	1902	genre^h	31	region	272	one-vs-all	confidence	pos, neg
			region^h	272	genre	31	one-vs-all	confidence	pos, neg
Neubarth et al. 2013a	Basque	1902	genre^h	31	content	17	one-vs-all	confidence	pos, neg
			region^h	272	content	17	one-vs-all	confidence	pos, neg
Neubarth et al. 2013b	Basque	1902	genre	5	content	19	one-vs-all	confidence	pos, neg
			region	7	content	19	one-vs-all	confidence	pos, neg
	European folk dances	3367	genre	9	content	19	one-vs-all	confidence	pos, neg
			region	6	content	19	one-vs-all	confidence	pos, neg
Edström 1999	European	n.s.	nation	2	content	1	one-vs-one	[narrative]	–
Conklin 2009	European	195	region	2	content	5	one-vs-all	confidence	pos
Conklin 2010a	European and Asian	432	region	3	content	9	one-vs-all	growth rate	pos
Conklin & Anagnostopoulou 2011	Cretan	106	genre^h	13	content	1	one-vs-all	growth rate	pos
		106	region^h	7	content	1	one-vs-all	growth rate	pos
Anagnostopoulou et al. 2013	European children's songs	505^s	region	7	content	3	one-vs-all	growth rate	pos
Conklin 2013	Basque	1902	genre^h	31	content	2	one-vs-all	p-value	neg

n.s. = not specified. ^{s} = tune segments. ^{h} = hierarchically structured attribute. ^{e} = examples reported. perform. = performance style. ^{g} = only global attributes counted.

Description To characterize groups within the datasets, the studies listed in Table 15.1 make use of metadata (Neubarth et al., 2012), global music content features which are extracted manually (Densmore, 1913, 1918, 1929) or automatically (Neubarth et al., 2013a,b; Taminau et al., 2009), or descriptors referring to the performance style of songs (Grauer, 1965; Lomax, 1962). Sequential patterns are either derived by computing the event feature sequence for predefined segments (Anagnostopoulou et al., 2013; Edström, 1999) or by discovering patterns of flexible length as part of the contrast mining process (Conklin, 2009, 2010a, 2013; Conklin and Anagnostopoulou, 2011). Many of the cited studies analyse one global or event feature at a time. The application of subgroup discovery to European folk music by Taminau et al. (2009) allows flexible conjunctions of two attribute–value pairs, while Grauer (1965) determines a fixed combination of four attribute–value pairs by inspecting individual songs of the target style; in a second step Grauer then considers the remaining 33 attributes for the covered songs. The study by Lomax (1962) presents style profiles using the complete set of 37 descriptor attributes, from which candidates for contrasting attributes can be suggested. Some sequential pattern studies extract several event features but treat each of these separately (Anagnostopoulou et al., 2013; Conklin, 2013); on the other hand, two of the listed analyses (Conklin, 2009, 2010a) mine for patterns using multiple features.

Contrast Mining Table 15.1 indicates the primary evaluation measure that the listed studies apply in the comparison. Analyses adopting contrast mining techniques, or explicitly referring to contrast data mining, use measures common in these techniques: weighted relative accuracy in subgroup discovery (Taminau et al., 2009), confidence in constrained association rule mining (Neubarth et al., 2012, 2013a,b), or growth rate from emerging pattern mining (Conklin, 2010a; Conklin and Anagnostopoulou, 2011). Conklin (2013) evaluates the p-value computed with Fisher's exact test to assess candidate patterns. Cited earlier studies consider occurrences of patterns in different groups, but the comparison itself is mainly narrative (Densmore, 1913, 1918, 1929; Edström, 1999) or to some extent visual (Lomax, 1962). Occasionally Densmore's textual description uses phrasings corresponding to growth rate (not illustrated in Table 15.1), for example: "The percentage of songs of a mixed form is more than twice as great in the Ute as in the Chippewa and Sioux" (Densmore, 1922, p. 53). Where group counts are included (Densmore, 1913, 1918, 1929), evaluation measures may be calculated post hoc (Neubarth, 2015). Most of the listed studies follow a one-vs-all strategy in comparing pattern distributions between groups. The publications by Densmore represent different comparison strategies: the analysis of Teton–Sioux music (Densmore, 1918) contrasts two chronologically ordered repertoires—old and relatively modern songs of the Teton–Sioux—presented as Group I and Group II (one-vs-one comparison); features of Pawnee music (Densmore, 1929) are presented against the cumulative support for the comparator groups (one-vs-all comparison); in the analysis of different genres among Chippewa music (Densmore, 1913) all groups are listed. Different comparison strategies, applied to the same dataset, may result in different contrast patterns (Neubarth, 2015).

15.4 Case Studies

In this section, three case studies will be presented in some detail to illustrate the different contrast mining methods applied to folk music. The first case study describes patterns by global features and discovers contrasting patterns as subgroups (Taminau et al., 2009). The second case study uses an event feature representation; candidate sequential patterns are evaluated as emerging patterns (Conklin and Anagnostopoulou, 2011). The third case study draws on two publications which apply constrained association rule mining to discover not only positive but also negative rules in folk music data (Conklin, 2013; Neubarth et al., 2013b); both global feature patterns and sequential patterns are considered.

15.4.1 Case Study 1: Subgroup Discovery in European Folk Music

The analysis of European folk music by Taminau et al. (2009) identifies global feature patterns which distinguish between folk songs of different geographical origin, through subgroup discovery. The authors explicitly set out to explore descriptive rule learning as an alternative approach to predictive classification, in order to find interpretable patterns. The following sections summarize the dataset, outline the data mining method and relate discovered subgroups.

15.4.1.1 Dataset and Global Feature Representation

The studied folk music corpus, called *Europa-6* (Hillewaere et al., 2009), contains 3470 folk music pieces from six European countries or regions; thus the dataset is partitioned into six groups: England (1013 pieces), France (404 pieces), Ireland (824 pieces), Scotland (482 pieces), South East Europe (127 pieces) and Scandinavia (620 pieces). All pieces are monophonic melodies, encoded in MIDI, quantized and with grace notes removed (Taminau et al., 2009). To represent melodies, global attributes are selected from existing attribute sets, resulting in a total of 150 global attributes: 12 attributes from the Alicante feature set (Ponce de León and Iñesta, 2004), 37 from the Fantastic feature set (Müllensiefen, 2009), 39 from the Jesser feature set (Jesser, 1991), and 62 from the McKay feature set (McKay, 2010). Numeric features are discretized in a pre-processing step, into categorical values low and high, using as a split point the attribute's mean value in the complete corpus. Consequently, melodies are represented as tuples containing 150 attribute–value pairs and the region.

15.4.1.2 Contrast Pattern Mining by Subgroup Discovery

Subgroup discovery is applied to find global feature patterns which are characteristic for a region compared to other regions. Subgroups are extracted for each region at a

Table 15.2 Contrast patterns discovered in the *Europa-6* corpus (based on Taminau et al., 2009). The table lists pattern X, group G, coverage $P(X)$, prevalence $P(G)$, sensitivity $P(X|G)$, confidence $P(G|X)$ and weighted relative accuracy *WRAcc*. Abbreviated attribute names: proportion of descending minor thirds (dminthird); proportion of dotted notes (dotted); proportion of melodic tritones (melTrit); interpolation contour gradients standard deviation (intcontgradstd). Bold *WRAcc* values mark the strongest subgroup among subsuming subgroups (details see text). Contrast patterns for South East Europe are omitted because of inconsistencies in the reported measures (Taminau et al., 2009)

X	G	$P(X)$	$P(G)$	$P(X\|G)$	$P(G\|X)$	*WRAcc*
mode:major, notedensity:low	England	0.36	0.29	0.54	0.43	**0.052**
mode:major	England	0.77	0.29	0.88	0.33	0.032
notedensity:low	England	0.50	0.29	0.63	0.37	0.038
dminthird:low, range:low	France	0.26	0.12	0.77	0.34	**0.059**
dminthird:low	France	0.52	0.12	0.83	0.19	0.036
range:low	France	0.43	0.12	0.93	0.25	0.058
dotted:low, compoundMetre:1	Ireland	0.23	0.24	0.62	0.65	0.093
dotted:low	Ireland	0.70	0.24	0.86	0.29	0.038
compoundMetre:1	Ireland	0.32	0.24	0.71	0.53	**0.093**
metre:3/4, melTrit:low	Scandinavia	0.14	0.18	0.62	0.78	0.086
metre:3/4	Scandinavia	0.15	0.18	0.63	0.75	**0.086**
melTrit:low	Scandinavia	0.94	0.18	0.96	0.18	0.004
metre:4/4, intcontgradstd:high	Scotland	0.17	0.14	0.62	0.52	**0.063**
metre:4/4	Scotland	0.38	0.14	0.77	0.28	0.054
intcontgradstd:high	Scotland	0.44	0.14	0.76	0.24	0.044

time, taking all instances annotated with the region under consideration as positive examples and all instances annotated with other regions as negative examples (one-vs-all comparison). The study uses the CN2-SD algorithm (Lavrač et al., 2004), which adapts the classification rule induction algorithm CN2 (Clark and Niblett, 1989) for subgroup discovery. In CN2-SD rule candidates are evaluated by weighted relative accuracy (see (15.1)) rather than predictive accuracy. Compared to classification rule induction, which seeks to create highly accurate rules, weighted relative accuracy trades off accuracy against coverage in order to find statistically interesting subgroups which "are as large as possible and have the most unusual distributional characteristics with respect to the target attribute" (Lavrač et al., 2004, p. 154). In the application to folk music (Taminau et al., 2009), rules are generated with a fixed length of two features in the antecedent in order to avoid overfitting the data and to increase the interpretability of discovered rules.

15.4.1.3 Discovered Contrast Patterns

The study by Taminau et al. (2009) presents the top contrast pattern for each of the geographical regions, ranked by weighted relative accuracy. To facilitate interpretation of these rules, additional evaluation measures are reported: the coverage and sensitivity for the pattern and for each of its global features individually as well as the confidence of the rule. The information on the individual features allows us to analyse pattern subsumption: given two sets of global features, a more specific set X is *subsumed* by a more general set $\widehat{X}$ if all pieces in the corpus which support set X also support set $\widehat{X}$. Syntactically, a subsumed global feature pattern X is a superset of a more general global feature pattern $\widehat{X}$ (see Fig. 15.5). For each group Table 15.2 first lists the two-feature pattern reported in Taminau et al. (2009), followed by the subsuming single-feature patterns. Bold values in the last column mark the highest weighted relative accuracy in each rule triple; if both the original specialized pattern and a more general single-feature pattern have the same measure value the more general pattern is marked, as the specialized pattern does not provide further distinctive information for the characterization of the region.

The results support several observations. Subgroup descriptions are simple expressions built from categorical (or discretized) attributes and their values. Different subgroups are characterized by different attributes; only the metre attribute appears in more than one subgroup. The rules, which link the global feature pattern with a region, are partial rules, which do not cover all instances of a group or pattern: for the originally reported rules, sensitivity $P(X \mid G)$ ranges between 54% and 77%, and confidence $P(G \mid X)$ ranges between 34% and 78%. The measure of weighted relative accuracy trades off confidence and coverage of the rule: for Scandinavia and Ireland, a more general subgroup reaches the same weighted relative accuracy, despite a lower rule confidence, because of the higher coverage $P(X)$ of the rule antecedent. These subgroups could already be sufficiently characterized by a single feature. Indeed, Taminau et al. observe that for Scandinavia the second component of the rule, the low proportion of melodic tritones, does not increase the reliability of the rule as the probability of this component in the Scandinavia group ($P(X \mid G) = 0.96$) is hardly higher than its probability in the total corpus ($P(X) = 0.94$). The subgroup is mainly specified by the metre feature, presumably relating to the large proportion of triple-metre polskas among the Scandinavian tunes (Taminau et al., 2009). By comparison, for the Ireland subgroup Taminau et al. comment that the addition of the second component substantially increases the rule's confidence, with $P(G \mid X)$ increasing from 0.29 to 0.65. In fact, in this case the second component, compound metre, dominates the subgroup, and adding the first component, low proportion of dotted rhythms, does not increase weighted relative accuracy: the main genre among the Irish tunes in the corpus is the jig (Neubarth et al., 2013b), typically in 6/8 metre. In the case of the French tunes in *Europa-6*, the low proportion of descending minor thirds only slightly increases the weighted relative accuracy of the subgroup (from $WRAcc = 0.058$ to $WRAcc = 0.059$). More characteristic is a low range, which may be related to the fact that all French tunes with known lyrics in the corpus are covered by this description; as sung melodies they would obey certain restrictions of the human voice compared to instrumentally performed tunes (Taminau et al., 2009).

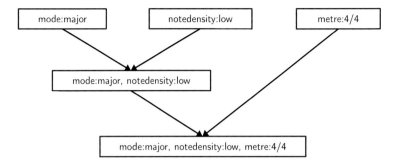

Fig. 15.5 Example of subsumption between global feature patterns

15.4.2 Case Study 2: Emerging Pattern Mining in Cretan Folk Tunes

As a second case study we present an example of sequential pattern discovery as emerging pattern mining (Conklin and Anagnostopoulou, 2011). Again, we summarize the data set, mining method and example results.

15.4.2.1 Dataset and Viewpoint Representation

For this study (Conklin and Anagnostopoulou, 2011), 106 Cretan folk tunes were selected from four printed sources which collate transcriptions of Cretan and Greek folk music. In preparation for computational analysis, the tunes were digitally encoded in score format and exported as MIDI files. The selected tunes represent eleven song types: four dance types and seven non-dance types. In addition, tunes are assigned to geographical regions: more specifically to one of five areas and more generally to Western or Eastern Crete. An idiosyncratic aspect of this dataset is that geographical area groups are not completely mutually exclusive: songs that are known to be sung in several areas of Crete were placed in all of the relevant area groups. In summary, the dataset is overlaid with four groupings (target attributes): type (11 groups), supertype (2 groups: dance vs. non-dance), area (5 groups) and superarea (2 groups: west vs. east).

Data instances are represented as sequences of intervals, using the viewpoint formalism of Conklin and Witten (1995): the melodic interval viewpoint calculates the interval between the current event and the previous event in semitones. As an example, $[-4, +2]$ describes a sequence of a descending major third followed by an ascending major second, which is supported by, for example, the note (event) sequence [A, F, G]. With a single viewpoint, the viewpoint name is often omitted from the individual components in the description.

15.4.2.2 Contrast Pattern Mining by Emerging Pattern Mining

The MGDP method (Conklin, 2010a) is applied to find maximally general distinctive patterns: emerging patterns which differentiate between the groups in the dataset. In previous work (Conklin and Bergeron, 2008), a pattern was considered interesting with respect to a corpus of music pieces if its frequency in the corpus was higher than expected, where expected frequency was computed from some statistical background distribution (see also Chap. 16, this volume). When applying the MGDP method for emerging pattern mining of a corpus organized into groups, the support of a pattern in a target group can be directly compared against its support in other groups, or more specifically in a one-vs-all approach: against its support in the rest of the corpus. Then pattern interest $I(X)$ is defined as the growth rate (see (15.2)), with the background dataset G' consisting of all groups but G (i.e., $\neg G$) to adapt the measure to the one-vs-all comparison: $I(X) = P(X \mid G)/P(X \mid \neg G)$. A pattern is distinctive if its interest $I(X)$ is greater than or equal to a specified threshold θ, with $\theta > 1$. Thus a pattern is distinctive for a group G if it is at least θ times more likely to occur in group G than in the other groups. For $P(X \mid \neg G) = 0$, pattern interest is infinite, $I(X) = \infty$, and pattern X is called a *jumping pattern*.

Among distinctive patterns the analysis is interested in maximally general patterns: patterns which are not subsumed by more general distinctive patterns. A pattern X is *subsumed* by a more general pattern $\widehat{X}$ if all instances supporting X also support $\widehat{X}$. In particular, a single-viewpoint sequential pattern is subsumed by any of its subsequences, and, vice versa, a pattern subsumes any pattern extended by one or more components (see Fig. 15.6). For example, the interval pattern $[-4, +2]$ subsumes the pattern $[-4, +2, -3]$, supported by the note sequence [A, F, G, E]. If both a pattern X and a more general pattern $\widehat{X}$ are distinctive (and no more general pattern subsuming $\widehat{X}$ is distinctive), only pattern $\widehat{X}$ is reported as a maximally general distinctive pattern: while X is distinctive, it is not maximally general. If, on the other hand, X is distinctive but $\widehat{X}$ is not distinctive, X is reported. In addition, a minimum support threshold can be applied to ensure a certain generality of discovered rules.

15.4.2.3 Discovered Contrast Patterns

Table 15.3 lists examples of discovered patterns which are distinctive (with a pattern interest threshold of 3) and maximally general. Only patterns with a minimum support count of 5 are presented (Conklin and Anagnostopoulou, 2011). From top to bottom the table includes two examples each for contrast mining by type, supertype, area and superarea. The results illustrate how local contrast patterns can overlap: of the dances described by the third and fourth rule in Table 15.3, twelve tunes support both patterns, $[+4, -4]$ and $[+4, +1, +2]$. Two of the listed patterns are jumping patterns: the sequence of a descending fourth followed by a descending major second found in the dance syrtos, and the pattern of two intertwined falling thirds found in Western Crete.

Table 15.3 Examples of maximally general distinctive patterns in Cretan folk tunes (Conklin and Anagnostopoulou, 2011). Columns indicate pattern X, group G, support count of the group $n(G)$, support count of the pattern in the group $n(X \wedge G)$, pattern interest $I(X)$ and p-value according to Fisher's exact test. The last column shows a schematic pitch sequence instantiating the pattern

X	G	$n(G)$	$n(X \wedge G)$	$I(X)$	p-value	
$[-5, -2]$	syrtos	22	5	∞	0.00032	
$[+1, +2, +3]$	malevisiotis	13	5	34.2	8.6e-5	
$[+4, -4]$	dance	51	16	19.1	8.4e-6	
$[+4, +1, +2]$	dance	51	19	11.4	3.3e-6	
$[-7, +4]$	lassithi	35	7	14.2	0.0017	
$[-4, +2, -3]$	rethymno	29	10	6.6	0.00028	
$[-4, +2, -3]$	west	64	14	∞	0.00023	
$[+1, +2, -2, +2, -2]$	east	47	13	5.9	0.00081	

While only maximally general distinctive interval patterns are included in Table 15.3 and thus no subsumed distinctive patterns are reported, the rules for the west of Crete and for Rethymno (in Western Crete) are related by subsumption (see Fig. 15.6). In Conklin (2013), the MGDP algorithm is extended to consider subsumption relations between groups and to exploit background ontologies in order to prune redundant rules. A rule linking a pattern and a group subsumes rules derived by specializing the pattern, specializing the group or both (see Fig. 15.6). If a more general rule is distinctive the search space underneath this rule can be pruned and specializations of the rule are not further explored. Thus, if the extended method was applied to the Cretan folk music corpus the pattern $[-4, +2, -3]$ would no longer be reported for both west and rethymno but only for west: as the pattern is already distinctive for the super-area the specialized rule for rethymno would not be generated.

pattern subsumption   **group subsumption**

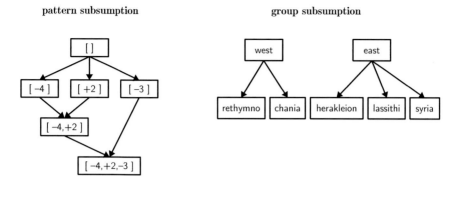

rule subsumption

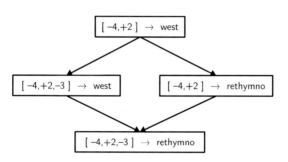

Fig. 15.6 Examples of subsumption between patterns, groups and rules. Group (region) subsumption from Conklin and Anagnostopoulou (2011)

15.4.3 Case Study 3: Association Rule Mining in Basque Folk Music

The two case studies presented above yield positive rules: sufficiently frequent global feature patterns or sequential patterns which are more likely to occur in one group than in the other groups. In comparison, the third case study gives examples of mining not only for patterns which are over-represented but also for patterns which are under-represented in one group relative to the remaining corpus, considering both global feature patterns (Neubarth et al., 2013b) and sequential patterns (Conklin, 2013).

15.4.3.1 Data

The *Cancionero Vasco* is a collection of Basque folk songs and dances, collated by the Basque folklorist and composer Padre Donostia. The digitized corpus, curated by the Basque Studies Society, consists of 1902 tunes. The tunes are annotated with geographical information on the location of collection and with genre information, organizing the dataset into seven regions and five genres, which are further specified into sub-regions and sub-genres, giving a total of 272 regions and 31 genres used to label tunes in the *Cancionero Vasco*. The tunes were represented by global features (Neubarth et al., 2013b), with continuous attributes discretized during pre-processing, and by viewpoints (Conklin, 2013). Contrasting global feature patterns were mined for region and for genre as target attribute, only considering the top-level regions and genres (Neubarth et al., 2013b); for the discovery of contrasting sequential patterns (Conklin, 2013) the genre was selected as the target attribute, taking into account the complete genre ontology.

15.4.3.2 Contrast Pattern Mining by Association Rule Mining

Conklin (2013) introduced the term *antipatterns* to denote (sequential) patterns which are rare in a corpus, corresponding to a target group G, but frequent in an anticorpus, corresponding to the complement of the target group $\neg G$. This chapter shows that, in the context of contrast pattern mining, conjunctions of global features can be treated as patterns; thus the term *antipatterns* can equally be applied to global feature patterns under-represented in a corpus relative to an anticorpus. Then antipatterns can be expressed as negative class association rules, $X \rightarrow \neg G$, where X is a global feature pattern or a sequential pattern.

In the analysis of global feature patterns (Neubarth et al., 2013b), constrained association rule mining is applied to find both positive and negative rules. Candidate rules are primarily evaluated by rule confidence (see (15.3)): $c(X \rightarrow G) = P(G|X)$ for positive rules and $c(X \rightarrow \neg G) = P(\neg G|X) = 1 - P(G|X)$ for negative rules. A minimum confidence threshold ensures that the pattern occurs mainly in instances of group G (positive rules) or mainly in instances of groups other than G (negative rules), and that group G is distinguished from other groups by a high or low number of data instances supporting pattern X. The mining is restricted to pairwise associations between one attribute–value pair in the antecedent and the target attribute in the consequent in order to reveal the fundamental relationships in the data before considering attribute interactions and in order to reduce the search space by syntactic rather than evaluation measure constraints: for negative rules with small or even zero rule support the pruning strategies of positive rule mining based on minimum support (Agrawal and Srikant, 1994) can no longer be applied. For rules meeting the confidence threshold, a *p*-value is calculated according to Fisher's one-tailed exact test, with right tail for positive and left tail for negative rules. The test measures the probability of finding at least (right tail) or at most (left tail) the observed number $n(X \wedge G)$ of instances supporting both X and G given the marginal counts in the contingency table (see Fig. 15.4); the lower the *p*-value the less likely it is that the number of co-occurrences can be explained by chance alone.

Sequential antipattern candidates in the *Cancionero Vasco* are primarily evaluated by their *p*-value (Conklin, 2013). In addition to Fisher's exact test in order to assess

Table 15.4 Positive and negative rules discovered in the *Cancionero Vasco*. Top: global feature patterns and antipatterns discovered with a minimum confidence threshold of 0.5 (based on Neubarth et al., 2013b). Abbreviated attribute names referring to attributes of the McKay (2010) set: primary register (register); repeated notes (repeated); average melodic interval (intervals). Bottom: sequential antipatterns discovered with a maximum *p*-value threshold of 0.01 (Fisher's test) and minimum *p*-value threshold of 0.001 (χ^2 test) (Conklin, 2013)

X		G or $\neg G$	$n(X)$	$n(G)$	$n(X \wedge G)$	confidence	p-value
register:high	$\rightarrow$	dances	249	495	179	0.72	≈ 0.0
repeated:freq	$\rightarrow$	life-cycle songs	7	477	5	0.71	0.012
intervals:narrow	$\rightarrow$	$\neg$ Araba	945	27	4	0.99	6.0e-4
notedensity:low	$\rightarrow$	$\neg$ Zuberoa	95	80	0	1.00	0.015
$[+1,-5,0]$	$\rightarrow$	$\neg$ historical songs	60	121	0	1.00	0.007
$[+1,-1]$	$\rightarrow$	$\neg$ children's songs	754	56	13	0.98	7.8e-5
$[2/1,3/2]$	$\rightarrow$	$\neg$ festive songs	164	82	2	0.99	0.005
$[3/1]$	$\rightarrow$	$\neg$ lullabies	883	98	29	0.97	2.3e-8

the reliability of the association between an antipattern and a group, a χ^2 goodness of fit test is applied to assess the distribution of a candidate antipattern in the anticorpus. The anticorpus $\neg G$ covers several groups. To be considered interesting, an antipattern candidate should be frequent across the groups of the anticorpus rather than being concentrated in only one group within the anticorpus; in the latter case it would be more appropriate to consider it as a pattern for that group instead of an antipattern for the target group (Conklin, 2013). Thus, antipatterns must satisfy two measure thresholds: a maximum p-value threshold in Fisher's test and a minimum p-value threshold in the χ^2 test.

15.4.3.3 Discovered Contrast Patterns and Antipatterns

Table 15.4 shows selected results of mining the *Cancionero Vasco* for positive and negative rules. The first four rules relate to global feature patterns, with two examples each for positive and for negative associations, covering both genres and regions as target attributes. The second part of the table lists examples of sequential antipatterns for genres: two melodic interval antipatterns and two duration ratio antipatterns. The last global feature antipattern and the first interval antipattern are jumping antipatterns, which do not occur at all in the target group.

Considering not only the top-level genres and regions but the complete taxonomies and thus exploring rule subsumption (Neubarth et al., 2013a) could provide additional insight and help the interpretation of general rules (see Fig. 15.7). For example, high register is particularly related to dances without lyrics (165 out of the 179 tunes) and thus presumably instrumental performance of these tunes. The primary register attribute of the McKay (2010) set is calculated as the average MIDI pitch of a piece; a high register corresponds to an average pitch of 73 or higher, that is, above C5 (see example in Fig. 15.8). The positive association between tunes with a high proportion of repeated notes and the genre of life-cycle songs is supported by repetitive melodies

group subsumption

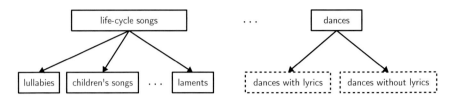

rule subsumption

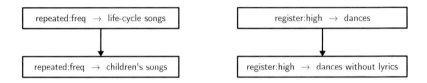

Fig. 15.7 Examples of group (genre) subsumption and rule subsumption for patterns discovered in the *Cancionero Vasco*. In the group taxonomy solid boxes refer to metadata annotations, dashed boxes refer to specialized groups of dances derived by evaluating the presence of lyrics

in children's songs, which include songs associated with children's games such as skipping songs, clapping songs or counting-out rhymes (see also Martí i Pérez et al., 2001). Figure 15.9 shows a children's song from the *Cancionero Vasco*, in which 70.1% of notes repeat the previous note, against a mean value of 19.2% in the complete corpus. For German folk songs, Steinbeck (1982) also observes a higher proportion of repeated notes in children's tunes than in other folk music samples.

Fig. 15.8 Untitled dance without lyrics (excerpt) from the *Cancionero Vasco*

Fig. 15.9 Children's song "Arri, arri, mandua" from the *Cancionero Vasco*

15.5 Conclusions

Contrast pattern mining aims to discover and describe patterns which differentiate subpopulations or groups in a dataset. This chapter has introduced the task and representative methods of contrast pattern mining and has reviewed work in quantitative and computational folk music analysis which can be phrased as mining for contrast patterns. Three case studies have been presented in detail, illustrating a variety of folk tune corpora, different groupings or partitionings of datasets, global feature and sequential representations of patterns, and different contrast pattern mining methods.

The analysis task of contrast pattern mining is related to classical methods in descriptive and inferential statistics, which describe the distributions of variables and differences between group means and variances for selected continuous variables. Statistical analysis has also been used in quantitative folk music analysis, generally restricted to analysing single variables (e.g., Freeman and Merriam, 1956; Gundlach, 1932; Kolinski, 1982; Sagrillo, 2010; Steinbeck, 1982). Methods of descriptive and inferential statistics are productively applied for testing variable distributions across the complete dataset, rather than for knowledge discovery (i.e., the discovery of previously unknown relations). In classic contrast pattern mining, on the other hand, pattern descriptions are based on discrete attributes, and discovered contrast patterns are local descriptive patterns which constitute binary predicates on music pieces in a corpus and are assessed by evaluating pattern support in different groups.

Contrast patterns are traditionally specified as combinations (sets or sequences) of attribute–value pairs. Previous work in computational folk music analysis has sometimes used attribute selection or classification to evaluate the discriminative power of single attributes or sets of attributes in the context of predictive model induction (e.g., Bohak and Marolt, 2009; Hillewaere, 2013; van Kranenburg and Karsdorp, 2014; van Kranenburg et al., 2013); the methods reveal attributes which can separate groups of music pieces but reported results do not give insight into which values or value ranges of the attributes are characteristic for which group.

For sequential pattern discovery in inter-opus music analysis, two ways of determining pattern frequencies have been proposed (e.g., Conklin and Bergeron, 2008): the piece count of a pattern is the number of pieces in the corpus which contain the pattern one or more times; the total count of a pattern is the number of all pattern occurrences including repetitions of a pattern within the same piece. The definition of pattern support in this chapter, and in the case studies presented in this chapter, corresponds to piece count; it follows general approaches in contrast data mining and classic sequential pattern mining (Agrawal and Srikant, 1995; Mooney and Roddick, 2013; Novak et al., 2009b). Some quantitative studies in folk music research have also considered total counts, or proportional frequencies, of event features (e.g., Gundlach, 1932; Sagrillo, 2010). Beyond folk music, examples of mining contrasting, or distinctive, melodic or polyphonic patterns using total counts include an analysis of Brahms' string quartet op. 51 no. 1 against the string quartets op. 51 no. 2 and op. 67 (Conklin, 2010b) and the analysis of Beethoven's piano sonatas in Chap. 17 of this volume.

As the name contrast data mining suggests, the analysis focuses on differences, rather than similarities, between groups. The notion of similarity has attracted considerable attention in music information retrieval and computational music research, including computational folk music research (e.g., Müllensiefen and Frieler, 2004; Scherrer and Scherrer, 1971); generally the comparison tends to be between pairs of individual folk tunes rather than at the level of groups of tunes. An early exception is an example study by Suchoff (1970), who compares support counts of interval sequences in folk music repertoires (Serbo-Croatian women's songs and Romanian winter solstice songs) against samples of 16th-century vocal and instrumental music and finds "interesting similarities [...] which seem to point toward folk-based or folk-styled characteristics of the art melodies" (p. 202). Similarity or overlap between folk music repertoires has also been studied in the context of clustering (e.g., Juhász, 2006; Juhász and Sipos, 2010). However, clustering itself is an unsupervised data mining method: information on groups is introduced manually by partitioning the mining input or during post-processing; groups are referenced by prototypical instances rather than generalized patterns (Juhász, 2006) or filtered visualization rather than symbolic description (Toiviainen and Eerola, 2001).

Compared to the unsupervised task of clustering, contrast pattern mining is a supervised data mining task, which evaluates instances from labelled groups within a dataset. The three case studies presented in this chapter have all used predefined groupings or partitionings of a folk music corpus based on metadata, for example, into folk music genres or regions of collection. Obviously there is no one "correct" grouping of a corpus appropriate for all analysis tasks, and there is no reason the grouping cannot use any available ontology, be specified flexibly by an analyst considering metadata or music content characteristics (e.g., Jesser, 1991) or result from previous computational analysis such as clustering (e.g., Steinbeck, 1982).

While this chapter has focused on applications in folk music analysis, quantitative comparative analysis and contrast pattern mining are not confined to this repertoire. Existing musicological research has applied quantitative methods to corpora of, for example, early music (Trowbridge, 1986), performance criticism of Beethoven piano sonatas (Alessandri et al., 2014), 19th-century music (VanHandel, 2009) and popular music (Huron and Ommen, 2006), as well as comparisons between folk and art music (Suchoff, 1970). Recent example studies in music data mining and music information retrieval include, for example, subgroup discovery in Haydn and Mozart string quartets (Taminau et al., 2010), corpus analysis of ragtime (Volk and de Haas, 2013) or visualization of contrapuntal module occurrences in different style periods (Antila and Cumming, 2014). Contrast pattern mining could be used where support counts can be determined for features or feature sets which are derived from metadata, such as instruments, genres or styles in music publication titles (Hess, 1953; Rose and Tuppen, 2014); extracted from music scores or digitized music content, such as tempo indications, tonal material or melodic patterns (Albrecht and Huron, 2014; Post and Huron, 2009; Suchoff, 1970); or compiled from contextual information, such as dates, locations and repertoire of concert performances (Kopiez et al., 2009) or performers, compositions and release dates of music recordings (Alessandri et al., 2014).

Contrast patterns are not restricted to the specific representations of melodic patterns used in the reported case studies: conjunctions of global features and sequences of event features. The general approach is very flexible, and numerous other pattern representations used in symbolic music analysis could also be considered, for example, vertical viewpoint patterns (Conklin, 2002), geometric polyphonic patterns (Meredith et al., 2002, see also Chaps. 13 and 17, this volume) and chord sequence patterns (Conklin, 2010a). Theoretically, any representation that defines a computable boolean predicate can be used for a pattern representation (Atzmüller, 2015), for example: patterns described by a conjunction of global and event features, feature set sequential patterns (Conklin and Bergeron, 2008), sequential patterns with gaps (Comin and Parida, 2008), patterns with variables (Angluin, 1980), and even patterns described by grammars or rewrite rules (Sidorov et al., 2014). With more powerful pattern representations would come additional challenges. First, the classical tradeoff between expressiveness and tractability in knowledge representation (Levesque and Brachman, 1987) would naturally be encountered, and compromises on the search of the pattern space would need to be accepted. Second, the results of contrast pattern mining may be more difficult to interpret as one moves to further levels of abstraction from the underlying music representation. Logical subsumption between patterns, as well as consideration of domain ontologies, offers one strategy to restrict the search space, organize the data mining output and facilitate the interpretation of discovered patterns.

Acknowledgements This research is partially supported by the project Lrn2Cre8 which is funded by the Future and Emerging Technologies (FET) programme within the Seventh Framework Programme for Research of the European Commission, under FET grant number 610859.

References

Agrawal, R. and Srikant, R. (1994). Fast algorithms for mining association rules. In *Proceedings of the 20th International Conference on Very Large Data Bases (VLDB 1994)*, pages 487–499, Santiago de Chile, Chile.

Agrawal, R. and Srikant, R. (1995). Mining sequential patterns. In *Proceedings of the 11th International Conference on Data Engineering (ICDE 1995)*, pages 3–14, Taipei, Taiwan.

Albrecht, J. D. and Huron, D. (2014). A statistical approach to tracing the historical development of major and minor pitch distributions, 1400–1750. *Music Perception*, 31(4):223–243.

Alessandri, E., Eiholzer, H., and Williamon, A. (2014). Reviewing critical practice: an analysis of *Gramophone*'s reviews of Beethoven's piano sonatas, 1923–2010. *Musicae Scientiae*, 18(2):131–149.

Ali, K., Manganaris, S., and Srikant, R. (1997). Partial classification using association rules. In *Proceedings of the 3rd International Conference on Knowledge Discovery and Data Mining (KDD-97)*, pages 115–118, Newport Beach, CA, USA.

Anagnostopoulou, C., Giraud, M., and Poulakis, N. (2013). Melodic contour representations in the analysis of children's songs. In *Proceedings of the 3rd International Workshop on Folk Music Analysis (FMA 2013)*, pages 40–42, Amsterdam, Netherlands.

Angluin, D. (1980). Finding patterns common to a set of strings. *Journal of Computer and System Sciences*, 21:46–62.

Antila, C. and Cumming, J. (2014). The VIS framework: analyzing counterpoint in large datasets. In *Proceedings of the 15th International Society of Music Information Retrieval Conference (ISMIR 2014)*, pages 71–76, Taipei, Taiwan.

Atzmüller, M. (2015). Subgroup discovery: advanced review. *WIREs Data Mining and Knowledge Discovery*, 5(1):35–49.

Baader, F., Calvanese, D., McGuiness, D., Nardi, D., and Patel-Schneider, P. F., editors (2003). *The Description Logic Handbook: Theory, Implementation and Applications*. Cambridge University Press.

Bay, S. D. (2000). Multivariate discretization of continuous variables for set mining. In *Proceedings of the 6th ACM SIGKDD International Conference on Knowledge Discovery and Data Mining (KDD-2000)*, pages 315–319, Boston, MA, USA.

Bay, S. D. and Pazzani, M. J. (2001). Detecting group differences: mining contrast sets. *Data Mining and Knowledge Discovery*, 5(3):213–246.

Bohak, C. and Marolt, M. (2009). Calculating similarity of folk song variants with melody-based features. In *Proceedings of the 10th International Society for Music Information Retrieval Conference (ISMIR 2009)*, pages 597–601, Kobe, Japan.

Bohlman, P. V. (1988). *The Study of Folk Music in the Modern World*. Indiana University Press.

Bronson, B. H. (1959). Toward the comparative analysis of British-American folk tunes. *The Journal of American Folklore*, 72(284):165–191.

Carter, T. (1986/1987). Music publishing in Italy, c.1580–c.1625: some preliminary observations. *Royal Musical Association Research Chronicle*, 20:19–37.

Chan, S., Kao, B., Yip, C. L., and Tang, M. (2003). Mining emerging substrings. In *Proceedings of the 8th International Conference on Database Systems for Advanced Applications (DASFAA 2003)*, pages 119–126, Kyoto, Japan.

Clark, P. and Niblett, T. (1989). The CN2 induction algorithm. *Machine Learning*, 3(4):261–283.

Comin, M. and Parida, L. (2008). Detection of subtle variations as consensus motifs. *Theoretical Computer Science*, 395(2–3):158–170.

Conklin, D. (2002). Representation and discovery of vertical patterns in music. In *Proceedings of the 2nd International Conference on Music and Artificial Intelligence (ICMAI 2002)*, pages 32–42, Edinburgh, UK.

Conklin, D. (2009). Melody classification using patterns. In *2nd International Workshop on Machine Learning and Music at ECML/PKDD 2009 (MML 2009)*, Bled, Slovenia.

Conklin, D. (2010a). Discovery of distinctive patterns in music. *Intelligent Data Analysis*, 14:547–554.

Conklin, D. (2010b). Distinctive patterns in the first movement of Brahms' String Quartet in C minor. *Journal of Mathematics and Music*, 4(2):85–92.

Conklin, D. (2013). Antipattern discovery in folk tunes. *Journal of New Music Research*, 42(2):161–169.

Conklin, D. and Anagnostopoulou, C. (2011). Comparative pattern analysis of Cretan folk songs. *Journal of New Music Research*, 40(2):119–125.

Conklin, D. and Bergeron, M. (2008). Feature set patterns in music. *Computer Music Journal*, 32(1):60–70.

Conklin, D. and Witten, I. H. (1995). Multiple viewpoint systems for music prediction. *Journal of New Music Research*, 24(1):51–73.

Cook, N. (2004). Computational and comparative musicology. In Clarke, E. and Cook, N., editors, *Empirical Musicology: Aims, Methods, Prospects*, pages 103–126. Oxford University Press.

Cornelis, C., Yan, P., Zhang, X., and Chen, G. (2006). Mining positive and negative association rules from large databases. In *Proceedings of the IEEE International Conference on Cybernetics and Intelligent Systems*, pages 613–618, Bangkok, Thailand.

Cornelis, O., Lesaffre, M., Moelants, D., and Leman, M. (2010). Access to ethnic music: advances and perspectives in content-based music information retrieval. *Signal Processing*, 90:1008–1031.

Csébfalvy, K., Havass, M., Járdányi, P., and Vargyas, L. (1965). Systematization of tunes by computers. *Studia Musicologica Academiae Scientiarum Hungaricae*, 7:253–257.

Densmore, F. (1913). *Chippewa Music II*. Smithsonian Institution Bureau of American Ethnology Bulletin 53.

Densmore, F. (1918). *Teton Sioux Music*. Smithsonian Institution Bureau of American Ethnology Bulletin 61.

Densmore, F. (1922). *Northern Ute Music*. Smithsonian Institution Bureau of American Ethnology Bulletin 75.

Densmore, F. (1929). *Pawnee Music*. Smithsonian Institution Bureau of American Ethnology Bulletin 93.

Densmore, F. (1932). *Yuman and Yaqui Music*. Smithsonian Institution Bureau of American Ethnology Bulletin 110.

Dong, G. and Li, J. (1999). Efficient mining of emerging patterns: discovering trends and differences. In *Proceedings of the 5th ACM SIGKDD International Conference on Knowledge Discovery and Data Mining (KDD-99)*, pages 43–52, San Diego, CA, USA.

Edström, O. (1999). From *schottis* to *bonnjazz* – some remarks on the construction of Swedishness. *Yearbook for Traditional Music*, 31:27–41.

Elscheková, A. (1965). General considerations on the classification of folk tunes. *Studia Musicologica Academiae Scientiarum Hungaricae*, 7:259–262.

Elscheková, A. (1966). Methods of classification of folk tunes. *Journal of the International Folk Music Council*, 18:56–76.

Elscheková, A. (1999). Musikvergleich und Computertechnik. *Croatian Journal of Ethnology*, 36(2):105–115.

Forrest, J. and Heaney, M. (1991). Charting early morris. *Folk Music Journal*, 6(2):169–186.

Freeman, L. C. and Merriam, A. P. (1956). Statistical classification in anthropology: an application to ethnomusicology. *American Anthropologist*, 58:464–472.

Fujinaga, I. and Weiss, S. F. (2004). Music. In Schreibman, S., Siemens, R., and Unsworth, J., editors, *A Companion to Digital Humanities*, pages 97–107. Blackwell.

Fürnkranz, J., Gamberger, D., and Lavrač, N. (2012). *Foundations of Rule Learning*. Springer.

Geng, L. and Hamilton, H. J. (2006). Interestingness measures for data mining: a survey. *ACM Computing Surveys*, 38(3):1–32.

Grauer, V. A. (1965). Some song-style clusters – a preliminary study. *Ethnomusicology*, 9(3):265–271.

Gundlach, R. H. (1932). A quantitative analysis of Indian music. *The American Journal of Psychology*, 44(1):133–145.

Hand, D., Mannila, H., and Smyth, P. (2001). *Principles of Data Mining*. The MIT Press.

Herrera, F., Carmona, C. J., González, P., and del Jesus, M. J. (2011). An overview on subgroup discovery: foundations and applications. *Knowledge and Information Systems*, 29(3):495–525.

Hess, A. G. (1953). The transition from harpsichord to piano. *The Galpin Society Journal*, 6:75–94.

Hillewaere, R. (2013). *Computational models for folk music classification*. PhD thesis, Faculty of Sciences, Vrije Universiteit Brussel, Belgium.

Hillewaere, R., Manderick, B., and Conklin, D. (2009). Global feature versus event models for folk song classification. In *Proceedings of the 10th International Society for Music Information Retrieval Conference (ISMIR 2009)*, pages 729–733, Kobe, Japan.

Hoshovs'kyj, V. (1965). The experiment of systematizing and cataloguing folk tunes following the principles of musical dialectology and cybernetics. *Studia Musicologica Academiae Scientiarum Hungaricae*, 7:273–286.

Huron, D. and Ommen, A. (2006). An empirical study of syncopation in American popular music, 1890–1939. *Music Theory Spectrum*, 28(2):211–231.

Járdányi, P. (1965). Experiences and results in systematizing Hungarian folk-songs. *Studia Musicologica Academiae Scientiarum Hungaricae*, 7:287–291.

Jesser, B. (1991). *Interaktive Melodieanalyse. Methodik und Anwendung computergestützter Analyseverfahren in Musikethnologie und Volksliedforschung: typologische Untersuchung der Balladensammlung des DVA*. Studien zur Volksliedforschung 12. Peter Lang.

Juhász, Z. (2006). A systematic comparison of different European folk music traditions using self-organizing maps. *Journal of New Music Research*, 35(2):95–112.

Juhász, Z. and Sipos, J. (2010). A comparative analysis of Eurasian folksong corpora, using self organising maps. *Journal of Interdisciplinary Music Studies*, 4(1):1–16.

Kavšek, B. and Lavrač, N. (2006). APRIORI-SD: adapting association rule learning to subgroup discovery. *Applied Artificial Intelligence*, 20:543–583.

Keller, M. S. (1984). The problem of classification in folksong research: a short history. *Folklore*, 95(1):100–104.

Klösgen, W. (1996). Explora: a multipattern and multistrategy discovery assistant. In Fayyad, U., Piatetsky-Shapiro, G., and Smyth, P., editors, *Advances in Knowledge Discovery and Data Mining*, pages 249–271. MIT Press.

Klösgen, W. (1999). Applications and research problems of subgroup mining. In Raś, Z. W. and Skowron, A., editors, *Foundations of Intelligent Systems*, pages 1–15. Springer.

Kolinski, M. (1982). Reiteration quotients: a cross-cultural comparison. *Ethnomusicology*, 26(1):85–90.

Kopiez, R., Lehmann, A. C., and Klassen, J. (2009). Clara Schumann's collection of playbills: a historiometric analysis of life-span development, mobility, and repertoire canonization. *Poetics*, 37:50–73.

Lampert, V. (1982). Bartók's choice of theme for folksong arrangement: some lessons of the folk-music sources of Bartók's works. *Studia Musicologica Academiae Scientiarum Hungaricae*, 24(3/4):401–409.

Lavrač, N., Kavšek, B., Flach, P., and Todorovski, L. (2004). Subgroup discovery with CN2-SD. *Journal of Machine Learning Research*, 5:153–188.

Levesque, H. J. and Brachman, R. J. (1987). Expressiveness and tractability in knowledge representation and reasoning. *Computational Intelligence*, 3:78–92.

Lincoln, H. B. (1970). The current state of music research and the computer. *Computers and the Humanities*, 5(1):29–36.

Lincoln, H. B. (1974). Use of the computer in music research: a short report on accomplishments, limitations, and future needs. *Computers and the Humanities*, 8(5/6):285–289.

Liu, B., Hsu, W., and Ma, Y. (1998). Integrating classification and association rule mining. In *Proceedings of the 4th International Conference on Knowledge Discovery and Data Mining (KDD-98)*, pages 80–86, New York, USA.

Lomax, A. (1959). Folk song style. *American Anthropologist*, 61(6):927–954.

Lomax, A. (1962). Song structure and social structure. *Ethnology*, 1(4):425–451.

Marsden, A. (2009). "What was the question?": music analysis and the computer. In Crawford, T. and Gibson, L., editors, *Modern Methods for Musicology: Prospects, Proposals and Realities*, pages 137–147. Ashgate.

Martí i Pérez, J., Cunningham, M., Pelinski, R., Martínez García, S., de Larrea Palacín, A., and Aiats, J. (2001). Spain. II: Traditional and popular music. In Sadie, S., editor, *New Grove Dictionary of Music and Musicians*, volume 24, pages 135–154. Macmillan, 2nd edition.

McKay, C. (2010). *Automatic music classification with jMIR*. PhD thesis, Schulich School of Music, McGill University, Montreal, Canada.

Meredith, D., Lemström, K., and Wiggins, G. (2002). Algorithms for discovering repeated patterns in multidimensional representations of polyphonic music. *Journal of New Music Research*, 31(4):321–345.

Mooney, C. H. and Roddick, J. F. (2013). Sequential pattern mining: approaches and algorithms. *ACM Computing Surveys*, 45(2):Article 19.

Müllensiefen, D. (2009). Fantastic: Feature ANalysis Technology Accessing Statistics (In a Corpus): Technical report v1.5. Technical report, Goldsmiths College, University of London, London, UK.

Müllensiefen, D. and Frieler, K. (2004). Optimizing measures of melodic similarity for the exploration of a large folk song database. In *Proceedings of the 5th International Conference on Music Information Retrieval (ISMIR 2004)*, pages 274–280, Barcelona, Spain.

Nettl, B. (1973). Comparison and comparative method in ethnomusicology. *Anuario Interamericano de Investigacion Musical*, 9:143–161.

Nettl, B. (1975). The state of research in ethnomusicology, and recent developments. *Current Musicology*, 20:67–78.

Nettl, B. (2005). *The Study of Ethnomusicology*. University of Illinois Press.

Nettl, B. (2010). *Nettl's Elephant: On the History of Ethnomusicology*. University of Illinois Press.

Neubarth, K. (2015). Densmore revisited: contrast data mining of Native American music. In *5th International Workshop on Folk Music Analysis (FMA 2015)*, Paris, France. (to appear).

Neubarth, K., Goienetxea, I., Johnson, C. G., and Conklin, D. (2012). Association mining of folk music genres and toponyms. In *Proceedings of the 13th International Society of Music Information Retrieval Conference (ISMIR 2012)*, pages 7–12, Porto, Portugal.

Neubarth, K., Johnson, C. G., and Conklin, D. (2013a). Descriptive rule mining of Basque folk music. In *Proceedings of the 3rd International Workshop on Folk Music Analysis (FMA 2013)*, pages 83–85, Amsterdam, Netherlands.

Neubarth, K., Johnson, C. G., and Conklin, D. (2013b). Discovery of mediating association rules for folk music analysis. In *6th International Workshop on Music and Machine Learning at ECML/PKDD 2013 (MML 2013)*, Prague, Czech Republic.

Novak, P. K., Lavrač, N., Gamberger, D., and Krstačić, A. (2009a). CSM-SD: methodology for contrast set mining through subgroup discovery. *Journal of Biomedical Informatics*, 42(1):113–122.

Novak, P. K., Lavrač, N., and Webb, G. (2009b). Supervised descriptive rule discovery: a unifying survey of contrast set, emerging pattern and subgroup mining. *Journal of Machine Learning Research*, 10:377–403.

Ponce de León, P. J. and Iñesta, J. M. (2004). Statistical description models for melody analysis and characterization. In *Proceedings of the 30th International Computer Music Conference (ICMC 2004)*, pages 149–156, Miami, Florida, USA.

Post, O. and Huron, D. (2009). Western Classical music in the minor mode is slower (except in the Romantic period). *Empirical Musicology Review*, 4(1):2–10.

Rhodes, W. (1965). The use of the computer in the classification of folk tunes. *Studia Musicologica Academiae Scientiarum Hungaricae*, 7:339–343.

Rose, S. and Tuppen, S. (2014). Prospects for a big data history of music. In *Proceedings of the 1st Digital Libraries for Musicology Workshop (DLfM 2014)*, pages 82–84, London, UK.

Sagrillo, D. (2010). Computer analysis of Scottish national songs. In *1st International Conference on Analytical Approaches to World Music (AAWM 2010)*, Amherst, MA, USA.

Savasere, A., Omiecinski, E., and Navathe, S. (1998). Mining for strong negative associations in a large database of customer transactions. In *Proceedings of the 14th International Conference on Data Engineering (ICDE 1998)*, pages 494–502, Orlando, FL, USA.

Schaffrath, H. (1992). The retrieval of monophonic melodies and their variants: concepts and strategies for computer-aided analysis. In Marsden, A. and Pople, A., editors, *Computer Representations and Models in Music*, pages 95–109. Academic Press.

Scherrer, D. K. and Scherrer, P. H. (1971). An experiment in the computer measurement of melodic variation in folksong. *The Journal of American Folklore*, 84(332):230–241.

Schneider, A. (2006). Comparative and systematic musicology in relation to ethnomusicology: a historical and methodological survey. *Ethnomusicology*, 50(2):236–258.

Sidorov, K., Jones, A., and Marshall, D. (2014). Music analysis as a smallest grammar problem. In *Proceedings of the 15th International Society for Information Retrieval Conference (ISMIR 2014)*, pages 301–306, Taipei, Taiwan.

Srikant, R. and Agrawal, R. (1996). Mining quantitative association rules in large relational tables. *ACM SIGMOD Record*, 25(2):1–12.

Steinbeck, W. (1976). The use of the computer in the analysis of German folksongs. *Computers and the Humanities*, 10(5):287–296.

Steinbeck, W. (1982). *Struktur und Ähnlichkeit. Methoden automatisierter Melodienanalyse*. Kieler Schriften zur Musikwissenschaft 25. Bärenreiter.

Suchoff, B. (1967). Computer applications to Bartók's Serbo-Croatian material. *Tempo*, 80:15–19.

Suchoff, B. (1968). Computerized folk song research and the problem of variants. *Computers and the Humanities*, 2(4):155–158.

Suchoff, B. (1970). Computer-oriented comparative musicology. In Lincoln, H. B., editor, *The Computer and Music*, pages 193–206. Cornell University Press.

Suchoff, B. (1971). The computer and Bartók research in America. *Journal of Research in Music Education*, 19(1):3–16.

Taminau, J., Hillewaere, R., Meganck, S., Conklin, D., Nowé, A., and Manderick, B. (2009). Descriptive subgroup mining of folk music. In *2nd International Workshop on Machine Learning and Music at ECML/PKDD 2009 (MML 2009)*, Bled, Slovenia.

Taminau, J., Hillewaere, R., Meganck, S., Conklin, D., Nowé, A., and Manderick, B. (2010). Applying subgroup discovery for the analysis of string quartet movements. In *Proceedings of the 3rd International Workshop on Music and Machine Learning at ACM Multimedia (MML 2010)*, pages 29–32, Florence, Italy.

Toiviainen, P. and Eerola, T. (2001). A method for comparative analysis of folk music based on musical feature extraction and neural networks. In *Proceedings of the*

VII International Symposium on Systematic and Comparative Musicology/III International Conference on Cognitive Musicology, pages 41–45, Jyväskylä, Finland.

Trowbridge, L. M. (1985/1986). Style change in the fifteenth-century chanson: a comparative study of compositional detail. *The Journal of Musicology*, 4(2):146–170.

Tzanetakis, G., Kapur, A., Schloss, W., and Wright, M. (2007). Computational ethnomusicology. *Journal of Interdisciplinary Music Studies*, 1(2):1–24.

van Kranenburg, P., Garbers, J., Volk, A., Wiering, F., Grijp, L., and Veltkamp, R. C. (2010). Collaborative perspectives for folk song research and music information retrieval: The indispensable role of computational musicology. *Journal of Interdisciplinary Music Studies*, 4(1):17–43.

van Kranenburg, P. and Karsdorp, F. (2014). Cadence detection in Western traditional stanzaic songs using melodic and textual features. In *Proceedings of the 15th International Society for Music Information Retrieval Conference (ISMIR 2014)*, pages 391–396, Taipei, Taiwan.

van Kranenburg, P., Volk, A., and Wiering, F. (2013). A comparison between global and local features for computational classification of folk song melodies. *Journal of New Music Research*, 42(1):1–18.

VanHandel, L. (2009). National metrical types in nineteenth century art song. *Empirical Musicology Review*, 4(4):134–145.

Volk, A. and de Haas, W. B. (2013). A corpus-based study on ragtime syncopation. In *Proceedings of the 14th International Society of Music Information Retrieval Conference (ISMIR 2013)*, pages 163–168, Curitiba, Brazil.

Webb, G. I., Butler, S., and Newlands, D. (2003). On detecting differences between groups. In *Proceedings of the 9th ACM SIGKDD International Conference on Knowledge Discovery and Data Mining (KDD-2003)*, pages 256–265, Washington, DC, USA.

Witten, I. H., Frank, E., and Hall, M. A. (2011). *Data Mining: Practical Machine Learning Tools and Techniques*. Morgan Kaufmann, third edition.

Wong, T.-T. and Tseng, K.-L. (2005). Mining negative contrast sets from data with discrete attributes. *Expert Systems with Applications*, 29(2):401–407.

Wrobel, S. (1997). An algorithm for multi-relational discovery of subgroups. In *Proceedings of the 1st European Conference on Principles of Data Mining and Knowledge Discovery (PKDD'97)*, pages 78–87, Trondheim, Norway.

Zimmermann, A. and De Raedt, L. (2009). Cluster-grouping: from subgroup discovery to clustering. *Machine Learning*, 77(1):125–159.

Chapter 16
Pattern and Antipattern Discovery in Ethiopian Bagana Songs

Darrell Conklin and Stéphanie Weisser

Abstract Pattern discovery is an essential computational music analysis method for revealing intra-opus repetition and inter-opus recurrence. This chapter applies pattern discovery to a corpus of songs for the bagana, a large lyre played in Ethiopia. An important and unique aspect of this repertoire is that frequent and rare motifs have been explicitly identified and used by a master bagana teacher in Ethiopia. A new theorem for pruning of statistically under-represented patterns from the search space is used within an efficient pattern discovery algorithm. The results of the chapter show that over- and under-represented patterns can be discovered in a corpus of bagana songs, and that the method can reveal with high significance the known bagana motifs of interest.

16.1 Introduction

Pattern discovery is a central component of music analysis, concerned with the induction of patterns, those that are perceptually salient, statistically distinctive, or interesting to an analyst, within a single piece of music (*intra-opus*) or in a corpus of pieces (*inter-opus*). In contrast to a *deductive* analysis, which proceeds from known or postulated patterns and queries for their occurrences within a corpus, an *inductive* analysis performs the converse inference, proceeding from the music surface to salient patterns. The identification of salient structures within a piece or a corpus is a

Darrell Conklin
Department of Computer Science and Artificial Intelligence, University of the Basque Country UPV/EHU, San Sebastián, Spain
IKERBASQUE, Basque Foundation for Science, Bilbao, Spain
e-mail: darrell.conklin@ehu.eus

Stéphanie Weisser
Université libre de Bruxelles, Brussels, Belgium
e-mail: stephanie.weisser@ulb.ac.be

© Springer International Publishing Switzerland 2016
D. Meredith (ed.), *Computational Music Analysis*,
DOI 10.1007/978-3-319-25931-4_16

central part of musical analysis. In contrast to current methods for pattern discovery in music (Conklin and Anagnostopoulou, 2001; Lartillot, 2004; Meredith et al., 2002), which rely to varying extent on a form of salience determined by intra-opus repetition and inter-opus recurrence, a recent study (Conklin, 2013) has considered the problem of discovering *antipatterns*: patterns that are surprisingly rare or even absent from a piece or corpus. This property, which Huron (2001) refers to as a *negative presence*, has so far seen little attention in the computational music analysis literature.

Since the virtual space of patterns may be large or even infinite (in the case, for example, of antipatterns), all pattern discovery algorithms must address the dual problems of efficiently searching this space, and of ranking and presenting the results. Subsequently, a second order evaluation process arises: are patterns that are highly ranked also interesting to the analyst? Therefore it can be extremely productive to deeply study pieces where prior motivic analyses are available (Collins et al., 2014), for example as performed by Huron (2001), and Conklin (2010b) in their computational validations of Forte's (1983) motivic analysis of the Brahms String Quartet in C Minor.

In this chapter we will present a study of pattern discovery in Ethiopian bagana songs. The study of a bagana corpus provides a unique opportunity for the evaluation of pattern discovery techniques, because there are known inter-opus motifs, both rare and frequent, that are significant for didactic purposes (Weisser, 2005). The aim of this study is to explore whether inductive methods for the discovery of significantly frequent and rare patterns in music can reveal the known motifs, and possibly others that have functional significance.

Sequences are a special form of data that require specific attention with respect to alternative representations and data mining techniques. Sequential pattern mining methods (Adamo, 2001; Agrawal and Srikant, 1995; Ayres et al., 2002; Mooney and Roddick, 2013) can be used to find frequent and significant patterns in datasets of sequences, and also sequential patterns that contrast one data group against another (Deng and Zaïane, 2009; Hirao et al., 2000; Ji et al., 2007; Wang et al., 2009). In music, sequential pattern discovery methods have been used for the analysis of single pieces (Conklin, 2010b), for the analysis of a corpus of pieces (Conklin, 2010a), and also to find short patterns that can be used to classify melodies (Conklin, 2009; Lin et al., 2004; Sawada and Satoh, 2000; Shan and Kuo, 2003).

Further to standard pattern discovery methods, which search for frequent patterns satisfying minimum support thresholds (Webb, 2007), another area of interest is the discovery of rare patterns. This area includes work on rare itemset mining (Haglin and Manning, 2007) and negative association rules (Wu et al., 2004) which have seen application in bioinformatics (Artamonova et al., 2007). For sequence data, rare patterns have not seen as much attention, but are related to *unwords* (Herold et al., 2008) in genome research (i.e., absent words that are not subsequences of any other absent word), and *antipatterns* (Conklin, 2013) in music (patterns that are surprisingly rare in a corpus of music pieces). Antipatterns may represent structural constraints of a musical style and can therefore be useful for classification and generation of new pieces.

Fig. 16.1 The Ethiopian lyre *bagana*. Photos: Stéphanie Weisser

This chapter is structured as follows. Section 16.2 provides some historical context on the Ethiopian bagana, the notation used to encode notes in bagana songs, the known motifs, and a description of the encoded corpus of bagana songs. Section 16.3 outlines the pattern discovery method, statistical evaluation of patterns, and an algorithm for pattern discovery. Section 16.4 presents the computational analysis of the bagana corpus, first for antipatterns, then for positive patterns. The method is able to reveal known bagana motifs in a small corpus of bagana songs. The chapter concludes with a general discussion on the role of inductive methods in computational music analysis.

16.2 Bagana Music and Notation

In this chapter known frequent and rare motifs proposed by a master bagana teacher are studied using pattern discovery methods. Before presenting the motifs and corpus, a brief introduction of the cultural context will serve to provide the relevant background in playing technique and notation used to encode pieces.

The Ethiopian lyre *bagana* is a large instrument (ca. 1.20m high), made of wood, cattle skin and gut strings (see Fig. 16.1). It is played by the Amhara, a people settled mostly in Central and Northern Ethiopia. As a stringed instrument with strings running to a yoke or crossbar held by two arms coming out of the resonator, the bagana is categorized by organologists as a lyre. While such instruments were largely

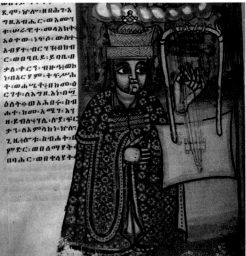

Fig. 16.2 Bagana representations from ancient manuscripts. Left: Illumination (detail) from Gospel of St. John (fol. 3v), Debre Bankol, Shire, Tigre Province, 19th century. Photo courtesy of Michael Gervers, University of Toronto. Right: Illumination (detail) from Life of St. Täklä Haymanot & Gäbrä Mänfäs Qeddus, Story of Archangel Mikael (fol. 119v), Samuel Za-Qoyetsa Monastery, Tigre Province, 18th century. Photo courtesy of Michael Gervers, University of Toronto

played in ancient Mesopotamia, ancient Egypt and ancient Greece, millennia ago, they are nowadays only found around the Nile and in East Africa.

The bagana plays a special role in Amhara culture: it is indeed the only melodic instrument belonging to the *zema*, the Amhara spiritual musical sphere. All the other instruments of the zema are percussive, producing sounds without definite pitch. The myth of its origin might explain such a specific status: according to Amhara belief, the bagana is the biblical King David's instrument, brought to Ethiopia together with the Ark of the Covenant by Menelik I, legendary son of King Solomon and Queen of Sheba. Such close association with the divine election and with the founder of the Solomonic dynasty explains why the bagana was historically an instrument played by pious men and women of the nobility (*makwannent*).

Even though it is not played during liturgical ceremonies, the bagana is considered as a sacred instrument, whose sounds are able to create a special connection with God, the saints and the Virgin Mary. For this reason, it is the only instrument traditionally allowed to be sounded during Lent (*Fasika Tsom*), the long fasting period before Easter. The bagana is also considered as a very powerful object, able to cast away the devil and to protect a house from evil spirits. This power against evil forces is linked to the biblical text of Samuel (1 Samuel 16:14-23), recalling the episode of King David playing the instrument to appease King Saul, tormented by an evil spirit. Indeed, the bagana is often depicted in iconographic representations being played by King David in majesty on his throne (see Fig. 16.2). The bagana is therefore a highly-respected instrument, inducing strong emotional states for players as well as for listeners (Weisser, 2012).

The bagana is a solo instrument accompanied by singing voice only and produces very low pitch sounds (from 50 to 200 Hz in general, which is close to the tessitura of a double bass). Bagana sounds are characterized by their very specific buzzing sound quality: indeed, due to a specific device named *enzira* and located at the bridge, the instrument generates extremely rich and harmonic sounds, perceived by the human ear as buzzing.

A bagana song is usually referred to as a *mezmour* (spiritual song), and it is built on repetition: a relatively short melody is repeated up to 20 times, with different lyrics each time except in the refrain (*azmatch*). Bagana songs are usually preceded by instrumental preludes, called *derdera* (pl. *derderotch*). Lyrics are an important part of the bagana repertoire, as they comprise prayers, praise to God, Jesus, the Virgin Mary and the saints, and elaborate poetry including *semenawork* (literally "wax-and-gold", a literary construct widely used by Amhara and characterized by double- or triple-meaning). Musical repetition is not strict: several modifications can be introduced by players in the course of the song, but they are usually subtle. The perceptual effect of the musical repetition, combined with the absence of dynamic variation (the buzzing sound colour makes it impossible to vary the loudness), the specific flowing rhythm and the softened voice tone induces a very meditative, introspective mood, distinct from other Amhara musical expressions (Weisser, 2012).

16.2.1 Bagana Playing and Notation

The bagana can be played by plucking the strings with the left hand fingers or with a plectrum (*girf*). The latter technique has nowadays almost disappeared, even though iconographic evidences (see Fig. 16.2: left) suggest that it was frequently in use. The bagana is a monophonic instrument; even when played with the plectrum, the musician selects the pitches by allowing to vibrate freely only the strings that are supposed to sound, and by blocking with the fingers the ones that are not supposed to sound. When plucked with the fingers, the strings are also played individually, even though, as the strings are left open and therefore sound until natural extinction, some superposition might be created when the plucking of several strings is fast.

The plucking technique of bagana consists in placing the left hand behind the strings, and performing a movement from a non-sounding string (a rest string) to the next one (a playing string), to pluck it with the flesh of the finger and then back to the rest string. Traditionally, the playing of the bagana was taught privately, by a master player to a pupil. The pupil placed his hand on the master's and understood that way how to proceed. The musical part of bagana repertoire was not written down: only lyrics were sometimes notated. However, the development of musical teaching inspired from Western music schools led to the opening of a bagana class at the Yared School of Music (Addis Ababa). The professor Alemu Aga, one of the most renowned and acclaimed bagana players of the country, who taught this class from

Table 16.1 Fingering of the bagana, with finger numbers assigned to string numbers

string	1	2	3	4	5	6	7	8	9	10
finger	1	r	2′	2	r	3	r	4	r	5

1972 to 1980, developed a new method in order to formalize the learning process, in cooperation with the professors of other instruments. He assigned a number for each finger, each sounding string and each pitch (see Table 16.1 and Fig. 16.3).

In Table 16.1, "r" (for "rest") indicates a string that is not played, but rather is used as a rest for the finger after it plucks the string immediately next to it. Strings 3 and 4 are both played by finger number 2 (string 3 being therefore notated as finger 2′), otherwise the assignment of finger number to string number is fixed.

Only six of the ten strings are playing strings, tuned according to a pentatonic scale. The two scales (*keniet*, pl. *kenietotch*) used for bagana performance are usually either anhemitonic (with all intervals larger than a tempered semitone), or hemitonic (containing one or more semitones). The anhemitonic scale is called *tezeta* and the hemitonic one is often named *anchihoye* (see Table 16.2). As in the rest of Amhara music, both secular and sacred, the scales are built on untempered intervals and the absolute pitch is irrelevant. Players usually adjust their pitch range to their taste and voice range, transposing the scale to the desired voice register.

To illustrate the notation in Table 16.2, for example, in the tezeta scale the ascending pentatonic scale (closest tempered degrees being C, D, E/F, G, A) would be notated by the sequence $[2,3,1,5,4]$. The scale degree notation is also useful for considering the intervallic relation between two strings, as will be used in Sect. 16.4. Figure 16.3 shows the placement of the left hand on the 10 bagana strings, along with the information from Table 16.2: the finger numbering used, and the notes played by the fingers (in the tezeta scale). Figure 16.4 shows an example of a fragment of a bagana song, encoded as a sequence of finger numbers, corresponding to the fingering of the song.

Table 16.2 Tuning of the bagana, in two different scales, and the nearest Western tempered note (with octave number) corresponding to the degrees of the scales. String 1 in the tezeta scale can be tuned to either E2 or F2

finger	1	2′ and 2	3	4	5
string	1	3 and 4	6	8	10
scale tezeta	E2 or F2	C2	D2	A2	G2
scale anchihoye	F2	C2	D♭2	A2	G♭2
scale degree	$\hat{3}$	$\hat{1}$	$\hat{2}$	$\hat{5}$	$\hat{4}$

Fig. 16.3 Placement of left hand on the strings of the bagana. Photo: Stéphanie Weisser, Addis Ababa, October 2012

16.2.2 Known Motifs

In the context of formal teaching, Alemu Aga wrote down with this numbered notation all of the melodic material of the songs he performed. He also designed specific exercises: based on an analysis of his personal repertoire, he developed several motifs (two to seven notes), to be used in an early stage of the learning process (see Tables 16.3 and 16.4). The student, after learning how to hold the instrument properly and placing the left hand in a correct position, is expected to practise these series of motifs regularly until moving on to learning a real song. To this day, Alemu Aga still uses these motifs in his teaching, considering that they familiarize the student with the playing technique, the numbered notational system, the pitch of each string, and the unique buzzing sound colour of the instrument.

In the teaching process, Alemu Aga requests the student to practise each exercise three times before moving to the next one. When the motif is short (such as the first and second of the rare motifs in Table 16.3, and the second and third of the frequent motifs in Table 16.4), repetition is usually performed without a break, which leads the student to practice both the motif and its retrograde. For example, the pattern $[1,4,1,4,1,4]$ (repeating the first rare motif three times) effectively comprises the pattern $[1,4]$ and its retrograde $[4,1]$. When the exercise is long (such as the third and fourth of the rare motifs, and the first of the frequent motifs), a pause is usually taken

Fig. 16.4 A fragment encoded in score and finger notation, from the beginning of the song *Abatachen Hoy* ("Our Father"), one of the most important bagana songs, as performed by Alemu Aga (voice transcription and lyrics not shown). Transcribed by Weisser (2006)

Table 16.3 The four rare motifs provided by Alemu Aga, from Weisser (2005, page 50)

	Motifs in numeric notation
First exercise	$[1,4]$
Second exercise	$[1,2]$
Third exercise	$[2,3,1,5,4]$
Fourth exercise	$[4,5,1,3,2]$

Table 16.4 The three frequent motifs provided by Alemu Aga, from Weisser (2005, page 50)

	Motifs in numeric notation
First exercise	$[4,5,4,5,4,5,1]$
Second exercise	$[4,2]$
Third exercise	$[3,1]$

after the final note, before starting the motif all over again. Therefore, it cannot be said that the bigrams $[4,2]$ and $[2,4]$ (which are the joining bigrams formed by the repetition of the third and fourth rare motifs) are rare, nor that the motif $[1,4]$ (which is the joining bigram formed by the repetition of the first frequent motif) is frequent. In fact, the opposite is true ($[1,4]$ is a rare motif: see Table 16.3) and this will also be confirmed by the pattern discovery results of Sect. 16.4.

16.2.2.1 Rare Motifs

Table 16.3 shows four motifs that correspond, according to the bagana master Alemu Aga, to motifs that are rarely encountered in his real bagana songs and are used during practice to strengthen the fingers with unusual finger configurations (Weisser, 2005). Referring to Fig. 16.4, it can be seen that the motifs of Table 16.3 are absent from the fragment. The first two motifs are bigrams, and in Sect. 16.4 it will be explored whether these two rare motifs can be discovered from corpus analysis. The third and fourth motifs correspond to longer pentagrams that form ascending and descending pentatonic scales and are also used for didactic purposes. Since most pentagram patterns will be rare in a small corpus, an additional question that will be explored in Sect. 16.4 is whether these two pentagram motifs are *surprisingly* rare.

16.2.2.2 Frequent Motifs

Table 16.4 shows three motifs that correspond, according to the bagana master Alemu Aga, to motifs that are frequently encountered in his real bagana songs. The first exercise works the independence of the little finger regarding the ring finger and increases the strength of the little finger. The ring finger and the little finger are particularly exercised because they pluck the tautest strings of the instrument. The final part $[5,1]$ of the first exercise also directly outlines the particular difficulty of the thumb, which plucks the string in the opposite direction compared to the other fingers. The second exercise focuses on mastering extreme notes of the ambitus of the bagana. This motif is very often used, particularly at the beginning and at the end of musical phrases (for example, see the final notes of the fragment of Fig. 16.4).

Finally, the third exercise of this category outlines the difficulty of plucking a string with the middle finger without moving the ring finger.

16.2.3 Bagana Corpus

The analysed corpus comprises 29 melodies of bagana songs and 8 derderotch (instrumental preludes) performed by seven players (five men, two women). These 37 pieces were recorded and transcribed by Weisser (2005) between 2002 and 2005 in Ethiopia (except for two of them recorded in Washington, DC).

It is important to note that in bagana performances, melodic variations are frequent, and the performance is rarely completely fixed. However, these modifications are not structural, as they do not undermine the identity of the song. Some musicians introduce these changes in a different way each time they are playing the song. In order to limit the impact of these variations on the results, non-structural variations were not included, nor were additional and optional ornamentations.

After removal of non-structural variations, a total of $N = 1906$ events (finger numbers) are encoded within the 37 pieces (events per song: $\mu = 51$, $\sigma = 30$, min $= 13$, max $= 121$).

16.3 Pattern Discovery Method

In this work we apply data mining to discover distinctive patterns in the bagana corpus. Here a pattern P of length ℓ is a contiguous sequence of finger numbers, notated as $[e_1, \ldots, e_\ell]$. The number of occurrences of a pattern P in the corpus is given by c_P (see Table 16.5).

In pattern discovery in music, the counting of pattern occurrences can be done in two ways (Conklin, 2010b): either by considering *piece count* (the number of pieces containing the pattern one or more times, i.e., analogous to the standard definition of pattern support in sequential pattern mining) or by considering *total count* (the total number of positions matched by the pattern, also counting multiple occurrences within the same piece). Total count is used whenever a single piece of music is the target of analysis. For the bagana, even though several pieces are available, total count is used, because we consider that a pattern is frequent (or rare) if it is frequently (or rarely) encountered within any succession of events. Therefore in this study c_P is the total number of events which initiate a pattern P.

Table 16.5 Glossary of notation and terminology used in this chapter

notation / terminology	meaning
pattern	a sequence of finger numbers
$P = [e_1, \ldots, e_\ell]$	pattern P of length ℓ
motif	a known frequent or rare pattern for the bagana
positive pattern	over-represented in a corpus
antipattern	under-represented in a corpus
c_P	total count of pattern P
c_e	total count of event e
N	total number of events in corpus
X	random variable modelling the total count c_P of pattern P
t_P	maximum possible total count of pattern P
b_P	analytic background probability of pattern P
$\mathbb{E}$	expected total count of pattern
$\mathbb{B}$	binomial probability density function
$\mathbb{B}_\le$	binomial cumulative distribution function
α	statistical significance level

16.3.1 Pattern Statistics

In this section two subtypes of pattern are introduced. A *positive pattern* is a pattern which is frequent in a corpus; an *antipattern* is a sequence that is rare, or even absent, in a corpus. For data mining, these definitions though intuitive are not operational. For positive patterns, very short patterns will tend to be highly frequent but usually are not meaningful because they may occur with high frequency in any corpus. For antipatterns, almost any sequence of events is an antipattern, that is, most possible event sequences will never occur in a corpus, and most are not interesting because it is expected that their total count is zero. Therefore we want to know which are the *significant* positive patterns and antipatterns: those that are *surprisingly* frequent or rare in a corpus.

Positive patterns and antipatterns can be evaluated by their *p-value*, which gives the probability of finding at least (for positive patterns) or at most (for antipatterns) the observed number of occurrences in the corpus. The binomial distribution, which can be used to compute the probability of obtaining an observed number of occurrences in a given number of sequence positions, is a standard model for assessing discovered motifs in bioinformatics (van Helden et al., 1998) and will be used here to compute pattern *p*-values as described below.

In studies where there is a set of pieces available to contrast with the corpus, it is possible to compute the *empirical background probability* of a pattern. This was the method used for ranking patterns in inter-opus pattern discovery studies of Cretan folk songs (Conklin and Anagnostopoulou, 2011) and antipatterns in Basque folk tunes (Conklin, 2013). For the bagana there is no natural set of pieces to contrast with the corpus, and the background probability of a pattern $P = [e_1, \ldots, e_\ell]$ must be estimated, for example using a zero-order model of the corpus:

$$b_P = \prod_{i=1}^{\ell} (c_{e_i}/N) , \qquad (16.1)$$

where c_{e_i} is the total count of event e_i, and N is the total number of events in the corpus. This *analytic background probability* b_P therefore estimates the probability of finding the pattern in ℓ contiguous events. In this study, a zero-order model of the corpus is used: a higher-order analytic model would not be able to detect bigram patterns because the expected total count of a bigram pattern would be equivalent to its actual count.

To define the *p*-value of a pattern $P = [e_1, \ldots, e_\ell]$, we define the random variable X that describes its total count c_P. This is modelled by the binomial distribution (see Appendix A for definitions):

$$\mathbb{P}(X = c_P) = \mathbb{B}(c_P; t_P, b_P) , \qquad (16.2)$$

where $t_P = \lfloor N/\ell \rfloor$ approximates the maximum number of positions that can be possibly matched by the pattern (this is a lower bound, as patterns with self-overlap have a higher maximum) and b_P is the background probability of the pattern.

Letting $\mathbb{B}_{\leq}$ be the binomial cumulative distribution function (see Appendix A for definitions), the *p*-value of P as an antipattern is the probability of finding c_P or fewer occurrences of the pattern in the corpus:

$$\mathbb{P}(X \leq c_P) = \mathbb{B}_{\leq}(c_P; t_P, b_P) , \qquad (16.3)$$

and the *p*-value of P as a positive pattern is the probability of finding c_P or more occurrences of the pattern in the corpus:

$$\mathbb{P}(X \geq c_P) = 1 - \mathbb{B}_{\leq}(c_P - 1; t_P, b_P) . \qquad (16.4)$$

Low *p*-values according to (16.3) or (16.4) indicate patterns that are statistically surprising and therefore potentially interesting.

16.3.2 Pattern Discovery Algorithm

The pattern discovery task can be stated as: given a corpus, find all patterns having a *p*-value ((16.3) and (16.4)) below the specified significance level α. Furthermore, for presentation we consider only those significant patterns that are *minimal*, that is, those that do not contain any other significant pattern (Conklin, 2013; Ji et al., 2007).

The discovery of minimal significant patterns can be efficiently solved by a refinement search over the space of possible patterns (Conklin, 2010a, 2013), using an algorithm similar to general approaches for sequential pattern mining (Ayres et al., 2002). The refinement search is also similar to the STUCCO (Bay and Pazzani, 2001) method for contrast set mining, here with a method for under-represented pattern pruning. A depth-first search (see Fig. 16.5) starts at the most general (empty) pattern. The search space is structured lexicographically so that no pattern is visited twice. If a pattern P at a particular node of the search tree is not significant (either as a positive pattern or an antipattern: see (16.3) and (16.4)), it is *specialized* to a new pattern P' by extending it on the right hand side by every possible event (finger number) and updating the pattern counts $c_{P'}$, and computing $t_{P'}$, $b_{P'}$, and both p-values ((16.3) and (16.4)). All specializations of the pattern are then added to the search queue. The search continues at a node if the pattern is significant neither as a pattern nor as an antipattern. Significant patterns are added to a solution list, with a filtering against other solutions found so far to ensure that the final pattern set contains only minimal patterns.

The runtime of the algorithm is largely determined by the specified significance level α, because with low α the search space must be more deeply explored before a significant positive pattern is reached. For positive patterns, the p-value (defined in (16.3)) rapidly decreases with pattern specialization, so unless α is very low the search for positive patterns will tend to terminate early. For antipatterns the situation is reversed, with the p-value tending to increase through a search path.

Nevertheless, for antipatterns it is possible to compute the minimal antipattern p-value (16.3) achievable on a search path. This can lead to the pruning of entire

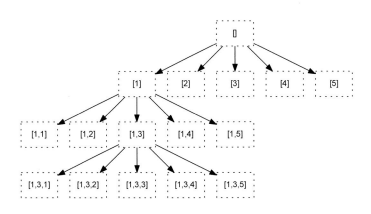

Fig. 16.5 A refinement search space of bagana patterns, through the pattern $[1,3]$ down to its specializations

search paths that cannot possibly visit an antipattern meeting the significance level of α:

Theorem 16.1. *For any pattern P, if* $\mathbb{B}(0;t_P,b_P) > \alpha$, *then* $\mathbb{B}_{\leq}(c_{P'};t_{P'},b_{P'}) > \alpha$ *for any specialization P' of P.*

Proof. Consider a pattern $P = [e_1,\ldots,e_\ell]$ and a specialization $P' = [e_1,\ldots,e_{\ell'}]$. Since $\ell' > \ell$, it follows that $b_P \geq b_{P'}$ (16.1) and that $t_P \geq t_{P'}$. This implies that $(1-b_P)^{t_P} \leq (1-b_{P'})^{t_{P'}}$. Therefore, $\mathbb{B}(0;t_P,b_P) \leq \mathbb{B}(0;t_{P'},b_{P'})$. Following the definition of the cumulative distribution $\mathbb{B}_{\leq}$ (16.6), $\mathbb{B}(0;t_{P'},b_{P'}) \leq \mathbb{B}_{\leq}(c_{P'};t_{P'},b_{P'})$. Therefore $\mathbb{B}(0;t_P,b_P) \leq \mathbb{B}_{\leq}(c_{P'};t_{P'},b_{P'})$, so if $\mathbb{B}(0;t_P,b_P) > \alpha$, then $\mathbb{B}_{\leq}(c_{P'};t_{P'},b_{P'}) > \alpha$. ☐

The impact of this new theorem is that if the pattern P at a search node is being tested only as an antipattern, and $\mathbb{B}(0;t_P,b_P) > \alpha$, the search does not need to continue at that search node. The theorem also provides an important way to use the algorithm above for efficient *unword* discovery, i.e., to find significant antipatterns where $c_P = 0$.

16.4 Results and Discussion

The pattern discovery method described in Sect. 16.3 was applied to the bagana corpus to find all minimal antipatterns and positive patterns at the significance level of $\alpha = 0.01$. In this section, first the discovered antipatterns, then the discovered positive patterns, are presented and discussed.

16.4.1 Discovered Antipatterns

Table 16.6 presents the antipatterns revealed by the discovery method. In the columns are the pattern P, the closest tempered interval (in the tezeta scale) formed by the components of the pattern, the pattern counts (both total count and piece count), the expected total count of P given by $\mathbb{E}(X) = b_P \times t_P$, and finally the p-value according to (16.3).

The method revealed exactly ten significant antipatterns: five antipatterns and their retrogrades. Interestingly, all are bigrams and all come in retrograde pairs. The two antipatterns $[4,1]$ and $[2,1]$ presented in the top part of Table 16.6 are the *most significant* antipatterns discovered, and correspond to the retrogrades of two of the didactic rare motifs (Table 16.3). As mentioned earlier, this discovery is valid as, for example, the first motif $[1,4]$ repeated three times will also play the motif $[4,1]$. It is therefore remarkable that both retrograde forms, not only the form listed in Table 16.3, are discovered.

The second column of Table 16.6 presents the closest tempered interval (in the tezeta scale) formed by the pattern. Note that antipatterns involving finger 1 can give

Table 16.6 Bagana antipatterns discovered (top and middle) at $\alpha = 0.01$. Intervals are measured in the tezeta scale. Top: corresponding to rare bigram motifs of Table 16.3; middle: novel rare patterns; bottom: the two pentagram motifs of Table 16.3. Partial horizontal lines separate retrograde pairs. Numbers in brackets indicate the number of distinct pieces containing the pattern

P	closest tempered interval	c_P	$\mathbb{E}(X)$	$\mathbb{P}(X \leq c_P)$
$[1,4]$	P4/M3	21 (14)	48	7.5e-06
$[4,1]$		2 (2)	48	6.3e-19
$[2,1]$	M3/P4	6 (5)	50	1.8e-15
$[1,2]$		13 (7)	50	2.6e-10
$[3,4]$	P5	3 (3)	30	4.0e-10
$[4,3]$		2 (2)	30	3.8e-11
$[2,5]$	P5	16 (9)	38	2.7e-05
$[5,2]$		17 (10)	38	6.6e-05
$[3,5]$	P4	5 (4)	26	5.7e-07
$[5,3]$		11 (8)	26	0.00077
$[2,3,1,5,4]$	ascending scale	8 (7)	0.11	1.0
$[4,5,1,3,2]$	descending scale	4 (3)	0.11	1.0

rise to two alternatives, depending on the tuning of string 1 to either an E or an F (see Table 16.2). Interestingly, all of the discovered antipatterns form a melodic interval of a major third or greater (intervals of P4, M3, and P5).

In addition to the two bigram motifs in Table 16.3, the three additional antipatterns $[3,4]$, $[2,5]$, and $[3,5]$ (with their retrogrades) are found by the method. It is worth noticing specifically the rarity of the interval of fifths (perfect in tezeta, diminished and augmented in anchihoye) outlined by antipatterns $[3,4]$ and $[2,5]$. According to authoritative writings in ethnomusicology (Arom, 1997), the perfect fifth and the cycle of fifths play a founding role in anhemitonic pentatonic scales such as tezeta. The rarity of perfect fifths (P5) in the songs is significant, and it can be speculated that this interval is a mental reference that is never (and does not necessarily need to be) performed. Similarly, the antipattern $[3,5]$, a perfect fourth (P4), is the inversion of a perfect fifth. The rarity of the fourth can be related to the rarity of the fifth, as intervals and their inversions are usually connected in several musical cultures, including Western art music.

For completeness with the results of Weisser (2005), at the bottom of Table 16.6 are the two pentagram motifs from Table 16.3. As expected, these motifs are not frequent, but it is notable that they are not significant as antipatterns according to their p-value (therefore they are not reported by the pattern discovery method). In fact, they occur in the corpus more than expected according to their background probability.

16.4.2 Discovered Positive Patterns

The method revealed fourteen significant positive patterns (Table 16.7): five patterns and their retrogrades (reversal), and four unison patterns (repetitions of the same finger number). Most of the significant patterns are bigrams, as with the antipatterns in Table 16.6. The unison patterns are not presented further: according to bagana musicians, the exact number of a repeated pitch is not important and may depend on other factors than the structure of music.

The three patterns [3, 1], [2, 4], [5, 4] (with their retrogrades, which are also significant) cover the frequent motifs in Table 16.4. As with the rare motifs, the discovery of the retrograde is valid, as the frequent motifs are also practised three times in a row. Regarding the discovered pattern [1, 5], which is not listed in Table 16.4, it is the retrograde of [5, 1] (which is the end of the first frequent motif of Table 16.7). It is worth noticing that the pattern [1, 5], though appearing in Alemu Aga's third rare motif (see Table 16.3), is only a small part of this motif: [1, 5] is therefore not practised as much as the other retrogrades. However, the fact that the discovered pattern [1, 5] is found among the rare motifs can be explained: it is mostly in songs studied in a more advanced phase in the learning process. Therefore, the practice of the [1, 5] motif in a familiarization phase is not really needed. Its discovery as a pattern is consistent with all discovered bigrams being in retrograde pairs.

In terms of melodic intervals, the discovered patterns represent conjunct melodic motion (one scale step), except for the pattern [2, 4], corresponding in the tezeta scale to a major sixth and the largest interval playable on the instrument. This pattern is also considered idiomatic of bagana playing. Interestingly, the two pentagram motifs of Table 16.3, presented according to their rarity in the songs of Alemu Aga, are composed entirely of frequent significant bigram motifs.

Table 16.7 Bagana positive patterns discovered at $\alpha = 0.01$. Top: frequent bigram motifs of Table 16.4; bottom: two novel discovered patterns. Partial horizontal lines separate retrograde pairs. Numbers in brackets indicate the number of distinct pieces containing the pattern

P	closest tempered interval	c_P	$\mathbb{E}(X)$	$\mathbb{P}(X \geq c_P)$
[3, 1]	M2/m3	195 (37)	34	1e-87
[1, 3]		148 (35)	34	4.6e-51
[2, 4]	M6	154 (35)	44	9.4e-41
[4, 2]		200 (37)	44	1.3e-71
[5, 4]	M2	127 (31)	37	3.7e-33
[4, 5]		112 (31)	37	8e-25
[1, 5]	m3/M2	160 (35)	41	6.4e-48
[5, 1]		139 (32)	41	4.9e-35
[2, 3]	M2	104 (35)	31	3.7e-26
[3, 2]		67 (28)	31	7.7e-09

It can be hypothesized that the favouring of patterns forming a conjunct melodic motion is linked with the singing voice. Indeed, as the lyrics are of great importance and mostly syllabic (each syllable is sung on one note), such a conjunct motion is easier for the musician to sing as well as easier for the listener to understand. It should be noted that the singing voice accompanying the bagana is not limited to a total range of a sixth: as an interval of an octave is not considered significant, the pattern $[4,2]$ can be also performed as conjunct, when the pitch of string 4 (A) is sung an octave lower than usual, meaning lower than the pitch of string 2 (C).

16.5 Conclusions

An inductive approach to computational music analysis holds great potential for revealing both *intra-opus* motifs from a single piece, or *inter-opus* motifs from a corpus of several pieces. In cases where motifs of functional significance are known, pattern discovery methods can be validated against prior knowledge, and new discoveries may gain potential musicological significance.

This chapter has developed an inter-opus pattern discovery method and applied it to the discovery of over- and under-represented patterns in bagana songs. From a small corpus of bagana songs, the method was able to find the rare and frequent motifs used by Alemu Aga for bagana teaching. The validation of pattern discovery on a known motif set is invaluable as it lends additional interest to novel motifs discovered, and even to future work with other corpora.

A zero-order background model for pattern discovery provided excellent results for pattern discovery in the bagana corpus, with few type I errors (discovered minimal patterns that are not bigram motifs) and no type II errors (bigram motifs that are not discovered as minimal patterns). As mentioned above, higher-order background models would not be able to detect the types of short motifs that are known for the bagana. The selection of a background model for pattern discovery, necessary in music analysis tasks where no explicit anticorpus is available, is always an issue in statistical hypothesis testing, being a tradeoff between tolerance of type I and type II errors. In the field of musicology, Huron (1999) refers to the reluctance to discard patterns as "theory-conserving skepticism", arguing that the application of statistical methods to musicology should have high statistical power to avoid overlooking any potentially interesting pattern.

Antipattern discovery in music, the process of discovering patterns that are surprisingly rare in a group of pieces, was introduced in the context of Basque folk tunes (Conklin, 2013), where each annotated tune genre is contrasted against remaining genres. This chapter shows that antipattern discovery can be carried out without an explicit set of contrasting pieces by setting up a background statistical model that produces expected counts in the corpus. Large deviations have low probabilities according to the binomial distribution, and are reported as significantly rare patterns.

From a musicological point of view, the analysis we present here can be characterized by its *emic* basis, based on a musician *within* the culture. Such ground provides the analyst with a very important clue regarding the way a musical piece is built and conceptualized. Influenced by linguistics and more specifically by phonology, (ethno)musicologists often search for "minimal units" in a musical repertoire, similar to phonemes in a language. In the case of the bagana, the use of such motifs *by the musicians themselves* is a precious indication towards the idea that the minimal units of bagana songs are not single pitches, but rather pairs (or triplets) of sounds.

Such formal principles made the computational analysis of the presence of motifs pertinent in this specific context. The analysis of non-Western, non-written (or partially non-written) repertoires is a complex task, mostly when it comes to the validation of hypotheses constructed by the analyst—often an outsider to the cultural and musical system being studied. Several researchers, including Arom (1997), developed methods allowing a kind of generation of the repertoire according to the hypothesis tested by the investigator (Fernando, 2004). Indeed, with such a method, the musician can therefore validate a result, instead of a concept. Pattern and antipattern discovery, with its inductive approach, paves the way for generating music according to structural and formal rules. Such an approach will be invaluable for the analysis of a repertoire, especially in the field of ethnomusicology.

Acknowledgements This research is supported by the project Lrn2Cre8 which is funded by the Future and Emerging Technologies (FET) programme within the Seventh Framework Programme for Research of the European Commission, under FET grant number 610859. Special thanks to Kerstin Neubarth for valuable comments on the manuscript.

A Binomial Distribution: Definitions and Notation

Binomial probability density function (probability of exactly k successes in n independent trials, each having probability p of success):

$$\mathbb{B}(k;n,p) = \binom{n}{k} p^k (1-p)^{n-k} . \tag{16.5}$$

Binomial cumulative distribution function (probability of k or fewer successes in n independent trials, each having probability p of success):

$$\mathbb{B}_{\leq}(k;n,p) = \sum_{i=0}^{k} \mathbb{B}(i;n,p) . \tag{16.6}$$

References

Adamo, J.-M. (2001). *Data Mining for Association Rules and Sequential Patterns.* Springer.

Agrawal, R. and Srikant, R. (1995). Mining sequential patterns. In *Proceedings of the Eleventh International Conference on Data Engineering*, pages 3–14, Taipei, Taiwan.

Arom, S. (1997). Le "syndrome" du pentatonisme africain. *Musicae Scientiae*, 1(2):139–163.

Artamonova, I., Frishman, G., and Frishman, D. (2007). Applying negative rule mining to improve genome annotation. *BMC Bioinformatics*, 8:261.

Ayres, J., Gehrke, J., Yiu, T., and Flannick, J. (2002). Sequential pattern mining using a bitmap representation. In *Proceedings of the International Conference on Knowledge Discovery and Data Mining*, pages 429–435, Edmonton, Canada.

Bay, S. and Pazzani, M. (2001). Detecting group differences: Mining contrast sets. *Data Mining and Knowledge Discovery*, 5(3):213–246.

Collins, T., Böck, S., Krebs, F., and Widmer, G. (2014). Bridging the audio-symbolic gap: The discovery of repeated note content directly from polyphonic music audio. In *Proceedings of the Audio Engineering Society's 53rd Conference on Semantic Audio*, London, UK.

Conklin, D. (2009). Melody classification using patterns. In *International Workshop on Machine Learning and Music*, pages 37–41, Bled, Slovenia.

Conklin, D. (2010a). Discovery of distinctive patterns in music. *Intelligent Data Analysis*, 14(5):547–554.

Conklin, D. (2010b). Distinctive patterns in the first movement of Brahms' String Quartet in C Minor. *Journal of Mathematics and Music*, 4(2):85–92.

Conklin, D. (2013). Antipattern discovery in folk tunes. *Journal of New Music Research*, 42(2):161–169.

Conklin, D. and Anagnostopoulou, C. (2001). Representation and discovery of multiple viewpoint patterns. In *Proceedings of the International Computer Music Conference*, pages 479–485, Havana, Cuba.

Conklin, D. and Anagnostopoulou, C. (2011). Comparative pattern analysis of Cretan folk songs. *Journal of New Music Research*, 40(2):119–125.

Deng, K. and Zaïane, O. R. (2009). Contrasting sequence groups by emerging sequences. In Gama, J., Santos Costa, V., Jorge, A., and Brazdil, P., editors, *Discovery Science*, volume 5808 of *Lecture Notes in Artificial Intelligence*, pages 377–384. Springer.

Fernando, N. (2004). Expérimenter en ethnomusicologie. *L'Homme*, 171-172:284–302.

Forte, A. (1983). Motivic design and structural levels in the first movement of Brahms's String Quartet in C minor. *The Musical Quarterly*, 69(4):471–502.

Haglin, D. J. and Manning, A. M. (2007). On minimal infrequent itemset mining. In *Proceedings of the 2007 International Conference on Data Mining*, pages 141–147, Las Vegas, Nevada.

Herold, J., Kurtz, S., and Giegerich, R. (2008). Efficient computation of absent words in genomic sequences. *BMC Bioinformatics*, 9:167.

Hirao, M., Hoshino, H., Shinohara, A., Takeda, M., and Arikawa, S. (2000). A practical algorithm to find the best subsequence patterns. In Arikawa, S. and Morishita,

S., editors, *Discovery Science*, volume 1967 of *Lecture Notes in Computer Science*, pages 141–154. Springer.

Huron, D. (1999). The new empiricism: Systematic musicology in a postmodern age. Lecture 3 from the 1999 Ernest Bloch Lectures. http://musiccog.ohio-state.edu/Music220/Bloch.lectures/3.Methodology.html. Accessed Mar 3, 2015.

Huron, D. (2001). What is a musical feature? Forte's analysis of Brahms's Opus 51, No. 1, revisited. *Music Theory Online*, 7(4).

Ji, X., Bailey, J., and Dong, G. (2007). Mining minimal distinguishing subsequence patterns with gap constraints. *Knowledge and Information Systems*, 11(3):259–296.

Lartillot, O. (2004). A musical pattern discovery system founded on a modeling of listening strategies. *Computer Music Journal*, 28(3):53–67.

Lin, C.-R., Liu, N.-H., Wu, Y.-H., and Chen, A. (2004). Music classification using significant repeating patterns. In Lee, Y., Li, J., Whang, K.-Y., and Lee, D., editors, *Database Systems for Advanced Applications*, volume 2973 of *Lecture Notes in Computer Science*, pages 506–518. Springer.

Meredith, D., Lemström, K., and Wiggins, G. (2002). Algorithms for discovering repeated patterns in multidimensional representations of polyphonic music. *Journal of New Music Research*, 31(4):321–345.

Mooney, C. H. and Roddick, J. F. (2013). Sequential pattern mining – approaches and algorithms. *ACM Computing Surveys*, 45(2):19:1–19:39.

Sawada, T. and Satoh, K. (2000). Composer classification based on patterns of short note sequences. In *Proceedings of the AAAI-2000 Workshop on AI and Music*, pages 24–27, Austin, Texas.

Shan, M.-K. and Kuo, F.-F. (2003). Music style mining and classification by melody. *IEICE Transactions on Information and Systems*, E88D(3):655–659.

van Helden, J., André, B., and Collado-Vides, J. (1998). Extracting regulatory sites from the upstream region of yeast genes by computational analysis of oligonucleotide frequencies. *Journal of Molecular Biology*, 281(5):827–842.

Wang, J., Zhang, Y., Zhou, L., Karypis, G., and Aggarwal, C. C. (2009). CONTOUR: an efficient algorithm for discovering discriminating subsequences. *Data Mining and Knowledge Discovery*, 18(1):1–29.

Webb, G. I. (2007). Discovering significant patterns. *Machine Learning*, 68(1):1–33.

Weisser, S. (2005). *Etude ethnomusicologique du bagana, lyre d'Ethiopie*. PhD thesis, Université libre de Bruxelles.

Weisser, S. (2006). Transcrire pour vérifier: le rythme des chants de bagana d'Éthiopie. *Musurgia*, XIII(2):51–61.

Weisser, S. (2012). Music and Emotion. The Ethiopian Lyre Bagana. *Musicae Scientiae*, 16(1):3–18.

Wu, X., Zhang, C., and Zhang, S. (2004). Efficient mining of both positive and negative association rules. *ACM Transactions on Information Systems (TOIS)*, 22(3):381–405.

Chapter 17
Using Geometric Symbolic Fingerprinting to Discover Distinctive Patterns in Polyphonic Music Corpora

Tom Collins, Andreas Arzt, Harald Frostel, and Gerhard Widmer

Abstract Did Ludwig van Beethoven (1770–1827) re-use material when composing his piano sonatas? What repeated patterns are distinctive of Beethoven's piano sonatas compared, say, to those of Frédéric Chopin (1810–1849)? Traditionally, in preparation for essays on topics such as these, music analysts have undertaken inter-opus pattern discovery—informally or systematically—which is the task of identifying two or more related note collections (or phenomena derived from those collections, such as chord sequences) that occur in at least two different movements or pieces of music. More recently, computational methods have emerged for tackling the inter-opus pattern discovery task, but often they make simplifying and problematic assumptions about the nature of music. Thus a gulf exists between the flexibility music analysts employ when considering two note collections to be related, and what algorithmic methods can achieve. By unifying contributions from the two main approaches to computational pattern discovery—viewpoints and the geometric method—via the technique of symbolic fingerprinting, the current chapter seeks to reduce this gulf. Results from six experiments are summarized that investigate questions related to borrowing, resemblance, and distinctiveness across 21 Beethoven piano sonata movements. Among these results, we found 2–3 bars of material that occurred across two sonatas, an andante theme that appears varied in an imitative minuet, patterns with leaps that are distinctive of Beethoven compared to Chopin, and two potentially new examples of what Meyer and Gjerdingen call *schemata*. The chapter does not *solve* the problem of inter-opus pattern discovery, but it can act as a platform for research that will further reduce the gap between what music informaticians do, and what musicologists find interesting.

Tom Collins
Faculty of Technology, De Montfort University, Leicester, UK
e-mail: tom.collins@dmu.ac.uk

Andreas Arzt · Harald Frostel · Gerhard Widmer
Department of Computational Perception, Johannes Kepler University, Linz, Austria
e-mail: {andreas.arzt, harald.frostel, gerhard.widmer}@jku.at

© Springer International Publishing Switzerland 2016   445
D. Meredith (ed.), *Computational Music Analysis*,
DOI 10.1007/978-3-319-25931-4_17

17.1 Introduction

The topic of borrowing, between composers or within a single composer's oeuvre, has long been a concern for musicologists studying various periods and genres (Burkholder, 2001). George Frideric Handel's (1685–1759) music has received much attention in this regard, so it seems appropriate to begin this chapter with an example of Handel's borrowing from Reinhard Keiser (1674–1739), given in Fig. 17.1 (Roberts, 1986; Winemiller, 1997). In Fig. 17.1(a), Keiser's seven-note pattern occurs first in the oboe and is then sung by Clotilde. Shown in Fig. 17.1(b), Handel uses this same sequence of pitches, again in the oboe, but with a different rhythmic profile. Whereas Handel is often mentioned in connection with borrowing between composers, a composer well known for reworking of his own compositions is Beethoven:

> More than a third of Beethoven's compositions reworked his existing music in some way.
>
> (Burkholder, 2001)

Lutes (1974) identifies a pattern from the first movement of Beethoven's Piano Sonata no. 5 in C minor, op. 10, no. 1 (Fig. 17.2(a)) that recurs in the first movement of the Piano Sonata no. 6 in F major, op. 10, no. 2 (Fig. 17.2(b)). Beethoven, however, was also apt to borrow from other composers and Lutes (1974) credits Radcliffe (1968) with identifying the pattern in Fig. 17.2(a) as an instance of borrowing from Joseph Haydn's (1732–1809) Symphony no. 88 in G major, Hob.I:88 (Fig. 17.2(c)).

What do the pattern occurrences in Fig. 17.2 have in common, and how do we define the term *pattern*? Commonalities first (and see Sect. 17.3 for a definition of

Fig. 17.1 (a) Bars 1–5.1 of 'Mit einem schönen Ende' from *La forza della virtù* by Keiser. Two occurrences of a seven-note pattern are highlighted. (b) Bars 1–4.1 of 'Must I my Acis still bemoan' from *Acis and Galatea* by Handel. An occurrence of a seven-note pattern is highlighted. Throughout this chapter, 'bar *x.y*' means 'bar *x* beat *y*'

Fig. 17.2 (a) Bars 233–240 of the first movement from Beethoven's Piano Sonata no. 5 in C minor, op. 10, no. 1. One occurrence of a twelve-note pattern is highlighted in blue. A second occurrence in bars 237–240 is not highlighted. Instead, a different ten-note pattern is highlighted in red and discussed later on with reference to Fig. 17.11(c). (b) Bars 18–26 with upbeat of the first movement from Beethoven's Piano Sonata no. 6 in F major, op. 10, no. 2. One occurrence of a twelve-note pattern is highlighted in blue. A second occurrence in bars 25–26 with upbeat is not highlighted. (c) Piano reduction of bars 1-4.2 with upbeat of the second movement from Symphony no. 88 in G major by Haydn. An occurrence of a ten-note pattern is highlighted in bars 1–2, followed by a second occurrence in bars 3–4

pattern): the bass moves from scale degree $\hat{1}$ to $\hat{2}$. Simultaneously, the melody—doubled at the octave—outlines a rising arpeggio, beginning on $\hat{3}$ and ending on scale degree $\hat{1}$, followed by a fall to scale degree $\hat{7}$. This pattern provides the antecedent of an antecedent-consequent formula typical of the period. In each excerpt, the consequent consists of the bass moving from $\hat{7}$ to $\hat{1}$, while the melody—still doubled at the octave—outlines a rising arpeggio beginning on $\hat{5}$ and ending on $\hat{4}$, followed by a fall to $\hat{3}$. Putting the octave arpeggio to one side, the bass movement of $\hat{1}$–$\hat{2}$–$\hat{7}$–$\hat{1}$ and melodic movement of $\hat{1}$–$\hat{7}$–$\hat{4}$–$\hat{3}$ was referred to by Meyer (1980) as a *schema*—instances of simultaneous bass and melodic movement to be found across many pieces. Gjerdingen (1988) identified numerous instances of this particular schema across the period 1720–1900, and then other different categories of schemata (Gjerdingen, 2007). So the subdiscipline of music analysis known as *schema theory* was born, and remains popular to this day (Byros, 2012). So prevalent was the use of Meyer's schema in the Classical period, and so abstract the definition, that to mix it with remarks on borrowing is perhaps inappropriate. It seems neither Meyer (1980) nor Gjerdingen (1988, 2007) were aware of the examples identified in the earlier work of Radcliffe (1968) and Lutes (1974), which are perhaps better described as *borrowing* rather than *schemata* due to the specificity of octaves and rising arpeggios in each case. Still, Radcliffe (1968, p. 38) cautions,

> it is very dangerous to attach too much importance to thematic resemblances of this kind, especially in music written at a time when there were so many familiar turns of phrase used by all and sundry. Haydn's tune is slow and majestic, and Beethoven's recollections of it all move at a quicker pace, sometimes with the suggestion of a dance.

Whether referred to as pattern or schema, evidently the highlighted content of Figs. 17.1 and 17.2 and surrounding discussion are of interest to music analysts and musicologists more broadly. Processes of musical variation (more about which below) are in evidence in these figures, but instances of literal borrowing—e.g., where a number of bars are reused more or less verbatim—are of interest also (Winemiller, 1997). This chapter explores computational methods for identifying resemblances between pieces of music (involving both literal borrowing and more complex variation). The methods are described, applied to 21 movements from Beethoven's piano sonatas (which, given the above discussion, seem a sensible place to begin), and the results are presented and discussed.[1] It is remarkable how much existing literature on Beethoven's piano sonatas focuses on intra-movement as opposed to inter-movement or inter-piece analyses (Caplin, 2013)—an exception being Marston (1995). Even so, Marston's (1995) mix of sketchbook, biographical, and Schenkerian analysis is quite apart from what follows here. The question of whether Beethoven intended any discovered resemblance will not be considered. We focus instead on the likelihood of the pattern occurring in other Beethoven sonatas, or in the piano works of another composer such as Chopin. If the pattern occurs more often in the works of Beethoven than some other composer(s), then it can be

---

[1] The movements used are: op. 2, no. 1, mvts. 1–4; op. 10, no. 1, mvts. 1–3; op. 10, no. 2, mvts. 1–3; op. 10, no. 3, mvts. 1–4; op. 26, mvts. 1–4; and op. 109, mvts. 1–3. Movements were selected on the basis of frequent mentions in the analytic literature.

said to be distinctive of Beethoven's style. Books and articles abound on the topic of Beethoven's sonatas, but one motivation for this chapter is to see what light can be shed on the sonatas from the point of view of computational music analysis.

It is also remarkable how much existing (predominantly non-computational) work on borrowing involves musical excerpts that are either at the beginning of pieces or already known to be themes (Barlow and Morgenstern, 1948). One of the advantages of taking a computational approach is that it can be made more democratic in terms of detecting borrowing beyond incipits and themes. The apparent bias towards incipits and themes in existing work also raises the question: is thematic material inherently more *distinctive* than excerpts drawn from elsewhere in a movement? This is a question that we also seek to address in the current chapter.

17.2 Select Review of Computational Pattern Discovery

While the current chapter focuses on the music of Beethoven, it is part of a wider literature on *inter-opus pattern discovery*. That is, given a corpus of music, define an algorithm that returns musically interesting patterns occurring in two or more pieces. With regards to work on inter-opus pattern discovery, the major contribution of this chapter is a method capable of being applied to polyphonic music—polyphonic in the most complex sense of the term, where any number of voices may sound at a given point in time. After processing of the symbolic representations in Fig. 17.1 to extract individual melodic lines, there are computational methods capable of retrieving the type of patterns shown (Conklin, 2010; Knopke and Jürgensen, 2009). At present, however, no computational method exists capable of discovering the type of patterns shown in Fig. 17.2. The lack of such a method goes some way towards explaining why musicologists do not, in general, employ computational methods as part of their research into borrowing: practitioners of music computing have tended to import algorithms from other fields such as bioinformatics, which work well for melodic representations but do not apply to polyphonic music where voices can appear and disappear. Should practitioners of music computing be in any doubt about the need to look beyond melody-only representations, then let us consider Caplin (2013, p. 39):

> Although it is easy to focus attention on the melody, it is important to understand that the basic idea is the *complete* unit of music in all of its parts, including its harmonic, rhythmic, and textural components. *The basic idea is much more than just its "tune".*

Broadly, there are two approaches to the discovery of patterns in symbolic representations of music: (1) string-based or *viewpoint* methods (Cambouropoulos, 2006; Conklin, 2010; Conklin and Bergeron, 2008; Knopke and Jürgensen, 2009; Lartillot, 2005) (see also Chaps. 11, 12 and 15, this volume); (2) point-set or *geometric* methods, such as those described in the current chapter and Chap. 13 in this volume (see also Collins, 2011; Collins et al., 2013, 2011; Forth, 2012; Janssen et al., 2013; Meredith et al., 2002). As the name suggests, the viewpoints approach involves treating musical events as *sequences* considered from different perspectives (e.g., sequences of MIDI note numbers, sequences of intervals, durations, etc.) and in different combinations. The geometric approach, on the other hand, involves representing numerical aspects of notes in a given piece as *multidimensional points*. The two approaches diverge when more than two notes sound at the same point in time, because in the viewpoints approach the sequential ordering of features of those notes becomes ambiguous. Viewpoints have been applied in both intra- and inter-opus pattern discovery scenarios, but up until this point, geometric methods have been applied in *intra*-opus discovery scenarios only.

In this chapter, we describe the first application of geometric pattern discovery algorithms in an inter-opus scenario. We discuss the challenges involved, present results from the piano works of Beethoven, and suggest possible directions for future work in this domain. The geometric method has some advantages over the viewpoint approach: first, the geometric method can be applied conveniently to both polyphonic and monophonic representations. Viewpoints have been applied to polyphonic representations before (Conklin and Bergeron, 2010), but rely on extracting a fixed number of voices from each piece in the chosen corpus; second, the geometric method is more robust to interpolated events in pattern occurrences. For instance, the six notes highlighted in red and labelled H_2 in Fig. 17.3(c) are a diatonic transposition of the six notes highlighted in red and labelled H_1 in Fig. 17.3(a). In between the C♯4 and A3 of H_2, however, there is an interpolated B3 (similarly, there is an interpolated G♯3 between the following A3 and F♯3). The sequential integrity of C♯4 → A3 is broken by the interpolated B3, compared with G♯4 → E4 of H_1, and so the viewpoint method will not recognize the evident similarity of the melodies in bar 1 of Fig. 17.3(a) and bar 21 of Fig. 17.3(c). We refer to this as the *interpolation problem* of the viewpoint method—a problem that also affects models of music cognition derived from the viewpoint method (e.g., Pearce et al., 2010).[2] The geometric approach is more robust to this type of variation (Collins et al., 2013, 2011). Therefore, the application of geometric pattern discovery algorithms in an inter-opus scenario described in this chapter constitutes an important advance for computational music-analytic methods.

17.3 Method

This section begins with a mathematical definition of the term *pattern*. As in Chap. 13 of this volume, in the current chapter we represent notes in a given piece of music as multidimensional points. For example, a note has a start time that might be assigned

---

[2] Advocates of the viewpoint method might say that defining a so-called threaded viewpoint to take pitch values only on quarter note beats would address this interpolation problem, but then offbeat notes that do belong to a pattern are overlooked also. Since we have mentioned an advantage of the geometric approach over the viewpoint approach, it is fair to state an advantage in the other direction also: if one is interested primarily in patterns that consist of substrings (as opposed to subsequences) in monophonic voices, then such patterns can be found more efficiently using string-based representations than they can be using point-based representations.

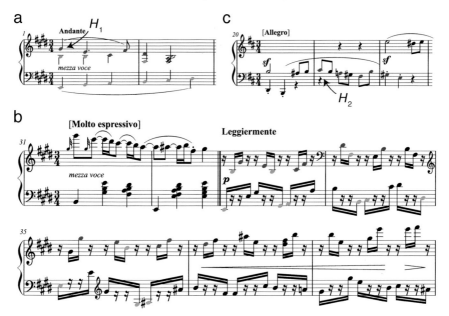

Fig. 17.3 (a) Bars 1–2 of the third movement from Piano Sonata no. 30 in E major, op. 109, by Beethoven. One occurrence of a six-note pattern is highlighted in red and labelled H_1. Taken together, the red and blue notes form a fifteen-note pattern that occurs inexactly in (b), which shows bars 31–37 of the same movement. In (b), one inexact occurrence can be seen in bars 33–34, and a second inexact occurrence in bars 35–36, with the same colour scheme as in (a) being maintained. (c) Bars 20–22 of the third movement from Piano Sonata no. 7 in D major, op. 10, no. 3 by Beethoven. An inexact occurrence of the six-note pattern from Fig. 17.3(a) is highlighted in red and labelled H_2

to the x-value of some point, and a numeric pitch value (e.g., MIDI note number) that might be assigned to the y-value of the same point, to give $\mathbf{d} = (x,y)$. (Using two dimensions is typical, but more are admissible, and later in the chapter we represent chord labels as points rather than notes.)

In a point-set representation of a given piece of music, there may be a collection of points P_1 that are perceived as similar to some other collection of points P_2, heard either elsewhere in the same piece or in another piece. In general, there could be m so-called *pattern occurrences* $P_1, P_2, \ldots, P_m$ across a corpus of pieces. Sometimes it is convenient to group these together into an *occurrence set*, denoted $\mathcal{P} = \{P_1, P_2, \ldots, P_m\}$. The term *pattern* is used rather loosely to refer to a member $P_i \in \mathcal{P}$, normally the member that is most typical of the occurrence set (often but not always the first occurrence, $P_i = P_1$).

17.3.1 Calculating the Distinctiveness of a Pattern

Rather than seeing viewpoint and geometric approaches to pattern discovery as two opposing camps, this chapter seeks to unify the methods to some extent, by developing geometric equivalents of the viewpoint technique for measuring pattern distinctiveness in inter-opus scenarios (Conklin, 2010). This technique is based on the concept of likelihood ratio. In statistics, the likelihood ratio test gives the best chance of occurrence of an observation under some null hypothesis, divided by its best chance of occurrence overall. Common uses include testing goodness of fit of observed data to some hypothesized underlying distribution (Pielou and Foster, 1962), and testing dependencies between variables such as crime and drinking (Pearson, 1909). In viewpoint pattern discovery, the likelihood ratio appears in various guises, e.g., for estimating the interest of an observed pattern in some corpus (Conklin and Bergeron, 2008). Conklin (2010) uses another likelihood ratio to measure the distinctiveness of an observed pattern P for one corpus of pieces Θ versus another *anticorpus* of pieces Θ', written

$$d(P, \Theta, \Theta') = p(P|\Theta)/p(P|\Theta') \, . \qquad (17.1)$$

In these settings, the statistics are based on either piece counts (the number of pieces in which the pattern occurs (Conklin, 2010)) or a zero-order model (Conklin and Bergeron, 2008). Piece counts can be problematic if a pattern occurs note for note (or feature for feature) in some pieces but only partially in others. Only counting exact occurrences leads to underestimation of the probability, whereas counting inexact occurrences on a par with exact occurrences leads to overestimation. In a zero-order model, a pattern is defined as a sequence of musical features, and its probability is proportional to the product of the relative frequencies of occurrence of the constituent features. Temporal order of features does not impact on the calculated probabilities in a zero-order model, which is a shortcoming (i.e., because B4, G4, C5 might be more probable in a certain style than the same pitches in different order, C5, B4, G4, say). We refer to this as the *zero-order problem* of the viewpoint method. An extension of these likelihood calculations to polyphonic textures has been proposed (Collins et al., 2011), but it too assumed a zero-order model.

To develop a geometric equivalent of the distinctiveness measure, it is necessary to calculate the empirical probability of a given pattern occurrence in a piece or across multiple pieces, $p(P|\Theta)$, preferably using a model that is: (1) less reliant on the sequential integrity of pattern occurrences and so addresses the interpolation problem, which is important since variation is such a central concept in music; (2) more realistic than one based on zero-order distributions, and so addresses the zero-order problem. Central to this development will be the technique of symbolic fingerprinting, which enables us to estimate the likelihood of occurrence of a pattern across one or more pieces of polyphonic music.

17.3.2 Symbolic Fingerprinting

Symbolic fingerprinting consists of calculating, storing, and retrieving differences between local pairs or triples from a point-set representation of a piece or pieces, denoted D (Arzt et al., 2012). It enables us to take some point-set query Q and find occurrences in D of Q that have been transposed, time-shifted and time-scaled. For readers familiar with music theory, the definition of a fingerprint will be reminiscent of Lewin's (1987, Chapter 4) generalized interval systems. Independently of Lewin's work, Wang and Smith (2012) developed an efficient fingerprinting storage and retrieval method that enabled automatic, fast recognition of music audio, known as Shazam.

In the general case, we have a piece of music represented as an ordered point set $D = \langle \mathbf{d}_1, \mathbf{d}_2, \ldots, \mathbf{d}_n \rangle$.[3] To begin with in this chapter, each point $\mathbf{d}_i \in D$ represents a note from the piece, and is a pair $\mathbf{d}_i = (x_i, y_i)$ consisting of an ontime x_i and a morphetic pitch y_i (MPN, see Meredith, 2006). Ontime is the time in the piece in quarter note beats, counting from zero for bar 1 beat 1, and MPN is the height of the note on the staff, with C4 = 'middle C' = 60, C♯4 = 60, D♭4 = D4 = D♯4 = 61, etc.[4] Other choices about how to represent time and pitch, and how many dimensions to include in one point set, have been explored (Collins et al., 2010), but for the sake of simplicity we will use ontime and MPN at present. As an example, Beethoven's op. 109, mvt. 3 (see Fig. 17.3(a)) would be represented as

$$
\begin{aligned}
D = \langle & (0,48), (0,59), (0,64), (1,50), (1,59), (1,62), \ldots, \\
& (192,48), (192\tfrac{1}{4},59), (192\tfrac{1}{2},64), (192\tfrac{3}{4},55), \\
& (193,57), (193\tfrac{1}{4},62), (193\tfrac{1}{2},59), (193\tfrac{3}{4},50), \\
& (194,51), (194\tfrac{1}{4},60), (194\tfrac{1}{2},63), (194\tfrac{3}{4},58), \\
& (195,59), (195\tfrac{1}{4},61), (195\tfrac{1}{2},56), (195\tfrac{3}{4},52), \\
& (196,53), (196\tfrac{1}{4},55), (196\tfrac{1}{2},59), (196\tfrac{3}{4},60), \\
& (197,61), (197\tfrac{1}{4},59), (197\tfrac{1}{2},56), (197\tfrac{3}{4},54), \ldots, \\
& (891,59), (891,62), (891,64) \rangle \, .
\end{aligned}
\tag{17.2}
$$

The first chord, consisting of pitches E2, B3, and G♯4, has ontime 0, and it can be verified that the MPNs of these pitches are 48, 59, and 64 respectively. The next excerpt of the piece given in (17.2) corresponds to bars 33–34 (the beginning of variation II, Fig. 17.3(b)). The beginning of bar 33 has ontime 192 (although calculating this is nontrivial, given some intervening repeat marks and first/second

---

[3] The order is called *lexicographic order*. It is most easily explained in relation to (17.2). For instance, $(0,64)$ is lexicographically less than $(1,50)$ because $0 < 1$. If there is a tie in the x-dimension, it is broken by the values in the y-dimension, which is why $(1,50)$ is lexicographically less than $(1,59)$. And so on.

[4] Note that Meredith (2006) defines the morphetic pitch of $\ldots$, A♭0, A0, A♯0, $\ldots$ to be 0, so that middle C has a morphetic pitch of 23.

time bars), and its first note is E2, or MPN 48. The movement ends on bar 293, beat 3, ontime 891, with a five-note chord, of which the top three notes are B3, E4, and G♯4, or MPNs 59, 62, and 64 respectively.

In what follows, we want to be able to perform matching that is invariant to time-shifting, time-scaling, transposition, or any combination of these operations, so we will use triples of points $(\mathbf{d}_i, \mathbf{d}_j, \mathbf{d}_k)$ (where i, j and k are the indices of the points in the lexicographically ordered dataset) such that:

1. the points are local, obeying $i < j < k$, with $j - i < 5$ and $k - j < 5$;
2. the ontimes are not simultaneous, i.e., $x_i \neq x_j$ and $x_j \neq x_k$;
3. the ontimes are proximal, with $x_j - x_i < 10$ and $x_k - x_j < 10$; and
4. the MPNs are proximal, with $y_j - y_i < 24$ and $y_k - y_j < 24$.

These criteria were selected based on previous work (Arzt et al., 2012). A *fingerprint*—that is, the information stored for each $(\mathbf{d}_i, \mathbf{d}_j, \mathbf{d}_k)$—is a quadruple, ⟨token, piece ID, ontime, ontime difference⟩, where each token is itself a triple:

$$\left\langle \underbrace{\left\langle y_j - y_i, \; y_k - y_j, \; \frac{x_k - x_j}{x_j - x_i} \right\rangle}_{\text{token}}, \; \underbrace{\text{“beethoven123”}}_{\text{piece ID}}, \; \underbrace{x_i}_{\text{ontime}}, \; \underbrace{x_j - x_i}_{\text{ontime difference}} \right\rangle. \quad (17.3)$$

For the three underlined points in (17.2), which form a legal triple according to criteria 1–4 above, the fingerprint is

$$\left\langle \left\langle 62 - 64, \; 60 - 62, \; \frac{194\frac{1}{4} - 193\frac{1}{4}}{193\frac{1}{4} - 192\frac{1}{2}} \right\rangle, \; \text{“beetOp109Mvt3”}, \; 192\frac{1}{2}, \; 193\frac{1}{4} - 192\frac{1}{2} \right\rangle$$

$$= \left\langle \left\langle -2, \; -2, \; 1\frac{1}{3} \right\rangle, \; \text{“beetOp109Mvt3”}, \; 192\frac{1}{2}, \; \frac{3}{4} \right\rangle. \quad (17.4)$$

For each legal triple $(\mathbf{d}_i, \mathbf{d}_j, \mathbf{d}_k)$ in the point set D, a fingerprint is calculated and stored in a so-called *fingerprint database*.

Given a query point set Q, which represents some known theme or otherwise-interesting excerpt (from the same piece or from another piece), the fingerprint database calculated over the point set D can be used to find ontimes $t_1, t_2, \ldots, t_m$ in D at which events similar to the query Q occur. First, it is necessary to calculate the fingerprints of triples $(\mathbf{q}_i, \mathbf{q}_j, \mathbf{q}_k)$ from Q, in an analogous fashion to the calculations over D. Then tokens from the query are matched against tokens from the database. When there is a match, the ontime u_l of the matching fingerprint in the database and the ontime v_l of the matching fingerprint in the query are recorded as a pair (u_l, v_l). These ontimes are readily accessible, being stored as the third element in a fingerprint (see (17.3)).

Let the set of ontime pairs of matching tokens be denoted

$$U(Q, D, \alpha) = \{(u_1, v_1), (u_2, v_2), \ldots, (u_L, v_L)\}, \quad (17.5)$$

where α is a parameter to be described in due course.

If the piece contains a transformation of the query Q, then an arbitrary point $\mathbf{q} \in Q$ will be expressible as $\mathbf{q} = (ax_i + b, y_i + c)$ for some $(x_i, y_i) \in D$, where a is the time scale, b is the time shift, and c is the transposition. Substituting this expression for some triple $(\mathbf{q}_i, \mathbf{q}_j, \mathbf{q}_k)$ from Q in (17.3), these operations will cancel, and so the query and database tokens will match:

$$\left\langle (y_j+c)-(y_i+c), \ (y_k+c)-(y_j+c), \ \frac{(ax_k+b)-(ax_j+b)}{(ax_j+b)-(ax_i+b)} \right\rangle$$

$$= \left\langle y_j - y_i, \ y_k - y_j, \ \frac{x_k - x_j}{x_j - x_i} \right\rangle. \tag{17.6}$$

While being able to match queries to instances that have undergone such transformations is useful, composers often write more complex variations of themes into their works than can be expressed in terms of the transformations considered above (i.e., time-shifting, time-scaling and transposition). As an example of more complex variation, let us take the opening two bars of Beethoven's op. 109, mvt. 3, as a query (Fig. 17.3(a)), the transition into the complex variation shown in Fig. 17.3(b) as database, and see what would be required to match the two via symbolic fingerprinting. The query is

$$Q = \langle (0,48), (0,59), (0,64), (1,50), (1,59), (1,62), (2,51), (2,60), (2\tfrac{1}{2},63),$$

$$(3,52), (3,56), (3,61), (4,53), (4,56), (4,58), (4,59), (5,54) \rangle. \tag{17.7}$$

Taking the underlined triple in (17.7), which corresponds to the underlined triple in (17.2), the fingerprint token would be $\langle -2, -2, 1 \rangle$. Comparing with $\langle -2, -2, 1\tfrac{1}{3} \rangle$ from (17.4), the disparity between the two is in the final element—the time difference ratio of 1 in the query token versus $1\tfrac{1}{3}$ in the database token. If however, we permit some percentage error, $\alpha = 40\%$ say, when matching tokens' time difference ratios, then the query token $\langle -2, -2, 1 \rangle$ would be considered a match to the database token $\langle -2, -2, 1\tfrac{1}{3} \rangle$, and the corresponding ontimes would be included in U from (17.5).

Plotted in Fig. 17.4(a) are the ontime pairs of matching tokens $U(Q, D, \alpha = 40)$ for the query Q from (17.7) and the point set D from (17.2). As there are coincident points, we use marker size to indicate the relative number of matches at a particular coordinate, with larger circles indicating more matches. The presence of approximately diagonal lines in this plot means that there are multiple subsequent matches between query and database (i.e., that there is a more or less exact occurrence of the query in the database). Two such occurrences are indicated by the two thick dashed transparent lines in Fig. 17.4(a). To summarize this plot properly, affine transformations are applied to the points (indicated by the arrows and straight vertical lines) and they are binned to give the histogram shown in Fig. 17.4(b). The histogram shows two peaks—one at ontime 192 (or bar 33) and another around ontime 198 (bar 35). There is an occurrence of the theme from Fig. 17.3(a) at each of these times,

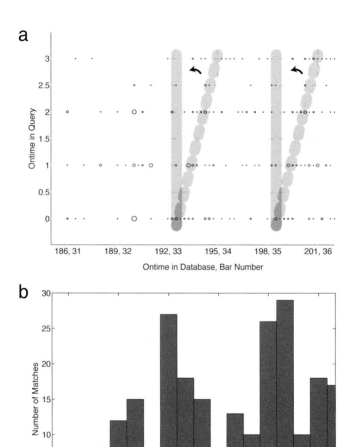

Fig. 17.4 (a) Plot of time stamps for matching query and database fingerprint tokens. Size of circular markers indicates the relative number of matches coincident at a particular point, with larger circles meaning more matches. Two occurrences of the query in the database are indicated by the two thick dashed transparent lines. The arrows and straight vertical lines allude to an affine transformation. (b) Fingerprint histogram indicating the similarity of the piece to the query as a function of time. This plot results from application of an affine transformation to the points in Fig. 17.4(a), followed by binning the transformed points to give the histogram. The rotation in the affine transformation is influenced by the value of the ontime difference, stored as the final element of a fingerprint (see (17.3), and, for more details, Arzt et al. (2012))

subject to quite complex variation as shown in Fig. 17.3(b) (where red and blue highlighting indicates likely contributors to the two peaks in the histogram).

In summary, symbolic fingerprinting can be used to identify occurrences of a given query in a point-set representation of a piece. The stronger the resemblance to the query at a particular time in the piece, the larger the number of matches in a fingerprint histogram such as Fig. 17.4(b). In what follows, we refer to the fingerprint histogram as $f(t)$, and use it as a measure of the similarity of the piece to the query as a function of time t. For the purposes of comparing different queries and different pieces, it is also convenient to normalize the fingerprint histogram so that the y-axis is in the range $[0, 1]$. For the purposes of analysing occurrences of a query across multiple pieces, we will also concatenate point sets $D_1, D_2, \ldots, D_N$ representing N pieces into one point set D. That is, we set $D = D_1$ and then for $i = 2, \ldots, N$, the set D_i is shifted to begin shortly after D_{i-1} ends, and then appended to D. To distinguish between the fingerprint histogram for a query calculated over some collection of pieces $\Theta = \{D_1, D_2, \ldots, D_N\}$ as opposed to some other collection $\Theta' = \{D'_1, D'_2, \ldots, D'_{N'}\}$, we will write $f_\Theta(t)$ and $f_{\Theta'}(t)$ respectively.

Among the advantages of symbolic fingerprinting are its speed and robustness (Arzt et al., 2012). As demonstrated, it is capable of identifying query occurrences that have had time shift, time scale, and transposition applied, as well as more complex transformations. Symbolic fingerprinting is not necessarily a definitive solution to the problem of modelling perceived music similarity, however. For example, based on the ontime-MPN representation, it is unlikely that the α-parameter could be increased sufficiently to identify Lutes' pattern occurrences without also returning many false positive matches. The concision of the fingerprint histogram can also be a double-edged sword. Especially with the α-parameter increased, sometimes there is a peak in the histogram (say, at ontime 190 in Fig. 17.4(b)), but, when referring back to the music, one is hard-pressed to justify the peak's existence.

17.3.3 Calculating the Probability of a Pattern Occurrence

To develop geometric equivalents of the distinctiveness measure, given in (17.1), we must be able to calculate the empirical probability of a given pattern occurrence in a piece or across multiple pieces. Symbolic fingerprinting, described in the previous section, will be central to this development. If we calculate fingerprints for a short pattern occurrence, as well as fingerprints for a whole piece or collection of pieces, it is possible to construct a histogram $f_\Theta(t)$ measuring the similarity of the pattern occurrence to the piece(s) as a function of time. Strong matches appear as large global peaks in the histogram, whereas partial/weaker matches appear as smaller local peaks or are indistinguishable from chance matches. Examples of such histograms are given in Fig. 17.5. The dashed curve shows $f_\Theta(t)$ for the query highlighted in red in Fig. 17.3(a). Intuitively, this is quite a specific query, with a relatively low likelihood of occurrence across Beethoven's piano sonatas (apart perhaps from its host piece, op. 109, mvt. 3). In accordance with this intuition, $f_\Theta(t)$ for this *specific* query is

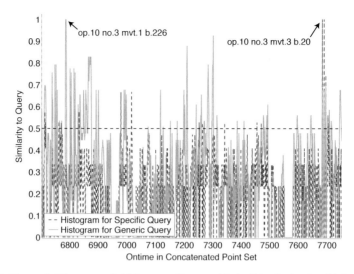

Fig. 17.5 Fingerprint histograms $f_\Theta(t)$ for a specific query (*dashed blue line*) and $g_\Theta(t)$ for a generic query (*solid green line*). The *x*-axis, time in the concatenated point set (database of Beethoven piano sonatas), extends from the end of op. 10, no. 3, mvt. 1, continuing through op. 10, no. 3, mvt. 2, and ending shortly after the beginning of op. 10, no. 3, mvt. 3

generally *below* the indicated similarity level of .5 in Fig. 17.5. For the sake of clarity, the time axis in Fig. 17.5 is restricted to a subset of our database, beginning towards the end of op. 10, no. 3, mvt. 1, continuing through op. 10, no. 3, mvt. 2, and ending shortly after the beginning of op. 10, no. 3, mvt. 3. Beyond op. 109, mvt. 3, two strong occurrences of the specific query stand out, in bars 18 and 20 of op. 10, no. 3, mvt. 3 (see arrow on the right of Fig. 17.5 and Fig. 17.3(c)).

The solid green curve, $g_\Theta(t)$, in Fig. 17.5 is the fingerprint histogram for a query consisting of a seven-note descending scale. Intuitively, this is quite a generic query, with a relatively high likelihood of occurrence across Beethoven's piano sonatas. That is, whilst listening to or studying Beethoven's piano sonatas, we would not be particularly surprised if a descending scale or scale fragment appeared. In accordance with this intuition, $g_\Theta(t)$ for the *generic* query in Fig. 17.5 is most often *above* $f_\Theta(t)$ for the specific query, and also quite often above the indicated similarity level of .5. A descending scale in the recapitulation of op. 10, no. 3, mvt. 1, is particularly noticeable (see arrow on the left of Fig. 17.5), but multiple other descending scale figures occur across these movements. Even though the generic query contains more notes than the specific query, the former appears to have a higher likelihood of occurrence than the latter.

In this chapter we use the superlevel set of a fingerprint histogram $f_\Theta(t)$ to formalize the intuitive sense of a query point set's likelihood. The superlevel set of $f_\Theta(t)$ is defined by

$$L_c^+(f_\Theta) = \{t \mid f_\Theta(t) \geq c\}, \tag{17.8}$$

which is the set of timepoints for which the histogram is equal to or exceeds some threshold similarity level c. The cardinality of the superlevel set (the number of timepoints it contains), divided by the total number of timepoint bins in the histogram, denoted $|L_0^+(f_\Theta)|$, can be used as a proxy for the empirical probability of observing the pattern occurrence across some piece or pieces.

Returning to the example queries and histogram excerpts shown in Fig. 17.5, the superlevel set (with parameter $c = .5$) for the specific query contains 638 timepoints, out of a total 13,003 timepoint bins. Thus the specific query has an empirical likelihood of $|L_{.5}^+(f_\Theta)|/|L_0^+(f_\Theta)| = 638/13,3003 = .049$. Meanwhile, the more generic query has an empirical likelihood of $|L_{.5}^+(g_\Theta)|/|L_0^+(g_\Theta)| = 1,345/13,003 = .103$. Thus the empirical likelihoods confirm our intuition: the highlighted note collection in Fig. 17.3(a) is less likely to occur in Beethoven's piano sonatas than a seven-note descending scale.

But what about *distinctiveness*? To bring this section to its natural conclusion, we turn back to Sect. 17.3.1 on distinctiveness, and substitute the above likelihoods into (17.1), writing

$$p(P|\Theta) = |L_c^+(f_\Theta)|/|L_0^+(f_\Theta)|\,, \tag{17.9}$$

where P is a point set representing some query, Θ is a collection of pieces in point-set representations, and $f_\Theta(t)$ is the fingerprint histogram of P across Θ. To measure how distinctive some pattern P is of some corpus Θ, relative to some anticorpus Θ', it follows that we can use

$$d(P,\Theta,\Theta') = \frac{|L_c^+(f_\Theta)| \times |L_0^+(f_{\Theta'})|}{|L_c^+(f_{\Theta'})| \times |L_0^+(f_\Theta)|}\,. \tag{17.10}$$

To avoid division by zero, we set $|L_c^+(f_{\Theta'})|$ equal to a minimum of 1.[5] Completing the worked example, we can take Chopin's piano sonatas as an anticorpus, and calculate the distinctiveness of the specific and generic patterns for Beethoven's piano sonatas, relative to Chopin's.[6] The specific query has empirical likelihood of .075 in Chopin's piano sonatas, and so the distinctiveness of the specific query for Beethoven's piano sonatas relative to Chopin's is $.049/.075 = .660$. The generic query has empirical likelihood of .117 in Chopin's piano sonatas, and so the distinctiveness of the generic query is $.103/.117 = .887$. Importantly, this example demonstrates that specificity and distinctiveness are not the same thing. According to intuition, the specific query has lower probability of occurrence in Beethoven's piano sonatas than the generic query. The specific query does not appear to be more distinctive of Beethoven's sonatas than the generic descending scale, however. This is because the specific query has a relatively high likelihood of occurrence in Chopin's compared to Beethoven's sonatas (cf. .075 and .049), and so its distinctiveness is low. Distinctiveness values

[5] Division by zero arises if $L_c^+(f_{\Theta'})$ is empty, either because c is too high and/or $f_{\Theta'}$ too low (Conklin, 2010).

[6] Chopin's sonatas are: op. 4, mvts. 1–4; op. 35, mvts. 1–4; and op. 58, mvts. 1–4. It is worth noting that even though there are allusions to Beethoven in these works (cf. Chopin, op. 35, mvt. 1, and Beethoven, op. 111, mvt. 1), the focus in this chapter is Beethoven–Beethoven resemblances, not Chopin–Beethoven resemblances.

greater than one indicate that a pattern is more probable in the corpus than the anticorpus, and so more distinctive of the corpus.

Choice of anticorpus will affect the results, so, for the first time here, we consider the impact of this choice by reporting results for a second anticorpus also: Chopin's mazurkas.[7] These corpora (21 Beethoven sonata movements, twelve Chopin sonata movements, 49 Chopin mazurkas) may appear to differ in size, but they are comparable (to within 1,000) in terms of number of notes.

17.4 Experimental Results

Although we were not necessarily expecting to detect instances of literal borrowing across Beethoven's piano sonatas (because they are not already known, suggesting perhaps there are none), it is prudent to at least check. Experiment 1 was designed primarily with this aim in mind. Experiment 2 increased the temporal inexactness parameter α to investigate less literal resemblances, and Experiments 3 and 4 were similar to 1 and 2 but for melodic rather than polyphonic queries. The last two experiments apply a pattern discovery algorithm SIARCT-CFP (Collins et al., 2013) to pairs of Beethoven sonata movements to find—in an unsupervised manner—inter-opus resemblances between note collections (Experiment 5) and chord sequences (Experiment 6). Apart from discovering resemblances, the experimental results also shed some light on: (1) patterns that are distinctive of Beethoven's piano sonatas compared to Chopin's; (2) whether thematic material is inherently more *distinctive* than excerpts drawn from elsewhere in a movement; and (3) the impact of anticorpus choice.

17.4.1 Experiment 1

In Experiment 1, we defined twelve-note queries using the full polyphonic representation of each movement, beginning at the start of each bar. This method of query definition is not exhaustive: if there are more than twelve notes in a given bar, then some content will be overlooked. Nor is the method always musically appropriate: if some phrase begins with an upbeat and/or contains fewer/more than twelve notes, then this will not be segmented appropriately. Taking a fixed number of notes is preferable, however, to taking a fixed time window and the (variable) number of notes appearing in this window, because the latter leads to variable-length queries, which could introduce biases in similarity calculations. In any case, our fixed-length queries are only intended to identify the *kernel* of some inter-piece resemblance, and then we can review the excerpts in question, to hear/see whether the resemblance extends

---

[7] Chopin's mazurkas include the following: op. 6, nos. 1–4; op. 6, nos. 1–4; op. 7, nos. 1–5; op. 17, nos. 1–4; op. 24, nos. 1–4; op. 30, nos. 1–4; op. 33, nos. 1–4; op. 41, nos. 1–4; op. 50 nos. 1–3; op. 56, nos. 1–3; op. 59, nos. 1–3; op. 63, nos. 1–3; op. 67, nos. 1–4; and op. 68 nos. 1–4.

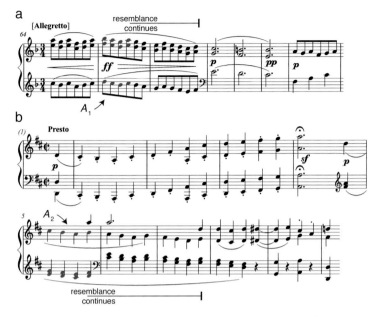

Fig. 17.6 (a) Bars 64–70 of the third movement from Piano Sonata in F minor, op. 2, no. 1, by Beethoven. One occurrence of a twelve-note pattern is highlighted. (b) Bars 1–10.1 with upbeat of the first movement from Piano Sonata in D major, op. 10, no. 3, by Beethoven. One occurrence of a twelve-note pattern is highlighted, indicating a second occurrence of the pattern from Fig. 17.6(a)

over a longer time period, and to consider other contextual factors that need to be taken into account. In inter-opus pattern discovery in general, rarely will it suffice to present the algorithm output and say nothing more. Reviewing and interpreting the excerpts in question are vital steps towards producing a musical analysis.

Each twelve-note query was subject to fingerprinting analysis against the database of Beethoven piano sonata movements (as well as two anticorpora— Chopin's piano sonatas and mazurkas). Taking the fingerprint histogram $f(t)$ calculated for a query over the Beethoven piano sonata movements (see Sect. 17.3.2), we could determine the location of the strongest match to the query (other than in the piece where the query originated), as well as the strength of this strongest match. Queries that provide strong matches to segments from *other* movements may indicate instances of literal borrowing. The strongest-matching query to a segment from another movement is indicated in Fig. 17.6, and some summary statistics for the pattern, labelled A_1 and A_2, are given in Table 17.1.

As alluded to above, it so happens that A_1 and A_2 comprise the kernel of resemblance that extends over a longer time period: bars 65–66 of Fig. 17.6(a) appear in bars 5–7 of Fig. 17.6(b). The query alone is not particularly distinctive, consisting of a first-inversion triad played at successively lower scale steps twice and then one scale step higher. It is more interesting, however, that the resemblance between the two pieces extends over two bars in the first instance and three bars (because of

Table 17.1 Distinctiveness of Beethoven patterns relative to two anticorpora

Figure	Label	Anticorpus of Chopin Sonatas	Anticorpus of Chopin Mazurkas	Query Definition, Time Tolerance $\alpha =$
17.6(a), 17.6(b)	A_1, A_2	0.430	1.376	Polyphonic segment, 15%
17.7(a), 17.7(b)	B_1, B_2	0.476	1.188	Polyphonic segment, 15%
17.7(c), 17.7(d)	C_1, C_2	0.536	3.557	Polyphonic segment, 15%
17.8(a), (b)	E_1, E_2	0.799	1.870	Polyphonic segment, 40%
17.8(c), (d)	F_1, F_2	0.660	0.957	Polyphonic segment, 40%
17.9(a), 17.9(b)	G_1, G_2	12.880	2.084	Melodic segment, 15%
17.3(a), 17.3(c)	H_1, H_2	0.660	1.953	Melodic segment, 15%
17.10(a), 17.10(b)	I_1, I_2	2.036	4.305	Melodic segment, 40%
17.9(a), 17.9(c)	J_1, J_2	5.400	8.663	Note discovery, 15%
17.11(a), 17.11(b)	K_1, K_2	0.193	44.101	Note discovery, 15%
17.2(a), 17.11(c)	M_1, M_2	41.092	78.121	Note discovery, 15%
17.12(c), 17.12(d)	N_1, N_2	1.515	2.544	Chord discovery, 15%

the differing time signature) in the second instance. Of what does this extended resemblance consist? The extension consists of A_1 heard twice more at successively lower scale steps. In op. 2, mvt. 3, this causes a strong hemiola effect, with six beats of music being perceived as three groups of two (as opposed to the prevailing two groups of three). Beethoven arrives on chord V in bar 67, V^7 in bar 69, and then the theme from the trio returns with chord I in bar 70 (Barlow and Morgenstern, 1948). The context of the borrowing in op. 10, no. 3, mvt. 1, is different. According to Barlow and Morgenstern (1948), the theme of op. 10, no. 3, mvt. 1, covers bars 1–4.1 with upbeat. Bar 5 with upbeat is likely heard as a variation of the theme's opening, with the melody D–C♯–B–A in both cases. Therefore, the instance of borrowing in op. 10, no. 3, mvt. 1, has a different function from that in op. 2, no. 1, mvt. 3. In op. 10, no. 3, mvt. 1, it is a variation of the theme, followed by a perfect cadence in bars 9.2–10.1. Taken as a whole, bars 5–10.1 with upbeat act as a consequent to the antecedent of bars 1–4.1 with upbeat, with bars 1–4.1 concluding on scale degree $\hat{5}$.

As we did not expect to find instances of inter-piece resemblance stretching 2–3 bars, the result shown in Fig. 17.6 is surprising and, to our knowledge, novel. Other results from the first experiment did not extend to create a longer period of resemblance, but two more are included in Table 17.1 (labelled B and C) and given in Fig. 17.7. The third movement of op. 2, no. 1, features in all three patterns A, B, C, suggesting it contains a stock of patterns—albeit not particularly distinctive according to Table 17.1—that appear in later compositions.

Fig. 17.7 (a) Bars 1–5 with upbeat of the third movement from Piano Sonata no. 1, in F minor, op. 2, no. 1, by Beethoven. One occurrence of a twelve-note pattern is highlighted. (b) Bars 8–10 of the first movement from Piano Sonata no. 30 in E major, op. 109, by Beethoven. One occurrence of an eleven-note pattern is highlighted, indicating a partial second occurrence of the pattern from Fig. 17.7(a). (c) Bars 24–28.1 of the third movement from Piano Sonata no. 1 in F minor, op. 2, no. 1, by Beethoven. One occurrence of a twelve-note pattern is highlighted. (d) Bars 15–16 of the fourth movement from Piano Sonata no. 7 in D major, op. 10, no. 3, by Beethoven. One occurrence of a twelve-note pattern is highlighted, indicating a second occurrence of the pattern from Fig. 17.7(c)

17.4.2 Experiment 2

The previous experiment aimed towards identifying instances of literal repetition or borrowing between movements, so in that experiment it was sensible to keep the temporal inexactness parameter α quite low ($\alpha = 15\%$). As symbolic fingerprinting can be used to identify non-rigid variations such as between Fig. 17.3(a) and (b), however, in the second experiment, α is increased to 40% to enable such discoveries. Everything else from Experiment 1 is kept the same.

Many of the patterns discovered in Experiment 2 were similar to or the same as those discovered in Experiment 1. But beyond these, two examples of the inexact inter-opus patterns discovered in Experiment 2 are given in Fig. 17.8. Pattern occurrence E_1 in Fig. 17.8(a) consists of a rising major triad, F3, A3, C4, with each note played

Fig. 17.8 (a) Bars 1–5 with upbeat of the third movement from Piano Sonata no. 6 in F major, op. 10, no. 2, by Beethoven. One occurrence of a twelve-note pattern is highlighted. (b) Bars 172–173 of the third movement from Piano Sonata no. 30 in E major, op. 109, by Beethoven. One inexact occurrence of the pattern from Fig. 17.8(a) is highlighted. (c) Bars 47–50 of the second movement from Piano Sonata no. 6 in F major, op. 10, no. 2, by Beethoven. One occurrence of a twelve-note pattern is highlighted. (d) Bars 1–4 with upbeat of the third movement from Piano Sonata no. 12 in A♭ major, op. 26, by Beethoven. One inexact occurrence of the pattern from Fig. 17.8(c) is highlighted

three times following a lower member of the triad. In occurrence E_2 (Fig. 17.8(b)), the three notes are D♯5, F♯5, A5, with each note played twice, and on this occasion they form the upper three notes of a dominant seventh chord that has B1 in the bass. There are fewer notes in E_2 than in E_1, and the time difference ratios between triples of notes in each occurrence are not always the same, but with $\alpha = 40\%$ the two occurrences bear sufficient resemblance to cause a local maximum in the fingerprint histogram. The same observation applies to pattern occurrences F_1 (Fig. 17.8(c)) and F_2 (Fig. 17.8(d)). This pattern consists of a chordal progression, with each occurrence having very similar voice-leading. The progression is I, I, Vb in Fig. 17.8(c), and i, i, V^7b in Fig. 17.8(d).

Fig. 17.9 (a) Bars 122–137.1 of the first movement from Piano Sonata no. 7 in D major, op. 10, no. 3, by Beethoven. One occurrence of a six-note pattern is highlighted in red. A different nineteen-note pattern is highlighted in blue. (b) Bars 43–44 of the second movement from Piano Sonata no. 7 in D major, op. 10, no. 3, by Beethoven. One inexact occurrence of the pattern from Fig. 17.9(a) is highlighted. (c) Bars 54–57.2 of the first movement from Piano Sonata no. 1 in F minor, op. 2, no. 1, by Beethoven. A second occurrence of the nineteen-note pattern from Fig. 17.9(a) is highlighted

17.4.3 Experiment 3

Since Handel sometimes borrowed melodies rather than full textures (see Sect. 17.1), it is sensible to make the same checks for Beethoven. Accordingly, Experiment 3 consisted of a melodic version of Experiment 1. We defined six-note queries using the highest-sounding notes in the right hand, beginning at the start of each bar. Everything else from Experiment 1 is kept the same.

The pattern H_1 from Fig. 17.3(a), recurring as H_2 in Fig. 17.3(c), is among the results of this experiment. In op. 109, mvt. 3, H_1 is the opening of a theme and variations. In op. 10, no. 3, mvt. 3, H_2 is imitative, passing between left and right hands at the beginning of the second section of the minuet. According to Table 17.1, however, pattern H_1 is not particularly distinctive of Beethoven's sonatas ($d = .660$) compared, say, to pattern occurrences G_1 and G_2 from Figs. 17.9(a) and (b), respectively ($d = 12.880$). The leap of six scale steps E3 to D4 in G_1 is the reason for this pattern's high distinctiveness. In op. 10, no. 3, mvt. 1, the first three notes of G_1 belong to a lower-octave repetition of the development's opening (see bar 125 with upbeat of Fig. 17.9(a)). This is the opening theme beginning on scale degree $\hat{5}$ instead of the original $\hat{1}$ (see Fig. 17.6(b)). The last three notes of H_1 belong to a minor statement of the opening theme, now beginning again on $\hat{1}$. Beethoven reuses these three-note scale fragments separated by a leap of six scale steps in the second movement of the same piece (Fig. 17.9(b)), just before the return of the main theme.

Fig. 17.10 (a) Bars 152–157 of the first movement from Piano Sonata no. 12 in A♭ major, op. 26, by Beethoven. One occurrence of a six-note pattern is highlighted. (b) Bars 126–128 of the third movement from Piano Sonata no. 30 in E major, op. 109, by Beethoven. One inexact occurrence of the pattern from Fig. 17.10(a) is highlighted

17.4.4 Experiment 4

Just as with Experiment 2, where we increased the temporal inexactness parameter of Experiment 1 from $\alpha = .15$ to $\alpha = .4$ to enable discovery of more complex variations on a pattern, so we did for melodic queries in Experiment 4. Many of the patterns discovered in Experiment 4 were similar to those discovered in Experiment 3, but an example of an additional pattern discovered in Experiment 4 is given as I_1 and I_2 in Fig. 17.10. Just as G_1 (Fig. 17.9(a)) was distinctive due to a large leap, so I_1 contains two compound sevenths. The inexactness of the relationships between notes belonging to I_1 and I_2, added to the large number of interpolated notes in I_2, make the resemblance between these passages difficult to discern. This was often the case for results from Experiment 4, inviting the observation that $\alpha = 40\%$ may be too high for melody-only queries.

Coming to the end of our experiments involving fixed-length queries, we address the issue of whether thematic material is inherently more *distinctive* than excerpts drawn from elsewhere in a movement. In each of the 21 Beethoven movements selected, it is the case that the first theme as annotated by Barlow and Morgenstern (1948) begins in bar 1. Therefore, to address the issue, we can calculate the distinctiveness of the opening six-note query from each movement, and compare this value to the distinctiveness of some other six-note query selected at random from the same movement. This procedure can be simulated many times for each movement to derive a proportion ρ of the times that the distinctiveness values of themes are significantly higher than those of randomly-selected queries. If a query Q belongs to piece D_i, then it makes sense to set the corpus Θ from (17.1) to this piece, $\Theta = \{D_i\}$, and the anticorpus Θ' to all other Beethoven movements apart from this piece, $\Theta' = \{D_1, D_2, \ldots, D_{i-1}, D_{i+1}, \ldots, D_{21}\}$. Then $d(Q, \Theta, \Theta')$ indicates how distinctive the query Q is for piece D_i, relative to its prevalence in other movements.

Following this procedure for $\alpha = 15\%$ and 1,000 simulations, we found that only on 18 occasions ($\rho = 1.8\%$) was distinctiveness of themes significantly higher according to the Wilcoxon signed-rank test than distinctiveness of queries selected at random from elsewhere in the same piece. The proportion ρ was still small (i.e., always below 5%), whether using $\alpha = 40\%$, twelve-note polyphonic queries, or Chopin as the anticorpus instead of other Beethoven movements. These results suggest that Beethoven's thematic material is not more distinctive of his style—at least quantitatively—compared to excerpts drawn from elsewhere in a movement.

17.4.5 Experiment 5

In the last two experiments reported in this chapter, we move away from predefined, fixed-length queries, and toward queries generated in an unsupervised manner by running the pattern discovery algorithm SIARCT-CFP (Collins et al., 2013) on concatenated pairs of movements $D = \text{conc}(D_i, D_j)$, where $1 \leq i, j, \leq 21$. That is, for instance, when running SIARCT-CFP on a point set consisting of the concatenation

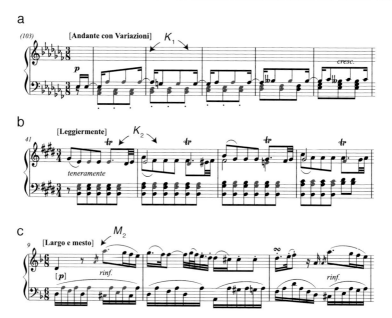

Fig. 17.11 (a) Bars 103–107 with upbeat of the first movement from Piano Sonata no. 12 in A♭ major, op. 26, by Beethoven. One occurrence of a 28-note pattern is highlighted. (b) Bars 41–44 of the third movement from Piano Sonata no. 30 in E major, op. 109, by Beethoven. A second occurrence of the pattern from Fig. 17.11(a) is highlighted. (c) Bars 9–11 of the second movement from Piano Sonata no. 7 in D major, op. 10, no. 3, by Beethoven. A second occurrence of the pattern from Fig. 17.2(a) is highlighted (in red)

of op. 10, no. 3, mvt. 1, and op. 2, no. 1, mvt. 1, the pattern occurrences labelled J_1 (Fig. 17.9(a)) and J_2 (Fig. 17.9(c)) are discovered, and we can calculate the distinctiveness of all such output patterns. Until recently, it would not have been feasible to run geometric pattern discovery algorithms across all pairs of movements from a 21-piece corpus, but Collins (2011) introduced a parallel version of SIA (Meredith et al., 2002) called SIAR, whose runtime reduces with the number of available processors.

Pattern occurrences J_1 and J_2 provide a kernel of resemblance that could point to a more pervasive Beethovian stylistic trait: both bars 133–137.1 of Fig. 17.9(a) and bars 55–57.1 of Fig. 17.9(c) consist of alternating octave eighth notes in the left hand; both consist of a global descending melodic contour in the right hand with a concluding upturn; both involve dynamic emphases at beginning and end; both excerpts appear early on in the development sections of op. 10, no. 3, mvt. 1, and op. 2, no. 1, mvt. 1 (although the latter has been heard before as the second theme). So it would be interesting to know whether further instances appear in other pieces by Beethoven, Haydn, etc. Potentially, this could be an example of a new Beethovian developmental schema.

Similar remarks about schematic potential could be made regarding K_1 (Fig. 17.11(a)) and K_2 (Fig. 17.11(b)), since both constitute chordal textures in theme and variations movements. An interesting aspect of this pattern is that while it does not appear to be distinctive of Beethoven's piano sonatas relative to Chopin's ($d = 0.193$ in Table 17.1), it is distinctive of Beethoven's sonatas relative to Chopin's mazurkas ($d = 44.092$). This trend in distinctiveness values was present across many discovered patterns (e.g., see M_1 and M_2 in Table 17.1 and Figs. 17.2(a) and 17.11(c) respectively), but it was most marked for K_1, K_2. Overall, the choice of anticorpus does not seem to create too much volatility in results: if pattern X has distinctiveness d_X for the Chopin sonata anticorpus and e_X for the Chopin mazurka anticorpus, pattern Y has distinctiveness d_Y for the Chopin sonata anticorpus and e_Y for the Chopin mazurka anticorpus, and there is some distinctiveness ordering for one of the anticorpora (e.g., $d_X < d_Y$), then apart from a couple of exceptions in Table 17.1, this ordering holds also for the other anticorpus (e.g., $e_X < e_Y$).

17.4.6 Experiment 6

The final experiment explored a new representation in the context of pattern discovery: geometric encoding of chord symbols. To create such a representation, the HarmAn algorithm (Pardo and Birmingham, 2002) was run on all pieces in our database. For given symbolic note input, HarmAn produces ontimes of chord labels, the root pitch classes, chord types, chord durations, and ratings of the confidence with which each label was assigned. It does not take into account modulations, inversions, or functional harmonic labels. Focusing on chord ontimes and root pitch classes, an example of HarmAn output is shown in Fig. 17.12(b) for the input of Fig. 17.12(a). SIARCT-CFP was used to identify collections of points that occur repeated and/or varied in the ontime-root space of Fig. 17.12(b), just as it had done in ontime-MPN space for Experiment 5.

An example of the type of harmonic pattern discovered is given in Figs. 17.12(c) and (d), where chord labels have been converted manually to Roman numerals for clarity. Both N_1 (Fig. 17.12(c)) and N_2 (Fig. 17.12(d)) begin by moving from i to V and back to i. Whereas N_2 then mimics this movement to reach the dominant minor (V, II, v), in N_1 the pattern occurrence finishes on V^7 and then cadences back on to i a bar later. Pattern discovery on a large scale in this harmonic space is still in its infancy, because robust algorithms capable of labelling chords to the standard of a human expert still do not exist (Collins, 2014).

17.5 Conclusions and Future Work

This chapter has described a computational method for discovering resemblances between excerpts from different pieces of polyphonic music, and summarized the results of this method applied to a collection of piano sonatas by Beethoven. The method combines formulae for calculating the distinctiveness of repeating patterns—

Fig. 17.12 (a) Bars 1–8.1 with upbeat of the first movement from Piano Sonata no. 1 in F♭ minor, op. 2, no. 1, by Beethoven. (b) Plot of root pitch class against ontime of chords, as estimated by the HarmAn algorithm. (c) Bars 72–77 of the first movement from Piano Sonata no. 6 in F major, op. 10, no. 2, by Beethoven. An occurrence of a six-chord pattern is highlighted below the staff. (d) Bars 18–22 of the first movement from Piano Sonata no. 30 in E major, op. 109, by Beethoven. A second occurrence of the six-chord pattern from Fig. 17.12(c) is highlighted. Chord labels were converted to Roman numerals in these plots to aid comparison

developed in the viewpoint approach to pattern discovery—with representations that apply conveniently to melodic or polyphonic (voiced or unvoiced) representations—developed in the geometric approach to pattern discovery. The combination or unification was made possible by symbolic fingerprinting, which enabled us to estimate the likelihood of occurrence of a music query across a piece or database of pieces.

Of particular interest among the results was an instance of literal resemblance between op. 2, no. 1, mvt. 3 and op. 10, no. 3, mvt. 1 (Fig. 17.6), a melodic resemblance between an andante theme in op. 109, mvt. 3 and an imitative passage in the minuet, op. 10, no. 3, mvt. 3 (Fig. 17.3), and two new candidates for schemata (Figs. 17.9 and 17.11). A quantitative analysis of the distinctiveness of Beethoven's thematic material versus material drawn from elsewhere in the same pieces found that the themes are not significantly more distinct. One should be wary of interpreting null effects, but this result is perhaps not so surprising when one considers the content of Beethoven's motivic designs. For instance, the themes in both Figs. 17.8(a) and 17.12(a) consist of rising triadic pitches followed by a descending scale fragment. Such musical building blocks have relatively high likelihood across many corpora, and so may not be distinctive of Beethoven. Based on this result, we might tentatively suggest that the apparent bias in existing analytic work toward discussing incipits and themes could be due to cognitive load (easier to remember and maintain incipits and themes than entire movements) rather than this material being particularly distinctive of a composer's style. Computational music analysis may serve to democratize intra- and inter-opus pattern discovery somewhat, giving equal consideration to less well-known passages from longer pieces, which could lead to interesting new findings.

At the beginning of the chapter, we stated that computational methods exist capable of discovering the type of melodic resemblance shown in Fig. 17.1, but that no computational method exists capable of identifying the more abstract resemblances in Fig. 17.2. As yet, therefore, music informaticians have not developed sufficiently flexible methods for identifying the types of patterns that musicologists find interesting (Burkholder, 2001; Byros, 2012; Gjerdingen, 1988, 2007; Lutes, 1974; Radcliffe, 1968; Winemiller, 1997). The method proposed and applied in the current chapter has made some progress in this regard, because it can handle melodies as well as any sort of polyphonic texture, and it addresses the interpolation and zero-order problems, which are simplifying and problematic assumptions about the nature of music made by previous approaches. If, however, the temporal inexactness parameter α of our fingerprinting method is increased to the point where occurrences of schema such as in Fig. 17.2 become detectable, then many false positive results are returned also. The method proposed in the current chapter is not a complete solution, therefore, and one idea for future work would be to query point-set representations of notes and chord labels simultaneously, to help filter out the number of false positives resulting from increases in the inexactness parameter.

Taking a step back, a more fundamental suggestion for future work is to create high-quality encodings in kern or MusicXML format, synchronized to audio recordings, of specific works that can support computational research into borrowing and distinctive pattern discovery. For instance, while there are a good number of Handel's works available in kern format, there are far fewer encodings of works by contemporaries such as Keiser, let alone encodings of human-annotated instances of borrowing between these works. If we want to rigorously evaluate methods for identifying borrowing and resemblances—so that these methods can be applied more widely and with more confidence to other music—then testing against known instances of borrowing is a sensible first step. This testing requires that digital encodings of specific works and annotations of those works exist. Synchronizing audio recordings achieves two things: first, while it may sound trivial, it makes browsing of the discovered patterns a far more enjoyable process, because the researcher can listen to a human performance while doing so, rather than, say, inspecting piano-roll plots without sound or (possibly worse for some individuals) listening to mechanical MIDI files. This is important when trying to engage musicologists with the technology. Second, if audio and symbolic representations of a piece are synchronized, and there exist expert music-theoretical annotations of the symbolic data (e.g., functional harmonic analyses, cadence locations, textural categories, occurrences of schemata, occurrences of motifs, themes, and other repetitive elements), then via the synchronization this can act as a ground truth for evaluating audio-based algorithms (in addition to symbolic-based algorithms) that attempt to produce these annotations automatically.

We would like to see more joint work between technologists and musicologists on the development of interfaces that make it possible to run and browse the output of such algorithms across corpora and for representations of interest. The results presented in this chapter suggest that our knowledge about music *can* be advanced by computational music analysis—the extent to which it *will* be advanced in coming decades depends on researchers in music informatics getting to grips with some higher-level music-theoretic concepts, and musicologists being prepared to help guide and engage with this work.

Acknowledgements We are grateful to KernScores (http://kern.ccarh.org/) for hosting high-quality symbolic music data. The musical figures in this chapter were made using MuseScore (http://musescore.org/). We are grateful to three reviewers for their comments on an earlier version of the manuscript, and to Kerstin Neubarth for additional insightful remarks.

Supplementary Material See http://www.tomcollinsresearch.net for code and data in support of the research reported in this chapter.

References

Arzt, A., Böck, S., and Widmer, G. (2012). Fast identification of piece and score position via symbolic fingerprinting. In *Proceedings of the 13th International Society for Music Information Retrieval Conference (ISMIR 2012)*, pages 433–438, Porto.

Barlow, H. and Morgenstern, S. (1948). *A Dictionary of Musical Themes*. Crown Publishers.

Burkholder, J. (2001). Borrowing. In Sadie, S. and Tyrrell, J., editors, *The New Grove Dictionary of Music and Musicians*. Macmillan, 2nd edition.

Byros, V. (2012). Meyer's anvil: Revisiting the schema concept. *Music Analysis*, 31(3):273–346.

Cambouropoulos, E. (2006). Musical parallelism and melodic segmentation. *Music Perception*, 23(3):249–267.

Caplin, W. (2013). *Analyzing Classical Form: An Approach for the Classroom*. Oxford University Press.

Collins, T. (2011). *Improved methods for pattern discovery in music, with applications in automated stylistic composition*. PhD thesis, Faculty of Mathematics, Computing and Technology, The Open University.

Collins, T. (2014). Stravinsqi/De Montfort University at the MediaEval 2014 C@merata task. In *Proceedings of the MediaEval 2014 Workshop*, Barcelona, Spain.

Collins, T., Arzt, A., Flossmann, S., and Widmer, G. (2013). SIARCT-CFP: Improving precision and the discovery of inexact musical patterns in point-set representations. In *Proceedings of the 14th International Society for Music Information Retrieval Conference (ISMIR 2014)*, pages 549–554, Curitiba, Brazil.

Collins, T., Laney, R., Willis, A., and Garthwaite, P. H. (2011). Modeling pattern importance in Chopin's mazurkas. *Music Perception*, 28(4):387–414.

Collins, T., Thurlow, J., Laney, R., Willis, A., and Garthwaite, P. (2010). A comparative evaluation of algorithms for discovering translational patterns in baroque keyboard works. In *Proceedings of the 11th International Society for Music Information Retrieval Conference (ISMIR 2010)*, pages 3–8, Utrecht, The Netherlands.

Conklin, D. (2010). Discovery of distinctive patterns in music. *Intelligent Data Analysis*, 14(5):547–554.

Conklin, D. and Bergeron, M. (2008). Feature set patterns in music. *Computer Music Journal*, 32(1):60–70.

Conklin, D. and Bergeron, M. (2010). Discovery of contrapuntal patterns. In *Proceedings of the 11th International Society for Music Information Retrieval Conference (ISMIR 2010)*, pages 201–206, Utrecht, The Netherlands.

Forth, J. C. (2012). *Cognitively-motivated geometric methods of pattern discovery and models of similarity in music*. PhD thesis, Department of Computing, Goldsmiths, University of London.

Gjerdingen, R. (1988). *A Classic Turn of Phrase: Music and the Psychology of Convention*. University of Pennsylvania Press.

Gjerdingen, R. (2007). *Music in the Galant Style*. Oxford University Press.

Janssen, B., de Haas, W. B., Volk, A., and van Kranenburg, P. (2013). Discovering repeated patterns in music: state of knowledge, challenges, perspectives. In *Proceedings of the International Symposium on Computer Music Multidisciplinary Research (CMMR 2013)*, pages 225–240, Marseille.

Knopke, I. and Jürgensen, F. (2009). A system for identifying common melodic phrases in the masses of Palestrina. *Journal of New Music Research*, 38(2):171–181.

Lartillot, O. (2005). Multi-dimensional motivic pattern extraction founded on adaptive redundancy filtering. *Journal of New Music Research*, 34(4):375–393.

Lewin, D. (1987). *Generalized Musical Intervals and Transformations*. Yale University Press.

Lutes, L. (1974). *Beethoven's re-uses of his own compositions*. PhD thesis, Department of Music, University of Southern California.

Marston, N. (1995). *Beethoven's Piano Sonata in E, op. 109*. Clarendon Press.

Meredith, D. (2006). The *ps13* pitch spelling algorithm. *Journal of New Music Research*, 35(2):121–159.

Meredith, D., Lemström, K., and Wiggins, G. A. (2002). Algorithms for discovering repeated patterns in multidimensional representations of polyphonic music. *Journal of New Music Research*, 31(4):321–345.

Meyer, L. (1980). Exploiting limits: creation, archetypes, and style change. *Daedalus*, 109(2):177–205.

Pardo, B. and Birmingham, W. P. (2002). Algorithms for chordal analysis. *Computer Music Journal*, 26(2):27–49.

Pearce, M., Ruiz, M., Kapasi, S., Wiggins, G., and Bhattacharya, J. (2010). Unsupervised statistical learning underpins computational, behavioural, and neural manifestations of musical expectation. *Neuroimage*, 50:302–313.

Pearson, K. (1909). On a new method of determining correlation between a measured character *a*, and a character *b*, of which only the percentage of cases wherein *b* exceeds (or falls short of) a given intensity is recorded for each grade of *a*. *Biometrika*, 7(1–2):96–105.

Pielou, E. and Foster, R. (1962). A test to compare the incidence of disease in isolated and crowded trees. *Canadian Journal of Botany*, 40:1176–1179.

Radcliffe, P. (1968). *Beethoven's String Quartets*. E.P. Dutton.

Roberts, J. (1986). Handel's borrowing from Keiser. *Göttinger Händel-Beiträge*, 2:51–76.

Wang, A.-C. and Smith, J. (2012). System and methods for recognizing sound and music signals in high noise and distortion. Patent US 8,190,435 B2. Continuation of provisional application from 2000.

Winemiller, J. (1997). Recontextualizing Handel's borrowing. *The Journal of Musicology*, 15(4):444–470.

Index

Abdallah, S., vi, 157–183
algebraic approach, 251–269
algorithmic information theory, 159, 337
ambiguity, 222, 253
anatomy, 16, 18
Andreatta, M., vi, 57–79
anticorpus, 412, 459, 460, 467, 469
antipattern, 412, 413
approximation, 9, 22, 25
architecture, 16, 18
artificial intelligence (AI), 192, 222
Arzt, A., viii, 445–472
association rule mining, 401, 412
atonal music, 37, 43, 75, 99
audio, 7, 8, 35, 36, 83, 118, 121, 123, 128, 131,
    137, 138, 140, 305, 336, 371, 373
auditory scene analysis, 34, 139
Automatic Timespan Tree Analyser (ATTA)
    (software), 23, 166, 221–247
automaton, 163
    finite state automaton, 163
    push-down automaton, 163

Bach, J. S., vii, viii, 6, 11, 24, 40, 42, 48, 69,
    70, 73, 75–77, 84, 91, 92, 103, 120, 121,
    123, 127, 128, 131, 137, 138, 149, 166,
    176, 177, 179, 182, 198, 202, 209, 211,
    213, 215, 254, 297, 303, 304, 315, 316,
    324, 329, 339, 349, 351, 353, 356, 357,
    360, 363, 369–371, 373, 374, 378, 379,
    381–383
    Das Wohltemperirte Clavier, 103, 122–124,
    128, 137, 138, 149, 297, 316, 349, 351,
    353, 356, 357, 360
backpropagation, 146, 148
bagana, viii, 425–441
Bartók, B., 48, 50

Bayes, T., 168
Bayesian inference, 168, 172, 182, 200
    naive Bayes, 370, 376, 383
Bayesian network, 172
beat tracking, 226
Beatles, The, 48, 50
Beethoven, L. van, viii, 41, 42, 242, 316, 323,
    360, 362, 363, 369, 370, 373, 374, 378,
    379, 445–472
Bellman, R., 141
Bent, I., 16, 335
Bigo, L., vi, 57–79
binding problem, 138, 139, 142
bioinformatics, 426
bits-back coding, 170, 178
black box model, viii, 369, 370
Boulez, P., 60
Brahms, J., 426
Bregman, A. S., 34, 139
Byrd, D., 9

C4.5 (algorithm), 202, 205, 209–212, 236, 373,
    377
Cambouropoulos, E., vi, 31–53, 117, 336
categorical perception, 33, 34
cellular complex, 62
Chomsky, N., 163, 252
Chopin, F., 24, 316, 360, 362, 445, 448, 459,
    467, 469
chorale, 6, 11, 40, 42, 48, 49, 69, 70, 73, 75–77,
    84, 91, 166, 176–182, 198, 202, 209,
    211–213, 215, 254
chord, v, vi, 8, 26, 31–53, 57–79, 99, 138, 139,
    141–144, 152, 163, 166, 192–194, 207,
    208, 252, 371, 417, 469, 470
chord complex, 57–79
chromatic pitch, 339

© Springer International Publishing Switzerland 2016
D. Meredith (ed.), *Computational Music Analysis*,
DOI 10.1007/978-3-319-25931-4